AERIAL VIEW.

MANTOVA

MODENA

BOLOGNA

MAX INFORMATION

THE AREA IT COMES FROM.

(LEFT BANK OF THE RIVER RENO). THE WAY WE MAKE IT IS STRICTLY DEFINITE TOO: IT'S AN ARTISAN PRODUCT, AS IT HAS ALWAYS BEEN, PRODUCED USING MILK COMING EXCLUSIVELY FROM COWS IN THE AREA OF ORIGIN, NO ADDITIVES ALLOWED. MATURED FROM 12 TO MORE THAN 24 MONTHS, IT IS CHECKED CHEESE BY CHEESE, DAY AFTER DAY. THE RESULT IS A UNIQUE CHEESE: HIGHLY DIGESTIBLE AND GUARANTEED BY THE CONSORTIUM'S SEAL. A 100% NATURAL CHEESE. FANCY ANOTHER PIECE OF PARMIGIANO-REGGIANO?

PARMIGIANO REGGIANO

ONLY FROM OUR COWS

In Maremma the feast goes on.
Along the wine routes, among unforgettable landscapes and cordial hospitality, discover the genuine flavours and the most charming atmospheres of this unique land. For further information: APT Grosseto +39 0564 462611.

La Maremma fa bene

APT GROSSETO

S.PELLEGRINO

BOTTLED AT THE SOURCE SAN PELLEGRINO TERME · ITALY

SPARKLING NATURAL MINERAL WATER

Prolonged socializing may result.

Whatever language you speak, *live in Italian.*

Typical regional products: the quality is a guarantee with a blend of aromas and tastes.

REGIONE LAZIO

MILANO
TORINO
VENEZIA
GENOVA
BOLOGNA
FIRENZE
ROMA
LAZIO
CAGLIARI
NAPOLI
BARI
PALERMO

The councillorship of the Agriculture department has placed the regional products as top priority to protect and promote them.
To defend and promote the "typical" means to preserve the entire territory rediscovering the history, the traditions and above all those good old fashioned tastes of which the regional product is the guardian angel.
To guarantee the quality means appreciating the time and goodwill of the producers to look after the consumers.

Councillorship of
the Agriculture
Via Rosa Raimondi
Garibaldi, 14
00145 Rome - Italy
Tel.:
0039.06.51684105

www.assagri.it

In accordance with new common rural policy, the regional programme has its foundations on the respect for the resources and peculiarities of the territory, enhancing their potential so as to benefit the community. The local economy will be able to survive thanks to the interaction between the producer and the consumer who, moved by the same objectives, will contribute to the preservation of the quality of life. On one side the producer will guarantee the quality of the product, and on the other the consumer will choose high quality typical products. To safeguard and promote "Typicality" means preserving the entire territory and appreciating again its history, traditions and true flavours of which the typical product is the faithful guardian.

This is the starting point of the Strategic promotional programme adopted by the Regional Department of Agriculture which has set aside 12 billion lira in 2001 alone for promotional and advertising activities. The programme also includes an evaluation system of the benefits deriving from the attendance to these events. This action plan will be supported by a targeted and thorough communication campaign which will reach out to the greater food outlets as well.

One of the main objectives is to create an umbrella trademark for the food production of the Region that guarantees quality and typicality, and which will be the key to the door to greater markets for our products.

The Lazio Product will be the main attraction of touristic-oenogra-stronomical itineraries where the people who work in the gastronomical sector will be involved in addition to those operating in the fields of trade, culture, handicraft and the environment. With this purpose in mind, the Lazio Region has passed a law which establishes the Roads of wine, oil and traditional and typical products and which provides regional funds to create touristic routes.

Antonello Iannarilli

Councillorship to the Agriculture of the Lazio Region-Italy

The oeno-gastronomical production

Lazio currently counts about 170 traditional products, 5 Protected Origin Denomination (DOP) products, 2 Protected Geographic Indication (IGP) products, 5 Typical Geographic Indication (IGT) wines and an impressive 33 Controlled Origin Denomination (DOC) wines.

All the DOPs and IGTs of Lazio

Established DOPs
Pecorino Romano Cheese - *Lazio*
Buffalo Mozzarella
from Campania - *Fr and Lt*
Genzano Casareccio Bread - *Rm*
Oil of Sabina - *Ri and Rm*
Oil of Canino - *Vt*

DOPs under examination
Caseus Romae cheese - *Lazio*
Roman Ricotta cheese - *Lazio*
Roman Caciotta cheese - *Lazio*
Fior di Latte cheese - *Rm, Ri and Vt*
Oil of the Tivoli Hills - *Rm*
Oil of the Roman Castles Hills - *Rm*
Extravirgin Oil of Mt. Soratte - *Rm*
Gaeta Olives - *Lt*
Latina Oil - *Lt*

DOPs about to be established
Oil of Tuscia - *Vt*

Established IGPs
White veal of the Central Appennins - *Ri and Vt*
Roman artichoke - *Rm and Lt*

The "Lazio Product"

REGIONE LAZIO

IGPs under examination
Roman Lamb - *Lazio*
Porchetta of Ariccia - *Rm*
Carrot of Fiumicino - *Rm*
Roman Hazelnut - *Vt*
Chestnut of Vallerano - *Vt*
Chestnut of Rieti - *Ri*
Chestnut of Segni - *Rm*
Kiwi of Lazio - *Lt*

All the DOCs and IGTs of Lazio

DOC wines
Aleatico di Gradoli, Aprilia,
Atina, Bianco Capena, Castelli
Romani, cerveteri, Cesanese del
Piglio, Cesanese di Affile,
Cesanese di Olevano Romano,
Circeo, Colli Albani, Colli della
sabina, Colli Etruschi Viterbese,
Colli Lanuvini, Cori, Est!Est!Est!
di Montefiascone, Frascati,
Genazzano, Marino,
Montecompatri - Colonna,
Orvieto, Tarquinia, velletri,
Vignanello, Zagarolo

IGT wines
Civitella D'Agliano, Colli Cimini,
Frusinate, Lazio, Nettuno

THE CULTURE IN CUTLERY

Alexander

1907

media Art&Ddesign group - ph. G. D'altoa

Alexander s.r.l.
Viale delle Industrie, 1
P.O. Box 120
33085 Maniago PN - Italia
tel. +39 0427 72538/9
Fax +39 0427 72082
www.alexanderitalia.com
e-mail: info@alexanderitalia.com

Alexander Italia inc.
6000 Metropolitain est.
Suite 304
Montreal Quebec
Canada H1S 1B1
tel. (514) 253-2539
fax (514) 253-3555
e-mail: info@alexanderitalia.qc.ca

AZIENDE AGRICOLE

CABERT

BERTIOLO (UD) FRIULI - ITALY
TEL. +39.0432.917434
FAX +39.0432.917768
bertiolo@tin.it
www.cabert.it

FRIULI GRAVE
CABERNET SAUV. RIS. 1993
ZURIGO 1997

FRIULI GRAVE
CABERNET FRANC 1996
LONDRA 1998

FRIULI GRAVE
SAUVIGNON 1998
TOKYO 1999

SAUVIGNON RISERVA
BARRIQUE 1997
VERONA 2000

Silver Award
FRIULI GRAVE
CABERNET SAUV. 1994
SAN FRANCISCO 2000

WINE
INTERNATIONAL
CHALLENGE
2001
LONDON
MERLOT RISERVA
BARRIQUE 1995
LONDRA 2001

The Italian Food Guide

The Ultimate Guide to the Regional Foods of Italy

Published in association with the Italian Ministry of Industry, Trade, and Handicraft - Department of Tourism

TOURING CLUB OF ITALY

Touring Club of Italy
President: Roberto Ruozi
Managing Director: Guido Venturini

Touring Editore
Chief Executive Officer: Guido Venturini
Editorial Director: Michele D'Innella

Senior Editor: Viviana Arrigoni
Editorial Coordination: Paola Pandiani
Editing: Guglielmo Martinello, Agostina Pizzocri, Giovanna Rosselli
Editorial Administration: Alice Ricci
Map Design: Cartographic Division- Touring Club of Italy
Design and cover: Federica Neeff with Mara Rold
Production: Vittorio Sironi

Curator of the publication: Francesco Soletti
Texts: Francesco Soletti, with Alessandra Oleotti; Teresa Cremona, Raoul Ciappelloni, Davide Di Corato, Luciano Revelli, Pier Luigi Grottola and Nadia Florimo, Giuseppe Lo Castro.
Gourmet association: Daniela Scrobogna for the Enoteca Italiana (Siena).
Production Editor: Buysschaert & Malerba (Milan) with Suna Erdem, Maurizio Zanuso; Anne Ellis, Elisabetta DaPra, David Stanton (translations from italian).
Text editing and practical information updating: Alessandra Oleotti
Cover photograph: "Twirling spaghetti on a Fork", Ph. Hunter, © Franca Speranza (Milan - Italy)

We would like to thank all those who have helped with the publication of this guide: the *Enoteca Italiana (Siena)*, the *Movimento del Turismo del Vino*, the *Associazione Nazionale Città del Vino*, the *Unione Ristoranti del Buon Ricordo*. In addition, the Tci fellows *Italo Arieti, Elio Torlontano* and *Pietro Liuzzi*; the *Associazione Italiana Collezionisti Etichette del Vino (Milan)*; the Agricultural Departments of the various regions; the *Archivio storico Barilla (Parma)*, *Cinzano* and *Zonin* for their permission to reproduce the objects of their collections.

The authors and publishers have done their best to ensure the accuracy of the information in this guide. However, because many of the details are subject to alteration, readers are advised to check opening hours, access conditions etc. of the places they intend to visit before making a journey. The publisher cannot take responsibility for any loss, injury or inconvenience caused as a result of the information contained in this guide.

Advertising Manager: Claudio Bettinelli
Local advertising: Progetto - Milan, piazza Fidia 1, phone 0269007848, fax 0269009334 -
Trento, via Grazioli 67, phone 0461231056, fax 0461231984 - www.progettosrl.it - info@progettosrl.it

Typesetting and color separations: APV Vaccani - Milan
Printing: Grafiche Mazzucchelli - Settimo Milanese (MI)
Binding: Legatoria Torriani - Cologno Monzese (MI)

Touring Club of Italy, corso Italia 10, 20122, Milan - Italy
www.touringclub.it
© 2002 Touring Editore - Milan

Distributed in the USA and Canada by Publishers Group West.
Distributed in Great Britain, Northern Ireland and the Irish Republic by Portfolio Books Ltd.

Code K6C
ISBN 88-365-2538-5

Printed in June 2002

SUMMARY

13

HOW TO CONSULT THIS GUIDEBOOK

Travel from region to region and find out about Italy's rural landscape and the agriculture that characterizes this country; the preservation of traditional agricultural activities and how their status has been raised; the gastronomy, presented in its geographical and historical contexts; and the restaurants which specialize in local flavors using both traditional and new recipes.

LIGURIA FLAVORS OF MOUNTAINS AND THE SEA

All the flavors of a cuisine that is at its best in Genoa and finds the origins of its most singular dishes in the history of commerce are concentrated between the Ligurian Sea and the Apennines.

Liguria is an "ethereal land," wrote Vincenzo Cardarelli. "Hot stones and clean clay are enlivened by vine leaves in the sun. Olive trees are gigantic. In the springtime mimosa blooms everywhere. Shadow and sun alternate in the deep valleys that run into the sea; in the steep cobbl....

fields of roses, wells and tilled earth; alongside farms and vineyards." A poetic but also realistic image of a coastal area protected from cold north winds by the Apennines. Liguria also crosses this mountain range into the Po Valley, where intensively cultivated land – often on narrow terraces – can be found alongside woods and pastures; where the indigenous Cabannina cow eats alongside the enormous Piedmont cow, enabling Ligurians to enjoy a wide variety of cheeses and meats.

Difficult to cultivate, the coastal area nonetheless produces a significant variety, if not quantity, of products including DOP (Denominazione di Origine Protetta) olive oil, vegetables and fruits from further inland , salamis, cheeses, mushrooms, truffles and chestnuts, while the sea abounds with fish and shellfish.

On the coast there is an excellent variety of restaurants. Inland the mountain economy is relatively closed so the foods served there are those found on the land. Tables in trattorie are laid with meats, particularly rabbit and poultry. Along the ance routes of commerce the tastes of Piedmont, E... and even Tuscany filter in.

At a crossroad...

20 REGIONAL SECTIONS

The guide is divided into 20 sections, one for each region, presented in order from North to South and West to East.
A brief overview introduces each region. Starting with the major characteristics, it introduces the reader to the food-and-wine peculiarities of each area.

REGIONAL MAPS

Each region includes a cartographic plate that, thanks to special symbols allows the reader to spot the areas where the main characteristic products are produced. These symbols are subdivided into the following categories: cheeses, charcuterie, meats, fish, fruit, vegetables, bread and sweets, grains, extra virgin olive oil, DOCG and DOC wines.

ROME

The capital is the Mecca for tourists and food lovers but the rest of this extensive and varied province should not be underestimated.

A common mistake of people staying in Rome is to exhaust their cultural and gastronomic curiosities within the city itself and underestimate the rest of the province. First of all, it has a long coastline with two interesting centers of seafood cuisine: Civitavecchia, bordering on Tuscany, and Anzio, bordering on Campania. Then there is the Campagna Romana running along the River Tiber, known for its beautiful countryside and its fruit and vegetables. Then there are the hills and some specific areas in between, such as the Monti della Tolfa to the north, the Sabatini around Lake Bracciano, and the Colli Albani with the Albano and Nemi lakes. The volcanic nature of the area, which favors agriculture, has also made it famous for producing wine (Frascati and Cerveteri being the most

widely-known), olive oil, fruit and vegetables. In the Apennines animal husbandry and cheese-making predominate. The cuisine is almost exactly that which is served in the most down-to-earth places in the capital: pasta flavored with vegetables or sauces made from meat or innards; suckling lamb or pig; fish from the sea or the lakes; peasant side dishes. Rome has an exceptionally high number and variety of restaurants; no less important are the more casual *trattoria* in the province.

Gourmet Tours

ROME. "If there is a city where you cannot possibly go and eat in a luxury hotel or a pretentious *trattoria*, it's Rome" says Paolo Monelli in the Ghiottone errante (The Misguided Glutton). "In Rome, you should only eat where the people eat; and if a tavern becomes fashionable, it would be better to find yourself another one. Rome, the capital of modern civilization, has the most plebeian cuisine in the world. However, this does not mean it is in-

sipid or bad. Roman cuisine is very tasty, aggressive, and varied but still rustic. And when the Rome of emperors, the Rome of Popes, the Rome of diplomats wants to eat well, it finds its recipes in the ghettos of the Jews and the alleys of the plebs." Taking up this idea, we have tried to find eating places which still have the *trattoria* atmosphere of fifty or a hundred years ago. Firstly, we recommend, for its history, the "Checchino dal 1887", which started life as a tavern for the old slaughterhouse and, as such, was the birthplace of the famous coda *alla vaccinara* (oxtail stewed with many seasonings and flavored

---

102 PROVINCIAL SECTIONS

102 provinces covered Italy is analyzed, province by province, based on Touring Club Italia's (TCI) 1:800,000 scale maps. This guide examines how the country's geography affects agricultural production, including the wines of noteworthy quality. You are taken from field to kitchen through a study of traditional gastronomy, the basic culinary themes of the area and the specialties contributed by groups such as ethnic minorities.

---

cuisine is dominated by Venice, and its ancient traditions remain, while the revival of the modern tourist boom has stimulated both the use of certain spices and innovative dishes. The cuisine is mainly based on fish but game and vegetables, the great resources of the lagoon and its islands, also play an important role.

Gourmet Tours

VENICE. This is a city that has a lot to offer the visitor, not just in terms of museums, churches and palaces, which are dealt with in other guides, but also in terms of its restaurants. Leaving aside the plethora of tourist restaurants, Venice's cuisine is among the most outstanding in Italy thanks to its culinary traditions and the quality of its local ingredients (especially fish than Chioggia and the vegetables grown in the area round the lagoon). The Rialto market should not be missed on any account: the fish market is held in a nineteenth-century loggia overlooking the Grand Canal, while the colorful fruit and vegetable one is located at one end of the Rialto Bridge.

This is where a visit to Venice's gastronomic highlight should begin; it could well commence with a tour of the *osterie*, the following are located at strategic points in the city: "La Mascareta", at Santa Maria Formosa, behind San Marco, the "Ca' d'Oro", near the Scuola Nuova, and the famous palace of the "Da Codroma", on the way from Piazzale Roma to the Campo Santa Margherita, the "Cantinone" right opposite the Squero di San Trovaso, at the Zattere, and the "Vecio Fritolin" between Rialto and Ca' Pesaro. Besides the various nursery emblem tin, these wine bars offer superb *cichéti* – tasty morsels, usually of fish. One of the best-known traditional dishes is *risi e bisi* (rice with peas).

PROVINCIAL GASTRONOMIC ITINERARIES

Beginning from each province's capital, which has its own specific information section, you are taken along one or more gourmet routes which pass through the most important places in the province. For each place, you are given information on the local produce and gastronomic traditions. The listings of restaurants and local food and beverage producers are compiled taking into account the extent to which each entry respects tradition and the restoration of historical surroundings.

THE FOOD-LOVER'S DIARY

Useful information is given to help plan your journey, from the dates of wine and food fairs to a selection of more than 500 of the most interesting restaurants in Italy. Also included are hotels, agriturismo establishments (rural accommodation), wine producers, olive oil producers and the best food stores.

The ★🛏 symbol indicates those establishments which give discounts to TCI members.

THE GRAND WINE AND FOOD TOUR

Centuries ago travelers from the other side of the Alps came to Italy for the Grand Tour of ancient sites, eager to admire the mossy atriums and crumbling forums of ancient Rome, the villas of Palladio, the churches of Florence and the many other areas of natural beauty enhanced by the hands of man. In other words the treasures of what was considered the 'Bel Paese' (beautiful country). However, when these travelers recounted their journeys, little or nothing was said of the small jewels set amidst ordinary abodes, along roadsides, scattered over the countryside – the churches, mansions, piazzas, castles, chapels, farms, monasteries - or of the landscape itself, the layout of the fields and the way crops were planted.

All this was discovered by a generation of travelers closer to our time and appreciated more when people realized that tourism did not just belong to the big cities. The tourist guides began dedicating space to the lesser-known arts and to everyday architecture. Attention was given to urban structure, the organization of the Alpine hut, the dairy farm, the farmhouses and even to industrial archaeology from medieval water mills to nineteenth-century factories. Much more detail was given about the surroundings but still nothing was said of the people who

lived in these surroundings, whether ancient or modern.
The subject of tourism was finally treated in full when it began
to cover handicrafts - which represent a certain continuity in our
civilization - and the production of food, which is often the main reason
for the conservation of the landscape from which it comes.

LOCAL PRODUCE - THE MYTH AND THE REALITY

The beauty of an Alpine hut is in the materials from which
it is made, its working structure and the way it fits into its
surroundings. These are fine words but do not whet your appetite. Stimulate the taste buds by adding a good cheese to
the description and it is a whole new story. Add to that the
knowledge that the cheese's flavor comes from the hay grown at
high altitudes and the cows that eat it are of an ancient breed,
and the whole story becomes a wonderful tale. At the opposite
end of the country, in Sicily, the walled baglio contains the story
of a full year's work in the fields, from the picking of the olives to the
grape harvest. Add to this rural microcosm the flavor of a farmer's afternoon snack - tomatoes, olives and salted capers, seasoned with olive oil
and hand-squeezed grape juice - and your trip is complete. These two examples covering north and south, mountain and sea, give an idea of the
wine and food aspect of tourism, which can either be the reason for the
trip or a complement to cultural interests. Whichever it is, it is an integral part of getting to know the traditions of a place. Do not let yourself
be too influenced by myths or you will be drawn into
the fashion of the moment. On the other
hand, those fighting the battle for
local produce need to in-

spire the so-called 'gastronauts'. Colonnata bacon is a case in point: without wishing to make it sound any less good than it is, who would have thought that this salami, nearly pure fat, would have become so sought after and talked about with such enthusiasm? Made using the right mixture of herbs and then matured in troughs of white Carrara marble, it deserves its reputation. It is made up of only a few ingredients - you can count them on the fingers of one hand - but the main reason for its elevated status is because it symbolises one of those many production processes which are endangered by food hygiene laws which are just too strict. Be that as it may, Colonnata, a little-known town in the Apuan Alps, is now a confirmed tourist destination thanks to the miracles of wine and food tourism.

TRADITIONAL AND CREATIVE COOKERY

It is a short step from local produce to local dishes. To tell the truth, local cooking has always fascinated even the most refined intellectuals: Hans Barth wrote a short literary masterpiece entitled, Osteria (Tavern), with an introduction by none other than Gabriele d'Annunzio; Paolo Monelli wrote Il Ghiottone Errante (The Misguided Glutton), a story about his alter-ego engaged in a gastronomic marathon, and supported by beautiful Novello illustrations. In any case, the subject was treated more with a spirit of hedonism than from the scientific point of view common today. Now that the view of the trattoria as just a place for cheap food is seen as old-fashioned, the critics' attention has turned to cooking traditions, local produce and an authenticity not always found in conventional restaurants.

Research at grass roots level has sometimes led to picking out the most minor of activities, like the fried-food shops or even the mobile tripe sellers, which are then held up as the stars of a region's gastronomy. Parallel to this, the wave of interest in local food has also drawn in the chefs who, having recovered from the dizzy heights of 'creativity at all costs' have come back to the traditional dishes, refining them or interpreting them in their own way or creating new recipes from traditional ingredients. This is how the farro (spelt) of Gargagnana, a very wholesome cereal, suddenly rose to fame and is now found in all the soups. The same goes for the Castelluccio lentil from the high Apennines, which provides an excellent protein base for all sorts of dishes. And finally, there has also been the 'discovery' of the dishes of ethnic minorities. You do not need to cross oceans or even the Alps to find new gastronomic horizons. From the Provençal in upper Piedmont to the Slovenians at the eastern borders, the arch of our major mountains represents a body of gastronomy which includes the cooking of the Walsers in the valleys leading up to Monte Rosa, the Tyroleans in Alto Adige, the Ladins, the Mocheni and the Cimbri, whose cuisine influences the gastronomy from Trentino through Veneto. The same can be said of the south with its ancient Albanian communities between Calabria and Basilicata, the North Africans in the Trapani area and the Island of San Pietro in Sardinia. For now, this is the final gastronomic frontier.

WINE ROUTES, FLAVOR ROUTES

The recent passing of the law on the Strade del Vino (wine routes) was like the foundation stone of wine and food tourism. Wine runs through the ages and draws you into a tourism of flavors - it is like a pass to good taste which leads you to the discovery of other delights of the land, particularly of olive oil. his is explicitly quoted by the law-makers, leaving a clear opening to routes for other products which could suitably represent their land. In Piedmont, they talk of the cheese routes in Monferrato and in Le Langhe, while there is similar talk of rice routes being set up between Novara and Vercelli. All this goes beyond simple gastronomic show and there are hundreds of such examples hidden in the shadows of Italy's bell towers, from the famous radicchio di Treviso (Treviso chicory) to the little-known but delicious foods such as pecorino di Filiano (pecorino sheep's cheese of Filiano, in the region of Basilicata), and n'-duja, a spicy, spreadable cold meat from Spilingo in Calabria. The concept of the flavor routes can be widened from the simply gastronomical aspect to encompass the land in all its forms, human and material, so that you enjoy the narrower dimension of local food and restaurants but also the more complex environmental dimension which makes up the whole landscape of your trip. So, you have the focus of your interest - the cheese or the sausage - which cannot be made anywhere else because of the combination of local earth, water and atmosphere which go into making it what it is, but you also have the dairy farm where the process is begun; the traditions surrounding it; the village which watches over it and the road which connects it to its neighbouring villages - and all this set in the complex of history and humanity. This dimension stretches to include towns, cities and regional capitals, each one with its own flavor to offer, a recipe to remember, perhaps linked to ancient domination or trade, or to a particular person who is now just a memory from the distant past.

WINE TOWNS, OLIVE OIL TOWNS, TRUFFLE TOWNS, ETC

The excitement and activity surrounding wine and food has given rise to the birth of so-called associations of 'class'. It is thanks to the Città del Vino (cities of wine), with 350 associates, big and small, and to the Movimento Turismo del Vino (Wine Tourism Movement) with over 700 wine companies, that gastronomic tourism has been breached, and they have shown that the road to success begins with a quality welcome. In both cases, being a member involves the responsibility of meeting certain standards regarding the organizational aspects of what is offered to the tourist and the etiquette of the wine cellar. The message is clear: out with improvisation because the guest may appreciate spontaneity but not a lack of professionalism, especially if he has invested money and expectation in the trip. In the wake of these two associations came 153 Città dell'Olio (Cities of Olive Oil), 21 Città dei Tartufi (Cities of Truffles), 15 Città del Pesce di Mare (Cities of Sea Fish) and 11 Città delle Lumache (Cities of Snails). Soon there will be others - and all with an unexpected wealth of recipes. The same goes for the restaurants even though the idea of an association was well-established long ago. One example is the Ristoranti del Buon Ricordo (happy souvenir restaurants), with the happy idea - already apparent in its name - of giving the gift of a collector's plate to anyone eating the selected local dish. In many places restaurants have clubbed together to offer the food-lover the local specialty prepared according to sacred custom, like the truffle restaurants in Le Langhe, the saffron restaurants in San Gimignano, the swordfish restaurants along the Stretto, to say nothing of the tasty scenes put together in various parts of Italy by the food-loving fraternity (which also do a lot to protect local foods and customs).

LOCAL SPECIALITIES VIA THE INTERNET

To close, let us take a look at the future. Wine and food tourism and trade now travel via the net. Have you been told of a cheese you have never heard of before? Try your luck on the Internet. Type in the mystery name, set the search engine in motion and you may be surprised to see appearing from the computer the answers to your question: name, place of origin, producer, preparation, taste, smell, texture, and even its price and how to buy it - obviously, because whoever takes the time to enter this information into the network is not doing it for encyclopaedic reasons but rather for commercial ones. This is one of the many aspects of the new economy. The computer screen is a virtual food shop window which does not, of course, attract you like the smells in a real store but certainly performs a small miracle in opening the door to a cheese factory lost in the depths of who knows where. The same goes for a growing number of restaurants: type in the name and you get to the relevant site then, window by window, you can visit the restaurant, leaf through its menu and wine list and even download the recipe of the restaurant's most popular dish. A recent slogan suggested that the flavor of a journey was in the desire for knowledge. We beg to differ.

THE LAND OF A THOUSAND FLAVORS

THE NORTH-WEST: VALLE D'AOSTA, PIEDMONT AND LIGURIA

This journey through the flavors of Italy begins at Mont Blanc, which stands out as the Old Continent's historical access route to the boot-shaped peninsular. The Valle d'Aosta stretches out before it - a region of meadows and Alpine pasture, of vines clinging to rock and fruit trees which soften the edges of the streams and rivers. The gastronomic symbol of these mountains is the fontina cheese - made from the milk of small dappled local cows - which tastes sweet and tempting. The cheese can be heated together with milk, butter and eggs to make a creamy fonduta, which is eaten by dipping bread into it or used as a sauce for one of the two dishes common to the whole of the Alps: gnocchi (soft dough balls made from flour and potatoes) and polenta (cornflour thickened in water and cooked in a copper pan).

At the end of the valley the view broadens out to the Padana plain, through which runs the Po river. The first important site you meet along its banks is Turin, once capital of Italy during the rule of the house of Savoy and now capital of the province of Piedmont, one of the most interesting regions for the food-lover. There is a quiet fascination in the city's 19th century royal palaces but also in its cafés and restaurants which frame its history in exuberant red velvet and mirrors. At table we find the best that hill farming can provide from two of the most famous of districts, Le Langhe and Monferrato. Their products include cheeses, such as the soft Robiola di Roccaverano, and the herby Castelmagno; the white truffle of Alba, a real gastronomic treasure; meat from huge white, Piedmont cattle; and the Barolo and Barbaresco wines. This is to name just the most famous of a group of foods which can hardly be rivalled anywhere in the world. In this land-locked province a few

Mediterranean ingredients pop up from time to time, such as olive oil and salted capers. We are then brought to the Apennine passes which take us through to Liguria - a unique, arch-shaped region squeezed between mountain and sea. It is a land of sailors who are also farmers and shepherds, and of travelers and merchants. Amongst Liguria' characteristic images is the view of the Cinque Terre, comprising villages huddled along the coast at one end of the arch, with their vines and vegetable gardens perching on steep mountain sides just out of reach of the waves. Then we pass through Portofino and San Remo, and finally Genoa which completes the picture with its palaces dating from the city's times at the center of a maritime republic, the alleyways down at the port and the famous focaccia stores. The dish that sums up the whole region is the trenette al pesto - a type of flat pasta with a sauce made from basil, garlic, pine nuts, cheese and olive oil blended together.

THE CENTER-SOUTH: LAZIO, CAMPANIA, PUGLIA, ...

All roads lead to Rome, according to the ancient proverb. This is still true today when referring to art and culture and, equally, as regards food and wine. The eternal city has an extraordinary gastronomy in terms of history and variety - it is cosmopolitan, as is only right for a modern capital, but also traditional. It is not difficult to eat Roman-style, especially if you find one of those trattoria which is a shrine to good, plain food. The dishes can be simple, like the spaghetti aglio, olio e peperoncino (spaghetti seasoned with garlic, olive oil and chili pepper); rich, like the bucatini alla carbonara (spaghetti-type pasta with a hole in the center served with a sauce made of pig's cheek, pecorino cheese bound together with egg) or the

abbacchio alla cacciatora (roast suckling
lamb seasoned with garlic, rosemary, wine,
anchovies and chili pepper); or unusual,
like the dishes from the Jewish community which has developed its own cuisine.
All can be washed down with white wines
of high standing which have long been
served at the tables of princes and popes,
like the Frascati of the Colli Romani
and the legendary Est! Est! Est! of Montefiascone.
Leaving Rome, the culinary horizons broaden to
embrace Mediterranean cuisine. The first stops are
Naples and the province of Campania where you find a cuisine divided between simple food and noble traditions. The pizza
springs to mind as an example of the former, that ubiquitous food where
dough is combined with San Marzano tomatoes grown in the volcanic
earth of Vesuvius and mozzarella cheese made from the milk of cows
and buffalo which graze on the plain around the Temple of Paestum. At
the other extreme, there are highly complex pastries made with filo pastry and filled with ricotta, candied fruit, cinnamon and vanilla. The cuisine of the south is filled with the sunshine of the Mediterranean and
the vigors of the Apennines, conjuring up images of lemons from the
Amalfi coast, the vines of famous red wines like Taurasi, tastes of sword
fish from the Tyrrheanian Sea and caciocavallo Silano, a stringy cheese
from the Calabrian mountains. Flavors range from delicate, such as the
Greco wine - a white wine with an ancient history - to strong, such as
the chili pepper which is used to spice up the charcuterie. On the opposite coast, the emphasis changes but the spirit remains the same. In
Abruzzo, there is the brodetto, a fish soup common throughout the
Adriatic but which is spicier the further south you go. In Puglia, where
the tourists go to admire the Romanesque cathedrals or the Gargano
countryside, the cuisine is of pasta and bread made with durum wheat,
vegetables, stringy cheeses, olive oil and rosé wines.

IN THE HEART OF THE MEDITERRANEAN: SICILY AND SARDINIA

These two large islands in the heart of the Mediterranean are two utter-
ly different worlds basking in the same sun. Sicily has been gradually
built up from many cultures: Greek, Latin, Arab, Norman and Spanish.
Sardinia is monolithic, still in touch with its ancient roots. One island
has Doric temples and baroque churches, the other has prehistoric monuments and a wild landscape. Their cuisines also reflect this: one has a
Mediterranean cuisine in the broadest sense of the word, and the other
has an island cuisine, more pastoral than sea-based. Sicily is a celebra-
tion of fruits from distant lands - blood oranges, pistachios from Etna,
fichi d'India (prickly pears or, literally, figs from India), and the raisins of
Malvasia and Zibibbo. Great importance is given to fish that follow the
currents,like tuna and swordfish. It is not mere chance that the symbolic
dish of the island is pasta with sardine sauce - served most prevalently

between Palermo and Cefalù. It is all summed up in the sauce whose cosmopolitan ingredients are found both on land and in the sea: capers, wild fennel, onion, salted anchovies, pepper, pine nuts and raisins. The pastries are just as eloquent, most being a variation on Arab ones. There are the cannoli - tubes of brittle pastry filled with sweet ricotta cheese, pistachios and candied fruit; cassata - a singular cold sweet with a pastry base covered in cream and green marzipan; Martorana fruits which get their name from a convent in Palermo - which are made of almond paste cleverly worked to look like fruit and are true works of art; ice-creams and granite (crushed ice drink) in the traditional flavors of pistachio, coffee and lemon, which are even eaten inside a brioche at breakfast. There is even a strange foreign element to the wine, in the sense that the most famous one, Marsala, was 'invented' in its liqueur form by an English merchant trying to find a way of conserving the wine for transportation overseas.

Sardinia is quite another story: it is introverted and looks more to the mountains than to the sea. It is a place where external influences - from Spain right up to Liguria in the north and down to North Africa in the south - have had little effect on the rock-solid traditions of the island. This ancient spirit comes across in the pastoral products (the pecorino cheese is the flagship of the island's gastronomy) and the meat which is grilled and seasoned with herbs which echo the Mediterranean, like myrtle and rosemary. The range of cereal products is also telling, the most well-known being the carasau bread, also known as carta da musica (music paper) because it is made in thin sheets and cooked on a hotplate like in ancient times. There are some important vinestocks, too, like the famous white Vermentino and red Cannonau, both originally from Spain. But most grapes are indigenous and offer an unequalled variety of flavors. This is an island of ancient flavors, a voyage of discovery, just beyond the borders of your dream holiday in the Costa Smeralda (the Emerald Coast).

GOURMET TOURS
OF ITALY

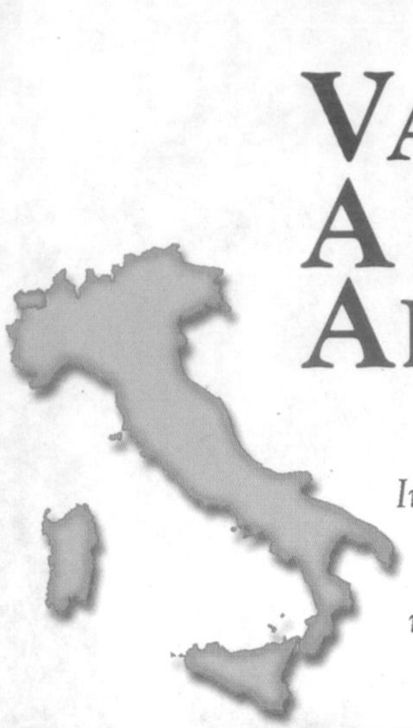

VALLE D'AOSTA
A TABLE SET WITH
ALPINE FLAVORS

*In the alpine region par excellence, animal farming
takes on a fundamental role that is reflected at the table,
where cheeses and meats are important components of
many traditional recipes.*

The Savoy king Emanuele Filiberto once said: "the Valle d'Aosta does not depend on us like the others. It has its own laws and traditions..." Today, this remark still holds true for a land that is heir to the proud civilization of the Salassi, in terms of both environment and people. It has always preserved a particular cultural identity that is the fruit of the peaceful cohabitation of many traditions.. Roman ruins, churches and castles testify to Aosta's thousand-year role as a crossroads of routes crossing the valley towards Switzerland and France and therefore as a meeting place of transalpine Europe with the Mediterranean. It is a role that is reflected in the region's gastronomy in more ways than one.

*Lake Blu,
by the Matterhorn
(Cervino)*

THE QUALITY OF MOUNTAIN PRODUCE
The territory of the Valle d'Aosta overlaps the Western Alps from Gran Paradiso to Monte Rosa and includes Mont Blanc and Cervino – all

elite European mountain resorts. Winding down from Europe's summit to the beginning of the Pianura Padana (Po Valley) is the Dora Baltea river. Starting at 1,200 meters at Courmayeur and ending at 300 at Pont-Saint-Martin, Dora Baltea is a major feature of the landscape. The main gully and the pattern of converging valleys shape the human settlements and productive land of a region where agriculture and animal husbandry are the main activities after tourism. Fruit is cultivated in the gullies, while grapevines grace the lower sunny slopes. Higher up, the woodland is a generous provider of a variety of wild products, and pastures sustain the breeding of cows and excellent cheese production.

Cup of Friendship

FONTINA: AN EXEMPLARY CASE

Mountain products have a very distinctive flavor. As far as the cultivation of fields and orchards go, this is the result of a drier climate where temperatures vary and neutralize mold and parasites. In cattle breeding it is a question of primary materials, particularly the rich, aromatic alpine hay. Another factor is the genetic heritage from native breeds such as Valdostana Pezzata Rossa, Pezzata Nera and Castana, which are less productive than others but better adapted to the climate. Given such a favorable base, the Regione Autonoma (Autonomous Region) authorities created a charter of quality best represented by *fontina*, one of the first mountain cheeses to obtain the DOP (*Denominazione di Origine Protetta*) recognition of quality. Today, *Valle d'Aosta Fromadzo*, a less fatty cheese, also has DOP recognition. The aim of the charter as regards the cheese is not so much the achievement of excellence – which is already guaranteed by the exclusive use of milk from Valle d'Aosta dairy cows and rigorous cheese-making practices – as the preserving of distinctive flavors that once separated one valley from another and even one *alpeggio* (summer mountain grazing area) from another.

QUALITY VITICULTURE AND THE PROTECTION OF SMALL PRODUCERS

The case for the ham Jambon de Bosses DOP and Lardo di Arnad DOP is different. The promotion of these products is aimed at preserving very small operations and stimulating them to the benefit of the small geographic regions involved. As for wines, their importance is linked more to protecting the environment and a small-scale economic fabric than to a purely mercenary interest. A single regional denomination Valle d'Aosta/Vallée d'Aoste has many sub-denominations that protect the local vines, from Picotendro (Nebbiolo grapes), used for Donnas and Arnad-Montjovet wines in the lower valley, to Petit Rouge and Vin de Nus grapes used in Chambave, Nus, Torrette and Enfer d'Arvier wines further up in the valley, and Prié Blanc grapes used in Blanc de Morgex et de La Salle, produced on the slopes of Mont Blanc. To complete the panorama of production, apples and honey are now awaiting their denomination; these are the Mela Renetta Valle d'Aosta apples, which are typical in the lower valleys, and Miele Valle d'Aosta honey, which is gathered at different altitudes in just about every village.

27

Valle d'Aosta - Typical products

Scale 1:800 000

0 ——— 15 km

CHEESES

1. **Fontina Dop.** Produced throughout the region.
2. **Valle d'Aosta Fromadzo Dop.** Produced throughout the region.

CHARCUTERIE

1. **Valle d'Aosta Jambon de Bosses Dop.** In Saint-Rhémy-en-Bosses, in the high valley of Gran San Bernardo.
2. **Valle d'Aosta Lardo di Arnad Dop.** In the Bassa Valle.

FRUIT

1. **Renetta Valle d'Aosta apples.** In the Dora Baltea valley.

2. **Martin Sec pears.** In the valley nearest to Piedmont.

VARIOUS

1. **Valle d'Aosta honey.** In the whole region.

LOCAL DOC WINES

1. **Valle d'Aosta Arnad-Montjovet**
2. **Valle d'Aosta Blanc de Morgex e de La Salle**
3. **Valle d'Aosta Chambave**
4. **Valle d'Aosta Donnas**
5. **Valle d'Aosta Enfer d'Arvier**
6. **Valle d'Aosta Nus**
7. **Valle d'Aosta Torrette**

AOSTA

Mountain cooking is at once simple and rich and ranges from rustic soups to hearty meat and cheese dishes.

In an alpine region where animal husbandry plays an extremely important role, meats and dairy products provide the basis of the cuisine. Bread, particularly rye bread, is also significant as it is an ingredient used in the vegetable and broth soups found in each valley with very few variations. *Polenta*, served with meat or cheese, is also widespread and is prepared *in umido*, or wet, as in the *carbonade*, which is made with red wine.

Gressoney.
Typical Walser
baite huts.

The valleys that run up to Monte Rosa are inhabited by people of Germanic origin, therefore certain dishes in this area recall those of Alto Adige. The simplest means are used to make every table rich with flavor. The *valligiani* (valley people) are tough and appear introverted; they remain reserved even at the table, where their hard-earned mountain products are served parsimoniously. Yet the ritual of the *coppa dell'amicizia*, or friendship cup, has become a token of every banquet: filled with a hearty blend of coffee and *grappa*, this cup with its many spouts, representing the inner warmth of this people, is handed around the table for all to drink.

HOTELS AND RESTAURANTS

Aosta
Le Foyer ❙❙
corso Ivrea 146
☎ 016532136
Vecchia Aosta ❙❙
piazza Porte
Pretoriane 4
☎ 0165361186
Vecchio Ristoro ❙❙
via Tourneuve 4
☎ 016533238
Trattoria degli Artisti ❙
via Maillet 5/7
☎ 016540960
Arvier
Café du Bourg ❙
via Lostan 14
☎ 016599094
Breuil-Cervinia
Cime Bianche ❙
at La Vieille
☎ 0166949046
Champoluc
Villa Anna Maria ★★★
via Croues 5
☎ 0125307128
⭐ ❙❙ **Le Petit Coq** ❙
at Villy (km 3)
☎ 0125307997
Châtillon
Privé Parisien ❙❙❙
at Panorama 1
☎ 0166537053
Cogne
Bellevue ★★★
via Gran Paradiso 22
☎ 016574825
Petit Dahu ★★
at Valnontey (km 3)
☎ 016574146
Lou Ressignon ❙❙
via Mines
de Cogne 23
☎ 016574034

Gourmet Tours

PONT-SAINT-MARTIN. The unusual bridge in the village of the same name dates back to the Roman era and the Via delle Gallie, a pilgrimage route once followed in the Middle Ages by the Saint who now stands next to the bridge. The bridge arches over the Lys river, which flows down from the valley of Gressoney. Nearby is the restaurant "Ponte Romano", which provides a fine introduction to the specialties the Valle D'Aosta has to offer.
GRESSONEY-LA-TRINITÉ. Before it became an alpine holiday resort, this land belonged to the Walser, a people of German stock who had established residence at the foot of Monte Rosa. This heritage is reflected at the table where *speck bollito con crauti, patate e carote* is served with *knolle* (boiled dried beef with potatoes and carrots served with *gnocchi*). Gressoney-St-Jean has two gastronomic highlights: "Principe", which devotes itself to keeping traditional cooking alive, and "Braciere", a mountain restaurant with a friendly atmosphere.
Here you should try *fromadzo*, a cheese similar to tome, creamy *reblec*, a cheese some eat with sugar and cinnamon, and *salignon*, which is basically *ricotta* blended with garlic, oil and aromatic herbs and then smoked.

Gressoney. Castel Savoia

DONNAS. This antique capital of the Bassa Valle (low valleys region) is made up of beautiful houses that line the Via delle Gallie, of which a stretch carved into the rock remains. The ancient tradition of terraced vineyards produces Nebbiolo grapes (locally known as Picotendro), which are transformed into a first-rate DOC wine that is considered the best in the valley. To sample this, stop by "Caves Coopératives de Donnas" where there is a wine tasting bar and restaurant. You could extend your visit to a nearby cheesemaker where an unsmoked *salignon* is produced. The farm "Chappoz Bonne Vallée" is also worth visiting for its old-fashioned *pane di castagne* (chestnut bread) that should be eaten with *lardo* (a kind of herbed salt pork) from the valley. Further ahead is Bard where Napolean demolished an austere castle that bothered him. It was later rebuilt by Carlo Alberto in 1831.

ARNAD. Continuing the ascent, you arrive at this village, known for its *lardo aromatico* pork as well as Arnad-Montjovet DOC, a red Nebbiolo wine. A good place to stop is "Lo Dzerby" an *agriturismo* (holiday farm) establishment that is reached by a pleasant walk. It sells typical regional products and it is also possible to have a hearty meal of meat and *polenta* accompanied by house wines (by reservation).

VERRÈS. The castle, one of the most beautiful in the region, overlooks the route from a rocky spur. Inside, a great staircase with flying buttresses leads to rooms with impressive fireplaces where feasts were held. The renowned restaurant "Pierre" in the village is a good place to find local and classic dishes. The excursion to Issogne, beyond the Dora River, is a must. There is another castle but this one became a noble residence with famous frescoes and an unusual pomegranate tree made out of wrought iron that graces the courtyard.

CHAMPOLUC. From Varrès you go back up the valley of a stream called the Evançon. The first stretch to Brusson, a village with old wood houses surrounded by fields, is called Valle di Challand. Further up, the name changes to Val d'Ayas, which is the capital of the area. At the top, majestically framed by Monte Rosa, is Champoluc. The *fontina* here is excellent and may be found in dishes of *polenta concia* (a rich *polenta* dish made with butter and cheese) and *fonduta* (cheese fondue).

SAINT-VINCENT. Beyond the strait of Montjovet (where you can find good wine), we enter the so-called Media Valle (middle valley). Travelers are received in the cultivated valley of Saint-Vincent where Renette apple and Martin Sec pear orchards can be found as

HOTELS AND RESTAURANTS

Cogne
Hostellerie de l'Atelier ❙
via Grappein 102
☎ 016574327
Lou Tchappè ❙
at Lillaz (km 3)
☎ 0165749291

Courmayeur
Gallia Gran Baita ★★★ 🏨
strada Larzey
☎ 0165844040
Grill Royal e Golf ❙❙❙❙
via Roma 87
☎ 0165846787
Dolonne ❙❙
at Dolonne (km 1)
via della Vittoria 24
☎ 0165846671
La Maison de Filippo ❙❙
at Entrèves (km 3)
☎ 0165869797

Gignod
La Clusaz ❙❙ 🏨
at La Clusaz (km 5)
☎ 016556075

Gressan
Hostellerie de la Pomme Couronnée ❙❙ 🏨
at Rosselin 3
☎ 0165251191

Gressoney-Saint-Jean
Il Braciere ❙❙ 🏨
at Ondrò
Verdebio 2
☎ 0125355526
Principe ❙
piazza Beck Peccoz 3
☎ 0125355117

VALLÉE D'AOSTE

DENOMINAZIONE D'ORIGINE CONTROLLATA

GAMAY

V.O.P.R.D
1992

Prodotto ed messo in bottiglia per
CASSOL ELIO
Villair/Morer - Verbès Saint (Aosta) Italia

0,75 l.℮   11,50% vol.

HOTELS AND RESTAURANTS

well as vineyards bursting with the local Petit Rouge grape. The village has been famous for its waters for a thousand years, and much more recently for the high life associated with its casinó. Locally, the refined "Batezar" restaurant is well-known, but we prefer "Del Viale" where a good young cook works. As for sweets, you should try the *torcettini di Saint Vincent*, which are made according to the original recipe of the historic pastry shop "Benedetto". "Morandin", a good candy maker with a small museum of dessert molds, is renowned for chocolates, marmalades and jellies.

CHÂTILLON. Sixteenth- and seventeenth-century houses and the Challant castle still stand in this village at the mouth of the Valtournenche river valley. Any visit here will have an important gastronomic flavor: "Privé Parisien", situated in a beautiful building decorated in French Provençal style, offers dishes of the Valle d'Aosta and France, as well as excellent *rigatoni mantecati all'amatriciana* (pasta with thick cream, fresh tomatoes and bacon). As for typical regional products, the area is known for *fontina* as well as *castagne* (chestnuts) and *noci* (walnuts).

BREUIL-CERVINIA. The journey back up the Valtournenche leads to one paradise after another. First to tempt you is the village of Antey-Saint-André, but immediately after comes Chamois which can only be reached by cable car. The village of Valtournenche follows; the route to climb Monte Cervinio (as the Matterhorn is known in Italy) begins there, and this has made a name for the village in the in the history of mountain-climbing. The goal for the day, however, is the Breuil valley. From here a cable car rises to the glaciers on Plateau Rosa or to the Cresta del Furggen, where the view of Cervinio is beautiful and outstanding. This is also where

Aosta, Piazza Chanoux.
The record-breaking pastry

some of the best *fontina* is made. For a gastronomic break go to the restaurant "Cime Bianche".

CHAMBAVE. "Crotta di Vegneron", which uses grapes from the town and surrounding vineyards to make 10 different DOC wines as well as table wines, is an interesting stop. Wine tasting, snacks and traditional dishes are available in the restaurant. Those who still have any energy left after a meal here can visit the seventeenth-century Casa Roncas and the Castello di Cly.

FÉNIS. The castle, with its turrets and embattlements, is one of the best known images of Valle d'Aosta. Peeking up through the ondulating hills at the bottom of the valley, its stern facade hides frescoes and beautiful glimpses of courtly life. Further along is Nus, the town that gives its name to Vin de Nus, one of the most interesting vine species in the valley.

In Quart, the well-known winery "Maison Vigneronne Frères Grosjean" offers wine tasting. Then, leaving the route to go to Saint Christophe, one arrives at the hotel-restaurant "Casale" which is bright and calm. This important stop on the wine and food tour serves the Buon Ricordo selection *pasticcio di fontina su letto di fonduta* (*fontina* on a bed of melted cheese).

AOSTA. Where the valley is at its widest we cross through the entry arch of *Augusta Praetoria*. Remains of the ancient city can be found within the walls. Then leaping forward a thousand years you come to the Middle Ages when pilgrims made their way to the Cathedral and the Collegiate

Gran Paradiso park: ibex

WINE
PRODUCERS

Arnad
La Kiuva
at Ville
☎ 0125966351
Chambave
Crotta di
Vegneron
piazza Roncas 2
☎ 016646670
Donnas
Caves
Coopératives
de Donnas
via Roma 97
☎ 0125807096
Morgex
Cave du
Vin Blanc de
Morgex et
de La Salle
at Les Iles
La Ruine
☎ 0165800331
Quart
Maison
Vigneronne
Frères Grosjean
at Ollignan 1
☎ 0165765283
Villeneuve
Renato
Anselmet
at La Crête 46
☎ 016595217

SHOPPING

Aosta
La Bottega degli
Antichi Sapori
via Porte
Pretoriane 63
☎ 0165239666
*Charcuterie and
typical cheeses;
wide selection of
distilled spirits.*

Church of Sant'Orso. It is here that, having fulfilled cultural obligations, you can stop for a rest: the *piazza* of the massive village church is also the home of "Taberna ad Forum", which is the headquarters of the *Enoteca Regionale* (Regional Wine Cellar Organisation). The restaurant was built in the fifteenth century and, as its name suggests, remains of the Roman Forum can be seen in the cellar; a nearly complete listing of regional wines may also be found to accompany a typical light meal. For a more substantial meal, we recommend "Vecchio Ristoro", which is located in a mill and where a young couple prepares elegant and creative dishes, some with Valtellinese influences (given the Valtellinese) origin of its owner. Anyone with a predilection for regional cuisine should make a note of the restaurant "Vecchia Aosta", which is set into the Roman wall. The shops carry all the regional products. Cheeses include *fontina*, but also the less common *reblec*. In the charcuteries you can find *boudin* (blood sausage made with *lardo* pork, boiled potatoes and herbs) and sausages in oil made from a blend of beef and pork meats; *mocetta* is a salt-cured meat, which can be either goat or beef. In the pastry shops you should buy *tegole* (thin layers of pastry with almonds), which are sometimes covered with chocolate. In Gressan, just outside the city, we recommend "Hostellerie de la Pomme Couronné". The place is straight out of a fairy tale, and apple is the main feature on the menu. For an excursion, we suggest the "Institut Agricole Régional", which was founded and is still run by Canons of Saint Bernard. The cellar (which puts its label on DOC and table wines from ancient grapevines) and the farm (with production and sale of cheese and fruit) are both open to visitors. Equally interesting is the Centro Agricolo Dimostrativo di Saint-Marcel, in the hamlet of Lillaz, for its medicinal herbs, honey and garden vegetables.

COLLE DEL SAN BERNARDO. The climb to the pass provides spectacular panoramas and several interesting places to stop and discover gastronomic treats. The first stop is at Gignod where we recommend the hotel-restaurant "La Clusaz" for its excellent Valle d'Aosta cuisine in the simplicity of an old-fashioned inn. On the menu are *crostini caldi con burro e mocetta* (hot crusts of bread with butter and dried goat's meat), *pancetta con castagne e pane di segale* (bacon with chestnuts and rye bread), *soupe valpellinentze* (soup Valpellinestyle, with bread, boiled cabbage, *fontina* and beef broth), *gnocchetti alla toma di Gressoney* (gnocchi with tome from Gressoney) and *carbonade con patate e polenta grigliata* (marinated beef stew with potatoes and grilled *polenta*). At Allein, *polenta* and homemade cheeses are always available at the *agriturismo* establishment "Lo Ratelé". By calling ahead it is also possible to try valley specialties and tasty meats from the farm. Finally, there are the old *baite* (Alpine huts) of Saint-Rhémy-en-Bosses. Locals are proud of *Jambon de Bosses*, a rare *prosciutto* that is the result of

summer mountain grazing. In the village we recommend the rustic hotel "Suisse", which has preserved the feel of the original inn that once hosted wayfarers in the seventeenth century. The excursion concludes with a visit to the *Ospizio*, a hospice founded by Saint Bernard, and its interesting archaeological museum.

SARRE. As we leave Aosta, Sarre's Savoy castle comes into sight among fields and terraced vineyards. Going off the road that leads to Cogne, we go up to Aymavilles to find the "Cave des Onze Communes", which is a treasure trove of information about the wines of the Valle d'Aosta. Wines may be tasted and bought here and it is possible to take walks through the vineyards. Conceived along the same lines, "Les Crêtes" is one of the most innovative farms in the region. Further ahead, in Saint-Pierre, the restaurant "La Tour" offers two good menus – gourmand and traditional – as well as a wide selection of wines. The store "Pain de Coucou" is the outlet for the Cooperativa dei Frutticoltori Valdostani (The Valle d'Aosta's fruit growers' cooperative). Here you will find Martin sec pears in syrup or wine, dried apples, medicinal herbs, cheeses,

SHOPPING

Aosta
Maison de la Fontine
via Monsignor De Sales 14
☎ 0165235651
Charcuterie and cheeses.
Pasticceria Nelva
via Porta Pretoria 42
☎ 0165363738
Pastries, cookies and sweets.
Arnad
Salumificio Bertolin
at Extraz
via Nazionale 11
☎ shop: 0125966212,
company offices: 0125699127
Charcuterie such as "lardo" from Arnad; "mocetta", "coppa" and "teuteun".
Cogne
La Cave de Cogne
via Bourgeois 50
☎ 016574498
Wines, distilled spirits (Genepy, aromatic "grappa"); honey, jam, candies; vinegar, goat's milk cheeses.
Pasticceria Perret
via Bourgeois 57
☎ 016574009
Typical pastries and cookies such as "Mecoulin", "tegole" and "cogneins".

Courmayeur. The village of Dolonne

SHOPPING

Courmayeur
Caffè della Posta
via Roma 51
☎ 0165842272
Donnas
Chappoz
Bonne Vallée
cascina Mamy
at Clapey
☎ 0125804098
*Local products
such as maize,
flour for "polenta",
chestnut flour for
biscuits, rye bread.*
Nicoletta
via Selve 1
☎ 0125806032
Typical cheeses.
Gressan
Centrale
Latière d'Aoste
at La Cure de
Chevrot 7/a
☎ 0165266101
*Milk, butter and
typical cheeses.*
La Salle
Macelleria
Salumeria Ottoz
via Gerbollier 1
☎ 0165861165
*Charcuterie
and cheeses.
Piedmont meat
and traditional
dishes.*
Morgex
Artari
via Valdigne 55
☎ 0165809707
*Famous for wines,
liquors and sweets.*
Nus
Maison Rosset
via Risorgimento 39
☎ 0165767176
*Good choice of
traditional breads.*

salamis and handicrafts. The *agriturismo* establishment "Les Ecureuils" is also worth a visit for its specialty goat's cheese, salamis and soup.

COGNE. This village has an important mining history but currently lends itself to tourism. It has maintained a genuine historical atmosphere in which the hunting lodge of Vittorio Emanuele II is key. As this is at the gates of the national park "Gran Paradiso", we recommend an inn at Valnontey called "Petit Dahu", which is well located for hiking in the mountains (self-organized). At the edge of the residential area is the hotel "Bellevue", which is elegant and secluded and offers delightful food at its restaurant "Le Petit Restaurant". "Lou Ressignon", with its antique furnishings and personnel in local dress, is also worth visiting for its cooking, which closely follows local tradition. Its offerings include *soupetta cogneintze* (a Cogne valley specialty made with cubes of rye

bread and *fontina* with beef broth and rice) and goat's meat with the buttery, cheesy *polenta concia*.

VILLENEUVE. In the shade of Châtel Argent is the farm "Renato Anselmet", renowned for its involvement in environmental causes and for its wines from a late grape harvest. A bit further along lies Arvier with its spectacular terraced "Enfer" (hell) vineyards, known as such because the sun beats down making it hotter than hellfire and giving force to the prized wine of the same name. In the village you will find "Café du Bourg", a pleasant wine bar with a kitchen that serves wine by the glass.

Prié Blanc

VALSAVARENCHE. At Introd two valleys, the Valsavarenche and the Val di Rhêmes, meet and penetrate into the heart of Gran Paradiso national park. Going up the Valsavarenche "A l'Hostellerie du Paradis" is a good place to stop for its vacation-house atmosphere and family-style cooking at good prices. *Carbonade* (a meat dish with red wine) and *fonduta* are not to be missed.

MORGEX. Beyond the Pierre Taillée strait is Alta Valle where Blanc de Valdigne, an exceptionally high quality type of grape, flourishes even at 1200 meters. Visit the "Cave du Vin Blanc de Morgex et de La Salle", a big, high-tech *baita* (mountain hut) with a restaurant. In the village it is worth seeking out the hundred-year-old colonial grocery store "Artari", where wine, liquors and sweets are sold, as well as the historic "Café Quinson", now called "Vieux Bistrot", which serves as a bar, wine bar and restaurant.

COURMAYEUR. In the Middle Ages, this village was the capital of the Alta Valle. Then, in the eighteenth century, the Alpinists of Mont Blanc and *the first* vacationers began to frequent it. Today, it is equipped with means for crossing the *Mer de Glace* glacier and going to Chamonix in France on one of the most classic excursions. In the center, "Caffè

della Posta (1911)" has a monumental seventeenth-century fireplace and mementos of illustrious names in Alpinism. The next stage brings us to "Glarey", a pastry shop famous for *baci di Courmayeur* (literally Courmayeur kisses, or pastries). For a good meal, "Grill Royal e Golf", at a hotel of the same name, is excellent. Two menus are offered: a traditional one that includes *medaglione di capriolo con sala al ginepro* (goat's meat medallions with juniper sauce), and a creative one with *petto di piccione con rösti di patate e cipolle al ragù di finferli* (pigeon breast with potato pancake and onions with wild mushroom ragout). A final word of advice to those who wish to take a break from civilization: go to "Beau Séjour" at Pré-Saint-Didier. This rustic inn offers an enchanting panoramic vista and excellent cooking.

Fontina

SHOPPING

Saint-Christophe
Coop. Produttori
Latte e Fontina
at Croix Noire 10
☎ 016535714
Shops at:
Brusson,
☎ 0125300223;
Cogne,
☎ 016574466;
Pré-Saint-Didier,
☎ 016587850
Fontina (exclusively produced using the milk from Valle d'Aosta dairy cows) and "fonduta".
Saint-Marcel
La Valdotaine
Zona Industriale 12
☎ 0165768919
Genepy, "grappa", distilled spirits and a wide range of specialties based on "grappa" (marrons glacés, chocolates, fruit preserves and jam).
Saint-Pierre
Pain de Coucou
at Cognein 6
☎ 0165903436
Cheeses, charcuterie, medicinal herbs, fruit preserves and jam.
Saint-Vincent
Pasticceria
Benedetto
via Chanoux 27
☎ 0166512177
Pastries and cookies such as the famous "torcettini" from Sain-Vincent.
Pasticceria
Morandin
via Chanoux 105
☎ 0166512690
Famous for candies, "fondants", fruit jellies.

Pezzata Rossa cows from Valle d'Aosta

TAKE WITH YOU THE TASTE OF THE MOUNTAINS

Buy Fontina at the chalets of the Cooperativa Produttori Latte e Fontina or in the best shops. From alpine pastures to your table: to remember how beautiful Valle d'Aosta is …. and how good.

Chalet outlets:
- Saint Christophe - Phone +39 0165 35714
- Pré Saint Didier - Phone +39 0165 87850
- Cogne - Phone +39 0165 74466

Warehouses:
- Issogne - 380 m asl: *42,000 cheeses*
- Montjovet - 420 m asl: *18,000 cheeses*
- Palleusieux - 1,200 m asl: *11,000 cheeses*
- Pré Saint Didier - 1,000 m asl: *11,500 cheeses*
- Saint Pierre - 730 m asl: *5,000 cheeses*
- Valgrisenche - 1,700 m asl: *6,000 cheeses*
- Valpelline - 1,147 m asl: *62,000 cheeses*

FONTINA COOPERATIVA PRODUTTORI LATTE E FONTINA Soc. Coop a r.l.
11020 Saint-Christophe (Ao) Italy Loc. Croix Noire, 10 - Phone +39 0165 35714-40551 Fax +39 0165 236467

Excitement rides on the river!

Tasting at the Morgex co-operative wine grower's association of the famous Fontina cheese and the Vin Blanc de Morgex La Salle, the white wine made from Europe's highest altitude vineyards.

Navigate with us… www.rafting.it

Morgex headquarters

Via St. Marc 5
11017 Morgex (AO)
Tel. (39) 0165 800088
Fax (39) 0165 809977

Valsesia headquarters

Via Isola 3
13020 Vocca (VC)
Tel. (39) 0163 560957
Cell. 348 0053978

E-mail: rafting@rafting.it

ITALIAN WINE TRAVELS
TRAVEL AGENCY - TOUR OPERATOR

Via S.G. Cafasso 41
CASTELNUOVO DON BOSCO (Asti)
Tel. +39 011 9927028
Fax +39 011 9927144
E-mail: iwt@castelnuovodonbosco.it

Discovering lands,
culture, tradition,
cuisine and wines
throughout Italy
and all over the world.

Group trips
organized on request.

JOURNEYS THROUGH THE HILLS

ASSOCIAZIONE "ALTO MONFERRATO"

Registered office
c/o the Town Hall, Via Torino, 69 - 15076 OVADA (AL)

Secretary's office:
via San Paolo 35/1 - 15076 OVADA (AL)
Tel. & Fax +39 0143 822102

PIEDMONT HAUTE CUISINE WITH TRUFFLES

In Piedmont, wine and food tourism is taken seriously, with great wines and truffles as the big attraction in a scenery that spans from mountains to the plane of river Po. An authentic pleasure for the real gourmet.

It is said that Piedmont comes into its own in fall, the time for truffles and for harvesting the Nebbiolo grapes which go into Piedmont's great reds. Featuring wild game, pheasants, partridge and hare, as well as *cardo gobbo* (thistle), Piedmont cooking is simple and tasty.

THE PASTURES, THE VINEYARD, THE RICE FIELDS

From the summits of Monviso and Monte Rosa to the banks of the Po, Piedmont is a region of great variety. The mountains run from the woods of the Apennines to Alpine glaciers and act as a backdrop to the production of beef and milk. The sector boasts valuable local breeds, from 'fat-thighed' Bianca Piemontese cattle to Langhe and Biellese sheep. The hills are covered with vineyards, vegetable gardens and orchards. To the east are the rugged areas of Le Langhe and Monferrato and to the west the rolling foothills of the Alps. Nebbiolo grapes are used for the outstanding wines such as Barolo, Barbaresco, Gattinara and Ghemme. The flatlands between Novara, Vercelli and Lombardy's Pavia constitute Italy's rice belt, where the most prized varieties – Arborio, Carnaroli, Vialone nano – are cultivated.

GREAT WINES, EXCELLENT CHEESES

The figures support Piedmont's reputation as a world wine region. Thanks to the high-quality and prolific Nebbiolo and Barbera grapes, there are seven excellent DOCG (*Denominazione di Origine Controllata e Garantita*) wines and 42 very good DOC (*Denominazione di Origine Controllata*) wines, as well as international wines including Pinot Bianco, Chardonnay, Müller Thurgau and experimental new blends. Cheese is important, with six exclusive DOP productions (*Denominazione di Origine Protetta*), but Piedmont is also famous for wild products, including truffles (especially white), mushrooms and snails.

THE FUTURE OF SMALL TOWNS LIES IN QUALITY

Piedmont is a mosaic of 1,209 small communities located in the hills and mountains. For these centers, agriculture is often the only viable economic means offered by the environment. But this market has also given rise to gourmet tourism inspired by the fine products found here. In 1995, Piedmont began a program for ecologically friendly agriculture to respect and protect the balance of nature.

A GASTRONOMIC TRADEMARK: THE TRUFFLE

Piedmont's gastronomy is so tied to the white truffle that any dish using it becomes *alla piemontese*, or in Piedmont style. Other top local products include, rice, vegetables and milk products, as well as meats, wild game and even wine, which come together in rich preparations, such as *fondute, risotti, bollito, fritto misto* (mixed fry), *lepre in civet* (hare stew) and *lumache al Barbera* (snails in Barbera wine sauce).

Monferrato countryside

Piedmont - Typical products

Scale 1: 1 500 000

0 _____ 40 km

🧀 CHEESES

1. **Gorgonzola Dop.**
   In the provinces of Novara, Vercelli, Cuneo and in Casale Monferrato. Also in Lombardia.

2. **Bra Dop.**
   In Bra in Roero and in general in the Cuneese valleys.

3. **Castelmagno Dop.**
   In Castelmagno, Pradleves and Monterosso Grana.

4. **Grana Padano Dop.**
   In the provinces of Asti, Cuneo, Novara, Torino and Vercelli.

5. **Murazzano Dop.**
   In Murazzano in the Belbo vallys and in various other parts of the Alta Langa

6. **Raschera Dop.**
   Throughout Cuneo province

7. **Robiola di Roccaverano Dop.**
   In 19 centers in Monferrato

8. **Taleggio Dop.**
   In Novara province.

9. **Toma Piemontese Dop.**
   Throughout the alpine valleys.

10. **Ossolano**

11. **Robiola d'Alba**

🥩 MEATS

1. **Fassone del Piemonte.**
   Throughout Piedmont and part of the Ligurian provinces of Imperia and Savona.

🫙 VARIOUS

1. **Nocciola del Piemonte.**
   Hazelnut from the Alta Langa and various other centers in the region.

2. **Marrone Valsusa.**
   Chestnut from the moutainous zones in the Susa valley

3. **Olio Essenziale di Menta Piperita Piemonte.**
   Peppermint essential oil from the Torino district of Pancalieri.

🍞 BREAD AND SWEETS

1. **Torrone Asti.**
   Nougat from Asti province.

🍇 DOCG WINES

1. **Asti**
2. **Barbaresco**
3. **Barolo**
4. **Brachetto d'Acqui**
5. **Gattinara**
6. **Gavi**
7. **Ghemme**

🍇 DOC WINES

8. **Albugnano**
9. **Barbera d'Alba**
10. **Barbera d'Asti**
11. **Barbera del Monferrato**
12. **Boca**
13. **Bramaterra**
14. **Canavese**
15. **Carema**
16. **Colli Tortonesi**
17. **Colline Novaresi**
18. **Colline Saluzzesi**
19. **Cortese dell'Alto Monferrato**
20. **Coste della Sesia**
21. **Dolcetto d'Acqui**
22. **Dolcetto d'Alba**
23. **Dolcetto d'Asti**
24. **Dolcetto delle Langhe Monregalesi**
25. **Dolcetto di Diano d'Alba**
26. **Dolcetto di Dogliani**
27. **Dolcetto di Ovada**
28. **Erbaluce di Caluso**
29. **Fara**
30. **Freisa d'Asti**
31. **Freisa di Chieri**
32. **Gabiano**
33. **Grignolino d'Asti**
34. **Grignolino del Monferrato Casalese**
35. **Langhe**
36. **Lessona**
37. **Loazzolo**
38. **Malvasia di Casorzo d'Asti**
39. **Malvasia di Castelnuovo Don Bosco**
40. **Monferrato**
41. **Nebbiolo d'Alba**
42. **Piemonte**
43. **Pinerolese**
44. **Roero**
45. **Rubino di Cantavenna**
46. **Ruché di Castagnole Monferrato**
47. **Sizzano**
48. **Valsusa**
49. **Verduno Pelaverga**
50. **Collina Torinese**

TURIN

A gastronomic tour in the province of Turin takes you from the city's cosmopolitan environment to the ethnic traditions of Alpine minorities.

More than half of the province of Turin is organized around the ridge of the Cottian and Graian Alps. Shaped by glaciers, the rough and rocky landscape spreads from the foothills of these Alps and is dotted with small lakes. The largest hill is the Serra d'Ivrea, which defines the Canavese district. Beyond the flatlands rise the Collina Torinese, a hill on the Po River, and the foothills of Monferrato, making for an interesting mix of natural and man-made landscapes. The Alpine lands are interesting for the vibrant sheep-rearing economy and the Provençal traditions followed the Valdesi and Susa valleys. Wine production brings life to the hills, which are varied by the terraced vines of the red Carema at the mouth of the Valle d'Aosta, the white Erbaluce di Caluso in the gentle landscape of Ivrea, the typically Piedmontese DOC Valsusa

Opposite: Turin.
The Mole Antonelliana

and Pinerolese vineyards, and the undulating vines of red Fresia di Chieri grapes. The flatlands are cultivated or used to rear cattle. As for a good meal, the regional capital offers both traditional Savoy cuisine and regional cooking from a wider area. The further one goes away from the city, the more local traditions take over in the many pleasant restaurants in the Piedmont mountains.

Gourmet Tours

TURIN. "A bit old, a bit provincial, but fresh with Parisian charm nonetheless..." This is how Guido Gozzano described the city in 1911, and his lines encapsulate all the nineteenth century charm of the capital of the Savoy kingdom. Starting with a visit to the Palazzo Madama, which traces the city's history, there are many places of cultural interest. We also recommend you visit the historic gourmet haunts dotted around the area. First on the list is the restaurant "Del Cambio" (established 1757), which was mentioned by Casanova and frequented by Count Cavour. Amid a décor of red velvet, stuccoes and gilding, this restaurant still offers what is considered to be the city's best cooking, impeccable service and

HOTELS AND RESTAURANTS

Turin
Grand Hotel Sitea ★★★
Carignano ¶¶¶¶
via Carlo Alberto 35
☎ 0115170171
Del Cambio ¶¶¶¶
piazza Carignano 2
☎ 011546690
Neuv Caval 'd Brôns ¶¶¶¶
piazza S. Carlo 151
☎ 0115627483
Turin Palace Hotel ★★★
via Sacchi 8
☎ 0115625511
Balbo ¶¶¶
via A. Doria 11
☎ 0118395775
Piemontese ★★★
via Berthollet 21
☎ 0116698101
La Prima Smarrita ¶¶¶
corso Unione Sovietica 244
☎ 0113179657
Victoria ★★★
via N. Costa 4
☎ 0115611909
Ij Brandé ¶¶
via Massena 5
☎ 011537279
L'Agrifoglio ¶¶
via Accademia Albertina 38/d
☎ 011837064
San Giorgio ¶¶
viale E. Millo 6
☎ 0116692131
Savoia ¶¶
via Corte d'Appello 13
☎ 0114362288
Antiche Sere ¶
via Cenischia 9
☎ 0113854347
Capannina ¶
via V. Donati 1
☎ 011545405

first-class wines. For those who prefer a picturesque setting, a stop at the restaurant "San Giorgio "(est. 1884), in the pseudo-medieval village of Valentino, is a must (a sampling menu is available at "Taverna del Borgo" downstairs). For a romantic stay, we recommend "Turin Palace" (est. 1872), with its good traditional restaurant where dishes include the classic *ravioli al plin* (*ravioli* with veal and pork). The city is famous for its pastries and candies – chocolates in particular – which have been produced on a large scale here since the eighteenth century. "Al Bicerin" (est. 1763) has a house specialty (coffee, chocolate and milk cream) of the same name and offers *zabaione al ratafià* (zabaione with a local fruit or nut-flavored liqueur). Then, listed chronologically, there are: the ice-cream shop "Firoio" (est.

Turin. *"Del Cambio" restaurant*

1780); the candy and pastry shop "Fratelli Stratta" (est. 1836); the pastry shop "Baratti & Milano" (est. 1875); the candy shop "Avvignano" (est. 1883); the cafe-restaurant "Torino" (est. 1903); and the cafe "Mulassano" (est. 1907). Modern gastronomy is represented by "Balbo", which offers traditional Piedmont cooking and creative dishes, many with fish. On the menu you can find *filetto di trota salmonata in carpione di Moscato* (salmon trout filet marinated in Muscat wine); *tagliatelle nere con cozze, vongole e brocoletti* (squid-ink *tagliatelle* with mussels, clams and broccoli); *triglie al Pinot Nero* (red mullet with Pinot Nero). The "Neuv Caval 'd Brôns" restaurant serves the great classics, with special attention to *lumache* (snails), but also has a well-priced sampling menu. "Grand Hotel Sitea", with its restaurant "Carignano", is

Bricherasio.
Pinerolese vineyard

an excellent choice for a night's stay and a good meal.

More affordable restaurants include "Savoia", a new restaurant with modern cooking and an *enoteca*, "Gli Infernotti dello Juvara". "Antiche Sere" is a traditional *trattoria* where guests are seated under a pergola and offered excellent regional wines and dishes. The traditional "Ij Brandé" is also a good bet. As for a bed for the night, two three-star hotels, the "Piemontese" and "Victoria", outshine all others.

If you want to buy typical products, go to the "Fratelli steffanone", founded in 1890, and the gourmet store "Baudracco", which offers anything from *antipasti* to sweets displayed across four windows on Corso Vittorio Emanuele. In the bakeries Turin's celebrated *grissini* – the unmistakable fragrant and slightly powdery handmade breadsticks – may be found alongside other typical breads such as *biova* and *mica piemontese* as well as the rare *gavasot*, which is hand made in the shape of a doll's neck and head, and *paisanotte*, shaped like an open book and brought to the city by workers from the mountains. Buy dreamy *gianduiotti* and other chocolates from "Peyrano".

1. The Susa Valley and the Chisone Valley

RIVOLI. The Savoy Castle dominates the hills formed by the ancient glacier that carved out the Susa Valley. In local pastry shops you can find *torcetti*, which are special puff pastry sweets, while nearby Pianezza offers the characteristic *paste meliga* (pasta made of corn flour). Beautiful routes lead to the Avigliana lakes, where a typical dish is *tinca* (tench, a European freshwater fish), and to Giaveno, which is known for its pears.

SACRA DI SAN MICHELE. One of Piedmont's most interesting monuments is this abbey, built into Monte Pirchiano. On the road again, we come to the DOC Valsusa vineyards. In Borgone, the winery "Carlotta" offers the inter-

WINE PRODUCERS

**Giaglione
Marco Martina**
at San Rocco 10
☎ 012231320
**Gravere
Vitivinicola Sibille**
regione Colfacero 1
☎ 0122622744
**Moncucco
Torinese
Bottega del Vino**
via Mosso 6
☎ 0119874765

SHOPPING

**Turin
Confetteria
Avvignano**
piazza Carlo Felice 50
☎ 011541992
"Confetto" pastries.
**Pasticceria
Baratti & Milano**
piazza Castello 29
☎ 0115613060
*Pastries, candies
and sweets.*
**Gastronomia
Baudracco**
corso V. Emanuele 62
☎ 011545582
Gourmet store.
Al Bicerin
piazza della
Consolata 5
☎ 0114369325
Pastries and sweets.
**Macelleria
Curletti**
corso Moncalieri 47
☎ 0116602177
Regional meat.
**Pasticceria
Falchero**
via S. Massimo 4
☎ 0118173077
Almond pastries.

esting red wine Rocca del Lupo that weds Barbera with the indigenous Avanà. SUSA. At the foot of Rocciamelone (3,538 meters/ 11,607 feet), where the routes of Moncenesio and Monginevro converge, is Susa. Although troops and pilgrims have constantly passed through here, it has preserved its Roman past in the Arch of Augustus and its medieval past in its Cathedral. You must take home some *toma* cheese from the Susa Valley. The Novalesa pass is recommended for an excursion: here, you can visit the Benedictine abbey and buy products from the Alpine pastures, including the Blu del Moncenisio, a soft cheese similar to Reblochon, and the rare Murianengo, or the buttery Muriennais, which is marbled with green mold.

SAUZE D'OULX. This small alpine village dates back to a time when a delicate rose preserve – possibly the legacy of the ancient Saracen rule – was made here. The hotels and villas portray the image of a lively ski resort. In the summer, *belgiunn*, a kind of straw-colored, granular *ricotta* cheese comes down from the pastures of San Sicario. The woods of Grande Bosco di Salbertrand are not far, and further up is the village of Bardonecchia, which is crowned by the woods and summits of the Cottian Alps. Here, we recommend two places: the hotel "Bucaneve" is good for a short stay in a friendly atmosphere, and for lunch, the restaurant "La Ciaburna" is characteristic of the region and serves traditional local dishes. SESTRIERE. From the route to

Monginevro go up to the depression between the summits rising from the Dora Riparia Valley and the Chisone Valley. Sestriere's most famous landmarks are the hotel towers built in 1928, when the elegant ski resort was founded. Here you can get cheeses from nearby Cesana, in particular Thures cheese, and from Pragelato comes excellent honey as well as *toma* cheese from Alpe Rocca del Grand Puj. Further down in the valley Perosa Argentina supplies wonderful cherries.

PINEROLO. The upper village at the peak preserves the memory of the Acaji, the branch of the Savoy dynasty that made it the capital of its lands. Here we find the late Gothic church of San Maurizio, with its tall campanile, and the *palazzi* attesting to the hundred-year-old rule of the Acaji. Further down, in the center of the old town is the Duomo, built in typical Piedmont style. *Funghi* (mushrooms), in particular the *porcini* (boletus) type, *lumache* (snails) and cheeses are to be found on every local table. Sannen goat's milk is made into creamy cheeses, some wrapped in chestnut leaves or aged in ashes (French-style). These are produced by "Capreria Occitana", which is located in the Abbadia Alpina and also manages a restaurant where dishes are made with *grano saraceno* (buck wheat), *farro* (spelt, a type of wheat), and other naturally cultivated products. Two dairy products worthy of mention are *seirass del Lausun*, a very fresh cheese made in cloth bags, and the *tomini del Talucco*, made in the Alps of the same name. In the local bakeries you can find *giaco*, a long-lasting bread shaped like a double triangle in the form of a book. We highly recommend an excursion to the Provençal valleys. The gastronomic highlight there is Vaudois cuisine in Torre Pellice at "Flipot", where creative dishes are painstakingly prepared. The menu is marked by *zuppetta d'orzo e porcini* (barley and boletus mushroom soup), *stufato di montone al timo serpillo* (stewed mutton with wild thyme), *trotella della Comba in crosta di funghi* (trout from the Comba covered with mushrooms), *bianco mangiare al latte di pecora* (blancmange made with sheep's milk). Other flavors may be discovered on short excursions from Pinerolo. In Cavour, you find excellent meat and an old tradition of *salame cotto con le verze* (salami cooked with Savoy cabbage), excellent apples and, in the pastry shops, there are *cavourrini al rum* (rum chocolates). Here, Silvio Brasda has perfected a series of original and unforgettable cured cichs ranging from *salami al Barolo* and *al Barbaresco* to *coppa di testa cotta nel Marsala* (a salami of pork cooked in sweet Marsala wine). In Cumiana, peaches and apples are stuffed with *amaretti* biscuits and spices and baked. In Pancalieri, peppermint is grown and liquors are produced locally. In Villafranca Piemonte, try the hard and tender Bra cheese.

2. The hill of Turin and Po

MONCALIERI. On the last peak of the Turin Hills, this village has preserved its castle and, further down, its historic center, which testifies to the attractive residences that once surrounded the Savoy capital. Good gourmet opportunities may be found here, particularly at "Rosa Rossa", which is also the headquarters of the "Confraternità della Trippa" (a sort of dining club of tripe lovers) and distributor of a special salami. Or you could continue to Carmagnola and take a seat at the elegant restaurant of the same name. On the way, admire the spectacle of locally-grown peppers laid out for sale on tables. Other excellent products include an early variety of Santena asparagus with pinkish-white tips called d'Argenteuil (available from mid-April to end-June). There are also Pecetto cherries at the June fruit fair. In Caringnano you will find tasty *zesti* – candied orange and lemon rinds.

CHIERI. At the foot of the eastern slopes of the Turin hill, looking across the plain you can glimpse the first ondulating hills of Monferrato. The landscape is marked by important Gothic monuments and the traces of the equally important wine production – particularly of Freisa wines. A tour of the museum and wine cellars at "Martini & Rossi", the historic producer of vermouth and liquors, is a must. In the surrounding area, we recommend two places to find wine: "Balbiano" winery at Andezano and the "Bottega del Vino" at Moncucco Torinese, which is paired with "Trattoria della Freisa". Another local specialty is *cardo* (thistle – a gigantic, tender,

Freisa grapes

SHOPPING

Turin
Emporio di Olivola
via Monte di Pietà 15
☎ 011541421
Regional specialties.
Gelateria Fiorio
via Po 8
☎ 0118173225
Ice-creams.
Florilegio
corso Dante 59/d
☎ 0116505511
Charcuterie.
Gastronomia G. Gallo
corso Sebastopoli 161
☎ 0111362597
Gourmet store.
Guido Gobino Cioccolato - Lab. Artigianale del Giandujotto
via Cagliari 15/a
☎ 0112476245
Since 1946, candies, chocolates, gianduja.
Caffè Mulassano
piazza Castello 15
☎ 0111547990
Cafe and pastry shop.
Pasticceria Peyrano
corso V. Emanuele 76
☎ 0111538765
Since 1915, pastries, chocolates and candies.
Salumeria F.lli Steffanone
via Maria Vittoria 2
☎ 0111546737
Since 1890, mushrooms, truffles, regional cheeses, wines, olive oil and vinegar.

49

white variety that is one of the best in the region for *bagna caôda*, a side dish made with anchovies and butter). If you wish to venture to the southern regions of the province, visit Pralormo. Here, the *trattorie* serve dishes made with *cardo* and the fish dish *tinche del lago della Spina* (tench from Lake Spina). *Pampavia* cookies can be found in the pastry shops.

SUPERGA. Leave the route which cuts through the hill to follow the line of the ridge that leads to Superga. At the Juvarra Basilica, a majestic jewel set into the hill, you can find a crypt with Savoy tombs dating back to the time of king Charles Albert. From here, go down to the Po, and on the way stop at "La Griglia", in Pino Torinese, or "Bontan" in San Mauro.

CHIVASSO. Following the Po river – if you have time make detours to Bosco del Vaj and the church of San Genesio – you arrive at this small, industrious city. The local specialty is *nocciolini*, or tiny,

sweet *amaretto* cookies. If you continue to Volpiano, visit the fish restaurant "La Noce", where the chef offers *battuto di pescatrice all'olio aromatizzato* (angler fish with aromatic olive oil), *linguine all'astice* (linguine with lobster), *mezzancolle e capesante con indivia e alloro* (shrimp and scallops with endive and bay leaf). Returning from the detour, you should try another gastronomic curiosity, *cipolle ripiene* (stuffed onions). The village of Settimo Torinese claims to have invented this delicacy, which is prepared with large yellow onions stuffed with chopped onions enriched with cheese, egg, butter pepper and *acquavita di pesca* (peach brandy).

3. The Canavese

CALUSO. Around this charming Citta del Vino (city of wine), which overlooks Lake Candia, spread the vineyards for "Erbaluce" – the village's exclusive white wine. We strongly recommend the restaurant "Gardenia", where traditional dishes are prepared with a modern twist. Also noteworthy are the *salami di*

SHOPPING

Turin
Confetteria
Pasticceria
F.lli Stratta
piazza S. Carlo 191
☎ 011541567
Confetto pastries and cookies.
Pasticceria Torino
piazza S. Carlo 204
☎ 011545118
Sweets and pastries.
Buriasco
Silvano Galfione
regione Canali 4
☎ 012156423
Sheep's milk cheeses such as tometti, caciotta and 'sairass d'l fen.
Giaveno
La Credenza dei Vecchi Sapori
via Coazze 109/bis
☎ 0119363724
Honey and fruit creams, apple fresh juices.
Ivrea
Macelleria Salumeria Gastronomia
F.lli Giordano
corso Cavour 78
☎ 012549037
Piedmont's meats; pork sausages; stuffed chicken, rabbit and duck. From October to April, the typical 'potatos salami'.

Lake Campagna near Cascinette d'Ivrea

patata, a blend of pork and potato, which are a tasty legacy from a more impoverished past.

IVREA. "The red towers reflect the beautiful Ivrea and dream of the sky-blue Dora in its ample bosom...," wrote the poet Giosue Carducci. The land is "excellent for mushrooms that last a day and absences of one night...," his fellow poet Guido Gozzano emphasized. Backed by such introductions, the city presents itself as an ideal starting point for discovering the Canavese, a hill district with well-defined aromas. At restaurants the cuisine is *alla Canavesane*, with rice bound by three kinds of cheese, soup thick with bread and cabbage, tender *coniglio con patate* (rabbit with potatoes) and *faseui a la tofeja* (beans cooked in a pot with pork rind). Shops have excellent salami, either with garlic or in oil, as well as cheeses: *tomini di Chiaverano* (cow's milk cheese) and *tomini Montaleghe* (sheep's milk cheese), *cavrin di Coazze* with its creamy center, and *tomini di Andrate*. Pastry shops purvey *amaretti eporediesi* and *polenta d'Ivrea*, a rustic cake made with corn flour and vanilla.

CAREMA. At the threshold of the Valle d'Aosta is this other Citta del Vino, wedged between terraced vineyards. Here, Nebbiolo battles with the harsh climate to produce a wine with an unforgettable rose flavor.

RIVAROLO CANAVESE. The Statale di Castellamonte crosses the Orco and goes to the castle of Malgrà, a thirteenth-century village keep. Here you can find excellent cheeses from Cuorgnè, made with milk from animals grazing in the Locana Valley and Gran Paradiso's summer alpine pastures.

CIRIÈ. The restaurant we recommend is "Dolce Stil Novo", where two young entrepreneurs offer delicate and creative dishes that reflect the restaurant's name. Higher up are the Lanzo Valleys, where you can get cherries and wild berries from Chialamberto, and a selection of butter and cheeses, including *toma di Balme* and *giunca*, which is a kind of salted ricotta.

SHOPPING

**Luserna
San Giovanni
Cooperativa
Agricola
Terranova**
strada Vecchia
S. Giovanni 65
☎ 0121909474
*Jam, wild berry
juice, honey.*
**Moncalieri
Azienda Agricola
San Matteo**
at Bauducchi 30 bis
☎ 0116409393
*Special jams and
marmelades produced
by the farm of the
same name located
at Giarre.*
**Pinerolo
Capreria
Occitana**
at Abbadia Alpina
via Nazionale 374
☎ 0121201139
Goat's cheeses.

ALESSANDRIA

A land of great wines, Alessandria is known for cooking with a strong regional flavor, accented by touches from across the border.

The province of Alessandria occupies the large south-eastern part of Piedmont, and is bordered to the north by the Po and in the south by the watershed of the Appenino Ligure. To the east, it is bordered by Lombardy (Oltrepò Pavese) and Emilia (the upper Trebbia Valley). Three quarters of the territory is hilly, and the terrain is characterized by a range of hills that runs from Casale Monferrato to Tortona, circling the plain of Alessandria.

These lands produce excellent wines,

including two DOCG wines – Brachetto d'Acqui and Cortese di Gavi – local DOC wines – Dolcetto di Acqui, Dolcetto di Ovada, Gabiano, Rubino di Cantavenna – and district DOC wines – Grignolino del Monferrato Casalese, Cortese dell'Alto Monferrato, Colli Tortonesi. The cuisine is influenced by cooking styles across the border, particularly in the Appenino where olive oil, garlic and anchovies are an old Ligurian legacy. In Valenza, one finds the flavors of Lomellina and in Tortona, those of Pavia and Piacenza. *Funghi* (mushrooms), *tartufi* (truffles), *salumi* (charcuterie) and cheeses are the distinctive features of the provincial cuisine. Everywhere, the tradition of small pastries is very much alive, with *baci di dama, amaretti*, chocolates and others.

Gourmet Tours

ALESSANDRIA. The center has the dignified air of the nineteenth century, with baroque details. The design of the city's walls, which have been replaced by wide tree-lined streets, and the citadel, which was built on the other side of the Tanaro in the eighteenth century, betray its military past. The hotel-restaurant "Alli Due Buoi Rossi" (established 1741) also dates back to this time. It is a temple to Pied-

Vineyard in the Basso Monferrato

mont cooking, with careful revisions, and has a predilection for *funghi* and *tartufi* (don't miss *coniglio in peperonata*, or rabbit in pepper sauce). Trademarks of Alessandrian cooking are the *agnolotti di stufato al sugo di stufato* (pasta filled with forcemeat and served with stewing juices), *rabaton di ricotta ed erbe* (ricotta and herb *gnocchi*), an ancient shepherds' dish, and *pollo alla Marengo* (chicken Marengo), of French ancestry. As for charcuterie, the city and the province are known for a cooked salami, which, as well as other fine products, can be bought from the reliable "Salumaio". "La Fermata" and "Il Grappolo" are also worth visiting. These restaurants offer dishes based on traditional flavors. For a good bottle of wine as well as wine tasting by the glass, stop by "Vineria al n° 1".

1. The Po and the lower Monferrato

VALENZA. This village rises on a plateau above the Po with the foothills of Monferrato as its backdrop. It is a city of gold and jewels, thanks to the plethora of goldsmiths that live there. As for local gastronomy, the Lombard

**HOTELS AND
RESTAURANTS**

**San Giorgio
Monferrato**
**Castello di San
Giorgio** ★★★ ¶¶¶
via Cavalli d'Olivola 3
☎ 0142806203
Tortona
**Cavallino San
Marziano** ¶¶¶
corso Romita 83
☎ 0131862308
Valenza
**Enoteca Antico
Caffè Verdi** ¶
piazza Verdi 5
☎ 0131941216

AGRITURISMI

Valenza
🏵 **Cascina Nuova**
Strada per Pavia 2
☎ 0131954763

**WINE
PRODUCERS**

Alfiano Natta
Fattorie Augustus
Castello di Razzano
at Casarello
☎ 0141922426
Gavi
**Castellari
Bergaglio**
at Rovereto 136
☎ 0143644000
**Ozzano
Monferrato**
Cantine Valpane
cascina Valpane 10/1
☎ 0142486713

influence is strong and nearby Lomellina has lent it recipes based on rice, frogs and snails. We recommend "Antico Caffè Verdi", a restaurant with atmosphere where traditional cooking, excellent wines and an interesting sampling menu are available. In Corso Garibaldi, the historic pastry shop "Barberis" (est. 1895) is a must. Everything from the elegant furnishing to the recipes dates from the shop's foundation. CASALE MONFERRATO. Medieval to the core, with its Duomo and synagogue and complex political and military history as a powerful stronghold and de facto capital of Monferrato. Today, the community takes greatest pride in the most typical product of the territory, its wine, Grignolino del Monferrato Casalese. The cooking is the same as that found throughout the foothills, and includes *gnocchi di patate* (potato gnocchi), *agnolotti* (pasta filled with forcemeat), *coniglio ai peperoni* (rabbit with peppers), *bollito misto* (boiled meat) and *fritti salati e dolci* (fried savories and sweets). You can see the inspiration from the Jewish culinary tradition in dishes based on turkey and geese. There are also the flatlands where vegetables are prevalent and the Po, where frogs and snails abound. The restaurant "La Torre" is worth trying: high on the Po, it offers a variety of dishes ranging from traditional to imaginative. In pastry shops you can find *Crumiri*, dry biscuits that are supposed to recall the mustache of Vittorio Emanuele II. *Grissia monferrina*, a hard bread that keeps well, comes

from Pontestura and is good with local salami and cheese.
GABIANO. At the borders with the province of Turin, this village also has its own DOC zone of the same name with 10 hectares that produce Barbaresca wines with a slight tinge of Freisa and Grignolino. This blend may also be found in *Rubino di Cantavenna*, which is produced in a village of the same name. From the banks of the Po, travel to Monferrato. In Cerrina, known for its fruit and vegetable production (asparagus, string beans, peas, strawberries), "Castello di Montalero" is a very pleasant restaurant with excellent wines and an interesting menu. As well as visiting Serralunga di Crea's noteworthy sanctuary, it is also worth taking the detour for "Tenuta la Tenaglia", a farm that is equipped for sampling wine and *agriturismo*. At Alfiano Natta, we recommend "Fattorie Augustus" for the castle-like ambiance and excellent Barbera d'Asti wines. During the cherry season, go to Cereseto.
SAN GIORGIO MONFERRATO. Here we recommend the Hotel "Castello di San Giorgio", which was created from the guest house of a fifteenth-century noble residence. Its elegant, intimate restaurant is one of the best in the province. At Orzano, "Cantine Valpane" offers outstanding Barbera wine and bed & breakfast hospitality. Further along, Rosignano Monferrato, with its historic center of steep and narrow streets, makes for a pleasant pause.
VIGNALE MONFERRATO. This village is remarkable for the "Enocoteca Regionale del Monferrato" that specializes in Barbera and Grignolino wines. Set in a his-

toric palazzo, its cellars – called *infernotti* – are dug into the voclanic rock and its restaurant has an affordable sampling menu. For a longer stop, go to the farm "Giulio Accornero", where you will find excellent wines and a room at the farmhouse.

2. The Colli Tortonesi

TORTONA. Cradled by one of the hills along the Scrivia in the flatlands, Tortona is a bridge to the Oltrepò Pavese. Lombard and Emilian influence are evident at the table in the dishes made with rice, filled pasta and stews, including *agnolotti con ripieno di erbe* (a kind of *ravioli* filled with greens) and *tagliatelle con agliata* (*tagliatelle* with ground walnuts, bread soaked in milk and crushed garlic). The Colli Tortonesi DOC wines are a source of local pride with Barbera and Cortese as the main types, betraying evident cross-border influence. Peaches and cherries usually come from Volpedo and the Grue and Ossona Valleys, vegetables and fresh cheeses from Caldirola, and white and black truffles from the woods feature in *polenta de siouri*, a gratin made with meat juices and cheese. Onions, spinach, different types of celery and melons come from Castelnuovo. In the town, the

Casale Monferrato.
The Torre civica

restaurant "Cavallino San Marziano" serves typical dishes such as *ravioli di zucca* (pumpkin *ravioli*), *carne cruda con fagioli* (raw meat with beans) and *arrosto al vino bianco* (roast with white wine). The restaurant "Forlino", in Montacuto, is in an outstanding setting and offers rustic dishes, including *cosciotto di cinghiale ai profumi di bosco* (leg of boar with specialties from the forest) and local cheeses. It is also possible to stay the night. In Carbonara Scrivia, we recommend the inn "Malpassutti", where delicious bread and *focaccia* baked in a wood-fired oven are just some of the flavors on offer.

3. The Appennino Ligure and Alto Monferrato

NOVI LIGURE. The name recalls the Genoese rule that lasted from 1447 to 1815, and which left its mark on the physiognomy of the village as well as the customs of the people. A typical dish of this mountain so close to the sea is *troffie*, made of durum wheat and chestnut flour, and served with *pesto al basilico* (basil pesto). Equally popular are *corsetti*, a type of round pasta, served with *sugo di funghi e salsiccia* (mushroom and sausage sauce). Soft *torrone al miele* (honey nougat) is excellent, as are *baci di dama* (almond based cookies flavored with vanilla). But the most typical product is *focaccia*

WINE PRODUCERS

Serralunga
di Crea
**Tenuta
La Tenaglia**
via Santuario
di Crea 5
☎ 0142940252
Strevi
Marenco
piazza
V. Emanuele 10
☎ 0144363133
Vignale
Monferrato
Giulio Accornero
Ca' Cima 1
☎ 0142933317

SHOPPING

**Alessandria
Pasticceria
Pittatore**
corso Roma 11
☎ 0131254022
*Pastries and
cookies such as
"Dolce del Convento",
"baci di dama"
and "amaretti".*
Il Salumaio
via Guasco 20
☎ 0131253624
*Local charcuterie,
Italian and French
cheeses; olive oil
and wines.*
Rovida Signorelli
piazza Garibaldi 23
☎ 0131252754
*Sweet and savoury
cookies.*
**Acqui Terme
Olivieri Funghi**
via Carducci 14
☎ 0144322558
*White truffles from
Alba and mushrooms;
truffles and boletus
mushroom paté.*

SHOPPING

Casale Monferrato
Fabbrica Krumiri
via Lanza 17
☎ 0142453030
Produces Krumiri biscuits since the eighteenth century.
Gavi
Traverso Amaretti
via Bertelli 3
☎ 0143642713
"Amaretti" cookies.
Olivola
La Collina Emporio Olivola
piazza Europa 2
☎ 0142928235
Regional specialties such as "bagna caôda". Jams, cookies and biscuits.
Valenza
Emmebi
piazza Verdi 5
☎ 0131941216
Restaurant and "enoteca", serves dishes based on wild game.
Pasticceria Barberis
corso Garibaldi 114
☎ 0131941041
Pastries and sweets.
Pasticceria Torti
Strada al Po 7
☎ 0131941090
Pastries and sweets.
Vignale Monferrato
Azienda Il Mongetto
cascina Mongetto 10
☎ 0142933469
Regional specialties such as "bagna caôda", "bagna du diaul" and "mostarda al vino".

di Novi. Chocolate is also a long-standing tradition. Arquata Scrivia is renowned for its salami production, while bakeries sell *grissini all'olio* (breadsticks) and *canestrelli* (sweet or savoury pastries). "Villa Pomela" is a good inn for spending the night.

GAVI. This is the city of Cortese, Piedmont's most important vine species producing white grapes. Here, it attains such results as to earn DOCG recognition for the Gavi denomination. The village lies along the route of the Bocchetta Pass and has an important Romanesque church and a Ligurian feel that you can also find at the table in *gnocchi al pesto* and *farinata di ceci* (chickpea flatbread). In pastry shops, look out for *canestrelli*, *savoiardi* and distinctive *amaretti di pasta di mandorle* (almond amaretti). "Castellari Bergaglio" is an excellent winery that has been making superb wines for four generations.

OVADA. This village is located on a narrow peninsula formed by the confluence of the Stura and Orba rivers and is one of the fortresses of Dolcetto, which has DOC specification. *Agnolotti in brodo di carne al vino rosso* (ravioli filled with forcemeat in beef broth with red wine) is a characteristic dish. The vegetable soups and a *minestra di cavolo* (cabbage minestrone) are Ligurian. Pastry shops offer Ovada's typical cookies, *farinata* and *castagnaccio* (chestnut cake), which come from the other side of the Apennines. In nearby Molare, *polenta*, *cotechini* (boiled, spiced pork sausage) and *funghi* are dominant during the spring festival.

ACQUI TERME. Here you find curative waters and excellent wines, including the DOCG wine Brachetto, which you can taste together with the DOC wine Dolcetto d'Acqui, at the "Enoteca Regionale del Brachetto", or at one of the best wine producers: "Marenco". In the area there is an abundance of *tartufi bianchi* (white truffles) as well as *mushrooms*, particularly the *porcini* (boletus) and *ovoli* (royal) varieties. A good local cheese is *tomini del Bec*, which used to be made only with goat's milk. Cooking is typically Piedmont, but the flavors that stand out are those with a Ligurian tendency, including aromatic herbs, salted anchovies, olives and pine nuts, all found with pasta and *focaccia*. Addresses to keep in mind are the "Enoteca Osteria la Curia", "Ca' del Vein" and "Antica Osteria da Bigat". Ancient local specialties include the *amaretti* and *baci*. In nearby Ponti, strawberries, peaches and apples are very good. Here, and throughout the Val Bormida, you can find *filetto baciato*, a salami made with the best cut of beef.

ASTI

From Basso to Alto Monferrato,
Girgnolino, Barbera and Moscato are
important players in the hills of Asti.

The prominent geographic element of the province of Asti is the Tanaro, which divides the mostly hilly land into two distinct parts: the Basso and Alto Monferrato which stretches from north of the Tanaro almost to the Po. Contrary to all logic, the Basso (low) Monferrato rises higher than Alto (high) Monferrato, which goes southward between the provinces of Alessandria and Cuneo. It is also more serene, while the Alto Monferrato is more rustic and almost prefaces the landscape of the Langhe. What the two districts have in common is their major wine production: Basso Monferrato is the domain of Barbera and Grignolino, warm wines that stand out among their drier Piedmont neighbors. In Alto Monferrato, the bubbly Moscato d'Asti dominates. In terms of protected productions, you have the DOCG Asti which uses only Moscato grapes, and

Astigiano countryside

the DOC wines Barbera d'Asti, Freisa d'Asti and Grignolino d'Asti. To these local productions you can add Albugnano, Loazolo, Malvasiadi Casorzo d'Asti, Malvasio di Castelnuovo Don Bosco and Rucé di Castagnole Monferrato. In Alto Monferrato animal farming and cheese production take on an important role with the cheese *Robiola di Roccaverano DOP* as the highlight. Fruit and vegetable cultivation is widespread, but locals specialize in *cardo* (thistle), the primary ingredient for *bagna caôda*, and peaches. The cuisine is first rate, improved by the abundance of mushrooms and truffles. Cooking is typically Piedmontese with a few local specialties. The network of restaurants is excellent with high points in "Gener Neuv", in Asti, and "Guido", in Costigliole.

Barbera grapes

Gourmet Tours

ASTI. The capital of Spumanti and Barbera wines, which are celebrated at the September festival "Douja d'or", this is also a Città del Tartufo (city of truffles), with a lively market held in October and November. While walking along the beautiful Corso Alfieri, you penetrate the oldest quarter, where you will find a Romanesque cathedral and the remains of over a hundred medieval towers. As for good food, typical dishes are the *costoletta di maiale all'astesana* (breaded and fried pork chop covered with truffles) or *frittura mista* (mixed fry with lamb chops, calves liver and kidneys, and asparagus tips). An obligatory stop is "Gener Neuv", just outside the center, where a relaxed country feel is spiked with professionalism and passion. Typical products include *mula*, a Monferrata sausage made with pork and tongue and preserved in lard in earthenware jars. From Azzano and San Marzanotto comes a rare turkey sausage. In the town, make purchases at "Gastronomia S. Secondo" in Corso Dante. Bakeries sell *papera*

del Monferrato, a kind of bread that is soft inside with a crunchy crust. In pastry shops, you can find *baci di dama, polentina mandorlata* (*polenta* made with almonds), *astigiani al rum* (chocolates with rum).

1. The Basso Monferrato
CASTELNUOVO DON BOSCO. The particular interest of this town lies in the religious complex connected with the life and deeds of the priest Giovanni Bosco. The vineyards that enliven the landscape are dedicated to Albugnano, a DOC wine made from Nebbiolo grapes blended with Freisa, Barbera and Bonarda. Black table grapes from here are also well known for their size, sweetness and strong flavor. Asparagus and the thistle-like *cardo* also grow here. Various cheeses include *robiola*, which is fatty and soft, and *bröss*, which is placed in jars to ferment with *grappa* or some other alcoholic beverage to obtain a very strong flavor. In nearby Moncucco, "Bottega del Vino", with its "Trattoria della Freisa" is worth a visit.
COCCONATO. Rising up in a valley off the beaten track is the Vez-

HOTELS AND RESTAURANTS

Asti
Gener Neuv ¶¶¶¶
lungo Tanaro
dei Pescatori 4
☎ 0141557270
**Angolo
del Beato** ¶¶
via Guttuari 12
☎ 0141557270
Da Aldo ¶
at Castiglione 22
☎ 0141206008
**Agliano Terme
San Giacomo** ★★★
via Arullani 4
☎ 0141954178
**Canelli
San Marco** ¶¶¶
via Alba 136
☎ 0141823544
**Cassinasco
I Caffi** ¶¶
at the Santuario
dei Caffi (km 2)
☎ 0141826900
**Castello di
Annone
La Fioraia** ¶¶
via Mondo 26
☎ 0141401106
**Costigliole d'Asti
Guido** ¶¶¶
piazza Umberto I 27
☎ 0141966012

zolano Abbey which played an important role in the medieval history of Monferrato. Its church is a noteworthy Romanesque-Gothic building. Barbera and Freisa vineyards spread out all around. In addition to the DOC wines produced here, there are other interesting experimental wines, and the producer "Bava" is worth investigating. Robiola, together with various sausages and cured meats, is produced here, and there is a good harvest of truffles.

MONCALVO. From its dominating position, Italy's smallest town, founded in 1705, has an aura that still reflects its strategic positioning, which was once so important. Gourmets are tempted by the lively calendar that follows wine production (Barbera, Grignolino, Freisa), truffle gathering and the celebrated *bue grasso* or fatted ox that contributes to the town's most characteristic dish, *polpettone alla moncalvese* (Moncalvo meatloaf). In Piazza Antico Castello is the restaurant "Ametista" where flavors of the hills join those of the sea. Not far away, in Cioccaro di Penango, "Da Beppe – Locanda del Sant'Uffizio" has gained a name for itself with its farm accomodation and typical restaurant. In shops, ask for *bresaola* (dried beef) and *salami di cavallo* (horse-meat salami) as well as *salami di'asino* (donkey meat salami).

MONTEMAGNO. High on the hill is the piazza with the theatrical church of Assumption, and further down, marked by a big sundial, is the popular restaurant "Braja", which specializes in mushrooms and truffles. *Cotechino* (boiled spiced pork sausage) and *fagioli* (beans) are traditional foods that often share the same plate. There are two exceptional DOC wines: Ruché di Castagnole Monferrato, a unique and rare wine with an unmistakable note of hyacinth, and Malvasia di Consorzio d'Asti, a bubbly and aromatic red or cherry-colored wine that is served at the end of a meal. From Refrancore come the famous asparagus, apples and peaches (these appear cooked with Barolo as a desert). In pastry shops you will find characteristic cookies called *finocchini*.

PORTACOMARO. This small capital of Grignolino has a historic tower that houses a "Bottega del Vino" and its restaurant. Visit the atmospheric *infernotto* cellar that has been dug into the volcanic rock to age the best bottles.

2. From the hills of Asti to the Langhe

SAN DAMIANO. This itinerary brings us into the green valleys of the Borbore, which are renowned

Asti. Colorful folk costumes

HOTELS AND RESTAURANTS

Isola d'Asti
Il Cascinalenuovo
S.S. Asti-Alba 15 ⦀
☎ 0141958166

Mango
Del Castello ⦀ ★ ⬛
piazza XX Settembre
☎ 014189141

Moncalvo
Ametista ⦀
piazza
Antico Castello 14
☎ 0141917423

Moncucco
Torinese
Trattoria
della Freisa ⦀
via Mosso 6
☎ 0119874765

Montegrosso
d'Asti
La Locanda del
Bosco Grande ⦀
at Messadio (km 5)
via Boscogrande 47
☎ 0141956390

Montemagno
Braja ⦀ ★ ⬛
via S. Giovanni
Bosco 11
☎ 0141653910

Penango
Da Beppe -
Locanda del
Sant'Uffizio ★ ★ ★
at Cioccaro (km 4)
strada S. Uffizio 1
☎ 0141916292

Revigliasco d'Asti
Il Rustico ⦀
piazza Vittorio Veneto 2
☎ 0141208210

for truffle hunting and peach orchards. We highly recommend a detour to Tigliole to go to the restaurant "Victoria", a splendid late eighteenth-century house with an excellent chef.

COSTIGLIOLE D'ASTI. The next stage brings us across the Tanaro for an unforgettable gastronomic experience at "Guido", which is one of Italy's finest restaurants. Choose from *filetti di tacchino* (turkey filets) with black *taggiasche* olives, *agnolotti di Costigliole al sugo di stinco* (meat-filled pasta Costigliole-style with cooking juices from roast shank) and *agnello di Roccaverano al forno con acciughe* (roast Roccaverano lamb with anchovies). We also recommend "Cascina Castlèt", with its nineteenth-century cellar, surrounded by 10 hectares of Barbera and Moscato vineyards. In the village, below the theater, is the "Enoteca Comunale". Renowned *amaretti* biscuits are to be found in the pastry shops. For those who would like to prolong their stay, we recommend "La Locanda del Bosco

Grande" in the midst of the Montegrosso d'Asti vineyards. The next day, head to the excellent restaurant "Il Cascinalenuovo", in Isola d'Asti, where popular old standbys are joined by innovatively combined and presented dishes.

CANELLI. One of the capitals of Italian *spumante* is to be found in the Belbo Valley, where the fortified castle "Gancia" looms over the village, providing the town's most enduring image. Wine tourists will want to stop by the "Enoteca Regionale delle Terre d'Oro". The more gourmet types will want to head to the restaurant "San Marco", which is well-known for the 40-yolk puff pastry of its excellent *Mariuccia*. In the area, the truffle harvest and market are also worth noting. Nearby there are other interesting opportunities for food and drink. In Calamandrana, go to the "Bottega del Vino" and the well-known producer "Michele Chiarlo". In Calosso, the *enoteca* "Crota 'd Calos" serves food including the local cooked salami which has gained renown.

Vineyards on the Astigiana hill

In Cassinasco, "I Caffi" is an elegant restaurant with regional dishes. Crossing into the Cuneo province, in Santo Stefano Belbo you can visit Cesare Pavese's birthplace and other places mentioned in the author's books. Not far away, in Mango, is the "Enoteca Regionale Colline del Moscato" with its restaurant "Del Castello".

ROCCAVERANO. This town has every right to be proud of its *robiola* cheese, made of blended milks, which has won DOP recognition (ask for the robiola made from the milk of Piedmont breeds). Do not miss the chance to try Loazzolo, a refined DOC wine made from Moscato grapes. At San Giorgio Scarampi, go to "Bottega della Langa Astigiana e della Val Bormida" where there is a wine-tasting counter and restaurant.

NIZZA MONFERRATO. The village made its old fortune from the *strada del Turchino*, the route that crosses Monte Turchino and effectively forms a border between Piedmont and Liguria, and the market that brought people together from Piedmont, Liguria and Lombardy. Here, too, the wine is very good, and you can find it at the "Vineria della Signora in Rosso" and the Museo Bersano delle Contadinerie, near the celebrated producer of the same name (tours and tasting). In the fall, celebrations are held in honor of the main local gastronomic players: the aforementioned *bue grasso, tartufo, cardo gobbo* (thistle for *bagna caôda*), and Barbera. From Mombaruzzo come the typical and famous *amaretti* biscuits At Castelletto Molina, try the *tartufo bianco* (white truffle) market.

ROCCHETTA TANARO. This village is a good stop for several reasons, one being the restaurant "I Bologna", which offers excellent cooking from the territory, suitably accompanied by first-rate wines. These include the celebrated Barbera from the winery "Braida", connected to the restaurant. The producer "Marchesi Incisa della Rocchetta" is excellent and receives house guests year round. Do not forget to ask bakeries for *lingua di suocera*, a thin, crisp pastry that is hand rolled and goes well with everything, but is also tasty by itself.

SHOPPING

Asti
Barbero Davide
via Brosserio 84
☎ 0141594004
"Torrone" and chocolate.
Torrefazione Ponchione
corso Alfieri 149
☎ 0141592469
Rare coffees; wines and pastries.
Gastronomia San Secondo
corso Dante 6
☎ 0141592415
Gourmet store.
Agliano
Panetteria Alciati
via P. Amedeo 17
☎ 0141954040
Bakery.
Liano d'Asti
Salumeria Truffa
via Mazzini 1
☎ 0141954284
Charcuterie.
Nizza Monferrato
Cascine Bongiovanni
strada Bossola 15
☎ 0141701140
Organic products.
Vineria della Signora in Rosso
Palazzo Crova
☎ 0141793350
Typical products.
Roccaverano
Caseificio Sociale
at Tassito 17
☎ 014493068
Typical cheeses.
Rocchetta Tanaro
La Curiona
Bossoleto 3
☎ 0141644781
Regional products
Mario Fongo
piazza Italia 2
☎ 0141644173
Bakery specialties.
San Giorgio Scarampi
Bottega della Langa Astigiana e della val Bormida
via Roma 6
☎ 014489230
Typical products.
Serole
Cascina Rocchino
at Rocchino 30
☎ 014494129
Typical products.

BIELLA

This province is characterised by the Pre-Alps, with their polenta, cheeses and red wines made from Spanna grapes.

The young province of Biella includes the valleys and hills of the Pre-Alps. These are located between the watershed of the Dora Baltea river to the west and the Sesia to the east, and part of the upper flatlands that stretch out at the feet of the pre-Alps, characterized by a heath known as *baragge*. In the province, cereal and vegetables are cultivated. Biellese sheep are raised for three products: meat, milk and wool, making them a main feature in the cuisine but even more so in textiles, which historically form the backbone of the local economy. The foothills of the Alps give rise to excellent wines. The main vine stock is Nebbiolo, with the denomination of Spanna; it is blended with juices from local Bonarda Novarese and Vespolina grapes, which give the wine its characteristic fragrance. The most prominent production is in the eastern part of the province. Here you find the DOC wines Lessona, in the center of the same name, and Bramaterra. One senses the closeness of the mountains in traditional cooking, and *polenta* is omnipresent in its many forms: with milk, enriched with butter and cheese (*cunscia*) or prepared as fritters with bits of cheese (*ballot de polenta*). Rice hails from the plains, and is cooked in milk as the base to many recipes.

Gourmet Tours

BIELLA. The town has two centers: on the bank of the Cervo stream is the Piano, where the most visible monuments stand out in a modern urban fabric, while higher up is the Piazzo which has preserved its medieval appearance. The two are joined by a funicular railway. Gourmets should go to "Prinz Grill – da Beppe e Teresio", which serves Piedmont classics such as fresh pasta with mushrooms, *tartufi*, or *Castelmagno* cheese. It also has an excellent wine cellar. The delicacies of Biella include *sargnon*, a creamy cheese with a strong character obtained by fermenting pieces of *gorgonzola* and other sharp cheeses in *grappa* or rum. *Salam d'la duja* is the sausage of choice and the lamb is excellent. Don't miss the hundred-year-old

shop "Giovanni Mosca". Pastry shops sell *canestrelli*, with their characteristic rectangular or square shape and wafer-like consistency. Having several times won the title of "best lager in the world", the Menabrea beer is considered a local glory.

1. The Zegna Vista

ANDORNO MICCA. Going up the Cervo Valley from the capital, the church of San Lorenzo, with its exquisite glazed terracotta ornamentation, marks the first stage of this journey. In the village you can buy *toma del Maccagno*, a typical mountain cheese. It is made from either whole or low-fat milk. The latter was once filtered using nettles, lichen and fern. Local tables are set with trout and *trippa alla savoiarda* (tripe cut into cubes

View of the Biellese mountains

HOTELS AND
RESTAURANTS

Biella
Prinz Grill -
Da Beppe
e Teresio ¶¶¶
via Torino 14
☎ 01523876
Le Premier
Cru ¶¶ ★
via Repubblica 46
☎ 015830820
Orso Poeta ¶¶
via Orfanotrofio 7
☎ 01521252
San Paolo ¶¶
viale Roma 4
☎ 0158493236
Baracca ¶ ★
via S. Eusebio 12
☎ 01521941
Bielmonte
Bucaneve ★★★
Panoramica Zegna
☎ 015744184
Candelo
Angiulli ¶¶¶
via Sandigliano 112
☎ 0152538998
Fuori le Mura ¶¶
via M. Pozzo 4
☎ 0152536155
Taverna
del Ricetto ¶¶
rua V del Castello
☎ 0152536066

and cooked in beef broth with lots of onions seasoned with butter, tomato, oil and spices). And here you can also get *ratafià d'Andorno*, a liquor made of black cherries that is the pride of the whole region. Taking a detour through Borgosesia, we arrive at Pettinengo which is also known as "Biella's balcony". The vista is outstanding and the *torcetti* cookies are famous. Continuing upwards, you arrive at Sagliano Micca, the native town of Pietro Micca, the hero of the siege of Turin in 1706. Further up, at the head of the valley is Piedicavallo, a starting point for excursions to surrounding summits. A traditional food is cow's 'teats' corned and then boiled together with *polenta moja*, which is so-called because it is left to soften (*amollare*) in *cacio* cheese.

BIELMONTE. From the Cervo Valley, go up to Bocchetta di Sessera, which is at the beginning of the Panoramica Zegna that takes its name from the Biellese fashion designer who sponsors parks here and is one of the most charming routes along the Alpine curve. Stop at Bielmonte, a winter sports resort and starting point for excursions in the woods of the Zegna oasis, a protected national park. From Trivero take a detour through Crevacuore, an old-style village with narrow streets lined with irregular doors, whose excellent cheeses are the products of the summer grazing pastures.

COSSATO. This is Biella's second largest community. In the town, you can find the much-appreciat-

ed DOC wine Lessona, a red with notes of violet produced from Nebbiolo (Spanna), Vespolina and Bonarda grapes. Nearby is Masserano, a gracious town in an area that flourishes thanks to its fruit and wine production. Here the DOC Bramaterra is made from the blend mentioned above.

2. The Oropa and Serra Valleys
OROPA. The Madonna di Oropa Sancturary, one of Italy's most important pilgrimage destinations, is a large and scenic complex of buildings arranged on a terrace in the valley. If you stop here, visit the restaurant "Croce Bianca". Rooms are available in the sanctuary's guest house and the menu includes the traditional *polenta concia* (a cheesy, buttery *polenta*), *capriolo al ginepro* (roebuck with juniper) and *tagliata al Barolo* (strips of beef in Barolo). In the area, milk from the indigenous Pezzata Rossa Oropa is used to make *tumet*, also called *beddu di Pralungo*, a fresh cheese used to make many local dishes, starting with the delicate *fonduta*. In Oropa's pastry shops visitors will find *mucroncini*, local sweets, and Oropa's own elixir made of Alpine herbs.

GRAGLIA. Another sanctuary in an enchanting location. Not far away is the ancient and pretty village of Netro with its houses and their porticoes arranged along the slope of the Serra. Ask for *tomino di Sordevolo*, which is made from either whole or low-fat milk. In Pollone, go to the restaurant "Faggio" where you will find innovative dishes made with *funghi* and *tartufi* (it is near the natural reserve "La Burcina", which is famous for its rhododendrons).

HOTELS AND RESTAURANTS

Cavaglià
Green Park Hotel ★★★
at Navilotto (km 4)
S.S. 143 n. 75
☎ 0161966771
Magnano
Le Betulle ★★★
near Golf Club Biella
☎ 015679151
Oropa
Croce Bianca ¶
via Santuario d'Oropa 480
☎ 0152455923
★ Fornace ¶
via Santuario Oropa 480
☎ 0152455922
Pollone
Faggio ¶¶
via Oremo 54
☎ 01561252
Il Patio ¶¶
via Oremo 14
☎ 01561568
Viverone
Marina ★★★
at Comuna (km 3)
☎ 0161987577
Rolle ¶
at Rolle
via Frate Lebole 27
☎ 016198668

MAGNANO. One of the reasons to visit this town is to see the Bessa, a quarry that was used by the Romans for its gold-bearing sand, but is now another natural reserve. On the horizon is the mass of the Serra, a hill of the Dora Baltea, which is covered with vineyards and woods. Nearby is Cerrione, where the *trattoria* "La Bessa" was already on the map as a stop for carriage drivers at the end of the 19th century. The original owner's grandson offers dishes that are in harmony with the *trattoria*'s history, from *lingua in salsa rossa* (tongue in red sauce) to *agnolotti*, (pasta filled with forcemeat), from *brasato* (braised beef) to *fritto misto* (mixed fry).

VIVERONE. In the *trattorie* around the lake, dishes are based on fish, particularly the prized *coregone* (whitefish). In the nearby castle of Roppolo you can find the headquarters of the "Enoteca Regionale della Serra", which specializes in wines from the eastern Pre-Alps ranging from the white wine Erbaluce di Caluso to the reds from Nebbiolo grapes, Gattinara and Ghemme. Here, in addition to wine-tasting, you will also find a restaurant and hotel.

Lake Viverone

3. The Baraggia Vercellese

CANDELO. South of the regional capital, a plain mostly cultivated with rice is divided into several parts of relevant environmental value. This town is special for the biggest and best preserved of Piedmont's medieval shelters, which are fortified agricultural depots that could also be used as refuges for the population. The one in Candello is a pentagonal group of buildings protected by walls and towers. Today, there is a traditional restaurant "Taverna del Ricetto" within the walls. "Anguilli", on the other hand offers creative cooking that alternates local products, such as *risotto alla robiola fusa e tartufo nero* (risotto with melted robiola cheese and black truffle), with seafood, such as *trancio di ombrina agli asparagi selvatici* (umbra with wild asparagus). Along the route to Vercelli, we come to three towns with beautiful monuments: Benna and Verone, then, on the return, Gagliancio.

AGRITURISMI

Cerrione
La Bessa - Ippica San Giorgio
cascina Pianone
☎ 015677156

SHOPPING

Biella
Giovanni Mosca
via S. Filippo 16
☎ 01523181
Meat, charcuterie, cheeses, olive oil and honey.
Andorno Micca
Distilleria Rapa
via Cantono 13
☎ 015473605
Distilled spirits.

CUNEO

The truffle and the great wines of Le Langhe are the spirit of this wine and food district that attracts gourmets from around the world.

The province of Cuneo occupies a large territory that runs from the French border and the Monferrato, which stretches from the Maritime and Cottian Alps to Monviso, on to the hilly district of Le Langhe. Vineyards and animal farming are the backbone of this food and farming economy, which is boosted by first-rate fruit and vegetable production and truffles. Wines are good quality and varied, and among the best are the DOCG Barbaresco and the DOC Barbera. You can also find Dolcetto and Nebbiolo d'Alba, the more local Roero, Dolcetto di Diano d'Alba, Dolcetto di Dogliani, Dolcetto delle Langhe Monregalesi, Colline Saluzzesi, and rarities such as Verduno Pelaverga. Cheeses that boast DOP recognition form another large group, including Murazzano, Bra, Castelmagno, Raschera and Toma Piemontese.

Opposite: vineyards in Grinzane Cavour

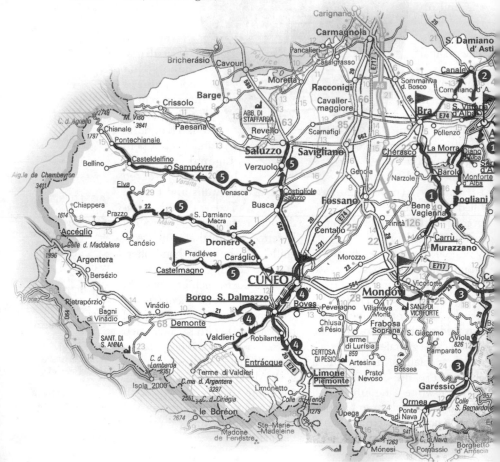

The direct result of this wealth of primary materials is a gastronomy with a wide variety of characteristics. In the mountains it is marked by meats and cheeses, products of the woods and exclusive products such as *grano saraceno* (*frumentino* or buckwheat). At lower altitudes the character remains the same, but the flavors are softened as vineyards, vegetable gardens and fruit orchards come into the picture. The restaurant sector, backed by the *tartufo bianco d'Alba* and the great wines of Le Langhe, is one of the most evolved in Italy, with "Rododendro", in Boves, taking the lead in a close-knit, well-defined network.

Gourmet Tours

CUNEO. The old city is located on a terrace formed by the confluence of the Gesso and Stura rivers. Its rich gastronomy contrasts with its austere appearance. In the background is the ring of the Maritime and Cottian Alps, harbingers of other flavors. In the town, the nineteenth-century cafe "Bruno" provides a nostalgic stop. Local pastry makers are proud of their *cuneesi al rum* (rum-flavored chocolates). For a good meal, you should try the traditional dishes *gnocchi alla bava con toma fresca, panna e tartufo* (gnocchi with fresh *toma* cheese, cream and truffle) and *polenta con lumache e salsiccia cotte nel vino* (*polenta* with snails and sausage cooked in wine). We strongly recommend "Osteria della Chiocciola", which offers a good synthesis of local cooking and creativity together with first-rate wines. Also noteworthy is "Le Plait d'Etain", where a Norman chef introduces the pleasures of northern French cuisine. If you want to go shopping, the excellent "Caud e Freid" offers a differ-

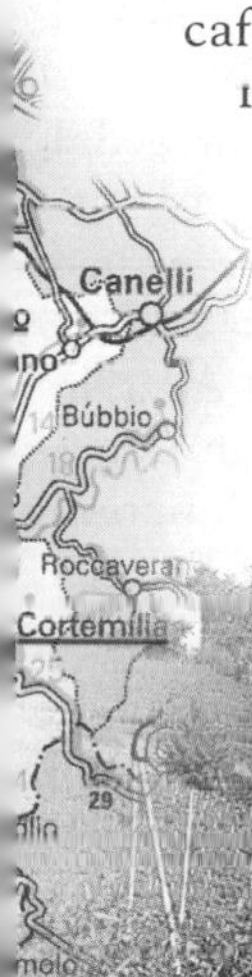

HOTELS AND
RESTAURANTS

Cuneo
Le Plat d'Etain ¶¶
corso Giolitti 18/a
☎ 0171681918
Osteria della Chiocciola ¶¶
via Fossano 1
☎ 017166277

Alba
Il Violetto ¶¶¶
via Bertero 6
☎ 0173363196
Albaretto della Torre Cacciatori - Da Cesare ¶¶¶
via S. Bernardo 9
☎ 0173520141

Barbaresco
Antica Torre ¶
via Torino 0
☎ 0173635170

Barolo
Brezza ¶¶
via Lomondo 2
☎ 017356191
Locanda del Borgo Antico ¶¶
piazza Municipio 2
☎ 017356355

Boves
Rododendro ¶¶¶¶
at S. Giacomo (km 5)
☎ 0171380372
Della Pace ¶¶¶
at Fontanelle (km 3)
via Santuario 97
☎ 0171380398

HOTELS AND
RESTAURANTS

Bra
Osteria
Boccondivino ¶
via Mendicità
Istruita 14
☎ 0172425674
Osteria
Murivecchi ¶
via G. Piumati 19
☎ 0172431008
Briaglia
Trattoria
Marsupino ¶¶¶
via Roma 20
☎ 0174563888
Canale
All'Enoteca ¶¶¶
via Roma 57
☎ 017395857
Carrù
Moderno ¶¶¶
via Misericordia 12
☎ 017375493
Centallo
Vittoria ¶
via Cavour 10
☎ 0171214100
Cervere
Corona Reale -
Da Renzo ¶¶¶
via Fossano 13
☎ 0172474132
Cherasco
La Lumaca ¶
via S. Pietro
(corner via Cavour)
☎ 0172489421
Osteria della
Rosa Rossa ¶
via S. Pietro 31
☎ 0172488133
Cortemilia
★ San Carlo ★★★
corso Divisioni
Alpine 41
☎ 017381546
Costigliole Saluzzo
★ Castello
Rosso ★★★
via Amm. Reynaudi 5
☎ 0175230030
Diano D'Alba
Antica Trattoria
del Centro ¶
at Ricca
via Cortemilia 91
☎ 0173612525

ent selection each day, as does "Ariano" which has *lonzardo provenzale* (Provençal sausage), *prosciutto d'alpeggio affumicato* (smoked cured ham from summer mountain grazing), and an interesting *salame di trota* (trout salami), all made on the premises from its own products. In bakeries, ask for *toponin*, Cuneo's most characteristic bread, particularly when it is hand made.

1. The Bassa Langa

ALBA. The capital of Le Langhe is also a Città del Vino e del Tartufo (city of wine and truffles) and holds festivals in honor of one or the other. The walled town in the triangle between the Tanaro and Cherasca streams still has medieval towers, churches and residences. Typical dishes are *tajarin conditi al brucio* (pasta with roasting juices) and *brasato al Barolo* (Barolo-braised beef). The *tajarin* is the only pasta Piedmont can call its own. In the city, "Il Vicoletto" is known for its *piccione al tartufo nero o bianco* (pigeon with black or white truffles depending on the season). *Robiola d'Alba* is one of the region's plentiful cheeses and is also made in Diano, Santa Vittoria, La Morra, Canale and Bra. If you stay in Alba, don't neglect the surroundings, which are also very interesting. In Piobesi d'Alba, "Locanda Le Clivie" is excellent for its invaluable chef, who reinterprets Piedmont cuisine with *risotto alle quaglie in salsa di zenzero* (risotto with quails in ginger sauce), *petto*

di fagianella in crepinette con sedano e marroni (pheasant breast and sausages with celery and chestnuts) and *granatina al Barolo Chinato con semifreddo alle pere caramellate* (pomegranate with Barolo Chinato and caramelized pear ice cream cake). Offering equal value and variety is "La Ciau del Tornaveneto" in Treiso with a beautiful terrace overlooking the hills of Le Langhe. In the same village is the winery "Villa Ile", which offers very good quality Barbaresco and Barbera in addition to the possibility of staying over in bed and breakfast accommodation.

BARBARESCO. The Torre del Brico stands as high as a lighthouse and dates back to a time when the municipality was being fought over by Asti and Alba. In the former church of San Damiano you can visit the "Enoteca Regionale del Barbaresco", which also has a restaurant. The town's wineries (in addition to the very expensive Gaja) include the noteworthy "Tenute Cisa Asinari dei Marchesi di Gresy" and its two crus: Barbaresco Camp Gros and Gaiun. In Neive, there are the "Bottega dei Quattro Vini" and two decent restaurants: "La Contea" (which has rooms) and "La Luna nel Pozzo".

DIANO D'ALBA. Today, Alba's historic rival for dominion over the lands of the Tanaro bases its reputation on "Dolcetto di Diano d'Alba", a DOC wine for which experts rigorously select each vine.

In the village of Ricca, you will appreciate "Antica Trattoria del Centro" for its atmosphere and home cooking. Going on to Grinzane Cavour, visit the manor that belonged to the Savoy statesman. Today it is the "Enoteca Regionale" and an ethnographic museum, in addition to hosting the activities of the Confraternità del Tartufo e dei Vini d'Alba (Alba's Truffle and Wine Brotherhood).

LA MORRA. This is one of the most charming villages in Le Langhe. From its plateau, there is a breathtaking view over villages and castles. Make it a point to stop at the restaurant "Belvedere", a famous old place with good dishes. In the village, you can visit the truffle market or purchase excellent *robiole*, *salumi* and preserves. Visit the "Cantina Comunale" and the "Museo Ratti dei Vini d'Alba" near the farm of the same name. Other highlights are the winery "Rocche Costamagna", which is located in the center, and "Fratelli Oddero", which has some excellent wines. In addition to the most celebrated wines in Le Langhe, Verduno Pelaverga DOC is also produced in the area from a local grape that gives the wine violet highlights and a certain spiciness. You can taste it at the hotel-restaurant "Real Castello", which has its own vineyard, in Verduno.

SERRALUNGA D'ALBA. Wine tourists will be very

interested in visiting the great winery "Tenimenti di Barolo e Fontanafredda", which used to be the hunting house of Vittorio Emanuele II and the residence of Countess Rosa di Mirafiori, better known as "Bella Rosin".

BAROLO. This town is full of alleys and characteristic little nooks. It is overlooked by the castle of the Marchesi Falletti, now the seat of "Enoteca Regionale del Barolo. Across from the castle rises the yellow building of the winery "Marchesi del Barolo" where the area's precious wine was "invented". Amid the vast production the historical crus stand out. They are the Cannubi, Sarmassa and Coste di Rose and can be tasted at the guest house, where groups can also dine. The town also offers several good eateries, including "Locanda nel Borgo Antico", which we recommend to both those in search of traditional food and the more adventurous. "La Cantinetta" and the *osteria* "Cantinella" are also good names.

MONFORTE D'ALBA. People flock to this gracious hill town in the summer when the lovely outdoor auditorium is filled with the notes of classical music concerts. The atmospheric hotel "Villa Beccaris" has an *enoteca* and is strongly recommended. On the other side of

La Morra

HOTELS AND RESTAURANTS

Dogliani
Albero fiorito ¶
piazza Confraternita 13
☎ 017370582

Grinzane Cavour
Trattoria del Castello ¶¶
piazza Castello
☎ 0173262172

La Morra
Belvedere ¶¶
piazza Castello 5
☎ 017350190

Limone Piemonte
Lu Taz ¶¶
via S. Maurizio 5
☎ 0171929061

Mondovì
Trattoria Mezzavia ¶¶
at Mezzavia
via Villanova 38
☎ 017440363
Croce d'Oro ¶
via S. Anna 83
☎ 0174681464

Monforte d'Alba
Villa Beccaris ★★★
via Bava Beccaris 1
☎ 017378158
Giardino - Da Felicin ¶¶¶
via Vallada 18
☎ 017378225
La Collina ¶¶
piazza Umberto 13
☎ 01738297
Trattoria della Posta ¶
piazza XX Settembre 9
☎ 017378120

Neive
La Contea ¶¶¶
piazza Cocito 8
☎ 017367126
La Luna nel Pozzo ¶¶
piazza Italia 23
☎ 017367098

HOTELS AND RESTAURANTS

Piobesi d'Alba
Locanda
Le Clivie ¶¶¶
via Canoreto 1
☎ 0173619261
Priocca
Centro ¶¶
via Umberto 1 5
☎ 0173616112
Saluzzo
La Gargotta
del Pellico ¶¶
piazza dei Mondagli 5
☎ 017546833
L'Ostu dij Baloss ¶¶
via Gualtieri 38
☎ 0175248618
Santa Vittoria
d'Alba
⭐▣ **Castello**
Santa Vittoria ★★★
via Cagna 4
☎ 0172478198
⭐▣ **Al Castello** ¶¶
via Cagna 4
☎ 0172478147
Treiso
La Ciau del
Tornavento ¶¶
piazza Baracco 7
☎ 0173638333
Verduno
Real Castello ★★
via Umberto 1 9
☎ 0172470125
Vezza d'Alba
La Pergola ¶¶¶
at Borgonuovo (km 2)
piazza S. Carlo 1
☎ 017365178

AGRITURISMI

Ceresole d'Alba
⭐▣ **Cascina Neri**
cascina Neri 39
☎ 0172574543
La Morra
Erbaluna
borgata Pozzo 43
☎ 017350800

the street is the "Antica Dispensa" where visitors will find truffle- and cheese-based gastronomic delights and many others. The restaurant "Giardino – da Felicin" has a menu that ranges from *tajarin al pomodoro e basilico* (tajarin pasta with tomatoes and basil) to *agnello alla monfortina* (Monforte-style lamb). "LaTrattoria della Posta", a long-standing traditional restaurant, and "La Collina", right on the village square, are also worth trying. The more adventurous might try continuing on to Albaretto della Torre where they will find the excellent restaurant "Cacciatori-da-Cesare" that serves a sublime *fritto misto* (mixed fry).

DOGLIANI. There is something aristocratic and elegant about this village that is confirmed by its own DOC production Dolcetto di Dogliani (also called *del presidente* because Luigi Einaudi was among its producers). This wine may be tasted at "Bottega del Vino". *Agnolotti* are a local favorite and can be tasted at "Albero fiorito", a fortress that upholds Le Langhe tradition.

CARRÙ. The seat of an important livestock market is also an important stop for those with a passion

Santa Vittoria d'Alba

for *gran bollito misto alla Piemontese* (mixed boiled meat Piedmont style). The place to eat *bue della coscia grossa* (the fat-thighed ox) is "Moderno", a restaurant with a strong local following. Ask for *rubata*, a prized variety of handrolled *grissini* (breadsticks).

CHERASCO. This is a "Citta delle Lumache" (city of snails), the capital of cooking based on the tasty gastropod. Along the colonnaded streets of the village there are many chances to verify this. "La Lumacha" and "Osteria della Rosa Rossa" are two pleasant, low-key restaurants that also serve good wine. In bakeries you will find the characteristic *stirate* breadsticks that go well with sliced sausages, cheese and the like, as well as with coffee at breakfast.

2. The Roero

BRA. The capital of the so-called Oltretanaro Albese area has a historic center with a baroque flavor and a commercial past. Traditional products are meat and a skimmed-milk cheese called *Bra*, although this cheese is more often produced in Alpine valleys. Two cheese cellars are still active: Cravero and Giolito. The latter produces *braciuk* (drunken Bra), which is aged in *vinaccia* (marc brandy)

from Barbera, Nebbiolo and Pelaverga wines. Also well-known is Bra sausage. This is the only sausage made from veal in all of Italy, by special permission from the Savoys, and flavored with spices, wine and *toma* from Le Langhe. It is eaten cold, grilled or even raw. In the city, go to the historic pastry shop "Converso" (est. 1901), or take a seat at one of the tables at "Osteria Boccondivino" (the name is a play on words, *bocconcino* meaning bite and *divino* meaning divine). "Cantine Giacomo Ascheri" is also good, thanks to two unblended wines made from Sirah and Viognier grapes. At its restaurant "Osteria Murivecchi", you can be sure of tasty home cooking and excellent house and other wines. Those who enjoy Savoy festivals will want to make the excursion to the Castello di Racconigi and return via Cavallermaggiore, a very pleasant village. On the way, stop at Sommariva del Bosco where there are two exceptional shops: the butcher-charcuterie "Raspo" and "Il Trovarebbe", a cafe-pastry shop that offers a thousand surprises.

CANALE. In the upper valley of Borbore, along the route to Colle di Cadibona, go to the "Enoteca Regionale del Roero" where "All'Enoteca" offers a rare variety of brilliant and imaginative food. The area is well-known for its fish and truffles. Connoisseurs of the white wine Arneis should go to the producer "Marsaglia" in Castellinaldo.

SANTA VITTORIA D'ALBA. Go up to the historic wine producer "Francesco Cinzano". Carved into the heart of the hillside, the cellars are extraordinary both for their size and atmosphere. A permanent exhibition of the historic archives tells of the house of Cinzano's exploits throughout the world. Groups may dine at the villa. To stay the night, try "Castello di Santa Vittoria", where there are many richly furnished rooms. Its restaurant "Al Castello" has a garden and terrace, and remains affordable.

Castelmagno cheese

3. The Alta Langa and the Alpi Liguri

MONDOVÌ. On the banks of the Ellero is the more modern nucleus of Breo; a hundred meters up (take the funicular) is Piazza, the medieval part of town embellished by baroque monuments. The backdrop of the Alpi Liguri means woodland and mountain flavors. The sophisticated restaurant "Mezzavia" and the traditional *trattoria* "Croce d'Oro" are both fine attractions. At Frabosa Soprana, in the heart of Raschera, ask for the creamy and tasty *bruss* which is made by fermenting leftovers from cheese-making.

CEVA. This village in the Tanaro Valley is a small mushroom capital with a big festival in September. Colonnades, galleries and high vaulted ceilings characterize the old town where you should look for local *robiola* and *toma*, which are sometimes kept in oil. Going down into the Belba valley, you arrive at Murazzano, a

WINE PRODUCERS

Barbaresco
Tenute Cisa Asinari dei Marchesi di Gresy
via Rabajà 43
☎ 0173635222
Barolo
Marchesi di Barolo
via Alba 12
☎ 0173564400
Fratelli Borgogno
at Cannubi
via Crosia 12
☎ 017356107
Bra
Cantine Giacomo Ascheri
via Piumati 23
☎ 0172412394
Castellinaldo
Emilio Marsaglia
via Mussone 2
☎ 0173213048
Castiglione Falletto
Gigi Rosso
via Alba-Barolo 20
☎ 0173262369
La Morra
Fratelli Oddero
at S. Maria
☎ 017350618
Rocche
Costamagna
via V. Emanuele 10
☎ 0173509225
Aldo Vaira
at Vergne
via delle Viole 25
☎ 017356257
Santa Vittoria d'Alba
Francesco Cinzano
S.S. 63
☎ 0172477111
Serralunga d'Alba
Tenimenti di Barolo e Fontanafredda
via Alba 15
☎ 0173613161
Treiso
Villa Ile
strada Rizzi 18
☎ 0173362333
Verduno
Castello di Verduno
via Umberto 19
☎ 0172470125

SHOPPING

Cuneo
Ariano
via Pascal 2
☎ 0171693522
Paté, smoked
fish and meat.
Caffè Bruno
via Roma 28
☎ 0171681950
Historic cafe.
Caud e Freid
corso Nizza 76
☎ 0171602490
Gourmet store.
Alba
De Stefanis
& Martina
via V. Emanuele 29
☎ 0173440118
Truffles and
mushrooms.
Drogheria
Enoteca Burdese
Giovanna
via V. Emanuele 13
☎ 0173362239
Good wines and
typical products.
Io, tu e i dolci
piazza Savona 12
☎ 0173441704
Pastries, cookies
and chocolate.
Gastronomia
Ugo
via Alfieri 4
☎ 0173441454
Regional specialties
and wines.
Gastronomia
Piero e Claudio
corso Piave 72
☎ 0173281615
Fresh pasta.
Vincafè
via V. Emanuele 12
☎ 0173364603
Wines, charcuterie
and cheeses.
Borgo San
Dalmazzo
I Piaceri
del Gusto
via Garibaldi 69/71
☎ 0171266189
Delicatessen.
Shops in Cuneo
(corso Nizza 16)
and Alba (via
V. Emanuele 23/a).

village that gives its name to the mold-streaked cheese that has obtained DOP recognition. This cheese is made by fermenting *bruz 'd Murazzan*, a strong cheese with many uses, in pottery jars. The route continues into Liguria at Millesimo, an interesting Città del Tartufo (city of truffles).

ORMEA. This village is reached from Ceva. Located near the springs of the Tanaro, it is a summer village with old houses and a medieval layout. Here you can find the DOP cheese Raschera as well as cheese from the Alps, made of cow's milk in Colle dei Termini, *soera* (or *sola*) made of Langhe sheep's milk, and *Valcasotto* from the area around Pamparato and Garessio.

CORTEMILIA. The two medieval quarters of San Michele and San Pantaleo face each other in the upper valley of Bormida di Millesimo. The surrounding areas produce mushrooms, *tartufi* and *nocciole* (hazelnuts) The traditional dish of the area is *grive*, small meatloaves made of liver and non-fat pork, wrapped in gauze and pan-fried. We recommend the hotel "San Carlo", which also has a good restaurant.

4. The Maritime Alps

BOVES. Some are encouraged by faith and others by their love for art to come to this village to visit the sanctuary of the Madonna dei Bosci, with its sixteenth-century frescoes. Others (probably even more) visit Boves on another pilgrimage: to "Rododendro", one of Italy's best restaurants with inspired cooking and an interesting cellar with transalpine influences. There are also many places to spend the night. Do not miss the *trattoria* "Della Pace". If you still haven't had your fill, many tempting shops line the streets. You will find a *tome* called *testun* as well as the characteristic little Boves cheeses that should be eaten fresh, and *robiola d'Alta Langa*, from Peveragno. And for a sweet ending, try Cuneo's celebrated whole *marroni* (chestnuts), which are excellent for making *marrons glacés*.

BORGO SAN DALMAZZO. This is the headquarters of the centuries-old Fiera Fredda (Festival of the Cold) on December 5, which honors the *lumaca* (snail)'s role in commerce and haute cuisine. The characteristic dish is *lumache alla borghigiana* (snails bourguignon), which is made differently in each restaurant.

Alta Langa countryside

LIMONE PIEMONTE. Over a thousand years old, this village has a new life as a touristic destination thanks to the ski-slopes and hiking. Most meals include trout and kid, and the honey is excellent. A traditional dish is toasted slices of *polenta di grano saraceno* (buckwheat *polenta*) served with *bagna caôda* and cream. "Lu Taz" is a restaurant with a fine ambiance and encapsulates the hearty flavors found in the territory.

ENTRAQUE. This town is at the entry to the National Park of Argentera, where chamois and ibex inhabit the mountain. In the cheese factories you will find a new fresh cheese called Pierino. Higher up at 1,368 meters are the Terme di Valdieri (Valdieri Baths), a well-known holiday resort and spa.

DEMONTE. Excellent cheeses are to be found on the way up the Sura Valley towards the Colle della Maddalena, including *tome*, *caprini*, which have their own special flavor thanks to the wild thyme growing in the pastures where animals feed. There is also the creamy *cachat*, and the similar *bruss*, which is made by fermenting milk with goat's cheese.

5. The Cottian Alps

VAL GRANA. The gourmet's first destination is Castelmagno, a small community in the upper valley. As well as the hunt for the local mold-streaked cheese produced in mountain huts from rich summer milk, the beauty of the place makes this a worthwhile trip. *Bruss* is made by fermenting leftovers from cheese-making into a sharp cream to be spread on toasted bread or mixed into *polenta*.

VAL MAIRA. Another paradise for Alpine cheese lovers. In Elva, the blue-stained, white cheese *caso* is produced, while Celle Macra produces the rare *tuma* and Aceglio produces its own cheese that is eaten very fresh. The mountain bread here keeps well.

VAL VARAITA. The route up from Costigiole Saluzzo leads to Sampeyre, the capital of this valley with a Provençal culture, and continues on to Castel Delfino and Pontechianale, at the foot of Monviso. Gnocchi with *toma*, *stracchino* and butter is a typical dish to be found in the *trattorie*. The *tomini* from Melle are particularly good. At Costigliole, spend the night at "Castello Rosso", a hotel with a spa.

SALUZZO. Once chosen as a capital by the local marquis, this village has maintained an aristocratic aura embellished by small *palazzi* and churches that blend the Gothic and Renaissance. Not far away is the castle of Manta, with its celebrated frescoes with courtly subjects. The traditional dish is in keeping with the theme: *quaietta*, or *costoletta alla castellana* (chatelaine's veal cutlet) is filled with a blend of meat, cheese, and truffle. We recommend "La Gargotta del Pellico", which is elegant without being ostentatious, and "Ostu dij Baloss", which is characteristic of the area and offers a wide choice of wines and cheeses. Shops offer well-known cheeses, with *tometta*, *tomini del Montuso*; *pecorino* and *caprini al pepe* from Barge and Bagnolo Piemonte and the soft, almost melted *paglierina* from Rifreddo. Wine tourists must not forget to ask for red wines made with Pelaverga and Quagliano grapes, which are the pillars of the DOC Colline Saluzzesi wines. Last of all, climb to Pian del Re to find the springs that feed the Po.

SHOPPING

Boves
La Bottega delle Carni
via Roma 7
☎ 0171380 2070
Piedmont's meats.
Il Forno a Legna
piazza Garibaldi 8
☎ 0171380208
Bakery specialties.
Bra
Pasticceria Converso
via V. Emanuele 199
☎ 0172413626
Pastries, candies and chocolates.
Cravero Giacomo
via Cacciorna 31
☎ 0172413608
Cheeses cellar.
Giolito Fiorenzo
via Montegrappa 6
☎ 0172412920
Cheese cellar.
La Morra
Mulino Sobrino
via Roma 108
☎ 017350118
Organic flours.
Monforte d'Alba
Antica Dispensa Bricco Bastia
via Bava Beccaris 3
☎ 0173787120
Fresh pasta with truffles or mushrooms; truffle pâté, preserves.
Sommariva del Bosco
La Genuina di Longhini e Bergese
via V. Emanuele 4
☎ 017254008
"Agnolotti del plin" and "agnolotti" filled with asparagus or artichoke.
Macelleria Salumeria Raspo Luigi
via Torino 4
☎ 017254215
Meat and charcuterie.
Strumia
Il Trovarobe
via V. Emanuele 9
☎ 017254230
Sweets and chocolates.

73

NOVARA

*Lakes, rivers and rice fields characterize the
landscape and influence the region's cooking with
flavors that suggest its proximity to Lombardy.*

The province of Novara is a long territory on a
north-south axis that is marked by the Sesia
and Ticino rivers. To the north are the
pre-Alps, where pastoral activities are embellished by lakes Orta and Maggiore. In the middle of the territory is a strip of hills defined by
glaciers and dedicated to viticulture. The
best quality wines are the DOCG
Ghemme and the DOC Sizzanto, Fara,
Boca and Colline Novaresi, in which
Nebbiolo (locally known as Spanna) profits
from the addition of Bonarda and Vespolina
grapes. Finally, to the south, lies the *pianura*,
or flatlands, where locals cultivate rice fields
and other fields inherent in animal husbandry
and cheese production The DOP *Gorgonzola*,
of Lombard origin, best expresses the produce of
the area. Such an environment gives rise to a
gastronomic tradition characterized by rice, as in
paniscia novarese (rice cooked in vegetable broth
with greens, beans and sausage, and served with a
generous grind of pepper), and by lake and river fish.
Lombard influence is also evident, especially in the
area neighboring Lomellina, where rice is prepared
with frogs and main dishes are based on goose meat. Going
into the mountains, Piedmont cooking is more prevalent, even
in the original use of donkey meat in *tapulon* (minced meat cooked in   *Lake Orta.*
wine with garlic) in Borgomanero. The network of restaurants is first-rate,   *Island of*
and a stop at "Al Sorriso", one of Italy's top restaurants known for its com-   *San Giulio*
plex dishes and poetic inspiration, is a must.

Gourmet Tours

NOVARA. Below the spire of the church of San Gaudenzo is the most Lombardian of Piedmont's cities. Within its horizons are the rice fields and the stables where DOP *Gorgonzola*, a cheese streaked with mold and developed in Lombardy, is produced. The most characteristic dish is *paniscia* (rice cooked in vegetable broth with greens, beans and sausage, and served with a generous grind of pepper). To taste the excellent wines of Novara's hills, go to "I Due Ladroni", where *prosciutto crudo affumicato* from the Vigezzo Valley, *paniscia*, *tapulon*, lake fish and a fine selection of cheeses including *Gorgonzola naturale* are served. At Lumellogno, we recommend "Tantris", a small, refined restaurant where cooking ranges from the best of tradition to new creations. In shops buy *salam 'd la duja*, which is kept in fat in earthenware jars. The shop "Moroni" is worth mentioning for its gastronomic counter filled with tempting salamis and cheeses from summer alpine grazing, including *Bettelmatt* from Val Formezza. Pastry shops sell Novara's famous *biscottini* (cookies).

1. Between the Sesia and the Ticino

CARPIGNANO SESIA. The westbound route goes by San Nazzaro Sesia, where there is a Benedictine Abbey, and then goes up to Carpignano, a farming town with a picturesque center of 15th-century houses. On the horizon you can see the hills. You then come across three wine-producing towns, renowned for their red wines made from Nebbiolo grapes.

These are Fara, Sizzano and Ghemme. In Sizzano the wine producer "Giuseppe Bianchi", active since the 18th century, produces organic wine and displays a fine array of labels. In Fara, you should seek out a particularly spicy and tasty *mortadella* made from liver. Further on in Cavaglietto, we recommend the restaurant "Arianna", where fish and meat are cooked with equal success.

BORGOMANERO. Borgomanero is located amidst the hills where the *statale* Biella-Arona crosses the Agogna stream. The beautiful Romanesque church of San Leonardo adorns the ancient center. One of the town's gastronomic attractions is *tapulon*, a tasty dish made of minced donkey meat marinated and cooked in wine. At the excellent restaurant "Pinocchio", the energetic Pietro Bertinotti offers great risottos and dishes of various regional inspiration. A stop at "Trattoria dei Commercianti" is less involving, as its good traditional menu has few creative options. "Trattoria del Ciclista" is pleasant with a laid back atmosphere. Typical products include *bresaola* (cured meat) made of horse-meat. In pastry shops look for *brutti ma buoni*, cookies that are "ugly but good". Those on the lookout for wine should take a detour to Boca, the homeland of another great red, while "Ori Pari" is a good place to try charcuterie and cheese together with great wines.

OLEGGIO. The route begins a short distance south of the Ticino river and ends in the beautiful colonnaded piazza at the center in the plain. "Il Gatto e la Volpe", a simple restaurant with good cooking by Daniele and Mercede, adds culinary interest to this stop.

HOTELS AND RESTAURANTS

Novara
Tantris ¶¶
at Lumellogno (km 5)
via Pier Lombardo 35
☎ 0321469153
I Due Ladroni ¶
via dell'Archivio 1
☎ 0321624581
Arona
Taverna del Pittore ¶¶¶¶
piazza del Popolo 39
☎ 0322243366
Vecchia Arona ¶¶
lungo lago Marconi 17
☎ 0322242469
Campagna ¶
via Vergante 12
☎ 032257294
Bellinzago Novarese
Osteria San Giulio ¶¶
at Badia di Dulzago
☎ 032198101
Boca
Ori Pari ¶¶
viale Partigiani 9
☎ 032287961
Boffalora Sopra Ticino
Osteria Croce Bianca ¶¶
via XXV Aprile 1
☎ 0297259008
Borgomanero
Pinocchio ¶¶¶¶
via Matteotti 147
☎ 032282273
Trattoria dei Commercianti ¶
via dei Mille 27
☎ 0322841392
Trattoria del Ciclista ¶
via Rosmini 34
☎ 032281649
Cavaglietto
Arianna ¶¶¶
via Umberto 4
☎ 0322806134
Momo
Macallè ¶¶¶
via Boniperti 2
☎ 0321926064
Oleggio
Il Gatto e la Volpe ¶¶
via Nebulina 22
☎ 0321998256
Orta San Giulio
Villa Crespi ¶¶¶
via Fava 8/10
☎ 0322911902

**HOTELS AND
RESTAURANTS**

Soriso
Al Sorriso ¶¶¶¶
via Roma 18
☎ 0322983228
Trecate
Caffè Groppi ¶¶¶
viale Mameli 20
☎ 032171154
Macrì ¶¶¶
piazza Cattaneo 20/a
☎ 032171251

AGRITURISMI

Castelletto
Sopra Ticino
⭐📷 **Cascina
delle Ruote** via
Beati 151
☎ 0331973158
Varallo Pombia
Cascina Bellaria
at Cascinetta
☎ 0321956805

**WINE
PRODUCERS**

Fara Novarese
Dessilani L. & F.
via C. Battisti 21
☎ 0321829252
Ghemme
**Antichi Vigneti
di Cantalupo**
via Buonarroti 2
☎ 0163840041
Sizzano
Giuseppe Bianchi
via Roma 27
☎ 0321820155

SHOPPING

Novara
**Pasticceria
Camporelli**
vicolo Monteriolo 3
☎ 0321620689
Pastries and sweets.
**Gastronomia
Moroni**
via Avogadro 1/b
☎ 0321611050
Gourmet store.
Borgomanero
**Il Tagliere
Macelleria Equina**
via Rosmini 26
☎ 0322841891
Horse meat.
Cavaglietto
Caseificio Oioli
piazza Castello 7
☎ 0322280655 1
Cheese producer.

Those who choose to spend the night instead of returning to Novara should use the time go to Galliate – where you will find *salam 'd la duja* and *pagnottelle con uva sultania* (rolls with sultanas) in the shops – and to Trecate for *salame d'oca* (goosemeat salami) and a characteristic dish of *anatra muta ripiena* (stuffed duck), with the idea of going on to the Boffalora bridge. Straying from the route, we suggest you go to "Osteria Croce Bianca", which offers updated Lombard cuisine in the setting of the Parco del Ticino. An alternative is to go west from Oleggio to the crossroads with the Statale 229 from Lake Orta. Here, at Momo, is the restaurant "Macallè" which offers a hybrid of hill and plains cooking: *risotto tartufato* (truffle risotto) and *gnocchetti al gorgonzola* (small gnocchi with gorgonzola), *stracotto d'asino al Barolo* (stewed donkey with Barolo wine), *quaglia farcita al fegato grasso d'Oca* (quail stuffed with fatted goose liver), *lumache* (snails) and *rane fritte* (fried frogs).

2. Lake Orta and Lake Maggiore
GOZZANO. The complex of the Castello, where the parish church, bishop's palace and other ancient buildings are located, provides the village with impressive monuments. However, gourmets should quickly take a detour to Soriso where one of Italy's best restaurants, "Al Sorriso", awaits. It is famous for the high quality of its cuisine and the almost poetic attention to detail. Running down the menu we find *galantina di volatili con fegato grasso e pere all'aceto balsamico* (galantine of fowl with fatted liver and pears with balsamic vinegar), *ravioloni verdi di formaggi freschi di capra al burro d'alpe* (large green ravioli with fresh goat's cheese and alpine butter), *gallina novella con composta di mele e purea al prezzemolo* (young hen with apple sauce and mashed potatoes with parsley), *rombo chiodato laccato al miele di tiglio con funghi galletti* (turbot with linden-honey glaze and chanterelle mushrooms) and *budino ai non-ti-scordar-di-me e profumo di Drambuie* (forget-me-not pudding flavored with Drambuie).

ORTA SAN GIULIO. The quiet lanes of the village, marked by traces of Baroque influence, stretch out on a peninsula into the lake's romantic waters. For an atmospheric stay enhanced by dining at a first-rate restaurant, check in at the nineteenth-century "Villa Crespi". Characteristic products include *mortadella di fegato* (liver *mortadella*) from the lower Sesia Valley.

ARONA. Protected by the hill of the Vergante, the village is a wealthy holiday resort on the Verbano. Its past is marked by commerce between Milan and Canton Ticino. In Piazza del Popolo is "Taverna del Pittore", which ranks at the top of the list of local restaurants.

VERBANIA

Monte Rosa and Lago Maggiore are the two extremes of Verbania's landscape and at the same time they are the symbols of the area's cuisine.

Below:
sheep farming
in the mountains
around Lake
Maggiore

The mountainous province of Verbano-Cusio-Ossola runs from the westernmost limits of Piedmont, for the most part wedged in between the Swiss Valese and Canton Ticino. The defining element of the landscape is the Toce River, which first opens the route between the Pennine Alps to form Val d'Osola and then runs into Lake Maggiore. Thus the natural backdrop is modulated between the two poles: Monte Rosa with its glaciers and the exotic Verbano. There is a similar contrast to the picture painted by human settlement.

On the one hand, the thousand-year-old pastoral economy of the Alpine valleys is still clearly seasonal and only recently enlivened by skiing and hiking. But on the other, since the 18th century, tourism has transformed the banks of Lake Maggiore into a backdrop of villas, palazzos and hotels. Thus, in the mountains rustic cuisine is closely tied to the traditions of the Germanic Walser people, who settled around Monte Rosa in the Middle Ages. But around the lake, you will find refined as well as Piedmont cuisine, which traditionally caters to a cosmopolitan and demanding clientele of tourists.

Gourmet Tours

HOTELS AND RESTAURANTS

Verbania
⭐📺 **Milano** ♦♦♦
at Pallanza
corso Zanitello 2
☎ 0323556816
⭐📺 **Piccolo Lago** ♦♦♦
at Fondotoce
via Turati 87
☎ 0323586792
Boccon di Vino ♦
at Suna
via Troubetzkoy 86
☎ 0323504039
Osteria del Castello ♦
at Intra
piazza Castello 9
☎ 0323516579
Baceno
⭐📺 **La Baita** ♦
Alpe Devero (km 11)
☎ 0324619190
Locanda Punta Fizzi ♦
Alpe Devero (km 11)
☎ 0324619108
Belgirate
Villa Carlotta
★★★ ♦♦♦♦
via Mazzini 121/125
☎ 032276461
Milano ★★★ ♦♦♦
via Mazzini 2/4
☎ 032276525
Cannobio
Del Lago ★★★ ♦♦♦
at Carmine (km 3)
via Nazionale 2
☎ 032370595
Lo Scalo ♦♦♦
piazza Vittorio Emanuele III 32
☎ 032371480
Crodo
Pizzo del Frate ★★
at Foppiano (km 4)
☎ 032461233

VERBANIA. There are two centers to this young provincial capital: Pallanza, to the west of the verdant point of Castagnola, facing the Borromeo Gulf, and Intra to the east, which faces Laveno. The first combines a medieval atmosphere with the feel of a prestigious health resort. Here you will find the restaurant "Milano", with its refined Art Nouveau room over-looking the lake and a menu that alternates between fresh – and salt –water fish and more typically regional fare. At Intra, a lively lake port, you will find the simpler "Osteria dell Castello", which offers products from the valleys and good dishes with *polenta*. Inland, at Ponte del Casletto, is the entry to Val Grande National Park, one of Italy's last true wild lands.

1. Lake Maggiore

STRESA. Walking along the lake, you discover the incomparable beauty of a place that is suspended midway between lake and mountain, embellished with villas and nineteenth-century hotels and lush with exotic plants. Don't miss out on a boat trip to the Isole Borromee, where you can see Isola Bella, with its grandiose Palazzo Borromeo and Italian garden spread over ten terraces, the Isola dei Pescatori, with its lake-side village and Isola Madre, with its large botanical garden animated by peacocks, pheasants and parakeets. In Stresa, there is an array of places to stay the night, beginning with the princely "Gran Hotel des Iles Borromees", a Gothic edifice built in 1861. More humble mortals might prefer to stay in Belgirate at the hotel "Villa Carlotta" which is set in the greenery of a large lakefront garden with a restaurant set across two elegant rooms on a large verandah. Here the dish that receives the Buon Ricordo listing is *filetto di pesce persico al cartoccio* (filet of perch baked in parchment). The "Piemontese" is a tranquil, refined, family-run restaurant, where you can dine under a pergola and try *agnolotti all'Ossolana* (Ossola-style *ravioli*) and *sformato di lumache al tartufo* (snail and truffle timbale).

Alpe Veglia.
Baite huts in
La Balma

The home-made *mostarda con l'uva fragola* (a spread made with strawberry grapes) is a curiosity. CANNOBIO. Situated at the mouth of the narrow Val Cannobina, which goes all the way to Ossola, the village boasts the medieval Palazzo della Ragione and sixteenth-century Santuario della Pietà as attractions, and faces Verbano. The town has earned itself a good name for food. In the center, "Lo Scalo" is a refined restaurant with a good wine cellar and interesting sampling menu. The restaurant "Del Lago" is located in Carmine and serves the evocative *insalata tiepida di astice con salsa di agrumi e burro fuso* (warm salad with lobster and citrus sauce and melted butter), *spaghetti neri ai gamberi, pomodori e asparagi* (squid ink spaghetti with shrimp, tomatoes and asparagus) and *rombo al caviale* (turbot with caviar).

2. The Val d'Ossola and the valleys

DOMODOSSOLA. In the large Toce Valley, this town is a thousand-year-old crossroads on the

HOTELS AND RESTAURANTS

Domodossola
Piemonte -
da Sciolla ❘ ★🚗
piazza Convenzione 4
☎ 0324242633
Formazza
Pernice Bianca-
Schneehendli ★★★
at Cascata del Toce
☎ 032463200
Ghiffa
Ghiffa ★★★ ★🚗
corso Belvedere 88
☎ 032359285
Macugnaga
Zumstein ★★★
at Staffa
via Monte Rosa 63
☎ 032465118
Chez Felice ★★ 🚗
at Staffa
via alle Ville 14
☎ 032465229
Mergozzo
Le Oche di
Bracchio ❘
via Bracchio 46
☎ 032380122
Santa Maria
Maggiore
Miramonti ★★★ ★🚗
piazzale Diaz 3
☎ 032495013
Stresa
G. Hotel des Iles
Borromées ★★★★L
corso Umberto I 67
☎ 0323938938
Piemontese ❘❘
via Mazzini 25
☎ 032330235
Varzo
Cuccini ★★
at San Domenico
(km 12)
☎ 0324706l

AGRITURISMI

**Santa Maria
Maggiore
Al Piano
delle Lutte**
at Lutte
via Domodossola 57
☎ 032494488
Varzo
⭐ 📷 **Ferrari
Orlando**
at Alpe Cortiggia
☎ 032472436
**Verbania
Monterosso**
at Cima
Monterosso 30
☎ 0323556510

SHOPPING

**Verbania
Bogogna**
at Intra
via S. Vittore 66
☎ 0323401571
*Charcuterie, cheeses,
wines and olive oil.*
**Baceno
Adolfo Olzeri**
via S. Antonio
☎ 032462140
*Local cheeses
and butter.*
**Crevoladossola
Alberto Mazzurri
Azienda
Agricola Bravi**
via del Ponte 5
☎ 0324338355
Bettelmatt cheese.
**Formazza
Nuova Formazza
Cooperativa**
at Valdo 36
☎ 032463169
Typical cheeses.

Sempione road. The Piazza del Mercato is surrounded by colonnades and ancient buildings, providing a beautiful picture of times gone by and capturing the austere fascination of the town. In restaurants we find the typical dishes of Ossola's gastronomy, including *gnocchi profumati di noce moscata* (gnocchi with nutmeg) or *lumache con ripieno di amaretti e noci* (snails stuffed with amaretti and walnuts). The period rooms and regional cooking – including an interesting method of cooking the *lumache all'amaretto* – are the strong points of the restaurant "Piemonte – da Sciolla", which also has a few rooms. In shops, look for *bresaola* (cured beef or venison) and smoked *prosciutto* with juniper berries, as well as *violini*, which are made of chamois and roebuck leg, but more often goat. From the mountain pastures come cheeses made of cow's milk (*nostrano d'alpe* and *spress* in the summer; *nostrano di latteria* in the winter) and of goat's milk (those from the Alpe Valle di Trasquera are well-known). The cheese *Bettelmatt* is also good and exploited by the Bernardini family.

MACUGNAGA. This small community is located at the top of the Valle Anzasca, below the rock – and ice-covered Monte Rosa. The town, which has been discovered by skiers and hikers, has interesting features from the culture of the Walsers. In Borca, you can visit a house-museum, and food takes on a different flavor here. The rustic restaurant "Chez Felice" closely observes lo-

cal tradition: don't miss the lamb shank with fried rice.

CRODO. A holiday resort and spa village, the primary gastronomic interest here is cheese from the upper valley. Milk from Bruna Alpina is used to make *grasso d'alpe* and *nostrano d'alpe* in the summer and *mezzapasta* in the winter. Goat's cheese, in 25 centimeter disks made from Chamois goat's milk, comes from Baceno. Foppiano is worth mentioning for its family-run hotel-restaurant "Pizzo del Frate".

SANTA MARIA MAGGIORE. Set in the Alpi Pennine, this village is a tourist attraction and spreads across the valley that marks the watershed between Val Vigezzo and the Swiss Centovalli. An excellent *prosciutto crudo* is produced here. It is aged in the mountain breeze for over a year and is also available smoked. The main cheeses are *nostrano d'alpe* and *caprini* (goat's cheese), while mushrooms abound. The traditional bread is made with buckwheat and rye. At the hotel "Miramonti" you will find good food.

FORMAZZA. Here, we are almost at the springs that feed the Toce. Beyond the mountains on one side is the Vallese and on the other the Swiss Canton Ticino. Along the border, around the local pasture, the cheese *Bettelmatt* is produced. Made in 8 – to 10 – kilo molds, the yellow buttery cheese is filled with fairly large holes. Characteristic of the same zone is *züfi*, a kind of *ricotta* that is fermented until it becomes a creamy spread. On the plain of the waterfalls of the Toce, stop at the hotel "Pernice Bianca Schneehendli" for the pleasure of tasting traditional Walser cuisine.

VERCELLI

The Sesia river defines the landscape, divided between pastures, woods, rice fields and poplar groves,and cuisine of Vercelli

The province of Vercelli includes the upper basin of the Sesia and, further downstream, a strip of the plain to the east of the river, growing wider as it approaches the Po. The northern portion is dominated by the hills of Monte Rosa, and marked by the many valleys that lead to the main gully. Cattle and goats are raised in this area, and cheese and charcuterie feature strongly. Further south is a strip of pre-Alpine hills, followed by hills blanketed with the Nebbiolo vine. Together with Bonarda and Vespolina, the Nebbiolo grape is used to make the excellent DOCG wine Gattinara. Rich with streams, the plain is the setting for the rice fields, which provide the primary raw material for meals in Vercelli. With Novara, Vercelli shares the traditional dish *paniscia* (rice cooked in vegetable broth with beans and sausage). Here you can find dishes similar to Lomellina's Lombard dishes, based on frogs, snails and fish. Beyond the Po, you come across new flavors and new wines at the foothills of Monferrato.

Below:
Vercellese
rice fields

Gourmet Tours

VERCELLI. The bulk of the Gothic basilica of San Andrea dominates a city with a medieval layout and dignified eighteenth – and nineteenth - century buildings. The Sesia flows nearby, and all around, dotted with poplars and inhabited by herons, you can see rice fields – the source of the province's wealth. Thus, tables are lavished with risottos, starting with the aforementioned *paniscia*, made according to the recipe of its native Novara. To try it at its best, together with grilled vegetables, meat and creative dishes, we recommend the restaurant "Giardinetto", which overlooks the garden of the hotel it belongs to. In the town, there is also the "Zaccone", which offers excellent traditional dishes. In Borgo Vercelli, just beyond the Sesia, "Osteria Cascina dei Fiori" is very good. Reworkings of traditional dishes are served in two rustic but elegant dining rooms. These include *risotto con rane e fiori di zucca* (*risotto* with frogs and pumpkin flowers), *gnocchetti bianchi e verdi al Castelmagno* (white and green *gnocchi* Castelmagno style), *trippa stufata con lenticchie di Castelluccio* (stewed tripe with Castelluccio lentils) and *budino al gianduia e amaretti di Sassello* (chocolate cream and Sassello amaretti pud-

ding). In Quinto Vercellese the restaurant "Bivio" is an excellent choice for *bollito misto* (boiled meats) and local cheeses.

1. The plain

SANTHIÀ. Not far from the rolling hills and vineyards of the Serra, you should stop on the way to Ivrea to visit this town's central piazza and admire a 16th-century polyptych in the parish church, before going down to the Po river. LIVORNO FERRARIS. The town's name pays homage to the its most celebrated son, the nineteenth-century scientist Galileo Ferraris, whose house-museum may be visited. Continuing to Castell'Apertolego, you will find "Da Balin", a warm and inviting restaurant created from an old barn in the middle of the rice fields. Freshwater fish, risotto with frogs or *tinca* (tench), and frogs and snails prepared in various ways feature as hors d'oeuvres.
TRINO. The old town still has the medieval layout of a French village. On the banks of the Po there are two good *trattorie* which reflect the flavors of both the rice fields, which come to an end at this point, and the hills of Monferrato, which rise up on the other side of the river. In Fontanetto Po you should try "La Bucunà", and at Due Sture di Morano sul Po visit "Tre Merli".

2. The Valsesia

GATTINARA. The celebrated wine from Nebbiolo grapes is a major feature of village life and just going to the shops and *osterie* is a joy for food and wine lovers. The ideal place to begin a tour is the "Bottega del Vino", in Piazza Italia (although this will later be promoted to "Enoteca Regionale" and transferred to the restored Villa Paolitti). Among the wine producers "Antoniolo" is an excellent place to taste great reds as well as the delicate white Erbaluce. In town, the restaurant "Nuovo Impero" offers fresh pasta, *brasato al Gattinara* (braised meat Gattinara style) and *fritto misto piemontese* (mixed fry).

VARALLO. Just beyond Borgosesia, the most populous center in the valley, lies Varallo. The village's best-known feature is the Sacro Monte, which has 44 chapels decorated with statues and frescoes. Gourmets, however, will also appreciate its vegetables: asparagus from Parone, leeks from Morondo, cabbage from Cervarolo. In the shops you can buy *toma* from Valsesia, *prosciuttini di pecora* (cured hams made from sheep), *mortadella di fegato* (liver

mortadella). From Rimella, in the parallel Mastallone Valley, comes soft *caprini* (goat's milk cheese) that becomes sharp with age. Creamy *frachet*, made by fermenting leftovers of *tomino* with grappa and spices, has become a rarity. There are many chances to taste good food, the most satisfying being in Carcoforo, 1,300 meters up the side of a valley, where the beauty of the place is only enhanced by the cosy restaurant "Scoiatolo", where you can feast on mushrooms, cheeses, wild game and desserts.

ALAGNA VALSESIA. The last stage of this itinerary brings us to the foot of Monte Rosa. Despite its recent popularity as a ski destination, the village has preserved some of its older areas, where the Walser lived. People of German stock, they came here in the thirteenth century from the Swiss valleys. In Pedemonte, you can visit the Museo Walser, in a wooden house dating from 1628 with original furnishings and tools. Honey from Monte Rosa is excellent. At Piode, the "Osteria del Muntisel" is very good.

WINE PRODUCERS

Gattinara
Antoniolo
corso Valsesia 277
☎ 0163833612
Bottega del Vino
piazza Italia 6
☎ 0163834070

SHOPPING

Vercelli
Zaccone
via Verdi 13
☎ 0161250457
Fresh pasta and traditional dishes.
Bianzè
Azienda Agricola Ferraris - Cascina Torrone Cagna
☎ 016149297
Rice producer (Carnaroli, Baldo and Arborio varieties).
Cigliano
Pasticceria Vittorio
via Umberto I 60
☎ 0161423128
Pastries and sweets.
Desana
Azienda Agricola Tenuta Castello
cascina Serrime
☎ 0161318297
Rice (Carnaroli and Vialone nano varieties) and other naturally cultivated products such as spelt (farro).
Piode
Caseificio Alta Val Sesia
via Varallo 5
☎ 016371154
Butter and cheeses.
Ronsecco
Azienda Agricola Lodigiana
strada delle Grange 20
☎ 0161816001
Wide range of rices.

Alagna Valsesia. Typical alpine houses

Piemonte

PROVINCIA DI NOVARA

The products and dishes of our land
six tasty reasons to come here...

Cheeses:
Gorgonzola D.O.P.
Toma del Mottarone

Wines:
Ghemme D.O.C.G.
Boca - Fara - Sizzano D.O.C.
Colline Novaresi D.O.C.

Flowers:
Azalee e
Rododendri

Acacia honey

Rice:
"Paniscia" a typical dish
with sausages and beans

Salami:
salamino della Duja
e fidighin

Piazza Matteotti, 1 - 28100 Novara - ITALIA
Tel. (+39) 0321 666466 fax (+39) 0321 666472 - www.provincia.novara.it

The Vercelli Province

Featuring one of the most varied natural environments in Piedmont, the province territory starts from the flat landscape between the Po and Sesia rivers, to rise then gradually to the first hilly slopes and, through the Prealps Mountains, finally come to the vast silence of high altitudes with *Monte Rosa*, in *Valsesia*.

On a clear summer day, the *Capanna Regina Margherita* (4,559 m a.s.l.) is surely the most breathtaking panoramic spot from which to enjoy the best view of the whole Vercelli territory.

Any tourist visiting the area will not be disappointed. The Vercelli province is uncommonly rich in art treasures and great masterpieces from different periods in history, starting with prehistoric times.

THE VERCELLI PLAIN is characterized by rivers and paddies. At the start of spring, when the rice fields turn into a vast expanse of water only broken by small villages and picturesque farmhouses, the plain acquires a certain enchanting quality, giving rise to a multitude of shades and undertones. The blue of rice fields mixes in with the waters of the Po and Sesia rivers and, as the season goes, the landscape changes with the colour of rice, growing and flowering in a long stretch of golden cobs. Vercelli, historical rice capital, is one of the main national production poles.
The rice varieties grown in the Vercelli area are over 100. From a nutritional and gastronomical point of view the most valued ones are *"S. Andrea"*, *"Baldo"*, *"Arborio"* and *"Nuovo Maratelli"*, soon to be covered by a quality trademark.

The Vercelli gastronomic tradition gives its best in dishes with a strong taste, often prepared with poor ingredients. So is *panissa*, a typical Vercelli dish, and the risotto with *fagioli di Saluggia or Villata*, pork rind, chopped lard, herbs and *salam d'la duja*, a small salami made only with pork meat and kept in fat or oil inside a terracotta jar called, precisely, *"duja"*.

LA VALSESIA is the land of *Walser*, people of German descent who in a distant past came to these mountains, bringing their language and traditions with them. Here we find typical mountain food, quite simple but full of surprise flavour combinations.

Typical dishes are the miacce, puff pastry made with milk and flour, and cooked using a red-hot iron spread with lard; the various kinds of *salami*, *marbled trout* from the clear waters of the Sesia river and *cheese*, in particular *tome and caprini* (goat cheese).

Such a rich territory cannot fail to have its own Regional Enoteca (wine collection), based in *Gattinara*, corso Valsesia 112 (tel. 39 163 834070), at Villa Paolotti. Some of the high quality wines produced in the Vercelli area: the prestigious *DOCG Gattinara*, the classic DOC *Bramaterra and Erbaluce di Caluso* and the new *DOC Coste della Sesia*

LOMBARDY
A PATCHWORK
OF FLAVORS

*From the Alpine valleys to the Bassa Padana, Lombardy has
an outstanding variety of unique products – meats, charcuterie,
cheeses, cereals, and even olive oil – as well as a strong
traditional cuisine.*

M ilan is a city of business and industry, where the
soccer teams Inter and Milan play under the
megastructure of the Meazza stadium; it is the
home of the Duomo (cathedral) and Leonardo's *Last Supper, panettone* and *cotoletta alla Milanese*. Lombardy is above all Milan, and it
is very difficult to consider one of Italy's most interesting regions in
gastronomic terms, with its first-rate farming industry, and a variety and wealth of raw materials.

FROM THE PASTURES TO THE RICE FIELDS
The journey begins at the Alpine ring, with the hills of the Pre-Alps
tempering the stark effect of the granite Alpine cliffs and great lakes
adding color to the region. The agricultural landscape ranges from terraced vineyards and orchards in the Valtellina to the olive orchards on
the banks of the lakes. Each area has its own appeal: the hills of Franciacorta and the morainic amphitheater of Garda are both linked to viticulture. But the territory is mostly covered with plains. In lower areas,
surface waters appear along a line that marks the beginning of the Bassa, which is rich with natural waters and vegetation.

A CUISINE OF MEAT AND CHEESE
With an area of nearly 24,000 sq. km, Lombardy is the third largest region of Italy, but in terms of population it is the biggest with nine million people. It accounts for over a fifth of the national revenue, contributing with industry, commerce and services as well as agriculture. Meat is an important part of Lombard cuisine – particularly pork. It is used to best effect in *cassoeula*, a stew with cabbage. As important as animal farming is local cheese production, one of the richest in Italy.

VINEYARDS, GARDENS AND ORCHARDS
Lombardy is the land of *risotto*, and the yellow *risotto* – the Milanese version with saffron – is the standard-bearer. Gardens and orchard produce is good, with some of them, such as the Valtellina apple, gaining renown – but the vineyard brings the most satisfaction to the farmer; the Oltrepò Pavese has gained national fame for the variety and production in Franciacorte, a land of excellent Spumante (a sparkling wine), while Garda is the land of a celebrated Chiaretto. There are many wild products, for instance truffles and wild asparagus;

VARIETY IN MILAN, TRADITION IN THE PROVINCES
Until World War II Milan still had its own unique gastronomy that was lost as the city became more cosmopolitan. Chefs arrived from all parts of Italy and from other parts of the globe, broadening the scope of Milanese cuisine. The increased competition meant quality improved so much that many believe Milan to be the Italian city offering the best food. In contrast, there are ten other Lombard provinces that have kept most of their own culinary tradition.

Cassinetta di Lugagnano. Villa Visconti Maineri

Lombardy - Typical products

Scale 1:1 250 000

0   15   30 km

🧀 CHEESES

1. **Bitto Dop.** Produced in alta Valtellina.

2. **Formai de Mut Alta Val Brembana Dop**

3. **Gorgonzola Dop.** A blue-streaked cheese produced in Lombardy and Piedmont.

4. **Grana Padano Dop.** A hard cheese produced throughout the region.

5. **Parmigiano Reggiano Dop.** The hard Parmesan cheese produced in Oltrepò Mantovano.

6. **Provolone Valpadana Dop.** Semi-hard cheese produced in the planes.

7. **Quartirolo Lombardo Dop.** Produced in the plains.

8. **Taleggio Dop.** Produced in the pre-Alps and the plains.

9. **Valtellina Casera Dop**

10. **Bagoss.** Produced in the Bagolino area.

11. **Caprini.** Produced in the pre-Alpine valleys.

12. **Casolet dell'Adamello**

13. **Crescenza.** Produced in the Bassa milanese and the lodigiana areas.

14. **Formaggelle di monte**

15. **Grana lodigiano**

16. **Mascarpone.** Soft cheese produced in Lodi and Abbiategrasso.

17. **Pannerone.** Produced in the bassa milanese and lodigiano areas.

18. **Silter.** Produced in Valcamonica and around Lake Iseo.

🌙 CHARCUTERIE

1. **Salame Brianza Dop.** Brianza salami.

2. **Salame di Varzi Dop.** Varzi salami.

3. **Bresaola della Valtellina Igp.** Cured raw beef from Valtellina cows.

7. **Salame Milano.** Milanese salami produced throughout the region.
8. **Salame e prosciutto d'oca.** 'Oca' salami and ham produced in Mortara.
9. **Salsicce della Valcamonica.** A sausage from Valcamonica.
10. **Violino.** Aromatic cured meat produced in Spluga and the lower Chiavenna valley.

FRUTTA

1. **Mela della Valtellina.** Valtellina apples.
2. **Melone di Viadana.** Viadana melons produced between Oglio and the river Po..
3. **Pera Mantovana.** Montovana pears.

VEGETABLES

1. **Asparagi di Cilavegna.** Cilavegna asparagus.
2. **Cipolla di Sermide.** Sermide onions.

EXTRA-VIRGIN OLIVE OIL DOP

1. **Laghi Lombardi Dop.** Produced around lakes Como and Isea.
2. **Garda Dop**

GRAINS AND CEREALS

1. **Riso della Lomellina.** Lomellina rice produced in Milan and Pavia.
2. **Grano saraceno.** Buckwheat produced in Teglio, in Valtellina.

VARIOUS

1. **Mostarda.** Spiced fruit chutney produced in Cremona and its province.

DOCG WINES

1. **Franciacorta**
2. **Valtellina Superiore**

DOC WINES

3. **Botticino**
4. **Capriano del Colle**
5. **Cellatica**
6. **Garda**
7. **Garda Colli Mantovani**
8. **Lambrusco Mantovano**
9. **Lugana**
10. **Oltrepò Pavese**
11. **Riviera del Garda Bresciano**
12. **San Colombano al Lambro**
13. **San Martino della Battaglia**
14. **Terre di Franciacorta**
15. **Valcalepio**
16. **Valtellina**

4. **Cotechino bianco.** A white spiced sausage, a Valtellina specialty.
5. **Prosciutto crudo della Brianza.** Brianza ham.
6. **Prosciutto crudo Colline Mantovane.** Ham from the Montavane hills.

MILAN

The city is a gastronomic universe in which the most disparate traditions come together, while in the provinces Lombard flavors prevail.

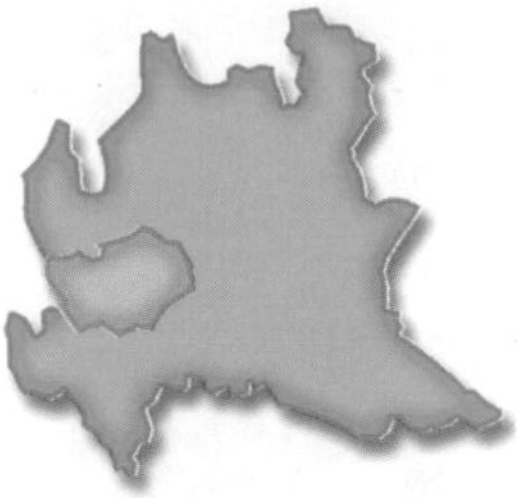

The province of Milan is the heart of Lombardy and covers the area between the valleys of the Ticino and Adda Rivers, and from the hills of Brianza to the dry plains which were once heathland. The city is in its center, with suburbs spreading out in every direction into the Bassa, an area verdant and rich with spring water. The countryside is well preserved thanks to a vast farming park, where large farms with courtyards and abbeys cultivated the lands around the year 1000. The network of canals and waterways created centuries ago feed the countryside, which in turn supplies a wealth of cheeses and charcuterie. As for gastronomy, Milan is the setting for an outstanding variety of regional and ethnic cuisines. Milanese tradition, which is made up of elements acquired during the Spanish and Hapsburg rule, can be found in a few historic restaurants and in the province.

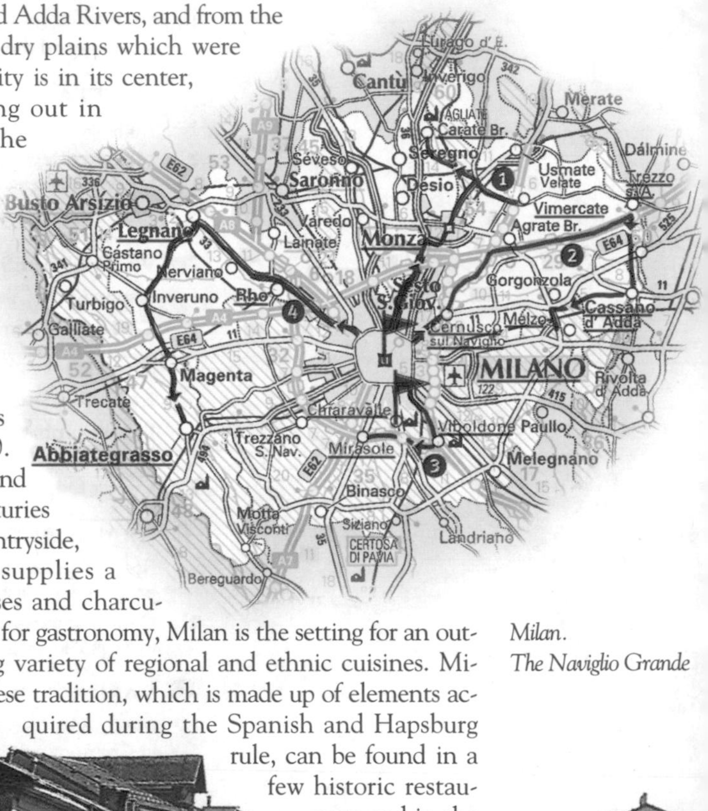

Milan.
The Naviglio Grande

Gourmet Tours

MILAN. A large pedestrian area links San Babila to Castello Sforzesco. It passes the Duomo (cathedral), beautiful buildings and elegant shop windows, making for a pleasant walk. A veritable melting pot of Italians and foreigners, Milan reflects many different cultures, as does its cuisine. It is one of the cities in which one eats the best, but here it is easier to find a true Tuscan or Chinese cook than a Milanese one. Our listing starts with establishments with long histories. In alphabetical order, "Bagutta" (established 1924) is a very central Tuscan restaurant that has hosted the a literary award of the same name since shortly after it was founded. Souvenirs from this event – book covers, caricatures – monopolize the decor. "Da Berti" (est. 1866), just outside Porta Nuova, is one of the last characteristic *osterie fuori porta* (outside the city walls). Dishes are rigorously Milanese, the wine cellar may be visited and, in the summer, there is a shady pergola. Back in the center is "Biffi Scala" (est. 1830) (now the Biffi Scala Toulà), located under a portico next door to Milan's temple to lyric opera. Here *risotto al salto* (sautéed risotto) is a post-theater tradition that has brought together generations of artists and lovers of opera. A veteran to city restoration is "Boeucc" (est. 1696), which began as a tavern frequented by Carlo Porta and the first members of the Carbonari secret society in via Durini and is now located in Piazza Belgioioso, where you can also visit Alessandro Manzoni's home.

Milan. The Galleria Vittorio Emanuele and the "Savini" restaurant

In the area around Porta Vittoria is "Giannino" (est. 1899), which began as a Chianti wine shop and later became a *trattoria* and over time became popular with influential people: today it boasts a good young chef who serves traditional and innovative dishes side by side. In the area around Corso Garibaldi, is "Antica Trattoria dela Pesa" (est. 1880) where the food is Lombard and the guest list ranges from the famous film director Pier Paolo Pasolini to the top journalist, the late Indro Montanelli. The historic "Savini" (est. 1867) in Galleria Vittorio Emanuele has tables on the walkway inside the shopping arcade and reserved salons upstairs. Milan also has a series of little gems waiting to be discovered. At the Piazza del Duomo side of the gallery is "Caffè Zucca" (est. 1867), originally called "Camparino", decorated with Art Nouveau mosaics from times past. In the same vein is "Cova" (est. 1817) on the elegant Via Montenapoleone, which has

HOTELS AND RESTAURANTS

Milan
Savini ⚑⚑⚑⚑⚑
galleria Vittorio Emanuele II
☎ 0272003433
Aimo e Nadia ⚑⚑⚑⚑
via Montecuccoli 6
☎ 0241 6886
Amì Berton ⚑⚑⚑⚑
via Nullo 14
☎ 0270123476
Boeucc ⚑⚑⚑⚑
piazza Belgioioso 2
☎ 0276020224
Biffi Scala & Toulà ⚑⚑⚑⚑
piazza della Scala
☎ 0286665 I
Giannino ⚑⚑⚑⚑ ⭐
via Sciesa 8
☎ 0255195582
Il Sambuco ⚑⚑⚑⚑
presso l'albergo
Hermitage ★☆☆
via Messina 10
☎ 0233610333
Hong Kong ⚑⚑⚑⚑
via Schiapparelli 5
☎ 0267071790
L'Ulmet ⚑⚑⚑⚑
via Olmetto 21
☎ 0286452718
Conte Camillo ⚑⚑⚑
presso l'albergo
Cavour ★★★
via P. Castaldi 18
☎ 0229522124
Jola ⚑⚑⚑
via P. Castaldi 18
☎ 0229522124
Malavoglia ⚑⚑⚑
via Lecco 4
☎ 0229531387
Tre Pini ⚑⚑⚑
via Morgagni 19
☎ 0266805413
Al Solito Posto ⚑⚑
via L. Bruni 13
☎ 026888310
Antica Trattoria della Pesa ⚑⚑
viale Pasubio 10
☎ 026555741

**HOTELS AND
RESTAURANTS**

**Milan
Bagutta** ¶¶
via Bagutta 14
☎ 0276002767
Da Berti ¶¶
via Algarotti 20
☎ 026694627
**Innocenti
Evasioni** ¶¶
via della Bindellina
☎ 0233001882
**Piccolo Teatro -
Fuori Porta** ¶¶
viale Pasubio 8
☎ 026572105
**Trattoria del
Nuovo Macello** ¶
via Lombroso 20
☎ 0259902122
**Cassinetta
di Lugagnano
Antica Osteria
del Ponte** ¶¶¶¶¶
piazza Negri 9
☎ 029420034
**Cernusco sul
Naviglio
Vecchia Filanda** ¶¶¶
via P. da Cernusco
☎ 029249200
**Concorezzo
Via del Borgo** ¶¶
via della Libertà 136
☎ 0396042615
**Cusago
Da Orlando** ¶¶
piazza Soncino 19
☎ 0290390318
**Gaggiano
Antica Trattoria
del Gallo** ¶¶
at Viganò (km 3)
via Kennedy1/3
☎ 029085276
**Garbagnate
Milanese
La Refezione** ¶¶¶
via Milano 16
☎ 029958942
**Melzo
Due Spade** ¶¶
via Bianchi 19
☎ 029550267
**Monza
De La Ville** ★★★
Derby Grill ¶¶¶
viale Regina
Margherita 15
☎ 039382581

survived the siege of designer shops and jewelers, as does "Lorenzi" (est. 1629), a shop descended from a knife-grinder from Val Rendena where knives, manicure sets and shaving tools sparkle like jewels in their presentation cases. Just around the corner, facing the gate to the austere Corso Matteotti is the exclusive "Sant'Ambroeus", a shrine to Milanese pastry. There are a few exceptional restaurants of more recent fame, including "Aimo e Nadia", located in a side street off the beaten track, universally acclaimed as one of the top Italian restaurants, with excellent products and rich, tasty traditional cuisine. Similarly good are "Giannino" and "Ulmet", another temple to regional tradition in an old building not far from the cathedral. New restaurants include "Joia", near Porta Venezia, where vegetarian and fish dishes are prepared by a creative chef with a love for Asia. For ethnic cuisine, the restaurant "Hong Kong", behind the Stazione Centrale, offers refined Cantonese and Szechwan cuisine. For totally covetable food you can take away with you, visit the three bountiful floors of "Peck", near Piazza del Duomo. Here you can also have a snack at the restaurant or bar.

1. The Brianza

MONZA. The Corona Ferrea, which crowned the heads of Italian kings from the Middle Ages

to Napoleon, is preserved at the cathedral of Monza, which was the seat of Theodolinda's Lombard court. The events of the Habsburg and Savoy dynasties live on at the Villa Reale and in the great park that is so dear to many Milanese. Not quite so magnificent, but appreciated nonetheless, is the sausage, also known as the *luganega*, that is used in *risotti*, *frittate*. The hotel "De la Ville", with its restaurant, "Derby Grill", is traditional and elegant with an English feel. In Concorezzo, we suggest the restaurant "Via del Borgo", located in an old courtyard, where *mondeghili* (meatballs) and Lombard-style chicken salad are served.

VIMERCATE. The fortified San Rocco bridge crossing the Molgora river and the many sixteenth- and seventeenth-century villas around it mark the ancient route *Vicus Mercati* that is still used today. At Ornago we recommend "Osteria della Buona Condotta" where you must not miss the *manzo all'olio con polenta* (beef with olive oil and *polenta*). There is also a well-thought-out list of charcuterie and cheese. The butcher "Carlo Sala", located in the central Via Cavour, sells cuts of famous Brianza veal and excellent charcuterie from Besana.

CARATE BRIANZA. The main attraction here is the Romanesque basilica of Santi Pietro e Paolo in Agliate, but the town also affords surprising and equally interesting glimpses of the Lambro Valley. For a gastronomic interval continue to Seregno, where "Osteria del Pomireu" is located in an old courtyard at the center of town, offering traditional cooking accompanied by an extensive wine list.

2. Along the Martesana and the Adda

CERNUSCO SUL NAVIGLIO. On the verdant banks of the Martesana lies the old resort town of Milan's nobility. In the shade of a smokestack is "La Vecchia Filanda", a restaurant that serves refined cuisine and typical Milanese dishes and fish. Next you come to Gorgonzola, famous for its blue-streaked cheese.

TREZZO SULL'ADDA. After a double loop between steep banks, the Adda first flows past the modern architecture of the Taccani power plant and then below the crumbling steps of what was once the castle of Bernabò Visconti. Here the restaurant "San Martino" offers classic cooking and dishes based on fish, mushrooms and truffles. On the opposite bank is Crespi d'Adda, a famous nineteenth-century working town.

CASSANO D'ADDA. The main aspects of the town are its medieval castle, a big neo-classical villa, old mills and power plants. A walk along the river banks offers picturesque views.

MELZO. The ancient city of *Melphum*, perhaps of Etruscan origin, still has its medieval layout and

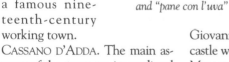
Typical breads "pan de mei" and "pane con l'uva"

boasts an ancient cheese-making tradition. We recommend the restaurant "Due Spade" where five diligent brothers run a kitchen that produces varied and meticulous cooking, including the excellent *piccione in casseruola* (pigeon casserole) and *gallinella nella lattuga* (young hen wrapped in lettuce). The wine list is very good. At Settala take a walk to the springs in Muzzetta.

3. A tour of the abbeys

CHIARAVALLE. In the countryside southeast of Milan rises the bell tower of the Cistercian abbeys that were founded in 1135 and which were responsible for cultivating the Bassa Milanese. After taking a tour stop to buy farm produce.

VIBOLDONE. Between Via Emilia and the Autostrada del Sole, the Gothic church and the campanile are all that remain of the monastery of the Umiliati (the humbled). Go to "La Rampina", an old *osteria* that today offers refined dishes, in addition to wild game and the traditional fried frogs. Further on at Melegnano, you will find the church of San Giovanni Battista and a Visconti castle with frescoed rooms.

MIRASOLE. The ancient monastic complex, now in the advanced stages of restoration, still has all the original elements of a farm, with cloisters and courtyards which were used for rural activities. The excursion ends in Zibido San Giacomo at "Antica

Ornago
Osteria Buona Condotta ¶¶
via Cavenago 2
☎ 0396919056
Pogliano Milanese
La Corte ¶¶ ★📷
at Bettolino (km 2)
via Chiesa 36
☎ 0293258018
San Giuliano Milanese
La Rampina ¶¶¶ ★📷
at Cascina Rampina
☎ 029833273
Seregno
Osteria del Pomireu ¶¶
via Garibaldi 37
☎ 0362237973
Trezzo sull'Adda
San Martino ¶¶ ★📷
via Brasca 49
☎ 029091978
Zibido San Giacomo
Antica Osteria Molrago ¶¶
at Mirago (km 3)
via Pavese 4
☎ 0290002174

SHOPPING

Milan
Antica Arte del Dolce
Sweets and pastries.
via Anfossi 10
☎ 0255194448
Coltelleria Lorenzi
via Montenapoleone 9
☎ 0276022848
Knives, manicure sets and shaving tools
Casa del Fungo e del Tartufo
via Anfossi 13
☎ 0255013179
Truffles and mushrooms.
Drogheria Gallina
via Caminadella 6
☎ 0286 1605
Delicatessen.
Gastronomia Peck
via Spadari 7/9
☎ 028053528
Delicatessen.

SHOPPING

Macelleria Ercole Villa
viale Brianza 11
☎ 026693118
Meat.

Pasticceria Clivati
viale Coni Zugna 57
☎ 0289400661
Pastries and sweets.

Pasticceria Confetteria Cova
via Montenapoleone 8
☎ 0276000578
Pastries and sweets.

Pasticceria Garbagnati
via Victor Hugo 3
☎ 02875301
Pastries and sweets.

Pasticceria Sant'Ambroeus
corso Matteotti 7
☎ 0276000540
Pastries and sweets.

Pasticceria Taveggia
via Visconti di Modrone 2
☎ 02791257
Historic cafe-pastry shop.

Salumeria Campagnoli
corso Vercelli 14
☎ 0248005361
Charcuterie and delicatessen.

Salumeria Garbelli
via Mameli 40
☎ 027388424
Charcuterie.

Zucca in Galleria
(ex Camparino)
galleria Vittorio Emanuele
☎ 0286464435
Cafe-pastry shop.

Concorezzo Boutique del Dolce
via de Giorgi 2
☎ 0396049251
Pastries and sweets.

Vimercate Macelleria Carlo Sala
via Cavour 20
☎ 039668467
Meat.

Osteria Moirago", which is set in a dairy farm and offers an extensive menu of fish, mushrooms and truffles Don't leave without trying the cakes from the adjoining pastry shop.

4. Towards the Ticino

RHO. Don't let yourself be influenced by the confusion of buildings on Rho's outskirts as you arrive there by the Statale Sempione. You do not have to go far from the traffic to make interesting discoveries. The Bosco di Vanzago, managed by the WWF, is a natural paradise. At

Cassinetta di Lugagnano.
The Antica Osteria del Ponte

Pogliano Milanese you will find the ever-improving "La Corte", a restaurant serving both a traditional and a more experimental menu, as well as good wines.

LEGNANO. This hardworking town, with the Bramantesque basilica of San Magno, is a point of reference for gastronomic exploration northwest of Milan. At Garbagnate, for example, "La Refezioneé" is a good place to go for Lombard cuisine. Then, further down the Ticino river you will find Castano Primo on the Villoresi canal, marking the entry into the river park. In Turbigo and Boffalora fish *trattorie* abound. And Magenta is the starting point for a visit to Cassinetta di Lugagnano, on the Naviglio Grande, where you will

see the beautiful villas of Milan's old guard, and the restaurant "Antica Osteria del Ponte", a rare find, with painstakingly prepared dishes and a wine cellar of international fame.

ABBIATEGRASSO. Once on the route taken by barges carrying marble from Candoglia to the Fabbrica del Duomo di Milano (the construction site for Milan's cathedral), this town has old colonnaded streets and a church, Santa Maria Nuova, that bears the mark of architect Bramante's genius. Abbiategrasso has a tradition of butter and cheese, *prosciutto* and *cresponi* (cured Milanese salami), and cherries. Nearby is the abbey Morimondo, and it is to the Cistercian monks here that the Lombardians owe the irrigation techniques that turned the Bassa Milanese into a small agricultural miracle. Built of brick, and deep in the countryside, the church is well preserved. Near Gaggiano, on the return route, the restaurant "Antica Trattoria del Gallo" is a convenient stop. Taking a detour to the north, Cusago offers another pleasant place to break your journey: "Da Orlando", where cuisine is seasonal and there is a good wine list. At Bareggio, the Fontanile Nuovo with its flowing spring water is beautiful.

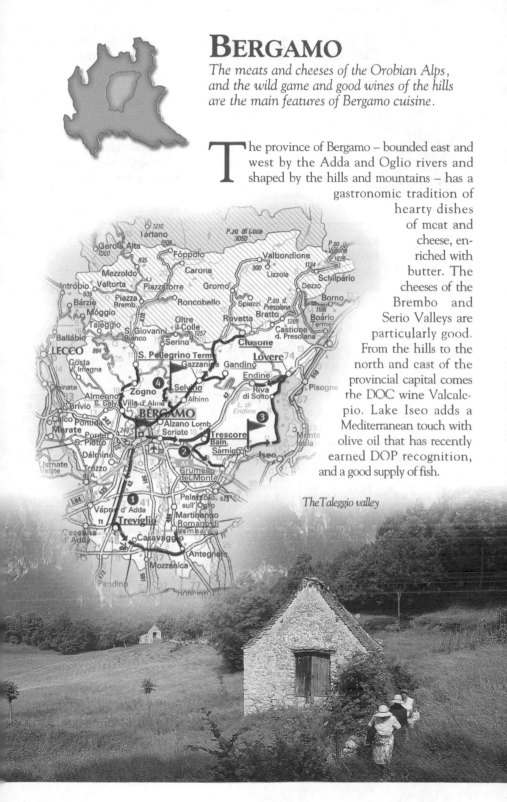

BERGAMO

*The meats and cheeses of the Orobian Alps,
and the wild game and good wines of the hills
are the main features of Bergamo cuisine.*

The province of Bergamo – bounded east and west by the Adda and Oglio rivers and shaped by the hills and mountains – has a gastronomic tradition of hearty dishes of meat and cheese, enriched with butter. The cheeses of the Brembo and Serio Valleys are particularly good. From the hills to the north and east of the provincial capital comes the DOC wine Valcalepio. Lake Iseo adds a Mediterranean touch with olive oil that has recently earned DOP recognition, and a good supply of fish.

The Taleggio valley

95

Gourmet Tours

BERGAMO. The city is a fascinating mix of Lombard Romanesque and Venetian Renaissance, with the legacy of Bartolomeo Coleoni, the fifteenth-century military leader, the paintings of the Accademia Carrara and the arias of Donizetti adding colour to the overall picture. To the north lies the Parco Regionale dei Colli di Bergamo (Bergamo Hills) – a pleasant rural area dominated by Canto Alto (1146 m/ 3760 ft). "Vittorio" is a top-notch restaurant on the main artery of the lower town. An elegant restaurant, many consider it the best in Italy for fish. "Lio Pellegrini" is also an excellent choice. Located in a seventeenth-century sacristy, it offers meticulous Tuscan cuisine. There are also three good historic eateries: the refined restaurant-bistro "Balzer" (est. 1850) opposite the Senterione passageway and in front of the Teatro Sociale, the "Taverna del Colleoni" (est. 1744), an exceptional place to try authentic Bergamo cuisine in the splendid Piazza Vecchia, and the nearby "Tasso" (est. 1476), an ancient tavern that bears the traces of 500 years of the city's history.

1. The Bassa Bergamasca

TREVIGLIO. The excellent restaurant "San Martino" – where a Lombard family offers first-rate regional cooking with interesting touches of French and vegetarian food – provides a good enough reason to stop in the busy town east of the Adda river. Nearby, along the Padana Superiore, is the town of Caravaggio with its celebrated Marian sanctuary.

ROMANO DI LOMBARDIA. On the other side of the Serio lies this village which has lived as much under the banner bearing the Visconti snake as that bearing the Venetian lion of San Marco. Along the way back to Bergamo, stop by the Malpaga castle that was once the sumptuous residence of Colleoni.

2. In the hills

TRESCORE BALNEARIO. At the top of Val Cavallina, in Bergamo's Pre-Alps, is a long-established spa center. At the church of Santa Barbara there is an admirable series of frescoes by Lorenzo Lotto. The excellent hotel "Della Torre", with a restaurant and well-stocked wine cellar, is a fine place to stop.

GRUMELLO DEL MONTE. This is the main center of Valcalepio, Bergamo's wine-producing area. The town's interesting medieval center has several wineries. You can find farms open to the public in nearby towns.

3. Between Lakes Iseo and Endine

SARNICO. At the point where the Oglio flows out of the Sebino river lies the village that grew up around the church of San Paolo. Along the lake there are some interesting early twentieth-century buildings. This is a good opportunity to try some fish-based dishes.

LOVERE. Where the Valcamonica runs into the lake, this fortified town was once dedicated to iron manufacturing, thanks to the mines of Upper Bergamo. Today tourism is the primary activity.

HOTELS AND RESTAURANTS

Bergamo
★★ Vittorio ⅲⅲ
viale Giovanni XXIII 21
☎ 035218060
Lio Pellegrini ⅲⅲ
via S. Tomaso 47
☎ 035247813
★★ Taverna del Colleoni e dell'Angelo ⅲⅲ
piazza Vecchia 7
☎ 035232596
Balzer ⅰ
portici Sentierone 41
☎ 035234083
Boario Terme
★★ Landò ⅱ
via Cavallera 1
☎ 0364535291
Branzi
Branzi ★★
via Umberto 123
☎ 034571121
Bratto-Dorga
★★ Milano
★★ Caminone ⅱ
at Bratto
via Silvio Pellico 3
☎ 034631211
Pian Camuno
Stube ★★
at Solato (km 3)
via Fane 12
☎ 0364590100
Trescore Balneario
★★ Della Torre ★★★
piazza Cavour 26
☎ 035941365
Treviglio
San Martino ⅲⅲ
via C. Battisti 3
☎ 036349075

Monuments include the basilica of Santa Maria in Valvendra and the neoclassical Palazzo Tadini, which has a major art collection. Leaving the lake, follow a brief stretch of the Val Cavallina where you will find Lake Endine. ENDINE. Situated at end of the lake, which is marked by tiny villages, Endine boasts many *trattorie* offering good fish dishes, with *tinca coi piselli* (tench with peas) as traditional fare.

4. In the heart of the Orobian Alps

SELVINO. Leaving Bergamo, you first arrive at Alzano Lombardo, a village at the start of the Val Seriana. Then a scenic route leads to Selvino, a vacation resort town in the mountains where you can find a comprehensive offering of traditional rustic fare, including *polenta e uccelli* (*polenta* with birds), *casonei* (pasta filled with salami, spinach, *ricotta* and eggs), *stracotto* (beef stew), salami and *cotechino*.

An Orobian goat on the Ugo Midali di Branzi farm

GANDINO. Another detour from the central valley leads to Gandino, an ancient wool-processing town with a well-preserved seventeenth-century center.
CLUSONE. This ancient village still has its famous Dance Macabre (Dance of Death) conserved by the Oratorio dei Disciplini. Further up, on one side is the top of the Val Seriana and on the other is the Presolana Pass that opens into the upper Scalve Valley and Schilpario village. At Bratto-Dorga we recommend the hotel "Milano" and its restaurant "Caminone".
SAN PELLEGRINO TERME. Follow the Val Brembana from Bergamo to this elegant early nineteenth-century spa town. In traditional restaurants you will find *tagliatelle alla brembana, casonsei alla Bergamasca* (pasta filled with salami, spinach *ricotta* and eggs), *lepre e capriolo in salmì* (jugged hare and roebuck) and *polenta e uccelli* (*polenta* with birds). A little further down the Enna gully take a detour at San Giovanni Bianco and head towards Val Taleggio, the home of the Taleggio cheese. Back along the Brembo to Cornello, a well-preserved medieval town, and further up is Branzi, the headquarters of the local cheese manufacturing cooperative. At the end of the route, Foppoli is nestled in a basin of fields and woods.

AGRITURISMI

Alzano Lombardo
Ardizzone ✈️🍴🏨
at Nese
cascina Grumello
☎ 035510060
Costa di Serina
La Peta 🍴🏨
at Gazzo, via Peta 3
☎ 034597955
Fonteno
Coop. Agrituristica
La Flora
at Monte I
☎ 035969115
Sotto il Monte Giovanni XXIII
Casa Clelia 🍴🏨
via Corna 1/3
☎ 035799133

WINE PRODUCERS

Grumello del Monte
Le Corne
via S. Pantaleone
☎ 035830215
Tenuta Castello di Grumello
Via Fosse 11
☎ 0354420817

SHOPPING

Bergamo
Bar del Tasso
piazza Vecchia 3
☎ 035237966
Bistro.
Pasticceria Cavour
via Gombito 7
☎ 035243418
Sweets and pastries.
Taleggio
Coop. Agricola S. Antonio in Valtaleggio
at Sottochiesa
☎ 034547021
Trescore Balneario
Pasticceria G. Pina
via Locatelli 14
☎ 035940344
Sweets and pastries.
Valtorta
Cooperativa Latteria Sociale
via Roma
☎ 034587770
Cheeses.

BRESCIA

A formidable list of raw materials in the hills, mountains, lakes and plains makes for a great culinary tradition.

An exceptional list of flavors hails from this province with its extremely varied landscape, which runs from the Valcamonica mountains to the Lower Po river, and from the hills of Franciacorta to those of Gardesana. Tables are laden with meats, cheeses and *polenta*, along with fish, olive oil and vegetables. Wine production is important and may be divided into two distinct zones: Franciacorta, to the west of the capital, and the Riviera di Garda to the east. The first produces a high quality Spumante, while the latter produces Chiaretto, a wine long celebrated by travelers.

Villa Bettoni
at Bogliaco di Gargnano

Gourmet Tours

BRESCIA. The iron-manufacturing industry, originally fed by Alpine mines, is the source of long-standing wealth reflected by unusual monuments and art collections. Piazza della Loggia, surrounded by Venetian-style architecture, is the starting point of a tour that covers the ancient Roman town of *Brixia* and ambitious Fascist urban developments. DOC wines produced in the hills around the city include Botticino, Cellatica and Capriano del Colle. Distilled products are also important, starting with the renowned Grappa di Malvasia. At Concesio, on the route to Val Trompia, is the excellent restaurant "Miramonti l'Altro", where creative Lombard cuisine is served and the wine list is high quality.

1. From Franciacorta to Valcamonica

ERBUSCO. From Brescia go to the hilly area of Franciacorta. The wine capital is Erbusco, where some interesting buildings still stand, but whose main point of interest lies in the restaurant "Gualtiero Marchesi" at the hotel "L'Albereta". In a converted villa one of the great masters of Italian cooking prepares classic dishes as well as inspirational modern food.

ISEO. To the north is Iseo, a village on the banks of a lake of the same name. Here, popular fish dishes feature *anguille* (eel), *tinche* (tench), *coregoni* (whitefish) and *trote* (trout). If you wish to spend the night, the inn "I Due Roccoli" offers a quiet and scenic sojourn and "Osteria il Volto" serves excellent fish from the lake. Further along are Monte Isola, a unique rural setting on an island, and Pisogne, an ancient commercial center and the last town on the Brescian banks of the lake.

BOARIO TERME. Located in the lower Valcamonica, this ancient spa resort town comes alive from June to September in the Parco delle Fonti, where theater and other events take place. It is here that you start to sample the gastronomy of the valley. Just beyond it, at Breno, you will find excellent charcuterie including *salsiccia di castrato in tegame* (fried mutton sausage) as well as *funghi* (mushrooms), *lumache* (snails), mountain products and *caicc* (local *ravioli*). At Capo di Ponte

HOTELS AND RESTAURANTS

Brescia
**Park Hotel
Ca' Nöa** ★★★
via Triumplina 66
☎ 030398762
Calvisano
Al Gambero ¶¶¶
via Roma 11
☎ 030968009
Concesio
Miramonti l'Altro
¶¶¶¶
at Costorio (km 1)
via Crosette 34
☎ 0302751063
**Desenzano
del Garda**
Esplanade ¶¶¶
via Lario 10
☎ 0309143361
Erbusco
L'Albereta ★★★ 🏨
via V. Emanuele 11
☎ 0307760550
**Gualtiero
Marchesi** ¶¶¶¶
via Vittorio Em. 11
☎ 0307760562
Gardone Riviera
G.H. Gardone
★★★ 🏨
corso Zanardelli 84
☎ 036520261
Iseo
I Due Roccoli
★★★ 🏨
at Invino (km 6)
via S. Bonomelli,
strada per Polaveno
☎ 0309822977

HOTELS AND RESTAURANTS

Iseo
**Osteria
Il Volto** ⅢⅢ
via Mirolte 33
☎ 030981462
**Salò
Laurin** ★★★ ⅢⅢ
viale Landi 9
☎ 036522022
Sirmione
G.H. Terme ★★★
viale Marconi 7
☎ 030916261
**Palace Hotel
Villa Cortine** ★★★
via Grotte 6
☎ 0309905890
Sirmione ★★★
piazza Castello 19
☎ 030916331
Catullo ★★★
piazza Flaminia 7
☎ 0309905811
La Rucola ⅢⅢ
via Strentelle 3
☎ 030916326
Vecchia Lugana ⅢⅢ
at Lugana (km 4)
piazzale Vecchia
Lugana 1
☎ 030919012

AGRITURISMI

Capriolo
⭐🛏 **Ricci
Curbastro & Figli**
via Adro 37
☎ 030736094
Monticelli Brusati
⭐🛏 **Villa Gradoni**
via Villa 12
☎ 030652329

homage is paid to the ancient Camuni people at the Parco Nazionale delle Incisioni Rupestri in Naquane.

EDOLO. This is the upper valley's main town. Leaving the route to Tonale, head up to Aprica. Tables here are laid with mountain salamis, wild game, and *capretto con polenta* (kid with *polenta*).

PONTE DI LEGNO. A sun-filled valley and the snows of Adamello make this one of the most appealing ski stations in Brescia. A characteristic dish is *uccelli scappati* (veal with *prosciutto*). There are also tender cheeses from the Alpine pastures of Tonale and Gavia. At Pezzo you will find home-made sausages.

2. The Brescian shores of Garda

DESENZANO DEL GARDA. In the tiny port and old center the atmosphere takes you back to the time of the Serenissima – Venetian rule – when the town was the seat of an important cereal market. Local products include *brodo di giuggiole* (literally broth of jujube berries), a delicate liquor made from a Renaissance recipe. The restaurant "Esplanade" serves excellent cuisine made from simple and sophisticated products combined in perfect harmony.

SIRMIONE. The small peninsula is embellished by the scenic Rocca Scagliera and the ruins ('grottoes') of the villa that perhaps once belonged to the Latin poet Catullus. Inland are the vineyards of the prized DOC wine Lugana and the tiny territory of San Martino della Battaglia. "La Rucola" is an excellent restaurant. There is a concentration of historic eateries, includ-

ing the cafe "Grande Italia" (est 1894), an amiable venue for illustrious events and the *trattoria* "Vecchia Laguna" (est. 1600), once a Venetian staging post and even earlier a Roman *hospitium*. Hotels include "Catullo" (est. 1888), set in a lakeside garden; "Sirmione" (est. 1892), Queen Margherita's favorite; "Terme" (est. 1922), one of the most prestigious on the lake and the neo-classical "Villa Cortine" (est. 1926).

SALÒ. Crossing the Valtenesi hills, stop at Calvagese della Riviera to visit the winery "Redaelli De Zinis", where you can get excellent Garda Classico DOC wines, as well as refreshments, olive oil and fine preserves. At Salò, which is steeped in history and touristic sites, try *pesce fritto del lago* (fried lake fish), *carpione* (Garda carp), and *trote* (trout), and buy liquors and syrups made with *cedro* (citron). For top-quality lodgings, stay at "Laurin", a splendid Art Nouveau villa.

GARDONE RIVIERA. Gardone brings to mind Gabriele d'Annunzio and his residence Il Vittoriale degli Italiani, where works and souvenirs of the eccentric poet may be seen. Those with a passion for beautiful places should stay at "Grand Hotel" (est. 1866), "Garda & Suisse" (est. 1866), on the shores of the lake, or the celebrated "Villa Fiordaliso".

LIMONE SUL GARDA. The town's name bears evidence of its Florentine past, when citrus trees were cultivated here and their fruits sold to transalpine countries. Today the old greenhouses still in use are only there for demonstrations, but they are monuments to the former industry of Garda citizens and are well worth a visit.

3. The Valley of the Chiese

GAVARDO. At the eastern edge of the Valtenesi hills, this town is renowned for *cotecchino* (sausages) served with *polenta*. At Barghe, "Da Benedetto", owned by the master of *bagoss* cheese, Benedetto Girelli, is worth a break in your journey. The cafe-pastry shop "Girelli" is next door.

ANFO. With its Venetian fortress, this village looks down on Lombardy's highest lake, Lake Idro (368 m / 1207 ft). After going up to the Maniva pass, you descend to the Val Trompia.

BAGOLINO. From the Chiese gully go up to this village through the Caffaro valley. It is the epicenter for production of the famous *bagoss* cheese. You will also see mushrooms, wild game, river fish and the spirit *grappa di genziana*.

4. The Bassa between Oglio and Chiese

ROVATO. At the foot of Monte Orfano, this village is known for its beef (used for *manzo sotto oil*, beef preserved in oil) and cheese (Stracchino and Quartirolo di Franciacorta, Taleggio di Rovato) Dishes made of horse meat are also well known and an elixir of herbs is traditional here.

CHIARI. The historic center consists of two squares joined by the sixteenth-century arcade of the Municipio (Town Hall).

ORZINUOVI. This town was founded in 1193 to mount a resistance against Soncino on the other side of the Oglio river, in the province of Cremona. The fortress and a square with old colonnaded buildings are reminders of the town's original function. *Anisone triduo*, a white anise liquor with a delicate flavor that has stood the test of time, is a typical local product.

VEROLANUOVA. This was the center of the Gambara fiefdom that made it into a small capital. The clan's sumptuous palace in the central Piazza della Libertà is indicative of the family's ambition.

MONTICHIARI. At the foot of the hills of the "Amphiteater of Garda", this village is recognizable by the towers of the Bonoris castle. A little beyond it is Calvisano, a center known for sturgeon farming. Don't miss the restaurant "Al Gambero", an established traditional family-run institution that offers pure Lombard cuisine.

Valvestino

AGRITURISMI

Piancogno
La Sognata
at Annunciata
via Ribalda 2
☎ 0364361218
Salò
Conti Terzi
via Panoramica 13
☎ 036522071

WINE PRODUCERS

Corte Franca
Barone Pizzini
via Brescia 1
Timoline
☎ 030984136
Lonato
cascina Spia d'Italia
via Cerutti 61
☎ 0309130233

SHOPPING

Brescia
Gastronomia di G. Creminati
via della Valle 10
☎ 030301306
Delicatessen.
Cigole
Caseificio Zani Fratelli S.p.A.
via Molino 6
☎ 0309959169
Cheeses.
San Gervasio
Caseificio Gervasina
via IV Novembre 1
☎ 0309934924
Cheeses.
Sirmione
Caffè Grande Italia
piazza Carducci 24
☎ 0309160006
Cafe-pastry shop.

COMO

Lake Como (also known as Lake Lario) on the foothills of the Alps unites the provinces of Como and Lecco at the table.

After its recent separation from Lecco, the province of Como includes the west of the Lario basin, and the *Triangolo Lariano*, a mountainous area between the two branches of the lake plus a portion of the basin of Lake Lugano, to the west along the Swiss border, and to the south the upper part of Brianza. The territory is mostly mountainous, and cattle and goat herding is less common now than in the past, but there is still a good amount of cheese production. The olive oil production is also significant, but very localized, and made within the framework of the DOP Laghi Lombardi. Advanced industrialization and tourism have deflated agriculture. Gastronomy in the province of Como is greatly inspired by the lake which offers fish in abundance – from the tiny *arborelle* fish that are *fritti* (fried) or *marinati in carpione* (soused, or pickled), to the more prized lavarelli (whitefish) and *agoni* (the latter, a type of shad fish, are sun-dried and preserved in barrels for the characteristic *missoltini*).

Lake Como.
A ferry with Comacina island in the background

102

Gourmet Tours

COMO. The grid of the Roman streets reflects the square wall that surrounds the city. It is worth visiting the monuments, which range from Romanesque to the rationalist architecture of the Fascist period. There is a significant amount of manufacturing – silk, in particular – which is reflected in shop window displays. To enjoy the lake, try the pleasant walk to Villa Olmo, or, better still, the smaller tour of the first basin aboard little steamboats. Fish is central to Como's gastronomy, and you can find it in *risotto con filetti di persico* (risotto with perch filets), *lavarelli alla salvia* (whitefish with sage), *frittura di alborelle* and the unusual *missoltini* (sun-dried shad) cooked over coals and served with *polenta*. A restaurant with a long history and well-priced food is "Osteria l'Angolo del Silenzio", while "Raimondi", at the charming hotel "Villa Fiori" overlooking the first basin, is a more sophisticated option. Outside the city, "Navedano" offers creative cuisine with a predilection for mushrooms and truffles. If you are looking for local products, the bread of Como, which is slightly acidic and cooked in a wood-fired oven, has a good reputation. For a tasty souvenir, choose from cured meats, cheeses, wines and liquors from "Moscatelli". The most typical local sweet is *resca* (fish bones) from the pastry shops "Franzi" and "Belli".

1. From Lario to Ceresio

CERNOBBIO. This gracious center is known for the periodic government and financial congresses that are held at the "Grand Hotel

Ossuccio. The bell-tower of the Maddalena with la Grigna in the background

Villa d'Este". The magnificence of this sixteenth-century villa is best admired from a ferry on the lake. The hotel has two restaurants: "La Veranda" and "Grill Villa d'Este". Leaving the town, take the old Strada Regina that runs along the lake between nineteenth-century villas and hotels. At Moltrasio stop in the pleasant piazza, onto which several restaurants open. We recommend the "Imperialino", which belongs to the "Grand Hotel Imperiale". Continuing to Brienno, you reach the historic "Crotto dei Platani" (est. 1855); do not miss *missoltini con alborelle in concia* (shad with marinated bleak) and *crostini di polenta* (polenta croutons).

ARGEGNO. The Telo stream runs down the lush Val d'Intelvi, passing under an arched medieval bridge. Take a detour to Lanzo d'Intelvi to go to "Locanda il Dosso" for *urgiada* (an old-fashioned barley soup), *trote di torrente* (river trout) and *selvaggina* (wild game). The road winds down to Lake Lugano.

HOTELS AND RESTAURANTS

Como
Navedano ¶¶¶
at Camnago Volta
via Pannilani
☎ 031308080
Villa Flori ★★★ ★
Raimondi ¶¶¶
via per Cernobbio 12
☎ 031573105
Osteria l'Angolo del Silenzio ¶¶
viale Lecco 25
☎ 0313372157
Albavilla
Il Cantuccio ¶¶¶
via Dante 36
☎ 031628736
Bellagio
G.H. Villa Serbelloni ♦♦♦
via Roma 1
☎ 031950216
Silvio ¶¶
at Loppia
via Carcano 12
☎ 031950322
Brienno
Crotto dei Platani ¶¶ ★
via Regina 73
☎ 031814038
Cernobbio
Villa d'Este ♦♦♦
La Veranda ¶¶¶¶
Grill Villa d'Este ¶¶¶
via Regina 40
☎ 0313481
Gatto Nero ¶¶
at Rovenna (km 4)
via Monte Santo 69
☎ 031512042
Lanzo d'Intelvi
Locanda il Dosso ¶¶
via Paraviso 4
☎ 031840401

Tremezzo: landing places on lake Como

HOTELS AND
RESTAURANTS

Lenno
San Giorgio ★★★
via Regina 81
☎ 034440415
Lurago d'Erba
★🛏 **La Corte** 🍴🍴🍴
via Mazzini 20
☎ 031699590
Mariano Comense
La Rimessa 🍴🍴🍴
via Indipendenza 10
☎ 031749668
Merone
Il Corazziere ★★★
at Baggero (km 2)
via Mazzini 7
☎ 031617181
Moltrasio
G.H. Imperiale ★★★
via Durini
☎ 031346111
★🛏 **Imperialino** 🍴🍴🍴
via Antica Regina 26
☎ 031346600
Sala Comacina
**Locanda
dell'Isola** 🍴🍴🍴
at Isola Comacina
☎ 034456755
★🛏 **Taverna Blu** 🍴
via Puricelli 4
☎ 034455107
Torno
Vapore 🍴🍴
via Plinio 20
☎ 031419311
Tremezzo
★🛏 **Rusall** ★★★
at Rogaro (km 2)
via S. Martino 2
☎ 034440408
La Fagurida 🍴🍴🍴
at Rogaro (km 2)
☎ 034440676

OSSUCCIO. Along the Strada Regina stands the famous bell-tower of the church Santa Maria Maddalena, which marks the start of Tremezzina, a district with a historically good cuisine. A little further up is the Santuario della Beata Vergine del Soccorso, a starting point for the climb to the beautiful Romanesque basilica church of San Benedetto. Turning towards the lake, you can see Isola Comacina. A ferry boat from Sala brings you to the ruins of Sant'Eufemia and "Locanda dell'Isola", which provide the setting for a pleasant summer evening. From the same dock, another boat goes to Villa Balbianello, one of the lake's dream houses. At Lenno, stay at the pleasantly old-fashioned hotel "San Giorgio" and buy local olive oil.

TREMEZZO. This town is very pleasant, with nineteenth-century hotels and colonnades dotted with cafes and shop windows. A stop at Villa Carlotta, in the midst of blooming azaleas and statues by Canova, is a must. Further inland, within the pleasant hamlet of Rogaro, the chefs at "Rusall" and "Fagurida" have strong reputations.

MENAGGIO. This village is the capital of the outer shore of Lake Como's western branch. It has a pleasant boardwalk and offers excellent hotels. In the pastry shops you will find the tasty *mataloc*, a sweet bread filled with dried fruits such as walnuts, hazelnuts, grapes and figs. At Loveno visit the splendid gardens at Villa Vigoni. Art enthusiasts should go on to Gravedona to see the unique church of Santa Maria del Tiglio with its octagonal campanile and two-color decoration. This is also where you should buy the traditional thick-crusted, slowly aged, uncurdled cheese with a sharp flavor, called *semuda*.

2. The Brianza and the Larian Triangle

CANTÙ. A splendid Romanesque church in the hamlet of Galliano is an artistic memento of the industrious Brianza village. Further on, at Mariano Comense, you can find a good restaurant called "La Rimessa", where creativity is skillfully blended with tradition.

INVERIGO. This is one of Brianza's most enchanting towns. Walk down from the Rotonda, a scenic villa at Cagnola, to Santa Maria della Noce. For a gastronomic stop at Lurago, "La Corte" is a pleasant restaurant in a villa.

Inverigo. S. Maria della Noce

ERBA. At the threshold of the mountainous Larian Triangle, this village has neo-classical villas and a series of pleasant little lakes. Restaurants worthy of praise in the area include "Il Corazziere", a rustic eatery on the banks of the Lambro at Merone, and "Il Can-tuccio", where there are a few fireside tables, at Albavilla. Take the Vallassina at Asso, where cow's and goat's milk cheeses have gained renown. At Canzo, you will find *amaretti Nocciolini*, biscuits made with hazelnuts and the liquor Vespetrò.

BELLAGIO. This town is located at the fork in the lake and it may also be reached by ferryboat from Tremezzo. It is a fascinating place with old colonnaded buildings, patrician residences and hotels from times gone by. Choose the "Grand Hotel Villa Serbelloni" for the overnight stay of your dreams. At Loppia, go to "Silvio" for typical *ravioli di pesce del Lario* (*ravioli* made with fish from Lario) and *fettuccine all'agone fresco* (*fettuccine* with twaite shad). Back in Como, at the gracious village of Torno, stop at "Vapore", a lakeside hotel-restaurant.

Olive trees by lake Como

AGRITURISMI

Bellagio
Azienda Clarke
at Visgnola
via Valassina 170/c
☎ 031951513
Nesso
Locanda Mosè
at Pian di Nesso
☎ 031917909
Sormano
La Conca d'Oro
al Pian del Tivano
☎ 031677019

SHOPPING

Como
Gastronomia Moscatelli
via Fontana 25
☎ 031270185
Delicatessen.
Pasticceria Belli
via V. Emanuele 7
☎ 031264287
Pastries and sweets.
Pasticceria Franzi
via Muralto 27
☎ 03127200
Pastries and sweets.
Canzo
Pasticceria Citterio
via Mazzini 30
☎ 031681330
Pastries and sweets.
Cortenova
Gildo Ciresa
at Bindo
☎ 0341901101
Local cheeses.
Erba
Erbadaltro
piazza V. Veneto 40
☎ 031644815
Natural products.
Lenno
Frantoio Osvaldo Vanini
via S. Pellico 10
☎ 034455127
Olive oil.
Menaggio
Pasticceria Manzoni
via Camozzi 6
☎ 034432532
Pastries and sweets.

CREMONA

Lower Cremona is traditionally dedicated to animal husbandry, but the Po River brings other flavors from nearby Emilia.

The Po River forms the province's southern border, while the Adda and the Oglio rivers define the limits more to the north of the strip of flatlands that go up to Crema and the border with Brescia. The land is given over to animal husbandry, charcuterie and cheese- making, while the gastronomy of its capital is influenced by the river and the nearby territories of Emilia. The river makes an outstanding contribution to the cuisine with its fish – don't miss *pez in aion* (soused fish), which is typical of the Po's Cremonese banks.

San Giovanni in Croce.
Villa Medici del Vascello

Gourmet Tours

CREMONA. Thanks to its Gothic bell tower, you can spot one of Italy's most beautiful medieval piazzas from afar. The town is renowned for the time-honoured craftsmanship of stringed instrument makers, boasting such names as Amati, Stradivarius and Guarneri. As for good food, *torrone* (nougat) and *mostarda* (fruit chutney spiced with mustard) are the trademark urban products, while the province also offers *provolone* and *grana padano* cheeses, and charcuterie, including *ciüta*, an excellent round *cotechino* (boiled spiced pork sausage). The Po adds to the mix by bringing other flavors with it. In the city, the *trattoria* "Porta Mosa" is worth trying and has a good wine list. Those travelling by car will enjoy an excursion to Scandolara Ripa d'Oglio, a small village with a beautiful castle and a good restaurant called "Al Caminetto". In Torre de' Picenardi, the restaurant "Italia" serves traditional cuisine with a fresh touch. PIZZIGHETTONE. The old center is crossed by the Adda river and set within star-shaped fortifications. At the end of the bridge is the Torre del Guado where a French king was once imprisoned.
CASTELLONE. The Torre del Leone testifies to the fortified town's history. Isolated in the countryside to the north of the town is the church of Santa Maria di Bressanoro. Along the route to Crema you will find the sanctuary of the

Madonna della Misericordia.
CREMA. Remnants of Venetian rule, walls built in 1488 enclose a web of ancient streets that converge at the Piazza del Duomo. Just outside the city, along the route towards Bergamo, is the sanctuary of Santa Maria della Croce, built in the style of Bramante. At Ripalta Cremasca, "Trattoria Viavai", an old restaurant has been revived with a passion for local foods, and deserves a visit.
PANDINO. With its square layout and towers, the Visconti castle is one of the most interesting in the region.
SONCINO. Near the Oglio river, the Sforza castle – one of the best preserved in Lombardy – and the medieval village take the visitor back in time. In the countryside a rare *radicchio* is cultivated.

Pizzighettone. The Adda river

SORESINA. Important neo-classical edifices testify to the fortune of this nineteenth-century agricultural and industrial center. Today butter and a high quality *grana* cheese are still being produced. Local specialties are *trippa* (tripe) and *cotechino*.
CASALMAGGIORE. Lying north of the Po, this village takes us back in time to the period of the Estes. You can see the beautiful nineteenth-century architecture of the Palazzo Comunale and the Cathedral. Restaurants serve *tortelli di zucca* (pumpkin *ravioli*).
PIADENA. Low, colonnaded houses surround the piazza, which showcases the Baroque parish church and the Palazzo Municipale. The Antiquarium Platina is worth visiting.

HOTELS AND RESTAURANTS

Cremona
Porta Mosa ✗✗
via S. M. in Betlem 11
☎ 0372411803
Ripalta Cremasca
Trattoria Viavai ✗✗
via Libertà 18
☎ 0373268232
Scandolara Ripa d'Oglio
Al Caminetto ✗✗✗
via Umberto I 26
☎ 037289589
Torre de' Picenardi
Italia ✗✗
via Garibaldi 1
☎ 0375394060

AGRITURISMI

Spino d'Adda
Cascina Fraccina
at Fraccina
☎ 0373965166

SHOPPING

Cremona
Coop. Agricola Iris
via Grado 1
☎ 037221415
Fruit and vegetables.
Augusto Fieschi
via dei Lanaioli 24
☎ 037222346
"Mostarda" and nougat.
Castelverde
Macelleria Ghiggi
via Garvinali 18
☎ 372427017
Meat.
Ostiano
Caseificio Zucchelli
via Osse 14
☎ 037285045
Cheeses.

LECCO

Rich tables are laid with an unusual variety of foods, including the charcuterie of La Brianza, lake fish and aged cheeses from Valsassina.

The young province of Lecco is made up of the eastern shores of Lake Como and the adjacent mountain district of Valsassina, which lies between the Grigna Mountains and the Pizzo dei Tre Signori, as well as the portion of Brianza between the valleys of the Lambro and Adda rivers. Agriculture, animal husbandry and cheese-making are the predominant activities, particularly in Valsassina. The production of charcuterie is of long standing renown, with the DOP Salame Brianza as the focal point. Olive growing also has a long history here, but the production of the DOP Laghi Lombardi olive oil is limited. This land of old vacation resorts offers excellent cuisine of lake and local products.

A lakeside walk

Gourmet Tours

LECCO. The cliffs of Mount San Martino with those of Resegone in the background provide the setting for Alessandro Manzoni's classic book, *I Promessi Sposi* (The Betrothed). In the town you can visit Manzoni's villa and the places mentioned in the book. The restaurant "Griso", at Malgrate, offers fabulous views and skillfully-prepared fish. It is worth staying over.

1. The lake and Valsassina

VARENNA. Once on the lakeside route, the first gastronomic stop is at the restaurant "Ricciolo", at Mandello del Lario, where you can try unusual dishes prepared with the fruits of the lake. Then comes Varenna where a ferryboat ride links the town to Bellagio and Tremezzo. Around the piazza, the small streets and steps provide a romantic atmosphere, while a tour on the lake is unforgettable. In a fifteenth-century building with a "lover's terrace", you will find the restaurant "Vecchia Varenna", where the menu includes *risotto al lavarello* (risotto with whitefish) and *salmerino alla boscaiola* (red char with mushroom and tomato sauce). For a taste of life in a villa, we strongly recommend "Du Lac". BELLANO. The *Orrido*, a cascade formed by the Pioverna stream in the gorge above the village, has long been a destination for excursions. The trip to the abbey of Piona, where the monks produce ancient liquors such as *Elixir San Bernardo* and *Gocce Imperiali*, is worth the effort. BARZIO. The winding roads up the mountain from Varenna or Bellano go through Valsassina,

where the production of *robiola* cheese aged in natural caves is renowned. The capital, Barzio, has been a resort town since the nineteenth century. At Crandola, go to "Da Gigi", where you must try large home-made *ravioli* called *scapinasc*. At Cremeno, go to "Clubino Montelago", a Buon Ricordo restaurant where the specialty is *pesce di lago in carpione tiepido* (warm soused lake fish).

2. The Brianza and Adda Rivers

OGGIONO. This village looks onto La Brianza's largest lake. Its backdrop is Monte Barro, which is now a natural park that can be entered via Galbiate. At Civate, you can climb to the basilica of San Pietro al Monte, one of the most important Romanesque buildings in Lombardy. At Oggiono, stop at the refined "Fattorie di Stendhal" or "Ca' Bianca". MERATE. Villa Belgioioso, one of the most beautiful residences in La Brianza, evokes the time when Manzoni was a schoolboy here. We recommend a detour to Montevecchia, where the landscape is well preserved and full of vineyards. High on a spur, the village is worth seeing and the old-fashioned cheeses are delicious. At Viganò the restaurant "Pierino Penati" has been well received by critics for its top quality cuisine and natural friendliness. Don't miss the risotto that is prepared with ingredients according to the season. At Casatenovo's "Fermata" you will get top-notch creative cuisine with four themed menus that are both creative and traditional. The area is also good for excellent charcuterie.

HOTELS AND RESTAURANTS

Casatenovo
Fermata ¶¶¶
via De Gasperi 2
☎ 0399205411
Crandola
Valsassina
Gigi ¶¶
piazza IV Novembre 4
☎ 0341840124
Cremeno
Clubino Montelago ¶¶¶
via Combi 15
☎ 0341996145
Malgrate
Il Griso ¶¶¶¶ ★🍴
via Provinciale 51
☎ 0341202040
Mandello del Lario
Ricciolo ¶¶
at Olcio (km 3)
via Statale 165
☎ 0341732546
Oggiono
Ca' Bianca ¶¶¶ ★🍴
via Alighieri 18
☎ 0341260601
Fattorie di Stendhal ¶¶¶
via Alighieri 16
☎ 0341576561
Varenna
Du Lac ★★★
via del Prestino 4
☎ 0341830123
Vecchia Varenna ¶¶
c.da Scoscesa 10
☎ 0341830793
Viganò
Pierino Penati ¶¶¶
via Trivulzio 8
☎ 039956020

SHOPPING

Missaglia
Pasticceria Magni
via Mozart 4
☎ 0396049251
Sweets and pastries.
Perledo
Gruppo Produttori di Perledo
via per Esino 28
☎ 0341830059
Laghi Lombardi Dop olive oil.

LODI

This beautiful city on the Adda river is known for first-rate cheese production and is influenced by Milanese gastronomy.

The territory of the young province of Lodi covers the strip of flatlands that includes the area between the lower Adda and the bed of the Lambro river, which extends to the valley of Milan. The area, with the Via Emilia running through it, is strikingly agricultural, and produces some of Lombardy's most renowned cheeses. Most representative of these is *Grana Lodigiano*, also known as *Granone*, which has been produced since the sixteenth century, but is now a rarity. Local gastronomy is strongly influenced by Milanese cooking, although with modifications. The hill called San Colombano al Lambro is worth mentioning for its production of the only DOC wine in the Bassa Milanese. It also boasts another distinction – the discrepancy between its geological position as an isolated splinter of the Apennine mountain that stands alone just north of the Po, and its administrative location as a Milanese enclave between Lodi and Pavia.

Cattle rearing in the Bassa Lodigiana

Gourmet Tours

LODI. Refounded on the Eghezone hills on the right bank of the Adda by Frederick Barbarossa in 1158, Lodi preserves its medieval heritage in its cathedral and the Broletto (Court of Justice), while the church of the Incoronata pays homage to its Renaissance past. Here *Grana Lodigiano*, or *Granone*, cheese is slivered into thin curls called *raspadura*, which are then used in *frittatine alla lodigiana* (Lodi omelets). There is also a wide variety of soft cheeses. We recommend you visit the restaurant "Tre Gigli-All'Incoronata", not far from the Duomo, where a young chef masterfully presents regional and contemporary dishes.

SANT'ANGELO LODIGIANO. West of the Lambro, the Visconti Castle houses the Morando Bolognini Museum of History and Art, the Lombard Museum of the History of Agriculture, and the Bread Museum. For dishes native to Lodi, go to the restaurant "San Rocco", which has been managed by the same family for many years. Pastry shops and bakeries sell their own local version of *amaretti*.

SAN COLOMBANO AL LAMBRO (MI). This village stands at the foot of a vine-covered hillside where the robust San Colombano DOC wine is made from Croatina, Barbera and Uva Rara grapes. Two wineries are open to the public for tasting, the "Pietrasanta-Poderi di San Pietro" and "Riccardi". There are two very pleasant restaurants, the "La Caplania" and "Osteria Sant'Ambrogio", a shrine to regional cooking.

CASALPUSTERLENGO. The Pusterla towers loom over a countryside dotted with farms. At Somaglia

San Colombano al Lambro

the Montichie WWF reserve is frequented by herons. Shops in the town carry the soft cheese *Bel Casale* and two kinds of local sweet, *calissoni* and *torta di Casale*.

CODOGNO. In the plain between the Po and Adda rivers, this village preserves some old monuments, including the parish church of San Biagio, the colonnades of the Mercato and the church of the Madonna delle Grazie, in addition to examples of early twentieth-century architecture such as Villa Biancardi. Pastry shops sell the renowned *biscottini*. Nearby, at Maleo, two restaurants boost the territory's gastronomic reputation, the "Del Sole" (which is also a hotel) and "Leon d'Oro", where you will find a fine selection of wines.

CASTIGLIONE D'ADDA. This ancient fortified town introduces the Parco fluviale Adda Sud (the riverside park of the southern Adda). The Statale 591 towards Crema crosses the Muzza canal and the river. Take one last cultural detour at Montodine.

ABBADIA CERRETO. The abbey church of San Pietro (twelfth-fourteenth century) is a Lombard Romanesque building with Cistercian-Gothic influence. Inside there is a canvas by Callisto Piazza.

HOTELS AND RESTAURANTS

Lodi
Tre Gigli-All'Incoronata ¶¶
piazza della Vittoria 47
☎ 0371421404
Maleo
Del Sole ★★★ ¶¶¶
via Trabattoni 22
☎ 037758142
Leon d'Oro ¶¶ 🔗
via Dante 69
☎ 037758149
San Colombano al Lambro (MI)
La Caplania ¶¶¶
via Serafina 11
☎ 0371897097
Sant'Angelo Lodigiano
San Rocco ¶
via Cavour 19
☎ 037190729

AGRITURISMI

Sant'Angelo Lodigiano
Az. F.lli Bottazzi
cascina Branduzza
☎ 0371935152

WINE PRODUCERS

San Colombano al Lambro (MI)
Carlo Pietrasanta - Poderi di S. Pietro
via Sforza 55
☎ 0371897540
Enrico Riccardi
via Capra 17
☎ 0371897381

SHOPPING

Lodi
La Bottega Casearia di G. Locatelli
corso Umberto 20
☎ 0371424979
Cheeses.
Pasticceria Nazionale
piazza d. Vittoria 44
☎ 0371421328
Pastries and sweets.
Pasticceria Tacchinardi
piazza della Vittoria 38
☎ 0371420677
Pastries and sweets.

MANTUA

Once the land of the Gonzagas, this province has a soothing cuisine with regular references to the flavors of the Veneto and Emilia.

The province of Mantua reaches from the hills in lower Garda to the lands around the part of the Po wedged in between the provinces of Verona and Emilia. It is a zone rich in water, with the Mincio river travelling right across it and the Oglio and the Po also running through. It is predominantly a river flatland that favors rice cultivation and fruit orchards. The gastronomy is typical of the Po valley with Venetian and Emilian influences. There are many kinds of condiments and *zucca* (pumpkin) adds a sweet note to many foods. Vineyards provide for the DOC Colli Mantovani del Garda wines and Lambrusco Mantovano, which is produced in the lands across the Po.

Along the Mincio river

112

Gourmet Tours

MANTUA. The ancient capital of the Gonzagas seems to have been protected from the toll of time by the embrace of the Mincio River and its lakes. A visit to Palazzo Ducale (with Mantegna's *Camera degli sposi* - newly-weds' room) and Palazzo Te (with Giulio Romano's Sala dei Giganti – giants' room) is obligatory. In the city we recommend "Cigno-Trattoria dei Martini", for many generations the best place to eat here. "Ochina Bianca" also has interesting

Fishing on Mincio

local dishes and "Aquila Nera" offers excellent cuisine in a historic setting. Don't miss this opportunity to purchase Mantuan charcuterie, particularly the *salamelle* and *salame*, the main features of the traditional *risotto con le salamelle*.

1. The Oltrepò Mantovano

SABBIONETA. The most beautiful of the small centers in the Bassa Padana, this ideal city was founded according to the specifications of its enlightened prince, Vespasiano Gonzaga. The area around Sabbioneta is known for its production of charcuterie and *grana* cheese, and a typical dish is *agnolotti con ripieno di carne di vitello mista a salumi* (*ravioli* filled with veal and charcuterie).
VIADANA. This agricultural and industrial center on the Po has a beautiful sixteenth-century church, Santa Maria Assunta di Castello, but owes its fame to melon farming.
SUZZARA. Bordering Emilia, this

town, with its low buildings and broad colonnaded streets, is a well-preserved example of a village along the Po. The Galleria Civica d'Arte Contemporanea (Municipal contemporary art gallery) displays paintings, and sculptural and graphic works centered on the theme of work, which were selected for the "Premio Suzzara" (Suzzara Awards) from 1948 to 1976 and again after 1989. In the village a historic restaurant called "Cavallino Bianco" – previously a post office – made the front pages in the 1940s for a famous literary prize hosted there. The atmosphere is delightful and the *tagliatelle con l'anatra* (*tagliatelle* with duck) excellent. Between Suzzara and Sermide is the ideal area for *tartufi bianchi* (white truffles).
SAN BENEDETTO PO. The village grew up around the Benedictine abbey of the Polirone (the area between the Po and its old tributary the Lirone) from the year 1000, and there is a museum of popular culture in the Po region. Charcuterie and *grana* cheese, vegetables and fruits have traditionally been produced locally, in addition to delicious preparations with an Emilian flavor, such as the *agnolini al ragù* (*ravioli* with meat sauce), *torta di tagliatelle* and the liquor *Nocino*.
QUISTELLO. In an old house in the town center, the inspired chef of the excellent "Ambasciata" restaurant is constantly seeking new uses for traditional local products. We highly recommend the *millefoglie di*

HOTELS AND RESTAURANTS

Mantua
Cigno - Trattoria dei Martini ⑪
piazza d'Arco 1
☎ 0376327101
Ochina Bianca ⑪
via Finzi 2
☎ 0376323700
Canneto sull'Oglio
Dal Pescatore ⑪⑪⑪
at Runate
☎ 0376723001
Goito
Al Bersagliere ⑪⑪
S.S. Goitese 260
☎ 037660007
Quistello
Ambasciata ⑪⑪⑪
via Martiri Belfiore 33
☎ 0376619169
Suzzara
Cavallino Bianco ⑪
via Menotti 11/a
☎ 0376531676

AGRITURISMI

Mantua
Corte Bersaglio
at Migliaretto
via L. Guerra 15
☎ 0376320345
Corte S. Girolamo
strada S. Girolamo 1
☎ 0376391010
Ostiglia
Arginino Piccolo
via Arginino 9
☎ 038631475
Solferino
Le Sorgive 🌟
via Piridello 6
☎ 0376854252
Viadana
Corte Lavadera
at Cogozzo
via Pangona 76
☎ 037588383
Volta Mantovana
Lucillo 🌟
at Bezzetti
☎ 0376838284

View of the Mantovani del Garda hills

SHOPPING

Castiglione delle Stiviere
Cherpesca
at Gozzolina
via Dottorina
☎ 0376639263
Fresh fish.
Goito
Salumificio Alto Mantovano
strada Levata 29
☎ 037660003
Charcuterie.
M.A.M. Macellatori Alto Mantovano
S.S. Goitese 194
☎ 0376604817
Meat
La Rinascita
S.S. Goitese 311
☎ 0376688248
Fruit and vegetables.
Quistello
Caseificio S. Fiorentino
at Nuvolato
via Europa 1
☎ 0376617133
Typical cheeses.
San Benedetto Po
Caseificio San Giovanni Apostolo
Gorgo 1
☎ 0376615331
Local cheeses.
Sermide
Latteria Agricola Mogliese
at Moglia
via Galvani 1
☎ 037661241
Milk and cheeses.
Suzzara
Caseificio Belladelli A. & C.
at Sailetto
via Zara Zanetta 150
☎ 0376527045
Typical cheeses.
Virgilio
Le Tamerici
at Pietole
via Romana 80
☎ 0376281005
Preserves.

trippe con polenta abbrustolita (mille-feuille of tripe with toasted *polenta*) and the menus made up of only *primi piatti* (first courses).

SERMIDE. This village is renowned for its fruit and vegetables, particularly onions, pears and apples. At Carbonar di Po and Borgofranco sul Po there are excellent opportunities to taste the fish of the great river. This is the area where *tartufi bianchi* (white truffles) are found and they appear in *agnolini* (*ravioli*) and other local dishes.

OSTIGLIA. On the left bank of the Po, this town marks the beginning of Lombardy's second largest rice growing area (Vialone Nano), after Lomellina. Roncoferraro is a reference point and rice is a common denominator at *trattorie* in the area.

2. Towards the hills of Garda

CANNETO SULL'OGLIO. From Mantua the lower Po leads quickly to the confines of the province of Pavia where this village shows strong traces of its military past. Those wishing to concentrate on culture should visit the Mortara collection at the Palazzo Comunale (Town Hall), where there are works by nineteenth- and twentieth-century Lombard artists as well as a permanent exhibition of toys, with exhibits in porcelain, wood, fabric and other materials. Afterwards, stop by "Dal Pescatore" where you will find excellent cooking with simple yet superb dishes ranging from *tortelli di zucca* (pumpkin *ravioli*) to *coscette di rana alle erbe fini* (frogs legs with fine herbes), from *pere alla lavanda e al pipasener* (a rustic sweet with pears and lavender) to a variety of small pastries.

CASTIGLIONE DELLE STIVIERE. Going through Asola, a lovely little town with many references to Venetian culture, we come to this village to the south of the hills of Garda. A baroque church pays homage to its most illustrious son, San Luigi Gonzaga. The museum at Palazzo Longhi is dedicated to the Red Cross, which the Genevan Henry Dunant had the idea of setting up while rescuing the wounded of the Battle of Solferino (1859).

SOLFERINO. Here a collection of relics recalls the French victory that took place here, and there are also mementos from the Piedmont victory on the same day at San Martino in the Second War of Independence.

GOITO. Another town full of memories from the Risorgimento (Resurgence – the period leading up to the independence and unification of Italy), this town now plays an important role in the Parco Fluviale del Mincio, housing the park's Centro visite delle Bertone (Tourist office). Stop along the Statale 236 at "Al Bersagliere", an excellent restaurant that has stood the test of time, and try the *risotto con le lumache* (*risotto* with snails).

PAVIA

A province with two sides to it, divided between Lomellina, the land of rice fields, and Oltrepò Pavese, famous for great wines and truffles.

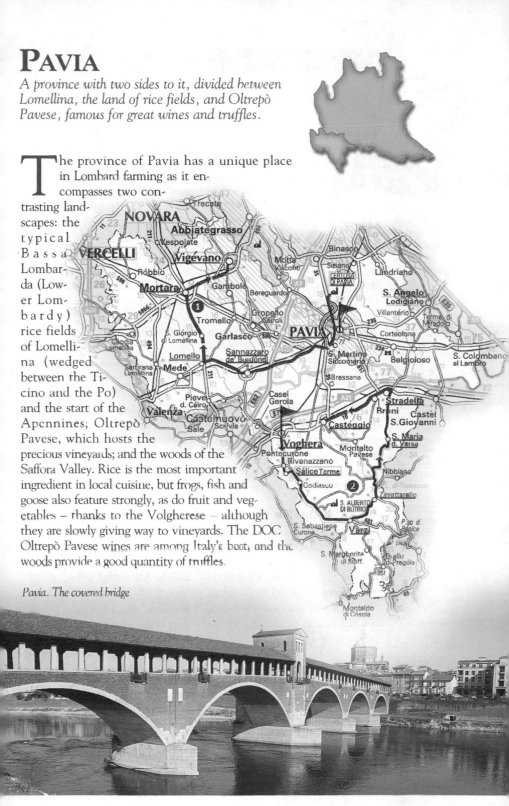

The province of Pavia has a unique place in Lombard farming as it encompasses two contrasting landscapes: the typical Bassa Lombarda (Lower Lombardy) rice fields of Lomellina (wedged between the Ticino and the Po) and the start of the Apennines; Oltrepò Pavese, which hosts the precious vineyards; and the woods of the Saffora Valley. Rice is the most important ingredient in local cuisine, but frogs, fish and goose also feature strongly, as do fruit and vegetables – thanks to the Volgherese – although they are slowly giving way to vineyards. The DOC Oltrepò Pavese wines are among Italy's best, and the woods provide a good quantity of truffles.

Pavia. The covered bridge

Gourmet Tours

PAVIA. In a city with a strong sense of community, the warmth of Lombard terracotta gives unity to important Romanesque churches and an urban setting where towers rise high and little squares, or *piazzette*, nestle among ancient residences. The Ticino river, with its typical Ponte Coperto, or covered bridge, beyond this the Borgo Ticino, and the Naviglio Pavese which flows into it, recall a past rich in river commerce. The best cuisine is to be found in the refined, creative "Al Cassinino" restaurant. A series of good traditional *trattorie* try hard to outdo it. "Antica Osteria del Previ", in Borgo Ticino, offers interesting dishes based on river fish as well as a good list of Oltrepavese wines. Don't miss two characteristic dishes: *anguilla alla borghigiana* (eel) and *zuppa alla pavese* (hot broth with egg, bread and cheese).

1. The Lombardy of the rice fields

CERTOSA DI PAVIA. A road leaves the Naviglio Pavese and soon arrives at this celebrated Lombard monastery. Beyond the arched entrance you can see the multicolored marble facade. Inside, the richness of the decor rivals the exterior – the fifteenth-century's greatest Lombard artists worked here. The 24 cells of the Carthusians surround the silent cloisters. "Il Vecchio Mulino", an historic restaurant with new and excellent management, is a good place to break for food.
SANNAZZARO DE' BURGONDI. This farming center lies near a branch

of the Po, and just a little to the north of it is the Scaldasole castle, one of the most beautiful in the Lomellina area.
LOMELLO. The remains of the castle and the late medieval church of Santa Maria Maggiore and its baptistery of San Giovanni ad Fontes indicate the former importance of the town.
MORTARA. The rectangular network of streets recalls the town's Roman origins. The Gothic parish has a centuries-old past as a center for farming and commerce. In late September the Sagra dell'Oca (Goose Festival) is celebrated in the piazza and on the tables. In restaurants, *risotto*, frogs, charcuterie made from goose and *prosciutto d'oca* (*prosciutto* of goose, a local specialty) must not be missed. There are also dishes from outside, such as *panissa* from Novara.
VIGEVANO. The Renaissance harmony of Piazza Ducale provides one of Lombardy's most beautiful images. "I Castagni", in a little villa off the beaten track, is unmisseable. Dishes are painstakingly prepared by a young chef in this famous restaurant.

2. The Oltrepò Pavese

VOGHERA. At the mouth of the Val Saffora the roads follow a winding route from the Padania area to the Ligurian coast. Excellent and unmistakable, peppers and celery come from the countryside here. "Antica Trattoria Lombardia" stands out for its home cooking, particularly the risotto and *malfatti* dumplings. At Cervesina, we recommend "Castello di San Lorenzo", a hotel with restaurant. At Codevilla you can taste wine at the ancient

HOTELS AND RESTAURANTS

Pavia
Al Cassinino ♙♙♙♙
at Cassinino km 4
☎ 0382422097
Antica Osteria del Previ ♙♙
via Milazzo 65
☎ 038226203
Certosa di Pavia
Locanda Vecchia Pavia Al Mulino ♙♙♙
via al Monumento 5
☎ 0382925894
Cervesina
Castello di S. Gaudenzio ★★★
at S. Gaudenzio (km 3)
☎ 0383333I
Montecalvo Versiggia
Prato Gaio ♙♙
at Versa (km 2)
☎ 038599726
Montescano
Pino ♙♙♙
via Panazza I I
☎ 038560479
Rivanazzano
Selvatico ♙♙
via Pellico I I
☎ 038394474
Salice Terme
Il Caminetto ♙♙♙
via C. Battisti I I
☎ 038391139I
Ca' Vegia by Musoni ♙♙
via Diviani 27
☎ 038394473I
Vigevano
I Castagni ♙♙♙
via Ottobiano 8/20
☎ 038142860
Voghera
⭐🛏 **Antica Trattoria Lombardia** ♙
corso XXII Marzo 139
☎ 038364 6186

116

tinaio, or wine cellar, of the winery "Montelio", which is also an *agriturismo* establishment.

SALICE TERME. Healthy waters bubble forth today in an establishment which was built "Pompeii style", in the early twentieth century. At the head of a list of good restaurants is "Il Caminetto", where two traditional dishes, *risotto alle vogherese* (Voghera-style *risotto*) and *rane fritte* (fried frogs), as well as the elegant *tagliata di petto di anatra* (sliced breast of duck), are served. At Rivanazzano the hotel-restaurant "Selvatico" offers a nineteenth-century setting and old-fashioned flavors. The charcuterie, pasta and bread are all made in-house. In the area, *tartufi bianchi, bianchetti e neri* (white, off-white and black truffles) are found in the woods. Excellent fruit, including pears, apples, peaches and cherries, come from the Staffora Valley.

VARZI. In past centuries this village became wealthy through commerce between the flatlands and the sea. Then its charcuterie gained fame, with its salami earning the title IGP (*Indicazione Geografica Protetta*), and other produce such as *coppa di Pietragavina* becoming famous alongside it. More energetic travelers should continue to Brallo di Pregola, set on a ridge, where you shouldn't miss *gnocchi con i funghi* (gnocchi with mushrooms), a mountain specialty.

ZAVATTARELLO. This is a charming ancient town with a castle. In shops you will find charcuterie, cheeses and fruit, particularly apples, pears and grapes. At Valverde there is a salami shop called "Porri" that specializes in *salame di Varzi*. Further on, at Ruino, "Il Boscasso" produces excellent *caprini*, or goat's cheese.

SANTA MARIA DELLA VERSA. This village takes its name from the seventeenth-century church that stands along the main road and is a center of expert vine-dressers. White truffles are gathered in this area, and cooking is based on hearty foods such as *ravioli al brasato*. Nearby, at Rovescala, the winery "Castello di Luzzano" has a tavern-restaurant and offers *agriturismo* lodgings. At Montevalco Versiggia, the hotel-restaurant "Prato Gaiao" offers variations on traditional themes, while at Montescano, "Pino" offers indigenous flavors with a creative angle.

STRADELLA. Passing through Montù Beccaria and Canneto Pavese – both *Città del Vino* (Cities of Wine) – the route leads to the far edge of the Apennines, where this fortified town was established to guard the route between Piacenza and Alessandria. White truffles and *cacciagione* (wild game) from here are famous. And the wines are excellent. At Zanevredo visit the "Tenuta il Bosco" to try the Oltrepò Pavese Bonarda.

CASTEGGIO. This town was called *Clastidium* in antiquity, and was the scene of a historic battle between the Romans and the Gauls. Come here for its charcuterie and truffles, and visit the eighteenth-century winery "Frecciarossa", which is well known for its prized reserve wines and distilled spirits.

AGRITURISMI

Borgo Priolo
Castello
di Stefanago
☎ 0383875227

WINE PRODUCERS

Casteggio
Frecciarossa
via Vigorelli 141
☎ 0383304465
Codevilla
Monteli
via Mazza 1
☎ 038373090
Rovescala
Castello Luzzano
at Luzzano 5
☎ 0523863277
Zanevredo
Tenuta il Bosco
at il Bosco
☎ 0385245324

SHOPPING

Pavia
Pasticceria
Medagliani
corso Cavour 37
☎ 038222740
Pastries and sweets.
Mortara
La Corte dell'Oca
via Sforza 27
☎ 038498397
Charcuterie and goose products.
Ruino
Il Boscasso
at Boscasso
☎ 0385955906
Goat's cheeses.
Valverde
Salumificio Porri
at Casa d'Agosto
☎ 0383589868
Charcuterie.

SONDRIO

*In the Valtellina the food consists of hearty
dishes with charcuterie, cheeses, mushrooms and
buckwheat accompanied by excellent red wine*

The province of Sondrio follows the upper
Adda river, from the springs to Lake Como.
The cooking of the Valtellina in Lombardy
has its own separate characteristics, starting with the use of exclusive
raw materials such as *grano saraceno* (buck wheat). Its cured meats are
unmistakable, the best being Bresaola IGP. The dairy industry produces
two superb cheeses, the Bitto DOP and Valtellina
Casera DOP. Other important products are apples,
which are distinguished by a special stamp of
quality, and mushrooms. Wine production
completes the picture with a red Nebbiolo,
which has four geographic sub-zones
– Sassella, Grumello, Inferno
and Valgella. The *Superiore* range was awarded
DOCG recognition.

*Sondrio.
The Madonna
della Sassella
sanctuary*

118

Gourmet Tours

SONDRIO. The most important economic center in the Valtellina is at the mouth of the Valmalenco, at the center of an area that produces excellent wines. In the city, go to the restaurant "Sozzani" at the inn "Della Posta" (established 1835), with its frescoed vaults and original decoration. At pastry shops buy Christmas *panon*, a kind of *focaccia* made of white flour enriched with chestnuts, walnuts, hazelnuts, dried figs, raisins and liquor. At Albosaggia, the restaurant-hotel "Campelli" has a panoramic view. From Sondrio a detour into the beautiful valley that goes up to the glaciers of Bernina and Disgrazia, with a stop at Chiesa in Valmalenco, is a must. Butter and cheese are products of the summer alpine pastures, while the valleys provide mushrooms and trout. The *bresaola* is excellent. Try the sweet version of *cicc* with milk, sugar and a little vanilla. Handmade earthenware pots made here are unbeatable for braising and stewing.

1. From the lower Valtellina at the Val Chiavenna

MORBEGNO. Just outside the city as you leave the provincial capital is the church of the Madonna della Sassella. Then cross the Adda and you arrive at Morbegno, at the mouth of the Val Gerola, the main sanctuary of Orobic goats. The cheese Bitto (DOP), indispensable in *pizzoccheri* and many other dishes, stands out among the wealth of other products from the rich dairy industry. Trade in fresh, dried and conserved

HOTELS AND RESTAURANTS

Sondrio
Della Posta ★★★
Sozzani ¶¶¶
piazza Garibaldi 19
☎ 0342510404
Albosaggia
Campelli ★★★
at Moia (km 3)
via Moia 6
☎ 0342510662
Bormio
Taulà ¶¶
via Dante 6
☎ 0342904771
Chiavenna
Cenacolo ¶¶
via C. Pedretti 16
☎ 034332123
Grosio
Sassella ▲▲▲ ¶¶
via Roma 2
☎ 0342847272
Teglio
Combolo ★★★
via Roma 5
☎ 0342780083
Villa di Chiavenna
Lanterna Verde ¶¶¶
at S. Barnaba 7
☎ 034338588

AGRITURISMI

Caiolo
Ribuntà
at San Bernardo
☎ 0342561297

119

WINE PRODUCERS

Tirano
Conti Sertoli Salis
piazza Salis 3
☎ 0342710404

SHOPPING

Sondrio
Il Camino s.r.l.
di Carlo Motta
piazzetta Rusconi 4
☎ 0342514590
Delicatessen from Valtellina.
Tognolina
via Beccaria 4
☎ 0342514673
Local delicatessen.
Chiavenna
Macelleria
F.lli Del Curto
via F. Dolzino 129
☎ 034332312
Meat.
Delebio
Latteria Sociale
Valtellina
via Stelvio 139
☎ 0342685368
Local cheeses.
Morbegno
Fratelli Ciapponi
piazza III Novembre 23
☎ 0342610223
Local cheeses.
Ponte in
Valtellina
Cooperativa
Ortofrutticola
via Stelvio 20
☎ 0342482103
Fruit and vegetable producer.
Cooperativa
Ortofrutticola
Alta Valtellina
via Nazionale 20
☎ 0342489021
Fruit and vegetable producer.
Villa di Tirano
Frutticoltori
Villa di Tirano
via Nazionale 1
☎ 0342795075
Fruit producer.

Teglio. The S. Giovanni church

mushrooms is considerable.

CHIAVENNA. At the western tip of Lake Como, we pass the Adda river once again. From a distance, the main center of the valley has the austere aspect of the mountains that surround it, but it is softened by churches, palaces and fountains. In the surrounding area, are the celebrated *crotte*, natural caves that have been set up as wine cellars and then transformed into *osterie*. In the area you will find products from the valley, starting with *violini*, or goat's legs cured like *prosciutto*. At Chiavenna go to "Il Cenacolo" where the specialty is *taròz*, a pureed soup of beans and potatoes cooked with cheese and seasoned with butter and pepper. At Villa di Chiavenna, you will find the excellent family-run restaurant "Lanterna Verde", where the wine cellar is well stocked. Further up, at Campodolcino, try the *grappa* from the Valle San Giacomo.

2. The Alta Valtellina

TEGLIO. In the village, visit the sixteenth-century Palazzo Besta.

The valley's best *grano saraceno* is produced in this area, meaning that the *pizzocheri* (buckwheat pasta) are excellent. The bakeries produce two kinds of rye bread – both soft and crusty – in addition to *brazzadella*, a doughnut-shaped bread made of the same grain. To stay in traditional lodgings, try "Colombo" hotel.

TIRANO. Before reaching the village, you arrive at an important Renaissance sanctuary dedicated to the Madonna, which also marks the road's departure from the Val Poschiavina. The nucleus, which straddles the Adda, has ancient buildings that include the Palazzo Salis, the seat of one of the most important wineries in the valley.

BORMIO. Going back towards the springs of the Adda, stop at Grosio. In the town center you will find the hotel restaurant "Sassella" At Bormio, a main center for the Parco Nazionale dello Stelvio, go to "Taulà", for modern cooking is in an historic atmosphere. Don't miss the local spirits: Braulio and Camomilla Alpina.

Tirano. Cantina Conti Sertoli Salis

VARESE

A province of lakes and wooded valleys, where good cooking skillfully combines the flavors of Brianza and the latest Piedmont trends.

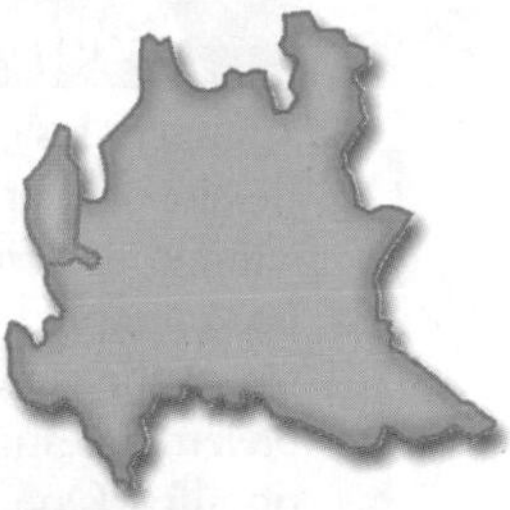

The province of Varese is located on the western edge of Lombardy, shaped by Lake Maggiore and the Ticino river, which flows out of the lake. On the eastern side it crosses the center of the Brianza, between Como and Milan. The territory consists of a broad strip of flatlands dotted with a few small lakes and a wide area of green valleys inland from Lake Verbano and Lake Lugano. The cuisine is similar to that of the provinces of Milan and Como, and there are many products in common. Meats, charcuterie and dairy products are all renowned, as are the freshwater fish, which still abound in the larger lakes. Many woodland products come from the valleys.

Angera. The fortress

121

Gourmet Tours

Varese. The Sacro Monte sanctuary

HOTELS AND
RESTAURANTS

Varese
Lago Maggiore ¶¶¶¶
via Carrobbio 19
☎ 0332231183
Il Gestore ¶¶¶
viale Aguggiari 48
☎ 0332236404
Busto Arsizio
Osteria Cinque
Campanili ¶¶¶
via Luigi Maino 18
☎ 0331630493
Cantello
Madonnina ★★★
largo Broggi 1
☎ 0332417731
Induno Olona
Villa Castiglioni ★★★
Al Bersò ¶¶¶
via Castiglioni 1
☎ 0332200201
★🍴 **Da Venanzio** ¶¶¶
via Olona 38
☎ 0332200333
Laveno
Il Porticciolo
★★★ ¶¶¶
via Fortino 40
☎ 0332667257
Luino
Camin Hotel
Luino ★★★
viale Dante 35
☎ 0332530118
Olgiate Olona
Ma.Ri.Na. ¶¶¶
piazza S. Gregorio 11
☎ 0331640463
Ranco
Il Sole di Ranco ¶¶¶¶
piazza Venezia 5
☎ 0331976507
Vergiate
★🍴 **Cinzianella** ¶¶¶¶
at Corgeno (km 3)
via Lago 26
☎ 0331946337

VARESE. This city lies on the gentle slopes that come down from Campo dei Fiori mountain and has preserved beautiful mementos of the time when it was the preferred destination of Lombard nobility. One of the attractions here is Sacro Monte, a place of devotion and art with thirteen seventeenth-century chapels. In the town go to the restaurant "Lago Maggiore" for a chance to taste rare dishes such as *rostin negàa* (veal browned in butter and cooked in white wine). Here you can also find the traditional dry biscuits *mostaccini* and *giromette*. The first are spicy and the latter are shaped like animals or warriors. At Induno Olona stay at the atmospheric hotel "Villa Castiglioni", which is complemented by the restaurant "Al Bersò". For a similar feel, try the "Madonnina" inn at Cantello, where the cooking is exceptional, particularly in asparagus season.

1. The Varesotto heath

CASTIGLIONE OLONA. This stop is a must in order to visit a fifteenth-century village filled by its humanist patron, Count Branda Castiglioni, with Tuscan art. A little beyond lies another detour for Castelseprio, where the church Santa Maria foris Portas is decorated with frescoes by an unknown Oriental master.

SARONNO. The history of this town is tied to the important sanctuary of the Madonna dei Miracoli, richly frescoed and built in 1498 according to plans by Tibaldi. Of more recent fame is the production of cookies (*Amaretti*) and liquors (*Amaret-*

to). Lovers of historical detail should visit the Lazzaroni factory's Museo del Biscotto.

BUSTO ARSIZIO. The church of Santa Maria di Piazza is an exceptional monumental presence in this historic center of manufactured textiles. The harmonious Renaissance construction is sumptuously decorated. For the Festa dell'Immacolata *machitt*, almond and sugar *torroncini*, or nougat, between two wafers, are traditional. We recommend you eat at "I 5 Campanili", where you can get *storione in camicia di lardo* (sturgeon wrapped in bacon). At Olgiate Olona, "Ma.Ri.Na" offers unusually prepared fish. Arsago Seprio is an artistic haven at the end of the route, with the important Romanesque basilica of San Vittore.

2. Lake Maggiore and Lake Ceresio

ANGERA. On the way to the lake, Vergiate is a good place to stop to eat at the Buon Ricordo hotel and restaurant "Cinzianella", where Lombard cuisine and creative cooking balance each other well alongside a first-rate wine list. Don't miss *scaloppa di salmeri-*

no al *Barbera* (red char scallop with Barbera wine). At Angera, stop on the shores of Verbano before heading up to the Rocca, which is a reminder of a time when the village was a lookout point for controlling lake traffic. A few kilometers further along, the "Il Sole di Ranco" is exceptional. At this beautiful inn everything is taken care of with great attention and the cuisine is beautifully elegant and expressive. LAVENO. Going up the shore, at the level of Leggiuno, take a detour for Santa Caterina del Sasso, a lovely convent set high above the lake. Then the road turns toward the gulf of Laveno, a pleasant town with a nineteenth-century feel. The restaurant "Il Porticciolo" is very good. It is well-located and serves good food – and not just fish. At pastry shops buy *Ossi*, dry candies typical of the area. Further inland, at Cittiglio and at Gavirate *Brutti e Buoni*, amaretto cookies made with hazelnuts have gained renown. In Valcuvia, which follows the northern border of Campo dei Fiori, turn off for Arcumeggia, a village with modern frescoes. LUINO. This old Lombard village has a lakeside boardwalk shaded by plane trees. Here the settings

The S. Caterina del Sasso sanctuary

of Piero Chiara's novels may be found. "Camin Hotel Luino", set in a beautiful Art Nouveau style villa, is worth trying. Further to the north is Maccagno, and rising above it the Valli del Luinese is home to excellent goat's cheese made with milk from the rare breed Nera di Verzasca. The honey production is also quite well known. From Luino take inland routes back to Varese. Go up the Tresa Valley and follow Lake Lugano or go along the green Valganna. VIGGIÙ. The visit to Lombardy ends between the hills of Viggiù and Bisuschio which are both pleasant vacation resorts. What better way to finish than with a stop at Induno Olona to go to "Da Venanzio", an elegant and pleasant restaurant. Here, *fegato d'oca con confettura di cipolle rosse* (goose liver with red onion jam) is astonishing, but the spirit of the place comes out in other pleasant offerings that are reasonably priced.

AGRITURISMI

Varese
Goccia d'Oro
Ranch
at Bizzozero
via dei Vignò 134
☎ 0332265389
Cassano Valcuvia
Albero Bianco
via Dante 569
☎ 0332995671
Daverio
Cascina
Fontana
cascina Fontana 11
☎ 0332948352

SHOPPING

Varese
Pasticceria Ghezzi
corso Matteotti 36
☎ 0332235179
Pastries and sweets.
Busto Arsizio
Incontro
via Lonate Pozzolo 87
☎ 0331635658
Ice-creams.
Casale Litta
Azienda Pasqué
at Bernate
☎ 0332948307
Local cheeses.
Maccagno
Caseificio
Lago d'Elio
at Musignano
☎ 0332561134
Local cheeses.

Cascina Capuzza

where art of fine wines meets good cooking.

wine makers since 1917

Cascina Capuzza - San Martino della Battaglia - Desenzano del Garda - Tel. **030/9910279**
www.tenuteformentini.com - **info@tenuteformentini.com**

THE VARESE HONEY

GOLD OF THE PRE-ALPS

CONSORZIO QUALITA' MIELE VARESINO

LOOK FOR
THIS QUALITY
MARK

PIAZZA MONTE GRAPPA, 5 VARESE · ITALY · PH +39 0332 295323
c/o Chamber of Commerce - Varese
www.mielevarese.it - e-mail:bruna@va.camcom.it

TRENTINO-ALTO ADIGE THE TWO FACES OF ALPINE CUISINE

Nowhere else in Italy does the border between two provinces mark such a clear division between cuisines. Trentino has rich dishes influenced by the Po Valley, while the delicate flavors of Alto Adige derive from the north of the Alps.

As he descended from the Brenner Pass, Goethe said: "I feel good, it is as if I had been born and bred here." That he was referring to South Tyrol should be no cause for surprise given the close affinity between this area and the German-speaking nations. Then, on the shores of Lake Garda, the poet was deeply moved by the sight of the lemon-trees in flower, reminding him of the fragrance and light of the Mediterranean world. You will experience similar sensations if you follow our routes – albeit in the opposite direction to Goethe – from Verona to the Brenner Pass: first the olive groves, the vineyards and orchards of the Trentino, which are still very Italian in appearance, followed by the timeless world of Dolomite farmhouses and the Hapsburg atmosphere of the small towns of Alto Adige.

A MOUNTAIN ECONOMY

However different their histories may be, the Trentino and Alto Adige are neighboring areas where change is progressive as the land rises up from the Po Valley plain to the Alpine peaks. You see farms on the hillsides and deep in the vallyes, where apples and vines are grown, while the terraces and plateaus are also devoted to cereals, fodder crops and vegetables – especially potatoes and cabbages – with the recent addition of berry fruits. Higher up, you find the summer pastures where milk, cheese and delicious honey are produced. Just about everywhere, the water of the mountain streams is used for the farming of trout and the small, trout-like char. Thus, this is a mountain economy that is ancient in its appearance and its ways but, at the same time modern in the attention it pays to the quality of the natural products and the care taken when working with them. The region is divided into two autonomous provinces, but they work together to protect the delicate environmental balance by supporting local agriculture. The way this strategy is implemented is, first and foremost, through cooperation: in both areas the producers' organizations are very active, and the Trentino and Alto Adige-Südtirol quality labels guarantee the adoption of environment-friendly agriculture based on traditional methods.

Prato Piazza. Green fields with the Dolomites in the background

POLENTA AND CHEESE, RYE BREAD AND SPECK

As far as the cuisine is concerned, Salorno, where the Adige Valley narrows, marks the transition, gastronomically speaking, from the Po Valley – or more precisely the Veneto – to the area of the Danube, with its evident Viennese influence. Thus, while in Trento it is *polenta* with everything, in Bolzano the favorite dish is *Knödeln*, large bread dumplings with various flavors. In the former area, they eat *pasta e fagioli* (pasta and beans), in the latter *Gulaschsuppe*. Both cuisines, however, require the conservation of the food for a long time, which is a typically Alpine need, given the difficulty of obtaining supplies. Hence the bread is baked to last for weeks, the meat is smoked and *sauerkraut* is made to accompany – together with potatoes – the numerous meat dishes. Both areas make ample use of mushrooms and game (especially rabbit, hare and venison) but, while the cuisine of the Trentino is robust, that of Alto Adige boasts more delicate flavors, including sweet and sour sauces made from apples, bilberries and other fruits. If you want to eat out, there are plenty of opportunities for a superb meal, particularly in towns such as Merano that have a long tradition as tourist centers. And there is no lack of pleasant surprises, from the first-rate restaurant hidden in the woods to the ancient *Stube* hidden under the portico of a piazza. Hospitality in the rural areas is traditionally excellent, especially in Alto Adige, where in every district at least one *maso* (farmhouse) – ancient or modern, they are always very comfortable – is open to vacationers. Unlike that in other regions, the *agriturismo* (accommodation on working farms) is in authentic, working farms, so guests can enjoy fresh milk and butter and apples from the orchard just behind the house.

The apple in all its colors is one of the region's main products

Terlago. The castle

Trentino-Alto Adige - Typical products

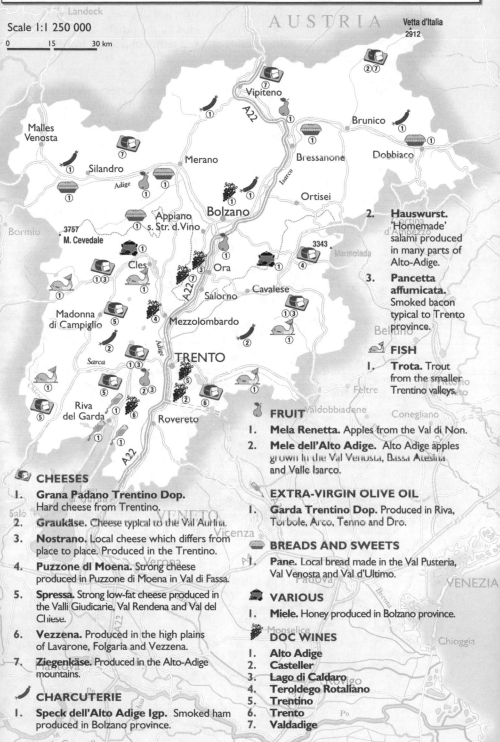

Scale 1:1 250 000

0   15   30 km

CHEESES

1. **Grana Padano Trentino Dop.** Hard cheese from Trentino.
2. **Graukäse.** Cheese typical to the Val Aurina.
3. **Nostrano.** Local cheese which differs from place to place. Produced in the Trentino.
4. **Puzzone di Moena.** Strong cheese produced in Puzzone di Moena in Val di Fassa.
5. **Spressa.** Strong low-fat cheese produced in the Valli Giudicarie, Val Rendena and Val del Chiese.
6. **Vezzena.** Produced in the high plains of Lavarone, Folgaria and Vezzena.
7. **Ziegenkäse.** Produced in the Alto-Adige mountains.

CHARCUTERIE

1. **Speck dell'Alto Adige Igp.** Smoked ham produced in Bolzano province.
2. **Hauswurst.** 'Homemade' salami produced in many parts of Alto-Adige.
3. **Pancetta affumicata.** Smoked bacon typical to Trento province.

FISH

1. **Trota.** Trout from the smaller Trentino valleys.

FRUIT

1. **Mela Renetta.** Apples from the Val di Non.
2. **Mele dell'Alto Adige.** Alto Adige apples grown in the Val Venosta, Bassa Atesina and Valle Isarco.

EXTRA-VIRGIN OLIVE OIL

1. **Garda Trentino Dop.** Produced in Riva, Torbole, Arco, Tenno and Dro.

BREADS AND SWEETS

1. **Pane.** Local bread made in the Val Pusteria, Val Venosta and Val d'Ultimo.

VARIOUS

1. **Miele.** Honey produced in Bolzano province.

DOC WINES

1. **Alto Adige**
2. **Casteller**
3. **Lago di Caldaro**
4. **Teroldego Rotaliano**
5. **Trentino**
6. **Trento**
7. **Valdadige**

TRENTO

Between Alto Adige and Verona are the valleys of the Trentino, where the flavors are from the mountains and red wines and spumanti abound.

The province of Trento corresponds more or less to the central part of the Adige Valley – between Avio and the Salorno pass – which, with the neighboring valleys of the Sarca, Chiese, Brenta and Noce, lies between magnificent Alpine ranges. To the west, on the border with Lombardy, soar the granite rocks of Adamello and Ortles-Cevedale; to the east, towards the Veneto, are the spectacular peaks of the Dolomites, such as the Sella Group, Marmolada and Lagorai. To the south, are the limestone massifs of Monte Baldo, overlooking Lake Garda, and Ortigara and Pasubio between Valsugana and the Asiago Plateau.

The landscape is, therefore, extremely varied, starting with the valley troughs, where orchards reign supreme with delectable reinette apples, and the lower slopes, which are covered with vines. The vast majority of the province's wines are produced in the Trentino DOC (*Denominazione di Origine Controllata*) zone, and comprise "Marzemino", a long-established red, the "Nosiola" white and the two muscats, "Giallo" and "Rosa", of the Valle dei Laghi. Other DOC labels are "Casteller", the wine synonymous with Trento, and "Teroldego", the famous red of Campo Rotaliano. Outstanding sparkling wines are produced under the "Talento" and "Trento Classico" labels. Further up the mountains are woods of broad-leafed trees and conifers, where chestnuts and mushrooms are plentiful, while on the cultivated terraces that interrupt them farmers grow numerous crops, especially potatoes and berry fruits. Highest up, you find the mountain pastures, where a wide range of cheeses are produced, including *nostrano* (which means local cheese), which varies from place to place, and the refined *vezzana*, made on the Lavarone Plateau. As far as cuisine goes, Trento and Rovereto, old cities situated on the road to the Brenner Pass, are the places most influenced by both South Tyrol, with goulash, and the Veneto, as may be seen in the *polenta* and the *pasta e fagioli* (pasta and beans). For the rest, the area's cuisine comprises soups, meat and game, with a great emphasis on cheese and the produce of the woodlands, particularly mushrooms. Also worthy of note is the cuisine of ethnic minorities of Germanic origin: for instance, those in the areas bordering on the Asiago Plateau (erroneously called "Cimbri") and the Mocheni, in the valley north of Pergine Valsugana. It is possible to eat very well in the area, where a major role is played by *agriturismo* establishments, often located on wine-growing farms and mountain pastures.

HOTELS AND RESTAURANTS

Trento
Chiesa ¶¶
parco S. Marco
☎ 0461238766
Osteria a
le Due Spade ¶¶
via Don Rizzi 11
☎ 0461234343
Pizzeria
Ristorante Doc ¶
via Milano 148
☎ 0461237489
Università ¶
via Prati 6
☎ 0461236524

Arco
Da Gianni ¶¶
at Chiarano (km 2)
via S. Marcello 21
☎ 0464516464
La Lanterna ¶¶
at Prabi (km 2)
via Legionari
Cecoslovacchi 30
☎ 0464517013
Lega ¶
via Vergolano 8
☎ 0464516205

Baselga di Pinè
Due Pini ★★★
at Vigo (km 1)
☎ 0461557030

Civezzano
Maso Cantanghel ¶¶
via della Madonnina 33
☎ 0461858714

Cles
Antica Trattoria ¶
via Roma 13
☎ 0463421631

Gourmet Tours

1. The Adige Valley

ROVERETO. Going up the Adige Valley from Verona, the beginning of the Trentino province is marked on the left by the castle of Avio, with its famous fourteenth-century frescoes of courtly scenes. A little further on, amidst the vineyards of the Val Lagarina, the small town of Ala is visible with its old quarter – known to the local people as Villa Alta – which has an enchanting medieval atmosphere. After this we come to Rovereto, an attractive city whose architecture distantly echoes that of Venice. On the river Leno stands the castle housing the largest and most interesting Italian museum of the First World War. Nearby, don't miss the Galleria Depero, devoted to the versatile Futurist artist Fortunato Depero, also famous for his advertising posters of the early twentieth century. Gourmets should stop at "Al Borgo", regarded by many as the best restaurant in the region. Here the friendly Dalsasso brothers make everything on the spot, bread included, and keep a first-rate cellar. The menu comprises the produce of both the mountains and the sea, with superb combinations, such as lasagna with the heavy-bodied grouper, turbot, sea bass and mushrooms, especially *porcini* (boletus). Also worth a visit is the warm and welcoming "Hotel Rovereto" and its restaurant "Novecento". In the food stores – for instance, the "Finarolli" *salumeria* and the established "Cooperativa Sav" – ask for the local *erborinato dolce* cheese, similar to Gorgonzola, and, when in season, the choice vegetables of the Gresta Valley (potatoes, cabbages, *radicchio* [red chicory], carrots and asparagus, 40 percent of which is grown organically), as well as the cherries and chestnuts of the Val Lagarina. There are excellent opportunities for tasting and purchasing

HOTELS AND RESTAURANTS

Levico Terme
Aurora ¶¶
at Compet 28
☎ 0461706467
Boivin ¶
via Garibaldi 9
☎ 0461701670
Malè
Conte Ramponi ¶¶
at Magras (km 1)
piazza S. Marco 38
☎ 0463901989
Mezzocorona
Cacciatora
¶¶ via Canè 133
☎ 0461650124
Mezzolombardo
Sole ¶¶
via Rotaliana 5
☎ 0461601103
Moena
Malga Panna ¶¶¶
via Costalunga 29
☎ 0462573489
Rifugio Fuchiade ¶¶
Passo San Pellegrino
☎ 0462574281
Nago-Torbole
Piccolo Mondo
at Torbole ★★★ ¶¶
via Matteotti 7
☎ 0464505271
Nogaredo
Le Strie ¶
piazza Centrale 10
☎ 0464412220
Ospedaletto
Va Pensiero ¶¶
via Pradanella 7/b
☎ 0461768383

Trento. The Neptune fountain in piazza del Duomo

wine, starting with the "Bossi Fedrigotti" winery, with its great reds (Cabernet and Merlot), located in a traditional farmhouse just outside the town. On the opposite side of the valley is "Isera", the center of production for "Marzemino", a red praised by Mozart, which here can be tasted and purchased at the "Casa del Vino della Val Lagarina". At Nogaredo, you can taste the wines and olive oil from the Letrari estate at the "Palazzo Lodron", while at the "Le Strie" *osteria* you will find a fine selection of local *salumi* (cured meat specialties) and cheeses.

TRENTO. Situated on the Adige river, at the point where the valleys of the Trentino converge, the town, once ruled by prince-bishops, has preserved its severe aspect and splendid architecture. A tour starts at Piazza del Duomo, from where the elegant Via Belenzani and Via Manci lead to the Castello del Buon Consiglio. Nearby, a splendid eighteenth-century building houses the excellent "Chiesa" restaurant, renowned for its menu based on apples, from hors d'oeuvre to the dessert. Classic dishes here include Bishop Bernardo Clesio's *talleri*, coin-shaped pasta served with meat sauce and vegetables (this is a "Buon Ricordo" dish). Another restaurant worth visiting is the "Osteria a le Due Spade", located in a late eighteenth-century *Stube*. In the food stores, look out for the local charcuterie, which includes *luganega* (sausage) made from meat minced fairly coarsely, smoked bacon, *carne salada* (salt beef) of the Valle dei Laghi, and horse-meat salami. Cheeses include the

Trentino version of *grana padano* and varieties produced on the Alpine pastures. In Piazza delle Erbe and Piazza Vittoria there are markets of fresh produce and, when in season, the mushrooms and excellent chestnuts of Sardagna. For wine enthusiasts, the "Università" is an *enoteca* serving wine and a variety of gastronomic specialties. Outstanding producers in the area include the "Ferrari Lunelli" winery, one of Italy's leading Spumante makers, and "Maso Bergamini", which offers *agriturismo* facilities. In the nearby village of Civezzano it is worth paying a visit to "Maso Cantanghel", a pleasant *trattoria* offering a splendid range of cheeses, wines and grappas.

2. The Valle dei Laghi, the Trentino shore of Lake Garda and the Valli Giudicarie

VEZZANO. The easiest way to reach the Sarca Valley is the Gardesana Occidentale highway (*statale* 45 bis), which climbs up to Lake Terlago and then descends to Vezzano. The alternative, with a series of hairpin bends and splendid views, is the road over Monte Bondone (1537 m/5043 ft). The two routes join up in sight of two adjoining lakes: Toblino, with its picturesque castle, and Santa Massenza, surrounded by olives. Here Nosiola vines stretch out as far as the eye can see. At Lon di Vezzano it is worth stopping off at the "Fior di Roccia" restaurant, a small family-run establishment where a young chef prepares local dishes, including delicious barley soup with Savoy cabbage and fresh Trentino sausage. At Pergolese visit the "Pisoni" winery. Found-

HOTELS AND
RESTAURANTS

Pergine Valsugana
Rifugio Capriolo ⊻
at Viarago (km 4)
at Masi Alti 11
☎ 0461551108
Riva del Garda
Luise ★★★ ⊻▦
La Limonaia ⊻⊻
viale Rovereto 9
☎ 0464552796
Al Volt ⊻⊻
via Fiume 73
☎ 0464552570
Piè di Castello ⊻⊻
via Diaz Cologna 55
☎ 0464521065
Ronzone
Orso Grigio ⊻⊻
via Regole 10
☎ 0463880625
Rovereto
Al Borgo ⊻⊻⊻
via Garibaldi 13
☎ 0464436300
Rovereto ★★★
Novecento ⊻⊻ ⊻▦
corso Rosmini 82/d
☎ 0464435222
**San Michele
all'Adige**
Silvio ⊻⊻ ⊻▦
at Masetto
di Faedo (km 1)
via Nazionale 1
☎ 0461650324
Spiazzo
Mezzosoldo ⊻⊻ ⊻▦
via Nazionale 196
☎ 0465801067
Strigno
Rifugio Crucolo ⊻⊻
Val Campelle
☎ 0461766093
Vezzano
Fior di Roccia ⊻⊻
at Lon (km 2)
via Nazionale 2
☎ 0461864029

ed in the seventeenth-century, it used to supply the prince-bishops and Austrian governors. Today it produces the celebrated "Trento Classico" spumante and various distilled drinks.

ARCO. Olives, oleanders and palms give a Mediterranean air to the resort that was a great favorite with the Hapsburg nobility in the late nineteenth century. The produce of the Valle dei Laghi may be purchased here, including "Vino Santo" and *carne salada* (salt beef or horse-meat, served thinly sliced, raw or heated on a griddle, with olive oil and lemon). When in season, the succulent Dro plums are available at the "Cooperativa Contadini Basso Sarca". The chestnuts of Drena are particularly good, and are used to make the stuffing for guinea fowl and rabbit. At Vignole the Bertamini oil-press produces first-rate

Lake Molveno

olive oil. At Chiarano, "Da Gianni" provides excellent food and accommodation.

TORBOLE. An elegant resort on the eastern shore of Lake Garda, it offers water sports and trips into the hills. Here we particularly recommend the "Piccolo Mondo". This is a hotel with a restaurant specializing in lake fish and *carne salada e fasoi* (salt beef and beans), a "Buon Ricordo" dish.

RIVA DEL GARDA. Surrounded by water, the castle is a reminder of the former strategic importance of the town, which was disputed between Lombardy and the Veneto. But its avenues, villas, and parks are a result of its more recent tourist development. "Al Volt" is a particularly fascinating restaurant located behind the port. Don't miss the *spiedino di coregone alla Nosiola* (skewered whitefish flavored with Nosiola wine), the most outstanding of various sophisticated dishes. Also worth visiting are the "Luise", a splendidly-located hotel with a restaurant, "La Limonaia", and the "Piè di Castello"

AGRITURISMI

Trento
Bergamini
at Cognola (km 3)
at Bergamini 3
☎ 0461983079
Lomaso
Maso Marocc
at Poia
☎ 0465702098
Tenno
Pizacol
at Cologna (km 3)
☎ 0464521701

WINE PRODUCERS

Trento
Ferrari Fratelli Lunelli
via del Ponte 15
☎ 0461972311
Lasino
Fratelli Pisoni
at Pergolese (km 4)
via S. Siro 9
☎ 0461564106
Lavis
Cantina La Vis
via del Carmine 7
☎ 0461246325
Sebastiani
via Clementi 31
☎ 0461246315
Mezzocorona
Cantina Rotari
Via del Teroldego 1
☎ 0461616300
Mezzolombardo
Cantina Rotaliana Mezzolombardo
corso del Popolo 6
☎ 0461601010
Le Brul Spumante
via Fiorini 19
☎ 0461603303
Villa De Varda
via Rotaliana 27/a
☎ 0461601486

trattoria, which serves excellent *carne salada*. The "Associazione Agraria" sells DOC wines, including "Nosiola" and "Moscato Giallo", and Garda Trentino DOP (*Denominazione di Origine Protetta*) extra virgin olive oil. From Riva you can make a short trip through the vineyards and olive groves to the village of Tenno and its picturesque lake. At Cologna, "Pizacol" is an *agriturismo* establishment serving the dishes, wines and distilled drinks of the valley.

PIEVE DI LEDRO. Southwest of Riva a road heads away from Garda into the Val di Ledro, with its own lake and the interesting Museo delle Palafitte at Molina, where you can see finds from Bronze Age pile-dwellings. The local *trattorie* serve trout (smoked or otherwise), risotto with perch fillets, and mixed grills. The *salumerie* have *salumi* made from game and the rare donkey-meat salami. From the very green Valle di Concei come mushrooms and berry fruits, as well as infusions and syrups of strawberries, raspberries, and bilberries, on sale in shops and pharmacies.

CONDINO. The Valli Giudicarie comprise the Valle del Chiese above Lake Idro and the upper Sarca Valley. This district was formerly governed, on behalf of the bishop of Trento, by a judge (*giudice*), hence the name. Adamello forms a backdrop to Condino, the first important village on the *statale 237* (Strada del Caffaro). Here you can buy *nostrano Valchiese*, a cheese matured for up to two years, giving it a pungent flavor. The summer cheese, from the mountain pastures, may be regarded as the local version of the Brescian *bagoss*. Another local cheese is the low-fat *spressa*, which is matured for 9-10 months and also has a strong flavor. Lastly, you may find the curious dairy product called *tara*, a piquant cream obtained by fermenting the leftovers of cheese-making in grappa. In this area, Darzo is renowned for its chestnuts, while Storo produces maize

WINE PRODUCERS

Roverè
della Luna
Gaierhof
via IV Novembre 51
☎ 0461658527
Rovereto
Conti Bossi
Fedrigotti
via Unione 43
☎ 0464439250
San Michele
all'Adige
Istituto Agrario
San Michele
all'Adige
via E. Mach 1
☎ 0461615111

SHOPPING

Trento
Bampi Andrea
Formaggi
via Calepina 33
☎ 0461239174
Cheeses and
charcuterie.
Pasticceria
Bertelli
via Oriola 29
☎ 0461984765
Strudel, Zelten
and cakes.
Gilli Ezio -
Alimentari
Salumeria
via Suffragio 132
☎ 0461987312
Local products
and charcuterie.
Gastronomia
Mattei
via Mazzini 46
☎ 0461238053
Salami, boletus
mushrooms, wines.

135

for *polenta* (the Marano variety, which is grown organically and stoneground by the Cooperativa Agri Novanta). A local specialty is *carbonera polenta*.

TIONE DI TRENTO. In a basin amidst pines and beeches, this is the chief town of the Valli Giudicarie. Beyond it, the Valle Rendena leads to Madonna di Campiglio and the Adamello and Brenta ranges. Gastronomic pleasures await visitors to Spiazzo, where the atmospheric "Mezzosoldo" hotel has a restaurant serving such local dishes as *tagliata di capriolo* (thinly-sliced roe deer) with mountain herbs, leg of lamb with potato polenta, smoked char fish with spinach, and wild onions and thistles. A specialty of the Valle del Banale is *ciuìga*, a sausage of pork and turnips eaten with polenta and sauerkraut. In the Valle Rendena the *salumi* are made from game and mutton, while *mocetta rendenera* is dried salt beef.

STENICO. With its castle dominating the valley and the Brenta Dolomites as a backdrop, this is an attractive mountain resort. On the opposite side of the valley, Bleggio and Lomaso produce meat, cheese, potatoes and delicious nuts. In a magnificent position, the "Maso Marocc" *agriturismo* offers accommodation and a range of tasty dishes. Another interesting trip is to Molveno, on the lake of the same name, and Andalo, with a cableway to the summit of Monte Paganella. The local restaurants serve lake fish – steamed trout and char – mixed fish grills, and mixed meat stew with *polenta* and mushrooms.

3. The Val di Non and the Val di Sole

SAN MICHELE D'ADIGE. For gourmets the Augustinian monastery is not just a splendid medieval building housing a remarkable ethnographic museum (Museo dei usi e costumi della gente trentina). As the premises of the "Istituto Agrario San Michele all'Adige", it is one of the top places in the world for the study of wine, a leading research center and also a winery producing superlative wines, Spumanti and distilled drinks. Nearby, other important distilleries include "Zeni", at Grumo, and Pojer and Sandri, at Faedo. At San Michele, Da Silvio is an interesting restaurant with a modern décor, noted for mixed meats grilled at the table.

MEZZOLOMBARDO. This is the most important village in the Piana Rotaliana, long famous for the red wine known as "Teroldego". After visiting the local wineries – such as "Cantina Rotaliana", "Le Brul Spumante" and "Villa De Varda" – those fond of whites should continue to Roverè della Luna, where the "Gaierhof "winery produces Müller Thurgau, Sauvignon, Traminer and Riesling. Particularly recommended at Mezzolombardo is "Al Sole", an established hotel with an excellent restaurant. At Mezzocorona, it is worth visiting the new winery of the "Rotari" spumante firm.

CLES. The chief town of the Val di Non, it stands on a terrace densely covered with orchards. Built in the Gothic and Renaissance styles with a Venetian flavor, the town's center is dominated by the castle that once be-

SHOPPING

Trento
Macelleria Ravagni
piazza Duomo 43
☎ 0461980061
Meat and game.
Vaiz
Piazza Vittoria
Fresh mushrooms and bilberries.
Arco
Cooperativa Contadini Basso Sarca
via Galas 37
☎ 0464518551
In season, plums from Dro.
Frantoio Ivo Bertamini
at Vignole
via Mazzini 12
☎ 0464517229
Excellent olive oil.
Campitello di Fassa
Bottega della Carne
piazza Centrale 4
☎ 0462750401
Smoked pork meat and smoked game.
Condino
Cooperativa Agri Novanta
via Regensburger 23
☎ 0465686614
Organically-grown maize for "polenta" (Marano variety).

longed to Bernardo Clesio, the famous prince-bishop of Trento. On sale here is the delicious *grana Trentino*, a hard cheese resembling Parmesan, which is produced in the area. Across the artificial lake of Santa Giustina lies Sanzeno, from where a road leads up to the spectacular sanctuary of San Romedio, a popular pilgrim shrine.

FONDO. Situated in the upper Val di Non amidst conifer forests, Fondo is divided by a river flowing through the village in a gorge. It makes an ideal starting-point for wonderful trips – for instance, to the Passo della Mendola and Monte Panegal (1737 m/5699 ft), where there are breathtaking views of the surrounding valleys and snow-clad peaks, and the more distant Dolomites. At Ronzone, we particularly recommend the family-run "Orso Grigio" restaurant, located in a beautiful villa on the fringe of the forest. It features dishes that showcase the good quality produce used and

boasts a well-chosen wine list. Try the potato *tortel* topped with *porcini* mushrooms and the saddle of lamb flavored with herbs.

MALÈ. This is the chief town of the Val di Sole. Extending from the bridge of Mostizzolo to Fucine, it is beautifully set in a long sequence of orchards, castles and ancient villages. On the main street you will find an ethnographical museum, the "Museo della Civiltà Solandra", as well as shops selling the valley's mouthwatering cheeses: the soft *casolèt*; the half-fat *nostrano*, mild or strong depending on how long it has been matured; *Solandro* from the Alpine pastures, sometimes slightly sharp; and the rare *poina enfumegada*, smoked *ricotta* with a strong tang. In the central piazza be sure to try the ice-cream for which this valley is renowned, with flavors including apple, herbs, and even Vino Santo. At Magras, a splendid palazzo houses the "Conte

The Val di Non. Apple trees in blossom

SHOPPING

Folgaria
Caseificio di Folgaria e Costa
at Costa (km 2)
via Maffei 269
☎ 0464720763
Typical cheeses (Nostrano, Asiago, Vezzena, "ricotta").
Macelleria Cappelletti
via Emilio Colpi 1
☎ 0464721109
Cured meats such as speck, würstel, salumi and Landyeger.
Isera
Casa del Vino della Val Lagarina
piazza S. Vincenzo 1
inf. APT di Rovereto
☎ 0464430363
Wines and DOC labels such as Marzemino.
Malè
Gelateria Roby
piazza Garibaldi 5
☎ 0463901126
Wide range of ice-creams made from apples, berries, wines and grappas.

Ramponi" restaurant, where the classic dishes of the valley's cuisine are served with the best of Trentino's wines. There are three options after Malé: either you can go to the left to the Val Meledrio, with the resorts of Folgarida and Madonna del Campiglio, or to the other side of of the river Noce, a few miles further on, to the Val di Pejo which terminates in the village of Pejo, or you can continue straight on, to the Val Vermiglio, which leads to the Passo del Tonale.

4. The Val di Fiemme, the Valsugana and the Val Lagarina

LAVIS. Its name derives from the river Avisio, which crosses it after flowing through vineyards and terraces down the Val di Cembra, where Müller Thurgau is the dominant grape variety. Absolutely unmissable is "La Vis", one of Trentino's leading wineries. The best wines from about 800 producers are on sale in the modern "Vinoteca". Also worth a visit is the Sebastiani winery, a family firm renowned for its outstanding Chardonnay Riserva. The local shops sell an unusual horse-meat salami and, from the Val di Cembra, the *nostrano de casèl* cheese, chestnuts, and berry fruits. At "Nave San Rocco" try the *persecche*, traditional fruit conserves (apples, pears, plums, and persimmons – mainly organically grown – sliced and dried with nothing added).

CAVALESE. From the majestic mountain ranges of the Lagorai and Latemar, you enter the Val di Fiemme, the name given to the middle part of the Avisio Valley. Cavalese is a resort that was already a favorite with the prince-bishops of Trento, who built what is now the Palazzo della Magnifica Comunità di Fiemme as their summer residence. A local specialty is *misto capra* (cow's and goat's milk cheese), which after maturing, is particularly sharp.

MOENA. The Val di Fassa – the upper part of the Avisio Valley – offers views extending from Sassolungo to Catinaccio. At Moena, Malga Panna is highly recommended for its friendly atmosphere and traditional cuisine, which includes *tagliata di cervo* (thinly-sliced venison) with potato *gnocchi*. On sale here is *puzzone di Moena* (known in Ladin, the language still spoken in the valley, as *spretz tzaorì*, strong cheese), a more traditional and pungent version of *nostrano de casèl*. At the Passo di San Pellegrino, you can enjoy good food at "Rifugio Fuchiade". Further up the main valley, "Canazei" is surrounded by some of the best scenery in the Dolomites.

SAN MARTINO DI CASTROZZA. After returning to Predazzo, take the *Statale* 50 up to the Passo Rolle where the Pale di San Martino gives way to the descent to the Valle di Cismon and the elegant resort of San Martino di Castrozza. Further down the valley you come to Fiera di Primiero, a resort renowned for its cheeses. In addition to *nostrano di casèl*, you can find *tosèla*, with a soft and elastic texture, which is fried in butter and salted.

BORGO VALSUGANA. Following the river Cismon, which flows through a long gorge to reach the Brenta, the *Statale* 50 crosses into

SHOPPING

Nogaredo
Letrari
palazzo Lodron
☎ 0464411093
DOC wines and olive oil.
Pergine Valsugana
Cooperativa Sant'Orsola
at Zivignago
via Lagorai 131
☎ 0461518111
Berries.
Riva del Garda
Associazione Agraria
via Lutti 10
☎ 0464552133
Trentino's DOC wines and Garda Trentino DOP extra-virgin olive oil.
Omezzolli
via Brione 9
☎ 0464551642
Organically-grown fruits.
Rovereto
Finarolli Alimentari
via Mercerie 7
☎ 0464434319
Local specialties.

the Veneto near Feltre to link up with the fast highway through the Valsugana. An alternative route from Fiera di Primiero is the scenic road that climbs, with innumerable hairpin bends, to the Passo del Brocon, before descending to Strigno. In the enchanting Val Campelle, "Rifugio Crucolo" is renowned for its excellent cuisine. Borgo Valsugana, with its imposing Castel Telvana, is set in a pleasant landscape of vineyards, pastures, and woods. Local produce include the chestnuts of Spera and Roncegno, as well as choice vegetables and berry fruits. At Ospedaletto, on the highway to Bassano del Grappa, the "Va' Pensiero" *trattoria* deserves a special mention.

PERGINE VALSUGANA. Passing between Lake Levico – in the village, the *osteria* Boivin is recommended – and the larger Lake Caldonazzo, the highway reaches this town with its old center towered over by a fifteenth-century castle. To the north is the Valle dei Mocheni, inhabited by the descendants of the German miners who settled there in the Middle Ages. There are numerous local specialties: at Sant'Orsola, pork and donkey-meat *luganega* (sausage); bacon cured in the smoke of juniper branches; roast leg of pork and the smoked donkey meat of Kamauz and Roveda. At Pergine there is the traditional beef or horse-meat *carne salada* and salami of mixed horse-meat and pork. The Valle di Pinè produces *zighera*, a hard smoked cheese, dark in color with a strong flavor. We have two suggestions for gourmets. At Viarago, try the "Capriolo" refuge (1300 m/4265 ft), and at Baselega, visit the "Due Pini" hotel and restaurant, where you will find traditional local dishes and a wonderful range of cheeses and wines. On the slopes of Panarotta, an Austrian stronghold in the First World War, is Vetriolo Terme, where the "Aurora" inn is good.

LAVARONE. From Levico Terme – and also from Rovereto, via Folgaria – a road climbs up to the Lavarone plateau. Meadows carpeted with flowers, fir and beech woods, and a small lake make this an ideal area for a vacation. The *malghe* (herdsmen's huts) around the Passo di Vezzana produce one of the Trentino's tastiest cheeses.

Typical Simmenthal cattle

SHOPPING

Rovereto
**Coop SAV
Soc. Agricoltori
Val Lagarina**
viale Trento 81
☎ 0464412111
Macelleria Stifan
via Mazzini 3
☎ 0464421263
*Meat and local
charcuterie.*
Strembo
**l'Artigiano
dei Salumi
e Formaggi
Trentini**
via Nazionale 31
☎ 0465804666
*Cured game meats,
cheeses, speck.*
**Vigo di Ton
Azienda
Agricola Andrea
Paternoster**
via Castel Thun 6
☎ 0461657582
*15 varieties of honey
and honey specialties
such as "mugomiel"
and honey with dried
apples.*

BOLZANO

The cuisine of this area in the heart of the Dolomites draws its strength from mountain flavors and refined Hapsburg traditions.

T he province of Bolzano borders Austria, extending along the upper Adige Valley from the watershed of the Alps to the Salorno narrows. Amidst the mountains, the great river and its main tributary, the Isarco, form a rough Y, whose arms meet at Bolzano, where they are joined by numerous valleys. The area is, therefore, particularly fascinating both for the spectacular peaks of the Dolomites and the extensive yet ordered human presence. Above the orchards and vineyards of the valleys, dotted with villages and farmsteads, are the terraces where crops are grown and animals grazed. Then come the mountain pastures, which form the seasonal vanguard of an economy that is essentially Alpine. The range of wines, especially the reds, of the Alto Adige provincial DOC (sub-divided into

Opposite: one of the 'contrada' settlements dotted around Val di Funes/Villnösstal

140

the Colli di Bolzano, Meranese di Collina, Santa Maddalena, Terlano, Valle Isarco and Valle Venosta sub-denominations) is remarkable both for its history and quality. The cultivation of apples is also of great importance and there are no less than four growers' associations. The livestock is also exceptional, and includes indigenous breeds of both cattle (Grigio Alpina, Pinzgauer, Pustertaler) and horses (Avelignese). The most notable of the cured meats is *speck*, which is protected by the IGP (*Indicazione Geografica Protetta*) classification. In addition there are such traditional cheeses as *Graukäse* and *Ziegenkäse*. The area has a very distinctive cuisine, due both to the original population – the Ladins, still present in the Val Gardena, Val Badia, and Val Marebbe – and to the lengthy period under Austrian rule. Thus, the simple cuisine of the Dolomites, where rye bread and *speck* are staple fare, has been enriched by specialties from the vast Hapsburg Empire, such as Hungarian *goulash* and the Viennese *Sachertorte*. The standard of the hotels in the towns is high, especially in Merano. Excellent tourist accommodation is also to be found in the rural areas, where the approach to vacationing has always been rather like that of present-day *agriturismo*. Then there is a wide range of restaurants varying from traditional to innovative – and some of them are truly outstanding.

HOTELS AND RESTAURANTS

Bolzano/Bozen
Parkhotel
Laurin ★★★ 🍴 🅿
Belle Epoque 🍴🍴🍴
via Laurin 4
☎ 0471311000
Magdalenerhof
★★★
via Rencio 48/a
☎ 0471978267
**Cavallino Bianco-
Weisses Rössl** 🍴
via dei Bottai 6
☎ 0471973267
Ca' de Bezzi 🍴
via A. Hofer 30
☎ 0471976103
Vögele 🍴
via Goethe 3
☎ 0471973030
**Appiano sulla
Strada del
Vino/Eppan an
der Weinstrasse**
Zur Rose 🍴🍴🍴
at San Michele
via Innerhofer 2
☎ 0471662249
**Bellavista-
Marklhof** 🍴🍴
at Cornaiano (km 2)
via Belvedere 14
☎ 0471662407
Turmbach 🍴
via Rio della Torre 4
☎ 0471662339
Bressanone/Brixen
Elefante ★★★ 🍴🍴🍴
via Rio Bianco 4
☎ 0472832750
Fink 🍴🍴
via Portici Minori 4
☎ 0472834883

141

Gourmet Tours

BOLZANO/BOZEN. Arriving from the north, Goethe was greatly impressed by the vineyards and, in the city, by the bustling market. Those arriving from the south, on the other hand, will be struck by the Gothic aspect of the old town, which stands at the confluence of the rivers Adige and Isarco. A meeting-point of the Germanic and Latin worlds, it reflects features of both in its architecture and cuisine. A tour of the city will inevitably start from Piazza Walther, dominated by the huge Gothic cathedral; while nearby is the lively Via dei Portici, with its balconied houses and elegant shops. Then the tour continues to the Piazza delle Erbe, where every day there is a colorful market selling fruit and vegetables, as well as local cheeses, *salumi* (cured meat specialties), and cereals. All around are cheerful beerhouses and, under a portico, the superb Vögele restaurant serving traditional local dishes: various versions of *Knödeln* (bread dumplings); goulash soup; *Gerstensuppe* (barley soup); *Frittatensuppe* (soup with strips of omelet); meat with or without sauerkraut; and an enticing selection of classically Austrian cakes and desserts. If you are looking for a cultural interlude, close by there is the Museo archeologico, housing Ötzi, the prehistoric mummy found on the edge of the Similaun Glacier in 1991,

and now Bolzano's greatest tourist attraction. Returning to gastronomic matters, the "Belle Époque" restaurant is worth a special mention. Located in the "Park Hotel Laurin" (founded 1910), it serves classic dishes and has an excellent wine list. In Via dei Bottai, the "Cavallino Bianco/Weisses Rössl" is much more informal. One of the city's oldest restaurants, it opens early in the morning to serve traders with such delights as tripe soup and *Bauernplatte*, "the peasant's dish," consisting of *Knödeln* and goulash. In the same street, but only open in the evening, is "Ca' de Bezzi", an old *osteria* on three floors, where the specialties include *polenta nera* (made from buckwheat) and red bilberries, washed down with local wine and accompanied by the sound of piped music. As regards shops, "Masè" in Via Goethe is specially recommended; it has its own *salumi* – such as traditional *speck* and *Hauswurst* ("homemade" salami) – as well as a whole host of cheeses, wines, and honey. The bakeries – such as "Franziskaner" (established 1776) next to the Franciscan monastery – have a huge variety of products on offer, including *Schüttelbrot* (crispbread), rye bread, sweet bread and fruit loaves. As for wines, a truly unique experience is a walk up the path that climbs from Via San Osvaldo or the end of Lungo Talvera Bolzano to the hill of Santa Maddalena through the

HOTELS AND RESTAURANTS

Bressanone/Brixen
Oste Scuro-Finsterwirt ⍾⍾
vicolo del Duomo 3
☎ 0472835343
Sunnegg ⍾⍾
via Vigneti 67
☎ 0472834760
Caldaro sulla Strada del Vino/ Kaltern an der Weinstrasse
Castel Ringberg ⍾⍾⍾
via S. Giuseppe al Lago 1
☎ 0471960010
Campo di Trens/ Freienfeld
Romantik Hotel Stafler ★★★
at Mules (km 4)
☎ 0472771136
Corvara in Badia/Corvara
Romantik Hotel La Perla ★★★
La Stüa de Michil ⍾⍾⍾
strada Col Alt 105
☎ 0471836132
Dobbiaco/Toblach
Santer ★★★
via Alemagna 4
☎ 0474972142
Falzes/Pfalzen
Schöneck ⍾⍾⍾
at Molini (km 3)
via Castello Schöneck 11
☎ 0474565550
Tanzer ⍾⍾
at Issengo (km 2)
☎ 0474565366
Laion/Lajen
Waldruhe ⍾⍾⍾
at Albions (km 6)
☎ 0471655882
Lana/Lana
Forsterbräu ⍾
via Maria Hils 17
☎ 0473561257

oldest vineyards in Alto Adige. Wine may be tasted and purchased at the "Cantina Sociale Santa Maddalena", while "Magdalenerhof" serves traditional Tyrolean fare. Another fascinating place is the suburb of Gries, where a renowned "Lagrein" wine is produced: don't miss a visit to the "Gries" winery, close to the Abbazia dei Benedettini. Take the cableway from Bolzano and then continue on the light railway to the beautiful Renon Plateau, and here visit the Museo dell'Apicoltura, with its working beehives and honey-tasting.

1. The Wine Route

APPIANO SULLA STRADA DEL VINO/EPPAN AN DER WEINSTRASSE. Created in the early twentieth century, the wine route winds for 22 miles through the villages on the west bank of the Adige, and their vineyards extending up the valley sides. The first of these is Cornaiano/Girlan, where the charming "Bellavista-Marklhof" restaurant, housed in an old monastery, has summer garden. You can taste the local wine at the "Cantina Produttori di Colterenzio" or the private "Niedermayr" winery. Next comes Appiano/Eppan, a scattered village with seven churches and a number of castles surrounded by vineyards. At the "Zur Rose" restaurant, a young but accomplished chef prepares mouthwatering delicacies: the varied cuisine includes roast pigeon breast with potatoes and onions and fried lasagna of zander (a large pikeperch native to central and Eastern Europe) in a sauce of mussels and clams. Those preferring more simple fare should stop

off at "Turmbach", which has been run by the same family for ten generations. For wine-tasting and purchases, visit the "Cantina Sociale San Michele di Appiano" and the centuries-old "Josef Brigl" winery.
CALDARO SULLA STRADA DEL VINO/KALTERN AN DER WEINSTRASSE. Overlooking the lake, it welcomes visitors with a row of hotels and old houses in the main street. The famous local red wine – made with Schiava grapes, to which small quantities of Pinot Nero and Lagrein is sometimes added – can be tasted at the "Cantina Sociale Erste & Neue" and the "Viticoltori Caldaro" winery, as well as at the "Di Pauli" winery, which is near an interesting wine museum. "Castel Ringberg", the residence of the Walch, a family of aristocratic wine-producers, provides a splendid setting for a restaurant where the refined cuisine is enhanced with traditional flavors. Every year in November, the *Törggelen* is a festival at which *speck* and chestnuts are washed down with new wine in the local *masi* (farmhouses). Further on is Termeno/Tramin, renowned for its fragrant Gewürztraminer. This can be tasted in the "Hofstätter" winery, which used to supply the Austrian emperor, or at the "Hofkellerei Walch", located in a medieval monastery. Then comes Cortaccia/Kurtatsch, with its numerous hamlets, and Niclara Castle, where the "Tiefenbrunner" winery makes Müller Thurgau from grapes grown at the remarkable altitude of 1,000 meters (3,280 ft). Finally, the *strada del*

HOTELS AND RESTAURANTS

**Malles Venosta/
Mals im Vinschgau**
Greif ★★★ ★🔲
via Gen.
Verdoss 40/a
☎ 0473831429
Moro ❢
at Burgusio (km 3)
☎ 0473831223
Merano/Meran
Palace ★★★
**Grillstube
Schloss Maur** ❢❢❢
via Cavour 2/4
☎ 0473271000
Sissi ❢❢
via Galilei 44
☎ 0473231062
Flora ❢
via Portici 75
☎ 0473231484
**Croce Bianca-
Weisskreuz** ❢
via delle Piante 2
☎ 0473232554
Rainer ❢
via Portici 266
☎ 0473236149
Naturno/Naturns
Steghof ❢❢ ★🔲
via Principale 123
☎ 0473668224
**Ortisei/
Sankt Ulrich**
Adler ★★★
via Rezia 7
☎ 0471796203
**Parcines/
Partschins**
**Onkel Taa
Bad Egart** ❢❢
via Stazione 17
☎ 0473967342
**Rasun
Anterselva/Rasen
Antholz**
Ansitz Heufler ❢❢❢
at Rasun di Sopra
☎ 0474498582

vino (wine route) brings us to Magrè/Margreid, where the old-established "Lageder" winery produces excellent Pinot Grigio and Chardonnay. On the way back, on the opposite side of the Adige Valley, stop off at Montagna/Montan to taste the Pinot Grigio at the "Franz Haas" winery.

2. Merano and the Val Venosta

TERLANO/TERLAN. This charming wine-producing center is located on the east bank of the Adige, just a few miles from Bolzano. Here the focus is on whites, especially Pinot Bianco and Chardonnay, which may be tasted at the "Cantina Prodottori di Terlano". An interesting excursion may be made by car – or by cableway from Vilpiano – to the Meltina Plateau, where a pleasant walk leads to the old

farm building housing the "Vivaldi Arunda" winery, specializing in sparkling wines.

LANA/LANA. Just before Merano, on the other side of the Adige, this village stands amidst orchards and vineyards at the mouth of the Val d'Ultimo. One reason for stopping in the village is to visit the interesting museum devoted to fruit-growing (Museo della Frutticoltura). From here it is easy to reach Foresta/Forst on the *Statale* 38 beyond Merano, where the restaurant adjacent to the Forst brewery (dating from 1857), serves various types of chilled freshly brewed beer.

MERANO/MERAN. Nestling in a sunny basin surrounded by hills covered with vineyards and orchards, Merano is a city of castles and palaces, hot springs, horse-racing, and

Bolzano. Spring procession

promenades along the Passirio, where the memory of Empress Elisabeth (Sissi) and the Austro-Hungarian Empire is still very much alive. Visitors come not only for the traditional grape therapy, which is both purifying and invigorating, but also for the wines. This is the domain of the Schiava grape, from which the eminently drinkable "Meranese di Collina" is made. Wines from the "St. Valentin" and "Schloss Labers" subdenominations may be tasted at the "Cantina Sociale di Merano". There is a vast choice of hotels, one of the most luxurious being the centrally-located Palace. Founded in 1909, it still has the aristocratic atmosphere described by Franz Kafka during his visit to Italy; in addition to a spa and beauty center, it has the "Grillstube Schloss Maur", a restaurant serving Tyrolean specialties

and a range of grilled meats. The best place to eat in town, however, is "Sissi" opposite the Castello Principesco, which features such delicacies as a flan of *porcini* mushrooms with fondue, *Knödeln* filled with *ricotta*, and duck cooked in red wine and honey. "Flora" in the 15th-century Palazzo della Giustizia, is especially worth mentioning for its traditional cuisine. For a more informal atmosphere, try "Rainer", a *trattoria* with a shady courtyard in the central Via dei Portici, and the "Croce Bianca/Weisskreuz", a typical *Burgenstube* with a garden serving local dishes and good wine. Lastly, "Café König" in Corso Libertà is renowned for its

HOTELS AND RESTAURANTS

Villandro/ Villanders
Steinbock ⁋⁋
at Santo Stefano
☎ 0472843111
Vipiteno/ Sterzing
Aquila Nera-Schwarzer Adler ★★★
piazza Città 1
☎ 0472764064
Gasteigerhof
★★★ ⁋ 🛏
at Casateia (km 3)
via Passo Giovo 52
☎ 0472779090
Kleine Flamme ⁋⁋
via Città Nuova 31
☎ 0472766065
Pretzhof ⁋⁋
at Tulve (km 8)
☎ 0472764455

AGRITURISMI

Badia/Abtei
Lüch d' Mozi
at La Villa
via Rottonara 14
☎ 0471817169
Chiusa/Klausen
Sonnegghof
at Verdignes 29
☎ 0472855476
Marebbe/ Enneberg
Lüch di Umbolt 🛏
at Fordora 31
☎ 0474501306
San Martino in Badia/Sankt Martin in Thurn
Lüch de Vanc 🛏
at Longiarù (km 7)
at Seres 36
☎ 0474590108

Viennese-style cakes. For wines, pay a visit to "Vinschger Tor", next to the church of the Cappuccini, an attractive *enoteca* that seems to belong to a bygone age, and the "Castello Rametz", a winery producing Riesling, Cabernet and Cesuret in a thirteenth-century castle. Just outside Merano is Castel Tirolo, which played a decisive role in the area's history, and the plateau of Avelengo/Hafling, where the sturdy Avelignesi horses are raised. Gourmets should also visit Parcines/ Partschins to enjoy the gastronomic delights of "Onkel Taa", a restaurant full of mementos of the Hapsburgs and located in the old "Bad-Egart" inn (established 1430); and to taste the Chardonnay, Pinot Nero, and Schiava wines at the "Stachlburg-Baron von Kripp" winery.

MALLES VENOSTA/MALS IM VINSCHGAU. The upper valley of the Adige, known as the Val Venosta, has various features of interest: Naturno/Naturns, with the archaic frescoes of San Procolo; Silandro/Schlanders, with its lofty campanile and its castle; Glorenza/Glurns, a well-preserved medieval walled village; and lastly Malles/Mals, the chief town of the valley, which displays a mixture of characteristics from the whole area. Sights of particular interest include the church of San Benedetto, housing the most important cycle of Carolingian frescoes in Europe, and, outside the town, the Benedictine abbey of Monte Maria. Moving away from spirituality

and onto food, the Val Venosta's specialties include *speck*, considered to be the best in Alto Adige; *Almkäse*, cheese from the Alpine pastures made from semi–skimmed milk, with a strong or even pungent flavor; and *Paarl*, bread made in the form of a pair of loaves, with variations made with whole-wheat, spelt wheat, and with natural yeast. DOC wine production, especially whites, extends as far as Silandro. The "Köfelgut" estate at Castelbello/Kastelbell is well worth a visit: it has 10 acres of vineyards, cultivated with environment-friendly methods around an eighteenth-century *maso* (farmhouse). In the center of Malles, the "Greif" hotel and restaurant is to be recommended, as is "Moro", standing amidst the meadows of Burgusio. At Naturno, Steghof is an old *maso* with two magnificently-decorated rooms that have been converted into a restaurant.

3. The Valle Isarco

CHIUSA/KLAUSEN. An old customs post on the road to the Brenner Pass, this small town dominated by the Torre del Capitano is noted for the picturesque houses on its main street. The area is also of interest for its gastronomy: it is worth going up to Villandro/Villanders to eat at the Steinbock, a hotel housed in a splendid old building. The restaurant serves not only Tyrolean specialties but also creative dishes, based on both local produce and fish. But that is not

all: at Laion/Lajen, near the beginning of the Val Gardena road, the "Waldruhe" (meaning 'the peacefulness of the woods') is another hotel with a restaurant which offers superlative cuisine in a simple setting. On the menu you can find tasty potato crescents filled with *porcini* mushrooms in juniper sauce, followed by a loin of lamb with thyme in a pastry crust, and a delicious *semifreddo* (refrigerated cake) of cherries in red wine to round off the meal. In Chiusa there is a long-established butcher's shop, "Gasser", from which one of Alto Adige's leading food firms has developed. BRESSANONE/BRIXEN. For eight centuries, from 1027 to 1803, this city was the capital of a vast ecclesiastical principality: which accounts for its austere appearance. To one side of the main square is the Baroque cathedral with a splendid Romanesque cloister frescoed with biblical scenes; to the other is the bishop-princes' fortified palace, surrounded by a moat. Not far away is the Via dei Portici Maggiore, a lively shopping street that has preserved its medieval character. This is where the "Pasticceria Heiss" is located – its specialties are *Sachertorte* and cake with wine-flavored cream – while nearby in Via Mercato Vecchio the "Pupp" café produces its own delicious cakes and pastries. Special mention must be made of the "Elefante"; founded in 1551, it was formerly a post house, but is now an exclusive and romantic hotel and restaurant famous for its enormous dish of mixed meats, vegetables, and rice known as the "Elefanten Platte." More informal is "Sunneg", an old *maso* in Via dei Vigneti with a panoramic terrace and a menu featuring game and mushrooms. In the local food shops look out for *Graukäse*, a traditional cheese made from semi-skimmed milk, which after maturing for only a short while acquires a distinctive sharp flavor. As far as wines are concerned, no one should miss the fascinating "Abbazia di Novacella", famed for its vineyards and a vaulted cellar where you can taste its wines and local specialties.

Bressanone. Festival of Schützen

WINE PRODUCERS

Caldaro sulla Strada del Vino/ Kaltern an der Weinstrasse
Cantina Baron Di Pauli
via Stazione 1
☎ 0471963133
Castelbello Ciardes
Tenuta Vinicola Köfelgut
Tre Canti 12
☎ 0473624142
Cortaccia sulla Strada del Vino/ Kurtatsch an der Weinstrasse
Tiefenbrunner Cantina Turmhof
at Niclara (km 2)
via Castello 4
☎ 0471880122
Magrè sulla Strada del Vino/ Margreid an der Weinstrasse
Alois Lageder
vicolo dei Conti 9
☎ 0471809500
Meltina/Mölten
Cantina Spumanti Arunda-Vivaldi
via Civico 53
☎ 0471668033
Merano/Meran
Cantina Sociale di Merano
via S. Marco 11
☎ 0473237734
Castello Rametz
via Labers 4
☎ 0473211011
Montagna/Montan
Franz Haas
via Villa 19
☎ 0471812280

VIPITENO/STERZING. The straight, colonnaded main street, which ends at the Torre della Città, is lined with large houses. Typically Germanic in style with flower-decked balconies, battlements, and elaborate wrought-iron signs, which take us back to the time when the town was home to merchants and bankers involved with trade through the Brenner Pass; the town is now packed with vacationers attracted by the beautiful valleys in the surrounding area. For accommodation, we particularly recommend the "Romantik Hotel Stafler" at Campo di Trens/Freienfeld; one of the oldest hotels in the valley, it has a restaurant serving excellent Tyrolean fare. In the town itself, "Kleine Flamme" prepares creative dishes in its open kitchen, while local specialties may be purchased at the Latteria Sociale Vipiteno. In the surrounding area, at Tulve/Tulfer in the Val di Vizze, the "Pretzhof" is renowned for its tasty traditional dishes and wonderful atmosphere; on the road to Monte Giove the "Gasteigerhof" has rooms in chalets and provides tasty food.

4. The Val Pusteria and the Val Gardena

RIO DI PUSTERIA/MÜLBACH. This route starts splendidly: just after the beginning of

WINE PRODUCERS

Parcines/
Partschins
**Tenuta Vinicola
Stachlburg –
Baron von Kripp**
piazza Mitterhofer 2
☎ 0473968014
Terlano/Terlan
**Cantina
Produttori di
Terlano**
via Silberleiten 7
☎ 0471257135
Termeno/Tramin
Josef Hofstätter
piazza Municipio 5
☎ 0471860161
**Hofkellerei
Walch**
via Zallinger 4
☎ 0471860215
Varna/Vahrn
**Az. Vinicola
Abbazia di
Novacella**
via Abbazia 1
☎ 0472836189

SHOPPING

Bolzano/Bozen
**Antica
Salumeria Masè**
via Goethe 15
☎ 0471978685
*Speck and home-
made Hauswurst;
cheeses, wines
and honey.*
**Panificio
Franziskaner**
via Francescani 3
☎ 0471976443
*"Schüttelbrot", rye
bread, sweet bread
and fruit loaves.*

the Val Pusteria -the valley of the Rienza – you come to the superb "Pichler", where the cuisine combines the best of tradition and creativity. The menu offers such delights as medallions of roe deer cooked with cherries in vanilla vinegar. In the center of the village, "De Gust" is a shop run by a gourmet selling all the finest specialties of Alto Adige, including a range of cheeses made by small-scale producers which is not available elsewhere. At Valles/Vals excellent accommodation is to be found at the "Masl", a hotel that also serves fine food.

BRUNICO/BRUNECK. As the name suggests, the town is believed to have been founded by Bishop Bruno in the thirteenth century. The center is divided by a street with houses in typical Tyrolean style, with flower-decked balconies, decorative signs, and gables. Behind the town the deep Valle di Tures, which changes its name to Val Aurina after Campo Tures, leads to the Vetta d'Italia (2919 m/9554 ft), Italy's northernmost point. It produces *Graukäse* and other delicious cheeses from the Alpine pastures. Nearby, at Teodone/Dietenheim, do not miss the "Museo Provinciale degli Usi e Costumi", located in a manor house and on its estate, where there are reconstructions of typical rural buildings of the area. In Brunico's Via Centrale, "Gastronomia Bernardi" has a remarkable range of local specialties. At

View of the Sella mountains

SHOPPING

Bressanone/ Brixen
Heiss Pasticceria
via Portici
Maggiori 20
☎ 0472836487
'Sachertorte' and the cake with wine-flavored cream.
Caffè Pupp
via Mercato
Vecchio 37
☎ 0472834736
Home-made pastries and cakes.
Brunico/Bruneck
Karl Bernardi
via Centrale 36
☎ 0171555172
Speck, roast shank, würstel, Gulash Suppe.
Dariz Delikatess
via Stuck 2
☎ 0474410177
Cheeses, charcuterie, mushrooms, wines delicatessen.
Stadtmetzger
via Centrale 36
☎ 0474555472
Vast range of local specialties like speck, salami, wild game meat, Gulash; good selection of wines and distilled spirits.

Falzs/Pfalzen, "Schöneck" is a superb restaurant offering creative dishes inspired by local traditions and made with the best ingredients – this goes for the bread too. There is also a good choice of wines. A typical meal starts with creamed barley in a sauce of kid and chanterelle mushrooms, pigeon breasts in raspberry sauce, and a soufflé of *ricotta* with berry fruits and white chocolate ice-cream. For a meal in attractive surroundings at Issengo/Issing, it is worth stopping off at "Tanzer", where tasty local dishes are served. Pleasant rooms are also available here. The road along the Val Badia, to the south of Brunico, gradually climbs up to Corvara and the Passo Gardena amidst magnificent scenery. At San Vigilio di Marebbe the Tabarel restaurant is recommended for its very special atmosphere and varied cuisine, including French dishes. After this detour from the main valley, we suggest you take another one along the Valle Anterselva to Rasun di Sopra/Oberrasen, where the restaurant at the "Ansitz Heufler", a hotel in a beautifully restored castle, offers a memorable gastronomic experience. DOBBIACO/TOBLACH. On the watershed between the Adige and Danube Valleys and strategically placed on the Strada di Alemagna (*Statale* 51) – the highway linking the Veneto to the Tyrol – this resort has an old center with a castle dating

from around 1500 and a Baroque parish church. A special attraction is the Museo Gustav Mahler, housed in Casa Trenker, where the composer spent several summers. Local specialties include the cheeses of the upper Val Pusteria – *Graukäse, Bergkäse, Ziegenkäse* – and rye bread baked in round flat loaves known as *Breatl*. In the restaurants be sure to try *Kaiserfleisch* (salted smoked pork served with sauerkraut). Splendidly located near the cross-country ski stadium, the "Santer" is the ideal hotel for a stay here. Other suggested hotels are the "Aquila/ Adler" at Villabassa/ Niederdorf, which has its own restaurant, and "Quelle", situated at Santa Maddalena Vallalta/Sankt Magdalena in the Valle di Casies. SAN CANDIDO/INNICHEN. The nineteenth-century "Parkhotel Sole Paradiso", a large chalet frequented by tourists from all over the world, bears witness to the fame of this mountain resort. The "Orso Grigio" is a charming hotel managed by a new generation of the Ladinser family. "Kugler", a typically Tyrolean inn with a well-stocked *enoteca* is the ideal place to stop by for a glass of wine. Traditionally-made *speck* produced by Senfter may be purchased at their shop, and cheeses at the "Latteria Sociale di San Candido". From Dobbiaco the *Statale* 51 goes up the Val di Lan-

SHOPPING

Castelrotto/
Kastelruth
**Azienda Agricola
Pfleger Hof**
at S. Osvaldo 24
☎ 0471706771
*Mountain
and medicinal herbs
grown organically.*
Chiusa/Klausen
**Macelleria
Gasser**
piazza Tinne 1
☎ 0472848492
Fiè allo Sciliar/
Völs am Schlern
**Macelleria
Pramstrahler**
piazza Chiesa 15
☎ 0471725038
*Charcuterie
and meat.*
Merano/Meran
**Café König -
Pasticceria**
corso Libertà 168
☎ 0473237162
Pastries and cakes.
Ortisei/
Sankt Ulrich
Pasticceria Alex
via Pedetliva 36
☎ 0471797760
*Strudel, Sachertorte,
Linzertorte and
a wide range
of chocolates.*
Rio di Pusteria/
Mülbach
De Gust
via C. Lanz 14
☎ 0472849873
*Local cheeses such as
Grigio, Rustico and
goat's milk "caprini";
olive oil and vinegar.*

dro to Carbonin/Schluderbach – in a magnificent setting – and then descends to Cortina d'Ampezzo in the province of Belluno. SAN CASSIANO/SANKT KASSIAN. From Cortina a road snakes up to the Passo di Falzarego, then descends into the Val Badia, where further gastronomic pleasures await the visitor. At San Cassiano, Ciasa Salares (an enchanting hotel) has "La Siriola", a restaurant and *enoteca* offering such Ladin specialties as *gnocchi* of *ricotta* and mountain cheese with buttermilk and smoked trout, as well as, on the creative side, coconut and mint soup with quenelles of duck. Another interesting restaurant in the village is "St. Hubertus", located in the Rosa Alpina, a comfortable hotel with a decent beauty center. CORVARA IN BADIA/CORVARA. Offering splendid views of the Sella Group, Corvara is the main resort of the upper Val Ba-

dia. It also has an outstanding restaurant, "La Stüa de Michil", in the "Romantik Hotel La Perla". Here décor is traditional, the welcome warm, and the cuisine innovative, with mushroom dishes taking pride of place. *Kaminwurzen* (smoked salami) are on sale in the village. ORTISEI/SANKT ULRICH. On the other side of the Passo Gardena the road descends between the peaks of the Sella and Sassolungo on the one side and those of the Odle on the other. Ortisei/-Sankt Ulrich is the main village of this Ladin valley, and is well known both for its wood-carving and as a mountain resort offering ample opportunities for hikes, rock-climbing, and skiing.

SHOPPING

San Candido/
Innichen
**Latteria Sociale
San Candido**
via Castello 1
☎ 0474913317
Typical cheeses.
Senfter
via Mercato
Vecchio 4
☎ 0474913139
Speck.
San Lorenzo
dI Sebato/
Sankt Lorenzen
Baumgartner
via Josef Kenzler 16
☎ 0474474018
*Meat, game and
charcuterie: rabbit,
lamb, beef, wild game,
cured ham, speck and
smoked cured ham.*
Sesto/Sexten
**Holzer
Alimentari e Vino**
via Heideck Moso 2
☎ 0474710599
*Wines and distilled
drinks; speck, cheeses,
honey, jam from
Valle di Braies and
boletus mushrooms.*
Vipiteno/Sterzing
**Latteria Sociale
Vipiteno**
via Città Nuova 18
☎ 0472765272
*Good local products,
yoghurt.*

The parish church of San Vigilio di Marebbe

151

VENETO FROM THE ADRIATIC TO THE DOLOMITES

The variety of landscapes in the Italian region most visited by tourists, and the contributions of past civilizations, are combined with a diversity of cuisine and wines. Veneto is remarkable for the way tradition has been kept alive.

The cuisine of the Veneto is at the same time aristocratic and popular. This is especially true of Venice, where the splendor of the *Serenissima* was evident in the banquets immortalized by Veronese, but was also reflected in the simple meals of the sailors and peasants who, day after day, helped to build up the grandeur of the Venetian Republic. This is the cuisine of the Venetian villas and *risi e bisi* (risotto with peas), which was served to the Doge on St. Mark's Day, and also that of the peasants with their *polenta* and pasta and beans: the patricians dipped refined *baicoli* (biscuits) into their *rosolio*, while the country folk washed down the more rustic *fugasse* (a type of cake) with the local wine.

A VARIETY OF LANDSCAPES AND A HOST OF FLAVORS

From Lake Garda to the Venetian Lagoon, from the River Po to the Dolomites, the Veneto forms a geographical entity with a variety of clearly defined characteristics. Starting from Venice, you first see the lagoon, where eels, bass, and mussels are cultivated in accordance with ancient traditions that are at the same time modern, since they are the only methods compatible with the fragile ecosystem. Then there are the broad horizons of the Po Valley, including the monotonous landscapes of recently reclaimed land, and cultivated areas further inland interrupted by hedges and trees. On the hills, vineyards are mixed with olive and cherry trees, higher up there are chestnuts and first pastures, where locals breed pigs and cure pork. Cattle-raising is widespread, and dairy farming is important to the region.

FROM THE LAGOON TO THE PLAIN

With such a variety of landscapes, it is hardly surprising that the food produced in the Veneto is some of the richest and most varied in Italy. The markets of Chioggia and Venice are a unique spectacle thanks to the vast assortment of fish they have on offer. In the lowlands, the most common crops are cereals, including maize and rice. The Vialone Nano Veronese rice is protected by the IGP (*Indicazione Geografica Protetta*) classification. Fruit and vegetables include the *radicchio rosso* (red chicory) of Treviso, together with the *radicchio variegato* (variegated chicory) of Castelfranco (also protected by the IGP classification) and similar varieties from Verona and Chioggia. The white asparagus of Bassano del Grappa is renowned, and there is a

Vicenza.
La Rotonda

long list of fruit and vegetables worthy of protection, including the apples, pears, peaches, and various vegetables of the Adige Valley and the Veronese plain, and the potatoes of the red lands of the Guà. Poultry farming is also strong, and the region is famed for the now rare Paduan hen.

Asiago

THE HILLS AND MOUNTAINS

The vine is the strongest feature of the hills from Lake Garda to the Marca Trevigiana, and it is a mainstay of the region's economy. The Veneto produces 20 percent of Italy's output of DOC wines, while the province of Verona alone produces as much DOC wine as the whole of Piedmont and more than Tuscany. There are several famous names such as Bardolino, Valpolicella, Soave, Conegliano and Valdobbiadene, and lesser-known wines such as the Colli Berici and Colli Euganei. Distilled drinks are also made here, particularly at the main center of Bassano del Grappa. Garda extra virgin olive oil is first-rate, and there will soon be a new denomination, Veneto. Elsewhere, the cherry tree adorns the hills at Marostica, the valleys of the Lessini and in the Berici Hills. There are two outstanding pork products: Prosciutto Veneto Berico-Euganeo, a DOC ham, and *soppressa*, a type of salami found all over the region. The region is also rich in wild foodstuffs, including mushrooms, truffles in Lessinia and the Berici Hills, and snails to the north of Verona and in the province of Vicenza.

THE VENETIAN TRADITION IN THE KITCHEN,

The cuisine of the seven provinces of the Veneto, although differing in many respects, is linked to two principal elements: the constant presence of *polenta* and the frequent use in the recipes of ingre-

Lessini Mountains

Chioggia Marina

dients (spices and raisins) originating from the eastern Mediterranean, a reminder of the sea trade of the Venetian Republic. Rice is
also used, but pasta is less common. Sea fish make up a large proportion of main courses, and the used of freshwater fish is also widespread. There is an emphasis on poultry and white meat in general,
while in the mountains game is the main course. There are three ethnic minorities – the German speakers of the Asiago Plateau (erroneously called "Cimbri"), the Ladins of the Valle d'Ampezzo, and the
Carinthians of the Comelico – that have enriched the cuisine with
flavors from north of the Alps.

THE PLEASURE OF VACATIONING AND ANDAR PER OMBRE

*Venice. The lion
of St. Mark*

The Veneto, a land of travelers, is also a region studded with villas. The people of the
Veneto may seem a little rustic to some,
but they have acquired the skills of hospitality due to the popularity of the province
as a destination. It is a pastime of the people
to *andar per ombre* – that is, go from one *osteria*
to the next in search of snacks, a glass of
wine, and someone to chat to. If you would
rather just sit down for a meal, there is a remarkable variety of restaurants in Venice.
Although *haute cuisine* is hard to find, there
are at least twenty establishments that merit a
visit. All the other large towns in the region provide a reasonable standard of hospitality, but visitors often do not realize that the less frequented
routes offer more pleasant surprises, from luxury accommodation in a villa to a simple but comfortable
hotel in the mountains.

Veneto - Typical products

Scale 1:1 250 000

0   15   30 km

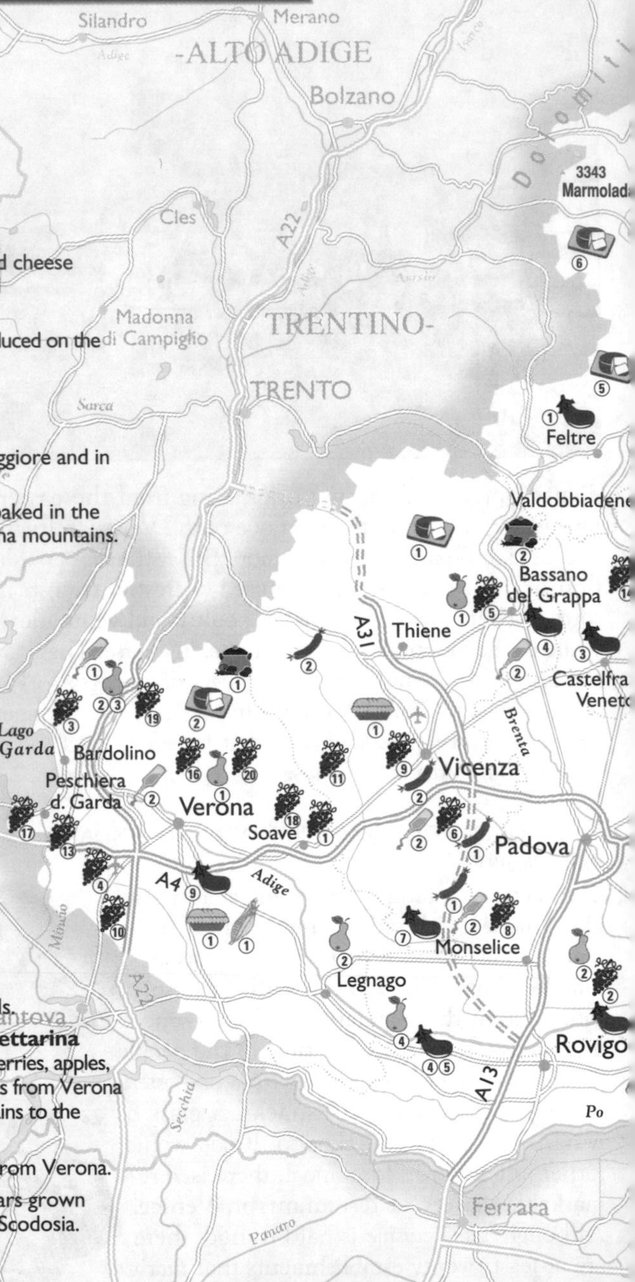

CHEESES

1. **Asiago Dop.** Matured or mild cheese produced in alto Vicentino and surrounding areas.
2. **Monte Veronese Dop.** Produced on the Monti Lessini.
3. **Casatella trevigiana**
4. **Malga bellunese**
5. **Piave.** Produced in Cesiomaggiore and in the Belluna valley.
6. **Schiz.** Fresh cheese served baked in the oven – produced in the Belluna mountains.

CHARCUTERIE

1. **Prosciutto Veneto Berico-Euganeo Dop.** Ham produced in the area between the Euganei and Berici hills.
2. **Sopressa vicentina.** Produced in the Pasubio valleys and throughout the province.

FRUIT

1. **Ciliegie.** Cherries grown in Marostica and the Verona hills.
2. **Fragola, Mela, Melone, Nettarina e Pesca di Verona.** Strawberries, apples, melons, nectarines and peaches from Verona grown in the area from the plains to the Garda hills.
3. **Kiwi di Verona.** Kiwi fruit from Verona.
4. **Pera del Medio Adige.** Pears grown in Castelbaldo and Casale di Scodosia.

VEGETABLES

1. **Fagiolo di Lamon Vallata Bellunese Igp.** Beans.
2. **Radicchio rosso di Treviso Igp.** Red chicory from Treviso.
3. **Radicchio variegato di Castelfranco Igp.** Variegated chicory from Castelfranco.
4. **Asparagi.** Asparagus grown in Bassano del Grappa, Cimadolmo and Castelbaldo.
5. **Aglio del Medio Adige.** Garlic from the Castelbaldo area.
6. **Patata americana.** Potatoes grown in Anguillara and Stroppare, in the Basso Padovano area.

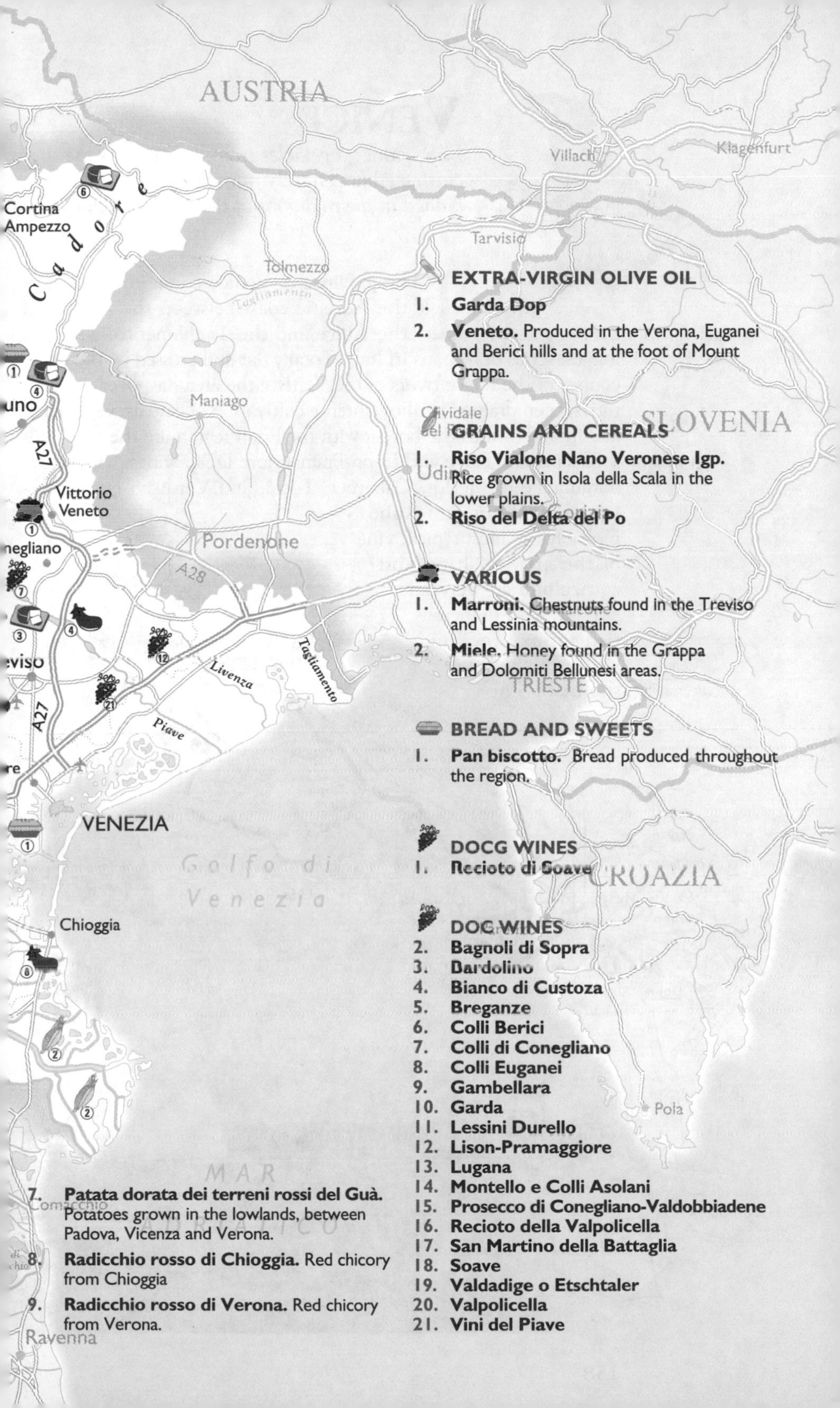

AUSTRIA

Cortina
Ampezzo

Tarvisio

Tolmezzo

Maniago

Cividale
del F...

SLOVENIA

Udine

Vittorio
Veneto

Pordenone

negliano

A28

veso

Livenza

A27

Piave

Tagliamento

TRIESTE

VENEZIA

Golfo di
Venezia

Chioggia

CROAZIA

Pola

MAR

Comacchio
TICO

Ravenna

EXTRA-VIRGIN OLIVE OIL

1. **Garda Dop**
2. **Veneto.** Produced in the Verona, Euganei and Berici hills and at the foot of Mount Grappa.

GRAINS AND CEREALS

1. **Riso Vialone Nano Veronese Igp.** Rice grown in Isola della Scala in the lower plains.
2. **Riso del Delta del Po**

VARIOUS

1. **Marroni.** Chestnuts found in the Treviso and Lessinia mountains.
2. **Miele.** Honey found in the Grappa and Dolomiti Bellunesi areas.

BREAD AND SWEETS

1. **Pan biscotto.** Bread produced throughout the region.

DOCG WINES

1. **Recioto di Soave**

DOC WINES

2. **Bagnoli di Sopra**
3. **Bardolino**
4. **Bianco di Custoza**
5. **Breganze**
6. **Colli Berici**
7. **Colli di Conegliano**
8. **Colli Euganei**
9. **Gambellara**
10. **Garda**
11. **Lessini Durello**
12. **Lison-Pramaggiore**
13. **Lugana**
14. **Montello e Colli Asolani**
15. **Prosecco di Conegliano-Valdobbiadene**
16. **Recioto della Valpolicella**
17. **San Martino della Battaglia**
18. **Soave**
19. **Valdadige o Etschtaler**
20. **Valpolicella**
21. **Vini del Piave**

7. **Patata dorata dei terreni rossi del Guà.** Potatoes grown in the lowlands, between Padova, Vicenza and Verona.
8. **Radicchio rosso di Chioggia.** Red chicory from Chioggia
9. **Radicchio rosso di Verona.** Red chicory from Verona.

VENICE

Fish, game, vegetables from the islands - the cuisine comes entirely from the lagoon, and is bathed in the traditions of the Venice Republic.

The province of Venice comprises the arc of the Adriatic coast between the mouths of the Adige and the Tagliamento, with the longest series of lagoons in Italy. Totally flat and crossed by the lower courses of the major rivers of the Veneto, the area has, over the centuries, been drained to allow intense cultivation of cereals, vegetables, and fruit. Towards the border with the Friuli region are the vineyards producing the Piave and Lison-Pramaggiore DOC wines, with a predominance of Merlot, Cabernet, Tocai, and Verduzzo grapes, followed by Pinot and Raboso – probably the most typical vine of the area. Fishing and aquaculture are very important, with numerous fish farms breeding white fish and shellfish. The

Venice.
Lateen sail

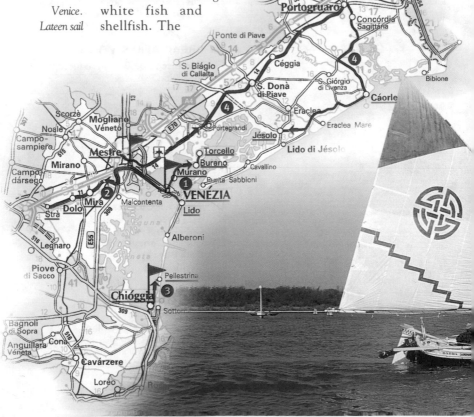

cuisine is dominated by Venice, and the ancient traditions are particularly noticeable in the use of certain spices and raisins, while the modern tourist boom has stimulated both the revival of old recipes and the development of innovative dishes. The cuisine is mainly based on fish, but game and vegetables, the great resources of the lagoon and its islands, also play an important role.

Gourmet Tours

VENICE. This is a city that has a lot to offer the visitor, not just in terms of museums, churches and palaces, which are dealt with in other guides, but also in terms of its restaurants. Leaving aside the plethora of tourist restaurants, Venice's cuisine is among the most outstanding in Italy thanks to its culinary traditions and the quality of the ingredients (especially fish from Chioggia and the vegetables grown in the areas round the lagoon). The Rialto markets should not be missed on any account: the fish market is held in a nineteenth-century loggia overlooking the Grand Canal, while the colorful fruit and vegetable one is located at one end of the Rialto Bridge.

This is where a visit to Venice's gastronomic highlights should begin. It could well commence with a tour of the *osterie*, and the following are located at strategic points in the city: "La Mascareta", at Santa Maria Formosa, behind San Marco, the "Ca' d'Oro", near the Strada Nova, behind the famous palace of the same name on the Grand Canal, "Da Codroma", on the way from Piazzale Roma to Campo Santa Margherita, the "Cantinone", right opposite the Squero di San Trovaso, at the Zattere; and the "Vecio Fritolin", between Rialto and Ca' Pesaro. Besides the customary *ombra de vin*, these wine bars offer superb *cicheti* – tasty morsels, usually of fish. One of the best-known traditional dishes is *risi e bisi* (rice with peas).

HOTELS AND RESTAURANTS

Venice
Danieli ✭✭✭
Castello 4196,
riva degli Schiavoni
☎ 0415226480
Antico
Martini ᵀᵀᵀᵀ
S. Marco 1983,
campo S. Fantin
☎ 0415224121
Cipriani ✭✭✭
Giudecca 10,
fondaco S. Giovanni
☎ 0415207744
Caffè
Quadri ᵀᵀᵀᵀ
piazza S. Marco 120
☎ 0415222105
Harry's
Bar ᵀᵀᵀᵀ
S. Marco 1323,
calle Vallaresso
☎ 0415285777
Londra
Palace ✭✭✭
Do Leoni ᵀᵀᵀ
Castello 4171,
riva degli Schiavoni
☎ 0415200533
Caravella ᵀᵀᵀ
S. Marco 1147,
calle larga XXII Marzo
☎ 0415208901
Osteria da Fiore ᵀᵀᵀ
S. Polo 2202/a,
calle del Scaleter
☎ 041721308
Gondolieri ᵀᵀ
Dorsoduro 366, S. Vio
☎ 0415286396
Osteria
Alle Testiere ᵀᵀ
Castello 5801,
calle del Mondo Novo
☎ 0415227220
Antica Besseta ᵀᵀ
Santa Croce 1395,
salizada de Cà Zusto
☎ 041721687

HOTELS AND RESTAURANTS

Venice
⭐🍴 **Le Bistrot deVenise** 🍴🍴
S. Marco 4685
☎ 0415236651
Corte Sconta 🍴🍴
Castello 3886,
calle del Pestrin
☎ 0415227024
Covo 🍴🍴
Castello 3968,
campiello Pescaria
☎ 0415223812
Harry's Dolci 🍴🍴
Giudecca 773,
fondamenta S. Biagio
☎ 0415224844
Aciugheta 🍴
Castello 4357, campo
Ss. Filippo e Giacomo
☎ 0415224292
Altanella 🍴
Giudecca 268
☎ 0415227780
All'Arco 🍴
San Polo 436, Rialto
☎ 0415205666
Ca' d'Oro detta Alla vedova 🍴
Cannaregio 3912,
calle del Pistor
☎ 0415285324
Cantinone- Vini al Bottegon 🍴
Dorsoduro 992,
S. Trovaso
☎ 0415230034
Da Codroma 🍴
Dorsoduro 2540,
fondamenta Briati
☎ 0415246789
La Mascareta 🍴
Castello 5183, calle
lunga S.M. Formosa
☎ 0415230744
Quattro Feri 🍴
Dorsoduro 2754,
calle lunga S. Barnaba
☎ 0415206978
Vecio Fritolin 🍴
Santa Croce 2262,
calle della Regina
☎ 0415222881
Lido di Venezia
Excelsior ★★★
lungomare mare
Marconi 41
☎ 0415260201

Served to the Doges on St. Mark's Day, it is made with peas from the vegetable gardens around the lagoon, while the rice is cooked in the broth obtained from their pods. Various kinds of risottos are made with fish, shellfish, pumpkin, and sausage. One of the most common types of meat is liver, especially prepared as *fegato alla veneziana* (calf's liver cooked in a pan with onions) and also as *figà col radeselo* (with sage leaves and butter) or as *figà garbo e dolce* (coated with breadcrumbs and fried with a little vinegar and sugar). Seafood dishes include *moleche* (baby crabs in the process of molting, without their shells).

A good place to begin a walk in search of the flavors of Venice is Piazza San Marco. Here do not miss the three historic cafés: "Florian" (established 1720), all velvet, mir-rors, and gilded frames, "Lavena" (est. 1750), which was frequented by Wagner and other composers, and "Quadri" (est. 1775), which also serves fish dishes upstairs. Nearby, where Calle Vallaresso leads onto the San Marco basin, you will find one of Venice's most celebrated restaurants, "Harry's Bar", lauded by Ernest Hemingway, where Arrigo Cipriani serves *carpaccio* (thinly-sliced raw meat) and other refined dishes. The tour proceeds along Riva degli Schiavoni, past the famous "Danieli Hotel" and the bridge of the Pietà, to a side street where you will find "Covo", a restaurant with a great menu and an excellent wine list. Further on, turn left towards the Arsenale dockyards and, after passing under the watchful gaze of the Greek lions guarding the entrance, continue along Calle del Pestrin. Here you will come across "Corte Sconta", with the bar and rooms of an old *osteria*, plus a secret garden for the warmer months. The cuisine is fish-based, with emphasis on good quality ingredients, but here Claudio also offers a few creative dishes to satisfy those wanting something different. It is, however, in the area of the Rialto Bridge and Campo di San Polo that the "Osteria del Fiore" is located. Considered by many to be the best restaurant in the city, it has earned this title with its strong emphasis on quality combined with the simplicity of its dishes. The menu includes *capesante al timo* (scallops with thyme), *fettuccine* with scampi and chards, and bass fillet in balsamic vinegar. Close at hand is another good restaurant, the "Antica Besseta", one of the oldest in Venice. Those wanting a change from fish would do well to head for "Gondolieri", not far from the Accademia Bridge, on the way to the church of Santa Maria della Salute. Here the cuisine is dominated by vegetables, as in the risotto made with early produce, and meat, particularly the superb beef fillet cooked in Barolo wine with *porcini* mushrooms. Last-

ly, we highly recommend three restaurants on the Giudecca island: the superb "Cipriani", in the hotel of the same name, the most exclusive in Venice; "Harry's Dolci", serving not only desserts but also dishes of the Veneto at lower prices than "Harry's Bar", in Calle Vallaresso; and "Altanella", with a friendly atmosphere and a splendid terrace. If you are interested in food shopping, it is worth paying a visit to some of the many *pasticcerie* (pastry shops). In addition to traditional biscuits (*baicoli*, *zaeti*, *fritole*, etc.), they also sell *caramei* or *golosessi*, pieces of candied fruit on long sticks. In the bakeries, look out for the bread rolls called *rosette* and in the area near the Ghetto, unleavened bread and cakes made according to the Jewish tradition. The "Rizzo" pasta shop, established in 1905, is located at San Giovanni Crisostomo, between Rialto and Strada Nuova. The *salumerie* have the typical *salumi* (cured pork products) of the Veneto, from the ubiquitous *soppressa* to the much rarer *bondola co'l lengual*, made with the meat from a pig's

Venice. A gondolier with Rialto bridge in the background
Opposite: the church of S. Giorgio on Giudecca island

HOTELS AND
RESTAURANTS

Lido di Venezia
Des Bains
Cigahotel-ITT
Sheraton ★★★
lungomare mare
Marconi 17
☎ 0415265921
Al Vecio Cantier ¶¶
via della Droma 76
Alberoni
☎ 0415268130
Trattoria
Favorita ¶¶
via F. Duodo 33
☎ 0415261626
Da Nane ¶¶
at San Piero in Volta
☎ 0415279100
Bar Trento ¶
via S. Gallo 82
☎ 0415265960
Burano
Da Romano ¶¶
piazza B. Galuppi 221
☎ 041730030
Gatto Nero -
da Ruggero ¶¶ ★
fondamenta della
Giudecca 88
☎ 041730120
Caorle
Airone ★★★
via Pola 1
☎ 042181570
Diplomatic ★★★
Duilio ¶¶ ★
via Strada Nuova 19
☎ 0421210361
Al Cacciatore ¶¶
at San Giorgio
di Livenza (km 12)
corso Risorgimento 25
☎ 042180331
Ceggia
Trattoria
al Trovatore ¶
via Noghera 31
☎ 0421329910
Chioggia
El Gato ¶¶¶ ★
campo S. Andrea 653
☎ 041401806
Osteria Penzo ¶
calle larga Bersaglio 526
☎ 041400992

head, lard from its cheek, and pork rind, together with cured tongue. One of the best-known of these shops is "Aliani", in the Ruga Vecchia San Giovanni, near the markets.

1. The islands of the lagoon

LIDO. The main interest of this island, which still has numerous bathing establishments dating from the early 20th century, lies in its two hotels – the "Grand Hotel des Bains" and "Grand Hotel Excelsior" – and the summer premises of the municipal casino. Beyond the sand dunes at the southern end of the island is the Alberoni beach, which can be reached with a pleasant walk along the *murazzi* (sea walls), or else by bus or rented bicycle. On the way, at Malamocco, amidst the vegetable gardens and wild vegetation, is "La Garzette", an *agriturismo* establishment, offering local dishes and its own wines, as well as a few rooms for those seeking an offbeat Venetian vacation. At the Alberoni beach, "Al Vecio Cantier" is a restaurant serving tasty fish dishes. As an alternative, on the way back, there is "Bar Trento", a popular *osteria* serving *cicheti* (snacks) and *ombre* (drinks) under a pergola, and also meals (at midday).

MURANO. The visit to the glass factories is a tourist ritual worth going through. And it is also a good idea to take a stroll along the Grand Canal dividing the island,

HOTELS AND RESTAURANTS

Dolo
Locanda alla Posta ¶¶
via Cà Tron 33
☎ 041410740

Lido di Jesolo
⭐🛏 **Casa Bianca al Mare** ★★★
piazzetta Casa Bianca 1
☎ 0421370615

Trattoria Laguna ¶¶¶
at Cavallino (km 10)
☎ 0421968058

Da Omar ¶¶
via D. Alighieri 21
☎ 042193685

Enoiteca Caneva ¶
at Jesolo Paese
via Antiche Mura 13
☎ 0421952350

Mestre
⭐🛏 **Dall'Amelia** ¶¶¶
via Miranese 113
☎ 041913955

Autoespresso ¶¶¶
at Marghera
via F.lli Bandiera 34
☎ 041930214

Caffè Concerto ¶¶
via Passo S. Boldo 21
☎ 041634100

Mira
Villa Margherita ★★★
via Nazionale 416
☎ 0414265800

Nalin ¶¶
via Novissimo
Argine Sinistro 29
☎ 041420083

Venice. Sunset on the lagoon

which is overlooked by the church of Santi Maria e Donato, the Museo dell'Arte Vetraria (Glass Museum), and splendid palaces and ordinary houses. A good place to eat is "Ai Frati", a seafood *trattoria* with tables outside in the summer.

BURANO. This is the island of lace, which the women still make as they chatter away on their doorsteps (the school and museum of lace-making are located in the square). Here, too, you can stroll by the canals lined with colorful fishermen's houses, and then stop off at "Da Romano", which has been the haunt of artists and the smart set since 1900, or else at "Gatto Nero da Ruggero", serving fish or game according to the season.

Burano

TORCELLO. This is the most solitary and fascinating of the islands in the lagoon. The splendid churches of Santa Maria Assunta and Santa Fosca are all that remains of a city of 20,000 inhabitants that was the heir to the Roman city of Altinum, on the mainland, before Venice was founded. One of the island's attractions is the "Locanda Cipriani", another of Hemingway's favorites. Today it offers exclusive accommodation, while the restaurant in the garden serves the traditional *riso alla torcellana* and a superb fish fry. More reasonably priced, but no less charming, is the nearby "Ostaria al Ponte del Diavolo".

2. The Riviera del Brenta

MIRA. On the road from Venice to Padua (Statale 11), turn off to the left at Mira to Malcontenta. The place takes its name from one of Andrea Palladio's most famous villas, which is well worth a visit. It is the first of over a hundred Venetian residences – ranging from sumptuous to run-down, but all interesting – lining the canal. After returning to Mira, which is made up of several villages, continue to Riscossa, where the Villa Widmann-Foscari is located. On the way, the road passes "Da Nalin", a restaurant noted for its fish-based cuisine. Those with more time available can proceed to Mirano, where "Al Paradiso" offers local specialties, especially (from November onwards) goose.

DOLO. The main town of the Riviera del Brenta, Dolo offers an interesting look at the past, with its mill located right over the canal. It is worth stopping off at the "Locanda alla Posta", a restaurant serving light modern fish dishes.

STRA. Visitors will not have any difficulty in finding the eighteenth-century Villa Nazionale (or Pisani). Virtually a palace, it is surrounded by a splendid park. For a buffet lunch or a full evening meal, try the "Villa Celin" *trattoria*, a pleasant mixture of old and new.

3. Chioggia and the Murazzi

CHIOGGIA. This is how the writer Giovanni Comisso described this

HOTELS AND RESTAURANTS

Mirano
19 al Paradiso ¶¶
via Luneo 37
☎ 041431939
La Ragnatela ¶
at Scaltenigo (km 4)
via Caltana 79
☎ 041436050
Murano
Ai Frati ¶¶
fondamenta Venier 4
☎ 041736694
Busa alla Torre ¶¶
piazza S. Stefano 3
☎ 041739662
Portogruaro
Antico Spessutto ★★★
via Roma 2
☎ 042171040
Alla Botte ¶¶ 🍴🏨
via Pordenone 46
☎ 0421760122
Valentino ¶
via Cavour 41
☎ 042172993
San Michele al Tagliamento
Mattarello ¶¶
via A. Venudo 2
☎ 043150450
Scorzè
Villa Soranzo Conestabile ★★★
via Roma 1
☎ 041445027

163

**HOTELS AND
RESTAURANTS**

Scorzè
San Martino ¶¶
at Rio San Martino
piazza Cappelletto 1
☎ 0415840648
Stra
Villa Celin ¶
via Venezia 99
☎ 049502034
Torcello
⭐ 🔟 **Locanda
Cipriani** ¶¶¶
piazza S. Fosca 29
☎ 041730150
**Ostaria al Ponte
del Diavolo** ¶¶
via Borgognoni 10/11
☎ 041730401

AGRITURISMI

Venice
Le Garzette
at Malamocco
lungomare
Alberoni 32
☎ 041731078
Chioggia
⭐ 🔟 **Ca' Rustica**
at Ca' Lino
via Ca' de Luca 15
☎ 0415200562
Mira
Santa Barbara
at Gambarare
via Seriola Veneta
destra 130
☎ 041428929

**WINE
PRODUCERS**

Annone Veneto
Bosco del Merlo
via Postumia 12
☎ 0422768167

lively fishing port on the south side of the Venice Lagoon: "The town is a rough oyster shell where, amidst glints of mother-of-pearl, the light seethes". The town is crossed by the wide Corso del Popolo and the parallel Canale della Vena, crammed with boats of all shapes and sizes. Halfway along this is the Granaio (granary) and, behind this, the old fish market, which should be visited early in the morning. On the other side of the canal are stalls selling the produce of the surrounding countryside, notably the delicious *radicchio rosso* of Chioggia and the popular *suca baruca*, a large round yellow pumpkin that is roasted in the oven. After touring the markets, you'll need to stop in one of the many *osterie* for a *cicheto*, a snack washed down by an *ombra* (glass of wine). Two local specialties not to be missed are the *broeto di pesce* (fish soup) and risotto with *gò*, the delicious gobies of the lagoon. They may, for instance, be savored at "El Gato", which also serves *biberesse in casopippa* (stewed mussels) and *luserna incovercià* (stargazer cooked in the pan). Another recommended restaurant, also near the market, is the "Osteria Penzo". On the other side of the bridge is Sottomarina. Facing the lagoon is a quay crowded with boats, while a wide beach looks out to the sea. Lastly, in the countryside bordering the

*Symbol of the Lison-Pramaggiore
wine consortium.*

province of Padua, at Pegolotte di Cona, not far from Cavarzere, you can find mild sheep's milk and mixed sheep's and cow's milk cheeses produced in the area (the cheese made from the milk of the Massese sheep is excellent).

PELLESTRINA. More enterprising visitors may wish to take the ferry to Pellestrina, a long, narrow island of sand between the sea and the lagoon, lying beyond the mouth of the port of Chioggia. From the ferry it is possible to take a bus or hire a bicycle to get to the Lido, or it can be reached by car. The first place to stop is Caroman, a lonely beach where little terns and Kentish plovers nest. This is now a bird sanctuary run by the LIPU (Lega Italiana Protezione Uccelli, the Italian Society for the Protection of Birds). Then, skirting the *murazzi*, the old sea walls, continue to Pellestrina and San Pietro in Volta. Either stop off in one of the island's *osterie*, or head straight for "Da Nane" at San Pietro.

4. From Mestre to the Tagliamento

MESTRE. Venice's mainland cousin has plenty to offer in the way of good cuisine. The most traditional restaurant is "Dall'Amelia", once a rustic inn, now the elegant haunt of gourmets and intellectuals. Particularly outstanding is "Caffè Concerto" with a cellar containing over 600 wines, excellent distillates, and a vast choice of cheeses and desserts. Less well-known, but certainly one of the best restaurants in the area, is "Autoespresso", at Marghera. The name indicates its location, near the Mestre bypass, and the cuisine is both meat- and fish-based. In the hinterland, at Scorzè, the "Villa Soranzo Conestabile" is a relaxing alternative to the crowds of Venice and its environs.

PORTOGRUARO. Rather than the *autostrada* (superhighway), the best route out of Mestre is the Statale 14, which skirts the northern part of the Venetian Lagoon, passing Portegrandi, where there is an old lock on the Sile overlooked by a boatmen's *osteria*. Then, after crossing the Piave and the Livenza, the road leads to Portogruaro, an old river port. One of the special attractions here is the antiques fair, held on the second Sunday of every month. It's well worth taking a trip to Concordia Sagittaria, heir to the Roman colony of Julia Concordia, with its fine cathedral and baptistery and remains of the ancient town. In the surrounding countryside there are around 2,500 acres of vineyards where the grapes for the Piave and Lison-Pramaggiore DOC wines are grown. The products of the best wineries accompany the meat- and fish-based cuisine of the "Valentino" *trattoria*, close to Porta Sant'Agnese. Those wishing to find out more about the local wines may wish to make a detour through San Stino di Livenza, An-

none Veneto, and Pramaggiore, where the "Enoteca Regionale del Veneto" has a display area of over 10,000 square feet devoted to wines, *grappa*, and other regional specialties. Those wanting direct contact with the producer should not miss the "Bosco del Merlo" winery at Annone, noted for its organic farming methods.

CAORLE. The cathedral's slender cylindrical campanile signals to those on both land and sea the presence of Veneto's third fishing port at the mouth of the Livenza river. The most outstanding restaurant is "Duilio", in the "Diplomatic Hotel". Also good is the "Cacciatore" at San Giorgio di Livenza, with generous helpings of waterfowl in the autumn and superb fish year-round. Fillets of marinated eel are prepared here.

JESOLO. The beach of this popular seaside resort is located on the spit forming the seaward edge of the Venetian Lagoon, between Porto di Piave Vecchia, at the former mouth of the Piave, and Porto di Cortellazzo, at the mouth of the Piave Nuovo. Gourmets should head for the Cavallino, the narrow strip of land extending with its vegetable gardens between the sea and the marshes. On the Pordelio Canal we recommend the "Trattoria Laguna" for its excellent fish grill and desserts. Don't miss "Enoteca Caneva", a celebrated haunt of lovers of great wines and tasty snacks.

SHOPPING

Venice
Aliani Gastronomia
San Polo 654
☎ 0415224913
Delicatessen.
Salumeria Gabriele Bianchi
Castello 1561,
via Garibaldi
☎ 0415221156
Charcuterie.
Caffè Florian
piazza S. Marco 56/59
☎ 0415285338
Historic cafe.
Caffè Lavena
piazza S. Marco
133/134
☎ 0415224070
Cafe and pastry shop.
Pastificio Rizzo
Cannaregio 5778,
S. Giov. Crisostomo
☎ 0415222824
Fresh pasta.
Lido di Venezia
Laboratorio di pasticceria Magghi Marren
via Dardanelli 46
☎ 0415260836
Pastries and sweets.
Lido di Jesolo
Pasticceria Roggio
piazza Trieste 16
☎ 0421380431
Pastries and sweets.
Mestre
Pasticceria Zanin
via Bissuola 81/h
☎ 0415343
Pastries and sweets.
Portogruaro
Pasticceria Caffetteria Toffolo
viale Matteotti 46
☎ 042171493
Cafe and pastry shop.

BELLUNO

In the setting of the Dolomites, the rustic cuisine of the province of Belluno is based on polenta, the faithful companion of game and cheeses.

The province of Belluno comprises almost all the upper valley of the river Piave, from its source down to the point where it flows into the Veneto plain. The central part is formed by the Val Belluna, to the north of which lies the Cadore and the Valle di Zoldo, to the west the Canale di Agordo, to the south the Feltre area. The largely mountainous terrain includes celebrated peaks of the Dolomites, such as Marmolada, the Tofane, and the Tre Cime di Lavaredo. At a lower level is a pleasant landscape of woods and pastures, abound-

The
Bellunesi
Dolomites

ing in rivers and streams, where cattle-raising and dairy farming thrive. Wild products such as mushrooms, berry fruits, and chestnuts are collected in the woods. The main crops in the valleys include potatoes (particularly renowned are the large white floury ones of the Cadore), beans, especially the Lamon variety, which is protected by the IGP (*Indicazione Geografica Protetta*) classification, and other vegetables. Both game and trout from the mountain streams play an important role in the area's cuisine. A notable feature of the cuisine of the province of Belluno is the way rustic mountain dishes are grafted onto the elegant, delicate base of traditional Veneto cooking. Thus, the first course may consist of barley soup or *gnocchi alla cadorina* served with smoked *ricotta*, while the main course could be roe deer or chamois on a spit or stewed in wine sauce. This is an area with plentiful tourist accommodation, especially in the resorts in the Dolomites.

Gourmet Tours

BELLUNO. A "little Venice in the mountains," it is located on a rocky terrace where the waters of the Piave river meet those of the Ardo. To the north there's a magnificent view of the Belluno Dolomites. The heart of the city is the splendid square where the Duomo, the Palazzo dei Rettori, and the Torre Civica are located. For a taste of the local cuisine, try *casunziei* (*ravioli* with pumpkin or spinach, ham, and cinnamon), *lasagne da fornèi* (lasagne served with a sauce of walnuts, raisins, dried figs, and poppy seeds), and roe deer stewed in wine sauce with *polenta*. Of the restaurants serving traditional fare, "Al Borgo" is especially good. It is housed in an eighteenth-century villa with a

HOTELS AND RESTAURANTS

Belluno
Delle Alpi ★★★ ▮▮▮
via J. Tasso 13/15
☎ 0437940545
Al Borgo ▮▮▮
via Anconetta 8
☎ 0437926755
Cortina d'Ampezzo
De la Poste ★★★
piazza Roma 14
☎ 04364271
El Toulà ▮▮▮▮
via Ronco 123
☎ 04363339
Park Hotel Faloria ★★★
at Zuel 46
☎ 04362959
Tivoli ▮▮▮
via Lacedel 34
☎ 0436866400
Beppe Sello ▮▮
via Ronco 68
☎ 04363236
Mel
Antica Locanda al Cappello ▮▮▮
piazza Papa Luciani 20
☎ 0437753651

splendid view. In the city center, "Delle Alpi" is a hotel with an excellent restaurant. Various stores, including "Il Paiolo", on the road to Feltre, sell the best produce of the province, especially the cheeses, which range from the celebrated Montasio to the various *latteria, nostrano prealpino, nostrano di malga, puina* (smoked *ricotta*) and *schiz* (fresh cheese served baked in the oven with butter and cream or milk). The more curious should also try *kodinzon*, an unusual apple conserve made at San Zenon di Sospirolo. In the *salumerie*, in addition to the local salami (made with pork and horse-meat), ask for *pastin, soppressa*, and *ossocolli de casada*. A specialty on sale in the pastry shops is the *fartaia*, a donut flavored with grated lemon peel, fried and dusted with sugar. Lastly, don't forget the various aromatic *grappa* produced locally.

1. The Alpago and the Cansiglio

PIEVE D'ALPAGO. The road up the Piave Valley above Belluno crosses the basin of Alpago, dotted with various villages. One of the first is Pieve d'Alpago, where you will find the "Dolada", one of Italy's most highly rated restaurants. A delightful establishment, it has been run for years by the De Prà family. Its simple, yet innovative, cuisine, is excellent, featuring, for example, trout in tartar sauce, venison cutlets and *polenta gnocchi*, and plum and pear strudel. A little further on, at Puos d'Alpago, the Locanda San Lorenzo offers comfortable accommodation and excellent local cuisine. Typical dishes of this area

include risottos with freshwater fish and smoked ham cooked in a pastry crust. Don't miss the local cheeses: *casalingo d'Alpago* and *nostrano prealpino*. Also well worth trying are the trout, snails, berry fruits, and bilberry-flavored grappa from the area.

PIAN DEL CANSIGLIO. Beeches, firs, and larches constitute the great forest that for centuries supplied timber to the Venice Arsenale. Thanks to the excellent way it was managed, it has survived intact. Suggested food purchases in the area include the smoked *ricotta* of the Cansiglio, produced on the Alpine pastures, and the mild but distinctive Cansiglio cheese, made from the milk of Brown Swiss cows and matured for up to a year.

2. The Cadore and the Belluno Dolomites

PIEVE DI CADORE. The noble aspect of the town reflects the wealth the local merchants acquired in their trade with Venice. The range of mountains to the north is the Marmarole, which Titian, a native of Pieve, depicted in his paintings. In the picturesque square stands the Palazzo della Magnifica Comunità di Cadore, and nearby is the house where Titian was born. Here you can visit the curious Museo dell'Occhiale, a museum devoted to the production of spectacles - an industry that has been the mainstay of the local economy for over three centuries. The cuisine comprises *polenta e osei* (*polenta* with birds), stewed roe deer, and various dishes based on mushrooms. The two local liqueurs are called Amaro di Cadore and Dolomiti.

SANTO STEFANO DI CADORE. Still

HOTELS AND RESTAURANTS

Monte Croce di Comelico (Passo di)
Passo Monte Croce-Kreuzberg-pass ★★★
☎ 0474710328

Pedavena
Birreria Pedavena ❘
viale V. Veneto 78
☎ 0439304402

Pieve d'Alpago
★ 🏨 **Dolada** ❘❘❘
at Plois (km 1)
via Dolada 21
☎ 0437479141
Rifugio Carota ❘
at Carota 2
☎ 0437478033

Puos d'Alpago
Locanda San Lorenzo ❘❘
via IV Novembre 79
☎ 0437454048

San Gregorio nelle Alpi
★ 🏨 **Locanda a l'Arte** ❘
via Belvedere 43
☎ 0437800124

further up the Piave Valley, the landscape becomes gentler. This area is known as the Comelico, where the traditional houses are built entirely or mainly of wood and a dialect similar to Ladin is spoken. At Santo Stefano, the chief village of the Comelico Inferiore, it is possible to purchase the excellent cheeses of the area, including the traditional Comelico, *nostrano di Costalta*, and *Carnia Dolce di Padola*. The Passo Monte Croce-Kreuzbergpass, a hotel and restaurant on the pass leading to the Val di Sesto, in Alto Adige, is particularly recommended.

SAPPADA. Located in the upper Piave Valley, this village is spread among meadows and fir woods. The excellent local cheeses include Sappada and smoked *ricotta*. In addition, there are delicious salamis and smoked cured meat similar to *speck*. Worth trying here is "Keisn", an intimate, romantic restaurant serving both traditional and creative fare, followed by superb desserts.

AURONZO DI CADORE. On the way back down the Piave Valley, turn into the Valle dell'Ansiei. Already a renowned resort at the end of the 19th century, Auronzo is located on the north shore of the Lago di Santa Caterina. Further up, near the head of the valley, is the celebrated Lago di Misurina and the start of the road leading to the Rifugio Auronzo, at the foot of the Tre Cime di Lavaredo.

CORTINA D'AMPEZZO. From the Passo Tre Croci the road descends into the basin of Cortina. Directly opposite is the mountain range of the Tofane, and, soaring at the sides, Cristallo and Sorapiss. The "pearl of the Dolomites" welcomes tourists in style. The smartest place to stay in Cortina is "De la Poste", established in 1866. A post office under the Austrians, it was then transformed into the resort's most fashionable hotel, with a grill-room serving tasty international fare. The most outstanding restaurant is the superb "Tivoli", where culinary skills combine with creativity to produce dishes that are both varied

Sappada. Typical house

HOTELS AND RESTAURANTS

San Vito di Cadore
La Scaletta ¶¶ ★ 🖼
at Chiapuzza (km 2)
via Calvi 1
☎ 0436890441
Sappada
Keisn ¶¶
borgata Kratten 8
☎ 0435469070
Vodo Cadore
Al Capriolo ¶¶
via Nazionale 108
☎ 0435489207

AGRITURISMI

Belluno
Fulcio Miari Fulcis ★ 🖼
Modolo Castion
☎ 0437927198
Colle Santa Lucia
Frena Luigi
via Pian 1
☎ 0437720084
Domegge di Cadore
Masi Alessandro
at Vallesella
via Milano 18
☎ 043572484

Dawn on the Dolomites

AGRITURISMI

Feltre
Meneguz Aurelia
at Villabruna
via Arson 113
☎ 043942136
Sappada
Zaine
via Soravia 32
☎ 043566057
Seren del Grappa
San Siro
via S. Siro 8/a
☎ 043944628

SHOPPING

Belluno
Molino De March
via Nongole 156
☎ 0437927633
*Vast range of
flours for "polenta".*
Pastificio Menazza
piazza Erbe 7
☎ 0437950245
*Traditional home-made
fresh pasta ("ravioli"
filled with red chicory
and "agnolotti" with
"speck" and potatoes).*

and delectable. The menu comprises such delicacies as a bowl of *porcini* mushrooms and potatoes with truffles, and mushroom strudel with game. Other recommended establishments are "Beppe Sello", a hotel with a friendly atmosphere offering excellent local cuisine, and "Meloncino" in the elegant "Hotel Faloria", which has a fitness center and other facilities. Also worth trying is "El Toulà", the first of the several restaurants of this name scattered around the world. Specialties on sale in the local food shops include *casunziei ampezzani* (*ravioli* with chard, *ricotta*, bread crumbs, and egg), mountain cheeses, smoked cured meats similar to *speck*, and sausages. In Corso Italia the "Piazzetta" delicatessen and the "Cooperativa di Cortina" are particularly recommended. In the bakers' shops look out for

puccia (rye and wheat bread with cumin seeds) and *carafoi*, rather like the Lombard *chiacchiere* (strips of fried or baked dough sprinkled with sugar).
SAN VITO DI CADORE. The road leading southwards from Cortina descends the Valle d'Ampezzo besides the river Boite to San Vito, a resort nestling between the spectacular slopes of Pelmo and Antelao. Here the "Cima Belprà Hotel" has a superb restaurant, "La Scaletta", offering simple, traditional fare. Don't miss the *casunziei alla cadorina* (large *ravioli* stuffed with beetroot) and beef fillet with *speck*. There is an excellent wine list, while meat dishes with *polenta* may be ordered without a first course. A little further down the valley, at Vodo Cadore, "Al Capriolo" is also worth trying.
ALLEGHE. Local specialties may be purchased here – the pastry

shops, in particular, are excellent. The village is reached from Cortina through the Passo Giau and Selva di Cadore, or by the road across the Passo Falzarego to Andraz. From here detours to Livinallongo del Col di Lana and Colle Santa Lucia are possible. The return route to Alleghe passes through Caprile. From Selva da Cadore, the road goes along the Val Fiorentina, dotted with traditional hay-barns, to Zoldo Alto. In this area, fresh and matured cheeses are produced on the mountain pastures. They include the mild Fodòm and the stronger Rènaz, goat's and cow's milk *ricotta*, and *spess*, cheese made from milk that has only just been curdled. There are also numerous *salumi* (cured meat specialties). The trout that are often found on the menus of the local restaurants are caught in the lakes and mountain streams of the area.

AGORDO. This is the main village of the Valle del Cordevole, it is also noted for the manufacture of spectacles (the museum of the Luxottica firm is located in the center). Superb celery and beans are grown locally, and the mountain pastures produce excellent butter, cheese, and mutton. South of the village, the road enters the Canale d'Agordo, a deep gorge formed by the river Cordevole, which flows through the mountains to the Val Belluna.

Cortina d'Ampezzo

3. The Val Belluna
MEL. On a hill overlooking the Piave, it has a compact nucleus, with imposing houses and churches adorned with works of art. In perfect harmony with its setting is the "Antica Locanda al Cappello" – established in 1730, it was formerly the premises of the Knights of Malta – which serves traditional fare.
FELTRE. The old nucleus derives its typically sixteenth-century appearance from the domination of the Venetian Republic. From Porta Imperiale, Via Mezzaterra climbs up through the center between decorated houses with overhanging roofs to Piazza Maggiore. Nearby is the cathedral. At Cesiomaggiore the "Busche" dairy produces the Piave cheese, which has recently become a commercial success. In this village there's the Museo Etnografico della Provincia di Belluno, with displays devoted to dairy products, and the area is renowned for its mushrooms, walnuts, and *grappa*. Nearby is Pedavena, noted for its brewery, with an adjacent bar.
LAMON. Near the border with the Trentino, this village is famed for its production of delicious beans. They are used in various tasty dishes, including the traditional *pasta e fasoi* (pasta and beans), and also in the Lamon risotto and soup, and in *minestrone alla montanara*.

SHOPPING

Belluno
Il Paiolo
via Feltre 104
☎ 04379404472
Regional products.
Cortina d'Ampezzo
Pasticceria Beduschi
2 shops:
largo Poste 32
☎ 01361823
via Zuel di Sotto 58
☎ 0436868054
Pastries, chocolates and pralines.
Cooperativa di Cortina
corso Italia 40
☎ 0436861245
Wide selection of regional products.
Enoteca - da Gerry
via del Mercato
☎ 0436862040
Good selection of wines.
Piazzetta
corso Italia 53
☎ 04363436
Delicatessen.

PADUA

The Paduan plain is interrupted by the Euganean Hills, which bring the flavors of the woodlands and a great variety of wines to the table.

The province of Padua occupies a large part of the lower Veneto plain. This is crossed by three rivers flowing to the Adriatic just south of the Venetian lagoon: the Brenta, the Bacchiglione, and the Adige. The only interruption to the broad horizon of the Po Valley is provided by the conical forms of the green Euganean Hills, which are of volcanic origin. Although the agriculture of the area is dominated by crop-growing, the raising of poultry is also important, especially of the distinctive Paduan hen, as is that of pigs, linked to the production of Prosciutto Veneto Berico-Euganeo, a ham with the DOP (*Denominazione di origine protetta*) classification. As far as viticulture is concerned the main output is of Colli Euganei DOC wines. In the area of Conselvano, towards the southern border of the province, is the zone of the Bagnoli DOC wine, which is made from the ancient Friularo grape. Unlike Venice and other cities of the Veneto that have developed traditions that can be termed aristocratic, Padua does not repudiate its peasant roots, hence the widespread use of poultry (especially hens and geese) and vegetables served simply, without adding spices or exotic ingredients. The most outstanding restaurants are to be found in Padua and the spa towns in the Euganean Hills, in particular Abano Terme.

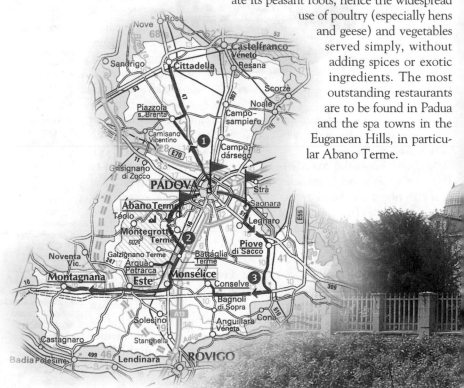

Gourmet Tours

PADUA. The city is noted, above all, for Giotto's frescoes in the Scrovegni Chapel, Donatello's sculptures in the basilica of Sant'Antonio, and early frescoes by Titian in the Scuola di Sant'Antonio. But it is also worth taking a stroll in the Prato della Valle, in the peaceful Botanic Gardens, or under the arcades of the old city. Not to be missed are the markets on both sides of the Palazzo della Ragione. Those fond of aristocratic milieux should visit what Stendhal described as "the best café in Italy," that is, "Pedrocchi" (established in 1772), which has recently been renovated, regaining its cultural role. In the city the great cuisine of the Veneto is well represented. In the area near the market, we recommend two inexpensive establishments: the "Anfora" *osteria* and the "Enoteca Leonardi", serving wine

and food. Those who prefer their eateries to be more upscale should make for the "Antico Brolo", also in the city center. Here they will find calf's head cooked in vinegar with onions (a "Buon Ricordo" dish) and an excellent wine list. Those staying for a longer period should try some of the interesting restaurants in the environs of Padua. The most outstanding is "Le Calandre" at Sarmeola di Rubano, where a young chef exhibits his notable skills in creative dishes, such as calf's tongue with ginger and apple mustard salad, multicolored gilthead *ravioli* with pilchard rolls, and rabbit with herbs cooked in a sealed pot. At Villafranca Padovana, "Dai Grandi" is strongly recommended, both for its atmosphere and its innovative cuisine drawing inspiration from tradition. The "Conte Umberto Emo Capodilista" winery, at Selvazzano Dentro, is a good place to try the wines.

1. The Euganean Hills

ABANO TERME. The volcanic origin of the Euganean Hills is not,

Padua. The Sant'Antonio basilica

HOTELS AND RESTAURANTS

Padua
Milano ★★★ 🍴📺
via P. Bronzetti 62
☎ 0498712555
Antico Brolo 🍴🍴🍴 🍴📺
corso Milano 22
☎ 049664555
Garibaldi ★★★ 🍴📺
at Ponte di Brenta
via S. Marco 63
☎ 0498932466
Sagittario ★★★ 🍴📺
at Ponte di Brenta
via Randaccio 6
☎ 049725877
Abano Terme
G.H. Orologio ★★★🍴
viale delle Terme 66
☎ 0498669111
Casa Vecia 🍴🍴
at Monterosso
via Appia 130
☎ 0498600138
Arquà Petrarca
La Montanella 🍴🍴🍴
via Costa 33
☎ 0429718200
Cittadella
La Filanda ★★★
via Palladio 34
☎ 0499400000
San Bassiano 🍴🍴🍴
via Palladio 34
☎ 0499402590
Loreggia
Locanda Aurilia 🍴🍴
via Aurelia 27
☎ 0495790395
Monselice
La Torre 🍴🍴
piazza Mazzini 14
☎ 042973752
Montagnana
Aldo Moro 🍴🍴🍴
via Marconi 27
☎ 042981351

HOTELS AND RESTAURANTS

Rubano
Le Calandre ¶¶¶¶
at Sarmeola, S.S. 11
☎ 049630303
Teolo
Al Sasso ¶¶
at Castelnuovo
via Ronco 11
☎ 0499925073
Torreglia
La Torre ★★★
piazza Capitello 27
☎ 0499930111
Villafranca
Padovana
★🍴 **Dai Grandi** ¶¶
at Taggi di Sopra
via Firenze 6
☎ 0499075220

AGRITURISMI

Baone
★🍴 **Le Pesare**
at Rivadolmo
via Ca' Bianche
☎ 0498803032
Bovolenta
★🍴 **Venturato**
at Fossaragna
via Argine Destro 29
☎ 0495347010

WINE PRODUCERS

Bagnoli di Sopra
Dominio di Bagnoli
piazza Marconi 63
☎ 0495380008
Praglia
La Pratalea
via Abbazia 12
☎ 0499900332
SelvazzanoDentro
**Conte Umberto
Emo Capodilista**
via Montecchia 16
☎ 049637294

as one might imagine, responsible for the hot springs accounting for the success of this famous spa town. The waters are, in fact, those that fall as rain on the Piccole Dolomiti, near Recoaro, at the head of the Val d'Agno in the province of Vicenza. After descending to a significant depth, the waters re-emerge in the Euganean Hills thanks to a strange quirk of geology. Known since Roman times, these springs allowed Albano to become, in the Belle Epoque, one of the most elegant resorts in Europe. In the restaurants, the tradition of using the produce of the hills is still very much alive. As well as delicious *soppressa*, there are risottos with mushrooms or quail, the famous *piccioni toresani allo spiedo* (pigeons on the spit) served with *polenta*, and small birds with *polenta*. We recommend the "Casa Vecia" restaurant at Monterosso. It offers a series of tasty dishes accompanied by first-rate wines and, to round off the meal, there is an incredible range of cheeses and desserts, all the more delectable for their elegant presentation. Nearby, the Benedictine abbey of Praglia, set in a hollow in the Euganean Hills, is well worth visiting. This trip also offers an opportunity to purchase some bottles of the excellent local wine at the Pratelea winery, a member of the Movimento Turismo del Vino. Local products include *maraschi-

Arquà. The statue of Petrarch

no, produced by the Luxardo distillery, which moved here from Zara (now Zadar, in Croatia) after World War II.

BATTAGLIA TERME. Already much appreciated by the Romans for the curative properties of its waters, this spa grew further in medieval times thanks to the trade on the Battaglia Canal. The patrician residences standing out against the backdrop of the hills attest to this. The most curious is the sixteenth-century Cataio, a complex surrounded by walls with battlements and a large park. Local specialties include *salumi* and pigeons on the spit.

ARQUÀ PETRARCA. It is not hard to see what persuaded Francesco Petrarch to retire here. The pleasant landscape of the Euganean Hills, perhaps the local wines, and certainly the peaceful environment are tempting enough. Little has changed. It is possible to visit the poet's house, surrounded by a shady garden of box trees, then one may explore the steep streets of the medieval village. Here we recommend the restaurant "La Montanella", where the specialties include pigeon on a spit and duck with fruit (a Paduan recipe of the seventeenth century).

MONSELICE. Its name derives from the Latin *Mons Silicis* (mountain of flint), referring to the trachyte that was quarried locally and sent by barge to Venice (it was twice used to pave St. Mark's Square). On the street winding up to the fortress, the town's most notable historic buildings are located – the castle, the old Duomo, the sanctuary of the Sette Chiese, and the Villa Duodo – all bearing witness to its glorious past. The surrounding countryside is renowned for its peaches, which are often sold at the roadside. Gourmets should head for "La Torre", a restaurant noted for its superb risottos and mushroom and truffle dishes.

ESTE. At the foot of the last offshoots of the Euganean Hills is the site of the ancient city of Ateste, important remains of which still exist. Today Este has the typical appearance of Venice's mainland possessions, with a castle dominating the town. In the surrounding area, white truffles are found and excellent raw ham is produced. Further on, this circular tour of the Euganean Hills continues to a couple of "wine towns": Cinto Euganeo, where we recommend "La Roccola", an *agriturismo* establishment, and Vò, with the "La Corte" *enoteca*. Teolo has mouth-watering figs.

MONTAGNANA. Set in the middle of the Veneto plain, this is one of the most famous and best-preserved walled towns in Europe. With its economy based on agriculture, it is the main production center of Prosciutto Veneto Berico-Euganeo, a DOP ham, and the location for the headquarters of the association that protects it.

2. On both sides of the Brenta

PIAZZOLA SUL BRENTA. The main point of interest here is the Villa Contarini. It contains the Sala della Musica – known as the "upturned guitar" – which, with its remarkable acoustics, is used for concerts.

CITTADELLA. Surrounded by medieval walls with towers and gates still intact, this town grew up around the intersection of the east-west road from Treviso to Vicenza with the north-south road from Bassano del Grappa to Padua. In the center, we recommend the hotel "Finlanda", with its "San Bassiano" restaurant, where the emphasis is on regional cuisine. Lastly, at Loreggia, nine miles south-east of Cittadella, the "Locanda Aurilia" serves delicious local dishes and excellent wines.

3. On the road to Chioggia

SAONARA. A leading nursery and gardening center, Saonara is also famed for its horse-meat specialties. In addition to salami and *bresaola* (salted and dried meat), there is also *sfilacci*, made by pounding the dried smoked meat.

PIOVE DI SACCO. Surrounded by medieval walls, the historic center has streets flanked by low arcades and buildings in the Venetian style. The fact that this small town is on the road to Chioggia is evident in the fish-based menu of the "Alla Botta" restaurant. Nearby is Polverara, noted for the breeding of Paduan hens and geese.

CONSELVE. An important cooperative winery is located here. Wine lovers will, however, want to visit the "Dominio di Bagnoli", at Bagnoli di Sopra, an estate with a long history. At its center is a large villa with fourteenth-century cellars. The milk of the Massese sheep is used in the sheep's milk cheese and mixed cow's and sheep's milk cheeses that are produced in the area.

SHOPPING

Padua
Caffè Pedrocchi
via VIII Febbraio 15
☎ 0498781231
Historic cafe.
Pasticceria Luigi Biasetto
via J. Facciolati 12
☎ 0498024428
Sweets and pastries.
Pasticceria Brigenti
piazza dei Signori
☎ 0498751560
Sweets and pastries.
Salumeria Guarnieri
via S. Francesco 48
☎ 0498750541
Charcuterie.
Antico Forno Vecchiato
piazza della Frutta 26
☎ 0498751873
Bakery.
Cinto Euganeo
Frantoio di Valnogaredo
via Mantovane 8/a
☎ 0429647224
Olive oil producer.
Legnaro
Pasticceria Belvedere
via Verdi 5/a
☎ 049790715
Sweets and pastries.
Montagnana
Bottega Mantoan
via Carrarese 35
☎ 042981653
Charcuterie and cheeses.
Montegrotto T.
Salumeria Bertin
Charcuterie.
piazzale Stazione 11
☎ 0497932527
Rubano
Pasticceria Le Calandre
at Sarmeola, via della Provvidenza 160
☎ 049630303
Sweets and pastries.

ROVIGO

The Polesine is a land created by water and its cuisine, as simple as the horizon of the Po Valley plain, is inspired by both the river and the sea.

The province of Rovigo, crossed by the lower courses of the Adige and Po rivers and numerous canals branching off these, comprises the southern part of the Veneto plain, known as the Polesine, which has become fertile thanks to centuries of reclamation work. From its most inland areas, wedged between the Oltrepò Mantovano and the border with the province of Ferrara, there is a gradual transition to the lands of the Po Delta. These lands were cultivated more recently, and the arable land alternates with reed-beds and shallow pools teeming with fish. Pig-farming is widespread, with a large output of salami and sausage, while in some areas sheep are reared, resulting in the production of sheep's milk cheese and *ricotta*. There is also no lack of wild products such as snails, mushrooms, and truffles, collected in the woods bordering the rivers. The cuisine of Rovigo is that of a well-watered land between river and sea. Therefore you find seafood risottos; fish from the marshland pools, such as eel, gray mullet, and sea bass; poultry, most notably guinea-fowl; and waterfowl, especially ducks and coot. In this youthful land, the restaurants are noted more for the quality of the ingredients used than for their inspiration or culinary virtuosity.

Gourmet Tours

ROVIGO. Between the Po and the Adige, in the very fertile land reclaimed from the marshes, Rovigo is a city with a modern look: the Corso del Popolo, dividing it into two, has, since the 1930s, occupied the former course of the Naviglio Adigetto canal. On one side is the seven-teenth-century Duomo and two towers of the medieval castle; on the other the main square, where the architecture of the buildings reflects four centuries of Venetian rule. They include the Palazzo dell'Accademia dei Concordi, housing the Pinacoteca, the city's picture gallery. The most outstanding local dishes comprise *faraona in tecia* (guinea-fowl cooked in an earthenware pot and stuffed with an onion pierced with cloves) and *risotto polesano*,

HOTELS AND
RESTAURANTS

Rovigo
Villa Regina
Margherita ★★★ 🚗 📺
viale R. Margherita 6
☎ 0425422433
Cristallo ★★★
viale Porta Adige 1
☎ 042530701
Belvedere - da
Romano ❚ 📺
viale Regina
Margherita 33
☎ 042531332
Cauccio ❚
viale Oroboni 50
☎ 042531647
Al Sole ❚
via Bedendo 6
☎ 042522917
Adria
Trattoria
al Naviglio ❚
via L. da Vinci 33
☎ 042623057
Ariano
nel Polesine
Due Leoni ❚❚
at Gorino Veneto
corso del Popolo 21
☎ 0426372129
Castelmassa
Portoncino Rosso ❚❚
via Matteotti 15/a
☎ 042581698
Crespino
Rizzi ❚❚❚
via Passodoppio 31
☎ 042577238

Rovigo. The Scardovari bay

cooked with eel and sea bass. The "Villa Regina Margherita", its Art Nouveau façade framed by tall plane trees, provides comfortable accommodation and, at the "Margherita" restaurant, delicious food. Those preferring the more informal surroundings of the *osteria* should pay a visit to "Al Sole", in Via Bedendo. More than a hundred years old, it has a friendly atmosphere, a splendid range of *cicheti* (snacks), and some tasty traditional dishes. The food shops – "Fratelli Piva", in Piazza Garibaldi, is especially good – sell *bondole*, large sausages typical of the lower Polesine, made with pork mixed with soft fat and lightly smoked.

LENDINARA. When leaving Rovigo, it is worth making a detour to pass through Fratta Polesine. The most interesting aspect of this village, frequented in the past by the landed aristocracy of the Venetian Republic, is the imposing Villa Badoer, built to a design by Palladio in 1570. Further on is Lendinara, a pleasant little town crossed by the Adigetto and boasting villas, churches, and Renaissance and Baroque palaces. Gourmets should continue to Lusia, where the "Al Ponte" restaurant is located. In an old house you can enjoy the delicious cuisine based on river fish and the local vegetables, used in risottos, *sformati* (pies), and fries.

BADIA POLESINE. This town is situated at the point where the Adige leaves its former course, now the Naviglio Adigetto. Its name derives from the abbey of Vangadizza, which promoted the reclamation of the area. The remains may be visited, while on display in the Museo Civico is the *Last Supper*, based on Leonardo's masterpiece, which formerly adorned the abbey's refectory. Once again on the road, head south to Castelmassa on the river Po. Here you will find a refined restaurant, the "Portoncino Rosso", renowned for its salami grilled in vinegar on bread with crackling. There is also a tempting range of meats and local vegetables. On the opposite bank of the Po, in Lombardy, is Sermide, the onion capital of the Oltrepò Mantovano.

Rovigo. Piazza Vittorio Emanuele

HOTELS AND RESTAURANTS

Lusia
Al Ponte ❢
via Bertolda 1
☎ 0425669890
Occhiobello
La Pergola ❢❢
at S. Maria Maddalena
(km 4)
via Malcantone 15
☎ 0425757766
Porto Tolle
Marina 70 ❢❢
at Scardovari (km 14)
via Belvedere 2
☎ 042680080
Brodon ❢
at Ca' Dolfin
(km 9)
☎ 0426384021

AGRITURISMI

Adria
⭐️🖈 **Scirocco**
at Voltascirocco 3
☎ 042640963
Rosolina
⭐️🖈 **San Gaetano**
via Moceniga 20
☎ 0426664634

178

OCCHIOBELLO. Returning eastwards along the Po you will find this riverside village where the traditional activities of eel-fishing (the sturgeon, however, is now rare) and the hunting of migratory birds still exist. Thus fish and game play an important role in the local cuisine, together with *stracotto d'asino* (donkey-meat stew) and, because Ferrara is close by, *salamina da sugo* (a large sausage that has to be boiled before it is eaten). We particularly recommend "La Pergola", where the menu offers pâté of pheasant or with truffles, *pappardelle al germano* (wide pasta ribbons with duck sauce), and marinated rabbit.

ADRIA. At Polesella leave the Statale 16 to Rovigo and follow the banks of the Po. A few miles further on is Crespino, with a restaurant, "Rizzi", where the cuisine is influenced by both the Veneto and Emilia, with the mouth-watering addition of mushrooms and truffles when in season. The next stop is Adria, an ancient trading station where Greeks and Etruscans did business. Such was its importance that it gave its name to the Adriatic Sea, which was considerably closer at that time. The Canal Bianco, which crosses the built-up area, is lined with handsome Venetian houses, attesting to the town's more recent function as an agricultural center. The cuisine is typical of the Po Delta: risotto with sea bass, *tagliatelle* with truf-

Polesine. The Po delta

fles, duck on the spit, coot with beans, grilled eel, and stewed snails. Local specialties on sale in the food shops include the *bondola di Adria*, a large sausage made of a mixture of pork and beef, with added lard, which is eaten boiled, like the Ferrarese *salamina da sugo*, and also the sheep's milk cheese from the reclaimed lands. "Da Danilo-al Naviglio" is a simple restaurant that won't disappoint those seeking tasty fish dishes, from the starter to the classic grill or mixed fry.

ARIANO POLESINE. After crossing the Po di Venezia, continue to the Goro branch of the river, where you will find the "Due Leoni". This traditional restaurant with a pleasant atmosphere also has a few quiet rooms. Its most notable offerings are *masurin* (mallard) with wild herbs, a Buon Ricordo dish, and barbecued eel from the Po Delta served with white *polenta*, which follow the tasty dishes of *pasta al torchio*. White truffles are found locally and the area is renowned for its production of *bondole* pork.

PORTO TOLLE. In the splendid setting of the recently formed Isola della Donzella, where the river Po flows into the Adriatic, the cuisine is based on a mixture of fish and migratory game-birds. There are two culinary outposts worth trying: at Ca' Dolfin, "Brodon" is a *trattoria* on the final stretch of the river, and at Scardovari, "Marina 70" has a panoramic terrace overlooking the sea.

AGRITURISMI

Trecenta
Ca' Pozza ★
via Tenuta Spalletti 41
☎ 0425700101

SHOPPING

Rovigo
Salumeria F.lli Piva
piazza Garibaldi 15
☎ 042524845
Charcuterie.
Badia Polesine
Pasticceria Sanremo
via S. Giovanni 26
☎ 042551042
One shop also in Lendinara, via Varliero 48,
☎ 0425600979
Pastries, ice-creams and candies.

TREVISO

A carefree land where good food is much appreciated, the province of Treviso is noted for its "red chicory", mushrooms and great wines.

T he province of Treviso comprises the plain flanking the lower course of the river Piave and a series of hilly areas, including the Colli Asolani and Colli di Valdobbiadene, the Montello, and the plateau of Cansiglio. Very well watered, the plain produces two types of chicory, protected by the IGP(*Indicazione Geografica Protetta*) classification: the *radicchio rosso* (red chicory) of Treviso and the *radicchio variegato* (variegated chicory) of Castelfranco. The southern part of the province is noted for the vines of the Piave and Lison-Pramaggiore DOC (*Denominazione di Origine Controllata*) zones, yielding excellent red wines from Merlot, Cabernet, and Raboso grapes. The hills produce whites, especially Prosecco, the sparkling wine dominating the three DOC zones of Montello e Colli Asolani, Colli di Conegliano, and Prosecco di Conegliano-Valdobbiadene. From the *prealpi*, the foothills of the Alps, come the renowned Montasio cheese, which has been awarded the DOP (*Denominazione di Origine Protetta*) classification, and mushrooms. This is one of the most interesting areas in Italy in terms of cuisine, favored by the remarkable quality of the foodstuffs available and a deep-

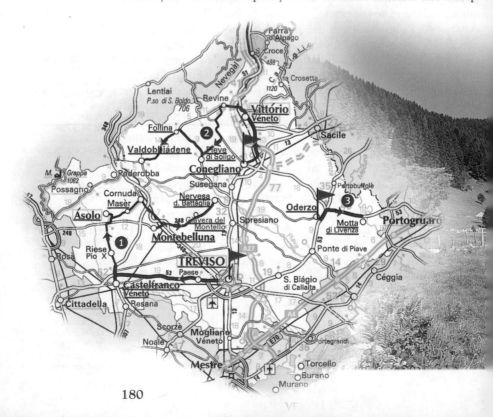

rooted culinary tradition. The radicchio is outstanding, but the rice, meat and fish are all excellent. In an area abounding in watercourses, river fish, especially eel, play an important role, while the plentiful supply of mushrooms and game has led to the Montello becoming one of the best-known gastronomic areas of the Veneto.

Gourmet Tours

TREVISO. This is what writer Giovanni Comisso had to say about his native city: "A very graceful medieval structure interacts bizarrely with the clear waters of the rivers crossing it." A tour of the city should start from the lively Piazza dei Signori. As well as churches and palaces, make sure your trip includes the Pescheria, the fish market standing on a small island that gives an accurate picture what Treviso was like in a bygone age. In this area, by the way, there's a very high concentration of *osterie*, where it is customary to stop for a chat and sip a glass of Fragolino or Clinton. When trying the city's cuisine, visitors should be ready to pay homage to the *radicchio rosso*, an essential ingredient in a unique risotto and a multitude of other delicious dishes.

Linked to the river are such local dishes as eel, served in various ways, and the *risotto al tajo*, made with prawns and eels. Dishes typical of the surrounding countryside are *risotto alla sbirraglia*, made with chopped chicken and its broth, and *sopa coada*, boned pigeon baked in the oven with slices of bread soaked in broth. This may be enjoyed in its original version at "Toni di Spin", a friendly *trattoria* just behind Piazza dei Signori. Because of its history, "Beccherie", established in 1875 and originally the favorite haunt of the local butchers (*bechèri*), is, however, the best place to try the popular *zuppa di trippa* (tripe soup) and other traditional dishes. Other restaurants worth trying include the elegant "Alfredo" (part of the "El Toulà" chain), as well as "Al Bersagliere" and "L'Incontro". "Al Fogher", a hotel with its own restaurant, provides particu-

Monte Grappa. Bocchette

HOTELS AND RESTAURANTS

Treviso
Al Fogher ★★★
viale della Repubblica 10
☎ 0422432950
Alfredo
via Collalto 26
☎ 0422540275
Al Bersagliere
via Barberia 21
☎ 0422541988
Beccherie - 1875
piazza Ancillotto 10
☎ 0422540871
L'Incontro
largo di Porta Altinia 13
☎ 0422547717
Toni del Spin
via Inferiore 7
☎ 0422543829
Asolo
Al Sole ★★★
via Collegio 33
☎ 0423528111
Villa Cipriani ★★★
via Canova 298
☎ 0423523411
Casier
Osteria alla Pasina
at Dosson
via Peschiere 15
☎ 0422382112
Castelfranco Veneto
Ca' delle Rose ★★
Barbesin
at Salvarosa
circonvallazione Est 33/a
☎ 0423490232
☎ 0423490446
Rino Fior
at Salvarosa
via Montebelluna 27
☎ 0423490462
Cavaso del Tomba
Locanda alla Posta
piazza XIII Martiri 13
☎ 0423543112

**HOTELS AND
RESTAURANTS**

Conegliano
Tre Panoce ¶¶¶
via Vecchia
Trevigiana 50
☎ 043860071
Al Salisà ¶¶
via XX Settembre 2
☎ 043831007
**Crocetta del
Montello**
★🛏 **Casa
Brusada** ¶¶
via Erizzo 117
☎ 042386614
Follina
★🛏 **Romantik
Hotel Villa
Abbazia** ★★★
via Martiri della
Libertà
☎ 0438971277
**Giavera del
Montello**
Agnoletti ¶¶
via della Vittoria 190
☎ 0422776009
**Gorgo al
Monticano**
Villa Revedin ★★★
via Palazzi 4
☎ 0422800033
Miane
Gigetto ¶¶¶
via De Gasperi 4
☎ 0438960020
Monfumo
★🛏 **Osteria alla
Chiesa - da Gerry** ¶¶
via Chiesa 14
☎ 0423545077
Montebelluna
Enoteca Marchi ¶¶¶
via Castellana 177
☎ 0423303530
**Nervesa della
Battaglia**
La Panoramica ¶¶
strada Panoramica
del Montello
☎ 0422885170

larly good accommodation. The local food shops offer a wide range of cheeses, from the most common, such as *castella, latteria*, and the fragrant *malga*, to more unusual products, such as the slightly sour *casalina* and the curious *formaio embriago* ("drunk cheese"), matured in the marc of Cabernet or Merlot grapes. Also on sale here is the famous *luganega trevisana*, a pork sausage made with meat from a pig's neck and lard from the animal's cheek tied up to form four segments and used to flavor risottos, or grilled. The following delicatessens are good: "Danesin", in Corso del Popolo, and "Cacciolato", in Vicolo Rialto, as well as the celebrated "Bottega del Baccalà". If you want desserts, especially the local *tiramisù,* go to the "Guiscardo Casellato" pastry shops. There are various interesting restaurants in the environs of Treviso. "Righetto" at Quinto di Treviso, is the undisputed temple of eel dishes and river fish in general. At Casier, we recommend the "Osteria alla Pasina". The "Castello di Roncade" offers excellent *agriturismo* facilities. At Zero Branco, renowned for its asparagus, we suggest a visit to "Ca'

Busatti". It may be a little difficult to find, but it's worth seeking out for the elegance of the villa set in a beautiful garden, and its superb cuisine, with the emphasis on risottos, fish, and white meats.

1. The Colli Asolani and the Montello

CASTELFRANCO VENETO. On the way to the Colli Asolani it's worth stopping off to visit this attractive little town in the plain, the historic center of which is still enclosed by the rectangular fortifications of the *castello*. In the Duomo there is the famous altarpiece by Giorgione, a native of the town, who began painting here (nearby, his house is open to the public). But Castelfranco is also well known for its *radicchio variegato* (variegated chicory), used in a wide range of dishes. It can best be enjoyed at "Rino Fior", which also offers accommodation in a country villa at the nearby village of Salvarosa. Admirers of Palladio should not fail to make a detour to Fanzolo di Vedelago, where the Villa Emo is located.

ASOLO. Visited by many illustrious travelers, including Robert Browning, Eleonaro Duse, and Eugenio Montale, its fame origi-

Maser. Villa Barbaro

nated with the legendary Caterina Cornaro, the former queen of Cyprus, who brought her court of poets and humanists here in the Renaissance. In addition to this fascinating past, the town has medieval buildings, fountains, flower-decked windows, antique shops, and olive groves and vineyards on the hills dotted with villas. And its hospitality is equal to its great fame. It has two exclusive luxury hotels, "Al Sole" and "Villa Cipriani", the latter with a refined restaurant. Also within the town walls, the "Hosteria Ca' Derton" is recommended for its wide choice of dishes, ranging from the popular *bigoli al ragù d'anatra* (*bigoli* in duck sauce) to the refined *zuppa di ovoli in crosta* (soup of *amanita Caesarea* mushrooms in a pastry crust). In the nearby village of Monfumo, the "Osteria alla Chiesa - da Gerry" is especially good for its cuisine based on local produce: radicchio, mushrooms, asparagus, and wild herbs. Not to be missed is the short detour to Possagno, the birthplace of Antonio Canova, where you can visit the great sculptor's house and his burial place, the Tempio. Then, at Cavaso del Tomba, you will find the "Locanda della Posta", a restaurant with a pleasant atmosphere and a few rooms for guests, where the female chefs prepare deliciously simple dishes, such as the home-made *tagliatelle* with *porcini* mushrooms, and snails with delicate herbs and *polenta*.

MASER. This village is universally renowned for the splendid Villa Barbaro, Palladio's masterpiece, and for Veronese's frescoes adorning it. Not everyone knows that it also houses a fascinating nineteenth-century winery with huge vaulted cellars, where the "Montello e Colli Asolani DOC" and other fine wines may be tasted.

MONTEBELLUNA. This little town, famed for its production of ski and hiking boots, is the starting-point for the road that circuits the Montello, the wooded upland area noted for its abundant mushrooms and numerous *trattorie*. Gourmets will find a visit to the "Enoteca Marchi" rewarding, while in the shops excellent honey is on sale, together with the produce of the woodlands. At nearby Crocetta del Montello, the Casa Brusada *trattoria* offers a menu in tune with the season, with asparagus and wild herbs in spring, mushrooms and game in autumn.

GIAVERA DEL MONTELLO. Following the southern slopes of the Montello, you come to Volpago, where the "Conte Loredan Gasperin" winery has 200 acres of vineyards around a large Palladian villa. At Giavera the main attraction is "Agnoletti"; established in 1780, it is a restaurant of historical importance where the Venetian nobility and the patriots of the Risorgimento (uprising that led to Italy's unification) used to meet. Today, sitting in the garden, you can start with the excellent local *soppressa* and then choose between various dishes made with mushrooms and game.

NERVASA DELLA BATTAGLIA. The battle in the name of the village is that of the Piave, which, during World War I, razed it to the ground. The event is commemorated by a memorial and a small museum. Today it is also noted for its fine restaurants. "La Panoramica", with its command-

HOTELS AND RESTAURANTS

Nervesa
della Battaglia
Roberto
Miron ¶¶ ⭐📠
via Brigata Aosta 26
☎ 0422885185
Oderzo
Gellius ¶¶¶
calle Pretoria 6
☎ 0422713577
Pieve di Soligo
Al Ringraziamento
¶¶¶
via S. Michele 2
☎ 043883699
Da Lino ¶¶
at Solighetto
via Brandolini 1
☎ 043882150
Portobuffolè
Villa
Giustinian ★★★
via Giustiniani 11
☎ 0422850244
Quinto di Treviso
Righetto ¶¶
via Ciardi 2
☎ 0422470080
San Pietro
di Feletto
Al Doppio
Fogher ¶¶ ⭐📠
at S. Michele di Feletto
via S. Michele 53
☎ 043860157
San Polo di Piave
Parco
Gambrinus ¶¶¶ ⭐📠
at Gambrinus,
via Capitello 22
☎ 0422855043
Tarzo
Il Capitello ¶¶¶
at Corbanese
via S. Francesco 1/e
☎ 0422855043
Valdobbiadene
Marianna ¶¶ ⭐📠
at S. Pietro
di Barbozza
☎ 0423972616
Trattoria
alla Cima ¶
via Cima 8
☎ 0423972711

ing position overlooking the hills and its own vineyards, is the best. "Roberto Miron" made its name with mushrooms, but makes an excellent impression all year.

2. The northern part of the province of Treviso

CONEGLIANO. In the Duomo is a beautiful altarpiece (*Virgin and Child with Sts. James and Jerome*) by the celebrated Renaissance painter Cima da Conegliano. From here proceed to the castle, where there is a magnificent view over the whole of the area producing Prosecco, the pride and joy of Treviso's viticulture. A town with solid gastronomic traditions, Conegliano boasts two first-rate restaurants. The first is the "Tre Panoce", a splendid villa on a hilltop, offering such traditional dishes as *pappardelle al radicchio* with *soppressa* and *polastro in tecia con parsemol* (chicken cooked in an earthenware pot with parsley, a Buon Ricordo dish). The other, "Al Salisà", close to the Fontana dei Cavalli, has a pleasant terrace and serves seasonal dishes, from *pasta ai profumi del bosco* (pasta with woodland flavors) to the *involtino di vitello con erbe spontanee* (veal roll with wild herbs). At Susegana, the "Conte Collalto" winery, a member of the Movimento Turismo del Vino, may be visited, with opportunities for tasting. At San Pietro di Feletto, "Al Doppio Fogher" offers excellent fish-based Veneto and Istrian cuisine.
VITTORIO VENETO. This was formed by merging two Venetian-style towns - Ceneda and Serravalle - located on the Strada di Alemagna, the highway linking Veneto to the Tyrol. The

mountains are close and this is reflected in the cuisine. In addition to the flavors of the Colli di Conegliano hills, there is roe deer and trout, the cheeses of the pre-Alps and the berry fruits of the Cansiglio. In the town, the "Postiglione" serves excellent traditional fare. At Corbanese di Tarzo, on the other hand, "Il Capitello" is a very successful restaurant run by a group of young people with a creative touch, where the ample menu offers delicious, impeccably-served dishes, both fish- and meat-based. At Carpesica wine buffs should not miss the "Cosmo Bellenda" winery.
PIEVE DI SOLIGO. The road leads through vineyards of Prosecco and Bianco dei Colli grapes to Pieve di Soligo. Here is a restaurant, "Al Ringraziamento", where an inspired and audacious chef prepares a range of tasty, well-presented dishes, including crispy lasagne with duck sauce and spinach on Gorgonzola sauce. Nearby, at Solighettto, the "Locanda da Lino" takes a more cautious approach. But the results here are also very satisfying, particularly the meat grill. Farra di Soligo is renowned for its production of goat's milk cheeses, both fresh and matured. Another local cheese is *mastela*, a slightly sharp cheese made from whole cow's milk. In addition, mushrooms and chestnuts are found in abundance here.
FOLLINA. The abbey of Santa Maria and a number of imposing fifteenth-century houses attest to the importance of this village, which was formerly a major center of the wool industry. An interesting excursion from here is to the Passo San Boldo (706 m/2316 ft).

A steep road winds up to the pass and then down into the Val Belluna. For those seeking accommodation, we particularly recommend the small but extremely refined "Romantik Hotel Abbazia". To find one of the best restaurants in the Veneto, however, it is necessary to make a short detour to Miane, where "Da Gigetto" has it all: a number of dining-rooms, a superb wine list, first-rate cuisine, and it is extremely good value.

VALDOBBIADENE. The vineyards sloping down from the hills to the broad bed of the Piave river are those of the celebrated Prosecco known as Cartizze, the leading attraction of this area. The main center of production is San Pietro di Barbozza, renowned also for its strawberries and excellent *trattorie*.

3. Between the Piave and the Livenza

ODERZO. It began as a market town on the Via Postumia, the Roman road across northern Italy, and such it has remained, with its porticoed Gothic houses and Renaissance palaces. Just a few miles away, at San Polo di Piave, the "Parco Gambrinus" is an attractive restaurant that started life as a pilgrims' inn. Now surrounded by a splendid park crossed by a river with fish ponds, it offers a range of carefully prepared creative dishes. Close by, at Piavon di Oderzo, the "Rechsteiner" winery is definitely worth a visit. Here you can taste the excellent Lison-Pramaggiore DOC wines in the setting of a seventeenth-century villa. At Gorgo al Monticano, the "Villa Revedin" is a very good hotel.

MOTTA DI LIVENZA. Now some distance away, the river Livenza once flowed by the original nucleus of the town - where the Duomo is located - which was the port for the produce of the surrounding countryside. Another center is the one that has grown up around the sanctuary of the Madonna dei Miracoli, built in 1510 on the spot where the Virgin Mary is said to have appeared (a marble altarpiece attributed to Jacopo Sansovino is located on the high altar). The "Casa del Bacco", on a vast estate devoted to wine-growing, is an *agriturismo* establishment offering accommodation and excellent cuisine, with such dishes as guinea-fowl with *peverada* (a sauce made with breadcrumbs, butter, ox marrow, parmesan cheese, salt and pepper) and *polenta*

Treviso red chicory

SHOPPING

Treviso
Bottega del Baccalà
via Pescheria 12
☎ 0422540818
Delicatessen.
Cacciolato
vicolo Rialto 25
☎ 0422545971
Delicatessen.
Pasticcerie G. Casellato
via Cadore
☎ 0422421342
Portico Oscuro
☎ 0422543332
S. Giuseppe
☎ 0422436399
borgo Cavour 6/a
☎ 0422544645
viale Cadorna 3/5
☎ 0422419390
Pastries and sweets.
Gastronomia Danesin
corso del Popolo 28
☎ 0422540625
Delicatessen.
Breda di Piave
Caseificio Tornasoni
at Campagne
☎ 0422686200
Cheeses.
Giavera del Montello
Dal Maso Mario Egidio
via Solstizio 10
☎ 0422775161
Honey.
Montebelluna
Pasticceria Bernardi
piazza Marconi
☎ 042322968
Pastries and sweets.
Oderzo
Acetificio Caramel
via Fabrizio 1/a
☎ 0422815445
Vinegar producer.

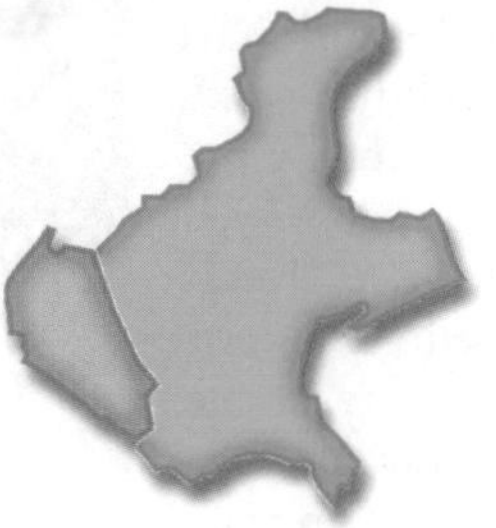

VERONA

A great cuisine with broad horizons, which range from Verona itself to Lake Garda, Valpolicella and the Po Valley plain.

The province of Verona is divided equally into the plain and the uplands. The northern part comprises the eastern shore of Lake Garda, the Adige Valley and the Lessini Mountains, an area with striking limestone features. The intermediate zone extends from the amphitheater of Garda to the rolling landscape of central Lessinia. The plain, crossed diagonally by the Adige river, is at first dry, then well-watered and eminently suitable for rice growing. The leading agricultural activity is, however, viticulture, which puts the province at the very top of the production of Italian DOC wines. Bardolino, the famous red wine made from the local Corvina and Rondinella grapes, is produced on the eastern shores of Lake Garda, while Custoza, a white made with Trebbiano Toscano and Garganega grapes, is produced in the area to the south-east of the lake. With similar grapes, the Valpolicella red and the Soave white are produced in the hills of Lessinia, as the whole area is called. Recioto Passito and Amarone are particularly outstanding wines in this area. Other important produce in the province of Verona comprises Garda extra virgin olive oil with the DOP (*Denominazione di Orig-*

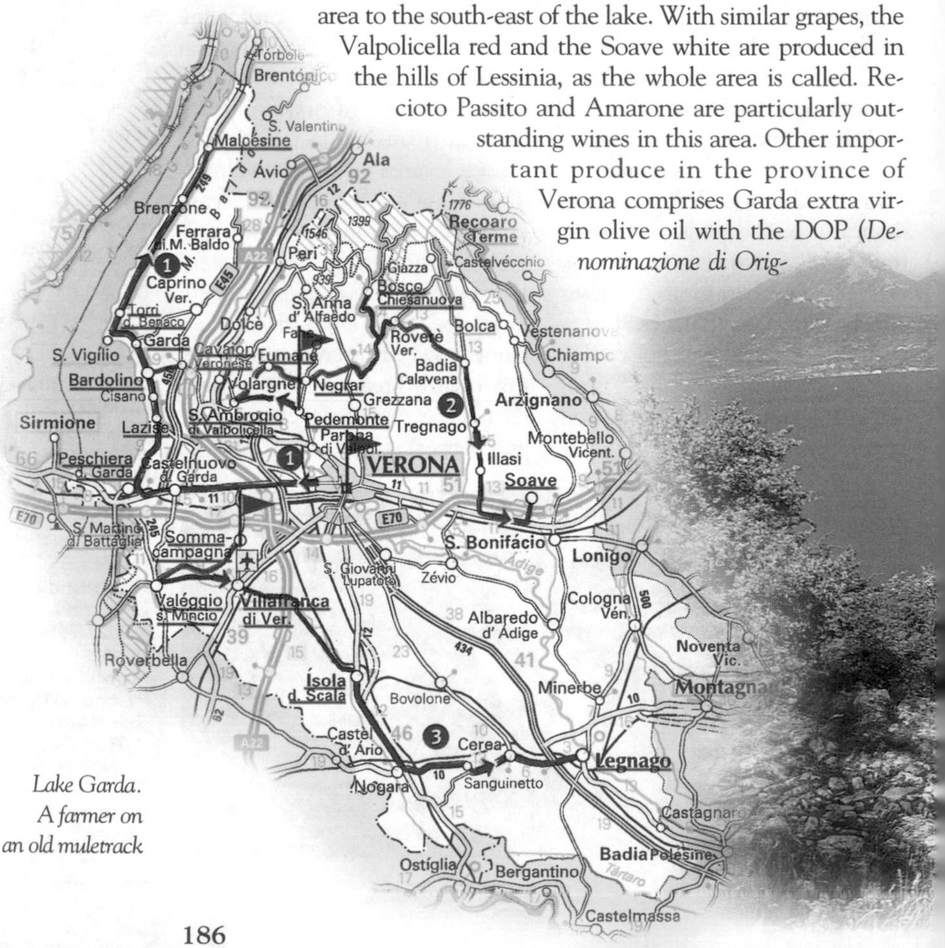

Lake Garda.
A farmer on
an old muletrack

ine Protetta) classification, Monte Veronese cheese (also DOP), and Vialone Nano rice with the IGP (*Indicazione Geografica Protetta*) classification. The remarkable variety of superb ingredients is enhanced by the great culinary traditions of Verona together with the influence of Lombardy and the Trentino. The city, in fact, has an extraordinary range of restaurants, the established ones vying with those that have made their name in recent years. The refined cuisine of Lake Garda is fish-based, the Lessini Mountains offer the fragrance of mushrooms and truffles, as well as the tastiest of snail dishes, and, in the plain, risottos are made with a whole host of ingredients.

Gourmet Tours

VERONA. "There is no world without Verona walls," says Shakespeare's Romeo, and well may we believe him. The city crossed by the Adige was the first point of contact with Italy for many travelers from northern Europe, and the influence of various epochs of the past have created an unforgettable townscape. In the Arena great operas are staged, while in the Romanesque church of San Zeno the faithful pray before Mantegna's altarpiece. A battlemented bridge leads to the Castelvecchio fortress, and Piazza dei Signori is dominated by splendid palaces and the Scaliger tombs. When sampling the cuisine, ask for *paparele* (*pappardelle*, wide pasta ribbons) with pea sauce, the delicious boiled meats with *pearà* (a sauce made with breadcrumbs, butter, ox marrow, parmesan cheese, salt and pepper), *pastissada di caval* (stewed horse-meat) with a sauce of aromatic herbs. The more adventurous should try the *zuppa scagliera*, where the pigeon, bread, and broth of the popular *sopa coada* has been ennobled by adding oth-

HOTELS AND RESTAURANTS

Verona
Arche ¶¶¶¶ ★
via Arche Scaligere 6
☎ 0458007415
Dodici Apostoli ¶¶¶¶
vicolo Corticella
S. Marco 3
☎ 045596999
Il Desco ¶¶¶¶
via Dietro
S. Sebastiano 7
☎ 045595358
Bottega del Vino ¶¶
via Scudo di Francia 3
☎ 0458004535
**Locanda
di Castelvecchio** ¶¶
corso Cavour 49
☎ 0458030097
Tre Marchetti ¶¶
vicolo 3 Marchetti 19/b
☎ 0458030463
Al Carro Armato ¶
via S. Pietro Mart. 2/a
⌂ 0458030175
Brigliadoro ¶
via S. Michele
alla Porta 4
☎ 0458004514
Garda
**Locanda San
Vigilio** ★★★
at San Vigilio
☎ 0457256688
Pino Due ¶
at Giare
☎ 0457255694
Isola della Scala
Gabbia d'Oro ¶¶¶¶
at Gabbia
☎ 0457330020
Isola Rizza
Perbellini ¶¶¶¶
via Muselle 10/11
☎ 0457135352
Lazise
Casa Mia ★★★
at Risare
☎ 0456470244

HOTELS AND RESTAURANTS

Montecchia di Crosara
⭐📺 **Baba Jaga** 🍴🍴🍴
via Cabalao 12
☎ 0457450222
La Terrazza 🍴🍴🍴
via Cesari 1
☎ 0457450940
Monteforte d'Alpone
Enoteca del Soave 🍴
piazza S. D'Acquisto 1
☎ 0457613422
Pedemonte
Villa del Quar ⭐⭐⭐
Arquade 🍴🍴🍴
via Quar 12
☎ 0456800681
Pescantina
Villa Quaranta Park Hotel ⭐⭐⭐
at Ospedaletto
via Brennero 65
☎ 0456767300
Alla Coà 🍴
at Ospedaletto
☎ 0456767402
Sant'Ambrogio di Valpolicella
Dalla Rosa Alda 🍴
at San Ambrogio di Valpolicella
strada Garibaldi 4
☎ 0457701018
San Zeno di Montagna
Taverna Kus 🍴
via Castello 14
☎ 0457285667
Torri del Benaco
Gardesana ⭐⭐⭐
piazza Calderini 20
☎ 0457225411
⭐📺 **Al Caval** 🍴🍴
via Gardesana 186
☎ 0457225666

er meats as well as white wine and spices. For a superb gastronomic experience, we suggest "Il Desco"; located in a sixteenth-century palace, it has a refined and innovative menu with such delights as a warm salad of marinated lobster, and *ravioli* with rosemary-flavored potatoes and crisp lard. We also recommend the "Tre Marchetti", a restaurant in a narrow street near the Arena that serves traditional, yet creative, dishes, and has an excellent wine list. Then there is the "Locanda di Castelvecchio". In an extremely elegant setting, it is particularly noted for its fresh pasta and roast and boiled meats. There are three other top venues for Veronese cuisine: "Arche", frequented since 1890 by the famous names in all the arts; "Dodici Apostoli", and "Antica Bottega del Vino" - established in 1890, it is an illustrious survivor from among the hundred wine bars that once populated the town. For a more informal meal, visit "Al Carro Armato", literally "At the Tank," a curious name for an *osteria*

with a wide selection of Veronese wines, as well as snacks, tripe, and various specialties of the Veneto. Great wines, and also delicacies of Lessinia and Garda, are served at the "Brigliadoro Enoteca". There are two outstanding food shops: "De Nunzio", in Piazza delle Erbe, and "Gastronomia Stella", in Via Stella, selling cheeses of Lessinia, Garda olive oil, and garlic-flavored salami. The "Istituto Enologico Italiano", on the banks of the Adige, has an excellent range of wines to choose from. The pastry shops have the fluffy *pandoro* sponge cake and also the traditional *nadalin* and *offella* (sweet focaccia made with flaky pastry). We also recommend "Brodo di Giuggiole" (literally, "soup of jujubes," although the expression "andare in brodo di giuggiole" means to go into raptures), an old liqueur revived by the Montresor winery, and pralines made from the same fruit. Just a few miles from the city center, at Sona, there are two wineries worth visiting: "Daniele Zamuner", which has a sparkling wine for connoisseurs, made with the same mixture of grapes as champagne, and "Sparici Landini", producers of prize-winning DOC wines.

Verona. The arena

1. The Veronese shore of Lake Garda

PESCHIERA DEL GARDA. The Riviera degli Olivi begins on the banks of the Mincio. In Roman times, the town was noted for eels, but over the centuries it has become famous primarily for its fortifications, which have left a military imprint on the rest of the town. Nearby, amidst the vineyards where grapes for the "Lugana" wine are grown, you come to "Combattente", a family-run *trattoria* serving delicious lake fish. LAZISE. An old port of the Venetian Republic, it retains its castle and other buildings linked to its former function. The area is renowned for olive oil - it may be purchased at the "Frantoio per Olive Veronesi" - and traditional *salumi*: raw and cooked ham, *mortadella*, and *cacciatorini* (small salamis). The "Casa Mia Hotel" is strongly recommended, not only for its comfort but also for its excellent cuisine. On the Riviera, the Museo dell'Olio illustrates the stages in the production of olive oil and makes direct sales. BARDOLINO. The village, with its narrow streets leading down to the lake, is renowned for the red wine that has delighted many visitors in the past. Try it first at the "Enoteca del Bardolino" in the Villa Carrara Bottagisio, and then visit a few producers. The most outstanding is the "Conti Guerrieri Rizzardi" *azienda*, which also produces first-rate olive oil. You can taste DOC wines, including a superb "Chiaretto", in the old *barchessa* (arcaded barn). For olive oil visit the producers "Giradelli" and "Costadoro". Near the church of San Severo, the "Aurora" has earned itself an ex-

cellent reputation. Featuring the produce of the lake, its menu includes *bigoli co' le aole* (*bigoli* with bleak, a small silvery fish).

GARDA. This is a small town with a special atmosphere and a beautiful tree-lined lakeside promenade. A nature trail skirting the shore links the town to the delightful Punta di San Vigilio, where you will find a villa and monastery converted into an inn serving sea fish. The "Pino Due" *trattoria* at Giare offers local dishes at moderate prices. TORRI DEL BENACO. There is a fascinating museum in the Scaliger castle illustrating the traditional systems of fishing as well as the most important aspects of the cultivation of the olive and the vine. By the port, we recommend the restaurant of the "Gardesana Hotel". In an enchanting setting it offers its own delicious version of local cuisine. "Al Caval", on the Gardesana highway, has a more modern atmosphere. The smoked pike with *radicchio* and balsamic vinegar is an example of its delightfully creative vein. Away from the lake, at Castion Veronese, olive oil and wine may be purchased at the "Pellegrini" *azienda*. An excuse for a trip up to San Zeno di Montagna, where there is a fine panoramic view of the lake, is the rustic "Taverna Kus". MALCESINE. In addition to olive oil, this town is renowned for the cheeses from the pastures of Monte Baldo (a cableway whisks visitors up to 1783 m/5850 ft), Monte Vespere and the unusual *casàt*, which is traditionally preserved in olive oil. In the town it is easy to get lost in the maze of

HOTELS AND RESTAURANTS

Valeggio sul Mincio
Al Cacciatore ★★★
via Goito 31
☎ 0457950500
Antica Locanda Mincio ¶¶¶
at Borghetto
via Michelangelo 12
☎ 0457950059
Eden ★★★
via don Beltrame 10
☎ 0456370850
Villafranca di Verona
La Filanda ¶¶
via Bixio 370
☎ 0456303583

AGRITURISMI

Illasi
Centro Ippico Agrituristico
at Cellore
at Deserto 1
☎ 0457834441
Lazise
Le Caldane
at Colà, Caldane 1
☎ 0457590300

WINE PRODUCERS

Verona
Vini Montresor
via Ca' di Cozzi 16
☎ 045913399
Bardolino
Conti Guerrieri Rizzardi
via Verdi 4
☎ 0457210028
Negrar
Le Ragose
at Le Ragose, Arbizzano
☎ 0457513171
Roberto Mazzi
at Sanperetto
via Crosetta 8
☎ 0457502072

narrow streets, but you won't miss the Scaliger castle on a rocky spur dominating the lake. At Porto di Brenzone, the "Taverna del Capitano" serves customary dishes of lake fish, but also the remarkable *aole in sisam* (dried bleak) with onion and vinegar. CAVAION VERONESE. The way back to Verona leads through this village, renowned for its olive oil. Olive groves and vineyards extend over the slopes of Monte San Michele, while asparagus and other vegetables are grown in the Adige Valley. Nearby, the "Affi, Poggi" *azienda* is housed in a handsome villa.

2. The Valpolicella and the Lessini Mountains

PEDEMONTE. This village is noted above all for Palladio's imposing Villa Serego. An additional reason for visiting this architectural masterpiece is that it houses the "Santa Sofia" *azienda*. Nearby is the "Villa del Quire", a splendid country hotel with its own restaurant, the "Arquade", and an *enoteca* in a sixteenth-century cellar.

SANT'AMBROGIO DI VALPOLICELLA. The village is renowned for its cheeses: especially a sheep's and goat's milk *caciotta*, and goat's milk cheeses made in the same way as the French *chèvre*. At San Giorgio, there is an interesting Romanesque church and a good *trattoria*, "Dalla Rosa Alda".

FUMANE. It is uncertain whether the "Villa della Torre", clearly displaying the influence of Roman architecture, was designed by Michele Sanmicheli or Giulio

Romano. Those wishing to debate the matter may do so in the welcoming surroundings of the "Enoteca della Valpolicella", which has a range of the area's best wines and serves seasonal dishes. Further up the valley of the Progno is the "Parco delle Cascate di Molina", a nature park with waterfalls - one of the loveliest spots in Lessinia.

NEGRAR. This celebrated winemaking center is also renowned for its cherries. Call in at "Le Ragose" winery, which obtains the grapes for a "Valpolicella Classico Superiore" and an "Amarone" for connoisseurs. Also recommended is "Roberto Mazzi", which produces wines from interesting mixtures of grapes and also provides meals and accommodation at the "Antica Corte al Mulino" *agriturismo* establishment. "Alla Ruota" is noted for home-made pasta and soup.

BOSCO CHIESANUOVA. Located on the edge of a plateau with a breathtaking view of the Veneto plain, Monte Baldo, and Lake Garda, this resort is surrounded by woods and pastures. The typical cheeses of the Lessini produced here include Monte Veronese, with a DOP classification, and *stracon*, a mild cheese produced from June to September. Black truffles and mushrooms are found abundantly in the area. The next stop is at Roverè Veronese, a pretty resort in the Squaranto Valley. A few miles further east, in the deep valley of the Illasi, is Sant'Andrea di Badia Calavena, renowned for its excellent snails.

WINE PRODUCERS

Pedemonte
Santa Sofia
via Ca' Dedè 61
☎ 0457701074
Villa Bellini
at Castelrotto
via dei Fraccaroli 6
☎ 0457725630
Sona
Sparici Landini
via Montecorno 10
☎ 0456081393
Daniele Zamuner
via Vallecchia 40
☎ 0456081090
Valeggio sul Mincio
Corte Marzago
at Le Bugne
☎ 0457945104

SHOPPING

Verona
Bottega del Baccalà
via Fincato 76
☎ 045525446
Delicatessen.
Bottiglieria Dal Zovo
viale della Repubblica 12
☎ 045918050
Wines .
Salumeria De Nunzio
piazza Erbe 36
☎ 0458002245
Charcuterie
Istituto Enologico Italiano
via Sottoriva 7
☎ 045590366
Excellent selection of wines.
Gastronomia Stella
via Stella 11
☎ 0458004998
Delicatessen
Affi
Giorgio Poggi
via Pigna 5
☎ 0457236222
Vegetables.

SOAVE. On the way back to the plain you can pass through Montecchia di Crosara, where there are two outstanding restaurants: "La Terrazza" and "Baba Jaga", the former specializing in fish, the latter featuring mainly local dishes. Close by are the vineyards of the Lessini-Durello wines. At Monteforte d'Alpone, the "Enoteca del Soave" is well worth a visit. The next stop will inevitably be at Soave, the well-preserved medieval town that has given its name to the celebrated DOC wine. Its hilltop castle dominates the Veronese plain.

3. The amphitheater and the Veronese plain

SOMMACAMPAGNA. Offering views over the hills of Lake Garda, where the grapes of the Bianco di Custoza are grown, this small town is known for its wineries and its associations with the Risorgimento.
VALEGGIO SUL MINCIO. The majority of visitors come here to see the Parco Sigurtà, 124 acres of gardens that can only be seen by car, but the fascination here also lies in the riverside scenery, with the Ponte Rotto, built by the Vis-

conti, the water-mills at Borghetto, and the castle. Perfectly in harmony with this setting is the "Antica Locanda Mincio", dating from 1600 and formerly a post-house. Taste wines at the "Corte Marzago" *azienda*, housed in a sixteenth-century monastery.
VILLAFRANCA DI VERONA. No one should miss a visit to the "Caffé Fantoni", established in 1842, which celebrated contemporary events in Italian history with such delicious inventions as the Umberto biscuits, named after Umberto I, King of Italy (1878-1900). Also recommended is "La Filanda", a small restaurant where the cuisine is first-class.
ISOLA DELLA SCALA. This is the main center of an important rice-growing area. In the *trattorie* the excellent Vialone Nano variety reigns supreme.
LEGNAGO. On the other side of the Valli Grandi Veronesi, a huge area of reclaimed land, is Legnago on the banks of the Adige. Beyond the river is Cologna Veneta, renowned for its production of almond cake.

SHOPPING

Bardolino
Azienda Agricola Costadoro
via Costadoro 5
☎ 0457211668
Olive oil producer.
Oleificio Cisano del Garda
c/o Cisano
Oil Museum
via Peschiera 54
☎ 0456229047
Olive oil producer.
Cologna Veneta
Gli Speziali di Cologna Veneta
viale del Lavoro 31
☎ 0442411380
Isola della Scala
Riseria Ferron
via Saccovener 6
at Pila Vecia
☎ 0457301022
Rice.
Isola Rizza
Pasticceria Perbellini
via Muselle 10/11
☎ 0457135899
Pastries and candies.
Lazise
Frantoio per Olive Veronesi
at Mata 3
via Gardesana
☎ 0457580030
Olive oil producer.
Pastificio Al Re del Tortellino
via S. Rocco 25
☎ 0457950523
Fresh pasta.
Vigasio
Riseria Gazzani
via Zambonina 40
☎ 0457363221
Rice.

Valeggio sul Mincio. The "Antica Locanda Mincio"

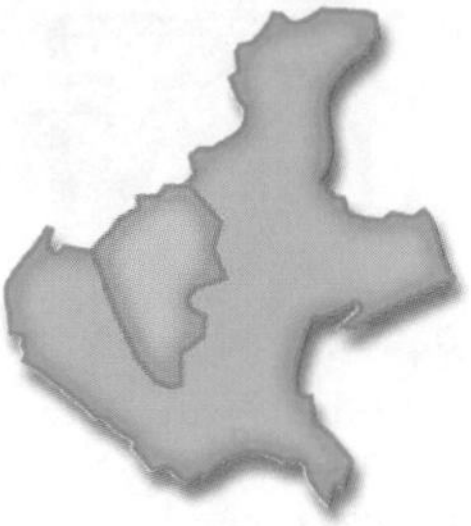

VICENZA

Vicenza extends from the Asiago Plateau, renowned for its cheeses, to Bassano, celebrated for its grappa and asparagus, and the Berici Hills

The province of Vicenza is very varied and is divided equally between the plain and the upland areas. The dominant feature of the latter is the Asiago Plateau (also known as the plateau of the Sette Comuni), flanked by the Pasubio and Grappa massifs, with Monte Ortigara lying to the north. An area where dairy farming is of primary importance, the plateau is particularly renowned for Asiago cheese, which has now been awarded the DOP (*Denominazione di Origine Protetta*) classification. Going southwards, there is an intermediate area of hills, favorable to the cultivation of vines, olives, and cherries, which extends from the south-eastern offshoots of the Lessini Mountains to the hilly areas around Marostica and Bassano. There are three DOC wine zones. From east to west, these are Lessini-Durello, shared with the province of Verona; Gambellara, producing white wines from Garganega grapes, including the celebrated Recioto Passito; and Breganze, with Torcolato Passito. Next comes the plain, crossed by the Bacchiglione and Brenta rivers, with a

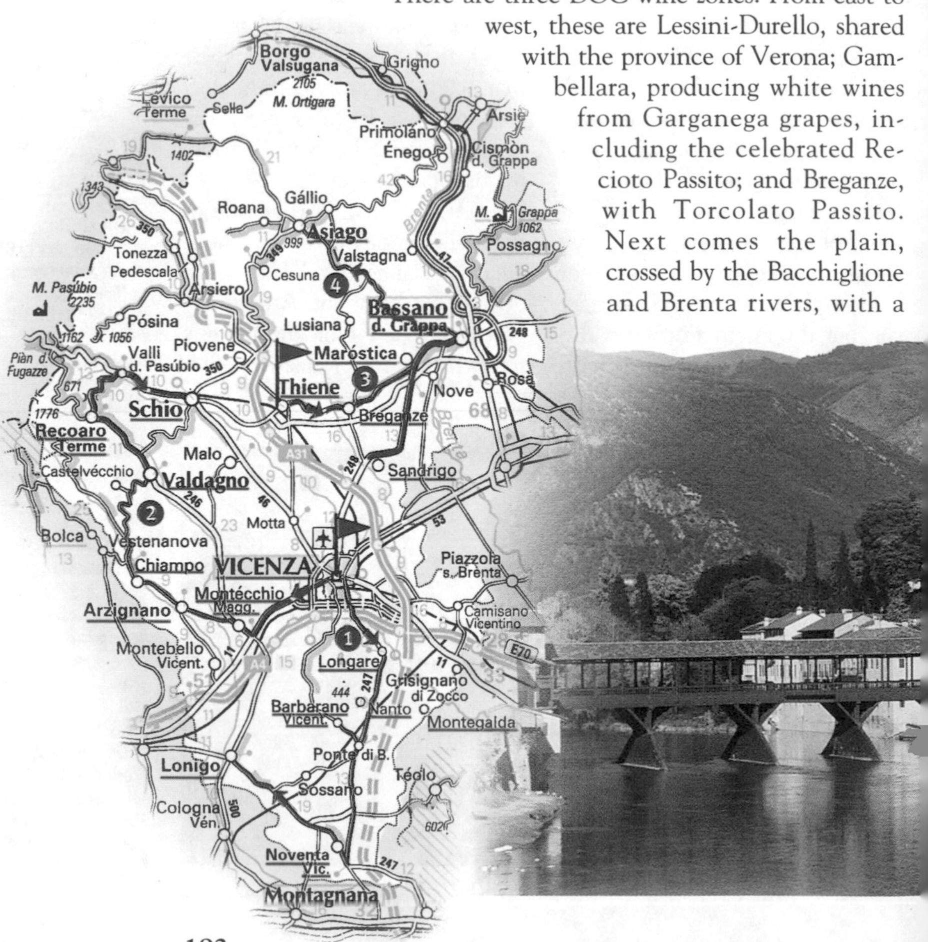

higher, drier strip where vines and asparagus are cultivated, and a lower well-watered area, where cereals and rice grow, especially Vialone Nano rice in the vicinity of Grumolo delle Abbadesse.
South of Vicenza soar the Berici Hills, where the climate suits both the olive and the vine. Here the Colli Berici DOC wines are produced, as well as a DOP ham, Prosciutto Veneto Berico-Euganeo. Rice plays a major role in the cuisine. In addition to the popular *risi e bisi* (risotto with peas), there is a wide range of risottos made with other ingredients, for example asparagus or pumpkin. Pasta is also frequently found, with the rustic *bigoli* (large spaghetti) and *tagliatelle*, or lasagne, served with duck sauce or the black truffles of the Berici. The most famous local dish is *baccalà alla vicentina* (Vicentine stockfish), which owes its origins to the area's long-standing trade links with northern Europe. Finally, there are the meat dishes, often featuring farmyard birds - pigeon on a spit and young turkey with pomegranate - and lamb raised on the hills. There is an interesting selection of restaurants, especially in the area around Bassano del Grappa.

Gourmet Tours

VICENZA. This is the city of Palladio, who designed numerous architectural masterpieces that have been included by UNESCO in its World Heritage List. The Basilica, the Teatro Olimpico, and the Palazzo Chiericati are located in the center. Just outside the city, on the Riviera Berica, visitors can admire the superb Rotonda, Palladio's most famous villa. The city's culinary specialty is *baccalà alla vicentina* (stockfish cooked with onions). Less well known are *bigoli* with duck sauce, *tagliatelle* with the black truffle of the Berici, young turkey with pomegranate, and pigeons on a spit, as well as the local wines, which are certainly underrated by the general public. In the city center, just behind Piazza dei Signori, you can taste

Bassano del Grappa

HOTELS AND RESTAURANTS

Vicenza
Nuovo Cinzia e Valerio 🍴🍴🍴 ★TCI
piazzetta Porta Padova 65/67
☎ 0444512796
Antico Ristorante Agli Schioppi 🍴🍴
contrà Castello 26/28
☎ 0444543701
Da Remo 🍴🍴
via Caimpenta 14
☎ 0444911007
Antica Casa della Malvasia 🍴
contrà Morette 5
☎ 0444543704
La Badessa 🍴
contrà Mura Corpus Domini 3
☎ 0444322185

Altissimo
Casin del Gamba 🍴🍴
at Roccolo Pizzati
☎ 0444687709

Arcugnano
Antica Osteria da Penacio 🍴🍴 ★TCI
al lago di Fimon
via Soghe 22
☎ 0444273081
Trattoria Zamboni 🍴
at Lapio
via S. Croce 14
☎ 0444273079

Arzignano
Principe 🍴🍴🍴
via S. Caboto 16
☎ 0444675131

Bassano del Grappa
Al Camin ★★★ 🍴🍴
at Cassola (km 7)
via Valsugana 64
☎ 0424566134
☎ 0424566409

**HOTELS AND
RESTAURANTS**

**Bassano del
Grappa**
⭐🏨 **Belvedere** ★★★
piazzale Generale
Giardino 14
☎ 0424529845
⭐🏨 **Belvedere** 🍽🍽🍽
viale delle Fosse 1
☎ 0424524988
**Bolzano
Vicentino**
⭐🏨 **Locanda
Grego** ★★★
via Roma 24
☎ 0444350588
Breganze
Al Toresan 🍽🍽
via Zabarella 1
☎ 0445873260
La Cusineta 🍽
via Pieve 19
☎ 0445873658
Brogliano
⭐🏨 **Locanda
Perinella** ★★★
via Bregonza 34
☎ 0445947688
Caldogno
⭐🏨 **Trattoria
Molin Vecio** 🍽🍽
via Giaroni 56
☎ 0444585168
Castegnero
Al Sole 🍽
via Roma 13
☎ 0444639028
**Cornedo
Vicentino**
Enoteca La Corte 🍽
via Volta 2
☎ 0445952910
Costozza
⭐🏨 **Taverna
Aeolia** 🍽🍽
piazza da Schio 1
☎ 0444555036
Gallio
⭐🏨 **La Lepre
Bianca** 🍽🍽
via Camona 46
☎ 0424445666

Vicenza cuisine at the "Antica Casa della Malvasia", a restaurant with centuries of tradition behind it. For those fond of grilled meat, the "Antico Ristorante agli Schioppi", in Piazza Castello, is an excellent choice. Two other excellent restaurants are located in the outskirts in the direction of Padua: "Nuova Cinzia e Valerio", renowned for its seafood, and "Da Remo", serving traditional fare. For those wishing to spend an evening sipping wine and sampling the local cheeses and *salumi*, there is no lack of *enoteche* (wine bars). "Berealto" is in a side-street off the central Corso Fogazzaro, and "La Badessa" is in the picturesque San Rocco quarter. Food shops worth a visit include "Il Ceppo", on Corso Palladio, which has *soppressa*, Asiago cheeses, wines and *grappa*, as well as *baccalà alla vicentina*, which makes a marvelous takeout dish. Those who have a taste for spicy food should try *mostarda vicentina*, a quince conserve flavored with generous quantities of mustard. In the environs of Vicenza, we highly recommend the "Trattoria Molin Vecio" ("Old Mill") at Caldogno. The water-wheel is still driven by the spring waters and inside you'll discover the fascinating world of Amedeo Sandri and Sergio Boschetto and his wife, experts on traditional recipes based on wild herbs and other wild produce. For a short trip to the Berici Hills, take the road to Monte

Berico. Shortly after the sanctuary of Monte Berico, built to commemorate an apparition of the Virgin Mary, is Arcugnano, where signs point the way to the "Antica Osteria da Penacio". Further on, at Lapio, the "Trattoria Zamboni" also offers tasty fare.

1. The Berici Hills and the south of the province of Vicenza

LONGARE. The main road (*statale* 247), linking Vicenza to Este, skirts the south-eastern edge of the Berici Hills, known as the Riviera Berica. Just outside the city, on a low hill overlooking the plain of the Bacchiglione, is Palladio's masterpiece, the Rotonda. A short walk away is the Villa dei Nani, decorated with a fresco cycle by Giambattista Tiepolo and his son Giandomenico. On the way to Longare, a short detour leads to Costozza, where the spectacular Villa Trento Carli is located. This houses the "Conti Alvise e Luigi da Schio" winery. Steps lead down from the square to an unusual wine store, while opposite is the Villa Aeolia, a frescoed pavilion with air conditioning provided naturally by ducts leading from the caves underneath. It is now an excellent restaurant, the "Taverna Aeolia". The road continues along the foot of the hills to Lumignano, which, thanks to the warmth reflected from the rocks above, is famous for its delicate peas, available very early in the season. Next comes Castegnero, renowned for its delicious cherries. Here the "Trattoria Al Sole" serves dishes that, according to the season, are made with peas, asparagus, mushrooms, truffles and even cherries.

MONTEGALDA. At Longare, the Bacchiglione meanders away from the hills and leads the way for a detour to the imposing castle of Montegalda. Here, Enrico Grandis's "La Capreria" offers *agriturismo* vacations and refined French-style organic cheeses; the "Fratelli Brunello" distillery produces excellent *grappa* and provides accommodation on the neighboring farm; and the friendly "Da Culata" *osteria* is very traditional. It is then possible to return to Vicenza through the ricefields of Grumolo delle Abbadesse, or via the Statale 247 along the Riviera Berica.

NANTO. Although the stone of Vicenza, used to excellent effect by Palladio in his buildings, is the mainstay of the local economy, this is also one of the most important olive-growing areas in the Veneto. Olive oil can be purchased from producers and presses. The area round Nanto is also renowned for the black truffle of the Berici: although mostly used by restaurants, truffles are sold locally, preserved in olive oil.

BARBARANO VICENTINO. This is the main center for the production of Tocai Rosso, which from now on - as a result of the Hungarian claim to have the exclusive rights to the name of the vine - will be known as Colli Berici Barbarano. For *agriturismo* vacations in style, there is "Il Castello", that is the Villa Godi Marinoni, built on the site of the castle belonging to the bishops of Vicenza in the eighteenth century. The farm here produces refined extra virgin olive oil and Colli Berici DOC wines. Also worth visiting is "L'Ape", a small firm with 1,200 beehives producing 27 different types of honey. Not far away, at "Toara di Villaga", visitors can taste the wines of the Alessandro Piovene Porto Godi estate, where 54 acres of vineyards surround a seventeenth-century villa in one of the areas of the Berici Hills most suited to viticulture. At San Germano dei Berici, the Villa Dal Ferro Lazzarini estate, with a sixteenth-century villa designed by Michele Sanmicheli at its hub, produces the superb Merlot di Campo del Lago

HOTELS AND RESTAURANTS

Grancona
Trattoria Isetta ⑪
at Pederiva
via Pederiva 96
☎ 0444889521

Lonigo
La Peca ⑪⑪
via Princ. Giovanelli 2
☎ 0444830214
Trattoria La Rocca Leonicena ⑨ 🔲
via Rocca 6
☎ 0444832117

Marostica
Rosina ★★★ 🔲
at Valle San Floriano
via Marchetti 4
☎ 0424470360
Al Castello Superiore ⑪
via Cansignorio della Scala 4
☎ 042473315

Montegaldella
Trattoria Cirillo ⑨
via Lampertico 27
☎ 0444636025

Mussolente
Villa Palma 🔲
★★★
La Loggia ⑪ 🔲
via Chemin Palma 30
☎ 0424577407

Roana
All'Amicizia ★
via Roana di Sopra 32
☎ 042466014

Romano d'Ezzelino
Ca' Takea ⑪
via Col Roigo 17
☎ 042433426

Sandrigo
Antica Trattoria Due Spade ⑨ 🔲
via Roma 5
☎ 0444659948

Vicenza.
La Rotonda

NOVENTA VICENTINA. This is the main agricultural center of the Vicenza plain, where the fertile countryside is dotted with large country houses. Important works by Andrea Palladio are the Villa Saraceno at Finale, and the Villa Pojana in the village of the same name. The area is noted for its dishes based on two local vegetables: the radicchio of Asigliano and the golden potato of the Guà.

LONIGO. The Rocca Pisana, standing isolated on a hill, welcomes visitors from afar. Then the road passes in front of the imposing Duomo, built on the site of the Scaliger castle, and beyond a portico lies the small Piazza Garibaldi, with the palazzo of the Venetian Pisani family. This bustling town has a centuries-old agricultural fair and is an important wine-producing center. It is also noted for its hams, especially the Prosciutto Veneto Berico-Euganeo, which has been awarded the DOP classification. The leading *azienda*, Brendolan, also produces the Parma and San Daniele types. Located near the Duomo, "Cestaro" is a major producer of almond cake. In the town center, "La Peca" is an innovative restaurant thanks both to its décor and the cuisine of a young chef who gives a modern touch to regional dishes. For more traditional fare try "Trattoria La Rocca Leonicena", where the specialty is horsemeat, grilled or in a *pastissada* (stew). At Pederiva di Grancona, in the hills on the way back to Vicenza, excellent local dishes are served at the Trattoria Isetta.

2. From Montecchio Maggiore to Schio

MONTECCHIO MAGGIORE. The castles of Romeo and Juliet, romantically paired, and the Villa Cordellina Lombardi, with Tiepolo's frescoes, grace the mouth of the Val d'Agno. This is an area of splendid vineyards: the "Zonin" and "Luigino Dal Maso" wineries are located at Gambellara. Take advantage of a visit to the "Cavazza" winery at Montebello to try the young turkey with pomegranate in the local *trattorie*. At Alte di Montecchio you can buy wine at the "Cantina Sociale dei Colli Vicentini".

ARZIGNANO. Tucked away in the industrial outskirts of this town is an unexpected culinary paradise, "Il Principe", where Andrea Sarni, the talented young chef, prepares such delights as thinly sliced scallops with lettuce and black truffle, and *bigoletti* with cuttlefish and radicchio of Verona with chives. With its varied menu, this restaurant offers very good value.

CHIAMPO. Renowned for its red-veined marble and leather, this small town is of interest to gourmets for its lamb, river trout, *salumi*, and locally grown cherries. In the upper Val Chiampo, Crespadoro is a town specializing in snails. The ancient market of the *corgnoi*, as they are known here, is held in December, but snails are always available in the restaurants. Over the border in the province of Verona, is Bolca, famed for the marine fossil bed of the Pesciara. It is well worth taking the winding road up to nearby Altissimo,

HOTELS AND RESTAURANTS

San Vito di Leguzzano
Due Mori ★★
via Rigobello 41
☎ 0445671635

Schio
All'Antenna
at Magrè
via Raga Alta 4
☎ 0445529812

Trissino
Ca' Masieri
via Masieri 16
☎ 0445962100

Valdagno
Hostaria a le Bele
via Maso 11
☎ 0445970270

AGRITURISMI

Barbarano Vicentino
Il Castello
via Castello 6
☎ 0444886055

WINE PRODUCERS

Vicenza
Enoteca Berealto
contrà Pedemuro S. Biagio 57
☎ 0444322144

Breganze
Franca Maculan
via Castelletto 3
☎ 0445873733

Longare
Conti Alvise e Luigi da Schio
at Costozza
villa Trento Carli
☎ 0444555032

Gambellara
Cantine Zonin
via Borgolecco 9
☎ 0444640111

Luigino Dal Maso
via Selva 62
☎ 0444649104

where we highly recommend "Casin del Gamba" for its pleasant atmosphere and superb cuisine.

VALDAGNO. This old center of the wool industry may be reached directly from Montecchio, or by crossing the hills. Although its development began under Venetian rule, its industry took off in the nineteenth century, when the Marzotto set up the first woolenmills and built a new town for the workers that is still admired today. Gourmets should head for the "Carlotto" distillery, founded in 1919 and famous for its Rosolio (a sweet liqueur). On a nearby hill is the "Hostaria a le Bele", serving delicious homemade pasta and risottos. Also recommended is the *tagliata di puledro* (thinly sliced horse-meat) and fondue with *polenta*. An outstanding restaurant at Trissino is "Ca' Masieri", which also has accommodation. Both traditional and innovative dishes are served, as well as excellent desserts.

RECOARO TERME. The spectacular peaks of the Piccole Dolomiti dominate the valley where this spa town is located. Its mineral water is used to make *chinotto*, an effervescent bitter-orange drink that was invented here. The pastry shops have cakes with strange names: Sorrisi di Recoaro ("Smiles of Recoaro") and Sassi dell'Agno ("Stones of the Agno"). The "Santagiuliana" butcher's shop sells superb local *salumi*. The best *soppressa*, however, is found in the upper Val Leogra, especially at Valli del Pasubio, where it is on sale at the "Salumificio Valpasubio".

SCHIO. The textile factories of Alessandro Rossi, who turned this town into "the little Italian Manchester" in the nineteenth century, now form part of a vast museum of industrial archaeology. Gourmets should try the *salumi*, honey, and a liqueur, Girolimino, from Monte Summano. At Magrè, just outside the town, the "Trattoria All'Antenna" serves a mouth-watering pasta dish, *gargati al consiero*, and superb rabbit and lamb. On the road to Vicenza, at San Vito di Leguzzano, the "Due Mori Hotel" has an excellent restaurant. Finally, at Motta di Costabissara, "Dolciara Loison" produces *pandori*, *panettoni* and biscuits.

Merlot grapes

WINE PRODUCERS

Montebello Vicentino
Cav. D. Cavazza
via Selva 42/a
☎ 0444649166
Sandrigo
Villa Magna
via Repubblica 26
☎ 0444659219
San Germano dei Berici
Villa Dal Ferro Lazzarini
via Chiesa 23
☎ 0444868025
Villaga
A. Piovene Porto Godi
at Toara, via Villa
☎ 0444885142

SHOPPING

Vicenza
Cose Buone
piazza delle Erbe 1
☎ 0444321867
Gastronomia Il Ceppo
corso Palladio 196
☎ 0444544414
Delicatessen.
Pasticceria Bolzani
corso Padova 146
☎ 0444300377
contrà XX Settembre 6
☎ 0444514267
Pastries and sweets.
Pasticceria Sorarù
piazzetta Palladio 17
☎ 0444320915
Pastries and sweets.
Arzignano
Pasticceria Da Venicio
corso Matteotti 41
☎ 0444670163
Pastries and sweets.

Trissino. Villa Trissino

3. On both sides of the Brenta

THIENE. In the town center stands the huge Villa Da Porto Colleoni Thiene, also known as the 'Castello'. While here try the local cake, the *treccia d'oro*, and pay a visit to the "Rizzato" bakery, which uses organic flour to make particularly tasty and long-lasting bread.

BREGANZE. That this was formerly a fortified village on the road to the Asiago Plateau is attested by the numerous towers, now used as dovecots. The local specialty is, in fact, pigeon on the spit. The Breganze DOC wines can be tasted at the "Maculan" winery: its Ferrata vineyard produces outstanding Sauvignon, Chardonnay, and Cabernet, while dessert wines include the celebrated Torcolato and Gran Riserva Acininobili. Restaurants of interest are "Al Toresan", serving local dishes, and "La Cusineta", a friendly *osteria*.

MAROSTICA. This well-preserved medieval town is surrounded by battlemented walls linking its two castles. The legend of the fair Lionora, whose hand was disputed by two rivals, is commemorated every two years by the famous chess match played with living pieces. The cherries grown on the nearby hills are considered to be among the best of the Veneto. In

Marostica. The Castello Superiore

the town center the "Caffè Centrale" serves superb wines and gourmet snacks. Two excellent pastry shops - "Chiurato", on the main street, and "Pigato", to the right of the Castello da Basso - offer other, sweeter delights. There are two recommended restaurants: "Castello Superiore", in a magnificent position, and "La Rosina", amidst the verdant hills.

BASSANO DEL GRAPPA. One of Italy's most attractive provincial towns, it has a long history, to which the churches, the palaces, the famous covered bridge over the Brenta, and the elegant villas in the surrounding countryside all bear witness. But Bassano is also renowned for its grappa. At the end of the Ponte degli Alpini is the "Nardini" distillery, founded in 1779, and nearby, in the Salita Ferracina, there is another distillery, "Poli", with its own grappa museum. The town's gastronomic specialty is asparagus, which is eaten with a simple egg sauce, or else used in various ways, for instance in a risotto. While eating out is generally a pleasure anywhere in Bassano, the "Hotel Belvedere" on Viale delle Fosse has a renowned restaurant and is especially good. Other hotels serving excellent food are

"Al Camin" at Cassola and the "Villa Palma", with "La Loggia" restaurant, at Mussolente. Finally, at Romano d'Ezzelino, "Ca' Takea", one of most innovative restaurants in the province, is highly recommended.

SANDRIGO. This stands on the border between the verdant strip irrigated by springs and the dry plain with soil that is particularly suited to the vine. First, stop at the "Villa Magna" *azienda*. Just outside the village the "Le Vegre" farm produces the Vespaiolo, Pinot Bianco, and Cabernet grapes used to make the firm's best wines. Said to be the birthplace of *baccalà alla vicentina*, Sandrigo is the venue of various gastronomic events featuring this dish. One of the restaurants specializing in this delicacy is the "Antica Trattoria Due Spade". At Bolzano Vicentino, on the road back to Vicenza, we also recommend the family-run "Locanda Grego"a former post-house.

4. The Asiago Plateau

ASIAGO. Totally rebuilt after the destruction of World War I, Asiago is the main town of the plateau of the Sette Comuni, which was colonized in the early Middle Ages by a people of Germanic origin, who left their mark on the local dialect and customs and, naturally, the food. Although tourism has brought prosperity to the area, animal rearing and forestry are still the mainstays of the traditional mountain economy. Dairy products are very important, especially Asiago cheese, which has been awarded the DOP classification. There are two types of Asiago: *pressato*, matured for a short time and mild, and *d'allevo*, which may be *mezzano*, *vecchio*, or *stravecchio*, depending on how long it is matured. More unusual is Morlacco, a cheese with a salty flavor, which is produced on Monte Grappa and owes its name to the fact that the cowherds who settled on the massif centuries ago came from Morlacchia in Dalmatia, and introduced the custom of maturing the cheese in manure. The lush pastures are also a source of excellent honey - it may be purchased at "Guoli", whose premises are at the end of Asiago's main street - and the essences used in the production of liqueurs such as Kumetto and Kranebet. Local dishes are based on game, mushrooms, and dairy products. At Gallio, "La Lepre Bianca" is recommended for its fresh interpretation of the area's old recipes. At Roana, the restaurant "All'Amicizia" serves more traditional fare.

SHOPPING

Pasticceria Pigato
piazza Castello 3
☎ 042472022
Pastries and sweets.
Montecchio
Maggiore
**Cantina Sociale
dei Colli Vicentini**
viale Europa 107
☎ 0444491360
Wines.
Montegalda
**La Capreria di
Grandis Enrico**
via Carbonare 45
☎ 0444634125
**Distilleria F.lli
Brunello**
via G. Roi 27
☎ 0444737253
Distilled drinks.
Mossano
**Azienda Agricola
A. Rigo**
via Olivari 1
☎ 0444886217
Nanto
Azienda Agricola
Arcobaleno
via Brazzolaro
at Monti
☎ 0444730125
Recoaro Terme
**Macelleria
F. Santagiuliana**
via Borromini 21
☎ 0445473787
Meat.
Rosà
Distilleria Capovilla
via Giardini 12
☎ 0424581222
Thiene
**Liquoreria
Carlotto**
via Garibaldi 32
☎ 0445401154
Valli del Pasubio
**Salumificio
Valpasubio**
via Fecchiera 1
☎ 0445590056

WINE AND... WINES
WINE SHOP IN VENICE
AT NUMBER 3301, CASTELLO
FONDAMENTA DEI FURLANI

TEL-FAX 041-5210184

Prestigious national and foreign wines
displayed on sale. Wide choice of
dessert wines and exclusive grappas.

Bed & Breakfast
and independent accommodation
in Venice, Veneto, and....

You will find an accommodation that suits your requirements among
the vast range of B&B or independent flats proposed.
It will bring you a perfect chance to experience the every day life of
the city's residents and the opportunity to gather useful information
and helpful suggestions about the most evocative places and corners
you are going to visit.

VACANZE IN FAMIGLIA

Via Casilina, 4 - 30030 CAMPALTO - VENEZIA (Italia), tel./fax 0039 041 455188 / 0039 041 900385
www.vacanzeinfamiglia.it - e-mail: info@vacanzeinfamiglia.it

Nicolis

The Azienda Nicolis Angelo & Figli is located in S. Pietro in Cariano, in the heart of
the "classic" zone. The art of viticulture is a
richness that the Nicolis family has passed
on for generations with a particular vocation
in the production of valuable wines.

AZIENDA AGRICOLA NICOLIS ANGELO & FIGLI

Via Villa Girardi 29 - 37029 S. Pietro in Cariano (VR) - Tel. e Fax +39 045 7701261 - E-mail: vininicolis@libero.it

---

Typical flavours and aromas of the
Pedemontana del Grappa area

The products made in the foothill area called Pede-
montana del Grappa today are safeguarded and
valued. They deserve to be enjoyed and acclaimed right where
they are produced. This is why we invite you to come and visit
our land, our culture, our traditions, our hospitality and above
all to taste our specialities and discover their flavours and
aromas while staying in a natural environment of rare beauty.

For further information: *Comunità Montana del Grappa*
(Grappa Mountain Community), tel. ++39 0423 53 036

DOLCIARIA A. LOISON S.r.l.
S.S. Pasubio, 6 - 36030 COSTABISSARA (VI) - Italy - Tel. +39 0444 557 844 - Fax +39 0444 557 869
E-mail: loison@loison.com - Web site: www.loison.com

FRIULI-VENEZIA GIULIA BETWEEN TWO WORLDS

This region – particularly Trieste – is where the Po culinary tradition, and the Latin one in general, meet that of Central and Eastern Europe, with its Austrian and Slavic lineage.

A region that has formed its own "Comitato per la Difesa delle Osterie Tradizionali" (committee for the protection of the traditional *osteria*) is particularly enviable: first of all because it still has many of these temples to good food; and secondly, because it means people still take pleasure in a chat over a glass of wine. And, being in the far northeast, a land of industrious people and of few words, this appreciation is in itself a declaration of how these people want to live.

A LAND OF MANY LANDSCAPES

Our journey begins in the Carnia Mountains, in well preserved areas where tradition lives on; places dedicated to animal husbandry and the production of Montasio cheese, which has a thousand-year history and gets its particular flavor from the milk of the local breed of cows, the Friu-

Cividale del Friuli. View from the Diavolo bridge

lian Pezzate Rosse. Then we visit the foothills of the Alps and the hills of the so-called "amphitheater", which curve along the Tagliamento and Isonzo rivers towards the flatlands. These lands have been inhabited for thousands of years and have given rise to the Prosciutto di San Daniele, a cured ham, and the wines that brought great fame to the region, such as the widely-produced Tocai and Merlot and the rare and prized Picolit and Ribolla. Then come the restless and bleak flatlands of the *magredi*, or uncultivated areas, and the immense riverbanks colonized by vineyards and orchards. The landscape changes color in the Bassa (the lowland), which is dotted with springs and green with irrigated fields of corn, rows of poplars and vines. Finally, we come to the sea, with the lagoons of the Adriatic and the rugged Carso plateau.

A MULTIETHNIC CUISINE

There are as many aspects to the gastronomy of Friuli-Venezia Giulia as there are types of landscape. In a way, the division of the region's cuisine echoes that of Trentino-Alto Adige: on the one hand, there is a heritage of dishes derived from the Veneto tradition with little variation, and on the other, a rich infiltration of Hapsburg, Slavic and Oriental flavors through the generous use of spices and a remarkable taste for sweet-and-sour. Gastronomic trademarks for Carnia are the *minestrone d'orzo e fagioli* (barley and bean soup) and *cialzons* (*ravioli* filled with meat and aromatic herbs), as well as *selvaggina* (wild game) and other dishes flavored with transalpine spices. The flatlands are marked by *risotto* enriched with garden vegetables, primarily asparagus. Coastal cuisine is characterized by *brodetto di pesce bianco di Grado* (Grado-style white fish broth), but also Dalmatian-style dishes. In Trieste and Goriziano, we find *iota*, a vegetable soup made of beans, cabbage and potatoes and flavored with cumin, which is common in many other dishes of Austrian origin. Then there is *Gulasch*, a hearty Hungarian stew, and *cevapcici*, a spicy Slavic sausage. But the unifying element is *polenta*, which is eaten with everything from cheese to fish and often used as a substitute for bread at mealtimes. Another common denominator is *muset con la brovada* (a kind of *cotechino* , or boiled sausage, made of various parts of a pig's head) served with *rape* (turnips) pickled in marc.

Cabernet Franc grapes

TWO HALLMARKS FOR A VERY CHARACTERISTIC REGION

Friuli-Venezia Giulia's food and agriculture are characterised by the Montasio DOP cheese and the cured ham Prosciutto di San Daniele DOP. These two products are truly enviable for their quality, fame and tradition. The first comes down from the mountains, from Carnia, the zone most representative of the region's gastronomic tradition. The second was born in the hills in the midst of the vineyards – another important economic resource and hallmark of the region. Other traditional products emerge in their wake, including cured meats and cheeses that used to be all but extinct, and others that have already found commercial success, such as the celebrated *grappa* (eau de vie).

Friuli-Venezia Giulia - Typical products

AUSTRIA

P.so di
M. Croce Carnico
1360

Scale 1:1 000 000

0   15   30 km

Pontebba

Tarvisio

Kranjska
Gora

Pieve
di Cadore

Forni
di Sopra

Tolmezzo

A23

Tagliamento

SLOVENIA

Tolmin

Gemona
d. Friuli

T. Cellina

Maniago

T. Meduna

S. Daniele
d. Friuli

Cividale
del Friuli

Belluno

Udine

Natisone

Isonzo

Gorizia

Vittorio
Veneto

Pordenone

A23

Cormons

Palmanova

A28

A4

Conegliano

A27

Latisana

Aquileia

Monfalcone

VENETO

Treviso

Grado

TRIESTE

Golfo di
Trieste

Piran

Koper

Mestre

VENEZIA

MAR ADRIATICO

Rovinj

Chioggia

CHEESES

1. **Montasio Dop.** Cheese of long-standing tradition produced throughout the region.

2. **Formaggio salato della Carnia.** Salty cheese found in alpine areas but also in Spilimbergo.

3. **Formaggio Tabor.** Produced primarily in Monrupino.

CHARCUTERIE

1. **Prosciutto di San Daniele Dop.** A cured ham.

2. **Prosciutto di Sauris.** A cured smoked ham.

3. **Prosciutto di Cormons.** Produced in the area bordering Slovenia.

4. **Peta della Val Cellina**

FISH

1. **Trota salmonata.** Salmon trout found in Pordenone and San Daniele del Friuli.

VEGETABLES

1. **Fagioli della Carnia.** Carnia beans found in the Chiarsò and Meduna valleys.

VARIOUS

1. **Grappa.** Spirit found throughout the region.

BREAD AND SWEETS

1. **Gubana.** Pastries with chocolates and nuts - specialty of Gorizia.

2. **Presnitz.** Sweet with nuts and raisins from the Natisone valleys.

DOC WINES

1. **Carso**
2. **Colli Orientali del Friuli**
3. **Collio Goriziano**
4. **Friuli Annia**
5. **Friuli Aquileia**
6. **Friuli Grave**
7. **Friuli Isonzo**
8. **Friuli Latisana**
9. **Lison Pramaggiore**

TRIESTE

The maritime region once under the rule of the Hapsburg dynasty became an important crossroads for a variety of cultures.

The province of Trieste is an unusual territory, defined on its coastal border by the Carso Plateau following post-war cessions. Yet it is steeped in ethnic and historical references because of its role as an administrative center during times that were momentous, not just for Italy, but for the whole European continent. The region's bare and chalky landscape has limited its agricultural production to the DOC Carso wines. These wines have been developed from indigenous white grapes such as Malvasia Istriana, Terrano and Vitouska. As for cuisine, Triestine gastronomy has Austrian, Hungarian, Jewish, Slavic and Oriental roots. While certain dishes are common to the entire region, in the city a variety of dishes dis-

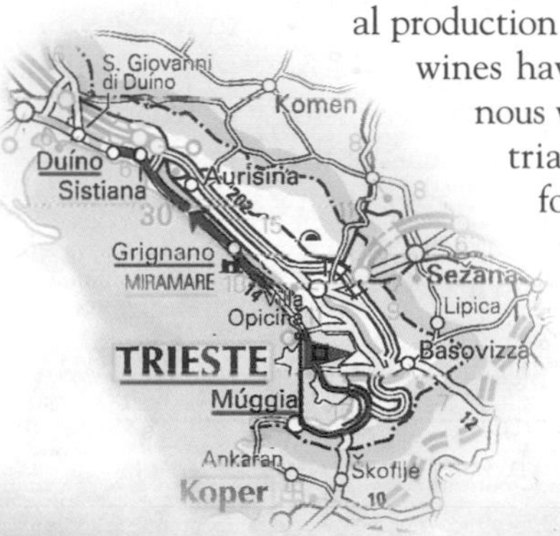

The bay of Sistiana

205

tinguish themselves by their broad and varied use of herbs and spices and a remarkable integration of sweet-and-sour flavors. The network of restaurants is exceptional, particularly in the regional capital. There is a good list of places to eat that are often a hundred years old, ranging from buffets to beerhouses in the port areas, and refined restaurants in government centers to *trattorie* just inland, where countryside and seaside flavors mingle with Po, Central European and Balkan traditions.

Gourmet Tours

HOTELS AND RESTAURANTS

Trieste
G.H. Duchi d'Aosta ★★★
piazza Unità d'Italia 2
☎ 0407600011
Antica Trattoria Suban ¶¶¶
via Cornici 2
☎ 04054368
Ai Fiori ¶¶
piazza Hortis 2
☎ 040300633
Bagatto ¶¶
via F. Venezian 2
☎ 040301771
★🍽 **Città di Cherso** ¶¶
via Cadorna 6
☎ 040366044
Harry's Grill ¶¶
piazza Unità d'Italia 2
☎ 040365646
Rondinelle ¶¶
via Orsera 17
☎ 040820053
Scabar ¶¶
erta di S. Anna 63
☎ 040810368
Birreria Forst ¶
via Galatti 11
☎ 040365276
Buffet da Pepi ¶
via Cassa di Risparmio 3
☎ 040366858
Buffet da Siora Rosa ¶
piazza Hortis 3
☎ 040301460
Spaten - Buffet Masè ¶
via Valdirivo 32
☎ 040639428
Trieste Pick ¶
via Pozzo del Mare 1
☎ 040307997

TRIESTE. The city of Italo Svevo and Umberto Saba is interesting for many reasons: the old town with the nineteenth-century Piazza dell'Unità d'Italia, the Romanesque church of San Giusto, and the view from the castle; the modern city, with the the typically Hapsburgian Maria Theresa neighborhood, the Grand Canal and the promenade along Corso Italia; and the port and the Rive, long quays overlooked by the dignified architecture of maritime companies. The city is a concentration of historic memories in gastronomic terms as well. Period cafes and pastry shops all have a story to tell, whether it be of literary or political turmoil. "Pirona", in Largo Barriera Vecchia, was frequented by James Joyce and is known for its excellent *cioccolata*,

Gubana

Vineyards in Carso

a rich hot chocolate. The winged lion at the Art Nouveau-furnished "San Marco" in Via Battisti has seen the passage of generations of Irredentists, plotting to reclaim all Italy's former territory. "Degli Specchi" is in the elegant heart of the city; "Tommaseo", in Riva Tre Novembre, is noted for its stuccoes and marble and cast-iron tables, while "Torinese", at the beginning of Corso Italia, displays intricate wood paneling. "Antica Trattoria Suban", one of the city's best restaurants, is also of historic renown. It was founded in 1865 and is still run by the same family. The table here is laden with all the classics of Triestine cuisine, from the bread and cheese *Knödeln* to the *Gulaschuppe* and *stinco di vitello* (veal shank). Also excellent, and providing a very warm welcome, is the elegant *trattoria* "Ai Fiori", with its offering of masterfully crafted seafood dishes both in classic style, for instance *sardoni in savor all'antica* (old-fashioned marinated anchovies), or in the form of new creations such as *filetti di branwino ai funghi e tartufi* (sea bass filets with mushrooms and truffles). As for where to stay, the "Grand Hotel Duchi d'Aosta", with its refined "Harry's Grill", deserves special mention. Up the hill, we also strongly recommend "Scabar", which serves inland and coastal dishes accompanied by a good wine list. Beer-houses such as "Forst" and "Spaten" offer a more relaxed Central European atmosphere, as do "buffets" – for instance "Pepi" in the heart of Trieste's business center and "Siora Rosa" behind the Rive - where you can eat *Luganeghe de Viena* (Vienna Sausages) and *carni bolliti* (boiled meat), as well as hearty soups and *Gulasch* at almost any time of day. You can also find a variety of interesting foods in the shops: from the well-known *cevapcici*, the slightly spicy Yugoslavian pork, beef and lamb sausages mentioned earlier, to *liptauer*, a Hungarian cheese mousse made spicy and red with the addition of paprika and mustard. The pastry shops,

Trieste. The Canal Grande

including the aforementioned "Pirona", offer all the sweets that are typical of Carso: *presnitz, putizza* and *pinza* - all full of goodies such as nuts and raisins. The small and elegant "La Bomboniera" is also worth a visit. As for wine, stop by the "Gran Bar Malabar", a very pleasant place with an extraordinary choice of wines *a mescita* (by the glass). If you want to

HOTELS AND RESTAURANTS

Duino-Aurisina
Alla Dama Bianca ¶¶
at Duino 61/c
☎ 040208470
Sardoc ¶
at Slivia 5
☎ 040200225
Grignano
Riviera & Maximilian's ★★★
strada Costiera 22
☎ 040224551
Monrupino
Furlan ¶¶
at Zolla
☎ 040327125
Muggia
★ 🏨 **Lido** ¶¶
via C. Battisti 22
☎ 040273338
Trattoria Risorta ¶¶
riva De Amicis 1/a
☎ 040271219

SHOPPING

Trieste
La Bomboniera
via XXX Ottobre 3
☎ 040632752
Cafe and pastry shop.
Caffè Degli Specchi
piazza dell'Unità
d'Italia 7
☎ 040365777
Cafe and pastry shop.
Caffè San Marco
via C. Battisti 18
☎ 040363538
Cafe and pastry shop.
Caffè Tommaseo
riva III Novembre 5
☎ 040366765
Cafe and pastry shop.
Gran Bar Malabar
piazza S. Giovanni 6
☎ 040636226
Cafe and pastry shop.
Caffè Pirona
Barriera Vecchia 12
☎ 040636046
Pasticceria
Torinese
corso Italia 2
☎ 040632689
Pastries and sweets.
Salumi Sfreddo
via Giarrizzole 37
☎ 040817357
Charcuterie.
Muggia
Pasticceria
Triestina Ulcigrai
at Noghere
via Petronio 1/a
☎ 040232335
Pastries and sweets.

explore the Carso don't miss the climb to Monrupino, where they make an excellent traditional *prosciutto*: it may be tasted on its own or in a crust of bread at "Furlan", which also serves other typical Carso dishes. Here you can also find some of the first *osmizze*, or seasonal restaurants, set up by farmers to sell the excess wine and other produce and authorized by an imperial decree in 1784.

MUGGIA. Across from Trieste, surrounded by ancient walls, this Istrian village has preserved a *piazza* that is in the perfect image of Venice, reflecting the village's long loyalty to the city they call La Serenissima. The established "Trattoria Risorta", where Venetian seafood cuisine meets Slavic cuisine with excellent results, is recommended locally. We also like the hotel "Lido" and its restaurant, which is a Buon Ricordo listing. The specialty dish here is *ravioli di mare con scampi alla busara* (seafood *ravioli* with prawns cooked in their shells). Nearby, sweets from the Venezia Giulia region such as *putizza, presnitz, pinza, favette* and marzipan may be purchased at the "Pasticceria Triestina Ulcigrai" factory outlet.

GRIGNANO. The Miramare Castle – the breathtaking final European residence of Maximilian of Austria – monopolizes the visitor's time with its great park that rises to Carso, and the maritime reserve just opposite. A little beyond it is Grignano, where there is a touristic harbor and seaside resort. Here, "Riviera & Maximilian's" is a fine hotel with a panoramic view of the area and good restaurant, "Le Terrazze".

DUINO. Just beyond Sistiana, a village surrounded by the tipical Carso woods, lies Duino, an ancient fishing village and one of the most striking places on the upper Adriatic. Here the Castello Vecchio, a ruin on a cliff, tells the tale of one Dama Bianca, an unhappy bride turned to stone, while the Castello Nuovo, with a powerful fourteenth-century tower and wall, celebrates the fortune of the Turn und Taxis family. Then, high above the coastline, is a footpath dedicated to the poet Rainer Maria Rilke, who was inspired by its beauty spots to write his celebrated *Duineser Elegien* (Duino Elegies). The cuisine here is primarily Triestine. Fish is exceptionally plentiful and there are also particularly good products from inland, such as salamis and *prosciutto*. On the waterfront you can find the restaurant "Alla Dama Bianca" where only fish is served, and it is also possible to stay. Inland in Slivia, "Sardoc", a family-run *osteria,* offers very typical Carsoline cooking.

GORIZIA

From Collio to the Grado lagoon
lies a gastronomic route spiked with
unusual flavors and excellent wines.

Although broken up during post-war territorial redistributions, the province of Gorizia retains a richness of landscape - encompassing the hills of Collio, which are part of the Giulie foothills, the wet flatlands of lower Isonzo and the Grado lagoon - which adds interest to the coastline. The agricultural production of the region is therefore varied, and is particularly noteworthy for the DOC Collio wines, which are produced from Gorizia to the border with Slovenia, and the Isonzo wines, which are shared with Udine. The Collio wines include excellent whites: Pinot, Tocai Friuliano, Sauvignon, and the native Ribolla Gialla and Picolit grapes, which are used to make unblended wines. Among the red Isonzo wines, Merlot is the undisputed leader, followed by indigenous wines such as the Refosco dal Peduncolo Rosso and Franconia. The region's fruits and vegetables complement the wine production with renowned produce such as Dolegna cherries and Sant'Andrea asparagus, as well as the *topinambur*, a tuber indigenous to the region. Animal farming is also significant, and provides good traditional cheeses and salamis. As in Trieste, the gastronomy here clearly reflects the simultaneous presence of different ethnic groups: in the risotto made with fresh garden vegetables and in

San Floriano
del Collio

HOTELS AND RESTAURANTS

Gorizia
Nanut ★★★
via Trieste 118
☎ 048120595
Alla Luna ❢
via Oberdan 13
☎ 0481530374
Ca' di Pieri ❢
via Codelli 5
☎ 0481533308
Da Sandra ❢
piazza De Amicis 7
☎ 048131644
Vito Primozic ❢
viale XX Settembre 138
☎ 048182117
Cormons
Cacciatore della Subida ❢❢❢
at Monte 22
☎ 048160531
Giardinetto ❢❢❢
via Matteotti 54
☎ 048160257
Gradisca d'Isonzo
Franz ★★★
viale Trieste 45
☎ 048199211
Il Melograno ❢❢
viale Trieste 47
☎ 048192882
Al Ponte ❢❢
viale Trieste 122
☎ 048199213
Grado
All'Androna ❢❢
calle Porta Piccola 4
☎ 043180950
De Toni ❢
piazza Duca d'Aosta 37
☎ 043180104
Mariano del Friuli
Le Dune ❢❢
via Dante 41
☎ 048169021
Monfalcone
Ai Campi di Marcello ❢❢
via Napoli 7
☎ 0481481937
Ai Castellieri ❢❢
via dei Castellieri 7
☎ 0481475272
San Floriano del Collio
Castello Formentini
piazza Libertà 3 ❢❢
☎ 0481884034
Savogna d'Isonzo
Gostilna Devetak ❢❢
at San Michele del Carso (km 4)
☎ 0481882005

the *minestra d'orzo e fagioli* (barley and bean soup) we find the Venetian spirit; the *gnocchi di patate alle prugne* (potato *gnocchi* with dried prunes) and the *Gulasch* are of Austro-Hungarian heritage; the cuisine along the shoreline and in Carso reflect exchanges with Dalmatia. The restaurants are excellent in the innately elegant city, and they are at their best in Cormons, Collio's capital. Otherwise, there are family *trattorie* in the hills and the countryside, with more fashionable eateries located in the tourist town of Grado.

Gourmet Tours

GORIZIA. The city's castle and the ramparts on the hilltop are over a thousand years old. Below is the great *piazza* named for the Victory of the Great War (Vittoria della Grande Guerra or World War I). The quest for fine cooking may begin with the customary *merenda da piron* (a snack eaten with a fork), which may be tripe, *Gulasch*, or something else accompanied by a glass of wine. The traditional epicenter is the market area: "Ca' di Pieri" is a *trattoria* worth inspecting, as are "Da Sandra" and "Vito Primozic". The nineteenth-century *osteria* "Alla Luna" serves hot and cold *stuzzichini*, or snacks, *risotto, minestrone*, and *gnocchi*, followed by *Gulasch*, or *baccalà*; when the season is right, try *frittatine alle erbe* (omelets with wild greens) and *funghi in umido con polenta* (*polenta* with mushroom sauce). Stay over at the small hotel "Nanut", which is simple and has a good restaurant with pure Gorizian cooking. For shopping, the covered market in Via Boccaccio and "Jerman" are good for cheeses and Friulian charcuterie, as well as mushrooms. If you go up to San Floriano del Collio, you will find Castello Formentini, a village with a wine producer,

wine museum, and an *agriturismo* tourist complex with an upscale hotel and restaurant.

CORMONS. Built on pre-Roman foundations, Cormons preserves a part of its medieval walls and seventeenth/eighteenth-century buildings, including the Duomo of Sant'Alberto. It is known as one of Collio's important towns and the main market for local wines. The "Enoteca di Cormons", located in a wing of Palazzo Locatelli, provides an excellent introduction to food with its light menus. "Cantina Sociale" is also a good choice; this is where *Vino della Pace* (wine of peace) originated and is bottled each year with artistic labels and sent with good wishes to important figures around the world. The restaurant "Giardinetto" boasts excellent Friulian and Slovenian cooking by the Zoppolatti twins. At the same establishment there are also rooms as well as the "Giardinetto Café", where you can taste pastries and wines from Collio. The "Cacciatore della Subida" has a fairytale atmosphere, refined and modernized *piatti poveri* (peasant meals) ranging from *pasta al sugo di cacciagione* (pasta with wild game sauce), *coscia di capriolo con mandorle e scaglione* (leg of roe deer with almonds and shallots), and excellent wines by the glass. At Capriva del Friuli, a few wine cellars belong to the *Movimento Turismo del Vino* (Wine Tourism Movement): *Schiopetto, Russiz Superiore* and *Villa Russiz*. Local products include smoked hams and charcuterie from the producer "D'Osvaldo".

GRADISCA D'ISONZO. This village originated as a Venetian bulwark against the Turks and took on its present appearance during the three centuries of Hapsburg rule. Beautiful architecture lies within the city walls and includes the Palazzo dei Provveditori Veneti (The Venetian Purveyor's Palace). The "Enoteca Regionale La Serenissima" (The Venice Regional Winery) is based here. We strongly recomment the hotel "Franz" and its creative restaurant "Il Melograno", while "Al Ponte" has good traditional fare. Sticking to the traditional, in San Michele del Carso there is the *trattoria-gostilna* "Devetek" where you can find *orzotto con verdure e ricotta affiumicata* (barley with greens and smoked ricotta), *tagliatelle con salsa di capriolo* (*tagliatelle* with roe deer sauce), *stinco di maiale con crauti*,

fagioli e patate (pork shank with sauerkraut, beans and potatoes), and *strudel di noci e uvetta al profumo di finocchio e cento distillati* (walnut and grape strudel flavored with fennel and herbal spirits).

GRADO. The road to Redipuglia passes through Monfalcone, a city of naval dockyards on the Gulf of Panzano. The seafood restaurant "Ai Campi di Marcello" is a worthwhile stop here. The route continues between the sea and the lagoon towards Grado, whose historic center, where the Early Christian Basilica of Sant'Eufemia stands, dates back to the founding of the city by the fugitives from Aquileia. The local culinary tradition is noted for its seafood dishes starting with the famous *brodetto alle delicate seppioline ripiene di granseola* (fish soup with small cuttlefish stuffed with crab). "All'Androna" is a fine gastronomic stop, and here you will find *capelunghe in boreto* (razor clams in broth), *sampietro in gremolata* (John Dory with chopped parsley, lemon and garlic), and *cacciagione* (wild game). Another well-known place is "De Toni", a low-key *trattoria* with a creative vein.

AGRITURISMI

Cormons
Kitzmüller Thomas
at Brazzano
via XXIV Maggio 56
☎ 048160853
Dolegna del Collio
Venica & Venica
via Mernico 42
☎ 048161264

WINE PRODUCERS

Capriva del Friuli
Schiopetto
via Pal. Arcivescovile 1
☎ 048180332
Russiz Superiore
at Russiz Superiore
☎ 048180328
Villa Russiz
via Russiz 6
☎ 048180047
Cormons
C. Produttori
Cormons
via Vino della Pace 31
☎ 048160579

SHOPPING

Gorizia
Pasticceria Bisiach
via Mazzini 15
☎ 0481530300
Pastries and sweets.
Jerman Salumi
e Formaggi
corso Verdi 32
☎ 0481534223
Cheeses and charcuterie.
Cormons
D'Osvaldo Salumi
via Dante 40
☎ 048161644
Charcuterie.
Giardinetto Café
via Matteotti 54
☎ 048160257
Cafe and pastry shop.
Iacuz Salumi
via Matteotti 39
☎ 048160312
Charcuterie.
Panificio Simonit
via Matteotti 88
☎ 048160216
Bakery.
Dolegna del Collio
Mulino Tuzzi
at Ruttars
☎ 048160546
Organic flours.

Monfalcone. Berthing in the Panzano gulf

PORDENONE

The transition from the banks of the Livenza to those of the Tagliamento marks the cultural and gastronomic change from the Veneto to Friuli.

The province of Pordenone is in the western part of Friuli and reaches from the Carnic foothills and the Cellina and Meduna valleys to the stretch of flatlands between the Livenza and the Tagliamento rivers. Cattle-breeding and the dairy industry make an important contribution to the economy in the mountains, while the valley, which is dry in the upper reaches and rich with spring water in the lower areas, hosts orchards and vineyards where the terrain is peppered with rocks, and fodder and corn in the coastal areas. The cuisine in Friuli's youngest province is derived from that of nearby Udine, where the only distinctive elements come from the omnipresent Venetian dishes in border towns. This can be seen in the prevalence of rice and *polenta* over pasta, the tendency to use the meat of farmyard stock, and the abundance of vegetables. Restaurants are at their best in the capital and its immediate surroundings and give way to very pleasant *osterie* and *trattorie* in smaller towns.

Gourmet Tours

PORDENONE. Corso Vittorio Emanuele is the main axis in the historic center and is lined with *palazzi* and churches that were built by the Venetian Republic when the city - then called *Portus Naonis*, or Port on the Naone, now called Noncello - traded by means of inland waterways connected to the lagoons on the Adriatic. Two excellent restaurants can be found at the "Palace Hotel Moderno" and "Villa Ottoboni". Still very good, and situated in historic buildings, are "Da Zelina" in Piazza San Marco in the town center and "Vecia Osteria del Moro" just a stone's throw away from the town hall. On the Corso, or main avenue, the cafe "Municipio" occupies a fine location. For gastronomic souvenirs, it is worth visiting "Al Tajer" in Via Grigioletti, and "San Marco" in Piazza San Marco. Many cheeses are also available: *Formella del Friuli*, a soft, pungent, sweet cheese made with slightly soured whole milk; *Frico Balacia*, typical of Borgo Meduna and Val Cellina, which is good for pan-frying or cooking on a griddle; *Pezzata Rossa*, an aged whole milk mountain cheese with a bite to it; and *Cit*, from a village of the same name in the Val Tramontina, which is a creamy cheese originally made from cheeses that did not mold properly but is now produced ad hoc in small quantities. In the surrounding area there are excellent places for tasting wine and culinary specialties. San Quirino lies on the route to Maniago, and its "La Primula Antica Trattoria" is very good. Here, a young chef skillfully prepares Friulian specialties with a skill that belies his age and appearance. Next to the hotel-restaurant is the *osteria* "Alle Nazioni", which has a more moderately-priced menu.

Pordenone. The S. Floriano park

HOTELS AND RESTAURANTS

Pordenone
Palace Hotel Moderno ★★★ ⬛
viale Martelli 1
☎ 043428215
Villa Ottoboni ★★★
piazzetta Ottoboni 2
☎ 043421967
Da Zelina ⅋⅋ ⬛
piazza S. Marco 13
☎ 043427290
Vecia Osteria del Moro ⅋
via Castello 2
☎ 043428658
Fiume Veneto
L'Ultimo Mulino ★★★
at Bannia (km 7)
via Molino 45
☎ 0434957911
Maniago
Vecchia Maniago ⅋
☎ 0427730583
Pasiano di Pordenone
Villa Luppis ★★★ ⬛
at Rivarotta (km 5)
via S. Martino 34
☎ 0434626969
Polcenigo
Cial de Brent ⅋⅋⅋
via Pordenone 3
☎ 0434748777
Sacile
Pedrocchino ⅋⅋⅋ ⬛
piazza IV Novembre 4
☎ 043470034

**HOTELS AND
RESTAURANTS**

San Quirino
⭐🍴 **La Primula**
Antica Trattoria 🍴🍴🍴
via S. Rocco 47
☎ 043491005
Alle Nazioni 🍴
via S. Rocco 49
☎ 043491005
San Vito al
Tagliamento
⭐🍴 **Griglia
d'Oro** 🍴🍴
at Rosa (km 2)
via della Dogna 2
☎ 043480301
Al Colombo 🍴
via Roma 4
☎ 043480176
Sesto al Reghena
Abate Ermanno 🍴🍴
piazza Aquileia 15
☎ 0434694950
Spilimbergo
La Torre 🍴🍴
piazza Castello
☎ 042750555
Osteria da Afro 🍴🍴
via Umberto I 14
☎ 04272264
Al Bachero 🍴
via Pilacorte 5
☎ 04272317
Valvasone
Alla Scala 🍴🍴
via C. Battisti 7
☎ 0434899366

AGRITURISMI

Morsano al
Tagliamento
La Privade
via dei Prati 3
☎ 0434697186
Vivaro
⭐🍴 **Gelindo
dei Magredi**
via Roma 16
☎ 042797037

Cordenons is renowned for the local production of smoked trout fillets. In Pasiano di Pordenone to the south, we recommend the hotel "Villa Lupis" - a former medieval convent surrounded by the foliage of a large park - and its prestigious restaurant. Equally good is Fiume Veneto's elegant and refined "L'Ultimo Mulino", a hotel that occupies a seventeenth-century mill and appears to be straight out of a period painting with its delightful little lake and functioning hydraulic machinery. In Prata di Pordenone, in the midst of the DOC "Grave" vineyards, is the wine producer "Vignetti Le Monde", with its aura of a time gone by combined with an avant-garde production highlighted by the "taglio bordolese Querceto" (a Bordeaux style wine produced by blending Merlot and Cabernet wines, and aged in oak barrrels).

1. The Grave

SPILIMBERGO. From the capital, the *Statale* 13 runs from Friuli to Casarsa della Delizia, a well-known wine making center. Here one turns north toward Tagliamento and soon arrives at Valvasone, a charming town with colonnaded streets and a Castello. We highly recommend the restaurant "Alla Scala" for its pleasant cooking with original dishes and a well-stocked wine cellar (rooms are also available for the night). Back on the road, the next stop is Spilimbergo, which overlooks the scenery of Le Grave, where vineyards and orchards alternate with the uncultivated areas known locally as *magredi*. The Duomo is a beautiful Gothic building and the Castello presents a frescoed façade onto its courtyard. In a wing of the manor is a good restaurant called "La Torre" with two rooms and a wine cellar offering a discerning selection from small vineyards. The village *osterie* "Afro" and "Al Bachero" are worth mentioning for their pleasant atmosphere and good dishes at fair prices. Fine cheese, wine, honey and delicious preserved green asparagus from Le Grave may be purchased at the "Cooperativa Tre Valli".

Pordenone. The S. Giorgio bell-tower

MANIAGO. Famous for its ancient knife-making industry, this town is a point of reference for an excursion to the Prealpi Carniche - Meduno and, further on, Clauzetto, for example - where there is an abundance of pleasant places to stop. The *osteria* "Vecchia Maniago" deserves mention with its *orzotto ai porcini* (barley with mushrooms) and *bollito affumicato* (boiled smoked meat) both of which are fine examples of the fare available.

SACILE. Just beyond Aviano, where there is a military airbase, you can make a stopover at Polcenigo to visit the restaurant "Cial de Brent" where a wood interior makes it cozy in winter, and meals are served outside in the summer. The kitchen serves a broad range of foods from *agnolotti ripieni di branzino con capesante* (*ravioli* filled with sea bass and scallops) and *fasolari alle pernici in casseruola* (clam and partridge casserole). The route opens onto the flatlands at Sacile - a city alive with activity and the arts since the Renaissance, and with colonnaded streets and Venetian-style palazzi crowding along the Livenza river. In the town center, the "Pedrocchino" is ranked by many critics as being among the best Friulian restaurants. The fish here is of the utmost freshness throughout the year and the menu is varied with *funghi* (mushrooms) and *tartufi* (truffles) when they are in season. Also in the area, the wine producer "Vistorta-Conti Brandolini d'Adda", known for the great Merlot from the farms surrounding the villa, should not be missed.

2. The Pianura

SAN VITO AL TAGLIAMENTO. The walls and gate of this farming town recall its intense history,

and the best culinary examples can be found at the "Griglia d'Oro", a rustic and simple place which has been run for five generations by the Benvenuto family. For those who prefer *osterie*, "Al Colombo" is good value.

SESTO AL REGHENa. Going through Cordovado, with its tiny old town enclosed by two turreted gates, you arrive at Sesto al Reghena, a farming center that grew up around the Benedictine Abbey of Santa Maria in Silvis. Once a fortified complex, all that remains now is the imposing Romanesque-Byzantine basilica. The hotel-restaurant "Abate Ermanno" – the name of which is inspired by the abbey's history – provides fine regional cooking. In the area, at Morsano al Tagliamento, the *agriturismo* establishment "La Privade" is reviving Friuli's gastronomic pride: the breeding of geese and their use in cooking.

Spilimbergo.
The "Palazzo dipinto"

WINE PRODUCERS

Prata di
Pordenone
Vigneti Le Monde
at Le Monde
via Garibaldi 2
☎ 0434626096
Sacile
Vistorta - Conti Brandolini d'Adda
at Vistorta
☎ 043471135

SHOPPING

Pordenone
Gastronomia Al Tajer
viale Grigoletti 30
☎ 043433005
Delicatessen.
Gastronomia San Marco
piazza S. Marco 15/a
☎ 043428376
Delicatessen.
Panifici Tomadini
corso Garibaldi 18
corso V. Emanuele 45
☎ 0434520606
Pastries and a vast range of bread varieties.
Claut
Macelleria Giordani
via E. Toti 15
☎ 0427878012
Meat and charcuterie.
Fiume Veneto
Caseificio Val Sile
at Bannia
via Manzoni 88
☎ 0434957853
Local cheeses.
Spilimbergo
Cooperativa Tre Valli
via Barbacane 10
☎ 042741387
Wines, cheeses, honey.

UDINE

A region and a culinary tradition that reaches from the mountains to the sea, and borrows traditions and flavors from across the border.

The province of Udine sweeps from the watershed of the Carniche and Giulie Alps, which marks the border with Austria and Slovenia, to the lagoons of the Adriatic. The mountainous area includes the upper basin of the Tagliamento, the designated zone for breeding the local breed of cattle *Pezzata Rossa*, and producing excellent cheeses in the DOP region of Montasio. A broad range of hills dotted

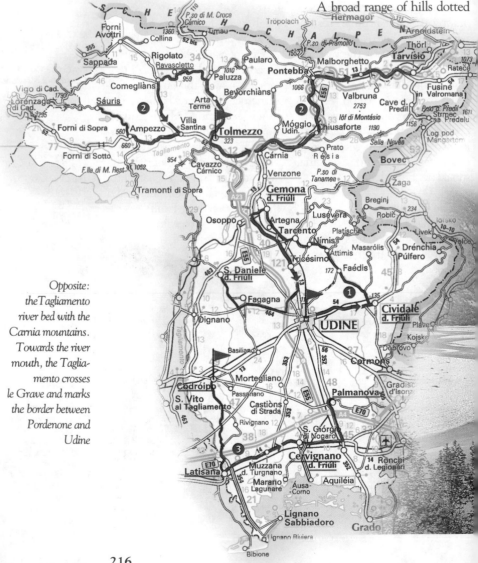

*Opposite:
the Tagliamento
river bed with the
Carnia mountains.
Towards the river
mouth, the Taglia-
mento crosses
le Grave and marks
the border between
Pordenone and
Udine*

with villages and castles sets the next scene. It would be a pity not to mention San Daniele del Friuli, the home of the cured ham Prosciutto di San Daniele DOP, and Cividale, the wine center for the DOC Colli Orientali , which include great whites, with Tocai Friuliano and the rare Picolit at the top of the list. The upland plain is a barren area of *magredi* (uncultivated areas), permeable and dry land that has been successfully converted into orchards and vineyards. Among the DOC Friuli Grave and, on the eastern side, the DOC Isonzo wines, whites prevail with Tocai Friuliano, Pinot Grigio, Chardonnay, and Pinot Bianco. The lowland plain has spring water, and irrigated cultivation is widespread. Vineyards are also common here; going from west to east along the coast, three DOC vineyards follow one another: Latisana, Annia and Aquileia, which boast red wines such as Merlot, Cabernet and Refosco dal Peduncolo Rosso. As for culinary tradition, rice is the common denominator and is prepared both *asciutto* (dry) and *in brodo* (in broth). *Polenta* is also commonplace, while pasta appears in *cialzons* which are a variation on *ravioli*. Main dishes range from meat and wild game in the mountains, often prepared with mushrooms, to fish in coastal areas. In the alpine regions, there is a significant influence from the culinary traditions of ethnic minorities of Germanic and Slavic descent. In terms of restaurants, although there is no shortage of finer places, the *osterie* and *trattorie* are good and are better represented in the hills and mountain regions than on the Adriatic.

HOTELS AND RESTAURANTS

Udine
Agli Amici ¶¶¶
at Godia (km 5)
via Liguria 250
☎ 0432256411
Là di Moret ★🏨
★★★ ¶¶¶
viale Tricesimo 276
☎ 0432545096
Ai Vecchi Parrocchiani ¶
via Aquileia 66
☎ 0432504506
Al Cappello ¶
via Sarpi 5
☎ 0432299327
Lepre ¶
via Poscolle 27
☎ 0432295798
Speziaria pei Sani ¶
via Poscolle 13
☎ 0432505061
Aquileia
Patriarchi ★★★🏨
Fonzari ¶¶
via Giulia Augusta 12
☎ 0431919595
Arta Terme
Salon ¶¶
at Piano d'Arta (km 2)
via Peresson 70
☎ 043392587
Cervignano del Friuli
🏨 **Internazionale**
★★★ **La Rotonda** ¶¶
at La Rotonda
via Ramazzotti 2
☎ 043130751
Cividale del Friuli
Locanda al Castello ★★★
via del Castello 20
☎ 0432733242
Al Monastero ¶¶¶
via Ristori 11
☎ 0432700808

Gourmet Tours

UDINE. Halfway between Venice and the Alpine passes lies Udine, which became Friuli's historic center when a thirteenth-century patriarch chose it over Cividale. The city, located at the bottom of the Castello hills, has an unusual *piazza* where Gothic and Renaissance elements blend

217

together with the masterly touches of Palladio and Tiepolo at the nearby Archbishop's Palace. Here we recommend the hotel-restaurant "Là di Moret" that was already an *osteria* in the early twentieth century. Is is now run by the fourth generation of the Marini family. Cooking is traditional with excellent risotto and *fiocco di manzo alla friuliana* (Friulian-style beef) as the dish recommended by Buon Ricordo. We also suggest "Agli Amici", which dates from 1887 and is located five kilometers out of town in the countryside at Godia. Here, too, the flavors are of local origin, and the culinary style moves freely between seafood and meat. The *tajut* is the local aperitif ritual that consists of a glass of Tocai served with *bocconcini di polenta* (pieces of *polenta*) and *muset* (a spicy salami) as well as other tasty morsels. We suggest you try this at "Speziaria pei Sani", "Ai Vecchi Parrocchiani", "Al Cappello" or "Lepre", where one may also take a seat and follow the *tajut* with soups, *risotto* and meats. "La Baita dei Formaggi" and "Troiano-Ven-

Udine. The Loggia del Lionello

turini" are good places to shop for cheeses and charcuterie from the entire region. Recommended cheeses are Montasio DOP, the widely produced Latteria e Malga, *ricotta* and sheep's and goat's milk cheeses from Carnia. Charcuterie include Prosciutto di San Daniele DOP, the cured smoked ham Prosciutto affumicato di Sauris, *salsicce di fegato* (liver sausage) and the popular, afore-mentioned, *muset*. The seasonal *Mercato dei funghi* (mushroom market) takes place in Piazza XX Settembre. "La Casa degli Spiriti" has a fine list of wines and spirits, while the historic "Farmacia Colutta" sells *Amaro di Udine*, a herbal digestive drink. In Tavagnacco, along the route to Gemona, "Grop" is a *trattoria* serving excellent soups and grilled meats accented by seasonal specialties such as asparagus, mushrooms and game. Along the Bassa Friulana *Statale* you can find "Blasut" in Mortegliano, where home cooking reflects the best of the market's products. At the wine-producer "Fratelli Pighin", in nearby Risano, you can taste excellent full-bodied red wines and whites from Collio, and guest rooms are available for the night. In Buttrio, along the Statale leading to Gorizia, the winery "Girolamo Dorigo" offers wine-tasting and snacks.

1. From Cividale del Friuli to San Daniele

CIVIDALE DEL FRIULI. There is a splendid view of the city from Ponte del Diavolo. This town is of great wine and culinary interest with its many typical *osterie* and *trattorie*, beginning with the historic "Alla Frasca", which is known for *funghi* (mushrooms). The restaurant "Al Monastero" is more refined; the "Locanda al Castello" is also a good place to spend the night. In the shops you can find Friulian salamis spiked with garlic; the pastry shop "Ducale" is the place to buy *Gubana* (pastries with chocolate and nuts). You can taste wine at the winery "Il Cantiniere Romano" where it is also possible to eat, or go directly to "Rubini", established in 1835. Tours are given here, and there is wine-tasting at the old villa, where you can sleep in the midst of vineyards with the romantic Bosco Romagno just outside. We cannot go to Premariacco without mentioning the wine producer "Rocca Bernarda", which is set within a castle of the Order of Malta and where the first mention of *Picolit* is recorded. In Stregna, which is on the border with Slovenia, "Sale e Pepe" is recommended for its regional cooking, full of dishes with strange names and memorable flavors.

GEMONA DEL FRIULI. Following the Statale 356, the first town you come to is Tarcento, a village on the banks of the Torre between the vine-covered hillocks and orchards of the so-called "amphitheater" of the Tagliamento. Further along is Gemona, with its Duomo that survived an earthquake in 1976, and its porticoed medieval-style streets. From here, take the Statale 463 to San Daniele, but do not hesitate to go down the Pontebbana, a road that follows a ravine to Tricesimo, where the restaurant "Boschetti" is a good place to make a break. From here, continue on to Pagnacco and Fagagna along the romantic Strada dei Castelli, or go to Colloredo di Monte Albano, whose beauty is combined with the refined promise of the restaurant "La Taverna".

SAN DANIELE DEL FRIULI. High on a hill, the architectural dignity and cultural traditions of this town are a must, although most are tempted here by the *prosciutto*. Places to shop and to taste products abound and range from outlets to specialist *prosciutterie*. As for restaurants, "Alle Vecchie Carceri" is typical of the region and dishes are prepared with great care. Cooking in the best traditions, and a pleasant atmosphere are to be found at "Al Ponte Antica Osteria" and "Al Tirassegno". Finally, "Al Cantinon", a restaurant in the Buon Ricordo listing, specializes in *filetto di trota salmonata e sformatino di verdura* (salmon trout filet with a vegetable timbale). Local products include trout derivatives such as eggs and *guancette* (cheeks).

2. The Carnia

TOLMEZZO. The capital of Carnia, this small city abounds with views and ancient surroundings. The Museo delle Arti Popolari is housed in the seventeenth-century Palazzo Campeis. "Cimenti", where the decor and cuisine are strictly Carnic, is the gastronomic choice. The Montasio DOP cheese, which originated here, as well as exceptionally good beef and lamb, trout and game, beans from Carnia and forest products

HOTELS AND RESTAURANTS

San Daniele del Friuli
Alle Vecchie Carceri ⑪
via G. D'Artegna 25
☎ 0432957403
Al Tirassegno ⑪
via Fagagna 16
☎ 0432957297
Al Ponte Antica Osteria ⑨
via Tagliamento 13
☎ 0432954909
Cantinon ⑪
via C. Battisti 2
☎ 0432955186
San Giovanni al Natisone
Campiello ⑪ ★🔲
via Nazionale 40
☎ 0432757910
Buco ⑪
at Dolegnano (km 2)
☎ 0432753317
Sauris
Pa' Krhaizar ★★
at Lateis (km 7)
via Lateis 5
☎ 043386165
Riglarhaus ★★
at Lateis (km 7)
via Lateis 3
☎ 043386049
★🔲 **Kursaal** ⑪
at Sauris di Sotto
piazzale Kursaal 91/b
☎ 043386202
Alla Pace ⑨
at Sauris di Sotto
via Roma 38
☎ 043386010
Stregna
Sale e Pepe ⑪
☎ 0432724118
Tavagnacco
Grop ⑪
via Matteotti 7
☎ 0432660240
Tolmezzo
Cimenti ⑨
via della Vittoria 28
☎ 0434332926
Tricesimo
Boschetti ⑪
piazza Mazzini 10
☎ 0432851230
Varmo
★🔲 **Da Toni** ⑪
at Gradiscutta (km 3)
via Sentinis 1
☎ 0432778003

PIGHIN

1991
GRAVE DEL FRIULI
DENOMINAZIONE DI ORIGINE CONTROLLATA
REFOSCO
DAL PEDUNCOLO ROSSO

IMBOTTIGLIATO DA AZIENDA
AGRICOLA VINICOLA DA
PIGHIN - S. - ITALIA
0.75l℮   12%vol.

AGRITURISMI

Nimis
★ 🏠 I Comelli
largo Diaz 8
☎ 0432790685
Povoletto
★ 🏠 La Faula
at Ravosa
☎ 0432666394

WINE PRODUCERS

Buttrio
Girolamo Dorigo
via del Pozzo 5
☎ 0432674268
Cervignano
del Friuli
Ca' Bolani
via Ca' Bolani 2
☎ 043132670
Cividale del Friuli
Cantina Rubini
at Case Rubini 4
☎ 0432716161
Premariacco
Rocca Bernarda
at Ipplis
☎ 0432716273
Risano
Fratelli Pighin
viale Grado 1
☎ 0432675444

SHOPPING

Udine
**La Baita
dei Formaggi**
via delle Erbe 1/b
☎ 0432510216
Cheeses.
**La Casa
degli Spiriti**
via Torriani 15
☎ 0432509216
Wine, distilled spirits.
Farmacia Colutta
piazza Garibaldi 10
☎ 0432501191
*"Amaro di Udine", a
herbal digestive drink.*

such as mushrooms are all to be found in shops and on every table. The more adventurous might enjoy the climb to Arta Terme where there is an excellent hotel and a restaurant that sticks closely to traditional cooking.
RAVASCLETTO. Stray from the Statale 52 Carnica into the Canale di Gorto, which leads into the most pleasant of Carnia's valleys. In Ravascletto, we recommend the hotel "Valcalda", which has been managed by the Giorgessi family since 1933, enjoys a beautiful setting and offers excellent fare. The famous *segala* (rye) bread can be bought at "Timau".
SAURIS. From Ampezzo, a pleasant resort town of wooden houses, the narrow Lumei valley leads up toward Sauris, a German-speaking town known for its *prosciutto affumicato* (smoked cured ham). As a place to spend the night we suggest "Riglarhaus", a refined and exclusive inn with a fantastic panorama. And near Lateis is "Pa' Krhaizar", an old house that has been restored and has a very good restaurant. In

Sauris di Sotto, "Kursal" is another good address for tasty traditional cooking with *gnocchetti* and *tortelli di patate alle erbe spontanee* (potato tarts with wild herbs). The restaurant "Alla Pace" is also worth mentioning. The celebrated *prosciutto*, *speck* (cured beef), and alpine cheeses can be found in the shops.
TARVISIO. The village is set in a dip of the Val Canale, making it a resort for holidays and sports. The best Carinzian food can be tasted at the 'Antica Tratoria Schönberg" in Malborghetto: charcuterie, *ricotta* and black bread, *minestra di orzo e fagioli* (barley and bean soup), *gnocchi* with prunes, *Gulasch*, smoked meat with *sauerkraut*, and apple or *ricotta* strudel. At the "Cooperativa Allevatore Valcanale" in Ugovizza, local cheese and honey are available.

3. From Tagliamento to Isonzo

CODROIPO. The main attraction in Passariano is the spectacular Villa Manin, the country house of the last Doge of Venice, which is complemented by long barns and, on the other side of the street, by a large, porticoed se-

mi-circular building. Still in the area, in Zompicchia, the 500-year old wine cellar "Vignetti Pietro Pittaro" is open to visitors. At Varmo di Gradiscutta, stop at "Da Toni", a Buon Ricordo restaurant, for their specialty: *filetto di maiale ai porri* (pork filet with leaks). Not far away, in Rivignano, "Al Ferarut" serves Friulian seafood.

LATISANA. The village greets its visitors with an artistic jewel: Veronese's *Baptism of Christ*, which may be admired in the Duomo. On the other side of the river is San Vito and the *osteria* "Al Colombo". The Tagliamento leads to Lignano Sabbiadoro, with a variety of gastronomic possibilities: the favorites are "Al Bancut", with its marine atmosphere, and "Bidin", with its wine shop.

CERVIGNANO DEL FRIULI. On the banks of the Ausa, a pleasant stay is possible at the hotel "Internationale" and at its restaurant "La Rotonda", there is a fine selection of fish dishes including *capesante con crema di piselli* (scallops with creamed peas), *zuppa di rombo* (turbot soup) and *boreto alla gradese con polenta* (Grado-style fish soup with *polenta*). Wines may be purchased from the producer "Ca'Bolani". An excursion to Aquilcia should not be missed: stay at the hotel "Patriarchi" and dine at "Fonzari". Grado lies further on.

PALMANOVA. This star-shaped fortress has nine points and was built by Venetians. Rather than go straight to Udine, a diversion through San Giovanni al Natisone will bring you to two noteworthy restaurants: "Campiello" for seafood accompanied by interesting wines, and "Buco", an excellent-value *trattoria*. The itinerary ends at Manzano, where "Il Borgo", a small hotel-restaurant, has made a name for itself. In Aielli del Friuli, the producer "Jolanda de Colò" offers refined goose products. Within the grounds of the Abbazia di Rosazzo (Rosazzo abbey), you can visit the wine producer "Walter Filiputti", heir to the cellar that was praised in 1438 by Marin Sanudo for its "perfettissimi vini" - its most perfect wines.

The Tarvisio forest

SHOPPING

Udine
Troiano-Venturini
via Sarpi 12/a
☎ 0432295269
Charcuterie, cheeses.
Aiello del Friuli
Jolanda de Colò
via Mameli 6
☎ 0432997733
Goose products.
Cividale del Friuli
Pasticceria
Gelateria Ducale
piazza Picco 18
☎ 0432730707
Pastries and ice-creams.
Pasticceria Vogrig
viale Libertà 136
☎ 0432730236
Pastries and sweets.
Percoto
Distilleria Nonino
via Aquileia 104
☎ 0432676331
Distilled spirits.
San Daniele del Friuli
La Casa del Prosciutto
Castellani
via T. Ciconi 32
☎ 0432941412
Charcuterie.
Prosciutteria
Dok Dall'Ava
via Gemona 29
☎ 0432940280
Charcuterie.
Prosciuttificio
Bagatto Rino
via C. Battisti 28
☎ 0432957252
Charcuterie.
Tarvisio
Gianni Macoratti
piazza Unità 13
☎ 04282319
Ice-creams.
Tolmezzo
Astori - Formaggi e Salumi Nostrani
via Cavour 3
☎ 04332372
Cheeses, charcuterie.

LIGURIA FLAVORS OF MOUNTAINS AND THE SEA

All the flavors of a cuisine that is at its best in Genoa and finds the origins of its most singular dishes in the history of commerce are concentrated between the Ligurian Sea and the Appenines.

L iguria is an "ethereal land," wrote Vincenzo Cardarelli. "Hot stones and clean clay are enlivened by vine leaves in the sun. Olive trees are gigantic. In the springtime mimosa blooms everywhere. Shadow and sun alternate in the deep valleys that run into the sea; in the steep cobbled roads; among fields of roses, wells and tilled earth; alongside farms and vine-yards." A poetic but also realistic image of a coastal area protected from cold north winds by the Apennines. Liguria also crosses this mountain range into the Po Valley, where intensively cultivated land – often on narrow terraces – can be found alongside woods and pastures; where the indigenous Cabannina cow eats alongside the enormous Piedmont cow, enabling Ligurians to enjoy a wide variety of cheeses and meats.

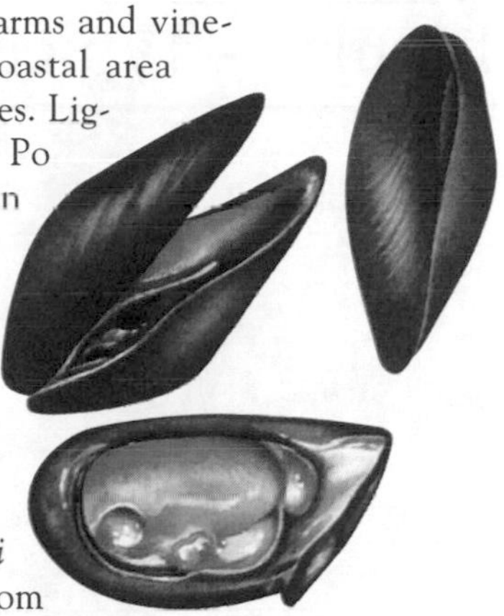

Difficult to cultivate, the coastal area nonetheless produces a significant variety, if not quantity, of products including DOP (*Denominazione di Origine Protetta*) olive oil, vegetables and fruits from further inland , salamis, cheeses, mushrooms, truffles and chestnuts, while the sea abounds with fish and shellfish.

On the coast there is an excellent variety of restaurants. Inland the mountain economy is relatively closed so the foods served there are those found on the land. Tables in *trattorie* are laid with meats, particularly rabbit and poultry. Along the ancient routes of commerce the tastes of Piedmont, Emilia, Lombardy and even Tuscany filter in.

At a crossroads for sea commerce, Liguria's cuisine has seen influences from Spain and the distant lands of the East. The difficult nature of land and the small-scale production of food has created an exacting people, carefully and skillfully using what nature offers – from humble greens and herbs to olives, basil and the wild foods of the forest – in harmony with the olive oil and wine made from fruits blessed by the sun.

The bay of Portofino

223

Liguria - Typical products

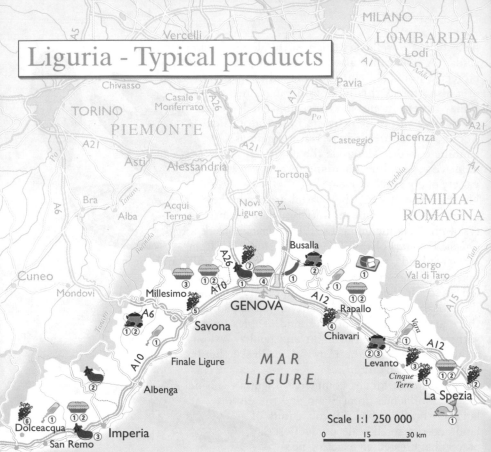

Scale 1:1 250 000

0   15   30 km

CHEESES

1. **Formaggio di Santo Stefano d'Aveto.** Produced in Rezzoaglio and Santo Stefano d'Aveto.

CHARCUTERIE

1. **Salame genovese.** Salami found in Val Polcevera, Orero and Sant'Olcese.

FISH

1. **Mitili del Golfo della Spezia.** Mussels found in the Gulf of Portovenere.

VEGETABLES

1. **Basilico genovese.** Genoese basil grown in Prà is the most renowned.
2. **Fagioli bianchi di Pigna e di Conio.** Haricot beans grown around Imperia.
3. **Oliva Taggiasca.** Olives grown inTaggia in Imperia.

EXTRA-VIRGIN OLIVE OIL

1. **Riviera Ligure Dop.** Produced throughout the region.

VARIOUS

1. **Castagna Gabbiana.** Chestnuts from around Savona and Imperia.
2. **Pesto**
3. **Acciughe sotto sale.** Salt-cured anchovies.

BREAD AND SWEETS

1. **Focaccia genovese.** Flat bread.
2. **Farinata.** Chick pea flour flat bread.
3. **Chinotti canditi.** Typical sweet with limited production in the Sassello area.
4. **Pandolce genovese.** Cake made in the regional capital, Genoa.

DOC WINES

1. **Cinque Terre e Cinque Terre Sciacchetrà**
2. **Colli di Luni**
3. **Colline di Levanto**
4. **Golfo del Tigullio**
5. **Riviera Ligure di Ponente**
6. **Rossese di Dolceacqua**
7. **Valpolcevera**

GENOA

*The great seaport is a melting pot in which
the territory's raw materials blend with
elements from other cultures.*

T he province of Genoa covers the Tyrrhenian
and the Po Valley slopes of the Ligurian Appenines, following the strip of coast from Co-
goleto to Moneglia. The Turchino and Giovi routes link the region to
Ovada and Novi Ligure in Alto Monferrato. The routes of Val Trebbia
and Colle di Cento Croci provide the
communication with

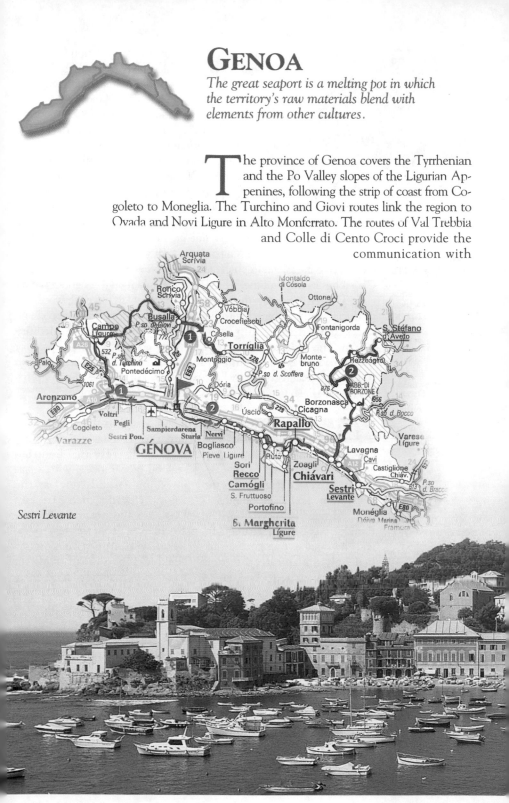

Sestri Levante

Piacenza and Parma in Emilia. Half of the population is concentrated in "grande Genova", which extends along 30 kilometers of coast from Voltri to Sant'Ilario. Inland, farmers grow fruit and vegetables, adding variety to a landscape of vineyards and olive groves. Golfo del Tigullio DOC is an important wine label of the area, with whites made of Vermentino, Bianchetta Genovese and Moscato grapes and reds made of Ciliegiolo and Dolcetto. Olive oil comes under the Riviera di Levante DOP classification. The mountains are dedicated to animal rearing, mainly of cattle, with the Bianca Piemontese and the indigenous Cabannina breeds. Dairy production is significant, with cheeses made of both cow's and goat's milk at Santo Stefano d'Aveto. There is also a fine production of charcuterie, including Genoese salami from Valpolcevra and widely distributed products such as *testa in cassetta* (a charcuterie) or *mostardella* (a kind of sausage). Genoa has its own cuisine, which has been taken up throughout the region. The territory's raw materials – fish, vegetables, olive oil, woodland products – are combined with imported products, such as salt cod and spices, that arrive by ship from Northern Europe and the Mediterranean. The archetypal symbol of Genoese cooking is *pesto*, a paste or spread made of basil, pine nuts, parmesan and olive oil that is used on *pasta di grana duro* (durum wheat pasta), another of the region's products, and to liven up vegetable minestrone or add to stuffing.

HOTELS AND RESTAURANTS

Genoa
Antica Osteria del Bai ¶¶¶¶
at Quarto dei Mille
via Quarto 12
☎ 010387478
Gran Gotto ¶¶¶
viale Brigata
Bisagno 69/r
☎ 010564344
La Bitta nella Pergola ¶¶¶
via Casaregis 52
☎ 010588543
Zeffirino ¶¶¶
via XX Settembre 20
☎ 010591990
Baldin ¶¶
at Sestri Ponente
piazza Tazzoli 20/r
☎ 0106531400
★🔲 **Bruxaboschi** ¶¶
at San Desiderio
via F. Mignone 8
☎ 0103450302
La Berlocca ¶¶
via dei Macelli
di Soziglia 45/r
☎ 0102474162
Da Guglie ¶
via S. Vincenzo 64/r
☎ 010565765
Sa Pesta ¶
via dei Giustiniani 16/r
☎ 0102468336
Le Rune ¶¶
vico Domoculta 14
☎ 010594951
Arenzano
Poggio
★🔲 **Hotel** ★★★
with its restaurant
La Buca ¶¶
via di Francia 24
☎ 0109135320

Gourmet Tours

GENOA. "A regal city leaning up against an Alpine hill," wrote Petrarch, in verses referring to the city's beauty and its proud inhabitants. Genoa "la Superba" – The Proud – has been a sea republic and the number one port of unified Italy. Its architecture runs from Romanesque to Baroque to modern, including the medieval Piazza San Matteo with the houses of the Doria family and the cathedral of San Lorenzo; Via Garibaldi, with its sixteenth/seventeenth-century *palazzi* of the aristocracy of merchants; Porto Vecchio, with the celebrated Lanterna lighthouse, the city's symbol; and the Aquarium. Some of the city's best restaurants are very old. "Antica Osteria del Bai" (established 1799) is the one we recommend most strongly. Splen-

didly located in the ancient outpost Quarto, today it is an elegant restaurant serving Ligurian seafood preparations, with *seppie in zemino* (squid stew) as the Buon Ricordo dish. In San Desiderio, the restaurant "Bruxaboschi" (est. 1862) integrates inland flavors, in particular *funghi*. "Baldin" is also worth trying. In addition to traditional food, there are innovative dishes made with fish, mushrooms, and truffles. For those who prefer to stay with the Buon Ricordo listing, "Gran Gotto" has earned renown with its specialty of *cappellacci di borragine in salsa di pinoli* (pasta filled with borage in pine nut sauce). "La Bitta nella Pergola", "Zeffirino", and the traditional "Le Rune" are also worth a try. If you want to explore simpler snacks, there are several places that serve the delicious *farinata* – a kind of *focaccia*, or flat bread, made of chickpea flour that is served plain or with rosemary, onions or even *bianchetti* (baby anchovies or sardines). You can also find typical dishes from fried food shops and places called *tavola calda* (snack bars). Right behind the Genova Brignole station is "Da Guglie". At the intersection of Via Giustiniani and Vico Sauli, shutters on the ground floor of a patrician *palazzo* open to reveal "Sa Pesta", which has a varied menu including the two classics *trenette al pesto* (pasta with pesto) and *stoccafisso 'accomodato'* (salt cod chopped and blended with boiled potato and onion, together with oil, garlic and parsley). For *trattoria* fare, try "La Berlocca". There are two sanctuaries for the sweet-toothed: the candy maker "Romanengo Pietro fu Stefano" (est. 1780), which uses ancient recipes for chocolates, candied fruits, pralines, petit-fours, and many other delights, and, slightly more recent, the cafe-pastry shop "Mangini" (est. 1876), a meeting place for writers that has preserved furnishings from its heyday. Try the cake *torta di pasta* and *biscotti del Lagaccio*, anise-flavored cookies that take their name from the port neighborhood. From the ovens come *focacce*, *panini a libretto* (small book-shaped breads) and *ciappe*, which are similar to *piadine* (round, flat bread), but are crusty because of the addition of olive oil. From fur-

ther inland you get charcuterie such as lightly smoked salami from Sant'Olcese or Orero, and the popular *mostardella*, a sausage made from pork and beef scraps. Preserved goods include marinated fish, *pignuetti*, or *novellame* (whitebait), or *boghe in scabeccio* (ox-eye bream, floured and fried, then marinated in sautéed onions, garlic, bay, sage and rosemary with olive oil).

1. From the Turchino Pass to the Giovi Pass

ARENZANO. This is the highlight of the small portion of the Genovese Riviera di Ponente where palm trees and tamarisk grow along the shore, and gardens and olive trees line the inland slopes up to the point where pine trees cover steeper lands. We recommend the "Poggio Hotel" and the restaurant "La Buca". From Voltri, head up to the Turchino Pass, stopping at Mele to go to "Osteria dell'Acquasanta", a family-run restaurant that serves excellent pasta dishes and very good wines and cheese.

CAMPO LIGURE. Beyond the crest, in the Stura Valley, is a center renowned for silver filigree. At the charcuterie shops you will find good *coppe di testa*.

BUSALLA. Good starting points for excursions in the Genovesato area are located in the upper valley of the Scrivia. At Savignone stay at the historic "Palazzo Fieschi". In Casella, relax over a

HOTELS AND RESTAURANTS

Bogliasco
Il Tipico ¶¶
at San Bernardo (km 2)
via Poggio Favaro 20
☎ 0103470754
Camogli
Da Paolo ¶¶¶
via S. Fortunato 14
☎ 0185773595
Rosa ¶¶¶
largo Casabona 11
☎ 0185773411
La Cucina di Nonna Nina ¶¶
at San Rocco (km 6)
via Molfino 126
☎ 0185773835
Campomorone
Da Iolanda ¶
piazza N. Bruno 6/7/r
☎ 010790118
Casella
Caterina ¶¶¶
at Cortino 5
☎ 0109677146
Leivi
Ca' Peo ¶¶¶
strada Panoramica
☎ 0185319696
Mele
Osteria dell'Acquasanta ¶
via Acquasanta 281
☎ 010638035
Ne
La Brinca ¶¶
at Campo di Ne 58
☎ 0185337480
Portofino
Splendido ★★★
viale Baratta 16
☎ 0185269551
Puny ¶¶¶
piazza Martiri dell'Olivetta 5
☎ 0185269037
Portofino
Da Ü Batti ¶¶
vico Nuovo 17
☎ 0185269379
Rapallo
Ü Giancu ¶¶
at S. Massimo (km 4)
☎ 0185260505
Recco
La Villa ★★★ ¶
via Roma 274
☎ 0185720779
Manuelina ¶¶¶ ¶
via Roma 278
☎ 018575364

meal at "Caterina", where they make the celebrated *mandioli de' seta* (literally, silk tissues), which are paper-thin lasagna noodles with greens, and *tomaxelle* (rich veal rolls filled with a host of ingredients including veal, garlic, mushrooms, pine nuts, cheese and egg, tied with string and cooked in a sauce of wine, tomatoes and meat). Then go downhill to the Giovi Pass, taking a detour through Campomorone to stop at "Da Iolanda", an old-fashioned *trattoria*. Heading through Pontedecimo, go to the "Antica Pasticceria Genovese Grondona". When you get to Sant'Olcese, you will find excellent charcuterie. At San Cipriano di Serra Riccò, there is a Buon Ricordo restaurant, "Ferrando", which serves *corzetti* from Valpolcevera. This very thin bow-tie pasta comes with butter, chopped pine nuts and herbs.

TORRIGLIA. From Busalla you could take the route through Valle di Scrivia followed by Fontanabuona, known for its hazelnuts, to Chiavari. If you do this, stop at Torriglia, which is known for an abundant supply of *porcini* (boletus mushrooms). The dairy industry here has achieved fame for *formaggette* and *ricotta*. At pastry shops try the local specialties, which include little *canestrelli* made of short pastry.

2. From the Gulf of Genoa to Tigullio

NERVI. This ancient town overlooks a small port. One of the pleasant excursions from here is a trip to Bogliasco, once a seafaring town, dominated by a castle. Go up to San Bernardo for a splendid panorama and good traditional and creative cooking at "Il Tipico". Try the *ravioli con il töcco genovese* (*ravioli* with Genoese meat sauce).

RECCO. The gourmand should head straight for *focaccia al formaggio* (flat bread with cheese, more specifically *prescinseua*, a semi-liq-

**HOTELS AND
RESTAURANTS**

Recco
⭐🍴 **Da Ö Vittorio** 🍴🍴
via Roma 160
☎ 018574029
**Santa Margherita
Ligure
Imperiale
Palace** ★★★
via Pagana 19
☎ 0185288991
**Trattoria
dei Pescatori** 🍴
via Bottaro 44
☎ 0185286747
**Savignone
Palazzo**
⭐🍴 **Fieschi** ★★★
piazza della Chiesa 14
☎ 0109360063
Serra Riccò
⭐🍴 **Ferrando** 🍴🍴
at San Cipriano (km 10)
via D. Carli 110
☎ 010751925
Sestri Levante
⭐🍴 **Fiammenghilla
Fieschi** 🍴🍴🍴
at Trigoso (km 4)
☎ 0185481041
Bottega del Vino 🍴
via Nazionale 530
☎ 018543349
**Uscio
Chiapparino** 🍴
via Colle Caprile 35
☎ 018591279

AGRITURISMI

**Arenzano
Argentea**
at Campo
via Val Lerone 50
☎ 0109135367
**Rossiglione
Monterosso**
at Valle Gargassa
☎ 010925866
**Santa Margherita
Ligure
Gnocchi Roberto**
at San Lorenzo
della Costa
☎ 0185283431

Camogli. Fish festival

228

uid curd cheese). "Manuelina", at the hotel "La Villa", is a restaurant with a solid reputation, run by the family of its now legendary founder. *Cappon magro* (scorpion fish) is a Buon Ricordo dish. "La Focacceria" is run by the same house, and offers an excellent version of the town's humble gastronomy. It is also an *enoteca*. Going up to Uscio, "Chiapparino", an authentic *trattoria* with good home cooking and flavors from the countryside and the woods, is a worthwhile stop.

CAMOGLI. The history of Camogli's celebrated shipyard past comes alive at the Museo Marinaro. The town's physiognomy is well preserved, with its tall fishermen's houses on the port and the church that was once on an island. A green dell filled with olive and citrus trees also provides wild herbs and greens for *preboggion*, a kind of rice soup with garden vegetables. At bakeries, look for *focaccia al formaggio* (with cheese) and *alle olive* (with olives), as well as *gallette da marinaio* (sea biscuits). The *Lasagne al pesto* at "Da Paolo" is exceptionally good. "Rosa" is well-known for its breath-taking terrace and good seafood dishes. Another celebrated restaurant is "La Cucina di Nonna Nina", at San Rocco, where you can eat *torte di verdure* (vegetable pies), *trofie col pesto* (hand-twisted noodles with pesto) and *pesce all'uso ligure* (Liguria-style fish with olives, potatoes, pine nuts and parsley). An excursion to the abbey of San Fruttuoso, a medieval jewel set into the promontory of Portofino, is a must, whether by boat or by footpath.

PORTOFINO. The boats anchored here show the reality of today's

Santa Margherita Ligure.
The "Imperiale Palace Hotel"

gilded tourism that beckons the rich and famous and crowds of the curious. The hotel "Splendido" (est. 1901), located up on the hills, is in keeping with the moneyed style of the place, and today it is renowned for its generous cuisine. Back down on the square, we recommend "Puny" (est. 1851)" with its two small rooms and *al fresco* dining for tasting dishes based mostly on fish. The owner personally entertains his clientele every evening.

SANTA MARGHERITA LIGURE. This town is made up of Corte, the fishermen's village facing the port, and Pescino, a rural district with its parish church dedicated to the martyr of Antioch. They were united under the name Santa Margherita and this helped develop tourism. The "Imperiale Palace"(est. 1889), with its frescoed rooms, has preserved its Belle Epoque splendor. "Trattoria dei Pescatore" has earned its renown for the past thirty years with *risotto di mare* (seafood risotto) and *pansoti con le erbe del monte di Portofino* (*ravioli* filled with greens from the hill of Portofino). Even more legendary is the ice-cream shop "Gelateria Simonetti". Try *scampi alla Batti* (house shrimp) at "Batti".

WINE PRODUCERS

Carasco
Roberto Noceti
at Dotta 1
at Paggi
☎ 0185350115
Ne
Fratelli Parma - Cantina e Distilleria
via Garibaldi 8
☎ 0185337073

SHOPPING

Genoa
Antica Pasticceria Genovese Grondona
discesa Torrente Verde 1
☎ 0107856134
Pastries and sweets.
Caffè Pasticceria Mangini
piazza Corvetto 3/r
☎ 010564013
Pastries and sweets.
Romanengo Pietro fu Stefano
2 shops:
via Soziglia 74/r
☎ 0102474574
via Roma 51/r
☎ 010580257
Pastries and sweets.
La Tavola del Doge
piazza Matteotti 80
☎ 010562880
Olive oil, "pesto", honey, cheeses, DOC wines.
Camogli
Cooperativa Pescatori Camogli
salita Priaro 14
☎ 0185772600
Fresh fish.
Carasco
Roberto Noceti
at Dotta 1
at Paggi
☎ 0185350115
Olive oil; wines.

SHOPPING

Chiavari
Barbieri
piazza Cavour 10
☎ 0185308665
"Focaccia" with onions.
Gran Caffè Defilla
corso Garibaldi 4
☎ 0185309829
Wines and hot dishes.
Rapallo
Tossini
via Venezia 6
☎ 018550414
One shop also
in Recco
via Assereto 7
☎ 018574137
"Focaccia" with olives and cheese.
Recco
Focacceria
Manuelina
via Roma 278
☎ 0185720019
"Focaccia" and wines.
Rezzoaglio
Caseificio Val d'Aveto
at Rezzoaglio Inf. 35
☎ 0185870390
Local cheeses.
Santa Margherita Ligure
Pinamonti
via dell'Arco 24
☎ 0185287552
"Focaccia" and pies.
Gelateria Simonetti
via Madonnetta 11
☎ 0185287186
Ice-creams.
Sant'Olcese
Salumificio Cabella
via Sant'Olcese 38
☎ 010709111
Traditional charcuterie.
Sestri Levante
Frantoio Bo
via della Chiusa 70
☎ 0185481605
Olive oil since 1867.

RAPALLO. The palm-lined boardwalk with big-windowed cafes and hotels, a centerpiece for the tourism of yesteryear, evokes the village's more recent transformation; while from its perch high on a cliff, the Castello takes us back to the town's seafaring golden age. We recommend you visit the restaurant "Ü Giancu", which is good for children (making it even more attractive is the cartoon decoration – Rapallo is a cartoonists' capital, and awards ceremonies are held here annually). Just inland, try traditional dishes at Tigullio, where mushrooms are plentiful. Nearby Zoagli is renowned for its figs and *focaccia all'olio*.

CHIAVARI. This town gained its fortune as Parma's and Piacenza's gateway to the sea. Its medieval center is rich with colonnaded streets. In Corso Garibaldi you will find the long-established "Gran Caffè Defilla", which functions as an *enoteca* and serves some hot dishes. Ask to hear about its history. Then, at Leivi you would be hard pushed to find bad cooking. "Ca' Peo", in the midst of olive trees, offers excellent cuisine along with top-notch oils and wines. The *tomaxelle* (rolls of sliced meat stuffed with ground meat) are the Buon Ricordo dish, while the *stracci di pasta al nero di seppia con sugo di ricci* (squid ink pasta with sea urchin sauce) and many other dishes are definitely memorable. It is also possible to lodge here. In town, buy *pane di Chiavari* flavored with black olive paste and *Sorrisi*, which are chocolate sweets. At Lavagna the olive oil production is renowned and fish is traditionally prepared *in ciappa*, or on slabs

of local slate. Another specialty is the old-fashioned *torta dei Fieschi*. Inland at Carasco, nestled among vineyards, olive groves and the green of hazelnut trees in Val Fontanabuona, is the winery "Noceti", with its excellent white wines and good farm cooking. At Ne, in Val Graveglia, we recommend "La Brinca" for traditional cooking with a touch of fantasy. *Ravioli*, roasts and desserts are all prepared on site. In the same town you can find the wine cellar and distillery "Fratelli Parma".

SANTO STEFANO D'AVETO. Take the long route up from Chiavari. This town has a reputation among gourmets for its good harvest of *porcini* (boletus mushrooms) and its cheeses, including *formaggiu de San Stè*, and sweet and salty *ricotta* (*sarassu*) of various ages.

SESTRI LEVANTE. The promontory, together with the town's original residential area, separates the Baia delle Favole (Bay of Fairy Tales) from the Baia del Silenzio (Bay of Silence). For good fish, remember the name "Fiammenghilla Fieschi", where you can get *scampi in pastella* (batter-fried shrimp), *taglierini al ragù di mare* (pasta with seafood tomato sauce) and *fricassea di pesce rospo con olive e pinoli* (monkfish fricassee with olives and pine nuts). In pastry shops look for *corsaretti*, sweets made of almond paste and covered with chocolate. Inland, the vineyards of the DOC wine "Golfo del Tigullio" also cover the land at Casarqa and Castiglione Chiavarese. At Sestri Levante go to "Bottega del Vino", where there is a broad selection of cheese, charcuterie and *bruschette*.

IMPERIA

*The Maritime Alps and the taste and aromas
of Provence remind visitors of the proximity
of the French border.*

The hilly and mountainous province of Imperia, one of Italy's smallest, constitutes the westernmost part of Liguria. The feel is that of the Maritime Alps, which are marked by the valleys of the Nervia, Argentina, Impero and Arroscia streams. The economy is based on cattle rearing and dairy farming, and the centers of Trioria and Medatica produce cheeses made of cow's and goat's milk. At lower altitudes, vineyards and olive groves take on major importance. The there are two DOC wine productions: Rossese di Dolceacqua – the only worthwhile red in the region – from inland Bordighera and Ventimiglia, and Riviera Ligure di Ponente, which crosses into Savona, but is made here under the sub-denomination of Riviera dei Fiori and is grown between Cervo and Ventimiglia. Olive oil production is particularly renowned in Oneglia and comes under the DOP Riviera Ligure denomination with the sub-denomination of Ponente. The olive oil is based on the local olive variety Taggiasca, which is one of the most appreciated. Horticulture is fairly widespread with white beans from Pigna, near France, and Conio, inland from the capital of the province, being the most significant product. The pasta and

*Cervo.
Typical houses
perched by the sea*

231

fish industries are also important. The cuisine is similar to Genoese traditional cooking, but distinguishes itself with its Provençal slant, which can be seen in the popular *piscialandrea*, a kind of *focaccia* derived from Nice's *pissaladière*, or in the *boiabesa*, a fish soup inspired by *bouillabaisse*.

Gourmet Tours

**HOTELS AND
RESTAURANTS**

Imperia
**Lanterna Blu-
da Tonino** ▯▯▯▯
via Scarincio 32
☎ 018363859
Dai Due Amici ▯
via Monti 30
☎ 0183292297
Pane e Vino ▯
via Des Geneys 52
☎ 0183290044
Arma di Taggia
Conchiglia ▯▯▯
via Lungomare 33
☎ 018443169
Bordighera
⭐▯ **La Via
Romana** ▯▯▯▯
via Romana 57
☎ 0184266681
Carletto ▯▯▯
via Vittorio
Emanuele 339
☎ 0184261725
**Circolo Porta
Sottana** ▯
via Dritta 20
☎ 0184260180
Magiargè ▯
piazza G. Viale
☎ 0184262946
**Borghetto
d'Arroscia**
Baita ▯▯
at Gazzo (km 6)
☎ 018331083
**Camporosso
Mare**
Gino ▯▯▯
via Braie 10
☎ 0184291493
Cervo
San Giorgio ▯▯
via A. Volta 19
☎ 0183400175
Dolceacqua
⭐▯ **Gastone** ▯▯
piazza Garibaldi 2
☎ 0184206577
Trattoria Re ▯
via Patrioti Martiri 26
☎ 0184206137

IMPERIA. Porto Maurizio and Oneglia, two villages with two very different histories lie at the mouth of the Impero stream, which gave its name to the town uniting the two from 1923 under a single administration. Porto Maurizio's most ancient nucleus, Parasio, perched up on a promontory, is intricate and picturesque. Gourmets will be tempted to make purchases here, as it is one of the capitals of native olive oil. At Oneglia, the famous *azienda* "Fratelli Carli", which has given us an olive oil museum, and "Frantonio di Sant'Agata" just inland are worth visiting. Following the Colla di Nava route inland to Chiusavecchia, "Torna- tore" – which boasts 2000 plants that are over 150 years old – is known for its refined olive oil, Fasce Lunghe. Finally, moving on to Dolcedo, you will find *extravergine sopraffino* at the oil master "Ranise" or, in the extremely limited selection, Primuruggiu (*primo fiore*, or first flower) from "Benza". Back in Oneglia, "Dai Due Amici" is a store that sells excellent *farinate*, while "Pane e Vino" is a well-stocked *enoteca* with *mescita* (wine by the glass) and snacks. Then, at Porto Maurizio you must not miss "Lanterna Blu –

Rossese grapes

da Tonino", where very fresh seafood and garden vegetables are made into creative dishes by Fiorello. At the bakeries you will find the typical *sciappa*, a bread that is a cross between a baguette and *grissini*, and *sardenaira*, a *focaccia* prepared with tomatoes, anchovies, olives and a drizzle of olive oil. At the butchers you can get *sanguinacci*, or *berodi* (blood sausage), and a local version of *testa in cassetta*. Going eastward, we arrive at Diano Marina, where *panserotti* are locally made and filled with jam, fried in olive oil and sprinkled with sugar. San Bartolomeo al Mare is well-known for its rabbit with oil and an abundant dose of herbs. At Cervo, an old town with white houses on a spur, you will find the restaurant "San Giorgio" with its beautiful sea-front terrace and a delectable offering of fish and mushrooms.

PIEVE DI TECO. In the valley of the Arroscia, which goes down to Albenga, this fourteenth-century village, built along the ancient Via del Sale, has remained virtually intact. Surrounding it is a landscape of olive groves with a few oak and chestnut trees. There are many interesting places to eat. At Borghetto d'Arroscia, we recommend the restaurant "Baita", which is typical of the territory and has a formidable sampling menu based on mushrooms. Nearby is Renzo, a Citta del Vino (city of wine) for the DOC "Riviera Ligure di Ponente", with excellent terraced vines planted at Pigato, Vermentino, Rossese and Dolcetto. On the opposite hill, at Rezzo, stop at the hotel "Negro" located in a medieval farm with a good restaurant. In the local stores you will find excellent cheeses from the hills, such as *ricotta di pecora* (sheep's milk *ricotta*) and *caprino di grattugia* (goat's cheese for grating), which is ideal for pesto. There is also the famous *toma di Mandatica* and other, lesser, cheeses made from cow's milk. Colle di Nava ends the excursion. Beyond it lies the valley of the Tanaro and the Alta Langa.

TAGGIA. At the mouth of the Valle Argentina, leaning up against a hill covered with olive trees, is one of the Ponente's most striking historic villages. A grandiose bridge with sixteen arches and streets lined with colonnades sets the medieval scene. To the south of the village is the important convent of San Domenico, which for centuries was a center for culture and art. On the seaside, at Arma di Taggia, the restaurant "Conchiglia" offers creative cooking based on fish and a wine cellar with over 250 labels. At

Badalucco, just inland, go to "Roi" a master oil maker and producer of excellent conserves. At the bakers you will find *carpasina*, a bread made of barley that keeps well.

TRIORA. In the Alpine landscape of the upper Argentina Valley, the *piazze*, flights of steps and tall houses with sculpted doorways give a historic feel to this village. Its ancient prosperity came from the forests and pastures, and locals continue to produce a variety of cheeses. These range from *formaggio di malga*, a cheese made from whole or semi-skimmed cow's milk and *bruzzu*, a sheep's milk *ricotta* that is served on toasted barley bread, to *caprino di malga*, goat's cheese aged for a few months in special cellars called *crotte*. The woods still provide large quantities of mushrooms and chestnuts that are to be found in many dishes. In the shops you will find the well-known *pane di Triora*, a soft, wholesome bread made from wheat and buckwheat flours. In the *trattorie*, *ravioli* and *coniglio alla cacciatora* (rabbit with tomato sauce) adorn the tables. We recommend you visit Molini di Triora, a celebrated Città delle Lumache (City of Snails), where they mostly use the Ligurian variety (*Helix aspersa*). According to ancient tradition, the tasty snails are cooked in their shells with olive oil, tomatoes and local aromatic herbs. Dishes you can taste here include *stoccafisso ripieno* (filled salt cod) and *torta*

Triora

HOTELS AND RESTAURANTS

Molini di Triora
Santo Spirito ¶ ⭐ 🅴
piazza Roma 23
☎ 018494092
Rezzo
Negro ★★
at Cenova (km 3)
via Canada 11
☎ 018334089
San Remo
Royal Hotel ★★★ 🅻
corso Imperatrice 80
☎ 01845391
Giannino ¶¶¶¶
corso Trento
e Trieste 23
☎ 0184504014
**Paolo
e Barbara** ¶¶¶¶
via Roma 47
☎ 0184531653
Maggiorino ¶
via Roma 183
☎ 0184504338
**Nuovo Piccolo
Mondo** ¶
via Piave 7
☎ 0184509012
**Osteria Vini
d'Italia Enoteca** ¶
corso Mombello 5
☎ 0184591747
Vallecrosia
Giappun ¶¶¶
via Maonaira 7
☎ 0184250560
Ventimiglia
Balzi Rossi ¶¶¶¶
at Ponte San
Ludovico (km 8)
☎ 018438132
Baia Beniamin ¶¶¶¶
at Grimaldi Inferore
(km 7)
corso Europa 63
☎ 018438002

verde di riso e bietole (green rice and beet pie). *Torrone di miele e noci* (honey and walnut nougat) is a local specialty. At "Santo Spirito", a simple, traditional restaurant, the Zucchetto family serves products from its own farm.

SAN REMO. San Remo's annual Festival della Canzone (Music Festival) and its casino are the only things anybody ever hears about this town. However, it has another side to it – its tasty cuisine. The old center, called *La Pigna* by locals, is a medieval hamlet set on a hill. The San Remo of the rich and wealthy is exemplified in the elegant Corso degli Inglesi and the Corso Imperatrice, where the "Royal Hotel (1872)" offers the elegance of well-preserved Art Nouveau furnishings and good old-fashioned service. If you are seeking the simple flavors of *farinata* (chickpea flour flatbread) and *sardenaira* (Ligurian *focaccia* with onions, olives and anchovies), stop in at places such as "Maggiorino" and "Vini d'Italia". For classics such as

stoccafisso alle olive (salt cod with olives), *trattorie* such as "Nuovo Piccolo Mondo" will fit the bill. "Paolo e Barbara" is in a class of its own, with a menu featuring such dishes as *uova affogate ai ricci di mare* (eggs with sea urchins), *trenette con triglie di scoglio* (trenette pasta with red mullet), *pansoti* (a transparent *ravioli* made of buckwheat flour and filled with *taleggio* cheese), *trippa croccante di stoccafisso con fagioli di Pigna* (crispy salt cod tripe with white Pigna beans) and *gamberoni flambate con pomodori secchi* (shrimp flambée with dried tomatoes). Another good restaurant is "Giannino", where the *antipasto* consists of *carpaccio di pesce e crostacei* (fish and shell fish carpaccio), followed by *trenette al nero di seppia* (pasta with squid ink) and excellent *misto alla griglia* (mixed grill).

BORDIGHERA. The old town is set on the promontory of Capo Sant'Ampelio, and below lies its renowned gardens full of palm trees. The network of restaurants is well regarded. "La Via Romana" is excellent and is also very elegant. Here dishes are based on

Dolceacqua. Bridge over the Nervia stream

fish, and range from Ligurian classics such as *ravioli di ricotta e spinaci con carciofi* (ricotta and spinach *ravioli* with artichokes) to the unusual *zuppa piccante di vongole e gamberi* (spicy clam and shrimp soup). A second suggestion is "Carletto", where a four-course gourmet menu is very tempting. Those who enjoy a good plate of pasta and maybe some salt cod will like "Porta Sottana" and "Magiargè". At pastry shops, don't miss the *torroncini* (nougats) called *cobaite*. Inland visit Vallebona, a well-preserved medieval town, and in Vallecrosia go to "Giappun", where the atmosphere is intimate and welcoming and the food strongly suggests nearby Provence. At San Biagio della Cima, "Maccario" is a good wine-producer, where wine is made from Rossese and Vermentino grapes, as well as rare local grapes such as Mossarda, which are harvested late and used for a hearty table wine. At Camporosso Mare go to "Gino", a family-run restaurant, and "Foresti", a respected winery.

VENTIMIGLIA. The old city is on the western side of the stream. It dates back to the Lombard conquest of Rotari and preserves ancient buildings and the remains of the old Genovese walls. Below, and across the river, is the modern city and the archaeological site of the Roman Albintimilium. The search for traditional flavors begins in the stores. Ask the bakers for *sardenaira*, and at pastry shops ask for *castagnole* and *canestrelli*. At the farm "Podere Bevera" buy extra-fine olive oil, and at the wineries get the good wine made from Rossese grapes. Excursions to Mortola Inferiore must not be missed for the extremely famous Hambury gardens, nor should you omit a visit to Balzi Rossi near the French border, where you can see prehistoric caves. You can also dine well in the village, as "Balzi Rossi" is also the name of an excellent restaurant at Ponte San Ludovico. The refined eatery offers a good menu and a terrace overlooking the sea. Not far away, at Grimaldi Inferiore, "Baia Beniamin" offers another beautiful view and the possibility of spending the night surrounded by a beautiful green park.

DOLCEACQUA. In the luxuriant setting of the valley of the Nervia, which you cross via an elegant medieval bridge, you can find excellent wines. This is the land of Rossese grapes, and our recommendations here begin with the wine producer "Terre Bianche", which is also an *agriturismo* establishment. The cuisine at the restaurant "Gastone", across from the Castello, invites the diner to discover the flavors of the valley. Next door is "Trattoria Re" where cooking is more Provençal and is accompanied by an excellent selection of wines and cheeses. In the upper valley is Pigna, renowned for its beans. Then, as you descend, you come to Vallecrosia, Apricale, Perinaldo and Baiardo. Finally, towards San Remo, you come to Ceriana with its baroque parish church at the center of an extraordinarily well-preserved nucleus of old houses, mills and remains of medieval walls.

SHOPPING

Imperia
Raineri
via Tommaso Schiva
☎ 0183290133
Olive oil, olive paté.
Badalucco
Olio Roi
di Franco Boeri
via Argentina 1
☎ 0184408004
Olive oil.
Chiusavecchia
Tornatore Oliveto
di Olivastri
☎ 018352888
Fasce Lunghe olive oil.
Dolceacqua
Azienda Agricola
Maccario
via S. Bernardo 23
☎ 0184206013
Organically grown fruit and vegetables, DOP olive oil, DOC wines.
Dolcedo
Benza Frantoiano
via Dolcedo 180
☎ 0183280132
Primuruggiu olive oil, olives and olive paté.
Azienda
Roberto Ranise
via IV Novembre 29
☎ 0183291615
Olive oil.
Ventimiglia
Podere Bevera
Abbo srl
at Saluzzo
via Gorla 3
☎ 017542600
Olive oil.

LA SPEZIA

This tiny area between the terraced vineyards of the Cinque Terre and the pastures in the Apennines is packed with good food.

The mountainous province of La Spezia is the smallest in Italy and runs from the Ligurian Apennines to the Tyrrhenian Sea. It is the strip of the Riviera di Levante that runs between Deiva Marina and Punta Bianca. The coast is so steep that even the Via Aurelia must follow a route further inland. The difficulty of the route is balanced by its exquisite landscape of terraced vineyards in the Cinque Terre, which has recently been added to UNESCO's World Heritage List. The wines produced here are made from the ancient *Bosco* and *Albarola* grape varieties and the legendary Sciacchetrà, as well as Vermentino, which was introduced more recently. These are all made in the sphere of DOC Cinque Terre and are close, in terms of zone and composition, to the denominations Colline di Levanto towards Genoa, and Colli di Luni bordering Tuscany. Inland locals rear cattle and make cheese in Varese Ligure, the upper valley of the Vara and the inland part of Bonassola. In the lower Lunigiana, in Sarzana, the cultivation of fruits and vegetables is gaining importance thanks to the successful harvest of peaches. Fishing is important and *mitili*, locally known as *muscoli* (mussels), are cultivated in La Spezia and Portovenere. The gastronomy follows Genoese traditions but also has some local influences. Fish-based dishes favor mollusks and shellfish, while increasingly the *mesciua*, or *minestra di ceci, fagioli e frumento* (chickpea, bean and wheat soup – also made with *farro*, or spelt, which is even better) – is seen as the mark of a good table,

Cinque Terre. Vineyards and terraces

even though it can hardly be found just outside the city. Restaurants are also good on the Gulf of La Spezia, while in the Apennine valleys you will find food that resembles the cuisine of Emilia and Tuscany.

Gourmet Tours

LA SPEZIA. The building of the Arsenale (dockyard) transformed the small walled town into a modern industrial capital, and you can learn about the history of the Italian Marines at the Museo Tecnico Navale (Naval Museum). In terms of food, La Spezia is known for excellent mollusks, especially *mitili*, or *muscoli* (mussels), which are raised all along the gulf. The restaurant "Parodi" is very good for seafood: among its most enticing dishes are *taglierini rosa su spuma di basilico con datteri di mare* (pink pasta with basil mousse and date mussels) and *triglie con asparagi, pinoli e maggiorana* (red mullet with asparagus, pine nuts and marjoram). A bit lower key, but no less good, is "Il Forchettone" where excellent fish is served alongside exceptional garden fragrances. In the same vein, "Antica Osteria da Caran" serves

Cinque Terre and Colli di Luni wines accompanied by *mesciua*, the traditional vegetable soup, or *stoccafisso in umido con polenta* (salt cod in a broth with *polenta*). For a slice of *farinata* (chickpea flat bread), go to "La Pia", a store in via Magenta that is more than 100 years old, or "Pomodoro", close to the Central Station. You should buy *acciughe in salamoia* and *formaggette* from Varese Ligure and Bonassola. Going up the winding roads you can findthe first of La Spezia's celebrated vineyards at Biassa and Campiglia.

1. The Gulf of the Poets and the Lunigiana

LERICI. D.H. Lawrence thought it was perfect. A tiny bay almost closed in by the rocks and lined with olive trees running into the

HOTELS AND RESTAURANTS

La Spezia
Parodi ‖‖
via Amendola 210
☎ 0187715777
Il Forchettone ‖‖
via Genova 288
☎ 0187718835
Antica Osteria da Caran ‖
via Genova 1
☎ 0187703777
Pomodoro ‖
piazza Saint Bon 5
☎ 0187739911
Ameglia
Paracucchi Locanda dell'Angelo ‖‖‖
viale XXV Aprile 60
☎ 018764391
Locanda delle Tamerlci ‖‖‖
at Fiumaretta
di Ameglia (km 4)
via Litoranea 106
☎ 018764262
Lerici
Miranda ‖‖
at Tellaro (km 4)
via Fiascherino 92
☎ 0187964012
La Barcaccia ‖‖
piazza Garibaldi 8
☎ 0187967721
Conchiglia ‖‖
via Mazzini 2
☎ 0187967331
Due Corone ‖‖
via Vespucci 1
☎ 0187967417
Vecchia Lerici ‖‖
piazza Mottino 10
☎ 0187967597
Levanto
Hostaria da Franco ‖‖
via privata Olivi 8
☎ 0187808647
Manarola
Marina Piccola ‖‖
via Lo Scalo 16
☎ 0187920103
Monterosso al Mare
Gigante ‖‖
via IV Novembre 9
☎ 0187817401

**ALBERGHI E
RISTORANTI**

**Monterosso al Mare
Il Pirata** ¶
via Molinelli
☎ 0187817536
**Ortonovo
Locanda Cervia** ¶¶
at Nicola (km 4)
piazza della Chiesa
☎ 0187660491
**Portovenere
Royal Sporting** ★★★
via dell'Ulivo 345
☎ 0187790326
**Taverna del
Corsaro** ¶¶¶
calata Doria 102
☎ 0187790622
**Riomaggiore
Da Aristide** ¶¶
via A. Discovolo 138
☎ 0187920000
**Vernazza
★⛴ Gambero
Rosso** ¶¶
piazza Marconi 7
☎ 0187812265

AGRITURISMI

**Castelnuovo Magra
★⛴ Cascina
dei Peri**
via Montefrancio 71
☎ 0187674085
**Maissana
★⛴ Giandriale**
at Tavarone
at Giandriale 5
☎ 0187840279
**Vernazza
Barrani Fabio**
at Corniglia
via Fieschi 14
☎ 0187812063

valleys, with just one pink fisherman's house with a yellow roof. From Shelley to James, and Italy's Mario Soldati, many poets were seduced by the magic of the place. To the village, with its ancient Castello and port, may be added the charming seafarer's hamlets of San Terenzo, Fiascherino, Tellaro and Montemarcello. The gastronomy is as interesting, and can be sampled in a range of restaurants, including "Miranda", "Conchiglia", "Vecchia Lerici", "Barcaccia" and "Due Corone". At pastry stores look for *ciambelon*, a kind of cake similar to *buccellato toscano*. Leave the route to Sarzana and head towards Arcola, an ancient village spread out on a hill. Here, go *Ligurian focaccia* to "Fattoria il Chioso" for its fine inventory of Colli di Luni wines.

SARZANA. The capital of Lunigiana holds many vestiges of a past full of battle and commerce. Further down, nearly at the border with Tuscany, is the archaeological site of the ancient city of Luni, which gives its name to the valley of the Magra and the DOC wines of its hills. *Spongata* (spiced Christmas cake with fruit and honey) is typical of the area, but in this transitional land you will also find Genoese *pandolce* and *buccellati* from Lucca. As for restaurants, going down to Ameglia you must not miss the excellent "Locanda dell'Angelo" ("Angelo" is the legendary *Paracucchi*, the owner of this refined hotel complex). Here

dishes range from *guazzetto di mare* (fish stew) to *filetto di manzo* (filet of beef) to *tartufo di mare* and *foie gras*. Locally, "Locanda delle Tamerici" is very pleasant, and is situated by the sea.

CASTELNUOVO MAGRA. This center in the hills has an interesting history and urban structure, with two high points – its church and its castle. A good reason to stop here is the "Enoteca Pubblica della Liguria e della Lunigiana" in the high-vaulted cellars of the seventeenth-century Palazzo Comunale. If you want to meet a producer of good Vermentino, you can also go up to "Cascina dei Peri", which is also an *agriturismo* establishment. At Castelnuovo you will find good table grapes and *focaccia dolce all'olio, con zucchero e pinoli* (sweet flat bread with olive oil, sugar and pine nuts). Continuing to Ortonuovo, in the green valley of Parmignone, you will find two good places to visit. First try "Locanda Cervia", where traditional simple cuisine is served, and then go to the "Cantine Lunae Bosoni", with its twenty hectares of vines, ranging from Vermentino to Merlot, which are harmonized in a fine collection of labels.

2. Cinque Terre and the hills of Levanto.

PORTOVENERE. The view of this town, which sprawls towards the Cinque Terre, with the church of San Pietro jutting out at the tip of

the promontery, is unforgettable. At the edge of the gulf of La Spezia, Portovenere shares with the capital its fame for mussels. They are served in broth, stuffed or in spaghetti sauce, in restaurants along the street Calata Doria, starting with "Taverna del Corsaro".

RIOMAGGIORE. This is the first of the Cinque Terre – five lands. It comprises tall houses leaning together into the cliffs, narrow winding streets and tiny squares, closed in by the vine-covered hills and precipitous cliffs above the sea. The celebrated Via dell'Amore leads the way among shrubs and agave plants to Manarola, a wine-making village opposite vines and gardens arranged on a hill like an amphitheater. You should try the restaurants "Da Aristide" at Riomaggiore, and "Marina Piccola" at Manarola. The area's main reference for wines is Manarola's "Cooperativa Cinque Terre".

VERNAZZA. Set into the rocks with stairs and narrow colonnaded streets leading everywhere, this is said to be the most beautiful of the Cinque Terre. A path through the brush leads to Corniglia, high above the sea, to the edges of a cove covered with vines – the less adventurous might prefer a short train ride. At Vernazza try the restaurant "Gambero Rosso", and go to the "Cantina del Molo" for shopping.

MONTEROSSO AL MARE. The sandy beach and the silhouette of the Punta Mesco promontary provide the setting for the most popular of Cinque Terre's villages. Inland, olive and lemon trees stand together with the last of the Cinque Terre vineyards. Go to the *cantina* "Sassarini" for wine purchases. "Gigante" offers the freshest of fish served grilled or baked while "Pirata" offers the imaginative *tortino di acciughe con moscardini e patate* (anchovy pie with miniature octopus and potatoes).

LEVANTO. Locked in between hills coverd with grapevines and olive trees, this ancient village gives its name to Liguria's youngest DOC wine production, a white made of Vermentino and Albarola grapes. Try the restaurant "Hostaria da Franco", and in the stores look for the *formaggette* from Bonassola and Varese Ligure.

Portovenere. The Romanesque church of S. Pietro

WINE PRODUCERS

Arcola
Fattoria Il Chioso
at Baccano
di Arcola
☎ 0187967110
Levanto
La Cantina Levantese
piazza Massola 3
☎ 0187807137
Manarola
Coop. Agricola Cinque Terre
at Groppo
☎ 0187920076
Monterosso al Mare
Cantina Natale Sassarini
at Plan del Corso
☎ 0187817034
Ortonovo
Cantine Lunae Bosoni
Via Bozzi 63
☎ 0187660187
Vernazza
La Cantina del Molo
piazza Marconi 16
☎ 0187821141

SHOPPING

La Spezia
Gastronomia Cerona Fragolina
via Vittorio Veneto 24
☎ 0187732933
Charcuterie and delicatessen.
Pizzeria La Pia
via Magenta 12
☎ 0187739999
"Farinata", "focaccia" with cheese and "castagnaccio".
Levanto
Coop. Agricoltori Vallata di Levanto
via delle Ghiare 20
☎ 0187800867
Olive oil and honey.

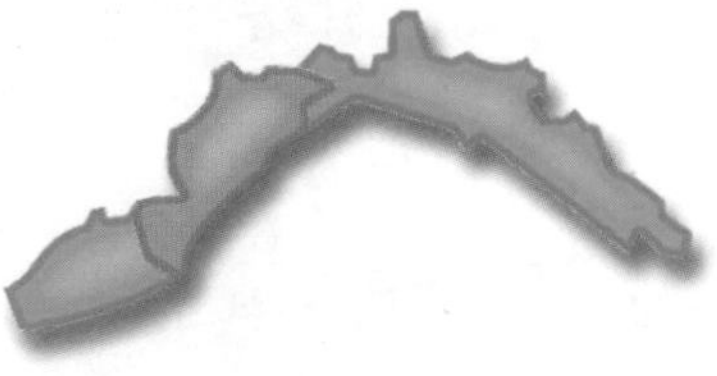

SAVONA

With its long history of exchanges with Piedmont, Savona is the Ligurian province that has best assimilated that province's gastronomic style.

The province of Savona is at the start of the Riviera di Ponente and stretches from the Tyrrhenian coast to the upper valleys of the Po.

The land lies in the transition area between the Maritime Alps and the Ligurian Apennines and is mostly mountainous with a forested area. At higher altitudes the primary activity is animal husbandry. There is a considerable production of meat from Piedmontese cattle and extensive dairy production including giuncata (a curd cheese) and many cow's, sheep's and goat's milk cheeses. The slopes facing the Po Valley, which borders Piedmont's Le Langhe at the upper Bormida Valley, are also rich with truffles, mushrooms and chestnuts. At lower altitudes, by the Tyrrhenian Sea, there is a stretch of vineyards and olive groves.

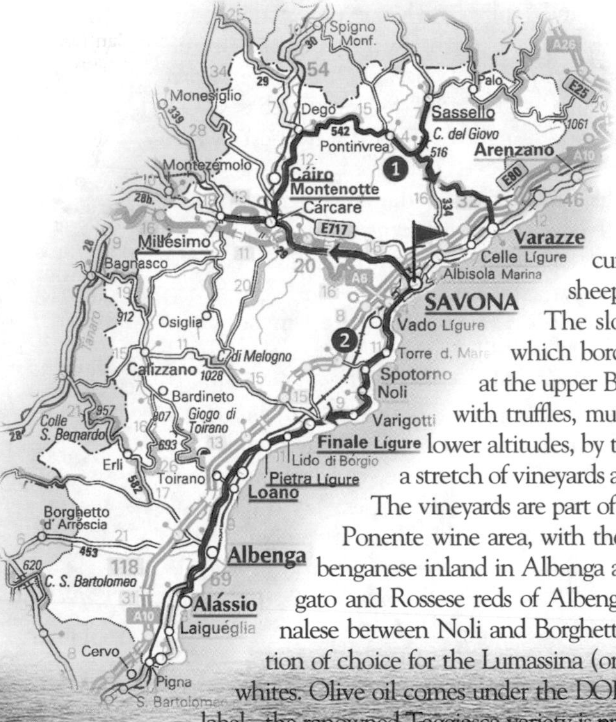

The vineyards are part of the DOC Riviera Ligure di Ponente wine area, with the sub-denominations of Albenganese inland in Albenga and Andora - where the Pigato and Rossese reds of Albenga predominate - and of Finalese between Noli and Borghetto Santo Spirito – the location of choice for the Lumassina (or Buzzetto) and Vermentino whites. Olive oil comes under the DOP Riviera Ligure di Ponente label - the renowned Taggiasca variety is predominant. The cultivation of citrus fruits is an ancient tradition and bitter orange is used in preparations of candied fruits and pastries. Along the coast fruit and vegetable growing is significant and the tomatoes, asparagus and artichokes of Albegna are renowned. The cuisine is close to that of Genoa with subtle variations in the preparation of the most typical dishes and considerable influence from Le Langhe as one gets closer to the border with Piedmont. The local restaurant tradition has its quintessential representative in "Palma" in Alassio and in several excellent restaurants along the coast. For places off the beaten track and more rustic in their offering head inland, where dishes are based on meats, mushrooms and truffles.

Gourmet Tours

SAVONA. Thanks to the route through the Cadibona pass, Savona is the historical gateway to the sea for the provinces of Turin and Piedmont. An aura of the past still exists in the colonnaded Via Paleocapa, the Duomo and the Fortezza Priamar (fortress) around the old dockyard. For room and board, we recommend "Molo Vecchio", where traditional dishes are served with a modern twist, including *risotto al granchio e zucchette* (risotto with crab and squash) and *guazzetto di pesce di scoglio e crostacei* (rockfish soup with shellfish). We particularly like "Il Rigolo", which has two fine gourmet menus featuring both meat- and fish-based dishes accompanied by fresh garden produce. Across the river "A Spurcacciun-a" offers a copious journey through a selection of *antipasti* that ends with a monumental grilled dish. To eat well without tempting ruin, head to "Vino e Farinata" near the port. In the same area, visit the covered market in Via Giuria: in the morning you may taste tripe in broth, the traditional mariner's breakfast. Good *funghi* are available inland. In pastry shops buy *amaretti del Sassello*, or taste the typical *chinotti al liquore* and candied fruit.

1. The Bormida Valley

MILLESIMO. From the capital of the province, take the route through the Cadibona pass. Near the pass, stop at Altare to get acclimatized and visit "Quintilio", a historic restaurant with a pleasant atmosphere that will introduce you to themes from Piedmont cooking, which you can find in *tortelli con fonduta* (cheese-filled pasta), *fritto misto* (mixed fry), *terrina di frutta* (fruit terrine) and *bonet* (a chocolate dessert). This is also a place where the craft of glassmaking is famous. Turning off to the left, go to Millesimo, which has earned the title of *Città del Tartufo* (City of Truffles) for the specialty found in its thirteen municipalities in the mountain community of the upper Val Bormida. Sausages and other cured meats are also available. CAIRO MONTENOTTE. Taking the route that heads toward Alba, you will come to this village to the west of the Bormida di Spigno and be transported back into the Middle Ages. Via dei Portici offers beautiful ancient views. The surrounding woods offer excellent *tartufi*, *porcini* (boletus mushrooms), *ovoli* (royal mushrooms), and *castagne* (chestnuts). In restaurants there is a fine blend of the cuisines of Liguria and Le Langhe, exemplified in the hearty

HOTELS AND RESTAURANTS

Savona
A Spurcacciun-a ¶¶¶ ★☎
via Nizza 89/r
☎ 019264065
Il Rigolo ¶¶
corso Mazzini 62/r
☎ 019856406
Molo Vecchio ¶¶
via Baglietto 8/r
☎ 019854219
Vino e Farinata ¶
via Pia 15/r
Alassio
Palma ¶¶¶¶
via Cavour 5
☎ 0182640314
Lamberti ★★★
via Gramsci 57
☎ 0182642747
Tre Mori ¶
passeggiata Italia 19
☎ 0182640495
Albenga
Antica Osteria dei Leoni ¶¶
via M. Lengueglia 49
☎ 018251937
Minispor l-ll
Pernambucco ¶¶
viale Italia 35
☎ 018253458
Altare
Quintilio ¶¶
via Gramsci 23
☎ 019580000
Andora
Casa del Priore ¶¶¶
via Castello 34
☎ 018287330
Bergeggi
Claudio ¶¶¶¶
via XXV Aprile 37
☎ 019859750
Borgio Verezzi
Doc ¶¶¶
via Vittorio Veneto 1
☎ 019611477

The "Baci di Alassio cookies"

HOTELS AND RESTAURANTS

Calizzano
Msè Tutta ⊞⊞
via Garibaldi 8
☎ 01979647
Laigueglia
Baia del Sole ⊞⊞⊞
piazza Cavour 8
☎ 0182690019
Noli
Lilliput ⊞⊞⊞
at Voze (km 4)
via Zuglieno 49
☎ 019748009
Pietra Ligure
Buca di Bacco ⊞⊞
corso Italia 113
☎ 019615307
Capanno ⊞
at Ranzi (km 4)
via Cappelletta 63
☎ 019625198
Varazze
Cavetto ⊞⊞⊞
piazza S. Caterina 7
☎ 01997311
Varigotti
Muraglia-
Conchiglia
d'Oro ⊞⊞⊞
via Aurelia 133
☎ 019698015

AGRITURISMI

Casanova
Lerrone
⭐ **Cascina il**
Poggio
at Marmoreo
via Poggio 97
☎ 018274040
Piana Crixia
La Celestina
at Gallareto
☎ 019570292

civet di cacciagione (wild game stew). *Torta di nocciole* (hazelnut cake) and *castagnaccia* (chestnut cake) are the popular choice in pastry shops. Continuing on to Dego, take the Pontinvrea *statale* that goes down to old Aurelia, a beautifully scenic route.

SASSELLO. A brief detour from the route to the Passo del Sassello brings you to the town center. The town is known for its production of soft *amaretti*, but it is also a valuable source of mushrooms, in particular *porcini* (boletus) and *ovoli* (royal) .

VARAZZE. All that remains of the medieval village of Varagine are bits of wall and a few towers, but the fame of *Ad Navalia,* a village of shipwrights, lives on in the local boat yard. Good local cooking hails from both the sea and inland where prized vines grow. We recommend the restaurant "Cavetto", where the cuisine is imaginative and meals are good value. At pastry shops, buy *panettone alla genovese* and *amaretti di Santa Caterina.*

2. The Finalese

FINALE LIGURE. Following the Via Aurelia through splendid landscapes, you find one good gastronomic offering after another. At Bergeggi, inland from Spotorno, "Claudio" is a hotel and restaurant with a good view. The village of Noli has gained renown for its production of *acciughe sotto sale* (salt-cured anchovies) and a restaurant, "Lilliput", at Voze. Then comes Varigotti, on a promontory with its terraced "saracen" houses. Here, *cozze e muscoli in zuppetta* (mussel soup) is the specialty at the restaurant "Muraglia-Conchiglia d'Oro". You then arrive at Finale, made up of three historic nuclei with beautiful monuments, and an inland zone divided into small cultivated upland plains. You can taste and buy good wines at the "Cooperativa Finalese". The olive oil production is also significant. At pastry shops you will find *amaretti*. If you venture inland along the Colle del Melogna route to Calizzano, in the upper valley of the Bormida di Millesimo, you can go to the restaurant "Msè Tutta", which we

Savona. The old dock

recommend for the house specialties of *ravioli* filled with *ortiche* (nettles) and *borragine* (borage), as well as roast goose.

PIETRA LIGURE. The *pietra* (stone) is that on which the medieval Castello still sits. All around this village there are vegetable gardens and Vermentino vineyards. "Buca di Bacco", in the center, and "Capanno", in Ranzi, are two good restaurants to try. Backtracking a few kilometers to Borgio, we recommend the restaurant "Doc", where dishes include *fazzoletti di pasta al Moscato con astice e zucchine* (pasta "tissues" with Moscato, lobster and zucchini), accompanied by a good selection of wines. If you have the time, go up to Verezzi where there is a breathtaking panoramic view from the theatrical *piazzetta*.

LOANO. The layout of this town is that of an ancient mariner's village with a waterfront and wharf, as well as an inland road running parallel to the beach and animated by the presence of stores.

ALBENGA. This is where you will find the most interesting old center on the Riviera di Ponente. The layout is Roman, the structures medieval, and the monuments remarkable. Inland there are some charming villages – Villanova, Campochiesa, Castelvecchio di Rocca Barbena – and the fruit and vegetables are renowned (artichokes, asparagus, tomatoes, peaches, apricots). In the center, we recommend the "Antica Osteria dei Leoni" where seafood dishes are prepared, including *ciuppin di crostacei al timo selvatico* (shell-

fish stew with wild thyme), *ravioli in salsa di mare* (ravioli with seafood sauce) and *pesce spada con melanzane e olive* (swordfish with eggplant and olives). Another good stop is "Il Pernambucco", a Buon Ricordo restaurant that prepares fish in Ligurian style. In pastry shops you will try the short pastry sweets *gubelletti,* and *baxin*. The well-known local wines, made from Pigato and Rossese grapes, can be tasted at "Cascina Feipu dei Massaretti" at Bastia d'Abenga, and the "Cooperativa Viticoltori Ingauni" at Ortovero.

VINO DA TAVOLA

PIGATO
di Ciamboschi

ALASSIO. The spirit of this ancient seafarer's village lives on in the lively street that runs parallel to the beach. Settle into the mood at the historic cafe "Balzola", which was once made pastry for the royal house of Savoy. Then comes "Palma", where an experienced chef skillfully prepares dishes that are extraordinarily light and filled with Ligurian flavors, and seafood such as *ravioli di maggiorana e gallinella* (ravioli filled with marjoram and gurnard), as well as refined dishes such as *piccione ripieno di foie gras al Madera* (pigeon stuffed with foie gras and Madeira). There are also other simpler restaurants such as "Tre Mori", which has a gazebo that overlooks the sea, or "Lamberti", which is also an inn located in a tranquil spot very close to the sea. Before leaving, pick up some *Baci di Alassio* (Alassio kisses) a soft filled cookie that is the local specialty.

WINE PRODUCERS

Bastia d'Albenga
Cascina Feipu dei Massaretti
regione Massaretti 7
☎ 018220131
Finale Ligure
Coop. Agricola Finalese
at Perti (km 3)
via Calice 112
☎ 019695246
Ortovero
Coop. Viticoltori Ingauni
via Roma 1
☎ 0182547127

SHOPPING

Alassio
Caffè Pasticceria Balzola
piazza Matteotti 28
☎ 0182640209
Pastries and cookies such us "Baci di Alassio".
Finale Ligure
Frantoio Magnone
via Calvisio 156
☎ 019602190
Dop olive oil and olives.
Finalpia
Apiario Benedettino
via Santuario 59
☎ 019601700
Honey and specialties produced from honey.
Loano
Oleificio Polla
Nicolò srl
via Ghilini 46
☎ 019668027
Olive oil.

LAND OF LIGURIA IS FOR CONNOISSEURS
Simply enjoy the real taste of the Riviera and discover our ancient traditions and precious treasures.

ATHENA AND DIONYSUS

Let yourself be tempted by the gastronomic treasures of Western Liguria and start on a tasty journey to the discovery of the Ligurian cuisine whose main characters have always been the goddess Athena – the godmother of extra virgin olive oil – and Dionysus – the god of wine – who managed to give rise to the real Mediterranean Diet.

THE MUSES OF THE RIVIERA

It is an extraordinary journey to the discovery of the most perfumed flowers and of the rarest plants which were a source of inspiration for the greatest artists of all times and are to be found in some of the most beautiful botanical gardens in Europe. It is not just a holiday since here you can enjoy the perfumes of the most beautiful roses, the colours of the most elegant orchids, the majesty of the rarest palms, and the silver-grey hues of the most ancients olive trees.

THE MERMAIDS OF MEDITERRANEAN SEA

It is an exciting journey to the discovery both of the sea fauna and of the story of the exploration of the seven seas thanks to marvellous aquariums and sea museums. During summertime you can also spend some time doing whale watching in the Sanctuary of Whales.
Your journey from Genoa to Antibes will follow the steps of the great explorers, like Jacques Cousteau, who worked hard to let people know what is hidden in the deep oceans – and make them love and respect the sea and the great cetaceans living there.

*To receive the catalogue **Divine Riviera: land of Liguria is for connoisseurs** please contact*
Nyala Wonder Travel· via Solaro, 134 – 18038 San Remo (IM) -Italy - tel: +39 0184 666 986- fax +39 0184 696 672
e-mail: info@rivieradivina.it - www.rivieradivina.it

FRANTOIO DI SANT'AGATA DI ONEGLIA sas

LIGURIA - RIVIERA DEI FIORI - IMPERIA

Via S. Agata - Incrocio Strada dei Francesi, 48
18100 IMPERIA - Tel. +39 0183 293472 - +39 0183 710963
www.frantoiosantagata.com - E-mail: frantoio@frantoiosantagata.com

PRODUCERS OF D.O.P. EXTRA VIRGIN OLIVE OIL (RIVIERA LIGURE - RIVIERA DEI FIORI) AND OTHER LIGURIA SPECIALITIES

FRANTOIO
DI SANT'AGATA
D'ONEGLIA®

OUTLET
Via V. Monti, 7
18100 Imperia
Tel. e Fax +39 0183 299703

MUNICIPALITY OF APRICALE

Imperia Province

Via Cavour, 2 - 18035 Apricale (IM) - Italy
web-site: www.apricale.org - E-mail: apricale@apricale.org

Year's Events:

January - May: Spring Festival
February: "A" for amore in Apricale - romantic
itineraries during St. Valentine's week
June - July: Elastic ball (Balòn) tournament
July: Classical music concerts at the Castle
1-15 August: Theatre season "The stars look down" with the Teatro della Tosse and the Puppet Festival
2nd Sunday in September: The Pansarola fair
24th December: Christmas vigil, with a bonfire on the main square, kept on burning until 6th January
St. Stephen's day: Christmas concert
All through the year, at the Lucertola Castle (in the afternoon), visits to the Museum, with different subject displays, and to Lele Luzzati's Theatre Gallery.
Great artists exhibitions at the Castel Hall.

You can find the full event timetable on the town's web site.

"THE REAL VOICE OF MY REGION IS THE ONE WHICH SINGS WITH ITS WINES."

"Our wine must be smelt and savoured : I once remember a landlord of Santarcangelo who boasted of having an exceptional wine and who, after his customers had tasted it, asked them : "Did you hear it ?"
I am convinced that all the world will soon "hear" it because of its strong and poetic essence."

Tonino Guerra
Poet, author and scriptwriter of worldwide fame.

Hours of opening

From Tuesday to Thursday	10-13	16-19,30
Friday	10-13	16-22,30
Saturday	10-13	15-22,30
Sunday and Bank Holidays	10-13	15-19,30

Closed on Mondays

ENOTECA REGIONALE EMILIA-ROMAGNA.

The temple of wines.

The Regional Wine cellar of Emilia-Romagna dating from 1970, is the only body officially recognised by the Region for developing and promoting the high quality, DOC and DOCG, wines produced in the local area. Inside the Sforzesca di Dozza Fortress, completely restructured in 1990 and now home to the Wine Cellar, over 800 wines are kept which are the results of the labours of more than 200 Associates and represent the very best of regional production. Before a wine is admitted, it has to undergo an examination on the part of the Technical Commission made up of oenologists, sommeliers and members of the Overseeing Authorities.
All the wines on show in the permanent exhibition are for sale and it is possible to taste them under the guidance of expert sommeliers.

Inside the Wine cellar with an exposition of more than 800 types of Regional wine.

ENOTECA REGIONALE EMILIA-ROMAGNA

For further information and the latest regional updates, contact our offices: Mr. Ambrogio Manzi

Rocca Sforzesca - 40050 DOZZA BO
Tel. +39 0542 678089 - Fax +39 0542 678073
E-mail enoteca@tin.it - http://www.enotecaemiliaromagna.it

GABRIELE UGOLINI / PROGETTOGRAFICO

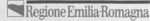
Regione Emilia-Romagna

EMILIA-ROMAGNA TWO SIDES TO GOOD EATING

The borderline separating the seductive dishes of Emilia and Romagna's fried gnocchi won't appear on any map, rather it is a meeting point for the two separate spirits of the same land.

The land bordered by the Po, Adriatic and Apennines is certainly Italy's richest in culinary terms. Its inhabitants are known for being big eaters and lovers of hearty cooking. The cult of the well-laid table is alive everywhere, with light pasta unifying a tradition fed by two different spirits. From Piacenza to Bologna lies Emilia and from Ravenna to Rimini is Romagna, separated at the Fall of Rome by a geographic and cultural borderline: the Longobards on one side, and the Byzantines on the other.

FROM APENNINES TO ADRIATIC

The Po's riverbed and the crest of the Apennines provide the characteristics of the landscape. The river shapes the horizon of the Bassa, with poplars and furrowed expanses dotted with farms built up around courtyards. Travelling west to east, you first come across the corn and medicinal herbs from the land of *culatello* and Parmigiano Reggiano, the great wines of Lambrusco, gardens and fruit orchards, and then the drained lands and fishing valleys of Comacchio. Flowing waters shape verdant mountains, the woods offer mushrooms and chestnuts and the pastures provide grazing for cattle and sheep. In the hills, vineyards spread from Trebbia to Marecchia and are blended with fruit orchards producing cherries and plums from Gutturnio to Albana. The coast is a thin strip of pine forests and sandy beaches.

"QC", THE LABEL FOR CONTROLLED QUALITY

With such a wide variety of produce, the region is deservedly known as a gastronomic paradise. Such renown is upheld by efforts to improve quality as well as preserve the traditional craftsmanship of its products. Thus labels such as "QC" for controlled quality have been instituted to identify products of integrated agriculture, which minimizes the use of chemicals. The region uses advanced organic agriculture methods. Local products are also protected by the DOP (*Denominazione di Origine Protetta*) and IGP (*Indicazione Geografica Protetta*) designations.

SUBTLE TASTES AND STRONG FLAVORS

The cuisine oscillates between the buttery, subtle tastes of Emilia, and the meatier, stronger flavors of Romagna, which are influenced by Central Italian cooking. Pork is widespread in Emilia, but there is a variety of alternatives – for example pigeon in Parma and rabbit in Modena. Mountain flavors are tinged with Ligurian and Florentine influences, while along the coast fish soups alternate with fried seafood. The cities offer first-rate restaurants – the Riviera eateries are well-known but the Apennines can throw up undiscovered gems. You can choose between abundant *trattorie*, *osterie* and *enoteche* serving meals and wine by the glass, back rooms of shops with tables and chairs offering snacks, *chioschi* (food kiosks) along the Riviera, offering "fast-food" in the form of the filled *piadina*, and shops full of charcuterie, soft cheeses and greens.

The Po, the main protagonist in Emilia-Romagna's landscape and cuisine

Emilia-Romagna - Typical products

CHEESES

1. **Parmigiano Reggiano Dop.** Parmesan cheese produced in Parma, Reggio nell'Emilia, Modena and Bologna.
2. **Grana Padano Dop.** Hard cheese produced above all in Piacenza.
3. **Provolone Valpadana Dop.** Produced in the province of Piacenza.
4. **Formaggio di fossa.** 'Pit cheese' produced in Sogliano al Rubicone, Ravennate and the high Valle della Marecchia.
5. **Pecorino dell'Appennino Reggiano**

CHARCUTERIE

1. **Coppa piacentina Dop.** Cured neck of pork.
2. **Culatello di Zibello Dop.** Zibello pork sausages.
3. **Mortadella Bologna Igp.** Bologna sausage
4. **Pancetta piacentina Dop**
5. **Prosciutto di Modena Dop**
6. **Prosciutto di Parma Dop.** The celebrated Parma ham.
7. **Salame piacentino Dop**
8. **Zampone di Modena Igp.** Stuffed pig's trotter.
9. **Ciccioli.** Bacon cubes – a regional specialty.
10. **Coppa di testa.** Cured pork produced in the Romagna hills.
11. **Cotechino di Modena Igp.** A spiced sausage from Modena
12. **Fiocchetto.** Produced in Parma, Piacenza and Cremona.
13. **Salame Felino**
14. **Pancetta Canusina.** Bacon produced in the Reggiano Apennines.
15. **Salama da sugo ferrarese.** A pork sausage.
16. **Spalla cotta di San Secondo.** Cooked shoulder of ham.
17. **Zuccotto di Bismantova**

MEATS

1. **Vitellone bianco dell'Appennino Centrale Igp.** Bullock raised in Bologna, Ravenna, Forlì and Rimini.
2. **Suino pesante padano.** Pork.
3. **Vitellone padano.** Bullock.

FRUIT

1. **Pera dell'Emilia-Romagna Igp.** Emilia-Romagna pears.
2. **Pesca e Nettarina di Romagna Igp.** Peaches and nectarines from Romagna.
3. **Ciliegia e Susina di Vignola.** Cherries and plums.

VEGETABLES

1. **Asparago verde di Altedo.** Green asparagus from Altedo.
2. **Scalogno di Romagna Igp.** Shallots from Romagna.
3. **Cipolla di Medicina.** Medicina onions.
4. **Cipolla di Parma.** Parma onions
5. **Aglio bianco piacentino.** White garlic.
6. **Patata tipica di Bologna.** Bologna potatoes.

EXTRA-VIRGIN OLIVE OIL

1. **Brisighella Dop**

VARIOUS

1. **Aceto balsamico tradizionale di Modena.** Traditional balsamic vinegar from Modena.
2. **Aceto balsamico tradizionale di Reggio Emilia.** Balsamic vinegar from Reggio Emilia.

3. **Fungo di Borgotaro Igp.** Mushrooms found in Val di Taro and Pontremoli.

4. **Marrone di Castel del Rio Igp.** Chestnuts from Castel del Rio.

BREAD AND SWEETS

1. **Coppia ferrarese**
2. **Erbazzone di Reggio Emilia**
3. **Gnocco fritto.** Fried *gnocchi* made in the Emilia area.
4. **Piadina.** Flat bread made in Romagna.
5. **Tortellino artigianale di Bologna**
6. **Cappelletto reggiano**
7. **Biscione reggiano**
8. **Ciambella reggiana**
9. **Spongata di Busseto.** Short pastry with nuts, honey and candied fruits from Busseto.
10. **Spongata reggiana.** Short pastry with nuts, honey and candied fruits from Reggio nell'Emilia
11. **Torta di riso reggiana.** Rice cake from Reggio nell'Emilia.

DOCG WINES

1. **Albana di Romagna**

DOC WINES

2. **Bosco Eliceo**
3. **Cagnina di Romagna**
4. **Colli Bolognesi**
5. **Colli Bolognesi Classico Pignoletto**
6. **Colli di Faenza**
7. **Colli d'Imola**
8. **Colli di Parma**
9. **Colli di Rimini**
10. **Colli di Scandiano e di Canossa**
11. **Colli Piacentini**
12. **Lambrusco di Sorbara**
13. **Lambrusco Grasparossa di Castelvetro**
14. **Lambrusco Salamino di Santa Croce**
15. **Pagadebit di Romagna**
16. **Reggiano**
17. **Reno**
18. **Romagna Albana**
19. **Sangiovese di Romagna**
20. **Trebbiano di Romagna**

EMILIA-ROMAGNA

PARMIGIANO-REGGIANO DOP
ONE PRODUCT, ONE REGION

A short history of a cheese envied the world over:
from its first appearance, deep in some Mediaeval monastery,
to the present-day DOP brand denomination protection.

Parmigiano-Reggiano takes its origin from a specific place and time: the place was the Enza valley, the dividing line between the modern provinces of Parma and Reggio Emilia; and the time was the Middle Ages, when certain monks dedicated themselves to the art of cheese making. It was during this period that the first matured Œgranal forms made their appearance, easy as they were to transport and which could be kept for a long time. Thus this unique cheese - excellent whether flaked or grated - came to be appreciated in the courts of Italy and the cities of Europe. For it to reach the rest of the world was by then merely a question of time.

CONSORZIO DEL FORMAGGIO PARMIGIANO-REGGIANO
Reggio Emilia
via Kennedy 18
☎ 0522 307741
Fax 0522 307748
e-mail: staff@parmigiano-reggiano.it
Internet: http://www.parmigiano-reggiano.it

The Consorzio organizes free visits to cheese-makers for school children and organized groups. The visits can cover the whole production cycle of the cheese.

From the river Po to the Appennines

The Parmigiano-Reggiano area now covers the provinces of Parma, Reggio Emilia, Modena and Bologna, the area to the left of the River Reno, and a small part of Lombardy in the Oltrepò Mantovano region. This is the territory which, in accordance with the Dop criteria, is responsible not only for the production of Parmigiano-Reggiano cheese but also of the milk from which it is made.

The milk. The excellence of Parmigiano-Reggiano (Parmesan cheese) is based on the milk from which it is made, which in turn depends on the quality of the cows' feed, made up mainly of local forage topped up with vegetable feed but nothing fermented as this could cause defects in the maturing process. The milk is worked from its natural, unpasteurized state, without thermal treatment, so the natural bacterial flora is respected. This allows the flavors of the forage to be passed on to the cheese and also allows the maturing process to begin naturally.

The human factor. The artisan cheese-maker who follows the milk's progress step by step is still the determining factor in the production of Parmesan cheese, even in the biggest and most important factories. The choices he makes, simple but vital, are based on his subtle knowledge and experience: he knows the milk and adapts the working of it to the

changing seasons, decides on the proportion of whey and rennet, and follows the cooking process every step of the way.

An unchanging technique. From the smallest cheese-makers to the most modern of factories, the production process still follows the traditional procedure. The milk comes from two milkings: the evening one, whose milk is partially skimmed, and the morn-

252

ing one whose milk is used as is i.e. full fat. The milk is put into copper heating vats and then whey from the previous day's milk is added. This is naturally enriched with milk enzymes which help turn the milk.

The wonder of this cheese.
Once the temperature reaches 34 °C, natural veal rennet is added to the milk which curdles it. It is then broken down into small granules. Next comes the cooking by slowly increasing the temperature until it reaches 55 °C. The curdled milk is then put into linen cloths and transferred to the cylindrical moulds the insides of which bear, by law, the words 'Parmigiano-Reggiano' in dotted letters, and the plate which unambiguously identifies the mould. The final step is to add the salt. This is done by immersing the cheese in a solution saturated with pure sea salt for 20-24 days.

A long maturing period.
The shortest period, as decreed by law, is 12 months but it is only from about 24 months that the cheese

really has that characteristic flavor. It is at this point that the milk enzymes have broken down most of the proteins into simpler molecules, making the cheese easily digestible and quickly turned into energy.

Very strict quality control.
Parmigiano-Reggiano is a Dop product (Denominazione d'Origine Protetta), in other words one whose area of origin is restricted, and recognized as such by the European Union. This means that 10 to 12 months after production, Consorzio (Parmesan Consortium) experts must examine every cheese form to check its quality and burn on the oval mark which, together with the words on the rind, show the cheese has been certified.

A food that goes well with everything.
When Parmigiano-Reggiano is at its best, it has a grainy, crumbly texture and a delicate but definite smell with vegetable overtones. It can be used in all sorts of ways: in the kitchen and at the table, eaten on its own or with walnuts, pears, honey, and many other things. From a nutritional point of view, it is particularly good for those needing energy quickly or who need easily digestible foods, so it is good for laborers, sportsmen, children, older people, and food-lovers of any age.

Parmigiano-Reggiano in numbers
16 liters of milk make 1 kg of cheese, 600 liters of milk are needed for each form of cheese
1 form of cheese weighs 38 kg
12 months minimum maturing period
20-24 months average maturing period
270,000 cows
6,500 companies
560 cheese-makers
108,235 tons produced
2,800,000 forms
1,700 billion lire sales at the production stage
2,400 billion lire sales at the distribution stage
Data is from the year 2000

Nutritional values
Water 30.8 g
Proteins (*) 33 g
Fats 28.4 g
Sodium chloride 1.39 g
(*) 23% free amino acids

Energy values
Kcals/100 g 392
Kjouls/100 g 1633
Calcium 1160 mg
Phosphorus 680 mg
Sodium 551 mg
Potassium 100 mg
Magnesium 43 mg
Zinc 4 mg
Cholesterol 83 mg
Vitamin A 270 µg
Vitamin B1 34 µg
Vitamin B2 370 µg
Vitamin B6 110 µg
Vitamin B12 4.2 µg
Vitamin PP 55 µg
Pantotenic Acid 320 µg
Colin 40 mg
Biotin 23 µg

Parmigiano-Reggiano does not contain any preservatives or other additives.

BOLOGNA

The city is Italy's true capital of good food; located at the center of an agricultural district, it has a cuisine that is unmatched in richness and variety

The province of Bologna is divided in two by the Via Emilia: to the north lies the broad plain bordered by the Reno river, which separates the province from the province of Ferrara: to the south are the calcareous Gessi Bolognesi hills, and then mountains that run to the crest of the Apennines. The flatlands are the setting for agriculture, animal rearing and fruit and vegetable growing. Major products include *Mortadella* di Bologna DOP and Asparago verde di Altedo IGP (green asparagus from Altedo) as well as the DOC wine Montuni del Reno, a product of the vines of the same name that grow along the river. Vineyards cover the hills which form the backdrop to the provincial capital. This is the zone for the DOC Colli Bolognesi. It has a variety of geographical sub-denominations, with the local Pignoletto worth noting from the whites, and the hearty

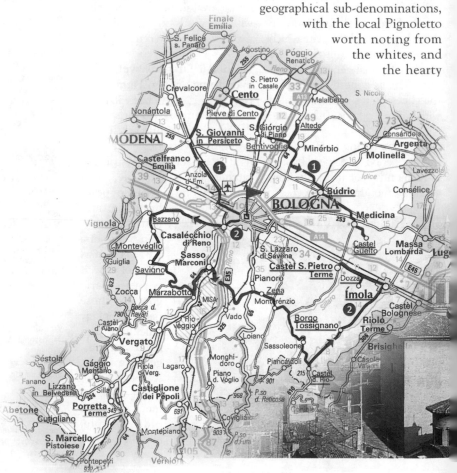

Barbera standing out among the reds. Towards the eastern border, the DOCG Albana di Romagna and the DOC Colli d'Imola offer a taste of Romagna. The mountains are fertile land for mushrooms, truffles and *castagne* (chestnuts), with an IGP production of chestnuts at Castel del Rio. The province offers the richest and most famous foods you can think of. The city is known as 'Bologna la Dotta' (Bologna the Learned) for its old university, but also 'Bologna la Grassa' (Bologna the Fat) because of its equally historical inclination towards the pleasures of food. The designation *alla bolognese* has become synonymous with rich flavors and generous servings of sauce the world over. Pasta made with eggs, whether plain or filled, is the city's gastronomic trademark, while *ragù* is the sauce that does it most justice.

Gourmet Tours

BOLOGNA. This is the city of the two towers – of Piazza Maggiore and San Petronio, of the University and the colonnades that line an old center rich with references, all in the shadow of nearby hills. One of the most astonishing visions for the stranger here are the *pizzicherie*, where all kinds of charcuterie are sold. These carefully-arranged stores are filled with a wealth of products that best represent the excellence of local gastronomy. The offerings in the city demonstrate just how provincial the food here is: the local tradition is so rich that there is no room for specialties from other Emilian or Romagnese towns. "Pappagallo", which is located in a fourteenth-century building on Piazza della

Bologna

HOTELS AND RESTAURANTS

Bologna
Pappagallo ¶¶¶¶ ★ TCI
piazza Mercanzia 3
☎ 051231200
Bitone ¶¶¶
via Emilia Levante 111
☎ 051546110
Rodrigo ¶¶¶
via della Zecca 2/h
☎ 051235536
Biagi
alla Grada ¶¶ TCI
via della Grada 6
☎ 051572063
Diana ¶¶
via Indipendenza 24
☎ 051231302
Argelato
L'800 ¶¶
via Centese 33
☎ 051893032
Borgo Tossignano
Locanda della
Colonna ¶¶¶¶
via Nuova 10/11
☎ 054291006
Castel Guelfo
di Bologna
Locanda
Solarola ¶¶¶¶
via S. Croce 5
☎ 0542670102
Castel San
Pietro Terme
Trattoria
Trifoglio ¶¶
at San Giovanni
dei Boschi (km 12)
☎ 051949066
Dozza
Monte
del Re ★★★ TCI
via Monte del Re 43
☎ 0542678400

Bologna. "Paolo Atti & Figli" pastry shop

**HOTELS AND
RESTAURANTS**

Imola
San Domenico ¶¶¶¶
via Sacchi 1
☎ 054229000
Pieve di Cento
**Buriani dal
1967** ¶¶¶
via Provinciale 2/a
☎ 051975177
San Giovanni in
Persiceto
**Osteria
del Mirasole** ¶¶
via Matteotti 17/a
☎ 051821273
San Lazzaro
di Savena
⭐🛏 **Le Siepi** ⭐⭐⭐
including restaurant
La Pietra Cavata
at Idice (km 2)
via Emilia 514
☎ 0516256200
San Pietro in
Casale
⭐🛏 **Dolce e
Salato** ¶¶
piazza Calori 16
☎ 051811111
Savigno
⭐🛏 **Amerigo** ¶¶
via Marconi 16
☎ 0516708326
Trebbo di Reno
**Sole - Antica
Locanda del
Trebbio** ¶¶¶
via Lame 67
☎ 051700102

Mercanzia, and "Diana" in Via Indipendenza are among the long-established restaurants of the town. The old-fashioned flavors available here include the sumptuous *fritto dolce e salato* (sweet and savory fry). "Biagi alla Grada" is famous for its excellent *lasagne*. Another unmissable venue is a store called "Paolo Atti & Figli", which sells pasta, pastry and other delicacies. Founded in 1880, the store in Via delle Capraie has preserved its original furnishings and atmosphere. In the search for something sweet, head for the café "Zanarini" (established 1919), which was founded under the colonnades of Bologna University, in the heart of the city. "Bitone" and "Rodrigo" are two restaurants worth visiting in town, while outside the city, in Trebbo di Reno, we recommend "Sole – Antica locanda del Trebbio", which offers meticulously prepared food and a good wine list. In San Lazzaro di Savena, eat at "Le Siepi", a plush hotel in an eighteenth-century *palazzetto* with a lively restaurant, surrounded by a big garden.

1. Bologna's plains

SAN GIOVANNI IN PERSICETO. Turning off the Statale 568 from Crevalcore, you come to Budrie, the native land of Santa Clelia Barbieri, founder of the *Suore Minime dell'Addolorata* order of nuns. Further along is San Giovanni in Persiceto, which has an ancient tradition of fruit cultivation. This tradition is continued today with the cultivation of watermelons and the San Matteo Decima melon. Other specialties are *Africanetti* cookies and *Ciabattine di San Antonio*. Locals are also proud of the characters Bertoldo and Bertoldino, created here by the sixteenth-century writer Giulio Cesare Croce, who was a native of this town. Good restaurants include "Osteria del Mirasole", with a menu listing dishes such as *tagliatelle con rigaglie* (tagliatelle with giblets), *torta di ciccioli a velo* (torte with pork rind) and *fegatelli all'alloro* (liver with bay leaf), all dishes evoking hearty country cooking.

PIEVE DI CENTO. Across the Reno, which marks the border with Ferrara, lies Cento, the native city of

Guercino, the seventeenth-century painter. On the same side of the river stands the Collegiate Church of Santa Maria Maggiore, which used to be a parish church, and the Bolognese-style colonnaded village that grew up around it. This stage in the journey is boosted by the excellent cooking at "Buriani dal 1967". Don't miss the *luccio in lattuga* (pike wrapped in lettuce) and the cheese cart.

BENTIVOGLIO. In the town of San Marino, visit the important Museo della Civiltà Contadina (Agricultural Museum). On the way there you will come across two appetizing restaurants: the "L'800", in Argelato, which is classic and modern at the same time, with a well-stocked wine cellar, and "Dolce e Salato" at San Pietro in Casale, where you can get Emilia's pasta in all its shapes and with all its fillings.

ALTEDO. After a few kilometers on the Porrettana heading towards Ferrara, you come to this village, a small center for green asparagus growing. The asparagus is also a fine excuse for a festival and competitions in mid-May.

BUDRIO. After passing through Minerbio, you reach Budrio, an ancient resort town where potatoes are the traditional cultivated product and mainstay of local gastronomy. Another symbol of the village is the *ocarina*, the humble wind instrument invented here in the mid-nineteenth century, and which even has its own museum.

CASTEL GUELFO. After passing through Medicina, continue between extensive fields of golden onions, which have been cultivated here since the thirteenth century and are being recommended for *Indicazione Geografica Protetta*. Then you arrive at the ancient Via degli Stradelli Guelfi, which was once the main road between Bologna and Romagna. In town you will get the best reception at "Locanda Solarola", a fascinating inn with comfortable rooms and particularly innovative Emilian cooking.

Bologna flatlands. Rice fields converted for breeding fish

AGRITURISMI

Fontanelice
Ca' Monti
at Sassoleone
via Montemorosino 4
☎ 054297666
Monte San Pietro
Tenuta Bonzara
at San Chierlo 37/a
☎ 0516768324
Monteveglio
Corte d'Albo
via Marzatore 15
☎ 051832583

WINE PRODUCERS

Imola
Tre Monti
via Lola 3
☎ 0542657116

2. The hills of Bologna and the Apennines

BAZZANO. Leaving the city via the Porta Saragozza, take the Statale 569 towards Vignola as far as Bazzano. In the springtime the blossoming cherry trees are spectacular. The vineyards are also important, with more than one Città del Vino (City of Wine) in the area, including Zola Predosa.

MONTEVEGLIO. High on a hill the ancient walled town hugs the abbey of Santa Maria. This is the nucleus of a natural park that lies between cultivated fields and small country roads. A brief detour leads to Monte San Pietro, a Città del Vino. This is a sub-zone of the DOC wine Colli Bolognesi. Wine tasting and *agriturismo* holidays are on offer at the excellent farm "Bonzara".

SAVIGNO. In the upper valley of the Samoggia lies this Città del Tartufo (City of Truffles), where an important festival and market are held in the fall. We recommend stopping by "Amerigo" for some excellent local food - featuring *tartufo bianco* (white truffles) and *funghi* (mushrooms) – and its remarkable wine cellar.

MARZABOTTO. Crossing over two ridges the road descends into the Reno Valley. Sadly the town is mostly known for the massacre carried out there by Nazis in 1944. Various sites within the historic Monte Sole park are memorials to the event. But near the river is the truly charming Etruscan town of Misa. Typical of the area is the cheese Pecorino di Vergato. Further down the valley you will find Sasso Marconi, where there is a villa-museum dedicated to the celebrated scientist Guglielmo Marconi. Near the springs are Porretta Terme and Castel di Casio, which is a small Città del Tartufo.

ZENA. Going down below the peak of Monte Adone, you arrive at the bridge crossing the Savena river. A turn to the right leads up to the Raticosa Pass. Loiano lies along the way and is the epicenter for the production of *furmajen*, (or *Semitenero di Loiano*), which is cheese – *formaggio* – in local dialect. Cutting across the peaks, you come to Idice, which is the start of a return route to the city through the unique landscapes of the Gessi Bolognesi and the Calanchi dell'Abbadessa.

CASTEL DEL RIO. Continuing to cut through the mountain tops, you reach the upper Valle del Santerno and the Montanara road, which winds its way between impressive peaks and areas of erosion to Tuscany. Stop in the Renaissance village there, which is a small center for chestnuts and *marron glacé*.

BORGO TOSSIGNANO. Passing through Fontanelice, a summer vacation spot and spa center, go down to the valley's main center. On the other side of the river, in an ancient construction at the foot of the Rocca di Tossignano,

SHOPPING

Bologna
Paolo Atti & Figli
via delle Capraie 7
☎ 051220425
Fresh pasta, bread and pastries; delicatessen.
Antica Salsamenteria Tamburini
via Capraie 1
☎ 051234726
Fresh pasta, Parmigiano reggiano, charcuterie.
La Baita Freo
via Pescherie Vecchie, 3/a
☎ 051223940
Typical cheeses.
La Caramella di Gino Fabbri
via Cadriano 27
☎ 051505074
Pastries and cookies.
Caffè Zanarini
piazza Galvani 1
☎ 051222717
Cafe and pastry shop.

is "Locanda della Colonna", which is known for creatively reinterpreting ancient recipes.

IMOLA. This town, with its impressive fortress, lies along the Via Emilia. Although it is part of the territory of Bologna, it is marked by the character and traditions of Romagna, with all the characteristics of its cuisine, ranging from the *piadina* (flatbread) to grilled *castrato* (mutton). We highly recommend the restaurant "San Domenico", where classic recipes alternate with original modern dishes. The pastries and wine cellar are excellent. The winery "Tre Monti" is fortunate enough to be part of the closed circle of "Viticoltori Italiani di Eccellenza" (Italian Vintners of Excellence).

DOZZA. Looking out over the plains from a delightful plateau, this Città del Vino (City of Wine) has an excellent DOCG Albana and a Regional Wine Cellar locat-

ed in the fifteenth-century fortress. We recommend stopping at "Monte del Re", a historic structure that now hosts guests in first-rate rooms and serves them with good cooking. Fruit (peaches, apricots, grapes) is cultivated in the area, and locals also gather truffles.

CASTEL SAN PIETRO. Located on the ancient border with Romagna, this is an important town noted for its hot springs. In addition to the wines of Romagna, some of the best Italian honey is produced in the hills. The cheeses are also highly regarded, and include *Squacquerone di Romagna, Rigatino, pecorino di Palesio, ricotta di pecora*. At pastry shops look for the renowned *'savoiardi' castellani* cookies. At San Giovanni dei Boschi leave the road for "Trattoria Trifoglio".

Flowering cherries in the lower Appennine hills

SHOPPING

Castel San Pietro Terme
Caseificio Comellini Ruberto & C.
via Flavio Gioia 6
☎ 051941376
Typical cheeses.
Savigno
La Dispensa di Amerigo
piazza XV Agosto 38
☎ 0516708528
Typical products from Bologna and Modena.
Silla
Macelleria Antoni
via Giovanni XXIII
☎ 053430027
Meat and charcuterie.

FERRARA

*The town of the Estes has some sumptuous
dishes, while the Po Delta offers pure flavors
from the river and the Adriatic*

T he province of Ferrara is very much shaped
by the waters that surround it. The Po and one
of its delta branches designate the confines to
the north, while the Reno river flows along its southern border. The east
is hugged by the lagoons and beaches of the Adriatic Sea. There is an order and uniformity to the landscape, and the streets and canals running
through the drained

*Below: Ferrara.
Palazzo comunale
(Town Hall)*

lands have a geometric layout. And where drainage was impossible, reeds and water lilies cover the land, and swampland birds fly overhead. Ingenious fishing methods have sprung up here, indicating a more promising future for these wetlands. The region of Ferrara is mostly an area of intensive agriculture, particularly for grains in the lands of the Delta, while around the capital the countryside is diversified by ploughed lands, orchards and vegetable gardens. The Bosco Eliceo DOC wines are quite unusual, and the red made from Uva d'Oro (the local name for Fortana grapes) is even more so with its grapes grown in sandy soil just inland from the Adriatic coast. Pig rearing is also quite widespread, and is represented among the gastronomic symbols of Ferrara with the *salama da sugo* (a pork sausage). Fish farming is also popular in the Valli di Comacchio, with *anguilla* (eel) a regular feature at the table. The gastronomy of the province of Ferrara is unique in terms of the variety of produce that can be found here. In the capital you will find dishes that revive the Renaissance feasts at the court of the Este as well as specialties derived from the Jewish community and even dishes with a certain Mantuan aspect to them. The culinary tradition of the province wavers between that of the land of the Reno, which is close to Bolognese cooking, and that of the younger lands of the Po, which is similar to the cuisine of the Veneto, dominated by fish from the river, lagoon, and the sea.

Gourmet Tours

FERRARA. Founded along a branch of the Po river, the town is divided in two by the main artery. On one side lies the oldest part of the town, with the Cathedral and a network of medieval streets, and on the other lies the area that was developed by Ercole I d'Este, with its straight streets and important Renaissance residences. First among these buildings is the Palazzo dei Diamanti, which today hosts important exhibitions. The Castello, surrounded by water, is center stage. The perimeter wall is planted with trees, framing it nicely. Palazzo Schifanoia plays an exceptional role in art with its unforgettable frescoes in the Sala dei Mesi (Room of Months). As for good food, the restaurant "Quel Fantastico Giovedì" is worth trying for its innovative, mostly fish-based cooking. If you wish to sample traditional dishes, such as *pasticcio di maccheroni tartufato* (truffled macaroni medley) and *salama da sugo* (a kind of pork sausage), try "L'Oca Giuliva", which has a very pleasant atmosphere. Jewish specialties are also worth tasting and range from *prosciutti d'oca* (goose *prosciutto*) to desserts for the fesval of Purim. Bakeries sell the famous *cornetti ferraresi*. At the city gates go to "Il Testamento del Porco", which has fantastic *chiocciole all'amatriciana* (pasta spirals with spicy tomato sauce). At Pontelagoscuro, a suburb on the Po, buy *mandorlini del Ponte*, candies made with almonds. Outside the city go to the restaurant "Don Giovanni" at Marrara, or "Lanzagallo" in Gaibana.

1. In the Po Delta

CODIGORO. Following the Po di Volano canal away from the capital, you come to Tresigallo and Massa Fiscaglia. Along the canal

HOTELS AND RESTAURANTS

Ferrara
Don Giovanni ¶¶
at Marrara (km 17)
via del Primaro 86
☎ 0532421064
Lanzagallo ¶¶
at Gaibana (km 10)
via Ravenna 1048
☎ 0532718001
L'Oca Giuliva ¶¶
via Boccanale
di S. Stefano 38
☎ 0532207628
**Quel Fantastico
Giovedì** ¶¶
via Castelnuovo 9
☎ 0532760570
**Il Testamento
del Porco** ¶
via Putinati 24
☎ 0532760460
Argenta
Villa Reale
★★★ [icl]
★
viale Roiti 16/a
☎ 0532852331
Bondeno
Tassi ¶¶ [icl]
viale Repubblica 23
☎ 0532893030
Codigoro
**La Capanna
di Eraclio** ¶¶
at Ponte Vicini (km 9)
via per le Venezie 21
☎ 0533712154
Comacchio
**Osteria
della Giulia** ¶
via Muratori 21
☎ 053381252
Lido di Spina
Aroldo ¶¶ [icl]
viale delle Acacie 26
☎ 0533330948

embankment you finally reach Codigoro, which is described in Giorgio Bassani's novel *L'Airone*. In keeping with that atmosphere is "La Capanna di Eraclio", a family-run *trattoria* with very interesting but simple dishes. Don't miss the *pesce in saor* (fish in an onion marinade) and, in season, *risotto con le folaghe* (risotto with coot).

POMPOSA. The bell tower of the celebrated abbey together with the cypress trees stands out in the Po valley, through which runs the Strada Romea. This is a stop for art lovers and is also interesting for the Bosco Eliceo DOC wines, the name of which recalls the landed property of the abbey.

MESOLA. The Castello, located where the Strada Romea crosses the Po di Goro, was the Estes' favorite residence during the deer hunts that were once held in the surrounding forests. For quite a long way this route follows the Gran Bosco della Mesola, now a nature reserve and a splendid remainder of that past.

GORO. After leaving the Strada Romea, follow the banks of the Po between the valleys. Goro and Gorino are the last inhabited villages, but it is possible to continue

by boat to the Faro (lighthouse) that marks the last bit of solid ground. To return to the town, cut straight through the Grande Bonifica Ferrarese and return to Tresigallo via Jolanda di Savoia. Otherwise, if you are not in a hurry, the route following the Po di Goro is punctuated by various towns -such as Guarda Ferrarese, which Giovanni Bacchelli used as the setting for *Mulino del Po*- which are quite charming.

2. Towards the Comacchio Valleys

OSTELLATO. As you go from Ferrara to Portomaggiore and on to Ostellato via the old parish of San Vito, we recommend you stop to try the refined cuisine of "Locanda della Tamerice", in which mostly valley fish are used. One of the chef's great successes is *zuppa d'aglio affumicato del Mezzano con coriandoli* (garlic soup with smoked Mezzano cheese and coriander), *luccio e pomodorini* (pike with cherry tomatoes), and *moriglione in salsa di mirtilli* (pochard, or dunbird, in blueberry sauce).

HOTELS AND RESTAURANTS

Mesola
Locanda Duo ‖
via Mazzini 60
☎ 0533993306
Ostellato
Locanda della Tamerice ‖‖
via Argine Mezzano 2
☎ 0533680795
Porto Garibaldi
Pacifico ‖
via Caduti del Mare 10
☎ 0533327169
Portomaggiore
La Chiocciola ‖
via Runco 94/f
☎ 0532329151
Sant'Agostino
Trattoria La Rosa ‖‖
via del Bosco 2
☎ 053284098

AGRITURISMI

Ferrara
Ca' Spinazzino
at Spinazzino
via Taglione 5
☎ 0532725035
Argenta
★ Prato Pozzo
Rifugio di Valle
at Anita
via Rotta Martinella 34/a
☎ 0532801058
Belfiore
via Pioppa 27
☎ 0533681164

Argenta. Campotto Valleys

Comacchio. Traditional sailboat in the city's canals

COMACCHIO. This fishermen's village is cut through by canals that connect the *valli*, expanses of lagoons converted through centuries of water cultivation. This is the main Italian homeland of the eel, which may be found cooked in soups, grilled or skewered. When marinated, the same fish is the source of a flourishing canned food industry. In the city, after having checked out all the staircases of the Trepponti – a unique bridge that links several inhabited islands – stop by the "Osteria della Giulia". The more energetic should continue on far as Porto Garibaldi, where they may taste good fish in classic recipes at "Pacifico". On the road again, cross the *bonifiche*, or drained lands, which made it possible to rediscover the Etruscan city of Spina. Then continue along the Strada Argine Agosta, which marks the internal limit of the Valli, and go along the Reno, pausing at Anita (the name refers to the death of Garibaldi's companion) and Longastrino.

ARGENTA. Located on the Statale Adriatica, this town is known above all for its natural heritage,

with a landscape made up of patches of valleys that escaped drainage. Those who love beautiful residences should spend a night at the elegant inn "Villa Reale". The route back to Ferrara goes through an area full of white truffles near San Bartolomeo in Bosco. At Portomaggiore, just outside the historic center, "La Chiocciola" specializes in frogs.

3. Near Bologna

BONDENO. Set amongst the willows that line the riverbanks, this land has a plentiful supply of white truffles. At the hotel-restaurant "Tassi" you can discover just how well they go with waterfowl.

CENTO. On the banks of the Reno at the edge of Bologna, this town has colonnaded streets and dignified seventeenth-century architecture. The 1600s was also the time of Guercino, the town's most illustrious son, who left several interesting paintings here.

SANT'AGOSTINO. In an area renowned for its *funghi* and *tartufi*, a stop at "Trattoria La Rosa" is a must. Try the *tortelloni di zucca* and the *faraona al cartoccio* (guinea hen baked in paper).

SHOPPING

Ferrara
**Enoteca
al Brindisi**
via degli Adelardi 11
☎ 0532209142
Wines, distilled spirits, olive oil and vinegar.
Comacchio
**La Bottega
di Fantinoli
Anna & C.**
via Pescheria 3
☎ 0533313040
Marinated eel.
**Pescheria
Trepponti -
F.lli Cavalieri**
via Trepponti 34
☎ 053381727
Fresh fish and seafood specialties.
Renazzo
Negrini Salumi
via Alberelli 28
☎ 051685001 1
Charcuterie.

FORLÌ-CESENA

The Adriatic Riviera supplies excellent fish to this province of Romagna, which sprawls between hills and mountains.

Below: Castrocaro Terme. The feudal castle

The province that unites Forlì and Cesena is divided by the Via Emilia, which splits it into an area of plains with a limited seafront in Cesenatico and an area of hills and mountains, such as the forested peak of Monte Fumaiolo. Agricultural production is quite varied. The hills are covered with vineyards and fruit orchards mostly full of peach trees. Fruit and vegetables are also cultivated in the plains. DOC wine production is also significant, with the quality of Vini del Passatore protected by a consortium of wine makers formed specifically for that purpose. The white wines of this area are Albana (DOCG), Pagadebit and Trebbiano, and the reds are Sangiovese and Cagnina, and are brought together under the

264

specification di Romagna. Poultry farming is an important activity in the plains, while the fish market of Cesenatico provides plenty of blue-fish. Back up in the valleys, truffles, *funghi*, and chestnuts are plentiful, and there is a wide variety of meats - from the big veal calves of the Bianca Romagnola breed to the *cinghiale* (wild boar) - cheeses and charcuterie (*salsiccia passita*). The cuisine is first rate and encompasses a range of flavors from those of the Romagna Riviera, which modulate between fish and special pastas, to the rustic dishes from the Apennines, in which both the historical and the geographical influence of nearby Tuscany can be seen. There is a dense network of restaurants, particularly along the coast, which includes two excellent eateries - "La Frasca" in Castrocaro Terme and "Paolo Teverini" at Bagno di Romagna.

Gourmet Tours

FORLÌ. The town's symbol is the bell-tower church of San Mercuriale, which stands in the large Piazza Saffi together with several old *palazzi*. The two main roads through Emilia start here, and many of the town's monuments are clustered around the square. Go to "Trattoria La Monda" for *piadine* (flatbread) and *tagliatelle* in the best homemade tradition. For a lunch fragrant with truffles and mushrooms from the Apennines, continue to San Martino in Strada, where you will find the elegant "Villa Merenda".

1. The hills of Forlì

CASTROCARO TERME. Follow the Statale 67 Tosco Romagnola up the Montone Valley. The first stop is at Terra del Sole, a Medici citadel with a Renaissance square that is still intact. Then you come to Castrocaro, with its me-dieval village nestled below a fortress, and thermal springs in a park. Here "La Frasca" is excellent, with nothing left to chance. The menus suggested by the establishments will lead you through a cuisine of seafood and vegetables based on the great traditions of the region, including *tortino di gamberi e melanzane* (shrimp and eggplant torte) and *strozzapreti leggerissimi ai crostacei e al pesto di scalogno* (very light pasta with shellfish and shallot pesto). A few recipes derived from the nineteenth-century cookery writer Pellegrino Artusi are particularly memorable. The area lends itself to gathering white truffles, and it is renowned for its cherry and peach orchards. There are also some good cured meats, and the rare *lombetto di maiale*, which is aged for three months, is of ancient fame.
ROCCA SAN CASCIANO. Upriver from Castrocaro we enter the Ro-

Castrocaro Terme. «La Frasca»

HOTELS AND
RESTAURANTS

Forlì
Trattoria
La Monda ¶
via Monda-Collina 72
☎ 054386372
Villa Merenda ¶
at San Martino
in Strada
via La Fontana 10
☎ 0543488131
Bagno di
Romagna
Paolo Teverini ¶¶¶¶
via del Popolo 2
☎ 543911260
Tosco
Romagnolo ★★★
piazza Dante 2
☎ 543911260
Castrocaro
Terme
La Frasca ¶¶¶¶¶
via Matteotti 38
☎ 543767471
Cesena
Casali ¶¶
via Croce 71
☎ 54727485
Cesenatico
Bistrot
No Code ¶¶
viale dei Mille 55
☎ 054782055
Lido Lido ¶¶
viale Carducci 12
☎ 547673311

magna Fiorentina, the area towards the Adriatic that from the fifteenth century to the fall of the Grand Duchy of Tuscany flew the banner with the Florentine *fleur-de-lis*. First is Dovadola, one of the capitals of mushrooms and white truffles in Romagna, followed by Rocca San Casciano, and it is here that the gastronomy of Romagna encounters that of Tuscany. Further upstream you will find two medieval towns, Portico di Romagna and Premilcuore, nestled among woods rich with mushrooms (*spugnole*, or morels, in the springtime, and *porcini*, or boletus mushrooms, in the autumn) and truffles. The prized cheese Ravaggiolo is produced in and around Portico (Tredozio, San Benedetto in Alpe, Premilcuore).

GALEATA. From Rocca San Casciano a panoramic road cuts through the Valle del Rabbi and goes down into the Bidente valley. In a dell lies

Galeata, a village with colonnaded streets and Tuscan-style architecture. A pleasant walk from here leads to the church of San Ellero. A little further down, in Santa Sofia, the tasty sausage *ciavarro*, or *salsiccia matta all'aglio*, is made of lesser cuts of meat (meat scraps, stomach, kidneys, etc.). A few kilometers away lies Civitella di Romagna. Here the traditional dish is *arrosto al lampeggio*, a roast that is basted with drops of burning lard. There are also many salamis and the usual abundance of truffles.

MELDOLA. Within its walls this village, with the long colonnaded, Bolognese-style Via Roma, the harmonious Piazza Orsini and the Palazzo Comunale (Town Hall), preserves its appearance dating from the time when it was an important center for silk trading. A detour is recommended at Predappio, the town where Benito Mussolini was born. Since 1957 he has been buried in the cemetery near the old church of San Cassiano

Cesenatico. The canal port with boats from the Museo della Marineria

HOTELS AND RESTAURANTS

Forlimpopoli
Al Maneggio ¶¶¶
via Meldola 1930
☎ 0543742042
Verghereto
Il Pentagono ¶
at Balze
via Nuova 64
☎ 0543906637

AGRITURISMI

Bagno di
Romagna
Bacino
at Vessa
☎ 0543912023
Bertinoro
Fattoria Paradiso
via Palmeggiana 285
☎ 0543445044

in Pennino, which has been largely rebuilt. Continuing along the beautiful route, in the Valle del Rabbi we come to Rocca delle Caminate, an ancient building that gained fame as the dictator's summer residence. At Predappio don't miss the Alta "Ca' de Sanzves" (Casa del Sangiovese), where you can taste the local *pecorino* (sheep's cheese) and much else.

BERTINORO. Its nickname 'Balcone di Romagna' refers to the town's fortunate position at the top of a hill among the vineyards that produce the most famous wines of Romagna. Each year the medieval town celebrates its tradition of hospitality with a festival. In the piazza a stairway leads down to "Ca' del Be'" (Casa del Bere), a small sanctuary for Vini del Passatore, Romagnese wines that are produced under the control of authorities. The Fattoria Paradiso offers wine-tasting in the cellar, and *agriturismo* farm stays.

FORLIMPOPOLI. This is the homeland of Pellegrino Artusi, the author of La Scienza in Cucina (The Science of the Kitchen), a milestone in Italian gastronomic literature. His memory is honored graciously at "Al Maneggio", a fine restaurant located in the seventeenth-century villa in which playwright Carlo Goldoni set *La locandiera*.

CESENA. The winding town walls and the fortress recall the fifteenth century and the Malatesta family. The old center offers a warm reception, well provided as it is by the surrounding area with fruit and vegetables, including the renowned local table grape. You can get fine lodgings and meals at "Casali", a traditional old inn. Just a few kilometers away, up on the hill dotted with villas, is the basilica of the Madonna del Monte with a collection of ancient ex-votos. We strongly recommend going on to Cesenatico, where traditional boats of the Adriatic are moored in the canal port and there is an important fish market. It is worth going to "Lido Lido" where the meat and fish dishes are simple and honest, and accompanied by good wine. For night-owls, "Bistrot No Code" offers a youthful atmosphere and good cooking.

2. In the Savio and Rubicone Valleys

SARSINA. The Statale 71 Umbro-Casentinese-Romagnola, which goes back up the Valle del Savio, first passes through Mercato Saraceno, where there are good opportunities for tasting the renowned local cheeses and charcuterie. Further up, stop at the interesting town of Sarsina. Founded in the Roman era, the Cathedral preserves archaeological remains and significant sacred architecture. The piazza is named after the native Latin comic poet Plautus, in whose name a theater revue is held each summer. The cuisine is equally interesting and includes excellent lamb, mutton,

AGRITURISMI

Castrocaro
Terme
Sadurano
via Sadurano 45
☎ 0543766643
Cesenatico
Ai Tamerici ★
via Mesolino 60
☎ 0547672730
Civitella
di Romagna
Ca' Bionda ★
at Cusercoli
via S. Giovanni 42
☎ 0543989101
Predappio Alta
Pian dei Goti ★
via Montemirabello 1
☎ 0543921118

Bagno di Romagna. The restaurant "Paolo Teverini"

dairy products and charcuterie (of which *coppone* is served with a *piadina*, or flatbread).

BAGNO DI ROMAGNA. Known for the quality of its waters, this town is located on the edge of the Parco Nazionale delle Foreste Casentinese e di Campigna. Such a position means that even the highest culinary expectations are met: beef, stream fish, *pecorino* (sheep's cheese), mushrooms and white truffles are the raw materials for a cuisine that is at its best in great roasts.

Here you must seek out the superlative restaurant "Paolo Teverini", at the hotel "Tosco Romagnolo", which offers cooking that is perfect to the last detail, with traditional menus that vary according to season. Don't miss the *ravioli di verdure saltate con frutti di mare* (vegetable *ravioli* sautéed with shellfish) and *lombetto di maialino marinato al ginepro con spugnole* (suckling pig loin marinated with juniper and morels). Further upstream at the foot of Monte Fumaiolo, lies the village of Verghereto, known for its abundant supply of *tartufo nero* (black truffles), wild boar and chestnuts. Visit the village of Balze di Verghereto, where the simple *trattoria* "Il Pentagono" offers hearty food and good local products.

SOGLIANO SUL RUBICONE. From Mercato Saraceno continue into the Valle del Rubicone (take detours here to Montefeltro, Pennabilli and Novafeltria). The town of Sogliano owes its gastronomic fame to *formaggio di fossa* (pit cheese), a local specialty that mobilizes the entire village to work on the unique ageing process for this cheese. Another typical local cheese is *Ravaggiolo*. A last stop before the Via Emilia is Longiano: a medieval walled village that offers plenty of art and theater to keep the visitor interested.

WINE PRODUCERS

Bertinoro
Ca' del Be'
piazza Libertà
☎ 0543445303
Predappio Alta
Ca' de Sanzves
piazza Cavour 41
☎ 0543922410

SHOPPING

Bagno di Romagna
Comero Funghi
via della Torretta 13
at S. Pietro in Bagno
☎ 0543917422
Mushrooms and truffles.

MODENA

Zampone, Lambrusco and balsamic vinegar are the stars in the very precisely-defined gastronomic identity of this province.

T he province of Modena is a long rectangle that runs from the Oltrepò Mantovano to the mountains of the Appennino Tosco-Emiliano. The lower strip is made up of the basin of flatlands around the Panaro, the site of ancient draining efforts and the subsequent cultivation of vegetables, grains and forage, and a place of flourishing cattle and pig breeding. To the north of the capital vines for making Lambrusco wines continue into the hills where they alternate with fruit orchards,

Modena.
Piazza Grande and
Palazzo comunale
(Town Hall)

which around Vignola are mainly full of cherry trees. An area of clay soil, wasteland and *salse*, or mud volcanoes, leads to the Apennines, corresponding to the historic region of Frignano. The landscape is characterized by the peaks of Monte Cimone and Corno alle Scale, where woods and fields offer wild produce, cheeses and beef products. Animal husbandry is an important source of food here, with the DOP Prosciutto di Modena and Zampone di Modena among the best-known charcuterie products. Wine production is also widespread, with the DOC wine Lambrusco, which is produced as Sorbara and Salamino di Santa Croce in the flatlands, and Castelvetro in the hills. But the most famous product from this area is Aceto Balsamico Tradizionale DOP, the balsamic vinegar produced with age-old skill in the flatlands and the hills. The purest of Emilian cuisine is prepared with produce from across the border – rice and *zucca mantovani* (Mantuan squash). Vegetable sauces are common in the flatlands to accompany boiled meats. Mountains are the source of lesser-known specialties such as *crescentine*, also called *tigelle* (a kind of light bread), and the local sweets *castagnaccio* (chestnut cake) and *ciaccio*.

Gourmet Tours

MODENA. The city's symbol, in terms of monuments, is the Torre della Ghirlandina, the soaring ornament of Modena's Romanesque cathedral, but those coming in search of the city's gastronomic offerings will quickly discover *zampone* (the celebrated pig's foot sausage), Lambrusco, and the Ferrari reds in the town of Maranello. In the center, "Giusti" is an excellent choice: located behind a historic *salumeria* is a small room where Laura prepares the best of Emilian cuisine, including *insalatina rinascimentale* (Renaissance salad), wonderful *ravioli*, *crostata* (pie) and wines from an interesting cellar. You should also visit "Fini", which began as a simple charcuterie business in 1912 and grew into a gastronomic legend. Don't miss the *gran bollito al carrello* (boiled meats served from a cart) accompanied by local vegetable sauces or *rafano* (radish). Lovers of "peasant food" will want to try *gnocco ingrassato*, or *rancido*, which are *gnocchi* baked in the oven with cubes of bacon or scraps of *prosciutto*. As for bread, throughout the province you will find *tigella*, which are simple *focaccia* of Latin origin made with water and flour – without yeast – and cooked on a griddle.

1. The Bassa Modenese

CARPI. Taking the Statale 413 Romana, stop first at Soliera, where another restaurant deserves the utmost attention: "Lancellotti" is a large *trattoria* run by three brothers and offers some of the best cooking in Italy in terms of organic greens and vegetables (from their own garden, which you can visit), meats and charcuterie. Just a few kilometers away is Carpi, unexpectedly steeped in the Renaissance thanks to its *signore*, the humanist prince Alberto III of the Pio family, who had commissioned the great town planner Baldassarre Peruzzi to give it this character. In the city it is possible to try out all forms of Modena's cooking, particularly the *bomba di riso* (a molded rice dish served with pigeon). Carpi's *mostarda* is also especially worth trying – this characteristic condiment for *bolliti* (boiled meats) is made with fermented black grape must that is concentrated and cooked together with pears, apples and quince. Continuing with the theme of conserved fruit, *prugne in aceto* (prunes in vinegar) and *marmellata di cocomero* (watermelon jam) are unique products you can find here. In terms of cured meats and sausages you will want to try *coppa, fiorettino, cotechini, zamponi, cappelli da prete*. Sweets include *spongata* (a kind of dessert made of two disks of short pastry filled with a blend of honey, walnuts, hazelnuts, almonds, pine nuts, candied fruits and raisins) and *torta di riso* (rice cake).

MIRANDOLA. The Pico governed for more than four centuries and the town owes its Renaissance physiognomy to them. The humanist Giovanni II (1464-94), the proverbial Pico della Mirandola with his encyclopedic knowledge, lived during the city's best period. The town's present-day renown is more down-to-earth and comes from its fruit canning industry and a few sausages known as *manicotti*, which are made of

Traditional balsamic vinegar

pork rind. Gavello, located along the confines with Mantua, is known for its melons and cucumbers. At Finale Emilia, closer to the region of Ferrara, liquors are produced, including Anicione.

BOMPORTO. This ancient river port on the Panaro used to be a resort town. Sorbara, which is a division of the town, lends its name to one of the denominations of Modena's Lambrusco. This is also the start of the area for balsamic vinegar and cheeses. San Prospero is renowned for its pear production.

NONANTOLA. The history of this town is linked to the abbey of the same name, where eloquent testimonials to the town's past wealth are preserved. The village, originally a medieval *castrum* with a Roman-style structure, has two towers and colonnaded streets. As for good food, the village is a member of the small group of Città delle Lumache (City of Snails) and boasts the region's only organic farm for raising the gastropod. In cooking the snail is combined with other local products such as *aceto balsamico* and *prosciutto*. Here you will also find good cheese and wine (this is where "Lambrusco Salamino di Santa Croce", which takes its name from a town north-west of the capital, is produced).

CASTELFRANCO EMILIA. On the route between Modena and Bologna, the parish church of this town houses a valuable *Assumption* by Guido Reni (1627). Legend claims this is the homeland of *tortellini* – whether true or not, excellent *tortellini* are certainly available here, as are *tagliatelle, tortelloni* and *zamponi*. The *grana* cheese and butter are also good.

AGRITURISMI

Guiglia
Ca' di Marchino
at Monte Orsello
via Buzzeda 4
☎ 059795582
Zocca
Ca' Monduzzi
via Vignolese 1130/d
☎ 059986206

SHOPPING

Modena
Acetaia Malpighi
via Pica 310
☎ 059465043
Traditional balsamic vinegar from Modena.
Antica Salumeria Giusti
via Farini 75
☎ 059222533
Historic delicatessen.
Forno S. Giorgio
via Taglio 6
☎ 059223514
Cafe and pastry shop since 1902; delicatessen.
La Tajadela
via S. Eufemia 11
☎ 059222598
Vast range of fresh pasta.

2. The Apennines and the Frignano

SASSUOLO. The Statale 486 to Montefiorino, which goes up to the Passo delle Radici, makes for a short trip to the threshold of the Apennines. The bustling ceramics capital gives the same name, *sassolino*, to a sausage similar to *zampone* and an anise-flavored liquor. White truffles proliferate, and the liquor *nocino* is everywhere. The route continues to Maranello, the home of Ferrari (see the factory museum), and Serramazzoni, a vacation resort.

PAVULLO NEL FRIGNANO. While taking the beautiful Via Giardini (named after the engineer who cut the road), go up to the area called Alto Modenese. This is the land of the ancient Liguri Friniati people, whose memory lives on in the dialect and customs. Good tables in the capital of this mountain district are laden with truffles, cheeses and *prosciutto*. "Parco Corsini" is a fine restaurant which will more than satisfy those who like mushrooms and good wine. Typical of this area is bread from Pavullo, which is made with special varieties of grain and natural yeast, as well as the *crescentina*, which is spread with lard and cooked on a griddle. Continuing on to the crest is Pievepelago near Abetone, where mountain flavors prevail.

ZOCCA. Going down to the Panaro, we come to the beautiful mountain towns of Sestola and Fanano. The descent down the other side leads to Zocca, another Città delle Lumache with its own unique and varied culinary offering. With this in mind, we recommend the inn "Panoramic". Other local products are cherries and the liquor *nocino*. Further downriver from the picturesque Sassi di Rocca Malatina lies the village of Guiglia, which offers cheese, *prosciutto*, chestnuts and *nocino*.

VIGNOLA. At the mouth of the Panaro in the plain, cherries are plentiful and are the reason for the town's renown. The fortress enhances the town center, the most illustrious sons of which are the architect Jacopo Barozzi, known as il Vignola (1507-73), and the historian Ludovico Antonio Muratori (1672-1750). In the courtyard of the manor is the praiseworthy *trattoria* "La Bolognese". In Tavernelle eat at "Antica Trattoria Il Moretto", where the *prosciutto* is excellent. If possible, continue to Castelvetro, the epicenter of "Lambrusco Grasparossa" area, and stop at "Casa dei Lambruschi Modenesi", in the Castello di Levizzano.

SPILAMBERTO. This town is one of the places where *aceto balsamico tradizionale* is produced. Here you can also find cherries and sausages such as *guancialino*, which is made in the same way as *zampone*, but is wrapped in the rind of the cheek (it is also produced in Russi, Mirandola and Carpi). Local production of *amaretti* is good.

Landscape in the Bassa Modenese

SHOPPING

Possidonio
Fondo Bordina
di Benedetto
Bonomi
via Matteotti 78
☎ 053539286
Pears and apples.
Rubbiara di
Nonantola
Azienda Agricola
Pedroni
via Risaia 2
☎ 059549019
*Balsamic vinegar and
"nocino" liquor.*
San Prospero
Azienda Agricola
Barbieri
Acetaia del Cristo
via Badia 41
☎ 059330383
*Traditional balsamic
vinegar from Modena.*
Savignano sul
Panaro
Punto Verde -
Azienda Agricola
A.M. Vitali
via Falloppie 1095
☎ 059796158
Preserves.
Solara di
Bomporto
Caseificio Coop.
Solarese
via Panaria Bassa 75
☎ 059901608
*Parmigiano Reggiano,
butter, fresh "ricotta".*

PARMA

From the banks of the Po to the hamlets in the Apennines, the region of Parma is an inexhaustible source of flavors.

The large rectangle of the province of Parma spreads from the Po to the watershed of the Apennines, and is closed in on either side by the territories of Piacenza and Reggio. Located in the heart of Emilia, it opens toward the Lombard cities of Cremona and Mantua. The flat terrain is intensely cultivated with vegetables – above all tomatoes – as well as cereals and forage, which are destined for use in cattle and pig breeding and food processing. There are two internationally recognized DOP products (Parmigiano-Reggiano and Prosciutto di Parma)

Torrechiara
View from the castle

and to these we must add the important pasta industry and some niche products, such as the rare Culatello di Zibello DOP pork sausages, Spalla di San Secondo (San Secondo shoulders of ham) and Salame di Felino (a salami made of prime cuts of lean meat, blended with bacon and aged for three months). The hills are covered with vineyards of the DOC zone Colli di Parma: whites predominate and there is an aromatic Malvasia, as well a Sauvignon that is often made into Spumante. Mountains account for about half of the territory and are heavily forested. There is much pastureland, providing wild products including the remarkably-flavored Funghi di Borgotaro DOP. As for gastronomy, it is enough to remember the popularity of the term *alla parmigiana*: local culinary tradition, which is marked by the richest of raw materials and full flavors, goes back to the time of Duchess Marie Louise of Austria, Napoleon's wife, who successfully governed the province for thirty years at the start of the nineteenth century. The main dish is *stracotto alla parmigiana* (Parma-style stew), which is also used to fill the celebrated *anolini in brodo* (meat-filled pasta in broth).

HOTELS AND RESTAURANTS

Parma
Daniel ★★★
Cocchi ¶¶
via Gramsci 16 and 16/a
☎ 0521995147
☎ 0521981990
La Greppia ¶¶¶
strada Garibaldi 39/a
☎ 0521233686
Parizzi ¶¶¶
via Repubblica 71
☎ 0521285952
Al Tramezzino ¶¶¶
at San Lazzaro
Parmense (km 3)
via Del Bono 5/b
☎ 0521487906
Antichi Sapori ¶
at Gaione (km 7)
strada Montanara 318
☎ 0521648165
Bedonia
Pergola ¶¶
via Garibaldi 19
☎ 0525826612
Borgo Val di Taro
Firenze ¶
piazza Verdi 3
☎ 052596478
Collecchio
**Villa Maria Luigia -
da Ceci** ¶¶¶
via Galaverna 28
☎ 0521805489
Fidenza
**Antica Trattoria
del Duomo** ¶
via Micheli 27
☎ 0524524268
Fornovo di Taro
**Trattoria di
Cafragna** ¶¶
at Cafragna (km 16)
☎ 05252363

Gourmet Tours

PARMA. Art enthusiasts come to the city to see the works of Antelami, Correggio, Parmigianino and many other masters at the Galleria Nazionale. The illustrious Farnese and the beloved Duchess Marie Louise beckon visitors into the various splendid *palazzi* built since the seventeenth century. As for good food, "Parizzi" is popular for its Buon Ricordo dish, *faraona in crosta di frutta secca con patate e cipollotti* (guinea hen with dried fruits and potatoes and green onions). Other noteworthy restaurants in the city are "La Greppia" and "Cocchi" at the hotel "Daniel", both of which are family-run and offer traditional cuisine. The shop windows at "Sorelle Picchi" will tempt you into purchases, while the shop's back room invites you to taste local dishes at midday. In the area, at San Lazzaro Parmense, the wine cellar at "Al Tramezzino" is a treat. At Gaione go to Davide Censi's *trattoria* "Antichi Sapori", while at Noceto "Aquila Romana" is an elegant dining room in a historic palazzo that has always been managed by the Petrini family.

1. In the lands of Verdi and Guareschi

COLORNO. Leaving the capital, we penetrate the land of *culatello* (cured pork rump). On the ancient hunting grounds near the Po the Palazzo Ducale brings alive the memory of the lovely vacation resorts of the Sanseverino, Farnese and Borboni families. Today it hosts splendid antique fairs, with an important event in May and smaller markets every last Sunday of the month. This is a prime area for gathering *tartufo bianco*, or white truffles, and the production of various sausages, salamis and cured meats – in particular, the *vescovo*, or bishop, which is the aristocratic version of the better-known *prete* (priest). For the *prete* the front shank of the pig is used, the rind is left on and it is cut and boned; but for the *vescovo*, in addition to the whole meat, the cut is filled with the blended ground meat for *cotechino*. Continue to Sissa, where charcuterie is produced; particularly outstanding is the *spalla cruda* (raw shoulder of ham), which is served with a Lambrusco-based pickle.

SAN SECONDO PARMENSE. Even more famous than the more conspicuous Castello,

Polesine Parmense. Massimo Spigaroli "Al Cavallino Bianco"

built in the mid-fifteenth century by Pier Maria Rossi, is the *spalla cotta*, or cooked shoulder of ham, a local specialty that found a devoted admirer in Giuseppe Verdi. ZIBELLO. Passing through Roccabianca, we come to the capital of *culatello*, the center of a production network that involves seven neighboring communities. Run by several generations of women, the *trattoria* "La Buca" is worth visiting and serves such hearty delights as *mariola*, or the ancient *cotechino della mietitura*. The "Antica Taverna San Rocco" in Ardola also has a rustic-elegant ambience and good food.

POLESINE PARMENSE. On the banks of the Po you will find "Al Cavallino Bianco", heir to a *trattoria* with a long history. Here Massimo Spigaroli offers the best of the river's flavors and *culatello* (which he makes himself). At the Buon Ricordo restaurant the signature dish is *luccio in salsa Farnese* (pike in Farnese sauce) and there is also an area where snacks are served. If your appetite first needs stimulation, rent a bicycle and go out to discover the lands of Verdi and Guareschi. It is also possible to purchase cured meats from the family-run farm "Antica Corte Pallavicina". In addition to *culatello*, discover the delights of myriad *salami tradizionali* (*strolghino di culatello, salame verdiano, salame gentile, crespone, crespometto, mariola*) as well as *pancetta, gola, fiocco di culatello, spalla cruda e coppe* (ageing in the rustic room next door).

BUSSETO. At the Rocca (fortress) the gracious Teatro Verdi pays homage to the great composer. In Roncole visit the maestro's birthplace, and at Sant'Agata you will see the villa where he lived at the height of his career. In town stop in at "Trattoria Campanini", where there has been a food store for several generations. A traditional local dessert is *spongata*, consisting of two disks of short pastry filled with a blend of honey, *mostarda*, dried fruits and spices, which is made at Christmas time and keeps well. At the bakery buy some *miseria*, which is raised naturally and served with refined lard.

SORAGNA. Another big turreted

HOTELS AND RESTAURANTS

Noceto
Aquila Romana ¶¶ ★ 🍴
via Gramsci 6
☎ 0521625398

Polesine Parmense
Al Cavallino Bianco ¶¶
via Sbrisi 2
☎ 052496136

Soragna
Locanda del Lupo ★★★ 🍴
via Garibaldi 64
☎ 0524597100

Antica Osteria Ardenga ¶¶ ★ 🍴
at Diolo (km 4)
via Maestra 6
☎ 0524599337

Varano de' Melegari
Castello ¶¶
via Martiri della Libertà 129
☎ 052553156

Zibello
Antica Taverna San Rocco ¶¶ 🍴
ad Ardola (km 2)
☎ 052499578

La Buca ¶¶
via Ghizzi 6
☎ 052499214

AGRITURISMI

Fidenza
Il Tondino
at Tabiano Castello
via Tabiano 58
☎ 052462106

Noceto
Il Cerreto 🍴
at Pieve di Cusignano
via Gabbiano 96
☎ 052462113

fortress with a sumptuous interior punctuates the tour. We have two recommendations here: for a stay in a special setting, go to the lovely "Locanda del Lupo", while "Antica Osteria Ardenga" offers a meal with pure local flavor. FONTANELLATO. One of Parma's most famous castles hosts travelers. In addition to its moat, there are walls with battlements and towers rise up in each corner, while inside is the refined beauty of Parmigiani-no's mythological frescoes. On the third Sunday of each month there is an antiques and collectors' market.

A dish of culatello, the number one charcuterie in the flatlands of Emilia

FIDENZA. The Duomo, dedicated to the martyr Donnino, was once one of the obligatory medieval pilgrimage stops on the Roman Way; after honoring the saint, the pilgrims faced the hard road through the Apennines. Today you can admire the sculptures by Antelami and his school and, while you are there, go to the family-run "Antica Trattoria del Duomo". The town produces fine charcuterie, cheeses and *nocino* liquor.

2. Salsomaggiore and the Apennines

SALSOMAGGIORE TERME. From Fidenza go back up the Valle dello Stirone, which is now a natural reserve for migrating birds. The well-known spa town follows soon after. The Terme Berzieri are housed in the spectacular Art Nouveau building, with its oriental style and frescoes by Galileo Chini. First-rate charcuterie, cheese and butter are available in this town.

PELLEGRINO PARMENSE. Near the sanctuary of the Madonna di Careno, the Fiera del Parmigiano Reggiano is held in July. In town pay homage to the incredible bread bakery "Lusignani". Then make a culinary stop at Varano de'Melegari. On the rise below the manor is "Castello", a rustic-elegant restaurant, with classic dishes and a creative variety you will appreciate.

BARDI. Set in the upper valley of the Ceno, this medieval town is quite picturesque, but owes its fame to the strong black *morelli* horses, called *bardigiani*, with their long manes.

BEDONIA. Mushrooms and berries, brook trout and wild game are the raw materials offered by the upper Apennines, while from the other side of the valley come Ligurian flavors with *torta* made with rice, beets, potatoes, savoy cabbage and squash. A sweet typical of the area is a cake made with chestnut flour and spread with *ricotta*. Stop at "Pergola", where *tortelli* and *pecorino con aceto balsamico* are served in a romantic dining room.

BORGO VAL DI TARO. The gathering of *porcini* (boletus mushrooms), in this town was mentioned in an account from the mid-eighteenth century, and it has given rise to more than one hundred years of commerce and

WINE PRODUCERS

Ozzano Taro
Monte delle Vigne
via Costa 25
☎ 0521809105

SHOPPING

Parma
Il Casale di Parma
S.S. Massese 264
☎ 0521649003
Typical cheeses and charcuterie.
Fattoria delle Delizie
via Cremonese 25
☎ 0521292757
Preserves and organic products.
Pasticceria San Biagio
via Garibaldi 41
☎ 0521286057
Pastries and cookies.
Sorelle Picchi
via Farini 27
☎ 0521233528
Regional specialties.

Branding Parma prosciutto

export, even to the Americas (the company "Bruschi Borgotaro" has stood the test of time). In addition to the mushroom market, make a note of the Settembre Gastronomico, a food fest that covers all the products in the valley: meats, wild game, trout and woodland products. *Tagliatelle con farina di castagne* (*tagliatelle* made with chestnut flour) is a local specialty. In nearby Albareto these are served in a broth of water, milk and cream.

BERCETO. This was the last station on the ancient Via Francigena before coming to the Cisa Pass. The village was established in the Middle Ages with rustic *palazzetti* from different periods. The memory of pilgrimages lives on in the church of San Moderanno.

FORNOVO DI TARO. Where the river flows into the plains, we recommend extending the route to go to "Trattoria di Cafragna" for the *risotto al tartufo bianco* (risotto with white truffles) and the *tagliatelle ai porcini, tartufi e ver-*

dure (*tagliatelle* with boletus mushrooms, truffles and vegetables). At Ozzano Taro, visit the *cantina* "Monte delle Vigne", which has gained renown for its sweet Malvasia wine.

SALA BAGANZA. The main attraction here is the Boschi di Carrega. The woods were once a ducal vacation spot and today form a regional park. Excellent *prosciutto* and charcuterie are available. At Collecchio we recommend the restaurant "Villa Maria Luigia - da Ceci", a Buon Ricordo restaurant in a nineteenth-century villa with period furnishings and a pleasant terrace. The specialty here is *guancialino di maiale in guazzetto al limone con riso selvaggio* (stewed pork cheek with wild rice). Nearby is Felino, renowned for its salami.

LANGHIRANO. This is a celebrated center for ageing Prosciutto di Parma. Just a few kilometers away are two interesting castles: Torrechiara, with its triple ring walls and splendid stores for Barbera wine, and Montechiarugolo near the boundary with Reggio. At Corniglio in the upper Parma Valley, look for chestnuts, cheese and *spongata*.

Parmigiano Reggiano Dop

SHOPPING

Borgo Val di Taro
Bruschi Borgotaro
via Caduti del Lavoro 5
☎ 052596430
Mushrooms since 1890.
Busseto
Trattoria
Campanini
Madonna dei Prati
via Roncole Verdi
☎ 052492569
Typical products.
Pellegrino Parmense
Panetterie
Lusignani
piazza Mazzini 4
☎ 052464126
70 qualities of bread.
Polesine Parmense
Antica Corte
Pallavicina
via Sbrisi 2
☎ 052496136
Regional charcuterie.

PIACENZA

This is a border land where the flavors of some of the region's purest cooking appear alongside Ligurian, Piedmont and Lombard elements.

The province of Piacenza is set in the north-westernmost part of the region between Lombardy, Piedmont and Liguria, which all influence its wine and food culture in a variety of ways. The plain produces vegetables, fruit, cereals and forage, on the province's few hills there are vineyards, fruit orchards and ploughed fields, while the Apennines are heavily forested and have a modest mountain economy. Animal rearing is important here, particularly the breeding of pigs, since pork is the basis of three DOP products: Coppa, Pancetta and Salame Piacentino. The province is filled with DOC Colli Piacentini wines that are represented first and foremost by the red Gutturnio, made with Barbera and Bonarda grapes imported from

Bobbio.
The Gobbo bridge

nearby Oltrepò Pavese, and by the white Trebbianino, made from Malvasia, Trebbiano and Ortrugo grapes. The gastronomic tradition reflects the town's border location. The flavors of Emilia come through due to its geographic closeness to the province of Parma, but flavors from further afield can also be found: from the Ligurian Riviera, from the hills of Piedmont and Lower Lombardy. Restaurants here are renowned and are well represented by Piacenza's "Antica Osteria del Teatro" and Farini's "Cantoniera".

Gourmet Tours

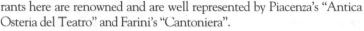

PIACENZA. This ancient city with its austere appearance is brushed by the Po and offers a thousand-year-old look at art in the Po Valley. You can trace the changes in art through the ages with the Duomo and other Romanesque churches, the Gothic Palazzo Pubblico, the Renaissance Madonna di Campagna and Baroque works from the era of the Farnese. The tradition of cuisine with a well-defined character is alive in the restaurants and *trattorie*. We recommend the "Antica Osteria del Teatro", located in a fifteenth-century building in the center. It is elegant, with a wine cellar made in heaven and varied cuisine. Neither the traditional *bomba di riso con piccione* (rice with pigeon) nor the avant-garde preparations should be missed.

1. The land of the Po

FIORENZUOLA D'ARDA. The town's name invokes Fiorenzo, a pilgrim saint, and the beautiful fifteenth-century Collegiata (collegiate church) dedicated to him. Further on, at Alseno, stop at "Giovanni", where you will find refined cuisine using *storione* (sturgeon) and *oca* (goose) and a table set with simple dishes with a noble history. Not far from the Via Emilia is the Cistercian abbey of Chiaravalle della Colomba. All

that remains of the old village are the church and the splendid Gothic cloister.

CORTEMAGGIORE THE name recalls a far-away Carolingian court, but the town's appearance is more that of the late fifteenth-century reconstruction by the Pallavicino family. Within this beautiful setting, on the first Sunday of each month there is an antique fair. The charcuterie here is excellent and, nearby in Besenzone, "Fiaschetteria" is a country house with refined offerings, including *caramelle di stufato con crema al tartufo bianco* (pasta "caramels" filled with stewed meat with white truffle cream), or *lumache in casseruola con scalogno e porcini* (snail casserole with shallots and boletus mushrooms).

MONTICHELLI D'ONGINA. Alongside the Po the fortress and the Collegiata recall the era of the Pallavicino family. Here, too, antiques collectors gather at the end of every month. Tourists with other interests will come here for the excellent charcuterie.

2. Towards the Ligurian Apennines

CASTEL SAN GIOVANNI. This ancient commercial center with its beautiful fourteenth-century collegiate church, is a Città del Vino hinging on Oltrepò Pavese and Colli Piacentini, as well as a production site for the *robiola piccante*

HOTELS AND RESTAURANTS

Piacenza
Antica Osteria del Teatro 🍴🍴🍴🍴
via Verdi 16
☎ 0523323777
Alseno
Giovanni 🍴🍴🍴
☎ 0523948304
Besenzone
Fiaschetteria 🍴🍴🍴
via Bersano 59/bis
☎ 0523830444
Bettola
Agnello 🍴🍴
piazza Colombo 53
☎ 0523917760
Bobbio
Enoteca San Nicola 🍴🍴
contrada dell'Ospedale
☎ 0523932355
Castell'Arquato
Maps 🍴🍴
piazza Europa 3
☎ 0523804411
Farini
Cantoniera 🍴🍴🍴
at Cantoniera
☎ 0523919313
Ponte dell'Olio
Riva 🍴🍴
via Riva 16
☎ 0523875193

AGRITURISMI

Borgonovo
Val Tidone
Il Corniolo
at Castelnuovo
☎ 0523869293
Ponte dell'Olio
La Torre
at Torre di Torrano
☎ 0523878244
San Pietro
in Cerro
La Valle
via Roma
☎ 0523839162

that shares its name. This is
where the Val Tidone climb begins, passing through Borgonovo
and Pianello. The fruit is excellent: apricots, plums, cherries and
table grapes in the traditional varieties of *moscatella, malvasia,
verdèa* (that from Ziano is famous)
and *besegana.*

BOBBIO. In basin of the Trebbia,
with the Pénice in view, go down
to the abbey founded by the monk
Colombano in 614. Ponte Gobbo
offers a well-known image of the
village that grew up around the
abbey, with its asymmetric arches
crossing the river. For gourmets,
Bobbio is a Città delle Lumache
(city of snails), with a fair each
December in the gastropod's hon-
or, in addition to the important
truffle market (mostly white). It is
also the city of *brachettone,* a pork
shank compressed between two
boards and cooked before serving.
Just behind the abbey, take a
break in the elegant rooms of
"Enoteca San Nicola", where
decor, cooking and wine are all
very good. Going down the valley,
you will find two excellent *cantine*
–"La Stoppa" in Rivergaro, and "Il
Poggiarello" in Travo – that offer
the best of DOC Colli Piacentini
wines. From Monteventano, located at the border with Liguria,
come alpine cheeses.

PONTE DELL'OLIO. From the banks
of the Trebbia go to those of the
Nure, stopping at Grazzano Visconti along the way. This "theme
park" was created ahead of its time
in the early 1900s by a Milanese
entrepreneur with an obsession
with all things medieval. Not far
away in Vigolzone, the major *cantina* is "Villa Peirano". Further up
is Ponte dell'Olio, an ancient
crossroads for the product of the

Ligurian olive presses. Here the
bread is soft and long-lasting and
has a trademark. We recommend
"Riva", a simple restaurant with
good local cooking.

BETTOLA. This center is renowned for its production of
salame and *coppa,* while restaurants offer wild game and trout. In
town, we recommend "Agnello" -
don't miss the *gnocchi di carote in
salsa di basilico e noci* (carrot *gnocchi* with basil and walnuts) - further along in Farini, we strongly
recommend "Cantoniera", a re-
treat for a Franco-Italian chef
who explores international cuisine with an innovative spirit.
Even closer to the border with
Liguria, Ferriere offers *funghi,
tartufi, selvaggina* and *salumi.*
Among these is a salami prepared
with the thigh, filet, loin, shoulder and neck of pigs. In the area
you should also seek out the delicious and rare *robiola di Morfasso,*
and also the hot *piccante sott'olio.*

CASTELL'ARQUATO. The Val
Nure leads into the Val d'Arda,
passing by Lugagnano, an important producer of *coppa piacentina.*
The starting point is in Castel-
l'Arquato, at the theatrical
square surrounded by small
streets. Created to promote the
local DOC wine Monterosso Val
d'Arda, the "Enoteca Comunale"
is located in the Palazzo del
Podestà. "Maps" is a fine place
with a menu based on products of
the sea and land and on items
from its well-stocked *cantina.* Try
the local almond *torta.* Then, going down to the Via Emilia, inland roads cut through minor
centers – Vigolo Marchese,
Carpaneto, San Giorgio – which
are active in the production of
coppe and other charcuterie.

RAVENNA

Stretching from the Adriatic to the hill of Brisighella and into the Apennines, Ravenna offers a full repertory of Romagna's flavors.

The entire province of Ravenna spreads out in Romagna between the Comacchio and Apennine valleys, without ever reaching the watershed (located in the Romagna Toscana area). The flatlands, which cover two-thirds of the territory, are situated along the Adriatic Sea, while the narrower inland strip nestles between the provinces of Bologna and Forlì. The province's economy is primarily agricultural, with first rate cattle and pig breeding. Among the major cultivations, fruit stands out – with pears, peaches and nectarines that come under the title DOP Romagna – as does DOP Brisighella

Ravenna. Church of S. Apollinare in Classe

olive oil. The wines range from productions shared with other provinces of Romagna – primarily the DOCG Albana – to more specific ones such as DOC Colli di Faenza. The latter are made by adding the fruits of international vines such as Pinot Blanc and Cabernet Sauvignon to traditional grapes – Pignoletto and Trebbiano for whites, and Ancellotta and Sangiovese for the reds. As for meats, we are in the land of the prized breed of Romagnola cattle, as well as that of excellent charcuterie and good fish, particularly what Italians call blue fish (sardines, anchovies, mackerel). Local gastronomy is Romagnese, with a touch of individuality injected by the fish and wild game from the Valli di Comacchio, Bolognese elements along the Via Emilia and Tuscan flavors in the Apennine Valleys. As for restaurants, there are several good ones on the Adriatic Riviera, while in the mountainous inland zone there are fewer, but high quality eateries.

Gourmet Tours

RAVENNA. The uniqueness of this city comes from its Byzantine art and the memory of the reign of Theodoric, the 'barbarian' educated in Constantinople. The gentle warmth of the terracotta and the lightness of the mosaics in Early Christian churches are an important part of a visit to Ravenna, which also offers good opportunities for food. In the city the are three names that will satisfy any palate: "Tre Spade" for fish lovers; "Ponte Nuovo" at the hotel "Romea" for grilled meats; "Trattoria Capannetti" for dishes based on truffles and *funghi delle pinete* (pine-forest mushrooms), asparagus and other wild products.

ALFONSINE. Rather than follow the Via Adriatica, take the Romea, which crosses the San Vitale pine forest and goes to the edge of the Valli di Comacchio. Here turn off towards Sant'Alberto (near Mandriole there is a memorial to Anita Garibaldi); then continue on to Alfonsine, a town which has gained a certain renown for white truffles. Following the banks of the Senio we come to Fusignano, where we

recommend a stop at the restaurant "Voglia Matta", with the annexed tavern "Ca' Ruffo". Here you will get excellent Romagnese cooking and fish in the elegant setting of a late-nineteenth-century palazzo and park.

LUGO. The thirteenth-century fortress is the most conspicuous monumental presence in the center of Ravenna's lowlands. Across from it is the Pavaglione, an eighteenth-century colonnaded quadrangle used as a marketplace. There are two house-museums, one the birthplace of the aviator Francesco Baracca and the other the birthplace of Gioacchino Rossini's father. The pears, apples and peaches of the surrounding countryside have earned renown, as have the extra-fine white and black truffles. Not far away is the Massa Lombarda, another celebrated name in Italy's repertoire of fruit- and vegetable-growers.

BAGNACAVALLO. This medieval village lies on the Statale 253 SanVitale. It has colonnaded streets and airy spaces such as the central Piazza Libertà, with the Collegiata di San Michele, and the elliptical Piazza Nuova, onto which craftsmen's workshops

HOTELS AND RESTAURANTS

Ravenna
⭐ 🛏 Romea ★★★
Ponte Nuovo ¶
via Romea Sud 1
☎ 054461247
Tre Spade ¶¶¶
via Faentina 136
☎ 0544500522
Trattoria Capannetti ¶¶
vicolo Capannetti 21
☎ 054466681
Bagnacavallo
Al Palazzo Tesoreri ¶¶¶
via Garibaldi 75
☎ 054561156
Osteria di Piazza Nuova ¶
piazza Nuova 22
☎ 054563647
Brisighella
Gigiolè ¶¶¶
piazza Carducci 5
☎ 054681209
Osteria la Grotta ¶¶
via Metelli 1
☎ 054681829
Strada Casale ¶¶
at Casale (km 7)
via Statale 22
☎ 054688054

open. Typical regional cooking may be found at the beautiful "Osteria di Piazza Nuova". Not far from the village is the Romanesque parish church of San Pietro in Silvis with noteworthy fourteenth-century frescoes. A gastronomic must is "Al Palazzo Tesoreri", a prestigious restaurant run by chef who is open to various regional cuisines; although one of the finest flavors in his creations is the locally-gathered *tartufo bianco*.

RUSSI. This is the most famous center for production of a special *cotechino* called *belecott*. Local cuisine uses *ciccioli* (bacon cubes), *salsicce* (sausages), *fagioli con le cotiche* (beans with pork rind) and *paste con goletta*.

CERVIA. After crossing the salt mines, now an important nature reserve, you come to the sea, where the port separates eighteenth-century Cervia Nuova from Milano Marittima, a garden city created in the early 1900s. From the beautiful *pineta* (pine forest) come mushrooms, truffles and pine nuts, while the best seafood dish is *canocchie in gratella* (grilled prawns). A typical sweet is *fritelloni* (a type of pancake). Fish is prepared in a wide enough variety of ways to satisfy any craving. "Al Teatro - da Sergio e Maura", in the first town, offers the delicious *cappelletti di rombo in salsa di gamberi* (turbot-filled pasta with shrimp sauce), and "Marinaio", in the second, has *tortelli di pasta nera al ripieno di granchio e ricotta* (squid ink pasta filled with crab and *ricotta*). Further along the Adriatic "Casa delle Aie" offers rustic home-made pasta and meats.

FAENZA. The town's history from the Middle Ages to the Renaissance is told in the contiguous Piazza del Popolo and Piazza della Libertà, while Corso Mazzini, the stretch of the Via Emilia as it goes through the town, has the dignified physiognomy of the papal era. The city takes pride in its ceramics, and there is a museum dedicated to the ancient tradition of making them. This Città del Vino is the best place for the DOC Colli Faentini wines. Meticulously-prepared territorial cuisine flavored with herbs is to be found at the restaurant "La Pavona", while "Sesto Conti-

Romagnola cattle bred

HOTELS AND RESTAURANTS

Casola Valsenio
Mozart ¶¶ ⚔ ▥
via Monte Fortino 3
☎ 054673508
Fava ¶
via G. Cenni 70
☎ 054673908
Cervia
Al Teatro - Da Sergio e Maura ¶¶
via XX Settembre169
☎ 054471639
Faenza
La Pavona ¶
via S. Lucia 45
☎ 054631075
Sesto Continente ¶
piazza Molinella 2
☎ 054620413
Fusignano
Ca' Ruffo ★★★
Voglia Matta ¶¶¶ ⚔ ▥
via V. Veneto 21
☎ 054550258
Milano Marittima
Marinaio ¶¶
via Puccini 8
☎ 0544975479
Casa delle Aie ¶
via A. Ascione 4
☎ 0544927631

nente", located in the space of the Circolo della Riunione Cittadina, is an old and interesting restaurant. Desserts typical of the area include *ravioli ripieni di castagne* (*ravioli* filled with chestnuts) and candied fruit. RIOLO TERME. From Castel Bolognese go up to this town with its medicinal waters, medieval center and fortress. The surrounding hills provide fruit and grapes, and the woods provide truffles and berries. *Selvaggina* (wild game) and *salumi* (charcuterie) regularly appear at mealtimes. The characteristic sweet is *cassata allo zabaione* (*ricotta* cake with *zabaione*).

CASOLA VALSENIO. Lavender blooms across the fields in this small Italian center know for its grasses. A Giardino delle Erbe (Garden of Grasses) covering four hectares has over 400 aromatic and medicinal essences. They are artfully employed together with unusual fruits such as *giuggiole* (jujube) or *pere volpine* (a rare type of pear). We recommend the refined restaurant "Mozart" or the simple *trattoria* "Fava".

BRISIGHELLA. A walk in the Valle del Lamone is punctuated by three spurs that rise up above the village and support the fortress, the clock tower and the sanctuary of Nostra Signora della Natività. The residential area has some ancient sections and a covered street called Via degli Asini, which recalls commerce with the upper Valle del Lamone. As a town where truffles are gathered and then honored at a market, Brisighella owes its most recent glory to its extra-virgin DOP olive oil. At the Cooperativa buy one of two excellent olive oils: Brisighello or Nobile Drupa. Choose from the following places to eat: in the city, go to "Gigiolè" or the "Osteria la Grotta", the first located in a convent (where it is also possible to get a comfortable bed for the night), the second in a real grotto. Out of town, in Casale, there is "Strada Casale", which stays true to the traditions of Romagnese cooking and has a good *cantina*. In Montemauro local *robiola* has gained renown; full of holes, it has a bitter-sweet flavor.

AGRITURISMI

Ravenna
⭐🅰 **L'Azdòra**
at Madonna
dell'Albero
via Vangaticcio 14
☎ 0544497669
Brisighella
Il Palazzo
via Baccagnano 11
☎ 054680338

SHOPPING

Brisighella
Cooperativa
Agricola
Brisighelese
via Strada 2
☎ 054681103
Brisighello and Nobile
Drupa olive oil.
Milano Marittima
Fratelli Bonanni
viale Matteotti
corner XXV traversa
☎ 0544948240
Typical "piadina"
flat bread.

REGGIO NELL'EMILIA

Cheese, sausages, wine, balsamic vinegar – all are products of an important province in terms of Italy's agriculture-based food production.

The province of Reggio nell'Emilia spreads from the great curve of the Po river to the Appenine crest at Guastalla, over which Monte Cusna (2120 meters/6955ft) rises. The territory's plains are used for agricultural production. In the lowlands, grains and forage are used for the breeding of cattle and pigs, which are in turn used for the production of Parmigiano Reggiano DOP and the salami *Fiorettino*. Vineyards predominate in the hills, making for the two DOC wines: Lambrusco Reggiano from Marani grapes, and Colli di Scandiano e Canossa, which has a white Sauvignon, and reds made from older grape varieties such as Malbo Gentile and Marzemino. In the cuisine the proximity to Lombardy is reflected in the *tortelli di zucca* (pasta filled with pumpkin), which are similar to those made in Mantua, and in the *salami d'oca* (goose salami), which recall those of Mortara in Pavia. Among the many dishes offered in restaurants and *trattorie* you will find *tortelli di erbette* (pasta filled with greens), *gnocco fritto* (fried gnocchi), *bomba di riso* (rice bomb), *coniglio alla reggiana* (Reggia-style rabbit) and *polpettone di tacchino* (turkey meatloaf). In terms of sweets, the specialty is *zuppa inglese*, in addition to those of regional interest.

Gualtieri. Piazza Bentivoglio

Gourmet Tours

REGGIO NELL'EMILIA. The hexagonal layout of the town was conferred upon it by the walls which once surrounded it and the Corso Garibaldi, which follows the ancient bed of the river Crostolo. Via Emilia divides it in half. In the heart of the town is Piazza Prampolini, with the Duomo and the Palazzo del Comune, from which point a network of medieval streets radiates like spokes on a wheel. Good food can be found in the restaurant "Cinque Pini - da Pelati", where Emilian cuisine is prepared using ancient recipes that have been revised, often with *funghi* and *tartufi*. "Trattoria della Ghiara", located in the center near the Chiesa del Cristo, is worth trying for its lovely *cappelletti* (pasta filled with *ricotta*, Romagna style) and the other food on offer is decent, and good value. We also suggest you try the *enoteca*-restaurant "Alti Spiriti" and the "Caffè Arti e Mestieri", which as well as serving food is a theater for cultural events. In the town and the immediate surrounding area, buy cheese and butter, as well as hand-crafted *salumi* (charcuterie). For Parmigiano Reggiano, at Aiola di Montecchio Emilia visit the Museo della Civiltà Contadina, an eighteenth-century road-keeper's house that was restored for cheese making. Still in the immediate area of the capital, at Campegine, "Trattoria Lago di Gruma" is worth visiting for its specialties of *lumache* (snails) and recipes based on greens and herbs.

1. In the lands of the Po

BRESCELLO. Taking the Statale 358 away from the capital, we come to the Po. Here lies the town that is the heir to ancient *Brixellum*, an important Roman river port whose most recent fame comes from the filming of stories starring the characters of Don Camillo and Peppone, created by the writer Giovanni Guareschi. *Tartufi* are gathered in the area and varieties of *salumi* are produced, including *culatello* and salami *Fiorettino*. Local *spongata* (short pastry with honey and dried and candied fruit) has been made and eaten here for more than one hundred years. For a meal, we suggest you try "Tavernetta del Lupo". Follow the river to Boretto, the main port on this stretch of the river. This is the native land of Marcello Nizzoli, a well-known graphic designer, who died in 1969 leaving ample traces of his activities behind him in the Sala del Consiglio comunale and in the local theater. A well-known local product is *cipolla 'borettana'* (a type of onion). River fish and lowlands cooking is to be found at the *trattoria* "Al Ponte".

GUALTIERI. The harmonious Piazza Bentivoglio pays homage to

A fishermen's cabin along the Po River

HOTELS AND RESTAURANTS

Reggio nell'Emilia
Caffè Arti e Mestieri ¶¶¶
via Emilia S.Pietro 16
☎ 0522432202
**Cinque Pini -
da Pelati** ¶¶¶
viale Martiri di
Cervarolo 46
☎ 0522553663
**Trattoria
della Ghiara** ¶¶
via del Folletto 1/c
☎ 0522435755
Alti Spiriti ¶
viale R.Margherita 1/c
☎ 05252922147
Boretto
Al Ponte ¶¶
via Argine 5
☎ 0522965002
Brescello
**Tavernetta
del Lupo** ¶
piazza Pallini 1
☎ 0522680509
Campegine
**Trattoria Lago
di Gruma** ¶¶¶
at Caprara (km 4)
vicolo Lago 7
☎ 0522679336
**Castelnovo
ne' Monti**
Bismantova ★★★
via Roma 73
☎ 0522812218
**Locanda
da Cines** ¶
piazzale Rovereto 2
☎ 0522812462
Cavriago
Picci ¶¶¶
via XX Settembre 4
☎ 0522371801
Gualtieri
**Antonio
Ligabue** ★★★
piazza IV Novembre 6
☎ 0522828120

the family that between the 1600s and 1700s drained the lands. The naïve artist Antonio Ligabue (1899-1969) was a humble son of this village. He animated the Po's woods with exotic animals and grotesque human figures in his paintings (in the Documentary Museum). "Antonio Ligabue" is also the name of a well-known inn. There are good opportunities in the area for collecting truffles. The Touring Club Italiano guide from 1931 mentions certain sweet melons called *ramparini*, in addition to *cocomeri* (watermelon).
GUASTALLA. This dignified town with its colonnades, rows of ancient houses and palazzos that were built here by a young branch of the Gonzaga family between 1532 and 1746 stands where the Crostolo flows into the Po. The area is full of truffles, watermelons, melons and squash. Poultry, and guinea hen in particular, is first rate, as is the *salumi* (*cappelli da prete, fagottini, bondiole*). Sweets include *biscione*, made of almond paste in the shape of a viper, with candied fruit for eyes.
LUZZARA. Further ahead, right at the border with Mantua, is Luzzara. This is the homeland of Cesare Zavattini, a broad-minded man of letters, and the local museum of naïve painting is dedicated to him. Local gastronomy is interesting, with fish from the Po, including *anguille* (eel), *carpe* (carp), *lucci* (pike) and *pesci gatto* (catfish), fried with *polenta* or in a sauce. Here you will also get good truffles and cheeses, as well as the walnut liquor *nocino*.
REGGIOLO. The fortress, a classic example of late medieval military architecture, evokes the town's an-

cient function of outpost for the community of Reggio. Stop at the elegant "Villa Nabila", with the annexed restaurant "Rigoletto", for refined cuisine that keeps to the territory's traditions. Taking the route towards the city, cross the Valli di Novellara, an area with wetlands that drainage has not fully deprived of natural interest.
NOVELLARA. The capital of a small independent state for nearly four centuries (1335-1728), this town has preserved images worthy of its past in the large colonnaded piazza and in the Rocca dei Gonzaga.
CORREGGIO. The celebrated painter Antonio Allegri was born here in 1489. Correggio preserves memories of him, and in the Palazzo dei Principi you learn of the Correggio family that ruled the town from the Late Middle Ages until 1635.
RUBIERA. Continue along the Via Emilia and the exertion is justified by the excellent "Arnaldo - Clinica Gastronomica", an old restaurant and *trattoria* in a fifteenth-century building. The restaurant, on the borders between Reggio and Modena, has a tradition of sumptuous roasts and mixed boiled meats accompanied by Lambrusco house wine.

2. The Matilde Appennines
CANOSSA. Go down to the Enza, where the Montecchio and Montechiarugolo castles have waterfront positions. The first good place to eat is at Cavriago, where you will find "Picci", which serves innovative territorial cuisine rich with *funghi* and *tartufi* –

HOTELS AND RESTAURANTS

Quattro Castella
Casa Matilde ★★★
at Puianello (km 8)
via Ada Negri 11
☎ 0522889006
Reggiolo
Rigoletto ¶¶¶ 🚩
piazza Martiri 29
☎ 0522973520
Villa Nabila ★★★
via Marconi 4
☎ 0522973197
Rubiera
Arnaldo - Clinica Gastronomica ¶¶¶
piazza XXIV Maggio 3
☎ 0522626124
Scandiano
Il Bosco ¶¶
via Bosco 133
☎ 0522857242
Al Portone ¶
piazza Fiume 11
☎ 0522855985
Viano
La Capannina ¶
via Provinciale 16
☎ 0522988526

AGRITURISMI

Castelnovo ne' Monti
Il Ginepro 🚩
at Ginepreto
via Chiesa 7
☎ 0522611088
Novellara
Nuova Agricola Riviera
at San Bernardino
via Riviera 7
☎ 0522668189

287

don't miss the *zuppa di spugnole* (morel soup). Continuing onward turn towards San Polo d'Enza, where the route that goes up into the Apennines crosses the foothills. Further on, at the vantage point for the Castello di Rossena perched high on a reddish crag, turn off for Canossa, a town associated with the energetic Contessa Matilde. A ruin isolated among spectacular erosions recalls a famous event featuring Pope Gregory IV and Emperor Henry IV. Henry humiliated himself in order to avoid excommunication, leading to the expression *"andare a Canossa"*, or "go to Canossa" that exists to this day. Here we recommend the inn "Casa Matilde", where there are a few elegant rooms that look out onto a big garden.

CASTELNOVO NE'MONTI. The climb, which at Casina continues along the Statale Cerreto, leads up to this beautiful mountain vacation resort, where the brooks are full of fish and the woods offer many products. Cheeses and charcuterie are also worth trying, including the salami enriched with *prosciutto* and bay leaves. The "Locanda da Cines" is a small family-run inn that serves good food made with *funghi* and *tartufi*. Nearby is Pietra di Bismantova, an unusual mountain topped by a plateau that dominates the landscape, further up the Parco dell'Appennino Reggiano spreads across the

ridge. "Bismantova" is also the name of a mountain inn whose restaurant serves *tortelli alla reggiana* (Reggia-style filled pasta), *rotolo di maiale farcito* (stuffed pork) and other hearty dishes.

VILLA MINOZZO. Start your return route from this town at the foot of Monte Cusna in the valley of the Secchia. Either follow the route through the bottom of the valley or take one of two alternatives: through Toano, which has panoramic views

The Reggian countryside

and the interesting parish church, Santa Maria di Castello; or go via Carpineti, situated in a cultivated dell dotted with large, elegant houses, rural centers and complexes with courtyards.

SCANDIANO. The fortress and the ancient city towers stand out in the gentle landscape of the hill that produces the appreciated DOC wine Bianco di Scandiano. As well as Matteo Maria Boiardo, who was a feudal vassal and poet at the court of the Estes, the city also pays homage to another illustrious son, Lazzaro Spallanzani, an eighteenth-century naturalist. At Scandiano two restaurants are worth trying, "Il Bosco" and "Al Portone". At Viano, as you climb up between the mountains, you come to "La Capannina", a traditional restaurant focused on seasonal fare, serving dishes such as *faraona all'aceto balsamico* (guinea hen with balsamic vinegar) and *bracioline fritte di agnello* (fried scallops of lamb).

SHOPPING

Reggio nell'Emilia
Consorzio per la Valorizzazione Prodotti Antica Razza Reggiana
Casello 101
c/o Istituto Agrario Zanelli
via F.lli Rosselli 41
☎ 0522294655
Parmigiano reggiano and typical cheeses .
Parmigiano Reggiano
via Kennedy 18
☎ 0522307741
Parmigiano reggiano.
Cavriago
Acetaia Picci s.n.c. di Piccirilli M. & B.
Via Roncaglia 29
☎ 0522371801
Traditional balsamic vinegar from Reggio Emilia.
Codemondo
La Vecchia Latteria di Miselli Dino
via Carlo Teggi 29/a
Parmigiano reggiano, charcuterie and preserves.

RIMINI

Bordering the Marche, the region of Rimini is a land of transition – something that is reflected in the flavors of the cuisine.

The province of Rimini runs along the shore from the mouth of the Rubicon river to the promontory of Gabicce, while inland it includes a narrow hilly strip sculpted by the Marecchia and Conca rivers. Bordering the province of Forlì-Cesena to the north and that of Pesaro-Urbino in the Marche to the south, the province of Rimini is a transitional territory between the upper and middle Adriatic, and also transitional from a gastronomic point of view. Here the bounty of the sea encounters vegetable and fruit cultivation and the oil and wine production. The latter comes under the title DOC Colli di Rimini, with whites based on Trebbiano and reds made from Sangiovese and Cabernet Sauvignon grapes. First courses and fish dishes are culinary highlights, often with a touch of spice in a nod to the flavors of the center-south. Best among seafood dishes is the soup *brodetto*, dense with tomatoes, strong with vinegar and black with pepper, the way it was once cooked on fishing boats. Inland, food has similar characteristics, which are at their fullest in the Montefeltro valleys in the Marche.

Rimini.
The Tiberio bridge

Gourmet Tours

RIMINI. The historic center, which was founded by Romans, lies at the mouth of the Marecchia river, between the bridge of Ponte di Tiberio and the Arco di Augusto, where the Via Emilia begins. Within the perimeter of the city wall lies the town of Sigismondo Malatesta, who in the fifteenth century wanted to give it the appeal of a real capital. Beyond the railway lies the "vacation city", with the "Grand Hotel" so dear to film director Federico Fellini, and the exuberant constructions so typical of the Riviera. Grateful to its seafaring past, Rimini continues to have the best Adriatic cooking, in which *brodetto* and *grigliate di pesce* (fish grills) abound. *Piadine* (flatbread) with charcuterie and runny cheese are also fairly common here. We recommend "Acero Rosso" for cooking that unites the land, the sea and the garden, accompanied by a good wine list.

1. The Valle della Marecchia

SANTARCANGELO DI ROMAGNA. Follow the Riviera from the capital through the pleasant towns of Viserba, Igea Marina and Bellaria, then cut inland to Santarcangelo, a traditional trading town on the Via Emilia. In the restaurants you will already get a taste of the Apennines. Worth trying is the "Osteria la Sangiovesa", a typical restaurant created in the stables of a patrician palace, with rooms carved out of the rock. It takes inspiration from the local poet Tonino Guerra, and pays homage to the great local wine and the *piadina* flat bread.

TORRIANA. Going back up the Valle della Marecchia, at Poggio Berni, we recommend the inn "I Tre Re", with old-fashioned rooms and good traditional cuisine. At Torriana stop by the "Osteria del Povero Diavolo", the kind of restaurant we would al-

HOTELS AND RESTAURANTS

Rimini
★ 🏨 **Grand Hotel** ★★★
parco F. Fellini 1
☎ 054156000
Acero Rosso ¶¶¶
viale Tiberio 11
☎ 054153577
Europa-Piero e Gilberto ¶¶
viale Roma 51
☎ 054128761
Cattolica
Lampara ¶¶¶
piazzale Galluzzi
☎ 0541963296
Monte Colombo
Villa Leri ★★★
al lago di Monte Colombo (km 5)
via Canepa 4
☎ 0541985262
Morciano di Romagna
Tuf Tuf ¶¶
via Panoramica 34
☎ 0541988770
Poggio Berni
★ 🏨 **I Tre Re** ★★★
via Roma 10
☎ 0541629760

Verucchio. View of the lower Valle della Marecchia

ways like to find, with good regional cooking and a few old, established recipes in addition to a breathtaking panorama.

VERUCCHIO. This village dominates the valley from between two hills that were once crowned by castles. Only the fortress of the Malatesta remains, a reminder of the origins of the family's fortune. At Villa Verucchio, along the way back to Rimini, is the Convent of San Francesco, with the cypress that the saint is said to have planted in 1251. Here you will also find "Zanni", a remarkable restaurant with excellent meat dishes.

SAN MARINO. An excursion into this autonomous republic in the heart of Italy is a must and offers good opportunities to sample the local cuisine. The beautiful walk up to the three fortresses, with museums and views to admire along the way, provides excellent preparation for the pleasures of local cooking. We recommend "Righi - la Taverna" in Piazza della Libertà right in front of Palazzo Pubblico, and the fairly new "La Grotta".

2. In the Valle del Conca

MONTEFIORE CONCA. Closed in by a ring of walls, in a landscape of high hills, this village offers a lovely, far-reaching view of the Adriatic from the Rocca Malatestiana fortress. At Monte Colombo, "Villa Leri" is a luxury hotel that offers great cooking. Further down is Morciano di Romagna,

where the *pastificio* (pasta-maker) "Chigi" boasts a long history of pasta production, while the creative cooking at "Tuf Tuf" should not be passed over. In Santa Maria di Pietrafitta, *crema di rosa canina* (rosa canina spread) and *prugne selvatiche sciroppate* (wild plums in syrup) are produced in small quantities.

SALUDECIO. In the basin of the Foglia, which flows toward Pesaro, you can see other towns belonging to the history of the Malatestas. Saludecio is a walled town with a medieval flavor, as are Mondaino and Montegridolfo—which host summer concerts.

CATTOLICA. The Riviera Romagnola ends with Gabicce Mare, which is part of Pesara. In addition to being a lively vacation resort, Cattolica is an ancient fishing port. Here, rich seafood-based cuisine may be best enjoyed at "Lampara", a port restaurant with nearly a hundred years of renown.

RICCIONE. This town's reputation for tourism began at the end of the nineteenth century and the garden city, which was created then, has preserved much of the charm and tranquility of yesteryear. Many restaurants stand among tree-lined streets and small villas. We recommend "Casale", a simple, pleasant restaurant you will want to go back to, and "Azzurra" for those looking for the best in Adriatic fish cuisine.

HOTELS AND RESTAURANTS

Riccione
Azzurra ⊗ 🖾
piazzale Azzarita 2
☎ 0541648604
Casale ⊗ 🖾
viale Abruzzi
☎ 0541604620
San Marino
Righi - La
Taverna ⊗⊗⊗
piazza Libertà 10
☎ 0549991196
La Grotta ⊗
via De Carli 2
☎ 0549906434
Santarcangelo
di Romagna
Osteria
la Sangiovesa ⊗⊗
piazza Simone
Balacchi 14
☎ 0541620710
Torriana
Osteria del
Povero Diavolo ⊗⊗
via Roma 30
☎ 0541675060
Verucchio
Zanni ⊗
at Villa
Verucchio (km 3)
via Casale 163
☎ 0541678449

AGRITURISMI

Saludecio
Torre 🖾
del Poggio
at Poggio S. Martino
via dei Poggi 2064
☎ 0541857190
Verucchio
Le Case Rosse
at Villa Verucchio
(km 3)
via Tenuta
Amalia 107
☎ 0541678123

SHOPPING

Ospedaletto
di Coriano
San Patrignano
Società
Coop. Sociale
via S. Patrignano 53
☎ 0541362362
*Typical wines
and cheeses.*

REPUBLIC OF SAN MARINO
MINISTRY OF TOURISM, COMMERCE AND SPORT

San Marino
the oldest Republic in the world

The excitement
of a holiday in
the heart of Italy

A land of
age-old flavours

Top-quality
wines

Mission Multimedia

Information: Consorzio San Marino 2000
Tel. (+378) 0549 885431/32/98/99 - Fax (+378) 0549 885433
e-mail: sanmarino2000@omniway.sm - www.sanmarino2000.sm

La tradizione
si rinnova
nei secoli

"IL TORRIONE"®

Antica Acetaia dei Carandini
CE
®

Aceto Balsamico di Modena

ACETO BALSAMICO DI MODENA
Antica Acetaia dei Carandini

Aceto
Balsamico
di Modena
da Agricoltura
Biologica

Carandini

"IL TORRIONE"
®

Contenuto
250 ml ℮

A *Modena*, cuore del Ducato Estense, nascono l'aceto balsamico Carandini classico e l'aceto balsamico derivato da coltivazioni biologiche, prodotti nel rispetto delle più antiche tradizioni accompagnate dalla garanzia del sistema qualità, ISO 9002.

Modena, heart of the Este Dukedom, is the home of classic Carandini Modena balsamic vinegar and balsamic vinegar from organic agricolture, produced in accordance with the most time-honoured traditions together with the ISO 9002 quality system guarantee.

SINCERT
CERTIFICATO N° 1576
NORMA UNI EN ISO 9002

CERTI AGRO

CISQ
CERTIFICAZIONE ITALIANA
DEI SISTEMI DI QUALITÀ
DELLE AZIENDE

CERTIFIED
IQ Net
QUALITY SYSTEM

ACETIFICIO CARANDINI EMILIO s.r.l.
Castelnuovo Rangone (MO) - Italia - Via per Formigine, 54 - Tel. 059.535.320 - Fax 059.536.306
http://www.carandini.it • E-mail: aceto@carandini.it

Acetaia Picci

Traditional Reggio Emilia Balsamic Vinegar

Consortium of Producers
of Traditional Balsamic Vinegar
of Reggio Emilia

Made using the must of "Spergola" and "Trebbiano" grapes cooked over a fire and then aged in barrels made of oak, chestnut, mulberry, cherry and juniper.

Picci

Acetaia Picci
Via Roncaglio, 29 Cavriago (RE) - Italy - Tel. 0039.0522/371801

PREMIUM

Welcome

Great Wine-glasses for the Professionals ideal for the Best Wines

How so? Well, because only professionals can tell the difference between just any glass and a really Great Glass. Premium is the latest tasters' line designed by Bormioli Rocco Professional in close co-operation with the Italian Association of Wine-waiters, to ensure that professionals have a product that truly meets their standards. Made of crystal that continues to sparkle after being washed many times, these distinguished goblets are the ideal receptacles out of which to enjoy the aromas and bouquets of famous wines.

Advanced technology and exclusive design are the hallmarks common to all products in the Bormioli Rocco Professional range, made specially for the catering business.

Bormioli Rocco
Professional

BORMIOLI ROCCO & FIGLIO S.p.A. - Viale Martiri della Libertà, 1 - 43036 Fidenza (PR)
Tel. (39) 0524 5111 - Fax: (39) 0524 527877 - web: www.bormiolirocco.com - e-mail: divcasa@bormiolirocco.com

TUSCANY
SIMPLE FLAVORS
OF THE HILLS

*Much appreciated by travelers of the past, the products
of the Tuscan hills shape a cuisine acclaimed for its
character and authenticity by gourmets the world over.*

The *trattoria* is, by definition, Tuscan, and the steak, Florentine.
This is a truth that was known to travelers the world over,
whether they were gourmets or not. Those who completed
the Grand Tour filled pages and pages with their tales, describing emotions, colors, the fragrances of their room looking over the Tuscan
countryside, with its cypresses and junipers, and their tables laden with
boar *prosciutto* and excellent wines.

MEDITERRANEAN LIGHT AND THE TUSCAN HILLS
Tuscany stretches over a vast area, encompassing a wide variety of landscapes. However, two elements, both of which are unknown to travelers
crossing the Apennines for the first time, give it unity: the Mediterranean light and the robust, sometimes dry, nature that is always rich in
odors and new flavors. Tuscany is mostly a hilly land with forests and
pastures, gardens and flowers, fields of wheat and herds of animals.

GREAT WINES, GREAT OLIVE OILS...
Dominating the hills are vines and olive trees, standing together in traditional farms, spreading over entire hills in modern ones. Wine cellars are
also attractive to tourists, and the
region takes the lead as far as
Strade del Vino (Wine

Routes) are concerned. Along these routes, there are hundreds of producers and restaurants who agree to welcome traveling gourmets. The olive
is rated equally highly for its excellent quality, nowhere better than in
Lucca, where the olive oil has been renowned for hundreds of years.

GREEN AGRICULTURE
Agricultural production in Tuscany is also known for being environ-
mentally friendly. An effort is being made to use low impact methods
that minimize the use of chemicals, and organic farming is also developing. Regional products, such as *pecorino*, *prosciutto* and extra-virgin
olive oil, are made by myriad medium and small producers and their
quality is protected by the denomination "Toscano".

THE UNCOMPROMISING SPIRIT OF THE TUSCANS
Tuscans are a simple, ironic people with a cuisine that reflects their un-
compromising spirit. A rustic table is refined by wholesome ingredients
and the well-judged way in which they are prepared: the cuisine is enlivened by ingenious combinations of farm and woodland flavors. A
highlight in Tuscan cooking is the blazing fire of aromatic wood over
which everything is cooked, from Florentine steaks to large mushrooms.
A thin drizzle of olive oil anoints every dish, appearing in its simplest
form on slices of bread and in soups and stews. It is country cooking,
which does not change in the cities – it is dressed up a little, but the spirit
is the same. Tuscans are said to be difficult about food, but with such traditions, they are right to be so.

A TRADITION OF EATING WELL
In this land where tradition reigns, excellence is widespread. To find a
great *ribollita* soup, there is no need to cross the threshold of a great
restaurant. Much of the food's merit comes simply from the abundance
of products and the hand of a careful cook.

*Farms and wild
maquis in the
Crete Senesi*

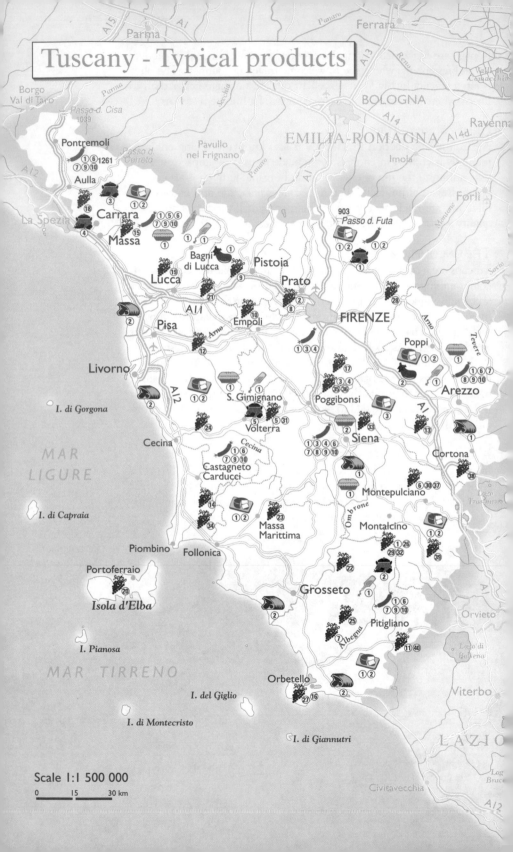

Tuscany - Typical products

🧀 CHEESES

1. **Pecorino toscano Dop.** Sheep's milk cheese made throughout the region.
2. **Caciotta toscana.** Cheese produced throughout the region.
3. **Marzolino del Chianti.** Cheese produced in the Chianti region.

🌶 CHARCUTERIE

1. **Prosciutto toscano Dop.** Ham.
2. **Bardiccio.** Product of Mugello.
3. **Buristo.** Produced in Florence and Siena.
4. **Finocchiona.** Fennel-flavored salamis produced in Florence and Siena.
5. **Lardo di Colonnata.** Fatty bacon from the Apuan Alps.
6. **Salame toscano.** Tuscan salami.
7. **Salsiccia.** Sausage.
8. **Sanbudello.** Produced in Siena and Arezzo provinces.
9. **Spalla toscana.** Shoulder of ham.
10. **Sopressata.** Produced throughout the region

🥩 MEATS

1. **Vitellone bianco Appennino Centrale Igp - Carne Chianina.** Bullock raised throughout the region but with a special 'Classica' production in the provinces of Arezzo and Siena.
2. **Carne di razza Maremmana.** Produced along the coast in the provinces of Livorno, Pisa, Grosseto and Alto Lazio.

🥬 VEGETABLES

1. **Fagiolo di Sorana.** Beans from Sorana.
2. **Fagiolo zolfino del Pratomagno.** Beans grown in the area surrounding Terranova Bracciolini and six other centers of Pratomagno.

🌾 GRAINS AND CEREALS

1. **Farro della Garfagnana Igp.** Spelt (wheat) from Lucca's mountains.

EXTRA-VIRGIN OLIVE OIL

1. **Toscano Igp.** Produced throughout the region.

🍯 VARIOUS

1. **Marrone del Mugello Igp.** Chestnuts from the Alto Fiorentino area.
2. **Castagna dell'Amiata.** Chestnuts mostly found on the Grossetto mountain slopes.

---

3. **Farina di neccio della Garfagnana.** Flour produced in Garfagnana in the Alto Lucchese
4. **Miele della Lunigiana.** Honey from the Magra valley.
5. **Zafferano di San Gimignano.** Saffron from San Gimigniano

🍞 BREAD AND SWEETS

1. **Pane toscano.** Tuscan bread produced throughout the region but particularly renowned at Lucchese.
2. **Panforte di Siena.** Siennese cake

🍇 DOCG WINES

1. **Brunello di Montalcino**
2. **Carmignano**
3. **Chianti**
4. **Chianti Classico**
5. **Vernaccia di San Gimignano**
6. **Vino Nobile di Montepulciano**

🍇 DOC WINES

7. **Ansonica Costa dell'Argentario**
8. **Barco Reale di Carmignano**
9. **Bianco della Valdinievole**
10. **Bianco dell'Empolese**
11. **Bianco di Pitigliano**
12. **Bianco Pisano di San Torpè**
13. **Valdichiana**
14. **Bolgheri**
15. **Candia dei Colli Apuani**
16. **Capalbio**
17. **Colli dell'Etruria Centrale**
18. **Colli di Luni**
19. **Colline Lucchesi**
20. **Elba**
21. **Montecarlo**
22. **Montecucco**
23. **Monteregio di Massa Marittima**
24. **Montescudaio**
25. **Morellino di Scansano**
26. **Moscadello di Montalcino**
27. **Parrina**
28. **Pomino**
29. **Rosso di Montalcino**
30. **Rosso di Montepulciano**
31. **San Gimignano**
32. **Sant'Antimo**
33. **Val d'Arbia**
34. **Val di Cornia**
35. **Vin Santo del Chianti**
36. **Vin Santo del Chianti Classico**
37. **Vin Santo di Montepulciano**
38. **Cortona**
39. **Orcia**
40. **Sovana**

FLORENCE

The "Città del Giglio" (from the city's emblem, the fleur-de-lis) inspires great emotions in every visitor – this is also true at table.

The province of Florence comprises the middle valley of the Arno. Centrally located, the capital occupies a broad valley closed in on three sides by hills covered with olive groves. Upriver is Valdarno Superiore, at the feet of Pratomagno mountain. Downriver, the Arno river runs past the capital of the Valdarno Inferiore - Empoli, which is set on the slopes of Monte Albano. To the north lies Mugello, a forested part of the Apennine district, and beyond the water-

Below, the Florentine countryside between Incisa and Rignano sull'Arno

shed are the lands of Romagna Toscana. Rising up to the south are the Colline del Chianti, which have a history of vine growing. The territory has a strong rural vocation, with renowned fruit and vegetable cultivation in the flatlands; wine and olive oil production in the hills; and pastures and forests at higher altitudes. Most quality labels here have been awarded to wines, such as the DOCG (*Denominazione di Origine Controllata e Garantita*) Chianti (Classico, Colli Fiorentini, Rufina, Montalbano and Montespertoli) and the DOC (*Denominazione di Origine Controllata*) wines Pomino, Bianco Empolese, Colli dell'Etruria Centrale and Vin Santo del Chianti (as well as Classico). Olive oil production falls under the denomination Toscana, while Marrone del Mugello has earned the distinction of Indicazione Geografica Protetta (IGP). The Florentine cuisine centers on the city, a melting pot for all the region's traditions as well as a repository for ancient methods. Mugello's cooking is particular to the mountains, while Chianti has farmhouse cooking with a hearty character. Restaurants offer great chances to eat well: Florence boasts one of Italy's finest in the "Enoteca Pinchiorri", but even lesser-known restaurants are excellent.

Gourmet Tours

FLORENCE. The "Città del Giglio" is a true gastronomic paradise, in which all the regional traditions and the most authentic of the city's customs are well represented. It is enough to wander the streets in the city's center, where the riverside markets exude colors and voices and perfumes that are all but forgotten in other cities. In the fall and winter the wandering tripe sellers seem to come from another era – as do the typical *lampredotto*, or offal sellers – to stand in the different piazzas throughout the city (at the Mercato di San Lorenzo, for example). In restaurants, you can begin with the better-known Tuscan dishes, ranging from *ribollita* (literally, re-boiled soup) to *bistecca alla fiorentina* (Florentine steak), from

HOTELS AND RESTAURANTS

Florence
**Helvetia
& Bristol** ★★★
via dei Pescioni 2
☎ 055287814
**Enoteca
Pinchiorri** ¶¶¶¶
via Ghibellina 87
☎ 055242777
Excelsior ★★★
piazza Ognissanti 3
☎ 055264201
Grand Hotel ★★★
piazza Ognissanti 1
☎ 055288781
**Grand Hotel Villa
Cora** ★★★
viale Machiavelli 18
☎ 0552298451
Regency ★★★
Relais le Jardin ¶¶¶¶
piazza D'Azeglio 3
☎ 055245247
**Grand Hotel
Baglioni** ★★★
piazza Unità Italiana 6
☎ 05523580
**Grand Hotel
Minerva** ★★★
piazza S. Maria
Novella 16
☎ 055284555
**Torre di
Bellosguardo** ★★★
via Roti Michelozzi 2
☎ 0552298145
Alle Murate ¶¶¶
via Ghibellina 52/r
☎ 055240618

pappa al pomodoro (tomato and bread soup) to *fritto misto* (mixed fry of offal, meat and vegetables), from *pappardelle sulla lepre* (wide pasta ribbons with hare sauce) to *pollo alla diavola* (grilled chicken with olive oil, ginger, onions and parsley). Then you can try dishes going back to Renaissance Florence, such as *pasticcio di carne tartufato* (pasta with a meat ragu flavored with truffles and baked in a pastry shell) or *cibreo di rigaglie* (sautéed chicken gizzards, livers and crests with a lemon sauce), as well as more commonplace dishes, such as *riso e fagioli* (rice and beans) and the so-called *stufatino* (little stew), which can be found in any good *osteria*. As for good restaurants, we must first cite "Enoteca Pinchiorri", firmly established as one of the top ten kitchens in Italy. On the menu you will find *ravioli di cavolo nero su salsa di zucca* (black cabbage *ravioli* with pumpkin sauce) and *sella di capriolo con cavolo rosso and castagne* (roe deer with red cabbage and

Florence. "Enoteca Pinchiorri"

chestnuts). For those who prefer fish, there is *filetti di triglia in pasta fillo con salsa di basilico* (fillets of red mullet baked in with pasta *in* basil sauce), and there is also an excellent variety of desserts. For those staying over in the city, we can offer two further excellent addresses: "Cibreo", a restaurant with a typical Florentine atmosphere and a good selection of regional soups; and "Alle Murate", an intimate place with fresh Mediterranean cuisine. In both cases, the *cantine* are especially good. Those who love a period

Florence. The restaurant "La Loggia," looking over the city

setting should try "Loggia", which looks out over the city from Piazzale Michelangelo, the "Osteria Caffè Italiano", in the historic Palazzo Salviati, or "Cantinetta Antinori" at the home of the celebrated winemaking dynasty. Then there is an array of historic cafes, including "Gilli" (established 1733), in Via Roma, not far from the Duomo (cathedral), "Giacosa" (est. 1815), in Via Tornabuoni, near Palazzo Strozzi, and "Rivoire" (est. 1882), just a quick walk from Piazza della Signoria, where, tradition has it, you may sip the best hot chocolate in the city. Also worth a try are "Giubbe Rosse" (est. 1890) and "Paszkowski" (est. 1846), in Piazza della Repubblica, which is the most widely recognised symbol of Florence, the capital.

Florence. "Hotel Helvetia & Bristol"

As for shops, one place to buy all the typical products is "Pegna", in business since 1860, which is situated to the right of the Duomo. It offers charcuterie and dairy products, wines, cookies and conserves of every kind. The entire center is a haven for the curious tourist, with its *vinaini*, or wine-sellers, who sell *mescite di vino* (wine by the glass), or *friggitorie*, which sell sweet and savory fried delights, and the *panifici* and *pasticcerie* (bread bakers and pastry shops) where you will find *schiacciata con l'uva* (flat bread with grapes) and many regional products, from *buccellato* (anise-flavored biscuits) to

brigidini (thin anise-flavored cookies). Last, but not least, we have a few suggestions for where to stay. Within Florence's vast offering of hotels, the following are some of the best in terms of atmosphere and history. "Grand Hotel Minerva" (est. 1848), in Piazza Santa Maria Novella, is a descendant of an old inn, while in Piazza Ognissanti you will find "Grand Hotel" (est. 1855), which has a dreamy winter garden. Settled along the Lungarno is the "Excelsior" (est. 1865), while "Helvetia & Bristol" (est. 1900) faces Palazzo Strozzi, and "Grand Hotel Baglioni" (est. 1903) is in Piazza Unità Italiana. "Gran Hotel Villa Cora" and "Torre di Bellosguardo" are worth noting for their verdant setting. Inn and restaurant cohabit well at the "Regency" and the "Relais le Jardin". For a stay in the hills, there are two names: "Villa Fiesole", for those looking for a room with a view, and "La Panacea del Bartolini", where tables are laid out on a very pleasant floral terrace.

1. The Upper Arno Valley, the Mugello and the Romagna Toscana

PONTASSIEVE. From Florence, follow the Arno up to Ponte Medicco which is where it meets the Sieve. This is where Chianti

HOTELS AND RESTAURANTS

Fucecchio
Vedute ⑪
at Le Vedute (km 7)
via Romana
Lucchese 121
☎ 0571297498
Montaione
Casa Masi ⑪
at San Benedetto-
Mura (km 4)
☎ 0571677170
Palazzuolo
sul Senio
Locanda
Senio ⑪ ★🏠
borgo dell'Ore 1
☎ 0558046019
La Bottega
dei Portici ⑫
piazza Garibaldi 3
☎ 0558046580
Reggello
Villa Rigacci ★★★
Le Vieux Pressoir
at Vaggio (km 5)
via Manzoni 76
☎ 0558656562
San Casciano
in Val di Pesa
Tenda Rossa ⑪⑪
at Cerbaia (km 6)
piazza del
Monumento 9
☎ 055826132
Albergaccio ⑪
at Sant'Andrea
in Percussina (km 3)
via Scopeti
☎ 055828471
Il Salotto
del Chianti ⑪
at Mercatale (km 5)
via Sonnino 92
☎ 0558218016
Vicchio
Villa Campestri
★★★ ★🏠
at Campestri (km 6)
via di Campestri 19
☎ 0558490107

AGRITURISMI

Greve in Chianti
Fattoria Casaloste
at Panzano (km 6)
via Montagliari 32
☎ 055852725
Montelupo Fiorentino
★ **Tenuta San Vito in Fior di Selva**
via S. Vito 32
☎ 057151411
Pontassieve
Tenuta Bossi
via Stracchino 32
☎ 0558317830
Rufina
Colognole
via del Palagio 15
☎ 0558319870
Santa Brigida
Castello del Trebbio
via S. Brigida 9
☎ 0558304900

WINE PRODUCERS

Carmignano
Tenuta di Capezzana
at Seano (km 3)
via Capezzana 100
☎ 0558706005
Pelago
Castello di Nipozzano
☎ 0558311325
Rufina
Fattoria Selvapiana
via Selvapiana 43
☎ 0558369948

OLIVE OIL PRODUCERS

Florence
Marchesi Antinori
piazza Antinori 3
☎ 0552359848
Barberino Val d'Elsa
Pasolini Dall'Onda Borghese
piazza Mazzini
☎ 0558075019

Rufina is made and the farms "Tenuta Bossi", "Castello del Trebbio" and "Colognole" all offer wine tasting in their *cantina*, as well as *agriturismo* holidays. At Sieci sausages are handcrafted for grilling or cooking with beans, and in Rosano there is a tradition of peach growing. From Pontassieve take a detour at Pelago, where you will find the charming *cantina* "Castello di Nipozzano". Go on to visit the celebrated abbey of Vallombrosa. From the woods of Pratomagno go down into the Valdarno Superiore (Upper Arno Valley). In Reggello, we recommend "Villa Rigacci", a lovely country inn with a busy restaurant, "Le Vieux Pressoir". Then stop in Figline, with its characteristic marketplace, and gastronomic fame earned by the *polli del Valdarno a cresta rossa* (Valdarno red-crested chickens). A final turn through Incisa closes the loop.

DICOMANO. Pork is processed here into *finocchiona*, *salsicce*, *prosciutti* (fennel-flavored salami, sausages, *prosciutto*). Take a detour right and head up to San Godenzo, a vacation resort set among the chestnut trees, and to the Passo del Muraglione, located in the forests of the Alpe di San Benedetto. Another possible outing from here is a trip to discover the wine-producing area of Pomino.

BORGO SAN LORENZO. This is the capital of the green Mugello Valley. In the beautiful church of the town's patron saint San Lorenzo, a fragment of the altarpiece (head of the Madonna) is attributed to the young Giotto. In the *trattorie*, you will find mountain specialties based on potatoes, *selvaggina* (wild game), *tartufi* (truffles) and *funghi* (mushrooms). In the shops, buy *pecorino di montagna*. There is a surprisingly abundant supply of sweets, including *torta in balconata*, with its richly filled layers; *cavallucci* (spiced biscuits with honey, walnuts and candied fruits); *bruciate ubriache* (roasted chestnuts conserved in *vin santo* wine) and *frittelle di riso e mele* (rice and apple fritters). Also worth trying is Gemma d'Abete, a distillate made by the Monte Senario monks. In Vicchio, "Villa Campestri" offers a pleasant stay and the Museo Beato Angelico should be visited. For a day-trip, go to Scarperia, a medieval village dominated by the towers of the Palazzo dei Vicari.

MARRADI. Taking a detour up to the Colla di Casaglia, cross the Apennine watershed and go into the Valle del Lamone, which is part of so-called Romagna Toscana. The dishes prepared at the restaurants here have a touch of Adriatic tradition, with its pasta and mutton, as well as *ricotta* and *selvaggina* (wild game). From the woods come excellent chestnuts and fruits that are used for making *frittelle* and conserves. On the route toward Firenzuola, we suggest stopping at "Locanda Senio" in Palazzuolo, where there are few, but pleasant, rooms and a decent restaurant. The alternative is "Bottega dei Portici", an attractive *enoteca* that also serves food. In the many food stores you can buy cheeses and good charcuterie (the ancient breed of Cinta Senese pigs is making a comeback in the area).

BARBERINO DI MUGELLO. Down in the Valle del Santerno, on the slope closer to the Adriatic, we come to Firenzuola, which is arranged around a central colonnaded street.When you reach the Strada della Futa, cross the watershed once again, and go down to Barberino, a transit town dominated by a castle. From the forest come truffles -black ones in particular as well as mushrooms. The Sieve produces trout. Visit the Villa Medicea di Cafaggiolo, a favorite of Lorenzo di Medici, and the Convento di Bosco ai Frati, where you can admire a crucifix attributed to Donatello.

SESTO FIORENTINO. Here visit the Museo delle Porcellane di Doccia and the Montagnola

Greve in Chianti

Etruscan tomb. The *trattorie* have curious dishes in store that change from season to season – in the summer, try *granchi inteneriti* (soft-shelled crabs) , and in the winter, go for *budella lessate di maiale* (boiled pig tripe).

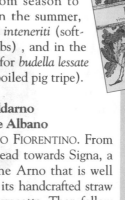

2. The Valdarno and Monte Albano

MONTELUPO FIORENTINO. From Florence head towards Signa, a town on the Arno that is well known for its handcrafted straw hats and terracotta. Then follow the river through the winding gully of the Golfolina to reach Montelupo, another center for ceramics, characterized by the fourteenth-century Palazzo del Podestà. In this area we recommend the organic wine producer "Tenuta San Vito in Fior di Selva", where farmhouses are set up for *agriturismo* with typical restaurants.

EMPOLI. Rising up on the Piazza is the beautiful white and green marble facade of the Collegiata collegiate church. Around it is the city, with an ancient market-

OLIVE OIL PRODUCERS

Impruneta
Sagittario
via Le Rose 81
☎ 0552374180
Pontassieve
Ruffino
☎ 05583605
San Casciano
in Val di Pesa
Fattoria Baggiolino
at La Romola
via della Poggiona 4
☎ 055768916
Tenuta Il Corno
via Malafrasca 20
☎ 0558248009
Tavarnelle
Val di Pesa
Carapelli
at Sambuca
via Basento Cellini 75
☎ 05580541

TRIPE SHOPS IN FLORENCE

Mario Albergucci
piazzale di Porta Romana
Orazio Nencioni
loggia del Porcellino
Palmiro Pinzauti
piazza de' Cimatori
Raul
via Gioberti
corner piazza Beccaria
La Trippaia
via dell'Ariento,
corner via S. Antonino
Il Trippaio
via de' Macci,
corner via Borgo la Croce

Vitiano
Chianti Classico

place and famous glassworks. Also very important is fruit and vegetable cultivation, with artichokes, peas and asparagus among the best in the region. The local cuisine reflects this, particularly with fried dishes. In addition to Chianti, the white wine Bianco dell'Empolese is produced in the vineyards in the foothills of Monte Albano. This DOC wine is a recent generation, but a descendent of the Trebbiani that were so well appreciated in Florence in the past. In the surrounding area, visit the spectacular Medici villa of Cerreto Guidi, and in Vinci visit the museum dedicated to Leonardo. At Fucecchio, the restaurant "Vedute" is worth trying for its cuisine that follows the market and the seasons of the old *trattoria di campagna*.

Chianti cellar

'Classica' zone, where the wine-producing tradition is the oldest, and is unified under the historic symbol of the Gallo Nero (Black Rooster). In Greve in Chianti, buy cheese and charcuterie, as well as the characteristic chocolate sweets called *africani*. In Panzano, the *agriturismo* establishment "Fattoria Casaloste" offers excellent local wines.

SAN CASCIANO IN VAL DI PESA. Crossing the border into the territory surrounding Siena, we come to Castellina and Poggibonsi. Here take the Via Cassia, the main route through the hills of Chianti. Cerbaia di San Casciano provides an extraordinary

3. Florentine Chianti

IMPRUNETA. The ancient feast day of San Luca (18 October), continues to be a moment of great emotion in the small village around the basilica of Santa Maria. Impruneta is also the birthplace of the chicken dish, *pollo alla diavola*. It also offers good charcuterie, including *finocchiona* (fennel-flavored sausage) and other cured meats. The *gelati* (ice-creams) are excellent.

GREVE IN CHIANTI. The Statale 222 Chiantigiana leads up to the

WINE SHOPS IN FLORENCE

Casa del Vino
via dell'Ariento 16r
☎ 055215609
De' Giraldi
via de' Giraldi 4r
☎ 055216518
Le Barrique
via del Leone 40r
☎ 055224192
Fuoriporta
via Monte
alle Croci 10r
☎ 0552342483
Le volpi e l'uva
piazza dei Rossi 1/r
☎ 0552398132
Zanobini
via S. Antonino 47r
☎ 0552396850

CAFES IN FLORENCE

Caffè Giacosa
via Tornabuoni 83 r
☎ 0552396226
Caffè Gilli
via Roma 1 r
☎ 055213896
Caffè Paszkowski
piazza della
Repubblica 6
☎ 055210236
Caffè Rivoire
via Vaccherecchia 4 r
☎ 055214412
**Gran Caffè
Giubbe Rosse**
piazza della
Repubblica13/14 r
☎ 055212280

culinary experience in "Tenda Rossa", a superb restaurant where the flavors of the sea and the land are adeptly balanced. Try the *tortelli di zucca con medaglioni croccanti di capesante alla salvia* (pumpkin-filled pasta with crisp scallop medallions with sage), *carré d'agnello rosolato nel lardo con verdure* (rack of lamb browned in bacon with vegetables) and the excellent bread. In Mercatale we recommend "Il Salotto del Chianti", a restaurant with just a few tables, but with creative cooking and a rich wine list. Here charcuterie is handmade and there is a long-standing tradition of clingstone peach growing. At Sant'Andrea in Percussina, we recommend the restaurant "Albergaccio" (est. 1450), which was the refuge of Niccolò Machiavelli during his tormented exile from the city. CERTALDO. At Poggibonsi you can take an alternative return route along the Statale 429 in the Val d'Elsa, which will lead to Certaldo, a medieval town in an area with abundant white truffles. Here you can visit Palazzo Pretorio, with frescoes by Benozzo Gozzoli, and the house of Boccaccio. Nearby, the eatery "Osteria del Vicario" (rooms available) is set around a Romanesque cloister.
MONTESPERTOLI. In Castelfiorentino turn off towards Montespertoli, a small town with a multitude of interesting elements. This is a Città del Vino (City of Wine) which gives its name to a sub-zone of Chianti DOCG. It has a well-equipped Strada del Vino, or wine route, (10 *cantine*, 4 *agriturismi*, 3 restaurants) and a major festival at the end of May.

The village of Montefioralle

SHOPPING

Florence
La Cantinetta del Verrazzano
via dei Tavolini 18/20
☎ 055268590
Wine tasting.
Fonte dei Dolci di Bruna Melai
via Nazionale 114
☎ 055294180
Pastries and cakes.
Gelateria Badiani
via dei Mille 202
☎ 055578682
Vast range of ice-creams.
Salumeria Pegna
via dello Studio 8
☎ 055282701
Regional delicatessen since 1860.
Carmignano
La Bottega d' Fochi
via Roma 10
☎ 0558712033
Pastries, cookies and biscuits.
Greve in Chianti
Antica Macelleria Falorni
piazza Matteotti 69
☎ 0558530229
Regional meat and charcuterie.
Antica Macelleria Cecchini
via XX Luglio 11
at Panzano (km 6)
☎ 055852020
Wide selection of regional meats.

AREZZO

The full flavors of this land are developed from the products of the forests of Casentino and the vineyards of the Val di Chiana.

The province of Arezzo is characterized by the Arno, which runs down from Monte Falterona, creating the woody mountain district of Casentino. Then, in a big curve, it carves out the Valdarno di Sopra, the area leading down toward Florence between the spurs of Pratomagno and the hills of Chianti. The Tevere river comes down from Monte Fumaiolo to create the verdant Alta Val Tiberina, between the Alpe di Catenaia and the Alpe della Luna. The Val di Chiana crosses a hilly range in the southern part of the province. Thus, this is a territory that is mostly hilly and mountainous and characterized by tree cultivation, with olive groves, vineyards and orchards, and animal hus-

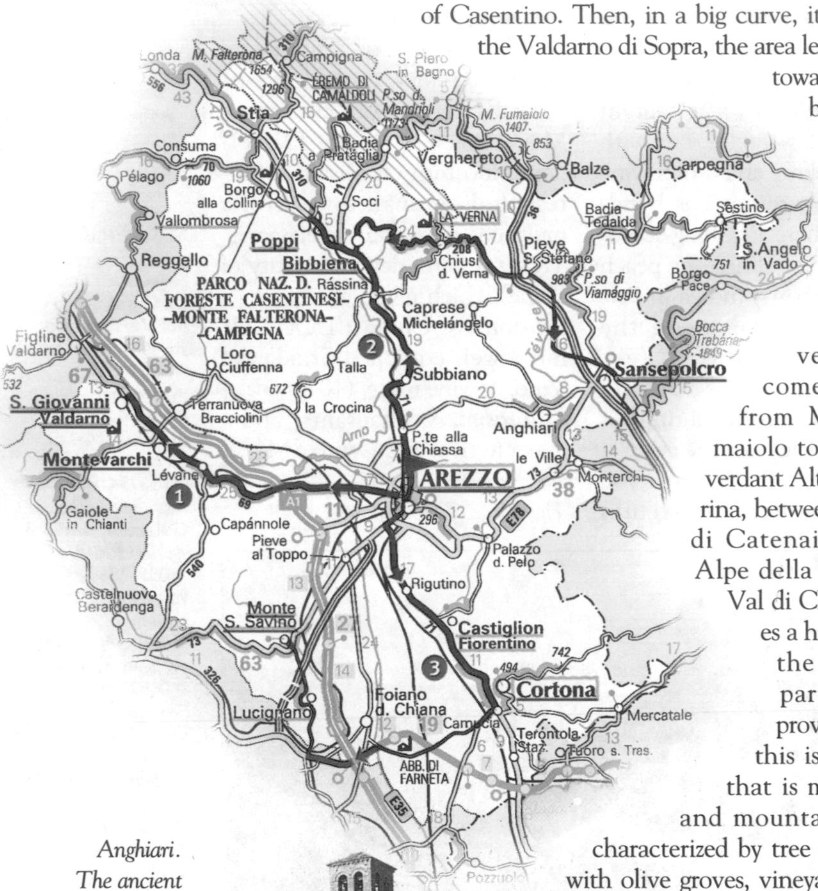

Anghiari.
The ancient
town center

bandry, specialising in the breeding of Chianina cattle. The Chianti Colli Aretini DOCG, the DOC Colli dell'Etruria Centrale and Valdichiana wines are all renowned. The gastronomy of the area is marked by dishes such as *pappardelle sulla lepre* (hare with pasta ribbons) or *fagiano tartufato* (truffled pheasant), which stand out for their hearty character within the already rustic framework of the region.

Gourmet Tours

AREZZO. Situated where the Valdarno, Casentino and Val di Chiana converge, this town may be appreciated for its medieval appearance and abundance of Etruscan and Romanesque references. The collection of art within sacred buildings and museums is extraordinary. Don't miss Casa Vasari, a jewel which the great Renaissance artist Giorgio Vasari built and decorated himself. Those fond of period settings will want to go to the Buon Ricordo restaurant "Buca di S. Francesco" (est. 1929), where there is a pleasantly imaginative medieval atmosphere. Some of the recipes are extremely old, such as the *sformato di fegatini con pollo* (liver and chicken flan). At bakeries you will find *panina unta* (bread made with bits of bacon).

1. The Valdarno di Sopra

MONTEVARCHI. The route leaving the capital and its beautiful river views leads to this ancient trading center, renowned for its black Valdarno chickens and the Chianti from the Colli Aretini. In the hills, just outside the residential area, we recommend "Osteria di Rendola", where the cooking of the area is interpreted in a modern and intelligent manner by a good young chef (there is a gourmet sampling menu). For an unusul sojourn, try the *agriturismo* establishment "I Selvatici",

where Chianti and other types of wines are produced by true connoisseurs. The surrounding area provides other opportunities to eat well. In Bucine, a charming, tranquil town, do not miss the restaurant "Le Antiche Sere", where everything is passionately and expertly home-made. In Mercatale Valdarno, it is possible to stay in one of the farmhouses at the wine producer "Fattoria Petrolo", where a swimming pool is set among the vines, olive groves and woods.

SAN GIOVANNI VALDARNO. Despite heavy renovations, Palazzo Pretorio preserves the ancient nobility of its original design attributed to Arnolfo di Cambio. The building is the main feature of the two squares that are the old center of the busy town. Once across the river, go up towards Pratomagno in the direction of Castelfranco di Sopra, partly enclosed by turreted walls. We recommend you stop at "Vicolo del Contento", an elegant restaurant with a prestigious wine cellar and a menu that offers a good balance of the classic and creative. For the return to Arezzo take the highway along a panoramic stretch, or follow a route cut into the hillside through Loro Ciuffenna, a charming medieval town, and Castiglion Fibocchi. If, instead you go down to Terranuova Bracciolini, you will find another good eatery, "Il Canto del Maggio", in Penna, a small medieval district with

HOTELS AND RESTAURANTS

Arezzo
Antica Trattoria al Principe ⚊
at Giovi (km 8)
piazza Giovi 25
☎ 0575362046
Buca di S. Francesco ⚊
via S. Francesco 1
☎ 0575233271
Le Tastevin ⚊
via de' Cenci 9
☎ 0575283046
Bibbiena
Borgo Antico ★★★
via B. Dovizi 18
☎ 0575536445
Bucine
Le Antiche Sere ⚊
at Sogna (km 5)
☎ 0559981149
Castelfranco di Sopra
Vicolo del Contento ⚊
at Mandri (km 1)
☎ 0559149277
Cortona
Il Falconiere ★★★
⚊
at San Martino
at Bocena (km 3)
☎ 0575612679
Monte San Savino
La Torre di Gargonza ⚊
at Gargonza (km 8)
☎ 0575847065

four houses and a little restaurant that is surprisingly warm and friendly. The simple dishes served here are full of memorable flavors.

2. The Casentino and the Alta Val Tiberina

BIBBIENA. From Arezzo take the route that climbs up to the Passo dei Mandrioli. The capital of Casentino rises up on a hill on the Arno. From here, fork right to go up to the Convento della Verna, linked to the memory of Saint Francis of Assisi, then go back down into the Valle del Tevere. At Bibbiena, we recommend "Borgo Antico", a small inn with typical local cuisine. Try the dish that symbolizes the area – *gnocchi di ricotta and spinaci* (spinach and ricotta gnocchi). Characteristic products are mutton and lamb and *pecorino di montagna* (mountain sheep's milk cheese). The breeding of Casentino pigs is traditional, and the hams are smoked with juniper wood.

POPPI. The Castello dei conti Guidi, colonnaded streets, towers and walls make up this town set against the backdrop of the Foreste Casentinesi, today a national park. A detour towards Camaldoli is a must, with its hermitage founded in 1012 by San Romualdo. In addition to providing spiritual comfort, the friars also provide herbal distillates.

SANSEPOLCRO. By crossing the Passo dei Mandrioli, which overlaps Romagna, or crossing Mount Verna, head into the Valle del Tevere. After Pieve Santo Stefano, go down to Sansepolcro, the native city of Piero della Francesca, whose great fresco of the Resurrection can be admired here. It is worth stopping in the center, crowded with *palazzi* and noble Renaissance houses, and set within walls and bulwarks. We recommend the inn and restaurant "Oroscopo di Paola and Marco", tastefully set within the owner's nineteenth-century house. In the area, *funghi* and *castagne* (chestnuts) abound at Caprese Michelangelo; white truffles and *bianchetti* at Badia Tedalda.

3. The Val di Chiana

CORTONA. Once past Arezzo, stop in Castiglion Fiorentino, a walled town with austere old houses, *palazzetti* and towers and soon one

Pieve di Sovara, in the Anghiari countryside

HOTELS AND RESTAURANTS

Montevarchi
Osteria
di Rendola ⁇
at Rendola
☎ 0559707491
Sansepolcro
Oroscopo di
Paola e Marco ⁇
at Pieve
Vecchia (km 1)
via Togliatti 66/68
☎ 0575734875
Terranuova Bracciolini
Il Canto del
Maggio ⁇
at Penna 30/d
☎ 0559705147

AGRITURISMI

Mercatale Valdarno
Fattoria Petrolo
at Galatrona
via Petrolo 30
☎ 0559911322
Montevarchi
I Selvatici
via Ricasoli 61
☎ 055901146

310

Bibbiena. The sanctuary of S. Maria del Sasso

can make out the medieval town of Cortona, the color of sandstone with steep slopes. Within the walls are two jewels of art collections: the Museo dell'Accademia Etrusca and the Museo Diocesano, which house works by Beato Angelico and other great Tuscans. Outside is the Madonna del Calcinaio, luminous with its Renaissance forms against a backdrop of the countryside. Cortona is the capital of *bistecca alla fiorentina* (Florentine steak), which is prepared here using the prized meat of Chianina cattle and honored by its own festival at Ferragosto (15 August). Producer of the appreciated Valdichiana DOC wine, Cortona is also a Città del Vino (City of Wine). Stay at "Il Falconiere", a refined inn in a verdant setting, decorated with frescoes and period furnishings. In the *limonaia* there is beautiful restaurant, with dishes ranging from meat to fish, and a respectable *cantina*.

MONTE SAN SAVINO. Once across the valley, go up to Lucignano, a village with an elliptical plan that is best viewed from the fourteenth-century Torre del Cassero. At the crossroads with the Senese-Aretina, go up a hill to a pass covered with olive trees and on to Monte San Savino. The beautiful Loggia dei Mercanti is attributed to the great sculptor Andrea Contucci, known as Sansovino, who was born here. In September there is a festival developed around *porchetta* (roast stuffed pork), the local specialty. Not far away is the Castello di Gargonza, which has been transformed into an elegant *agriturismo* location.

Chianina cattle

OLIVE OIL PRODUCERS

Loro Ciuffenna Grappolini
via Turati 26
☎ 0559172015
Il Gentile olive oil.

SHOPPING

Arezzo
La Bottega dell'Alveare
via N. Aretino 19
☎ 057520769
Rich selection of honeys and honey specialties.
Macelleria Gastronomia Aligi Barelli
via della Chimera 22
☎ 0575357754
Regional meat, typical charcuterie and cheeses.

311

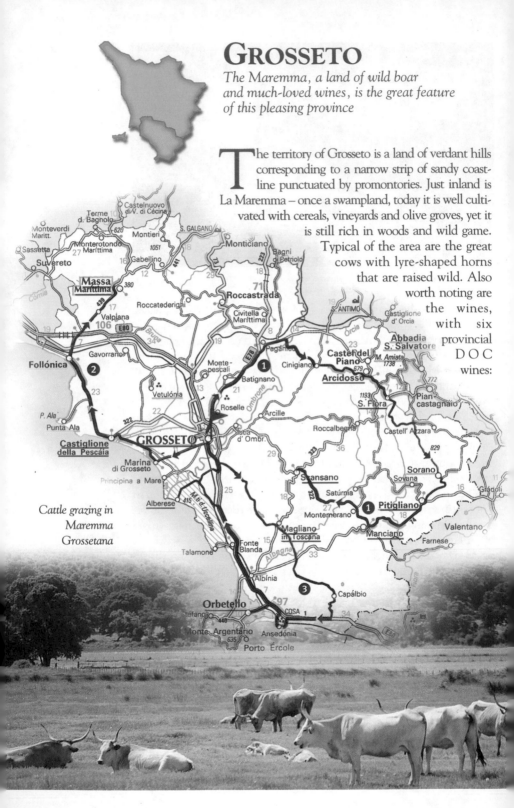

GROSSETO

*The Maremma, a land of wild boar
and much-loved wines, is the great feature
of this pleasing province*

The territory of Grosseto is a land of verdant hills corresponding to a narrow strip of sandy coastline punctuated by promontories. Just inland is La Maremma – once a swampland, today it is well cultivated with cereals, vineyards and olive groves, yet it is still rich in woods and wild game. Typical of the area are the great cows with lyre-shaped horns that are raised wild. Also worth noting are the wines, with six provincial DOC wines:

*Cattle grazing in
Maremma
Grossetana*

Ansonica Costa dell'Argentario, Bianco di Pitigliano, Monteregio di Massa Marittima, Morellino di Scansano, Parrina and Montecucco (plus Sovana and Capalbio which are awaiting formal recognition). Inland you come to the southern face of the wooded Colline Metallifere, which to the south gives way to the volcanic spurs of Monte Amiata, studded with chestnut trees. As for cuisine, the province is divided in three: the coastal zone, where there is a strong affinity with Livorno, the inland zone, influenced by Siena, and the intermediate zone of La Maremma, with its strong pastoral character and use of lamb and wild game – boar in particular – plus charcuterie, mushrooms and cheeses such as *ricotta* and *pecorino piccante*. The dishes that best represent Grosseto are the simple *acquacotta* (tomato and mushroom broth with egg and Parmesan on toast) and *brodo di fagiano* (pheasant broth), *cinghiale in agrodolce* (sweet and sour boar) and *zuppa d'agnello* (lamb soup). The offering of restaurants is good – although there are no particularly famous ones – and they are well distributed. They are often located in attractive settings such as farmhouses and small rural villages.

Gourmet Tours

GROSSETO. The capital of La Maremma Toscana preserves the atmosphere and appearance of times past within its hexagon-shaped ramparts. An ancient trading town, today it is still the center for agriculture and food production in the province. There is aged *pecorino* cheese with a slight bite to it, made further inland, and *toscanello della Maremma*, made of cow's and sheep's milk, which is sweet, but develops a bite with age. At bakeries, buy *pagnotta maremmana*, a traditional sourdough bread. Set into the walls, "Buca di San Lorenzo-da Claudio" is a fine restaurant.

1. Monte Amiata and the Valle del Fiora

ARCIDOSSO. From the capital, the Statale 223 Paganico leads to the junction with the route up Monte Amiata. Crossing the Ombrone you come to Cinigiano, a small Città dell'Olio (City of Olive Oil), and harbinger of the district of Amiata, where excellent olive

oil is produced. Travel though the beautiful landscape to Arcidosso, dominated by the Rocca degli Aldobrandeschi.Go around the mountain or make the climb up among the chestnut trees. To the north, visit Castel del Piano and Seggiano – the latter has gained renown for the cultivation of cherries and the production of a mountain *pecorino* cheese.

SANTA FIORA. Turning south, you reach this village which grew up around the ancient parish of Sante Fiora e Lucilla. The woods in the area offer a fine harvest of *funghi ovoli* and *porcini* (royal and boletus mushrooms) as well as chestnuts. On the slopes of Monte Labbro an animal reserve covers over 2000 hectares, where you can see many Apennine animals in addition to the *miccio dell'Amiata*, one of the rarest donkey breeds in Italy. In Roccalbegna, we strongly recommend the "Osteria del Vecchio Castello", a small restaurant with a passion for rich cuisine, perfect to the last detail, with traditional and innovative dishes of La Maremma, more than

HOTELS AND RESTAURANTS

Grosseto
Buca di San Lorenzo - da Claudio ¶¶
via Manetti 1
☎ 056425142
Terzo Cerchio ¶¶
at Istia d'Ombrone
piazza del Castello 2
☎ 0564409235
Ansedonia
Pitorsino ¶¶
Via Aurelia km 140
☎ 0564862179
Castiglione della Pescaia
Corallo ¶¶
via Sauro 1
☎ 0564933996
Pierbacco ¶¶
piazza Repubblica 24
☎ 0564933522
Follonica
Piccolo Mondo ¶¶
lungomare Carducci 2
☎ 056640361
Manciano
Caino ¶¶¶¶
at Montemerano
(km 6), via Chiesa 4
☎ 0564602817
Villa Acquaviva ★★★
at Montemerano
(km 6), at Acquaviva
☎ 0564602890
Massa Marittima
Bracali ¶¶¶¶
at Ghirlanda (km 2)
☎ 0566902318

600 wines and 300 distilled spirits.
PITIGLIANO. Along the Valle del
Fiora we come to two fascinating
medieval villages: Sorano, with
the Rocca degli Orsini, and Pitigliano, where the houses are the
color of the cliffs they stand on,
and have Renaissance features. In
this area Bianco di Pitigliano
DOC is produced and the rustic
zuppa called *buglione* is popular.
MANCIANO. This beautifully atmospheric town offers excellent
options for an overnight stay, the
best being "Villa Acquaviva", a
nineteenth-century farm which
has been rejuvenated as a family-
style inn. Once on the Statale
delle Collacchie, you will soon
pass through the walls of Montemerano. Stop here for the restaurant and rooms at "Caino". The
ravioli are excellent, the pigeon irresistible, the *enoteca* wonderful
and the typical products on sale
here are also very good. This
town, and the Alta Valle dell'Albegna (Upper Albegna Valley) in
general, are renowned for their
particular methods for curing
pork, such as *cotenne sott'aceto*
(pickled pork rind), *fegatelli sotto
strutto* (livers in lard), *polpa sott'o-*

lio (lean meat in oil). From here
take a quick detour towards Sat-
urnia, known for its thermal baths
as well as for its *pecorino* cheese.
SCANSANO. This is the land of
Morellino di Scansano DOC, a
red wine with a fine character
made mostly from Sangiovese
grapes, which are called Morellino
grapes here. The village is a point
of reference on the Strada del Vino through the Colli di Maremma,
which extends to the southern
part of the province, encompassing
four DOC zones and 140 wine-
producing and tourist regions.

2. The Colline Metallifere

MASSA MARITTIMA. The Duomo,
a true masterpiece of Pisan Romanesque-Gothic, gathers the *città vecchia* – the old city – around
it. Further up on the hill, beyond
beautiful Piazza Matteotti, lies the
città nuova – the "new" city – laid
out on a rectilinear plan in 1228.
"Bracali", a restaurant with a
strong family tradition, is excellent, offering fine cuisine that is at
its best in the autumn. Tradition-
alists should taste the *tagliata di
chianina con fagioli all'occhio* (*chianina* beef strips with cow-peas),

Sheep grazing in Maremma

while the more adventurous should go for *code di gambero saltate con porcini, carote and olio al basilico* (shrimp tails sautéed with boletus mushrooms, carrots and basil oil). Massa is also a Città del Vino, where Bianco, Vermentino, Rosato and Vin Santo Monteregio DOC wines are produced. The *cantina* "Morisfarms", offers wine tasting near the Duomo. For wine tourists, there is also a Strada del Vino, which crosses the Colline Metallifere and involves more than 40 wine producers and *agriturismo* operations.

3. Maremma and Argentario

MAGLIANO IN TUSCANY. Leaving the city on the Via Aurelia, take the turn-off to Montiano. At the crossroads with the Statale dell'Amiata lies Magliano, surrounded by fifteenth-century walls. Today it is a Città del Vino in the Morellino di Scansano DOC area. Further along, once on the Via Maremmana, continue on to Capalbio, which is heralded by a small hill covered with greenery. It is a land of *cinghiali* (boars), marked by a festival in September. ORBETELLO. After stopping at Ansedonia to visit the Etruscan digs, look back up the hill and you will see Orbetello, rising up amidst lagoons. Behind it rises a promontory. In town try the hearty cuisine of mariners, which has Spanish influences thanks to the city's previous rulers. Lagoon fish prevails on menus – *spigole* (bass), *orate* (gilthead), *cefali* (gray mullet) and *anguille* (eel) – featuring in *grigliate* (grilled dishes) and typical *spaghetti all'Ammiraglia*. An unusual custom in the town is a *merenda* (snack) based on preserved fish, in particular *anguilla scavecciata or sfumata*

(both eel dishes) and *tonno*, or *tonnina* (small tuna). Typical in Talamone is *marmellata di corbezzolo* (arbutus berry jam). At Ansedonia, we commend the chef at "Pitorsino", who is faithful to a tradition that incorporates coastal cuisine with that of the Maremma, but also open to innovation. In Orbetello stay at the inn "Vecchia Maremma", which is tranquil and family-run. At the "Tenuta Parrina" you will find excellent wines, as well as sheep's and goat's milk cheese as part of a good *agriturismo* holiday. ALBERESE. This small center stands at the gates of the Parco dei Monti dell'Uccellina, a sanctuary in La Maremma, where you can see big white cows grazing under the umbrella of domestic pines. In the marshes of the Ombrone, you will find wild horses and migratory birds. CASTIGLIONE DELLA PESCAIA. The pines on the Tombolo lead up to the gates of this walled city. The gastronomic offering is varied, with fish taking the lead, featuring in dishes such as *cappelletti di pescatrice alla mediterranea* (Mediterranean-style monkfish-filled pasta) at "l'Erbaccio" and *branzino in sfoglia di zucchine* (bass wrapped in zucchini slices) at "Corallo". Further along, beyond Punta Ala, lies Follonica, which is the last stop before the return from this tour. But first, stop at "Piccolo Mondo" for lunch – the specialty here is *risotto con scampi, aragosta, gamberetti e radicchio rosso* (risotto with prawns, lobster, shrimp and red *radicchio*) – then head off toward Gavorrano to make a last stop at the Etruscan necropolis in Vetulonia.

AGRITURISMI

**Marina di Grosseto
Femminella**
at Principina a Mare
via S. Carlo 334
☎ 056431179
**Orbetello
Azienda Agricola
Club le Cannelle**
at Talamone
☎ 0564887020
Grazia
at Orbetello Scalo
at Provincaccia 110
☎ 0564881182
**Scansano
Borgo de' Salaioli**
at Salaioli 181
☎ 0564599205

WINE PRODUCERS

**Massa Marittima
Morisfarms**
via Butini 1
☎ 0566919135
**Orbetello
Tenuta La Parrina**
at Parrina
☎ 0564862626

OLIVE OIL PRODUCERS

**Magliano
in Toscana
Le Pupille**
☎ 0564505129
Le Pupille olive oil.

SHOPPING

**Grosseto
Enrico
Ombronelli**
via Telamonio 61
☎ 05644943327
Regional meat and charcuterie from Castel del Piano.

LIVORNO

Gastronomy in Livorno means great fish from the capital to the island of Elba, but also the strong flavors from the area of Maremma Pisana.

The province of Livorno occupies a narrow strip of coastline that runs from the capital to Piombino and includes the Tuscan archipelago. The local economy is linked to the sea and so is the cuisine. . . so much so that the capital, which is renowned for its *cacciucco* (fish soup), is one of the leading members of the association Città del Pesce (Cities of Fish). This old port is also outstanding for the signs of other cultures, such as the Arab culture, to which it owes *cuscus di mare* (seafood couscous), and the Hebrew culture, which inspires certain sweets. The culinary panorama of Maremma Pisana is different, and includes the lands that go down towards the Grossetano, at the base of the Colline Metallifere. Here inland flavors prevail, with *selvaggina* (wild game) and *funghi di macchia* (a type of Mediterranean mushroom), cheeses, in particular *pecorino da serbo* and *toscanello*, and gar-

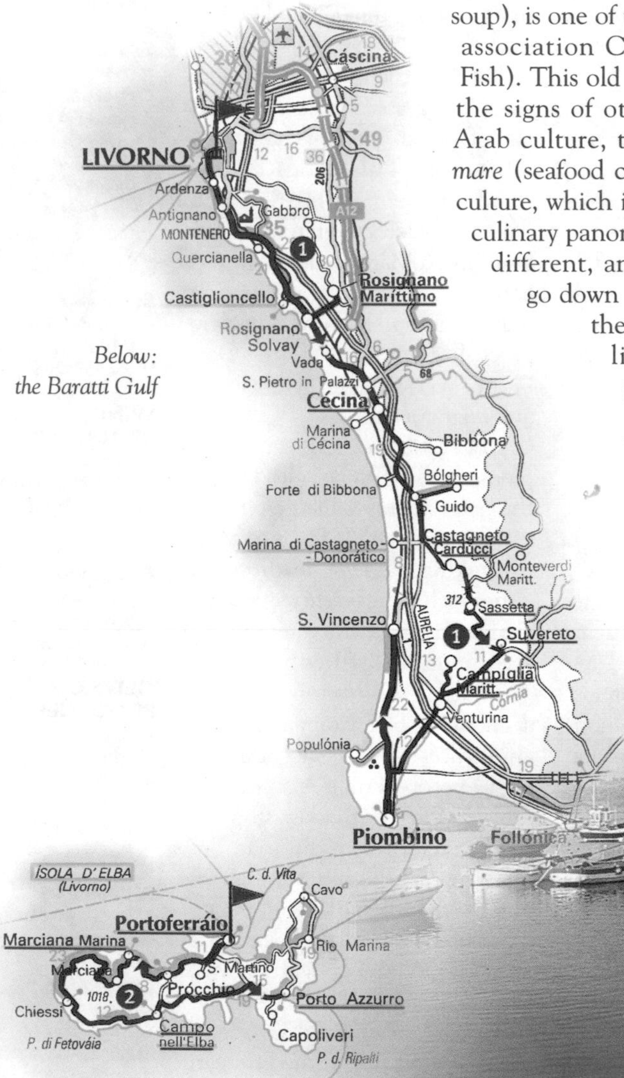

Below:
the Baratti Gulf

LIVORNO
Ardenza
Antignano
MONTENERO
Quercianella
Castiglioncello
Rosignano Solvay
Vada
S. Pietro in Palazzi
Cécina
Marina di Cécina
Forte di Bibbona
Marina di Castagneto - Donorático
S. Vincenzo
Campíglia Maritt.
Venturina
Populónia
Cáscina
Gabbro
Rosignano Maríttimo
Bibbona
Bólgheri
S. Guido
Castagneto Carducci
Monteverdi Maritt.
Sassetta
Suvereto
Cornia
Piombino
Follónica

ÍSOLA D'ELBA
(Livorno)
Marciana Marina
Marciana
Chiessi
P. di Fetováia
Portoferráio
S. Martino
Prócchio
Campo nell'Elba
C. d. Vita
Cavo
Rio Marina
Porto Azzurro
Capoliveri
P. d. Ripalti

den vegetables. Livestock breeders take pride in the *galline Livornesi* (Livorno hens) in their white, black and golden varieties, with yellow claws and exquisite meat. The fame of local wines is only recent. In the north, we find a descendent of the Pisan DOC wine Montescudaio; Bolgheri, in which Cabernet Sauvignon plays a major role; and the Val di Cornia, which blends Sangiovese with Cabernet and Merlot, and Trebbiano with Vermentino. There is also Elba, with unblended wines made from the ancient grapes Biancone, Moscato and Aleatico. The network of restaurants is also good, with particularly excellent food at "Gambero Rosso" in San Vincenzo. The restaurants in Elba are also pleasant.

Gourmet Tours

LIVORNO. The Medicean city, surrounded by moats and with two fortresses and the Venezia Nuova neighborhood, has charming views. In the modern part, you can take a pleasant walk along the sea if you follow the Viale Italia. Here you can also visit the museum dedicated to Giovanni Fattori, the Florentine expressionist painter of La Maremma landscapes and the battles of the Risorgimento. You can taste the good food of the city of *bavettine sul pesce* (thin noodles with fish) and *cacciucco* (fish soup) at "Ciglieri", which uses the best ingredients, has a gifted and competent owner and a great *cantina*. Dishes invented here include the *timballo di pesce con vellutata di fagioli* and *tartufo bianco*

Livorno. The port

HOTELS AND RESTAURANTS

Livorno
Ciglieri ¶¶¶
via O. Franchini 38
☎ 0586508194
Gennarino ¶¶ 🛏
via S. Fortunata 11
☎ 0586888093
Cantina Nardi ¶
via Cambini 6/8
☎ 0586808006
Da Galileo ¶
via della Campana 2
☎ 058688909
Enoteca Doc ¶
via Goldoni 40/44
☎ 0586887583
Castagneto
Carducci
Bagnoli ¶¶
at Bagnoli
☎ 0565763630
Da Ugo ¶
via Pari 3/a
☎ 0565763746
Cecina
Scacciapensieri ¶¶¶
via Verdi 22
☎ 0586680900
Bagatelle ¶¶ 🛏
at Marina di
Cecina (km 3)
via Carlo Ginori 51
☎ 0586620089

(fish timbale with a bean and white truffle mousse), *millefoglie di rombo in salsa di basilico* (turbot millefeuille in basil sauce) and *suprême di branzino al vino bianco con crema di carciofi* (supreme of bass with white wine and cream of artichoke). We also recommend "Gennarino", a Buon Ricordo restaurant. At "Cecco" and "Torteria Gagarin", try the traditional *farinata*, while at the pastry shops, sample marzipan fruits, Jewish sweets, *schiacciata all'acqua di fior d'arancia* and *all'anice* (flatbread flavored with orange flower water or anise). Don't miss a visit to the attractive market Scali Sassi for charcuterie, cheese, meats from La Maremma, and many other goodies.

Bolgheri. The chapel of S. Guido

HOTELS AND RESTAURANTS

Elba (Island of)
Emanuel ⚓
at Portoferraio
at Enfola
☎ 0565939003
**Osteria
del Noce** ⚓
at Marciana Marina
via d. Madonna 14
☎ 0565901284
**Marina di
Bibbona**
⭐ 🛏 **La Pineta di
Zazzeri** ⚓⚓
via Cavalleggeri Nord
27
☎ 0586600016
**Marina di
Castagneto
Carducci**
I Ginepri ★★★
viale Italia 13
☎ 0565744027
⭐ 🛏 **Nuovo Hotel
Bambolo** ★★★
at Donoratico (km 3)
at Il Bambolo 31
☎ 0565775206
Rosignano Solvay
⭐ 🛏 **Il Ducale** ⚓⚓
at Vada (km 5)
piazza Garibaldi 33
☎ 0586788600

1. The Etruscan coast

ROSIGNANO MARITTIMO. Pines and holm oaks cover the promontory of Castiglioncello, which juts out into the sea between cliffs and small beaches. The pleasant, traditionally elegant, village is near the Via Aurelia. Further south at Vada, the restaurant "Il Ducale" is worth a try. Refined and romantic, it is set in an eighteenth-century palazzo. Don't miss the delicious shellfish dish.

CECINA. The long pine-edged beach is the pleasant touristic annex of a recent city. Good vegetables and a small harvest of truffles are delivered from further inland.

Worth a visit is "Scacciapensieri", a refined restaurant, that serves *risotto con asparago di macchia e scampi* (risotto with wild asparagus and prawns), *piccione disossato al rosmarino con fagioli del purgatorio* (boned pigeon with rosemary and beans). At the Marina, we recommend "Bagatelle", which serves excellent fish prepared in a variety of interesting ways. In Marina di Bibbona go to "La Pineta di Zazzeri", where seafood is prepared delicately and intelligently (and the *cantina* is good).

BOLGHERI. The chapel San Guido and the double rows of cypresses in honor of the Nobel-prize-winning poet and literary critic Carducci herald a town that has earned exceptional fame for its wines. We like Sassicaia, a Cabernet Sauvignon with great character that represents the new direction in which Tuscan vine cultivation is heading. Few *cantine* are open to the public, but the old town is starting to catch on.

CASTAGNETO CARDUCCI. Located on the first slopes of Colline Metallifere, the village, with the Castello della Gherardesca, has an ancient aspect and interesting mementoes of Giosuè Carducci. As a Città del Vino, the town is a point of reference along the Strada della Costa degli Etruschi, which unites over 50 producers, *agriturismo* operations, restaurants and craft shops. At Marina, the "Hotel Ginepri", with its veranda, and thicket growing down to the sea, is renowned for its good cooking. In Donoratico, try "Nuovo Hotel Bambolo", located in an old *posteria*, or grocery shop.

SASSETTA. The route climbs through the picturesque landscape of Maremma Pisana. The town is high on a precipice, with houses built of stone and surrounded by chestnut trees and oaks. Local products include mushrooms and *selvaggina*, and *cinghiale* (wild boar), and best

Cypresses. A symbol of Tuscany

HOTELS AND RESTAURANTS

San Vincenzo
Gambero Rosso ¶¶¶¶
piazza della Vittoria 13
☎ 0565701021

AGRITURISMI

Castagneto Carducci
Podere Grattamacco ★
at Grattamacco 129
☎ 0565763840
Cecina
Elisabetta ★
at Collemezzano
via Tronto 10
☎ 0586661392
Elba (Island of)
Agricoop Isola d'Elba ★
at Seccheto
at Vallebuia
☎ 0565987035

**WINE
PRODUCERS**

Elba (Island of)
Portoferraio
Acquabona
at Acquabona
☎ 0565933013
Suvereto
Gualdo del Re
at Notri 77
☎ 0565829888

**OLIVE OIL
PRODUCERS**

Bolgheri
**Tenuta
dell'Ornellaia**
via Bolgherese 191
☎ 0565762140
*Tenuta dell'Ornellaia
olive oil.*
Cecina
**Ass. Interprov.
Prod. Olivicoli
di Pisa e Livorno**
via XXIV Maggio 12
☎ 0586686099
Lentisco olive oil.

of all the sweet figs, which are, according to the labels, preserved "sotto'olio" (in oil), but actually kept in honey. SUVERETO. Isolated in the woods of Monte Calvi, this Città del Vino produces the DOC Val di Cornia wine. Try the farm "Gualdo del Re", where excellent whites are made of pure Pinot and Vermentino and a red is made from Cabernet, Merlot and Sangiovese aged in barrels.

CAMPIGLIA MARITTIMA. In the Middle Ages, this town was the capital of Pisa – a distinction borne out by the surviving Rocca (fortress), *palazzi* and churches. It grew rich from mining marble in Rocca di San Silvestro, which today is an extraordinary museum of industrial archaeology. The town is noteworthy for its wines and excellent harvest of mushrooms, which are a fine excuse for a festival in the fall.

PIOMBINO. The historic port of embarkation for Elba is a city of industry and trade. Many are, therefore, surprised to discover the rural vocation of its more inland areas,

where there are renowned productions of wines and vegetables, particularly artichokes. In Baratti, the excavations of the Etruscan city of Populonia are extraordinary.

SAN VINCENZO. On the return route along the coast, a Pisan tower marks the site of the beach, the pines, and a restaurant that steals the heart of all gourmets. "Gambero Rosso" is located on the sea and run by a chef of few words but great professionalism. Choose from *spaghetti ai crostacei* (spaghetti with shellfish), *ravioli di zucca* (ravioli filled with pumpkin), *risotto alla pescatora* (fisherman's *risotto*), *piccione con puré di patate* (pigeon with mashed potatoes) – dishes we've seen everywhere, but rarely so good. Cheeses from La Maremma and France are carefully researched; the *cantina* and list of distilled spirits are also excellent.

2. The island of Elba

PORTOFERRAIO. Napoleon stayed here in exile for little less than a year, but left behind him a lasting record of his pres-

Campiglia Marittima

ence. Visit his residences, with their Empire-style furnishings and various other memorabilia of a curious nature. This, however, is not the only cause for interest in a seafaring city that was in its heyday in the sixteenth century. The island setting is not particularly inspiring, but it has its highlights, including "Emanuel", a pleasant restaurant shaded by a century-old fig tree and situated at the former tuna fishing zone in the Bay of Enfola. In keeping with this theme, you can try *tagliolini alla bottarga* (pasta with smoked tuna-fish eggs), or branch out with *cacciucco all'elbana, or sburrita* (Elba-style fish soup). The wine producer "Acquabona" is also good, and is the biggest on the island with 14 hectares of terraced vines. The best wines here are the Aleatico and Ansonica.

MARCIANA MARINA. After following the verdant coast northward, go ashore at this beautiful coastal town. Further up, on the slopes of Monte Capanne, in the midst of stands of chestnut trees, lies the capital. The restaurant

"Osteria del Noce" is located in the panoramic village of Castello, and offers seafood dishes with a Ligurian flavor.

CAMPO NELL'ELBA. Continuing the sail around the island, go down the western coast, which gets sunnier and sunnier, and enjoy the beautiful beaches of Fetovaia and Cavoli. This minute community includes Marina di Campo, a lively vacation village set around the small port, and San Piero situated among the greenery further inland.

PORTO AZZURRO. Facing the Golfo di Mola, this town is a point of reference for trips to the eastern part of the island. Take a day trip to Rio nell'Elba, the main mining town on the island, which is now a tourist center, and to Capoliveri, pleasantly situated on the Baia della Stella.

SHOPPING

Livorno
Azienda Bioagricola Marcantoni Sante
via del Vecchio Lazzaretto 110
☎ 0586500669
Organic pigeons grow.
Cecco
via Cavalletti 2
☎ 0586881074
Macelleria di Bonelli Paolo
via Monte Grappa 7/9
☎ 0586006044
Meat, olive oil, typical cheeses and delicatessen.
Torteria Gagarin
via d. Cardinale 24
☎ 0586884086
Traditional "farinata".
Castagneto Carducci
Progetto Natura srl
at Donoratico
via Aurelia 1/f
☎ 0565773010
Products by the Cooperativa Produttori Agricoli Livornesi.

LUCCA

The fashionable Versilia area and the rustic Garfagnana are gastronomic opposites joined within a province.

The province of Lucca is mostly mountainous, with the Apuan Alps and a stretch of the Apennines marking out the upper basin of the Serchio, (that is, the Garfagnana. Flat lands surround the Lucchesia area) a branch of the Valdarno and, near the sea, Versilia. The mountains are given over to the breeding of cattle and sheep, for both milk and meat, and to the products of the woods, as well as to farro (spelt), a rustic and healthy cereal, recently distinguished by the IGP (*Indicazione Geografica Protetta*) label. Going down to the plains, you cross the olive grove that brought Lucca its fame, which is still very much alive today. Its grapes are also good, and as testimony there is the DOC production Montecarlo, which comes from a town that is celebrated for its Trebbiani, as well as Colline Lucchesi. Lucca's cuisine distinguishes itself for its soups, which provide the ideal platform for tasting the olive oil. They range from the so-

Lucca. Piazza del Mercato

called *magro*, or thin soup, that is made with pork rind and salt pork, to *garmucia*, which is a spring vegetable *minestra* (soup) made with beans, peas, artichokes, asparagus and chopped meat. The restaurants are excellent, from the historic "Buca di S. Antonio" in Lucca to the evergreen "Lorenzo" in Forte dei Marmi in upmarket Versilia. More friendly, and no less appreciable, is the offering in Garfagnana.

Gourmet Tours

LUCCA. Within the rose-colored walls, this provincial capital preserves its original character. A tour of Lucca should include the Duomo and the tomb of Ilaria del Carretto. There is also a series of churches and *palazzi*, as well as medieval residences that are still intact, not to mention museums. The most moving experience, however, is the Piazza del Mercato, framed by ancient houses around the ellipse of a Roman ampitheater. Outside the gates, the river Serchio flows by and the fertile plain fills the gap between the Pizzorne plateau and Monte Pisano. Olive trees dominate the landscape and give

the town its gastronomic fame. We recommend you taste the local fare at the "Buca di S. Antonio" (established 1782). The restaurant is typical of Lucca; the owners are friendly and the traditional dishes are fairly priced. Don't miss the *zuppa frantoiana* (soup with beans and freshly-pressed olive oil) For those who love period decor, "Antico Caffè Di Simo" (est. 1846), in the central Via Fillungo, is decorated with Art Nouveau furnishings that recall a time when the literati gathered here for animated meetings. For pastries, one shop beats them all: "Taddeucci", behind San Michele, which sells *buccellato*,

HOTELS AND RESTAURANTS

Lucca
Buca di S. Antonio 𝄞𝄞𝄞 ★
via della Cervia 3
☎ 058355881
La Mora 𝄞𝄞𝄞
at Ponte a Moriano (km 9)
via Sesto di Moriano 1748
☎ 0583406402
Solferino 𝄞𝄞𝄞
at San Macario in Piano (km 6)
☎ 058359118
Antico Caffè delle Mura 𝄞𝄞
piazza Vittorio Emanuele 2
☎ 058347962
Camaiore
Locanda Le Monache ★★★
piazza XXIX Maggio 36
☎ 0584989258
Emilio e Bona 𝄞𝄞𝄞
at Lombrici (km 3)
☎ 0584989289
Castelnuovo di Garfagnana
Osteria Vecchio Mulino 𝄞
via Vittorio Emanuele 12
☎ 058362192
Forte dei Marmi
Byron ★★★
La Magnolia 𝄞𝄞𝄞
viale Morin 46
☎ 0584787052
Barca 𝄞𝄞𝄞
viale Italico 3
☎ 058489323
Lorenzo 𝄞𝄞𝄞
via Carducci 61
☎ 058466961

the typical anise-flavored sweet in Lucca. As for nearby towns, at San Macario in Piano, on the route towards Versilia, go to "Solferino", a restaurant with many a tale to tell, where some dishes date back generations. Finally, wine tourists leaving Monte San Quirico will want to go beyond Serchio, where the Strada del Vino delle Colline Lucchesi unravels.

1. The Valdarno and the Pizzorne plateau

CAPANNORI. One of the best olive oils in the region comes from this town. Capannori also takes pride in its fruit and vegetables, which include peaches and cherries, the celebrated *cardi gobbi* (thistles) and beans, both white and so-called *scritti*, which are boiled and dressed with local oil. "Fattoria Maionchi", in Tofori, is a must for wine tourists, and offers tastings, snacks, and *agriturismo* holidays.

ALTOPASCIO. On the outskirts of Valdinievole, this town lies on the route of the ancient Via Francigena and preserves a variety of images linked to medieval pilgrimages, starting with the central Piazza Ospitalieri. In the old center, buy the famous *pane casereccio* (wholemeal bread), which is exported a great deal. You can also get good charcuterie.

MONTECARLO. The Trebbiani wines of this walled town are of long-standing renown. They have been appreciated by popes and rulers in the past, and today are recognised by a DOC qualification and a Strada del Vino. A sta-

ple event for the local wine industry, the much visited Mostra Mercato, is held here in early September. The *agriturismo* establishment "Da Baffo", which is an annex to an *azienda*, is worth trying. On the menu here are charcuterie, *zuppa frantoiana* (soup with beans and olive oil) and *coniglio alla cacciatora con olive* (rabbit with tomato sauce and olives). Elsewhere you will find the traditional *tordi con un'oliva nel becco girati allo spiedo* (spit-roasted thrushes with an olive in their beaks). In Villa Basilica, climbing towards the Pizzorne, is the pleasant *trattoria* "Da Aldo", with a shop that sells charcuterie, including *lardo* (salt pork) and *biroldo*, as well as their own olive oil. You can also get excellent *cinghiale con le olive nere* (wild boar with black olives).

2. The Garfagnana

BORGO A MOZZANO. Further up the Serchio, the Buon Ricordo restaurant "Mora", in Ponte a Moriano, has long produced the best in traditional local cuisine, including one dish not to be missed: *fracosta al rosso lucchese* (meat with red wine from Lucca). In Borgo a Mozzano, there are good opportunities for buying charcuterie and cheeses. Then turn towards Bagni di Lucca, a spa town with a good reputation, in a land of black and white truffles.

BARGA. Visit the Città Vecchia, a quiet neighborhood stretching up the hillside. Then, from the Arringo, where the cathedral rises up, there is a broad panorama. In the *trattorie* there are the traditional *infarinata* (a flour-based dish that is a hybrid of *polenta* and *minestrone*)

HOTELS AND RESTAURANTS

Massarosa
★ 🍽 **La Chandelle**
via Casa Rossa I 🍴🍴🍴
☎ 0584938290
Pietrasanta
★ 🍽 **Pietrasanta**
via Garibaldi 35 ★★★
☎ 0584793726
Marcucci 🍴🍴
via Garibaldi 40
☎ 0584791962
Nonsolovino 🍴
vicolo S. Biagio 5
☎ 058470510
Seravezza
Osteria Ulisse Enoteca 🍴
via Campana 63
☎ 0584757420
Viareggio
Oca Bianca 🍴🍴🍴🍴
via Coppino 409
☎ 0584388477
Romano 🍴🍴🍴🍴
via Mazzini 122
☎ 058431382
Principe di Piemonte ★★★
piazza Puccini I
☎ 058450122
Darsena 🍴
via Virgilio 154
☎ 0584392785
Osteria n. I 🍴
via Pisano 140
☎ 0584388967
Villa Basilica
Da Aldo 🍴
via Cartiere 175
☎ 057243008

and dishes pungent with truffles. In Alpe di Sant'Antonio, visit the *agriturismo* operation "La Betulla", try soups, cheeses and Garfagnana *salumi*. The more adventurous should head up the beautiful Valle del Turrite on a day tip to the Grotta del Vento.

CASTELNUOVO DI GARFAGNANA. The Rocca (fortress), with its towers and corbels, serves the Apuan Alps on one side and the Apennines on the other. Don't miss the "Osteria Vecchio Mulino", where you will find all the local specialties and excellent wines. In the village buy local products, including *farro* (spelt) and other grains, chestnuts and mushrooms, walnuts and honey, cheeses and charcuterie. From here, climbing up towards the Passo delle Radici, we come to Castiglione di Garfagnana, where the usual abundance of products from pastureland is accompanied by black truffles and mushrooms, woodland berries and *trote di torrente* (brook trout). Continue towards the springs of the Serchio, and in Camporgiano stop at "Mulin del Rancone", an *agriturismo* operation where it is possible to spend the night and have dinner. On the menu are *tortelli* and *maiale con polenta di castagne* (pork with chestnut *polenta*).

3. The Versilia

VIAREGGIO. Originally, in the twelfth century, this town was a seaport with a tower near Via Regia. Today the city of fishermen and boat builders continues to thrive around the port, but it now gains its fame from its pine trees and beaches, which have turned it into the fashionable capital of Versilia. The *cacciucco viareggino* (fish soup Viareggio style) on the menu rivals that of Livorno for fame, and it is *più piccante* (spicier). Other characteristic local dishes are *zuppa di arselle*, or *nicchi*, (clam soup), and *scampi*, or *sparnocchi serviti con fagioli bolliti and pomodori freschi* (prawns served with boiled beans and fresh tomatoes), *cieche fritte con la salvia* (elver, which is a type of young eel, fried with sage). The network of restaurants is top class, starting with "Romano". Here the pleasant atmosphere combines with professionalism in a restaurant that has not lost any of its original sparkle and sets a fine example to others. The Buon Ricordo dish is *minestra di farro, verdure and pesce* (soup with spelt, vegetables and fish). "Oca Bianca" is a close second. In a beautiful and captivating setting, this restaurant serves dishes that have prominent flavors, in·

AGRITURISMI

Camporgiano
Mulin del Rancone
at Mulin del Rancone
☎ 0583618670
Molazzana
La Betulla
all'Alpe di S. Antonio
☎ 0583760052
Montecarlo
Da Baffo
via della Tinaia 7
☎ 058322381

WINE PRODUCERS

Capannori
Fattoria Maionchi
at Tofori
☎ 0583978194
Offers tastings, snacks, and "agriturismo" holidays.

SHOPPING

Lucca
Antico Caffè
Di Simo
via Fillungo 58
☎ 0583467148
Taddeucci
piazza S. Michele 34
☎ 0583494933
Typical pastries
and sweets.
Camaiore
Claudio
via Provinciale 45
☎ 0584989069
Wines and
delicatessen.
Da Lando
via V. Emanuele 41
☎ 0584983416
Typical delicatessen.
Salumeria
Bonucelli
via V. Emanuele 9
☎ 0584989680
Charcuterie.
Casciana
Agricola Bravi
via Sorbi 1
☎ 0583696182
Spelt and spelt flour.
Castelnuovo
di Garfagnana
Il Vecchio Mulino
via V. Emanuele 12
☎ 058362192
Good selection
of flours.
Lido di Camaiore
Giannoni
viale Colombo 444
☎ 0584617332
Charcuterie, cheeses
and savoury pies.
Pieve San Paolo
Il Cerro
via del Tiglio 92
☎ 0583981105
Charcuterie, cheeses
and typical specialties
("zuppa garfagnina").

cluding the excellent *linguine alla tracina* (*linguine* with weever fish) and *tagliata di rombo ai funghi porcini* (slices of turbot with boletus mushrooms). Those who prefer a period setting might try the hotel "Principe di Piemonte", a monument to Art Nouveau that has been the venue for the awarding of Viareggio's literary prize. At the *trattoria* "Darsena", a *frittura di paranza* is served at affordable prices, and the popular "Osteria n. 1" serves a fine selection of purely local dishes. From Viareggio, head out on a day trip to Torre del Lago Puccini, visit the composer's home and take a boat ride on Massaciuccoli Lake.

FORTE DEI MARMI. The Apuan Alps rise up behind the pines. Blocks of marble for sculpting statues used to be taken down from the quarries to the port for embarkation. The Grand Duke Leopold I had the Fort built in the middle of the *piazza* to store the marble, and an elegant vacation city grew up around it. An excellent place for a meal is the restaurant "Lorenzo", which has had much success with its great quality offerings thanks to the skill of the owner, who knows his wines and fish well. We also strongly recommend the hotel "Byron" and its restaurant "La Magnolia", which is decorated in Art Nouveau style, as well as "Barca", where the grilled fish is excellent. In Seravezza, the *trattoria* "Ulisse" – for *farro* (spelt), *chianina* beef, mushrooms and truffles – is a fine place to stop

along the beautiful route leading to the Pania della Croce.

PIETRASANTA. The historic capital of Versilia has its roots in the Middle Ages, when it was a stop along the Via Francigena. The thirteenth-century cathedral and the tall fortress are proof of its former ranking. The surrounding countryside has earned a good name for its olive oil, wines and fruit. The "Hotel Pietrasanta" is a charming stop. Set in an historic building, it offers every modern comfort. Two *enoteche* that serve food are interesting for the gourmet: "Marcucci" covers the range from Versilia to Garfagnana with wines, cheeses and *affettati* (charcuterie), and "Nonsolovino" is pleasant and affordable. The pastry shops at the Marina are renowned for *torta con becchi* (short pastry with a pinched border filled with chocolate cream).

CAMAIORE. Up in the hills, Camaiore is renowned for its olive oil and strawberries. Along the long road that divides the town are two good places to try the food: the *salumeria* "Bonucelli", which sells masterfully prepared meats, and "Lando", which offers a wide variety of local products. Stay at the "Locanda Le Monache", a characteristic house in the old center, with a typical restaurant that is elegant without losing its family feel. In Lombrici, you could try "Emilio and Bona", which is set in an ancient olive mill and specializes in mushrooms and truffles.

MASSA-CARRARA

A province with a split personality, as the flavors of Liguria come through near the Tyrrhenian Sea and trans-Alpine flavors take over in Lunigiana.

T he province of Massa-Carrara, wedged in between Emilia and Liguria, looks onto the sea, but is mostly mountainous. It includes the southern spurs of the Tuscan-Emilian Apennines and the north-western Apuan Alps, which are on the edge of the Valle del Magra. This is also called the Lunigiana Valley in memory of the an-cient Etruscan city of Luni. Agriculture is the main player in the local economy, and is focused on olive and vine culti-vation in the hilly areas, and fruit and vegetable grow-ing in the flatlands by the coast. Animal hus-bandry and dairy farming are the main features of the mountains, but there are also wild products, particularly mushrooms and chestnuts. The famous *lardo di Colonnata*, a niche product that has be-come a symbol of endangered methods, is a source of local pride. The province has two DOC wines – the Candia dei Colli Apuani, and Colli di Luni, which it shares with Liguria. The first is the title for white wines made from blends of grapes from Liguria (Vermentino and Albarola) and Tuscany (Trebbiano and Malvasia). The second is reminiscent, in both the landscaping of the terraced vines and the types of grapes, of the great wines of

View of the Massese countryside

the Cinque Terre. The cuisine is influenced by Liguria in coastal areas and Lunigiana elsewhere. Thus, on the one hand, the cuisine is based on seafood and vegetables near the Tyrrhenian Sea, with fish, vegetable *torta*, *testaroli con il pesto* (spongy flatbread "pasta" served with pesto) and *ravioli ripeni di erbe* (ravioli filled with greens), and on the other, more inland cooking such as the *bomba di riso*, *ripiena di carne di piccione* (rice bomb filled with pigeon), which is of Po heritage. As for restaurants, there are no greats, but the *trattorie* are pleasant and comfortable places to discover local products and traditional dishes.

Gourmet Tours

MASSA. On the sheltered side of the hill, where the Rocca dei Malaspina rises up, stands a small medieval nucleus. The sixteenth-century part of the city surrounds the contiguous Piazza degli Aranci. Here in the cellar of an ancient palazzo you will find the *trattoria* "Il Passeggero", which introduces local flavors with the typical *tordelli al sugo di funghi* (woodthrush with mushrooms). In the countryside there are excellent fruit and vegetable producers (of peaches, apples, figs), in addition to the vineyards that produce DOC Colli Apuani. At

the Marina, for an alternative evening, we suggest the small restaurant at the "Circolo della Vela", where all dishes are based on fish. In Montignoso, you will find excellent food at the restaurant "Bottaccio", set in an eighteenth-century olive mill at the inn of the same name.

CARRARA. Surrounded by olive trees, against a backdrop of Apuan Alps (here called the *panie*), Carrara has been the "town of marble" for two thousand years. Fine–grained white marble for statues, bardiglio, purple marble, Italian white and green cipolin marble and many others – all types are on display in

HOTELS AND RESTAURANTS

Massa
Il Passeggero ¶
piazza Aranci
☎ 0585489651
Bagnone
La Lina ¶
piazza G. Marconi 1
☎ 0187429069
Carrara
Enoteca Ninan ¶¶
via Bartolini 3
☎ 058574741
Venanzio ¶¶
at Colonnata (km 7)
piazza Palestro 3
☎ 0585758062
Locanda Apuana ¶
Via Comunale di
Colonnata (km 7)
☎ 0585768017
Fivizzano
Il Giardinetto ★★
via Roma 151
☎ 058592060

Massa. Rocca dei Malaspina

the Romanesque Duomo. In the town the small "Enoteca Ninan" is worth a visit. In addition to a wide variety of important wines, it also offers good local food, with both meat and fish. In the bakeries, you will find an unusual variety of products, including *manine*, a refined bread made for holidays and enriched with the best olive oil; the dark *marocca*, made with a blend of corn and wheat, raisins, pine nuts and anise; and *pane alle erbe*, made from an old recipe, with nettles, camomile, lemon balm, and a variety of other herbs, as well as a pinch of red pepper. Then climb up to Colonnata to see the quarries and also to buy the famous *lardo*, which develops its flavor in marble. Stop for a meal at "Venanzio", a fascinating eatery that serves simple, tasty cooking, for example *cotiche and fagioli* (pork rind and beans), *lasagnette verdi con funghi* (green lasagna with mushrooms), *agnello in casseruola* (lamb casserole). For *lardo* and other characteristic products, go to the "Locanda Apuana".

FOSDINOVO. Across the Parco delle Apuane, a winding road with sharp climbs and drops leads to this land of ancient flavors. From the castle it is possible to look out beyond the vineyards for the DOC Colli di Luni wine and far out into the sea of La Spezia. Here try a fairly spicy and tasty *mortadella*. The *trattoria* "Il Cucco", a family run eatery that has always come up to standard throughout its long history, offers home cooking and local wines.

AULLA. At the converging point of the routes through the Apennine passes –Cisa, Lagastrello and Cerreto – you will find the gateway to the Lunigiana surveyed by the Fortezza della Brunella . Olive oil from the olive press and *salumi* (charcuterie) are the major products here. Typical dishes include *torte d'erbe e cipolle* (tarts made with greens and onions), *minestrone* (vegetable soups), *lasagne verdi* (green lasagna) and *tortelli* (filled pasta).

FIVIZZANO. Surrounded by Florentine walls, this ancient trading town lies on the route leading to Reggiano. Here you can find authentic *pecorino* cheeses from Cerreto and the Capanne del Giovo, as well as mushrooms and chestnuts. The surrounding area offers olive oils and wines. For a pleasant stay and local food, go to "Giardinetto", where the menu includes *bomba di riso al piccione* (rice bomb with pigeon), *coniglio farcito* (stuffed rabbit), *polenta incatenata* (winter dish of *polenta* with fresh borlotti beans and black cabbage), and *polenta and funghi* (summer dish of *polenta* with mushrooms).

VILLAFRANCA IN LUNIGIANA. Here the hundred-year-old *salumeria* "Drovandi" has excellent *mortadella*, sausages and shoulders of ham. In the hamlet of Mocrone, "Gavarini" is a simple restaurant that offers an exquisite welcome for its guests, serving

HOTELS AND RESTAURANTS

Fosdinovo
Il Cucco ⑪ ★ 🏨
via Cucco 26
☎ 018768907

Marina di Carrara
Muraglione ⑪⑪⑪
at Avenza (km 1)
via Fivizzano 13
☎ 058552337

Marina di Massa
Circolo della Vela ⑪
viale Vespucci 84
☎ 0585244544

Montignoso
Bottaccio ⑪⑪⑪⑪
via Bottaccio 1
☎ 0585340031

Pontremoli
Da Bussé ⑪
piazza Duomo 31
☎ 0187831371

Villafranca in Lunigiana
Gavarini ⑪
contrada Mocrone
via Benedicenti 50
☎ 0187493115

Lunigiana. View from the Lagastrello Pass

AGRITURISMI

Fivizzano
Il Bardellino
at Soliera
at Bardellino
☎ 058593304
**Montignoso
Karma**
via Guadagni 1
☎ 0585821237
Pontremoli
⭐ ▦ **Costa
d'Orsola**
at Orsola
☎ 0187833332

SHOPPING

**Pontremoli
Cooperativa
Il Bosco**
at S. Giustina
☎ 0187833628
*Honey from
Lunigiana.*
**Villafranca in
Lunigiana
Salumeria
Drovandi**
piazza Vittoria 8
☎ 0187493019
*Charcuterie and
cheeses.*

dishes which include *pasta di farina di castagne* (pasta made with chestnut flour) and *chicchere*, a kind of green *gnocchi*, and *agnello* (lamb), *coniglio* (rabbit) and *cinghiale* (boar), in season. In Bagnone, you may stay at "La Lina", where a restaurant decorated in Art Nouveau style offers appetizing dishes, starting with tarts made with greens and garden vegetables. PONTREMOLI. This is the capital of the upper valley, near Cisa, which gains its fame from the literary award "Bancarella" (this award is promoted by the local bookstores in memory of booksellers of the past who, according to a deeply rooted custom, sold their wares in Italy's *piazze*). Don't miss the museum with its enigmatic prehistoric stelae from the Lunigiana at the Castello del Piagnaro. We espe-

Pontremoli

cially recommend the restaurant "Da Bussé", an *osteria* that is as traditional as the food eaten there – this includes *testaroli* (a spongelike pancake-pasta that is boiled and served with pesto or a cheese sauce) and all the local dishes, plus irresistible *torte alle erbe* (tarts with greens). Nearby is the century-old "Caffè degli Svizzeri", where the local sweet *amor* is produced. In the shops you will find various products from other centers in the upper valley, including sheep's and cow's milk cheeses, prized meats and charcuterie, beans, potatoes and other garden vegetables, *castagne*, *funghi* and *frutti di bosco* (forest fruits). Instead of bread, there is *carsenta*, a kind of *focaccia*, made with a variety of flours – wheat, corn or chestnut.

PISA

The sea, rivers and hills of Pisa ensure that fish, wild game and woodland flavors – particularly truffles – grace the tables here.

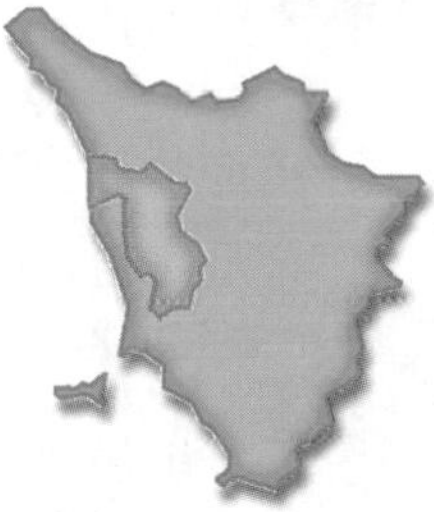

The province of Pisa has a mostly hilly territory, with a glimpse of the Tyrrhenian Sea, where the Arno and Serchio rivers create fertile plains. The ridge that runs from north to south includes Monte Pisano, a section of the Pre-Apennines and the northern section of the Colline Metallifere, which are wooded and almost uninhabited. The coastline is sandy, and bordered by pines. The hills are mostly given over to vineyards. The best typical wine is Chianti Colline Pisane DOCG, made in the same territory as the DOC wines Bianco Pisano di San Torpè, Colli dell'Etruria Centrale and Vin Santo del Chianti. By the borders with Livorno you will find the DOC wine Montescudaio, which has a red similar to Chianti, but softened by the maritime climate, and a white made from Trebbiano, Malvasia and Vermentino grapes.

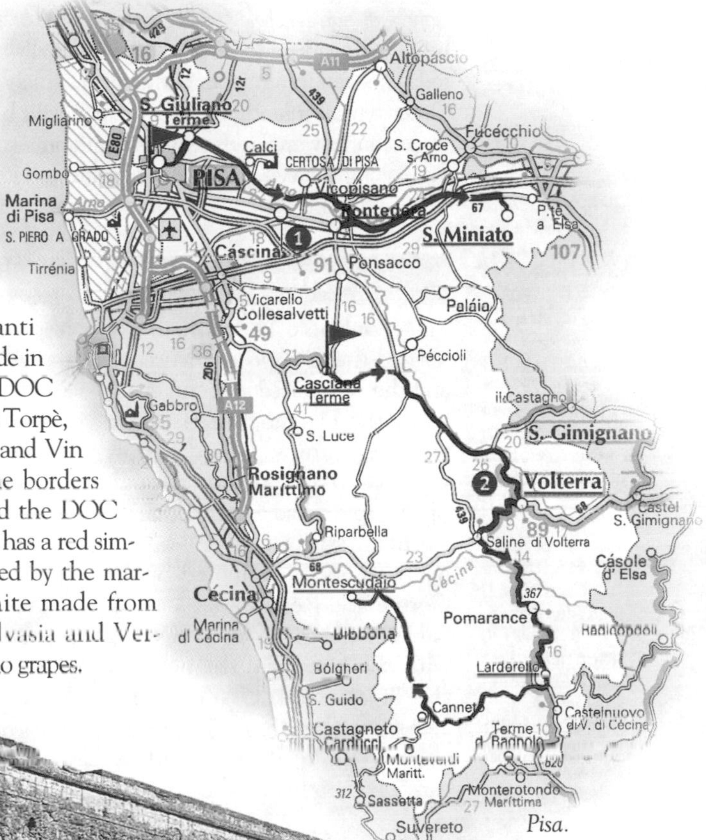

Pisa.
Medicean
aquaduct

Completing the picture is the production of olive oil, flatland vegetables and fruit, and sheep and cattle breeding for both meat and dairy products (Pecorino toscano da serbo and Toscanello). Traditional cooking is influenced by the products of both the water (fresh and salt) and the land. In Pisa, river and sea cooking is strong, with typical products ranging from *cieche fritte alla salvia* (baby eels fried with sage), and *muggini di foce d'Arno alla griglia* (grilled mullet from the mouth of the Arno), to *bavettine sul pesce* (thin noodles with fish), *zuppa di riso con le arselle* (rice soup with clams) and *baccalà bollito con i ceci, in agrodolce o in teglia* (boiled salt cod with chick peas, in sweet and sour sauce, or baked). Other dishes make use of inland resources – these include *minestra di fagioli bianchi di San Michele* (white bean soup), or *fagioli al fiasco* (slow-cooked beans with garlic and savory herbs, originally cooked in flasks in fire ashes, today cooked in terracota containers), which are both countryside dishes. Other typical inland products include wild boar and duck from the vast woods and swamplands. Many restaurants can be found in and around Pisa, along the coast and on the route to Florence. There are fewer, but more authentic, restaurants towards Volterra and the Metallifere hills.

HOTELS AND RESTAURANTS

Pisa
Artilafo ♚♚
via Volturno 38
☎ 05027010
Osteria dei Cavalieri ♚
via S. Frediano 16
☎ 050580858
Calcinaia
Calamidoro ★★★
via del Tiglio 143
☎ 0587297111
Marina di Pisa
L'Arsella ♚♚
via Padre Agostino
☎ 05036615
Toto ♚♚
via da Montefeltro 32
☎ 05036605
Montaione
Casa Masi ♚♚
ad Alteri (km 4)
☎ 0571677170
Montescudaio
⭐🍴 **Il Frantoio** ♚
via della Madonna 9
☎ 0586650381
Montopoli Val d'Arno
⭐🍴 **Quattro Gigli** ★★★
Quattro Gigli ♚♚
piazza Michele da Montopoli 1
☎ 0571466878
Trattoria dell'Orcio Interrato ♚
piazza S. Michele 2
☎ 0571466878
Pontedera
⭐🍴 **Aeroscalo** ♚♚
via Roma 8
☎ 058752024
⭐🍴 **La Polveriera** ♚♚
via F.lli Marconcini 54
☎ 058754765

Gourmet Tours

PISA. Gabriele D'Anunzio described the Campo dei Miracoli and the Romanesque scene created by the Duomo, the Baptistry and the Leaning Tower as holy marbles rising up as though singing spirits had breathed life into them. His awe is just one of many emotions prompted by the Gothic and Renaissance city divided by the Arno river. Keeping with the historical theme, visit the "Caffè dell'Ussero" (est. 1794), at the fifteenth-century Palazzo Agostini along the Lungarno Pacinotti (a route that follows the Arno river), which displays souvenirs from its many illustrious visitors. For good food, try "Artilafo", which is hidden in an alley but well worth hunting down for its painstaking and creative cooking. Easier to find is the "Osteria dei Cavalieri", where good wine accompanies an intelligent menu that balances out Pisan specialties and Tuscan classics with a dash of fantasy. Those with a passion for city color shouldn't miss the market in Piazza delle Vettovaglie, where tables of fruit and vegetables mingle with a variety of other products. For a more

San Miniato.
View of the Serra

sedate experience, go to the old cafe-pastry shop "Salza", in Borgo Stretto, with its rosewood panelling and Middle European atmosphere. A specialty in this town – in addition to the Easter sweet, *schiacciata di Pasqua* , is *torta coi bischeri* (a short pastry filled with rice, pine nuts, raisins and candied fruit). Just outside the city is the beautiful farm of San Rossore (the park may be visited on Sundays). At the seaside, you will find the Marina di Pisa and Tirrenia, beaches, pine trees, and tables heaped with fish.

1. Monte Pisano and the Valdarno

SAN GIULIANO TERME. Along the route toward Lucca, this town is renowned for its waters, but also for the produce of the lands that run down to the Serchio river, in particular fruit (cherries, peaches, table grapes) and vegetables (peas, cabbage, artichokes). "Sergio a Villa di Corliano", in the village of di Rigoli, is good – rustic and set in a hundred-year-old park, it offers traditional dishes and an affordable gourmet menu at midday.

CALCI. Amid the olive trees set at the feet of Monte Pisano, a belltower is the first thing you see of the Romanesque parish and the great Carthusian monastery embellished with Baroque volutes.

The town is well-known for its olive oil, which is celebrated with festivities in the square in early May. Sweet duck is an ancient traditional dish you should try here, and in the bakeries you should try the handcrafted biscuits.

VICOPISANO. Follow the series of charming routes to Buti (exceptional olive oil and chestnuts) and beyond to the Arno river. The Torre delle Quattro Porte lead into the old quarter of Vicopisano, which boasts the fourteenth-century Palazzo Pretorio and other medieval fortified buildings. At Bientina, watermelons and melons are grown in an unusual setting by what used to be the ancient Serto Lake. In Calcinaia, we recommend the elegant inn "Calamidoro", set in an eighteenth-century villa and its rustic outbuildings.

PONTEDERA. This name has been known for generations for the production of the legendary Vespa motorcycle, but it also has good food. We recommend the restaurant "La Polveriera", a simple and naturally friendly place that serves healthy and creative seafood dishes. At "Aeroscalo", on the other hand, the tendency is for more inland dishes, with *pappardelle al ragù di lepre* (wide pasta ribbons with hare ragout),

HOTELS AND RESTAURANTS

San Giuliano Terme
Sergio a Villa di Corliano ¶¶
at Rigoli (km 3) S.S.12
☎ 050818858
San Miniato
Taverna dell'Ozio ¶
via Zara 85
☎ 0571462862
Santa Croce sull'Arno
Beppe ¶¶¶
at Staffoli (km 10)
via Livornese 35/b
☎ 057137002
Tirrenia
Dante e Ivana ¶¶
viale del Tirreno 207/c
☎ 05032549
Martini ¶¶
via dell'Edera 16
☎ 05037592
Volterra
Trattoria del Sacco Fiorentino ¶¶
piazza XX Settembre 18
☎ 058888537
Il Vecchio Mulino ¶¶
at Saline (km 9)
via del Molino
☎ 058844060

AGRITURISMI

Lari
Le Macchie
at Usigliano
via delle Macchie 1/2
☎ 0587685327
San Miniato
Podere Canova
at Corazzano
via Zara 186
☎ 0571460120

**WINE
PRODUCERS**

**Morrona
Fattoria Badia
di Morrona**
via di Badia 8
☎ 0587658505

**OLIVE OIL
PRODUCERS**

**Peccioli
Tenuta di
Ghizzano**
at Ghizzano
via della Chiesa 1
☎ 0587630096
Cru Podere Torricella.

SHOPPING

**Pisa
Caffè dell'Ussero**
Palazzo Agostini
lungarno Pacinotti 27
☎ 050581100
Historic cafe.
Pasticceria Salza
Borgo Stretto 44
☎ 050580144
Sweets and pastries.
**Casale Marittimo
Camerini**
via V. Veneto 31
☎ 0586652081
Honey and honey
specialties.
**San Miniato
Norcineria
Falaschi**
via Conti 16
☎ 057143190
Meat and charcuterie.
**Volterra
Da Pina**
via Gramsci 64
☎ 058887394
Olive oil, truffles and
"pecorino" cheese.
**Fattoria di
Lischeto**
via del Monte
Volterrano
☎ 058830403
"Pecorino" cheese, olive
oil and preserves.

cinghiale in dolce e forte (wild boar with bitter cacao) and castagnaccio (chestnut cake).

SAN MINIATO. Surveying the plains of the Arno from pleasant hilltops, this town offers the visitor a medieval setting and the scent of truffles. Added to this, you can also enjoy the Chianti and the wines of the Colline Pisane, the olive oil, excellent artichokes and peas. These are among the wares plied by "Taverna dell'Ozio", an out-of-the way eatery which is well worth the effort. Here try insalata di funghi e tartufi (mushroom and truffle salad), agnolotti con asparagi e pecorino (meat-filled pasta with asparagus and pecorino) and spezzatino al pepe nero (stew with black pepper). At "Norcineria Falaschi", you can get good chianina beef and red wine salami. At the base of the Cerbaie hills in Santa Croce sull'Arno, "Beppe" is excellent, and offers spectacular compositions.

2. The Colline Pisane and Volterrano

CASCIANA TERME. In the Colline Pisane district, a land of excellent wines and truffles, this is a center of major environmental interest. Not far away is the wine producer "Badia di Morrona", set in 450 cultivated and wooded hectares. The cantina stocks Chianti Colline Pisane DOCG and Bianco Pisano di San Torpè DOC as well as a few innovative blends. The producer is located along the Strada del Vino Colline Pisane (currently being established), which straddles the Val d'Era from San Miniato to Chianni. Good venues along the route include Terricciola, a Città del Vino which holds festivals for its

wine and hares in the fall, and Lari, a place where excellent pasta is produced, and which takes credit for inventing fagioli al fiasco (slow-cooked beans).

VOLTERRA. A severe-looking harsh town in the rough landscape in the Val d'Era, Volterra boasts a medieval monument, Etruscan finds and fine paintings in the museums. The visit begins in the medieval Piazza dei Priori and ends at the Balze (cliffs) where you can contemplate the force of the erosion that has been swallowing up necropolises, buildings and churches as it advances. The surrounding countryside offers the strong flavors of pecorino cheeses, mutton, lamb, salamis, prosciutto, and plentiful truffles. At Saline , you should visit "Il Vecchio Mulino", a Buon Ricordo restaurant (and small inn) whose typical dishes include cinghiale alla volterrana (Volterra-style wild boar).

LARDERELLO. After Pomarance we come to the main industrial center of the Colline Metallifere (with its boric acid fumaroles and the geothermal power stations). Further along lies Castelnuovo di Val di Cecina, a town with a singular location, surrounded by ancient chestnut trees, in the middle of a field of fumaroles.

MONTESCUDAIO. This Città del Vino has a DOC wine named after it. It is situated on a hill and the view from there encompasses the Valle del Cecina and the sea surrounding Elba. In the old center, we recommend "Il Frantoio", where a meal begins with cured meats and proceeds with beef and wild boar, often with mushrooms (but there is also good fish). The cantina holds fine wines from the coast of Livorno.

PISTOIA

*Set in the pleasant Valdinievole area, Pistoia has
a culinary tradition marked by the products of
the mountains and the hills.*

The province of Pistoia reaches up the
southern slopes of the Tuscan-Emilian
Apennines and beyond the watershed at
the top of the Valle del Reno. Here the landscape is quite varied and picturesque, with
deep, wooded valleys. The landscape of the
southern part of the area is completely different, and includes the rough Valdinievole, the
flat lands around Pistoia and vine-covered Monte
Albano, near Florence. The main flavors around
Pistoia are, therefore, those linked to the mountains and hills, such as cheeses, meats and products of the woods, in addition to olive oil and
wine. The latter, in particular, includes remarkable products including Chianti Montalbano
DOCG (with the DOC wines Colli dell'Etruria
Centrale and Vin Santo del Chianti) and Bianco
della Valdinievole DOC, a long-established wine
that handsomely blends Trebbiano grapes with Malvasia, Canaiolo bianco and Vermentino. The area is also well
known for its fruit and vegetables (asparagus, potatoes, cherries).
The culinary offering recalls that of nearby Florence, although cured
and cooked pork is more common, as are products from the mountains
such as chestnut flour. The Valle del Reno provides a meeting point for
Tuscan and Emilian cooking, resulting in a cuisine that includes *costate
alla fiorentina* (Florentine steaks) as well as *tagliatelle al prosciutto*. Top
restaurants are concentrated in the capital and Montecatini Terme, but
the rest of the province also con-
tains good local eateries.

*Pistoia Hills.
Pietrabona*

Gourmet Tours

PISTOIA. The story of this ancient town, near the buttresses of the Apennines, and surrounded by fourteenth-century walls, is told by the *piazza* where the cathedral stands (with a splendid San Jacopo altar-frontal), the Baptistry and the Palazzo del Comune. Everything is interwoven with history. The café "Valiani", for example, has been in business since 1864, but its walls, with their delicate Giotto-esque frescoes, were part of the oratory of San Antonio Abate. Many great musicians of the past number among its important guests, and in the basement is an art gallery. Even the *osteria* "Lo Storno" has a long history and began as a medieval hostelry. Modern visitors can try Tuscan classics, such as *pappa al pomodoro* (a type of tomato soup), *ribollita* (reboiled vegetable soup) and *trippa alla fiorentina* (Florentine-style tripe), but there are also dishes with a

more summery appeal, using ingredients such as shrimps and eggplant. At Piteccio (12 km/8 miles away), the restaurant "Castagno di Pier Angelo" is excellent. Focusing on mushrooms and fish, the regional cuisine on offer appears simple, but is in fact backed up by much research and culinary talent. In town buy *brigidini* (famous thin round cookies flavored with anise), as well as *castagnaccio* (chestnut cake) and *necci* (chestnut-meal cakes served with fresh cheese or *ricotta*).

1. Valdinievole and Monte Albano

SERRAVALLE PISTOIESE. From the provincial capital, go up to Passo di Serravalle, the entrance to the Valdinievole. In this village there are a some delicious customs, including *arista* (chine of pork) and *tordi sott'olio* (thrush in oil) in addition to *necci con la ricotta fresca* (chestnut cakes with fresh *ricotta*). In the town of Ponte, the *trattoria* "Da Marino 1920" offers Tuscan fare such as *maccheroni con cicche*

**HOTELS AND
RESTAURANTS**

Pistoia
**Castagno di
Pier Angelo** ¶¶¶
at Castagno di Piteccio
(km 12)
via del Castagno 46/b
☎ 057342214
**Casa degli
Amici** ¶¶
via Bonelllina 111
☎ 0573380305
Manzoni ¶¶
corso Gramsci 112
☎ 057328101
Lo Storno ¶
via del Lastrone 8
☎ 057326193
**Trattoria
dell'Abbondanza** ¶
via dell'Abbondanza 10
☎ 0573368037
Abetone
**Locanda
dello Yeti** ¶
at Le Regine (km 3)
via Brennero 324
☎ 0573606974
Collodi
**Osteria del
Gambero Rosso** ¶
via S. Gennaro 1
☎ 0572429364

Montecatini Terme. "Grand Hotel & La Pace"

di carne ai funghi porcini (macaroni with bites of meat and boletus mushrooms) and *tagliata di chianina* (strips of *chianina* beef), as well as fish dishes such as *gnocchi ai frutti di mare* (*gnocchi* with shellfish) and a *grande fritto* (a large mixed fry, which appears on the gourmet menu). At "Le Poggiola", a farm in the middle of 20 hectares of vineyards and olive groves, you can taste wine, or even stay over, as part of an *agriturismo* holiday. The *cantina* offers Chianti Montalbano DOCG in addition to Colli dell'Etruria Centrale-DOC white and rosé wines.

MONSUMMANO TERME. This town is at the entrance to the southern part of Valdinievole, on the slopes of Monte Albano. "Slitti", a shrine to chocolate created by an excellent chocolate-maker, is a major gastronomic attraction. The village of Lamporecchio is known for its production of *brigidini* (thin ring-shaped cookies flavored with anise) and *berlingozzi* (ring-shaped cakes with a crisp exterior and soft inside). You can also find excellent olive oil here, as well as in Larciano. Further down is the Padule di Fucecchio – once a source of wild game, today it is a natural reserve. Beyond the summit of Monte Albano, the village of Quarrata is a wine tourism center where you can try Bianco della Valdinievole DOC at the "Fattoria di Lucciano".

MONTECATINI TERME. The great Parco delle Terme is the green heart of this spa town, and it is punctuated by architecture ranging from Neoclassical to Art Nouveau. The network of hotels is headed by the "Grand Hotel & La Pace" (est. 1870), with floral furnishings and frescoes (and a good restaurant). Also good is the turn-of-the-century "Gourmet" restaurant, which offers creatively prepared fish dishes. "La Torre", in Montecatini Alto, is a completely different kind of restaurant – set in a medieval building, it offers simple home cooking.

Collodi. Pinocchio's garden

PESCIA. Capital of Valdinievole, this town is known for its olive oil and vegetables – in particular large green asparagus and white Sorana beans cooked in an earthenware pot. The town, divided into "fifths" and split by a stream, has a medieval layout and distinguished monuments. For a good meal, try "Cecco", which has a good solid tradition behind it. Otherwise, climb up to Uzzano and choose from two good eateries. The first one is "Mason", a rustic but elegant place with dishes based on mushrooms, wild game and fish. The second is "Bigiano", in the charming Contrada Castello, that offers some of the most typical dishes of the region,

HOTELS AND RESTAURANTS

Montecatini Terme
Grand Hotel & La Pace ★★★
via della Torretta 1/a
☎ 0572758011
Gourmet ❙❙❙❙
via Amendola 6
☎ 0572771012
La Torre ❙❙
at Montecatini Alto (km 6)
piazza Giusti 8
☎ 057270650
Pescia
Cecco ❙❙
via Ford 96/98
☎ 0572477955
Serravalle Pistoiese
Da Marino Trattoria Enoteca ❙
at Ponte
via Lucchese 101
☎ 057351042
Uzzano
Mason ❙❙❙
via F. Parri 56
☎ 0572451363
Bigiano ❙
contrada Castello
via Bardelli 5
☎ 0572476341

AGRITURISMI

Cutigliano
Fattoria La Piastra
at Pian degli Ontani
at La Casetta 19
☎ 057368443

Mountain in Pistoia. Acquerino Nature Reserve

WINE PRODUCERS

Quarrata
Fattoria di Lucciano
via delle Gorga 38
☎ 0573750209
Serravalle Pistoiese
Fattoria Le Poggiola
via di Treggiaia 13
☎ 057351071

SHOPPING

Pistoia
Caffè Pasticceria Valiani
via Cavour 55
☎ 057323034
Sweets, cakes and pastries such as the "cassata Valiani".
Agliana
Arte del Cioccolato
via Provinciale 378
☎ 0574718506
Wide range of chocolates and pralines
Tripoli Forno
via Garibaldi 21
☎ 0574751092
Cookies and biscuits.
Salumificio Macelleria Marini
via Selva 313
☎ 0574718119
Typical meat and charcuterie.
Monsummano Terme
Andrea Slitti
via Pastrengo 13
☎ 0572952335
"Chocolate sculptures" and pralines.

starting with *cioncia* (a stew made with various parts of a calf's head, with hot pepper, spices and black olives). A trip up to Collodi is a must, partly because of Pinocchio, who was born here of the quill of Carlo Collodi, and partly for the gardens of Villa Garzoni that are said to be the some of the most beautiful in Italy. A curiosity here is "Osteria del Gambero Rosso", designed by Giovanni Michelucci in 1963, and set within a park dedicated to the marionette.

2. The Montagna Pistoiese

SAN MARCELLO PISTOIESE. Climb up into the Apennines following Statale 66 Pistoiese and 12 Abetone, which were carved out in the late 1800s. From Capostrada the route leads to the Passo del Poggiolo mountain pass, and then descends into the Valle del Reno. From Pontepetri take the turn-off for San Marcello Pistoiese, the capital of this mountain district. This is an excellent place to buy *funghi*, *castagne* and other woodland products. In the winter you can also get traditional *frittelle di farina di castagne* (chestnut pancakes).

CUTIGLIANO. This is the best-preserved town of the area. The *piazza* where Palazzo del Pretorio stands is beautiful, and the streets surrounding it are charming. Here you can get fresh and dried *porcini* mushrooms and other wild products, including chestnut. At the *trattorie* the main features are *lepre* (hare) and *trota* (trout). From the town climb up to Pian degli Ontani, near the Apennine crest, where "Fattoria La Piastra" offers *agriturismo* holidays within a friendly family atmosphere, and simple, carefully prepared meals including *zuppe di pane e verdure* (bread and vegetable soup) as well as excellent local cheeses.

ABETONE. The interest here, aside from the monuments that commemorate the opening of the route through the valley, lies in the surrounding forest, which provides an abundant harvest of mushrooms and *frutti di bosco* (forest fruits). Try the "Locanda dello Yeti", in Le Regine for its *porcini* mushrooms, which feature with *tagliatelle* and *polenta*, *tagliata di manzo* (strips of beef) and in every sauce.

PRATO

Florence is just around the corner, but you won't miss out if you stay here, as excellent wines and remarkable flavors on offer.

The young province of Prato, snuggled in between Pistoia and Florence, comprises the basin of the river Bisenzio, which flows along the Calvana Mountains, through the capital and into the Arno river near Signa. Further south are the northern spurs of Monte Albano, with its precious vineyards. Wine is an important product in the region of Prato, with two DOCG wines – one shared with Chianti Montalbano, and Carmignano, exclusive to the province, which is made with the addition of Cabernet to the traditional Chianti blend of Sangiovese and Canaiolo grapes. The same area produces Rosso, Rosato, Vin Santo and Vin Santo Occhio di Pernice wines under the title of DOC Barco Reale di Carmignano. The land's other flavors are produce from the hills, such as olive oil and vegetables, and the mountains, where animals are reared and wild products grow in abundance. The cuisine is predominantly Florentine with a few local specialties such as *minestra di pane alla rustica* (rustic bread soup), *sedani ripieni alla pratese* (celery stuffed with ground veal and chicken liver, then fried) and *polpette all'uva passa* (small meatloaves with raisins). There are no great names among the restaurants and places to stay, but they are an innovative part of the Strada del Vino Carmignano, which unites a fine network of *cantine* open to the public, *enoteche*, restaurants and inns.

The village of Carmignano

CHIANTI
1970
RISERVA del GRANDUCA
FATTORIA
ARTIMINO

Gourmet Tours

PRATO. Set within a hexagon of fourteenth-century walls, lapped by the waters of the river on one side, this is a city of commerce and old industries. The wool industry brought the city fame and wealth, which has been displayed in the form of major monuments. In the Romanesque Duomo, frescoes by Filippo Lippi enrich the apse. Donatello's *Dance of the Putti* is in the Museo dell'Opera. From the same period is the Castello dell'Imperatore, built at the request of Frederick II, while the adjoining church of Santa Maria delle Carceri is a Renaissance jewel. The city has two creative restaurants of note. "Piraña" has some fascinating fish dishes, such as *guazzetto di frutti di mare sul crostone* (shellfish stew on toast), *bavettine in cacciucco bianco* (noodles in fish chowder) and *calamaretti con zucchine all'aceto balsamico* (cuttlefish with zucchini and balsamic vinegar). "Osvaldo Baroncelli" offers not just a taste of the sea, but also inventions from the land such as *pasta avvolta alla nizzarda con ragù di piccione* (Nice-style rolled pasta with pigeon ragu) or *lombo di coniglio alle erbe aromatiche con peperoni dolci* (loin of rabbit with aromatic herbs and sweet peppers). For a simpler approach, try the *enoteca* "Barni", where well-priced, traditional dishes are served at lunchtime, and more refined preparations are served at dinner. In the town, buy charcuterie, starting with salami and *mortadella cotta di Prato*. Seek out the celebrated *cantucci* at two pastry shops which may well have invented them: "Nuovo Mondo", which is centrally located in Via Garibaldi, and "Luca Mannoni".

POGGIO A CAIANO. This town draws its fame from the Villa Medicea, originally a medieval

Artimino. View of the Medicean Villa

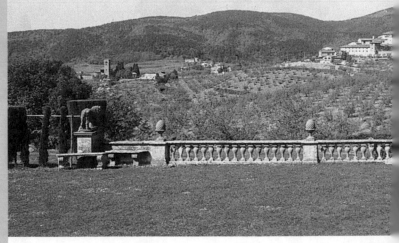

HOTELS AND RESTAURANTS

Prato
Osvaldo Baroncelli ¶¶¶
via fra Bartolomeo 13
☎ 057423810
Piraña ¶¶¶
via Valentini 110
☎ 057425746
Enoteca Barni ¶¶
via Ferrucci 22
☎ 0574607845
Carmignano
Paggeria Medicea
★★★
★
Biagio Pignatta ¶¶
at Artimino
viale Giovanni XXIII 3
☎ 0558718081
☎ 0558718086
Delfina ¶¶¶
at Artimino
via della Chiesa 1
☎ 0558718074
Osteria Enoteca
Su pe'l'Canto ¶
piazza Matteotti 25/26
☎ 0558712490

AGRITURISMI

Carmignano
Fattoria di Artimino
at Artimino
via 5 Martiri 29
☎ 0558718081

fortress, which was commissioned by Lorenzo the Magnificent from plans by Giuliano da Sangallo. Tour the frescoed interiors and visit the vast romantic park.

ARTIMINO. Nearby you will find another important Medici villa, the Ferdinanda, built by Bernardo Buontalenti in 1594, with a white facade between the two banked corner towers. Enjoy a splendid view from the terrace of the timeless Buon Ricordo restaurant "Delfina", which many consider to be the best place for true Tuscan cooking. *Coniglio con olive e pinoli* (rabbit with olives and pine nuts) is the house dish, and the *ribollita* and *spiedo* (spit-roasted dishes) are incomparable. If you wish to spend the night, we recommend "Paggeria Medicea", which is located in a sixteenth-century building among the olive trees and grapevines and has an annexed restaurant, "Biagio Pignatta". Not far away is the town, surrounded by medieval walls. A little further towards Carmignano you come to the Romanesque parish church of San Leonardo. In Comeana visit the Etruscan tomb of Montefortini.

CARMIGNANO. A fine attraction is the superb local wine, which the seventeenth-century writer and scientist Francesco Redi has already extolled in his poetic work *Bacco in Toscana*. A much praised Strada del Vino leads the wine tourist on a discovery of the *cantine* and villas, with 22 farms, 12 restaurants, 3 hotels and 2 *enoteche* to choose from. We particularly recommend "Tenuta di Capezzana" in Seano, which has the splendid atmosphere of a Medici residence with rural annexes (restaurants and overnight stays with reservations). The wine list is excellent, and includes DOCG Carmignano and Chianti Montalbano wines, as well as the innovative Ghiaie della Furba, made from Cabernet and Merlot and aged in barrels. In town go to the *enoteca* "Su pe' i' Canto", a friendly place serving wine by the glass and a variety of dishes.

WINE PRODUCERS

**Carmignano
Tenuta di
Capezzana**
at Seano (km 3)
via Capezzana 100
☎ 0558706005

SHOPPING

**Prato
Biscottificio
Antonio Mattei**
via Ricasoli 20/22
☎ 057425756
Biscuits from Prato since 1858.
**Pasticceria
Luca Mannoni**
via Lazzerini 2
☎ 0574216228
Pastries and cakes such as Setteveli, Abbraccio di Venere, Orient Express.
**Pasticceria Caffè
Nuovo Mondo**
via Garibaldi 23
☎ 057427765
Pastries, sweets and chocolates.

SIENA

From Chianti to Monte Amiata the province of Siena offers the best flavors of the hills, including wild game, truffles, cheeses, wine and olive oil.

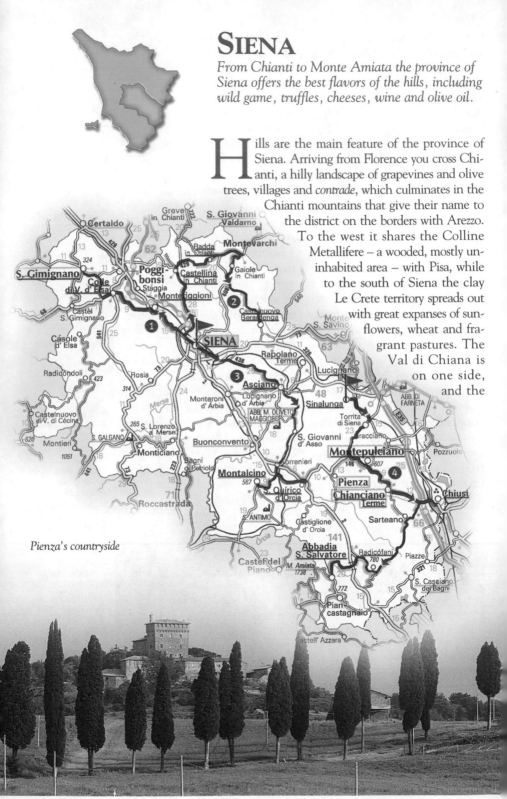

Hills are the main feature of the province of Siena. Arriving from Florence you cross Chianti, a hilly landscape of grapevines and olive trees, villages and *contrade*, which culminates in the Chianti mountains that give their name to the district on the borders with Arezzo. To the west it shares the Colline Metallifere – a wooded, mostly uninhabited area – with Pisa, while to the south of Siena the clay Le Crete territory spreads out with great expanses of sunflowers, wheat and fragrant pastures. The Val di Chiana is on one side, and the

Pienza's countryside

spurs of the volcanic Monte Amiata on the other. Over-all, it is a territory that profits as much from the cultiva-tion of vineyards and olive groves as from the breeding of sheep and cattle. It is exceptional in terms of wine, with five of Tuscany's six DOCG wines – Chianti (both Classico and Colli Senesi), Brunello di Montal-cino, Vino Nobile di Montepulciano and Vernaccia di San Gimignano – plus 11 DOC wines. Animal rearing is excellent, with Chianina leading the way for beef-based cuisine and Cinta Senese, which is currently regaining popu-larity, bringing fame to traditional charcuterie. *Pecorino* is the cheese here – flavored by aromatic herbs, its taste is matchless. Truffles and wild game – particularly wild boar – are readily available. The cuisine reflects the materials available and includes all the regional dishes, making them its own with an emphasis on garlic and herbs such as tarragon, mint, basil and thyme. The most typical dishes are *zuppa di lentic-chie col fagiano* (lentil soup with pheasant), *zuppa di fagioli alla senese* (Siena-style bean soup), *ribollita* (reboiled soup), *pasta e ceci* (pasta with chick peas), *pappa al pomodoro* (tomato soup), followed by *lepre* (hare) and *cinghiale in agrodolce* (sweet and sour wild boar), *pollo con le olive* (chicken with olives) and *fricassea di carne o funghi* (meat or mushroom fricassee). There is an excellent network of restaurants and *cantine* open to tourists.

Gourmet Tours

SIENA. Rivers of ink have been used to describe the city of the *Palio*. To see it from a different an-gle, climb the 88-meter Torre del Mangia, and look down at the Pi-azza del Campo. The pattern of the roofs makes the Via Francige-na easy to pick out as it crosses the medieval city, guiding pilgrims and merchants. The cathedral, set higher up on a rise, stand out in black and white, while stretching out around the town you can see the countryside. You can see the same countryside in a room near the top of the tower in the Buon Governo (The Effects of Good and Bad Government) fresco by Ambrogio Lorenzetti. In the cen-ter of the town, there is a whole variety of eateries. Just a few steps away from the cathedral, "Osteria Castelvecchio" offers strictly tradi-tional Sienese food. "Hosteria il

Siena. The "Enoteca Italiana"

Carroccio", behind Piazza del Campo, is a good *trattoria* with a reasonably priced gourmet menu. For an interesting setting (and good food, of course), try "Antica Osteria da Divo", among Etruscan and medieval remains, and "Oste-

HOTELS AND RESTAURANTS

Siena
Villa ★★★
Scacciapensieri
via di Scacciapensieri 10
☎ 057741441
Anna Siena
Nord ★★★
S.S. to the Chianti
at Fontebecci 1
☎ 057751371
Antica Torre ★★★
via Fieravecchia 7
☎ 0577222255
Antica Trattoria
Botteganova ❚❚
via Chiantigiana 29
☎ 0577284230
Antica Osteria
da Divo ❚
via Franciosa 25
☎ 0577286054
Enzo ❚
via Camollia 49
☎ 0577281277
Hosteria
il Carroccio ❚
via del Casato
di Sotto 32
☎ 057741165
Osteria
Castelvecchio ❚
via Castelvecchio 65
☎ 057749586
Osteria
Le Logge ❚
via del Porrione 33
☎ 057748013

343

![CHIANTI CLASSICO SAN FELICE RISERVA]

**HOTELS AND
RESTAURANTS**

Asciano
Da Ottorino
via Ss. Marie 114
zona industriale
☎ 0577718770
Castelnuovo
Berardenga
Da Antonio
via Fiorita 38
☎ 0577355321
**Relais Borgo
San Felice** ★★★
at San Felice
(km 10)
☎ 0577359260
Villa Arceno ★★★
at San Gusmé
(km 5)
at Arceno
☎ 0577359292
Bottega del 30
at Villa a Sesta (km 6)
via S. Caterina 2
☎ 0577359226
**La Vecchia
Osteria**
at Ponte a Bozzone
(km 15)
☎ 0577356809
**Bistrot La Stalla
e La Terrazza**
c/o Dievole
at Vagliagli
at Dievole 6
☎ 0577322613
**Enoteca
Bengodi**
via della Società
Operaia 21
☎ 0577355116
Cetona
**Frateria di
Padre Eligio**
at the Convento di
S. Francesco (km 1)
☎ 0578238261

ria Le Logge", within the walls and with the furniture of a late nineteenth-century food shop. The most interesting places, however, are to be found just outside the city, on the Via Chiantigiana. Here try "Antica Trattoria Botteganova", where time-honored traditional recipes have been updated to make the best use of each season's products. Don't miss the *tortelli di pecorino gratinati con fonduta di parmigiano and tartufo* (pasta filled with *pecorino* in a gratin with melted parmesan and truffle). Not far from the city, turn off the Statale di Montevarchi for the Certosa di Pontignano. Here "La Vecchia Osteria", which Luigi Cremona praises for its attentive management and the way wines are recommended according to dishes (a good sign). Back in the city, there are two good places to stay: "Antica Torre", which has just a few charming rooms, and "Villa Scacciapensieri", which has a nineteenth-century feel to it. Elegant, with an open-air restaurant and garden, the Villa looks onto the old center. As for pastries, don't

miss the chance to taste the celebrated sweets of Siena. *Panforte* (a sweet bread made with candied fruits) is the city's leading sweet, but you can also get *cavallucci*, with honey, candied fruits and spices, *ricciarelli* (lozenge-shaped descendants of ancient marzipan cookies) and white or black *copate*, which are flat disks with a crisp center between two wafers, fragrant with honey, nuts and anise. An excellent sweet producer is "Betti & Sinetti", at San Rocco in Pilli. For other kinds of purchases, try "Palazzo della Chigiana", a store in Via di Città with a tempting window full of charcuterie, cheeses and other delectables, or "Il Magnifico", an old grocery with a baking oven in Via dei Pellegrini. Finally, don't miss a visit to "Enoteca Italiana", the main national organization for the promotion of quality wines: the products of 400 companies are presented by professional sommeliers within the charming spaces of the Fortezza Medicea. There is also a variety of extra virgin olive oils. In the first ten days of June, the traditional Settimana dei Vini (Wine Week) takes place.

Siena. View from the Torre del Mangia

San Gimignano. The old town with its medieval houses and towers

1. The Cassia and San Gimignano

MONTERIGGIONI. The walls of this town, punctuated by fourteen towers, appear today just as Dante described them and the pilgrims on their way to Rome saw them. Walk around the center among the olive trees and then lose yourself pleasantly in the alleyways inside. Here, "Pozzo" is a good family restaurant that offers *salumi* and *crostini*, an excellent *zuppa di fagioli* and more refined *tortelli al cartoccio con tartufo* (*tortelli* pasta baked in foil with truffles), and grilled meats or a special duck dish with mushrooms and olives. Pastry shops are renowned for *panforte* (sweet bread with candied fruits). Outside the walls, there are two good restaurants: the refined "Casalta" and the delightful "Antica Osteria La Leggenda dei Frati".

COLLE DI VAL D'ELSA. In the upper part of the village, go through the gates to the Palazzo Campana, and enter the Castello quarter, which is medieval in appearance but has fifteenth- and sixteenth-century additions. The culinary interest here is centered on "Arnolfo", an exceptional restaurant that owes much of its success to the elegant and refined cuisine of one of Italy's best, and most modest, young chefs. The menu is full of excellent dishes, such as *taglierini di semola con ragù di capretto marinato alle erbe* (pasta with a ragout of kid marinated with herbs) and *sella di coniglio ai fichi con patate all'aceto balsamico* (loin of rabbit with figs and potatoes and balsamic vinegar). The *cantina* is also first rate. "L'Antica Trattoria", a family-run restaurant in a historic building, is also good.

SAN GIMIGNANO. Just the sight of

HOTELS AND RESTAURANTS

Chiusi
Osteria
La Solita Zuppa ¶
via Porsenna 21
☎ 057821006
Colle di Val d'Elsa
Arnolfo ¶¶¶¶
via XX Settembre 50
☎ 0577920549
L'Antica Trattoria ¶¶¶
piazza Arnolfo 23
☎ 0577923747
Gaiole in Chianti
Badia a Coltibuono ¶¶
at Badia a Coltibuono (km 6)
☎ 0577749424
Il Carlino d'Oro ¶
via Brolio
☎ 0577747136
Montalcino
Poggio Antico ¶¶¶
at Poggio Antico (km 1)
☎ 0577849200
Taverna dei Barbi ¶¶
at Podernovi (km 5)
☎ 0577849357
Osteria di Porta al Cassero ¶
via della Libertà 9
☎ 0577847196
Montepulciano
La Grotta ¶¶
at San Biagio
☎ 0578757607
Tiziana ¶
at Tre Berte
S.S. 326, n. 156
☎ 0578767760

CHIANTI COLLI SENESI

DENOMINAZIONE DI ORIGINE CONTROLLATA

Podere TAVERNACCE
PROD. FALCOLINI-REINSCH
SIENA - ITALIA

12% VOL

0,720 LITRI

HOTELS AND RESTAURANTS

Monteriggioni
Casalta ★★★
at Strove (km 6)
☎ 0577301002
**Antica Osteria
La Leggenda
dei Frati** ❢❢
ad Abbadia
Isola (km 4)
piazza Garfonda 7
☎ 0577301222
Pozzo ❢❢
piazza Roma 2
☎ 0577304127
Murlo
Osteria La Befa ❢
at La Befa
☎ 0577806255
San Gimignano
★❢ **Villa San
Paolo** ★★★
strada per
Certaldo, km 4
☎ 0577955100
**Osteria delle
Catene** ❢
via Mainardi 18
☎ 0577941966
**San Quirico
d'Orcia**
**Osteria
del Leone** ❢
at Bagno
Vignoni (km 5)
via Bagno Vignoni
☎ 0577887300
Sinalunga
★❢ **Locanda
dell'Amorosa** ★★★
**Locanda
dell'Amorosa** ❢❢❢❢
at L'Amorosa (km 2)
☎ 0577679497
Torrita di Siena
Chiusa ❢❢❢❢
via della
Madonnina 88
☎ 0577669668

this village in the distance stirs many emotions. Follow the ancient pilgrimage route that crosses Piazza della Cisterna, running straight up to the the Collegiata (collegiate church). A climb to the top of a tower (there zere 72 of these in San Gimignano's heyday) or onto the bastions of the fortress, offers a glimpse of ancient beauty. The gourmet will appreciate San Gimignano as a Città del Vino and a place where charcuterie is made of wild boar. Food stores and wine shops are not wanting, but make a point of visiting "Osteria delle Catene" for its *ribollita* (literally, reboiled vegeable soup), *stracotto di manzo chianino* (stewed *chianino* beef) and *coniglio alla Vernaccia* (rabbit with Vernaccia wine). If you want to visit a *cantina*, try the producer "Montenidoli", where wine is made strictly according to tradition. The same goes for the celebrated Vernaccia, as well as Chianti Garrulo, which is prepared according to the method of the nineteenth-century politician Baron Bettino Ricasoli. Typical regional meals are available on request at "Poderino la Fidanza", and *agriturismo* farm stays are pos-

sible. Along the route to Certaldo, we recommend staying at "Villa San Paolo", in a nineteenth-century atmosphere surrounded by an old garden.

2. The Chianti Classico

CASTELLINA IN CHIANTI. Whether you travel from Poggibonsi, the territory in which you will come across the first Chianti Classico vines, or straight from Siena, following the charming Chiantigiana route, you will reach Castellina. The town still has much of its Renaissance character. In the surrounding countryside, farmhouses from the grand-ducal era and earlier have been transformed into residences.

RADDA IN CHIANTI. Following the Statale di Val d'Elsa you come to this town that from 1425 was at the head of the Lega del Chianti (a consortium of wine producers) under the title of Gallo Nero, a name which refers back to a fifteenth-century military alliance of Chianti villagers (today it has been turned over to Chianti Classico wines). Not far away is an area that is a dream come true for wine tourists, the "Fattoria Castello di Volpaia". Here the entire village participates in wine production and rural hospitality, and you can visit

The Crete Senesi

the *cantina* and the *vinsantaia* (where vinsanto is made), *frantoio* (olive press) and *acetificio* (where vinegar is made), taste great bottles of Chianti Classico and stay in the appartments and *rustici* (cottages), where meals are available upon request for groups and there are also cookery demonstrations. We also recommend continuing to Badia a Coltibuono in the heart of Monti del Chianti. Here the ancient monastery, transformed into a villa and farm, is the headquarters of the wine producer of the same name. The itinerary continues on to Gaiole in Chianti, where you will find excellent sausages. You can eat at the *trattoria* "Il Carlino d'Oro", with a few very good dishes of meat, wild game and mushrooms. The fried chicken and rabbit should not be missed.
CASTELNUOVO BERARDENGA. From the Statale leading down to Siena turn on to the route leading to Castello di Brolio, the distinguished residence of Baron Bettino Ricasoli, minister of the Kingdom of Italy and 'inventor' of modern Chianti. From the bas-

tion, you will see an unforgettable panorama of vineyards framed by rows of cypresses. Below are the "Cantine Ricasoli". Go on to Castelnuovo, a town renowned for its wild boar charcuterie – salami, sausage, salt-cured filet – and excellent places to eat and drink. We strongly recommend "Da Antonio", where only the freshest fish is served, together with top wines. We similarly like "Bottega del '30", with its superlative offering of soups, fresh pasta and meats, as well as dishes prepared with frogs and snails. For a simpler experience, in the *piazza* is the *enoteca* "Bengodi", where wine is served by the glass and homemade pasta and Tuscan classics are available. As for wine, among the authoritative producers in the area is "Dievole", where it is possible to sip the *grandi riserve* Chianti Classico and table wines with evocative names such as Broccato or Rinascimento Toscano. Dine at "La Terrazza" and "La Stalla". The "Diavole" villa's farm offers *agriturismo* holidays amid 400 hectares, 90 of which are planted with vines. For upmarket stays try the wine-oriented "Relais Borgo San Felice" and "Villa Arceno". For a more family atmosphere, stay at

AGRITURISMI

Castelnuovo
Berardenga
**Fattoria
di Pacina**
at Pacina
☎ 0577355044
Trequanda
**Fattoria
del Colle**
☎ 0577662108

**WINE
PRODUCERS**

Castelnuovo
Berardenga
Dievole
at Vagliagli
at Dievole 6
☎ 0577322613
Gaiole in
Chianti
Barone Ricasoli
at Brolio
☎ 05777301
Montalcino
Banfi
Castello di Poggio
alle Mura
☎ 0577840111
**Fattoria dei
Barbi**
at Podernovi
☎ 0577849421
Montepulciano
Redi
via di Collazzi 5
☎ 0578757166
Radda in
Chianti
**Fattoria Castello
di Volpaia**
at Volpaia
☎ 0577738066
San Gimignano
Montenidoli
at Montenidoli
☎ 0577941565

the "Fattoria di Pacina", a small farm that offers *agriturismo* holidays in an old residence. Here Giovannina Tiezzi creates snacks to suit one of the best Chianti Colli Senesi wines and olive oil from the farm.

3. From the Crete to the Val d'Orcia

ASCIANO. The town has Etruscan origins and a medieval appearance. From the capital, take the Statale Lauretana across the fascinating landscapes of Le Crete. Not far away is the restaurant "Da Ottorino", with a relaxed atmosphere, the restaurant's own charcuterie and rustic dishes starting with delectable *pici con pancetta e fagioli* (meaty spaghetti with bacon and beans). The itinerary continues via the atmospheric abbey of Monte Oliveto, which is home to the celebrated cycle of frescoes by Luca Signorelli and Sodoma, narrating episodes from the life of Saint Benedict.

Nearby, Chiusure offers an unforgettable view of Le Crete and one of the best *pecorino* cheeses in the region. Moving towards the Val d'Orcia, stop at Trequanda, a pleasant medieval village known for *mortadella* and excellent *pecorino* cheese. We recommend "Fattoria del Colle", a splendid *agriturismo* operation in the middle of 300 hectares of vineyards, olive groves and forests full of truffles. House guests and visitors can dine at its *osteria*, where they can sample typical local dishes and excellent house wines. San Giovanni d'Asso, a Città del Tartufo, is noted for its truffle market. Buonconvento, an ancient town on the Via Francigena, offers white truffles, *prosciutto*, *mortadella*, fresh and dried sausages, and honey. At Murlo, go to "La Befa", which is a little out of the way, but the dirt roads you must take to get there provide a taste of adventure. This classic meeting place offers rustic dishes, such as *zuppa di porcini* (boletus mushroom soup), *tagliatelle al sugo di cinghiale* (tagliatelle with wild boar sauce).

OLIVE OIL PRODUCERS

Gaiole in Chianti
Castello di Cacchiano
at Monti (km 15)
☎ 0577747018
Terre del Chianti Classico olive oil.
Montepulciano
Tenuta Valdipiatta
via della Ciarliana 25
☎ 0578757930
Tenuta Valdipiatta olive oil.
Radda in Chianti
Fattoria di Monte Vertine
at Monte Vertine
☎ 0577738009
Monte Vertine olive oil.

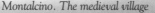
Montalcino. The medieval village

MONTALCINO. The city of Brunello stands on a hill, with its medieval walled city. Its fortress was the last Sienese bulwark against Florence. Wine is important here, and there are too many greats to choose from, so we give two recommendations strictly in alphabetical order. First there is "Banfi", one of the most renowned producers, which has an *enoteca* and restaurant. The second is "Fattoria dei Barbi", which combines cultural and food and wine activities. In the *cantina* you can taste and buy from the great reserves of Brunello al Bianco del Beato. At the "Taverna dei Barbi", traditional local dishes are prepared with the products from the farm (primarily charcuterie, including the exclusive *salame bastardo*). In the eighteenth-century villa, apartments are available for *agriturismo* stays. The restaurant "Poggio Antico" is excellent. Here a great chef works passionately and inventively even with the simplest of products, embellishing them with a variety of flavors. The menu includes *tagliatelle con pioppini e speck d'anatra* (*tagliatelle* with cured duck) *agnello*

in salsa all'aceto balsamico (lamb in balsamic sauce) and *semifreddo di formaggio al caffè* (soft coffee-flavored cheese ice-cream). For a snack or a rustic bowl of soup, try "Osteria di Porta al Cassero". Those in search of period settings should try "Fiaschetteria Italiana" (est. 1888), an exquisite example of Art Nouveau in the town's piazza, and rub shoulders with top winemakers and other illustrious Brunello connoisseurs. At pastry shops, buy *cavallucci* and *panforte* (a sweet bread made with candied fruits).

SAN QUIRICO D'ORCIA. In the ancient center, the beautiful collegiate church is a reminder of the medieval pilgrims who passed through here on their way to Rome (inside there is a triptych by Sano di Pietro, of the *Madonna and Child with Saints*). An outing to Pienza is a must. This ideal city was admired by Pope Pious II and partly built by Bernardo Rossellino. More prosaically, the town also has some excellent fresh *pecorino* cheese, which has a

SHOPPING

Siena
Azienda Agricola Belsedere
via Camollia 25
☎ 057747090
Charcuterie, typical cheeses and organic olive oil.
Il Magnifico
via dei Pellegrini 27
☎ 0577281106
Grocery with a baking oven.
Montalcino
Azienda Agricola La Macina
at Macina 80
☎ 0577847059
Cheeses and honey.
Caffè Fiaschetteria Italiana
piazza del Popolo 6
☎ 0577849043
Historic cafe; wine tasting.
Montepulciano
Antico Caffè Poliziano
via Voltaia
nel Corso 25
☎ 0578758615
Cafe and pastry shop.

Strada del Vino
Nobile di
Montepulciano

slight bite to it. Don't miss a visit to Bagno Vignoni, a tiny thermal town built up around a great basin of sulfurous water. Stop at "Osteria del Leone", a friendly, no-frills eatery with a well-stocked *banco di mescita* (wine bar) and a fine menu of Tuscan dishes.

4. Val di Chiana and Monte Amiata

SINALUNGA. This town stands on a rise and looks down on the Val di Chiana from the west. You should visit its beautiful collegiate church. Then, within 20 kilometers (13 miles), there are two good places to eat. The first is the "Locanda dell'Amorosa", in a fortified old farm that is also a fine inn. At the table you will find the best of traditional regional cooking and a careful selection of wines. At Montefollonico, the exclusive and elegant "La Chiusa" offers lodgings and dining.

MONTEPULCIANO. One of Tuscany's magic places, this town located on a ridge between Orcia and Chiana is made up of narrow streets, arches and vaults, with surprising Renaissance features. Follow the Corso, then go up to Piazza Grande, with its cathedral

and Palazzo Comunale, and finally descend the Via del Poggiolo, facing the valley below. Here, splendidly isolated, is the church of S. Biagio in the solemn form of a Greek cross, a masterpiece by Antonio da Sangallo the Elder, built in travertine against a backdrop of hills. Once you have seen all the sights, you can seek out the celebrated Vino Nobile di Montepulciano, which has its own, very recent, Strada del Vino. A visit to the "Redi" wine cellars within the Renaissance *palazzo* in the center is unforgettable: the cellars are located under very high cross-vaults resting on the bare rock. In the city, don't forget to stop at "Antico Caffè Poliziano" which serves pastries, aperitifs and a small selection of hot dishes. Buy *pecorino*, *ricotta* and sausages. We recommend the restaurant "La Grotta", set in a sixteenth-century building with a garden and a view of San Biagio. The menu has traditional dishes as well as good innovations. In the hamlet of Tre Berte, the family restaurant "Tiziana" is popular, and offers *pici*, *ribollita* and various roasts of poultry and rabbit raised by the restaurant – which has an adjoining inn (inexpen-

SHOPPING

Pienza
**Da Marusco
e Maria**
corso Rossellino 17
☎ 0578748222
*Charcuterie and
cheeses..*
San Gimignano
**Azienda Agricola
Officinalia**
at Cortennano 46
☎ 0577941867
Organic honey.
San Giovanni
d'Asso
Az. Agr. Vergelle
at Vergelle 135
☎ 0577834046
*Good selection of
"pecorino" cheese.*

sive and spotless) and grocery (the charcuterie and cheeses are excellent).

CHIANCIANO TERME. The curative waters were already appreciated by the Etruscans and Romans, but the village's golden age came in the early 1900s, as can be seen in the style of many buildings, the elegant shops and the great Parco delle Fonti. It is worth a visit but there are no particularly good restaurants. A couple of miles suffice to reach a better gourmet location.

CHIUSI. Set on a hillock dense with olive trees, this village bears the marks of its Etruscan and Grand Duchy past. In the center, try "Osteria La Solita Zuppa", a pleasant place where, as its name suggests, soup is the main attraction. The town is also known for its fish, from the nearby lake, that is used as the base for tasty *tegamaccio*. In Cetona, on the slopes of the mountain, is "Frateria di Padre Eligio", set in a Franciscan convent. Here the dish-

es are creatively prepared and the rooms, though few, are lavish.

RADICOFANI. The Statale 321 del Polacco leads to San Casciano dei Bagni, an ancient and beautiful spa town. Then climb up Monte Calcinaio until you cross the route to Sarteano. You quickly arrive in Radicofani, where the medieval town is set in the shade of the cliffs and the fortress. Here *pane dolce*, made with flour, honey, grapes and pepper, is a harves tradition.

ABBADIA SAN SALVATORE. The abbey that gives this town its name was founded in 743 by Rachis, a Lombard, and was the richest in Tuscany. The town is admirable for the extraordinary state of preservation of the medieval mountain-castle, with its Gothic and Renaissance additions. From here, follow the hairpin curves to the peak of Monte Amiata, or go to Pian Castagnaio, known for its excellent sausages in oil, and sweets made of honey and nuts.

SHOPPING

Sovicille
Betti & Sinatti
at San Rocco, Pilli (km 10)
via Grossetana 140
☎ 0577348196
Famous for "ricciarelli" cookies.

Trequanda
Azienda Agricola Belsedere
☎ 0577662307
Organic products such as charcuterie, cheeses and olive oil.

Ville di Corsano
Azienda S. Margherita
☎ 0577377101
Goat's milk cheeses.

Fattoria Il Colle di Nicola Zanda
☎ 0577377024
Meat, local charcuterie and a good selection of olive oils.

Your holiday
in the land of
the Etruscans

terretrusche.com

farmhouse holidays
restored period houses
country villas
apartment rentals
wedding planning

in Tuscany

terretrusche srl vicolo Alfieri 3, Cortona AR 52044 Italy
phone: +39 575 605287 - fax: +39 575 606886
website: www.terretrusche.com - email: info@terretrusche.com

VILLA
VIGNAMAGGIO
GREVE IN CHIANTI (FIRENZE)

Via Petriolo, 5
50022 Greve in Chianti (FI)
Tel. +39 055 854661 - Fax +39 055 8544468
www.vignamaggio.com
E-mail: agriturismo@vignamaggio.com

Vignamaggio is a Renaissance villa, birthplace of the famous Monna Lisa portrayed by Leonardo, and situated in the heart of the Chianti area, between Florence and Siena, at about 4 km from Greve in Chianti. The farmhouses closed to the villa have been restored according to the best Tuscan tradition and turned into farm holiday residences, with spacious rooms and apartments, all with air conditioning and independent heating. Wide open spaces, tennis court, two swimming pools, table tennis room, equipped children playground and gym are available for our guests. Horse back riding and golf are not far away. Painting courses are run at the villa by a famous local artist. Dinner are organized twice for week only for the guests. The farm products, wine, vinsanto, grappa and oil can be tasted and bought at the wine shop.
Guided visits to the cellars with wine tasting, and to the villa's famous Italian garden are possible upon reservation.

the finest
olive oil
comes from a unique land

[terra toscana]

Castello di Tornano

53013 Gaiole in Chianti, Siena
www.castelloditornano.it
Castellotornano@chiantinet.it
Tel. +39 0577 746067
Fax +39 0577 746094

In a magnificent Medieval hamlet dated back in the 11th century, we offer hospitality in the 6 exclusive and charming suites inside the Castle and in the 8 apartments inside the farmhouse nearby the Castle. The restaurant offers in a friendly atmosphere the best of the local cuisine. The pool is made from the moat of the Castle. There is a horse riding facility to ride

among vinyards and olive groves. Other armenities are the tennis court and the fishing lake. On site is possible to organize wine tasting and cooking class in a relaxed atmosphere. In the estate there is production of Chianti Classico wine and Olive oil. Open all year round. Highway A1, exit Valdarno. direction Siena-Gaiole in Chianti State Road n. 408 km 20.

At the heart of Montepulciano is one of the most famous historical Cafés in Italy.

RISTORANTE del CAFFÈ

Inside the Caffè Poliziano you will find the "Ristorante del Caffè" and its sophisticated yet warm atmosphere, where the kitchen puts forward new proposals next to the great dishes of local tradition, all accompanied by a selection of the most prestigious Vino Nobile labels.

Open (evenings only) from Monday to Saturday, it also has a splendid terrace overlooking the Valdichiana and the Trasimeno lake.

Via di Voltaia nel Corso, 27 - 53045 Montepulciano (Siena)
Tel. +39 0578 758615 - Fax +39 0578 752856
www.ec-net.it/site/caffepoliziano - E-mail: caffepoliziano@libero.it

the Tuscan Olive oil Consortium:
means quality.

Toscano extra virgin olive oil, labelled with the Protected Geographical Indication and branded with the Consorzio dell'Olio Toscano trademark, comes from high-quality Tuscan olives. The whole process, from cultivation to pressing, to packaging, is carried out in the region of Tuscany.

Tuscany holds first place among the different areas of the Mediterranean basin for olive growing. In order to safeguard and protect this unique and Incomparable products appreciated all over the world, the Consorzio dell'Olio Toscano checks and certifies their quality and characteristics, guaranteeing only the finest ones with its trademark.

Consorzio dell'Olio Toscano Via di Villa Demidoff, 64/D - 50127 Firenze
tel. 055 3245732 - fax 055 3246110 - e-mail: constoscana@tin.it - www.consorziooliotoscano.it

An elegant simplicity of all that surround you, on purpose designed for you. An excellent cooking careful of seasonal products and tradition. A severe selection of Tuscan wines.

Restaurant, Stock of vintage wines, meating room, tipical products, 14 suites, fitness center and suimming-pool. Murlo, Siena tel.0577814605 - fax.0577814606 www.boscodellaspina.com-bsturist@boscodellaspina.com

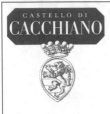

The Cacchiano Castle is situated in the southern part of the Gaiole-in-Chianti territory and therefore in the south Classic Chianti area.

The main product of the Castello di Cacchiano estate is wine (since the XII century), with an outstanding Chianti Classico DOCG – also as Millennio Vintage – and the Chianti Classico Vin Santo. Much appreciated is also the Chianti Classico DOP extra virgin olive oil. The Castle offers comfortable accommodation for seven people, and spectacular views.

Castello di Cacchiano (a Ricasoli - Firidolfi Estate)
Monti in Chianti - Gaiole (Siena) - Tel. +39 0577 747018 - Fax +39 0577 747157 - cacchiano@chianticlassico.com

Hotel VILLA SAN GIORGIO

VILLA SAN GIORGIO, in the heart of Tuscany, know as VAL d'ELSA over-looking the Classic Chianti area. The villa, surrounded by beautiful vineyards and olive groves, is located in an exceptional panoramic position from which it is possible to enjoy a fabolous view of the towers of SAN GIMINIANO and the incomparable Tuscan countryside. The hotel is a typical country farmhouse, recently renovated and dating back to the early 1900's. Swimming pool, restaurant and private carpark. Hotel VILLA SAN GIORGIO has rooms, all with private bath/shower, satellite TV, direct dial phone and heating. At Villa san Giorgio it is possible to take advantage of BREAK-FAST and BAR services and enjoy meals, wines and typical Tuscan produce in its natural green park.

**Loc. Cinciano 53036 POGGIBONSI (SI) - ITALIA
Tel. 0577 989190 - 938318 - Fax 0577 989194
E-mail: damatirr@cyber.dada.it**

"AL MARSILI"
Ristorante Enoteca
Gallo Nero

Since 1980 the "Al Marsili" has been one of the most prestigious restaurants of the area. Its spacious rooms, located on the ground floor of the historical Palazzo that once belonged to one of the illustrious families of medieval Siena, have been furnished in harmony with their architectural surroundings: Impruneta fired tiles, the chestnut wood of the old barrels and panelling, the Venice crystal of the light fixtures, the Siena clay bricks of the arches and vaults. All of these precious materials contribute in creating the special atmosphere that exalts the tastes of Tuscany's and especially Siena's wines and dishes. The wide selection of Tuscan wines, including the four DOCG wines produced in the province of Siena – Chianti Classico, Vernaccia di San Gimignano, Vino Nobile di Montepulciano and Brunello di Montalcino – reposes in the restaurant's cellars, excavated in the Middle Ages into the tufaceous rock of Siena using the same technique introduced long before by the Etruscans. The Al Marsili wine list, continuously refreshed so as to best match the dishes of the season, is made complete by a selection of 'Great Tuscan' wines and of other celebrated Italian wines.

The cuisine proposed by Al Marsili is classical Tuscan and mostly from Siena. It is based on local products and on the seasons of the year, without forgetting some of the traditional historical dishes such as guinea fowl alla Medici or the extra-large Fiorentina steak of the best Chianina beef available, selected specifically for the restaurant. The hors-d'oeuvres include Tuscan salamis, bruschette and the famous black crostini (types of toast served with savouries). Among the more requested pasta dishes on the menu are the zuppa di farro (spelt soup), spaghetti primavera (Spring-style spaghetti) and the more substantial conchiglie alla rustica (shell-shaped pasta with country-style sauce). The entrées consist of a wide selection of Tuscan meats, such as beef, veal, boar and fowl. Especially favoured are the Siena-style cutlets cooked with tarragon, one of the very few totally Siena derived second courses offered. The Marsili menu also offers classical vegetable side dishes cooked as Tuscan tradition demands, such as Cannellini white beans, oven-baked tomatoes with wild spices, pan-sautéed spinach and, when in season, mushrooms from Monte Amiata and truffles from San Giovanni d'Asso. Vegetarian guests will find in the Marsili menu a wide range of interesting choices for

their enjoyment. To top it all off, the desserts that obviously showcase the ancient tradition of Siena's typical medieval sweets, first among which the Panpepato, without shadowing Tuscany's equally representative desserts such as fruit pies, pine-seed cakes and the Zuppa Inglese (trifle) here embodied in the Dolce Marsili.

The restaurant, located in downtown Siena near the Duomo and next to Palazzo delle Papesse that hosts the city's contemporary art collection, is the perfect complement to a visit to Siena's historical and artistic beauties.

53100 Siena - Via del Castoro, 3
Tel. +39 0577 47154 - Fax +39 0577 47338

GRAND HOTEL TERME
★★★★

Piazza Italia, 8
53042 Chianciano Terme (SI)
tel +39 0578 63254
fax +39 0578 63524
www.wel.it/GHTchianciano
e-mail:
ghotelterme@ftbcc.it

Location: central
Parking:
supervised uncovered car park
50 parking spaces
Rooms: 65 + 7 suites
Banqueting room:
up to 200 people
Hotel Chain: Medea Hotels
(Chianciano Terme)

FACILITIES:
Sport & Fitness:
• 2 in-outdoor swimming pool
• sauna
• beauty center
• solarium
• special arrangement
  with Terme SpA

TRANSPORTATION:
• Florence Airport (120 km)
• Chiusi-Chianciano Terme
  railway station (12 km)
• Motorway (7 km)

SHOPPING:
• Piazza Italia
• Viale della Libertà

POINTS OF INTEREST:
Museums:
• Archaeological Museum
  (Museo delle Acque)
Theatres:
• Teatro Verde Fucoli

CULTURAL EVENTS:
Evergreen Festival

★★★★
GRAND HOTEL TERME

NEW OPENING

**Relais
Castello di Leonina**

Franchisee:

JOLLY HOTELS
www.jollyhotels.it

AVELLINO
tel +39 0825 25922
fax +39 0825 780029
avellino@jollyhotels.it
MESSINA
tel +39 090 363860
fax +39 090 5902526
messina@jollyhotels.it
SIRACUSA
tel +39 0931 461111
fax +39 0931 461126
siracusa@jollyhotels.it

*Medea
Hotels*

RELAIS ★★★★
CASTELLO DI LEONINA

Strada di Leonina
53041 ASCIANO (SI)
tel +39 0577 716088
fax +39 0577 716054
www.castellodileonina.com
e-mail:
info@castellodileonina.com

Location: Crete Senesi
Parking:
uncovered supervised car park
150 parking spaces
Rooms: 15 + 6 suites + 1 apartment
Banqueting room:
up to 200 people
Hotel Chain: Medea Hotels
(Chianciano Terme)

FACILITIES:
Sport & Fitness:
• outdoor swimming pool
• sauna
• beauty point
• Turkish bath

TRANSPORTATION:
• Florence Airport (50 km)
• Siena railway station (7 km)
• Motorway (30 km)

SHOPPING:
• Siena old town centre

POINTS OF INTEREST:
Siena city of art

Theatres:
• Teatro dei Rozzi

CULTURAL EVENTS:
International Video
Festival (Siena)
Palio (Siena)

*Special discount of 15 % on official prices
(minimum 2 nights) for guide possessor*

FARM HOLIDAYS		TENNIS COURT
ROOMS AND APARTMENTS		2.5 KM AWAY
RESTAURANT		
CELLAR BAR (WITH MUSIC)		18 HOLE GOLF COURSE
SWIMMING POOL		30 KM AWAY
RIDING ARENA		

Villa

Il Crocicchio

Il Crocicchio Is an old farmhouse lovingly restored and managed by the owners, Sonia and Fabrizio Gonnelli. Surrounded by vineyards and olive groves and deep in the beautiful Tuscan landscape it is the ideal place to enjoy a really relaxing holiday.

The villa is located at the centre of the Florence-Siena-Arezzo triangle. It has a choise of rooms and different sized apartments, all fully equipped.

Adult and children alike can enjoy the swimming pool and attractive garden during the spring and summer and children can spend many happy hours in the play area.

Throughout the year specialised personnel are ready to accompany guests on horse rides in the country or to give lessons to beginners.

The Farm produces and sells white and red wine and an excellent cold-pressing olive oil. Other delights include honey, home-made jams and vinsanto.

There is a small restaurant serving mostly typical Tuscan cuisine in the evening and a charming little bar available to guests.

Forget that diet for a while!

50066 REGGELLO (FI) - Via S. Siro 133
Tel. +39 055 8667262 - (home) +39 055 868970 - Fax +39 055 869102
E-mail: info@crocicchio.com - Internet: www.crocicchio.com

CASTELLO DI MODANELLA

53040 Serre di Rapolano (Siena) - Italy
Tel. 0577704604 - Fax 0577704740
E-mail: info@modanella.com – www.modanella.com

"A place for all seasons."

*Modanella
is the ideal destination
for an unforgettable
holiday and offers
its guests its own
excellent production
of olive oil and wine.*

VILLA GRAZIANI
Agriturismo

Villa Graziani, will be a paradise to its guests, situated in the lush green surrunding the farm "Il Pino". Your enjoyment of your stay will be enhanced by exquisite hospitality of the proprietor: he likes his guests to feel totally relaxed so that the holiday can be enjoyed to its fullest. So, there are a wealth of activities to choose from, such as taking a ride on a mountain bike, shopping in the nearby town, taking a leisurely walk along the beach or visiting one of the cultural centers for which Tuscany is so famous, such as Florence, Pisa, Volterra or Siena. Upon your return in the evening, the chef will be delighted to offer you either simple yet traditional Tuscan food, or more sophisticated and adventurous cusine. The meal is accompanied by products such as wine, oil and fuits which have all been produced organicly at Il Pino farm.

Fattoria "Il Pino" - Via per Rosignano, 14 - 57018 VADA (LI)
Tel. +39 0586 788244 - Fax +39 0586 785998 - E-mail: ilpino@tin.it - www.villagraziani.com

Castello di Lamole

Lamole Castle has been overlooking the Chianti hills since the 13th century, in a panoramic spot at 600 m altitude, surrounded by vineyards, chestnut and oak woods. The apartments have been made out of castle rooms with a special attention for the character and charm of the old fabric and they are all furnished with antique furniture. In the lovely small restaurant in the castle you can taste the typical dishes of Tuscany tradition, made as they used to, all the old country recipes with their simple ingredients, accompanied by the most prestigious, select wines from the Chianti area and the whole of Tuscany, including the renowned Castello di Lamole wines, the "Brando della Mole" Sangiovese, made as a pure wine and refined in oak carats and the white "Lauro di Lama" Chardonnay, together with the castle grappas, honey and extra virgin olive oil.

**50022 Greve in Chianti
(Florence - Italy)
Via di Lamole 80/82, Loc. Lamole
Tel. +39 055 630498
+39 055 8547006
Fax +39 055 630611
E-mail: info@castellodilamole.it
www.castellodilamole.it**

CASTELVECCHI

In the heart of the peaceful countryside the farm offers: bedrooms and apartaments for 70 persons, two swimming pools and tennis court.
A typical restaurant where our guests can taste the famous Tuscan cooking and Chianti wine.

Our restaurant, built in an ancient oil-mill, has a typical Tuscan architecture with its brick arches and its wooden beam ceiling. Our kitchen is essentially simple country cooking, rich in flavours due to the excellent use of herb, garlic and onion. It offers a few international dishes and typical Tuscan dishes like "bruschetta" amongst the antipasti or "Ribollita" amongst the soups. Amongst the meat dishes: poultry, rabbit or chicken.

Then our kitchen offers many home-made desserts like "salame dolce" or "cantucci".
Reservation is required.
Chianti Classico DOCG wine and Chianti Classico Riserva wine, extra virgin olive oil and grappa are produced on the farm and are available for purchase. Wine tasting and enological tour of the ancient historic cellars are also possible.

C.a.p. 53017 - Radda in Chianti - Siena - Italia
Tel. +39.577.738050 - Fax +39.577.738608
www.castelvecchi.com - E-mail: castelvecchi@castelvecchi.com

HOTEL ★★★★
RESTAURANT

"Villa le Rondini"

The beautiful view overlooking Florence!

- 43 Bedrooms
- Meeting Facilities
- Banqueting
- Fashion Shows
- Concerts
- Exhibition Areas

- 22 Hectar Park
- Tennis Court
- Swimming pool
- Helyport
- Golf 18 km
- Mountain bike

50139 FIRENZE - VIA BOLOGNESE VECCHIA 224
TEL. 055/400081 - FAX 055/268212 - WWW.VILLALERONDINI.IT

AGRITURISMO

"Villa Belvedere"

800 hundred Villas merged in a panoramic green areas on a hill, 25 minutes away from Florence center offers 3 Apartments nicely furnished for weekly stay and an open air swimming pool. It is the ideal place for a holiday in Tuscany.

For your inquiry: c/o "Villa le Rondini"

la frateria di padre Eligio

La Frateria, located in Cetona among the wonders of Italy, is a miracle created by Mondo X within the walls of the first Convent founded by S.Francesco d'Assisi in 1212. For 40 years Mondo X has been working in Italy and abroad to defend and to dignify Man overcome and humiliated by the turmoil of emptiness. Mondo X Communities have been created in carefully chosen places for people going through life crisis, for drug addicts, for those for whom life is an everlasting search.

In the most beautiful of these Communities the young people of Mondo X have restored and opened a small hotel and a sublime restaurant. Within few years some very determined people, in their quest and search for themselves, have discovered and loved this place - a space to stay and rest. At La Frateria you will find the warming welcome that you may no longer know: rooms full of fragrance, of love and wonders, as well as a refined cuisine. There you will find all the products of Italy made by all the Mondo X Communities. There you will find works of arts, olive oil from the Convent's oil press, jams, but above all you will be able to find thoughts. At the Frateria it might be possible for you, albeit for one night or for one day only, to feel again the joy of being a Man. And you'll come back to us .... the long-awaited for brother.

To Cetona: motorway "A1" FI/ROMA - 9 Km. from Chiusi/Chianciano exit.
All year open except
from 7/01 to 10/02
Credit Cards: Carta SI - VISA - MASTER - EURO
Phone: +39/0578/238261 - Fax +39/0578/239220
E-mail: frateria@bcc.tin.it - www.mondox.it

www.chiantigeografico.it

AGRICOLTORI del CHIANTI
GEOGRAFICO

Radda
Gaiole
Castellina

The territory is our treasure

...and the messagge is into the bottle.

53013 Gaiole in Chianti, Siena.
Tel. +39 0577 749489 r.a. - Fax +39 0577 749223
info@chiantigeografico.it

MARCHE BETWEEN APENNINE MOUNTAINS AND ADRIATIC SEA

A ripple of hills between the blue Adriatic and the Apennine mountains, where the flavors come from the land: pasta, meat, cheese, charcuterie, olive oil, etc.

The Marche (Marches), a land of many peoples, is one of Italy's show-case regions which is richly steeped in art and culture throughout.

A HARMONIOUS LAND

The fortress at San Leo

The region faces the Adriatic sea, with a narrow strip of densely-populated sandy coastline that is tourist-oriented and punctuated by important fishing ports. There is hardly any lowland before the land rises to

Senigallia.
Countryside

the rolling hills dotted with characteristic rocky outcrops which have been transformed into fortresses. The hills nearest the sea are full of olive groves and grape vines. The land used to be the realm of white wine but now also produces important reds, and boasts eleven DOC (*Denominazione di Origine Controllata*) wines. The mountainous area, famed for its mushrooms and truffles, has a lot of pasture. Sheep are prevalent, with their ability to adapt themselves to the sparsest of areas, and some of the great Italian cheeses are produced here.

THE TRADITIONS OF LAND AND SEA

The gastronomy of the Marche is a mixture of seafood and food from the land, and its dishes are mainly simple and homemade, with flavors influenced by the outside world and neighboring regions. The seafood is of excellent quality, including some of the best *vongole* (clams) in Italy, and *triglia* (mullet) which is called 'rosciolo' here. There are many restaurants along the coast but also some good ones to be found inland, in the less touristy areas. You can find the *vincisgrassi* throughout the region – a pasta dish cooked in the oven and made with paper-thin sheets of pasta. There are many theories about the origins of the name, including Windischgrätz, the Austrian prince who triumphed in the siege of Ancona. Other regional dishes include the slow-cooked *bue brasato* (braised beef), fish broth and *coniglio* (rabbit) from the lowlands, and there are also many local specialties. The sweet dishes are not very rich, and most have *sapa* (twice-cooked must, or partially-fermented grape juice), aniseed and dried fruit as their basic ingredients.

Carpegna ham

Marche - Typical products

Scale 1:1 250 000

0   15   30 km

CHEESES

1. **Casciotta di Urbino Dop**
2. **Formaggio di fossa di Talamello.** 'Pitcheese'.

CHARCUTERIE

1. **Prosciutto di Carpegna Dop**
2. **Ciauscolo.** A pork salami made with garlic, herbs, thyme and fennel produced inland.
3. **Salame di Fabriano.** Pork sausage.

MEATS

1. **Vitellone Bianco Appennino Centrale Igp.** Bullock raised in the central Apennine area.
2. **Cavallo del Catria.** Horse meat.

FRUIT

1. **Albicocche di Sassoferrato e Macerata.** Apricots from Sassoferrato and Macerata.
2. **Pera Angelica di Serrungarina.** Pears from Serrungarina.
3. **Pesche della val d'Aso.** Peaches from the Aso valley.
4. **Mele rosa di Amandola.** Pink apples from Amandola.
5. **Pere a cucuccetta di S. Emidio.** Pears.

VEGETABLES

1. **Broccoli.** Regional product.
2. **Carciofo Monteluponese.** Artichokes from Montelupone.
3. **Carciofo precoce di Jesi.** Artichokes from Jesi.
4. **Cavolfiori di Jesi e Fano.** Cauliflower from Jesi and Fano.

EXTRA-VIRGIN OLIVE OIL

1. **Olio extravergine di oliva Colli Pesaresi-Cartoceto Dop**

VARIOUS

1. **Miele dei Colli delle Marche Igp.** Honey from the Marche hills.
2. **Tartufi: Bianco, Nero e Nero pregiato.** Truffles.

DOC WINES

1. **Bianchello del Metauro**
2. **Colli Maceratesi**
3. **Colli Pesaresi**
4. **Esino**
5. **Falerio dei Colli Ascolani**
6. **Lacrima di Morro d'Alba**
7. **Rosso Conero**
8. **Rosso Piceno**
9. **Verdicchio dei Castelli di Jesi**
10. **Verdicchio di Matelica**
11. **Vernaccia di Serrapetrona**

ANCONA

Known for its fish cuisine, there is brodetto (fish broth) with everything, while the farmhouse flavors are found even in the towns.

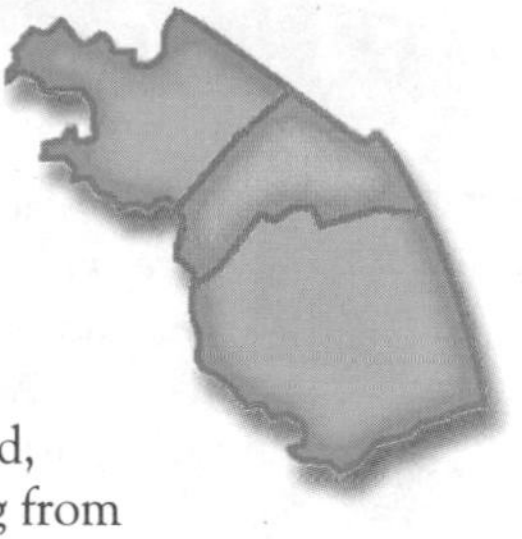

The cuisine of this province is mostly sea-based, with its fish soup and all kinds of fish, ranging from *sogliole* (sole) through *spigole* (sea bass) to *tartufi di mare* (Venus clams). But there is also a land-based gastronomy, with the *vincisgrassi* dish being the most important. These are the lands of the Verdicchio wine, from the region's historical vine. DOC wines include Verdicchio dei Castelli di Jesi, Rosso Conero, Esino and Lacrima di Morro d'Alba produced near Jesi.

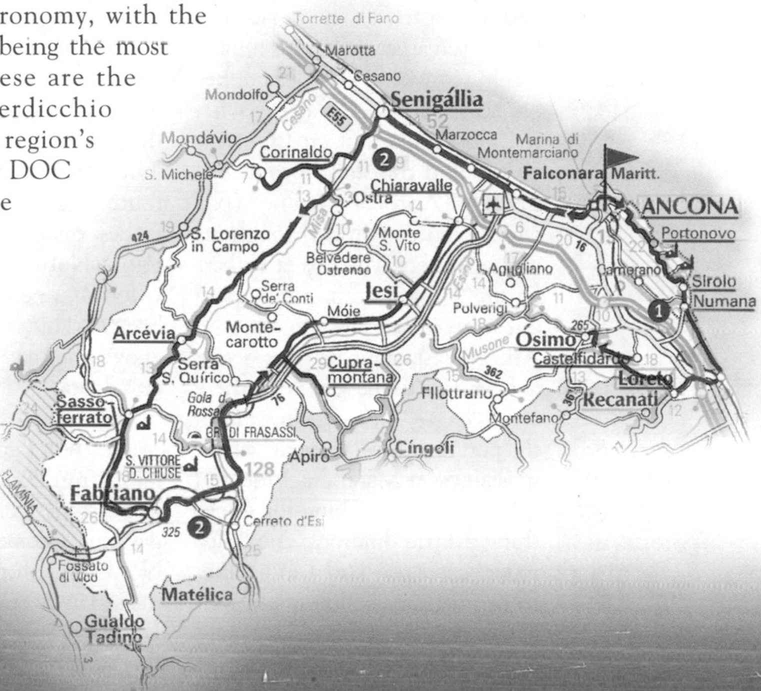

Ancona.
Portonovo

369

Gourmet Tours

ANCONA. A powerful vanvitellian (ancient *lazaretto*) structure which almost seems to rear up out of the sea marks the entrance to the town. The old part is up on the hill, around the town's greatest monument, S. Ciriaco, a bright church facing the port to which Ancona owes its existence. The Pinacoteca Civica (civic art gallery) is a must see. In terms of food, typical dishes are seafood-based, starting with the most important *brodetto* (fish broth) and the *stoccafisso all'anconetana* (Ancona-style dried cod) which you can find throughout the region but which is at its best here. As for restaurants, a good one to try is the "Passetto" a classic Ancona restaurant perched above a sheer drop to the sea. Then there is the "Corte", just steps away from the port, and the "Moretta" which specializes in Marche cuisine and fish. For those looking for something a little different, the "Moroder" *cantina* is based in a nineteenth-century building and welcomes people to the old servants' quarters amongst the vines as part of its agricultural tourism activities. Its cuisine is based on local products and wine. In town, the "Turchetto" – a liquor of bitter coffee, black rum and a hint of lemon – is not to be missed. It is served piping hot.

1. The Conero

PORTONOVO. In the area surrounding this seaside town you will find the church of S. *Maria di Portonovo*, a small gem of Roman architecture. In the town itself the hospitality is excellent. There is the ancient "Fortino Napoleon-

ico" (small Napoleonic fortress) which has been transformed into a hotel, and which has an exceptional restaurant, while "Emilia" is a very good hotel-restaurant, and the "Laghetto" restaurant serves really fresh fish. The landscape is shaped by the Conero headland, which rises up from the flat coast, is thickly covered with woods, and has precipitous drops into the sea. In the *comuni* (municipalities) surrounding the mountain, the Rosso Conero is produced. A red DOC wine, it is the star of Marche wine-making. The Strada del Vino (wine route), which leads you through its best *cantine*, winds through the Parco Naturale Monte Conero (Monte Conero park).

SIROLO. This village, perched high above the sea, has medieval origins. If you are looking for a peaceful time, visit the "Conchiglia Verde" hotel and restaurant. The family-run "Locanda Rocco", set in a historic building, will give you a warm welcome.

NUMANA. Numana Alta is immersed in greenery whilst Numana Bassa has a small port and extensive beaches. It is the home of the "Cantina del Conte Leopardi" and the "Fattoria Le Terrazze". "Il Saraghino" restaurant is an excellent and welcome surprise.

LORETO. This hillside town is formed around a sanctuary for the Virgin Mary, a place of pilgrimage that contains many works of art. The *bostrengo* cake, associated with the Madonna di Loreto festival, is made with corn and wheat flours, stale bread, raisins, dried figs, chopped walnuts, rice and either apples or pears. For a gastronomical stop, there is the ancient "Andreina" restaurant known for its excellent grills; for wine-tasting, try the "Cantina Garofoli". CASTELFIDARDO. On a wooded hill, you will find the monument commemorating a famous battle of the Risorgimento. It is worth paying homage to it, if only for the splendid view of the coast. The little town, renowned for its musical instruments, also has some gastronomic delights and some good bottles of Rosso Conero, especially in the *trattorie* in the immediate area. For your stay, there is the hotel "Parco". OSIMO. The little town is laid out on a hill with broad views towards the sea and the high valley of Musone. Although it is largely Roman, it also has examples of seventeenth- and eighteenth-century architecture. The local "Latini" farm is very painstaking with its dough, which is drawn through bronze and has a nice rough edge to it, and has won a place in the best restaurants in Italy for its quality. The "Umani Ronchi" *cantina* produces excellent wines. Further along is the Rocca di Offagna, built up as a defense against Osimo, and host to medieval festivals in the summer.

2. The valleys of Misa and Esino

SENIGALLIA. Before arriving here, you should stop at Falconara Marittima and take a break at the "Villa Amalia", built at the beginning of the twentieth century and now transformed into a hotel and restaurant, and also see the "Dell'Angolo" and "Scortichini" *enoteche* (where good wines are sold and can be tasted). Senigallia stretches along the sea, at the mouth of the River Misa. Its claim to fame is its Fort dating back to 1480. The town's gastro-

nomical attractions include the "Uliassi" restaurant which offers successful combinations of fish with whatever is available at the market. The "Duchi della Rovere" is a very comfortable, modern, functional hotel with restaurant. Not far away, in Marzocca, you will find the excellent "Madonnina del Pescatore" restaurant serving *millefoglie di coda di rospo* (angler fish millefeuilles) and tremendous desserts. CORINALDO. This is a town with a medieval feel, situated on a hill amongst the famous Verdicchio vines. In the Cantina Sociale Valnevola (wine producers' co-operative of Valnevola) you will find wines from a long and noble tradition, whilst in the "Bellavista" restaurant you will be served *girelle di coniglio* (topside of rabbit), *tagliolini con fave fresche* (*tagliolini* pasta with fresh broad beans), *funghi* (mushrooms) and *tartufi* (truffles). ARCEVIA. This is the impregnable town of Braccio da Montone, with its beautiful collegiate church of St Medardo. The "Co-operativa Buona Usanza" (based in Serra de' Conti) grows chickling, or grass peas, and serves some of the classic dishes of Marche cuisine, including *lonzini di fico*, a sweet made from aniseed, *sapa* (a cooked concentrate of must, or partly-fermented grape juice), dried figs, walnuts and almonds. SASSOFERRATO. This ancient *Sentinum* is made up of a lower, modern quarter, and the upper, old medieval center. The "Società Monterosso" specializes in products made with *farro* (spelt – a kind of wheat), doughs and flours. FABRIANO. Between the four-

HOTELS AND RESTAURANTS

Jesi
Forno Ercoli ¶
piazza Nova 8
☎ 073156960
Loreto
Andreina ¶¶
via Buffaloreccia 14
☎ 071970124
Numana
Il Saraghino ¶¶¶
at Marcelli (km 2)
via Litoranea
☎ 0717391596
Senigallia
Duchi della ★🏨
Rovere ★★★
via Corridoni 3
☎ 0717927623
Madonnina
del Pescatore ¶¶¶
at Marzocca (km 7)
lungomare Italia 11
☎ 071698267
Uliassi ¶¶¶
banchina di Levante 6
☎ 071659327
Cucinamariano ¶¶
via O. Manni 25
☎ 0717926659
Serra de' Conti
Hotel de' Conti ★★★
via S. Lucia 58
☎ 0731879913
Sirolo
Conchiglia ★🏨
Verde ★★★
via Giovanni XXIII 12
☎ 0719330018
Locanda Rocco ¶¶
via Torrione 1
☎ 0719330558

AGRITURISMI

Arcevia
Il Piccolo ★🏨
Ranch
at San Pietro
☎ 0731982162
Fabriano
Gocce di ★🏨
Camarzano
at Moscano
☎ 0732628172

teenth and fifteenth centuries, there were 40 workshops in the town making paper. The town is now known first and foremost for its pork sausage: Salame di Fabriano, then the well-matured *soppressato* and *mazzafegati* ('liver-killers'). A typical local dish is the *lumache in porchetta* (snails stuffed in the same way as *porchetta* – stuffed suckling pig roast). For a gastronomical stop, there is the "Pergola" restaurant, part of the "Janus Hotel Fabriano", serving *tagliolini di Campofilone con ragù di pesce* (Campofilone *tagliolini* pasta with fish ragout), and *guazzetti di carni bianche e vongole* (white meat and clam stew). A little further out, but not to be missed, is the "Old Ranch", a fish restaurant which also serves mushrooms and truffles when in season. There are two places worth seeing as you go down the Esino valley: Genga with the abbey of S. Vittore delle Chiuse, and the "Grotte di Frasassi" (Frasassi grottos) a few kilometres further along.

CUPRA MONTANA. The Verdicchio capital is high up in the Esino valley. Do not miss the Museo dell'Etichetta (label museum) in the ancient Leoni palace. Two *cantine* will give you a pleasant break: the "Vallerosa Bonci" and the "Colonnara" with its restaurant, the "Antiche Fonti della Romita", situated in an old convent. Not far off is Staffolo, with its Museo del Vino (Wine Museum) and an *enoteca* where you can taste the

wines of "Castelli di Jesi". The town is also host to the Festa del Verdicchio (Verdicchio festival) at the end of the summer. Visit the "Ciminiera 1846" restaurant and the "Zaccagnini" *cantina*.

JESI. This walled town is built tightly around the old center. Federico II was born in one of the tents of a Swabian encampment in the main square, one of the most beautiful in the Marche. Foodwise, the cuisine celebrates the cauliflower but other specialties include the artichoke, *brodetto* prepared the Ancona way (*all'anconetana*) with vinegar flavoring, *stoccafisso* (dried cod), *spuntature di maiale* (a pork dish), and a strange dish called *pollo-pesce* (chicken-fish) which is young cock cooked with olives, tuna, capers and anchovies. A specialty of the area is *'ciarimboli'* (local term for innards) flavored with garlic, salt, pepper and rosemary. To stay, there is the "Federico II" hotel, and the "Hostaria Santa Lucia" has excellent fish dishes. Also not to be missed are the "Forno Ercoli" *osteria*, the "La Serva Padrona" wine bar and the "Trieste" bar. From the medieval walls of Jesi, you look out on the valley of the Verdicchio Castles ("Castelli del Verdicchio"), with the castles of Castelplanio, Rosora, Mergo, Maiolati Spontini, Monte Roberto, Montecarotto and Morro d'Alba. At Montecarotto, there are the "Terre Cortesi Moncaro" and "Sebastiano Chessa" cheese factories.

CHIARAVALLE. A last cultural detour: the Chiaravalle abbey, which is one of the oldest Gothic-Cistercian buildings in Italy.

FOCUS

BONCI
Verdicchio
dei Castelli di Jesi
Classico

ASCOLI PICENO

*A border province which gives a foretaste
of the flavors and style of the Abruzzi cuisine
in its specialties from both land and sea.*

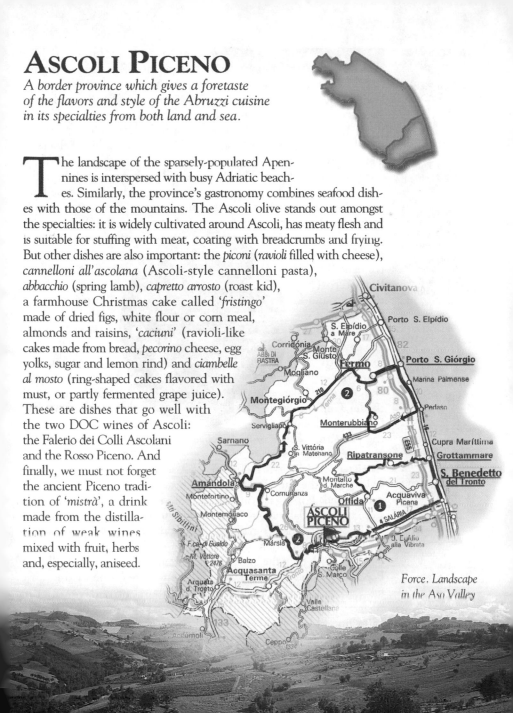

The landscape of the sparsely-populated Apennines is interspersed with busy Adriatic beaches. Similarly, the province's gastronomy combines seafood dishes with those of the mountains. The Ascoli olive stands out amongst the specialties: it is widely cultivated around Ascoli, has meaty flesh and is suitable for stuffing with meat, coating with breadcrumbs and frying. But other dishes are also important: the *piconi* (*ravioli* filled with cheese), *cannelloni all'ascolana* (Ascoli-style cannelloni pasta), *abbacchio* (spring lamb), *capretto arrosto* (roast kid), a farmhouse Christmas cake called '*fristingo*' made of dried figs, white flour or corn meal, almonds and raisins, '*caciuni*' (ravioli-like cakes made from bread, *pecorino* cheese, egg yolks, sugar and lemon rind) and *ciambelle al mosto* (ring-shaped cakes flavored with must, or partly fermented grape juice). These are dishes that go well with the two DOC wines of Ascoli: the Falerio dei Colli Ascolani and the Rosso Piceno. And finally, we must not forget the ancient Piceno tradition of '*mistrà*', a drink made from the distillation of weak wines mixed with fruit, herbs and, especially, aniseed.

*Force. Landscape
in the Aso Valley*

Gourmet Tours

ASCOLI PICENO. The town is situated in a green plain at the confluence of the Tronto and Castellano rivers. It is still set out in the medieval town pattern which is itself almost certainly the same as the previous Roman design. The Arringo square is beautiful and preserves the rectangular shape of the Foro (forum), with the Palazzo Comunale (Town Hall) the Duomo (cathedral) and the Battistero (Baptistry) around it. Not far off is the Piazza del Popolo, the town's "parlor", with the church of S. Francesco, the Palazzo dei Capitani del Popolo, and, under the porticos, the famous (now ex-) café "Meletti", built in Art Nouveau style, where the famous Anisetta was served. For a gastronomic stop, try the "Gallo d'Oro" near the Duomo, and the "Tornasacco" on the first floor of an ancient building which faces the Piazza del Popolo. From this provincial capital, you can take a trip out to the heart of the Monti Sibillini (Sibylline Mountains). The first stop is at Acquasanta Terme which dominates the Tronto valley from on high; the healing properties of its sulphurous waters were already renowned in Roman times. The Grotta Cratere Orsini is also famous: it is a large, natural swimming pool with water pumping out at 38 degrees centigrade. In the nearby Castello di Luco, still inhabited by descendants of

Ripatransone

the owners of long ago, the chapel houses a refined restaurant. At the "Terme" hotel and restaurant, you will find barbecued meats and home-made pasta in a rustic environment. At the "Tre Lanterne", which belongs to the Troiani brothers, you will be served freshwater crayfish, truffle risottos and dishes based on mushrooms. The second stop is Arquata del Tronto, the town of two parks – the parks of Monti Sibillini and Gran Sasso – and the starting point for excursions up the Monte Vettore. At the "Paolini" *trattoria* you will be served Ascolastyle fried dishes and the cuisine of the area.

1. Between Aso and Tronto

SAN BENEDETTO DEL TRONTO. This is a seaside town and fishing port, set between the Tronto and Tesino rivers. The town opens out onto one of the most beautiful stretches of coastline of the Adriatic. It is also in the "Rosso Piceno" area, one of the most abundant producers of the Marche vines. For a place to stay, try the "Arlecchino" hotel and its "Pescatore" restaurant facing the sea. For somewhere to eat, choose between: the "Trattoria del Molo Sud", a down-to-earth, very busy place that serves fish starters and first courses; the "Stalla", a colonial house transformed into a restaurant with a panoramic terrace; and last but not at all least, the "Ristorantino da Vittorio". For wine tasting and buying, there is the "Enoteca Internazionale Fratelli Bulgari". GROTTAMMARE. This seaside town is situated at the foot of the Castello hill and has a medieval town center. There are various food and wine choices: at the "Osteria dell'Arancio", a simple, pleasant place, offering a good choice of local produce which you can also buy in their neighboring shop; and at the "Borgo Antico" restaurant set in an old mill with a view of the sea, where the cuisine is innovative but does not forget old traditions. Continuing along the Adriatic, you reach Cupra Marittima which is part modern (on the sea side) and part medieval. Along the sea front there is a mollusc museum containing seven million exhibits of shells, mother-of-pearl and coral. For a stopover, there is the "Europa" hotel with restaurant. RIPATRANSONE. The so-called "Belvedere del Piceno" has endless panoramic views. It is surrounded by city walls and has retained much of its medieval aspect. There are important monuments in its historic center. Two events not to be missed in August are the "Sagra del *prosciutto* e del vino Rosso Piceno (Rosso Piceno wine and ham festival)", and the Puzzle Gastronomico. As a wine town, it has many *cantine*, the best ones being: "Cantina dei Colli Ripani", "Cocci Grifoni", "Cantina Le Caniette"; and an "Enoteca" of wines produced locally. The local specialty is the '*ciavarro*', a lightly spiced dish based on vegetables and cereals. OFFIDA. Situated on the Rosso Piceno Superiore hills, it is also famous for its lace, its Carneval cakes, and its '*chichi*', a *focaccia*

filled with tuna, capers and peppers. It has preserved its remarkable town hall (fifteenth-century) and fourteenth-century tower. The "Cantina Vinea" is a company *enoteca* (wine-seller where there is also wine-tasting) set in an old convent. It also organises the Banco d'Assaggio (tasting) of local wines and produce, at San Benedetto del Tronto, in the summer. Have a break at the "Taverna degli Artisti" where you can savor innovative cuisine within seventeenth-century walls.

2. From the Sibyllines to the sea
AMANDOLA. This is a holiday destination with a view of the Sibylline Mountains, famous for its ham, *ricotta* cheese and apples. The dish not to be missed is the *polenta con i tordi selvatici* (*polenta* with wild thrush). The "Paradiso" hotel, which serves local dishes, can be found in the historic center. It is worth popping over to Montefortino to try their excellent '*ciauscolo*' (a type of *salami* made from pork, garlic, herbs, thyme and fennel). Just a little further on, there is Montemonaco, famous for its truffles, snails in *porchetta* and chestnuts, and also for its *funghi peveracci arrosto* (roasted peveracci mushrooms). As you go down the Aso Valley into the Montelparo Valley, you can stay at the "Ginestra" hotel, which is made up of lots of small buildings that sit well in the landscape, and is good for families. FERMO. The scenic route from Amandola to Fermo follows the Tenna valley and has views of the Sibylline mountain chain. The first stop is at the Roman abbey of Saints Ruffino and Vitale, con-

HOTELS AND RESTAURANTS

Porto San Giorgio
Damiani & Rossi ¶¶
via Misericordia 2
☎ 0734674401
Davide ¶¶ ★▤
lungomare
Gramsci S. 503
☎ 0734677700
San Benedetto del Tronto
Arlecchino ★★★
Il Pescatore ¶¶
at Porto d'Ascoli
viale Trieste 22/27
☎ 073585635
☎ 073583782
Molo Sud ¶¶
via Tamerici
☎ 0735587325
Ristorantino da Vittorio ¶¶
via Manara 102
☎ 0735583344
La Stalla ¶ ★▤
contrada Marinuccia 35
☎ 0735587344

AGRITURISMI

Ascoli Piceno
Conca d'Oro
at the Abbazia di Rosara
via Salaria Superiore 137
☎ 0736252272
Amandola
Pelloni ★▤
via S. Lorenzo 3
☎ 0736847535
Lapedona
Casa Vecchia ★▤
via Aso 11
☎ 0734933159
Montemonaco
La Cittadella ★▤
at Cittadella
☎ 0736856361
Servigliano
Cascina degli Ulivi ★▤
contrada Commenda 4
☎ 0734710235

WINE PRODUCERS

Ripatransone
Cantina
dei Colli Ripani
contrada Tosciano 28
☎ 07359505
Cocci Grifoni
contrada Messieri 11
☎ 073590143
Le Caniette
via Canali 22
☎ 07359200

PASTA PRODUCERS
Campofilone
L'Antica Pasta
di G. Marcozzi
via Borgo
S. Patrizio 10
☎ 0734933156
La Campofilone
di Enzo Rossi
via XX Settembre 41
☎ 07343294
La Pasta
di Ivana Maroni
via S. Maria 17
☎ 0734931165
Il Laboratorio
di Sabina Salvatori
via S. Maria 14
☎ 0734932850

SHOPPING
Ascoli Piceno
Caffè Meletti
via Trivio 56
☎ 0736259966
Historic cafe.
Enoteca Internaz.
Fratelli Bulgari
via Montello 18
☎ 073583075
Wines.
Gastronomia
Migliori
piazza Arringo 2
☎ 0736250042
Delicatessen.
Monte Vidon
Combatte
Passamonti srl
via Leopardi 12
☎ 0734656109
Typical charcuterie.
Offida
Vinea
via Garibaldi 75
☎ 0736880005
Local olive oil, honey and DOC wines.

taining frescos from the fifteenth century. Moving on, we recommend a brief detour to Monte San Martino where you can get excellent *pecorino* and *ricotta* cheeses. A little further on, there is Servigliano, an eighteenth-century village built according to the urban rules for an ideal town. Apart from *porchetta*, which, it is said, was invented here, the area is known for its good charcuterie producers. Finally, there is Fermo itself, situated on a hill overlooking the sea, its Duomo (cathedral) dominating the town's skyline from the Girfalco esplanade which faces the medieval village. Not far from the Piazza del Popolo, the lively heart of the town, there is the very decent hotel "Astoria", and not far away, at Lido di Fermo, is the "Royal" hotel with its restaurant "Nautilus".

PORTO SAN GIORGIO. Previously called Castel San Giorgio, today this town is a seaside destination and an active fishing port. The Guelph Fort, which you can now visit, used to protect the area inland from raids by Turkish pirates, and the port was a sea outlet for Fermo. Not to be missed here are the *papaline*, which are small, fried sardines in *salmi* (a casserole). They were called *papaline* in honour of the Papal State which ruled here for a long time. In the summer, both the fishing and seaside activities are celebrated in a triumphal, gigantic fish fry-up. To stay over, we recommend the modern, "Tritone" hotel with its restaurant, "Da Mario". As a place to eat you

could also try the good value "Damiani e Rossi" restaurant, with its predominantly meat cuisine or the "Davide" restaurant, which belongs to the "David Palace", with its terrace overlooking the sea. Once by the sea, it is worth popping over to Pedaso, famous for top quality *mitili* (mussels). Possible gastronomic stops here include the "Valdaso" and "Perotti" restaurants, both with well-established reputations. Alternatively, there is the "Covo", an old farmhouse which has recently been turned into a restaurant. All three specialize in seafood.

MONTERUBBIANO. In the immediate Capofilone hinterland, once a land of cloth dyers, this town is today known for its excellent *maccheroncini* and *capelli d'angelo* pastas, made by local pasta factories. Small, local firms include "La Campofilone", which organises guided tours (advance telephone reservation required), and the "Antica Pasta". In the Santa Maria *contrada* (quarter), you will also find "La Pasta" and "Il Laboratorio", where the *maccheroncini* are still cut by hand. Monterubbiano, situated in a scenic spot in the Aso valley, is of Roman origin and was revived by Benedictines. Marked by sackings and bitter fighting, it was also occupied and fortified by Francesco Sforza. A few medieval churches survive today. Here, you will find the "Pazzi" restaurant (and hotel) which serves family fare steeped in tradition. A slight detour will allow you a visit to Moresco, an oval-shaped town, enclosed within its city wall.

MACERATA

A place for the refined palate: Matelica for Verdicchio wines, Camerino for cured meats, Cingoli for olive oil, and Porto Recanati for fish.

The land surprises you with its countryside which is cultivated as though it were a garden. The share-cropping, with tenant farmers paying the landowner with produce, was once common in this area and is still reflected in the flavours of its cuisine, especially in the popular dishes based on farmyard animals. So you get chicken and rabbit in *potacchio* – in other words cooked plain in an iron frying-pan with only garlic, rosemary and white wine – *papere in umido* (stewed young goose) and also lamb and suckling pig. The Macerata province is also the home of the "Marchigiana Gentile", a top breed of cattle. The best first courses are the *pinciarelli*, a pasta of flour and water served with fresh broad beans or tuna, and *cioncioni*, *tagliolini* pasta made from wheat flour and broad bean flour. By the sea, you get *clams* dishes and *sogliole dell'Adriatico in gratella* (grilled Adriatic sole). DOC wines include the famous Bianco dei Colli Maceratesi, Verdicchio di Matelica and Vernaccia di Serrapetrona.

Cereal farming and vineyards are the highlights of the hills in Marche

Gourmet Tours

MACERATA. High up in the Chienti and Potenza hills, this town's historical center is the model of elegance. It was developed mostly during the sixteenth century next to the Roman ruins of *Helvia Ricina*. As far as food is concerned, dishes not to be missed are the *pollo alla maceratese* (Macerata-style chicken) and the frittelle all'anice (aniseed flavoured griddlecakes). At the "Osteria dei Fiori", they cook what is in season and are aided by the owners who also act as sommeliers. There is also the "Enoteca Simoncini". For somewhere to stay, try the "Claudiani" hotel set in a beautiful building, and run by the same family for over a century.

1. Along the Adriatic

CIVITANOVA MARCHE. This is a busy seaside town on the Adriatic coast. On a hillock inland, there is Civitanova Alta which dates back to medieval times. The cuisine is dominated by shellfish: clams, razor clams, small shrimps and mussels. In addition to the town's own restaurants, it is worth mentioning "Il Pontino" in nearby Porto Potenza. It is very simple but refined, serving imaginative fish dishes, and wine from a very respectable cellar. In Montecosaro, a small inland town, we can highly recommend the "Luma Hotel" with its very good restaurant, and the "Due Cigni" for that really special meal.

PORTO RECANATI. This ancient port is, today, a renowned seaside town. It claims to use one of the original versions of the recipe for

brodetto (fish broth), which is prepared here with the extra ingredient of wild saffron found in the nearby hills. The Accademia del Brodetto defends and protects this tradition. The "Mago del Brodetto" restaurant, belonging to the "Vincenzo Bianchi" hotel, is very simple but nicely situated on the beach. The "Enzo", on the other hand, is an elegant hotel in the center with its own restaurant, the "Torcoletto". Another choice would be the "Fatatis", a gracious restaurant with a good wine cellar.

RECANATI. Between the Musone and Potenza valleys, this little town dominates a vast landscape of hills and valleys, the very ones found in the beautiful lyrics of Giacomo Leopardi who was born here in 1798. In the historical center, near the public gardens, you will find the family-run "La Ginestra" hotel, with its restaurant serving the food of the region. The countryside yields an abundance of good figs.

2. Up in the Macerata hills

TOLENTINO. The town is situated in the Chienti valley in charming countryside. The most important monument is the basilica of S. Nicola da Tolentino, rich in works of art. This is the country of the Vernaccia de Serrapetrona, the rare DOC dessert wine. The gastronomic specialties are the cannelloni which are also known as '*canne d'organo*' (organ pipes). Castello della Rancia is situated along the *statale* to Macerata. It was a Benedictine farm and grain store before being transformed into a castle in 1354. For a stopover, there is the "Hotel 77", with its busy restaurant.

HOTELS AND RESTAURANTS

Macerata
Claudiani ★★★
via Ulissi 8
☎ 0733261400
★ **Arena** ★★
vicolo Sferisterio 16
☎ 0733230931
★ **Osteria dei Fiori** ¶¶
via Lauro Rossi 61
☎ 0733260142
Cingoli
★ **Diana** ¶
via Cavour 21
☎ 0733602313
★ **Antica Taverna alla Selva** ¶
at San Vittore (km 12)
via Cicerone 1
☎ 0733617119
Civitanova Marche
Miramare ★★★
viale Matteotti 1
☎ 0733811511
Palace ★★★
piazza Rosselli 6
☎ 0733810464
Il Gatto che ride ¶¶
viale V. Veneto 117
☎ 0733816667
Enzo ¶
via Dalmazia 213
☎ 0733814877
Matelica
Al Teatro ¶
corso Umberto 17
☎ 0737786099
Montecosaro
★ **Luma** ¶¶¶
via Bruscantini 1
☎ 0733229701
★ **Due Cigni** ¶¶¶
via SS. Annunziata 19
☎ 0733865182
Porto Potenza Picena
★ **Il Pontino** ¶¶
via IV Novembre 13
☎ 0733688638

SAN GINESIO. This town, with its beautiful collegiate church and an art gallery/museum, squats on the top of a hill. You should try the *torta nociata* made of walnuts ground up with olive oil and flavoured with orange and lemon. To stay over, there is the "Centrale" hotel. To eat, there is the "Piergentili" restaurant in the main piazza.

CAMERINO. This little town, set between the gentle hills and the steep Apennine passes, has an ancient feel to it. It is known for its sausages, home-cooked duck, the *torta di Pasqua* (Easter cake), *torrone* (normally meaning nougat but here, a type of *panettone* – a light sponge-type cake with candied fruit and sultanas), and *panpociato*, a type of sweet bread *polenta* or must *polenta*. They hold a cheese fair here during the first two days of May. The "Rocca dei Borgia" restaurant is set in a fortress of the same name.

MATELICA. Its art is in its medieval and baroque monuments, and its gastronomic heritage finds expression in its *pinciarelli* (see above) with fresh broad beans or tuna, *crescia fogliata*, a type of strudel, its charcuterie (*ciauscolo* and *ciaringolo*) and its *pecorino* (from ewe's milk) cheeses. The town's famous DOC wine, the Verdicchio di Matelica, is fruity with overtones of almond and hazelnut. For wine tasting and buying, you have the "Enoteca della Cantina Sociale Belisario"

and the "Fattoria La Monacesca". To stay overnight, there is the "La Loggia" hotel, and to eat, the restaurant, "Il Teatro", both in the historical center.

SAN SEVERINO MARCHE. The heart of the town is the Piazza del Popolo, an ancient place of commerce. The traditional dish is *lumache al forno e in porchetta* (baked snails, stuffed in the same way as for *porchetta*). The "Due Torri" restaurant, with its traditional air, has been run by the Severini family since 1932. Attached to the restaurant is the "Bottega dell'Africano" which sells local specialties.

Olive trees

CINGOLI. It is known as the balcony of the Marche due to its views which stretch as far as the sea. Specialties of the land include celery and the extra-fine extra-virgin olive oil of Treviggiano (in the neighbourhood of Cingoli). *Parmigiana di gobbi* (thick, thistle-like plants – with parmesan) is the culinary highlight. For those staying overnight, there is the "Diana" restaurant and hotel in the historical center. For wine, try the "Cantina del Palazzo". Not far away, in San Vittore, there is also the "Antica Taverna alla Selva".

TREIA. It is renowned for its town wall complete with towers and gates. In the historical center, there is the simple and welcoming hotel "Grimaldi", with restaurant, or the local specialty cuisine of the "Antiche Mura".

HOTELS AND RESTAURANTS

Porto Recanati
Enzo ★★
Torcoletto ⁋⁋
corso Matteotti 21/23
☎ 0717590734
☎ 0717590196
V. Bianchi ★★★
via Garibaldi 15
☎ 0719799040
Fatatis ⁋⁋
at Scossicci (km 2)
via Vespucci 2
☎ 0719799366
Recanati
La Ginestra ★★★
via Calcagni 2
☎ 071980355
San Severino Marche
Due Torri ⁋
via S. Francesco 21
☎ 0733645419
Tolentino
Hotel 77 ★★★
viale Bruno Buozzi 90
☎ 0733967400

AGRITURISMI

Camerino
La Cavallina
at Polverina
S.S. 77 (km 48,9)
☎ 073746173
Civitanova Marche
Campolungo
contrada Migliarino 30
☎ 0733709504

WINE PRODUCERS

Cingoli
La Cantina del Palazzo
via Garibaldi 87
☎ 0733602531
Matelica
Belisario-Cantina Sociale Matelica e Cerreto d'Esi
via Merloni 12
☎ 0737787247
San Biagio
via S. Biagio 32
☎ 073783997

SHOPPING

Macerata
Enoteca Simoncini
galleria del Commercio 14
☎ 0733260576
Wines.

PESARO-URBINO

In the land of the Montefeltro, the truffle and the flavors of the Romagnole cuisine combine for the more robust cuisine of Central Italy.

R omagna, Tuscany and the Adriatic Sea border this province and have influenced and inspired it. Nature is the star here, playing among the hills which rise from the sea and reach as high as Mount Catria. The hills are good for vines, and the gentle sea air brings out delicate flavors in the wines, which are mostly white. (The production of red wines has developed in a few sub-areas like Focara and Roncaglia.) Bianchello del Metauro is produced in the area near the coast. This wine probably originates from the Metauro Valley; it goes very well with seafood cuisine. Nearby Romagna inspired the creation of the Colli Pesaresi red wines which go well with the *formaggio di fossa* (matured cheese made mostly from sheep's milk, with sometimes the addition of cow's milk) and the farmhouse dishes spruced up with Acqualagna and Sant'Angelo in Vado truffles. Moreover, the microclimate has allowed the flourishing cultivation of olives which produce a fruity oil that goes well with fish. The whole province produces excellent cheeses. The cuisine includes inland and coastal dishes: delicate soups, *guazzetti* (stews) of fish and pasta in a red sauce and *polenta* with a variety of mushrooms – *prataioli* (field mushrooms), russola mushrooms, *gallinacci* (chanterelle mushrooms) and *vesce* (puff-ball mushrooms). There are some excellent restaurants, and the traditional dishes are always made with impeccable skill.

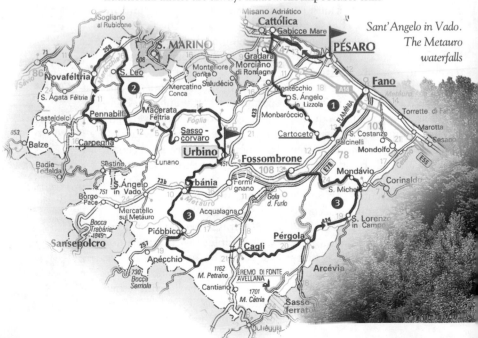

Sant'Angelo in Vado.
The Metauro
waterfalls

Gourmet Tours

PESARO. There are two sides to this town situated on the coast where the Foglia valley opens out: it is both a modern seaside resort and an ancient and industrial town. Gioacchino Rossini was born here, and the town now hosts a famous opera festival, in the summer months. The entrance to the town is watched over by the Laurana fortress. On a nearby hill stands the Villa Imperiale, the sumptuous Gonzaga residence. The heart of the town is the Piazza del Popolo where you will find the Palazzo Ducale. There is a choice of hotels: the "Vittoria" with its Art Nouveau feel; the "Villa Serena" set in a quiet park; and the fascinating "Locanda di Villa Torraccia". Restaurants include the "Scudiero", set in the stables of a sixteenth-century building, which serves fish dishes and makes the most of the Acqualagna truffle when it is in season. Along the seafront, there is the "Teresa" fish restaurant, which is part of the "Principe" hotel. Sheer above the sea, there

is the panoramic "Alceo" restaurant. Finally, in Candelara, there is the "L'Orto di Famiglia", a small farm where you can pick your own delicious organic vegetables 'by the basket'.

1. Amongst the beaches and villages

GABICCE MARE. A very busy modern seaside resort, this town still has an unspoilt corner down at the canal port. The lovely sandy beach, one of the busiest in the Marche, stretches out at the feet of the Gabicce Monte headland. The elegant and comfortable "Grand Hotel Michelacci", complete with a modern beauty center, is set in a beautiful spot. The "Cavalluccio Marino" hotel, facing the sea, has recently been renovated and offers a carefully chosen menu. On the other side of the canal, there is the "Stazione", a small hotel with simple rooms and a well-run restaurant. The "Antico Vico" is an excellent restaurant.

GRADARA. This is a castle with crenellated walls and ramparts enclosing within them a tourist

HOTELS AND RESTAURANTS

Pesaro
Vittoria ★✦★ 🏨
piazzale Libertà 2
☎ 072134343
Alceo ｜｜｜
via Panor. Ardizio 101
☎ 072155875
Lo Scudiero ｜｜｜
via Baldassini 2
☎ 072164107
Principe ★★★
Teresa ｜｜｜
viale Trieste 180
☎ 072130222
☎ 072130096
Villa Serena ★★★
via S. Nicola 6/3
☎ 072155211
Acqualagna
La Ginestra ★★★
at Furlo (km 5)
via Flaminia 17
☎ 0721797033
Furlo ｜｜
at Furlo (km 5)
via Flaminia 66
☎ 0721700096
Borgo Pace
**Oasi San
Benedetto** ★★ 🏨
at Lamoli (km 5)
via Abbazia 7
☎ 072280133
Cagli
La Guazza ｜
piazza Federico
da Montefeltro 1
☎ 0721787231
Cartoceto
Symposium ｜｜｜｜
Quattro Stagioni
via Cartoceto 38
☎ 0721890320
Fano
Corallo ★★★ 🏨
via L. da Vinci 3
☎ 0721804200
**Ristorantino
da Giulio** ｜｜
viale Adriatico 100
☎ 0721805680
Pesce Azzurro ｜
viale Adriatico 48
☎ 0721803165
Fossombrone
Al Lago ★★★
at San Lazzaro (km 2)
via Cattedrale 79
☎ 0721726129

Truffle zappette (hoes)

HOTELS AND RESTAURANTS

Gabicce Mare
⭐🏨 **Grand Hotel Michelacci** ★★★
Giardini Unità d'Italia 1
☎ 0541954361
⭐🏨 **Cavalluccio Marino** ★★
via V. Veneto 111
☎ 0541950053
Gradara
Hosteria la Botte ¶¶
piazza V Novembre 11
☎ 0541964404
Montemaggiore al Metauro
⭐🏨 **La Locanda del Borgo Antico** ¶¶
via Panoramica 4
☎ 0721896553
Pennabilli
Piastrino ¶¶
via Parco Bagni 9
☎ 0541928569
San Leo
Castello ★★
piazza Alighieri 11/12
☎ 0541916214
La Corte ¶
via M. Rosa 74
☎ 0541916145
⭐🏨 **La Rocca** ¶
via Leopardi 16
☎ 0541916241
San Lorenzo in Campo
⭐🏨 **Giardino** ¶¶¶
via Mattei 4
☎ 0721776803

village that lives off the nostalgic story of the sad love affair between Paolo and Francesca. An ancient olive tree in the village reminds us that the production of olive oil is an ancient tradition here. The *piadine* flat breads arrived here from nearby Romagna. You can also admire medieval architecture and the "Hosteria alla Botte, which is carved out of volcanic rock.

CARTOCETO. A pleasant journey over the hills takes you to the south of Pesaro, where you will find plenty of opportunities to eat well. In Monteciccardo, the small firm of "Irmo Falcioni, Salvatore Manca e Luigi Nobili" sells tasty *pecorino* cheeses. A very quick detour to Sant'Angelo in Lizzola will allow you to taste the hams of the "Sauro Geminiani" *salumificio* (charcuterie factory), and the tasty peaches which are also grown in nearby Montelabbate. In Montegaudio, the "Walter" restaurant serves simple, local dishes. In Serrungarina, note the rare Angelica pear, ready at the end of August. Here you will also find the "Villa Federici", built in 1683 by Abbott Federici, and today a welcoming little place with five rooms, good hospitality and cuisine prepared very carefully and professionally by a young cook. For wine buying and tasting there is the "Cantina Fiorini" in Barchi or the "Cantina Solazzi" in Saltara. When you see the Adriatic you have arrived at Cartoceto, which is famous for its light and fruity olive oil. Here, you will find the excellent "Symposium-Quattro Stagioni", famous for its cuisine using local produce in a nicely innovative way, e.g. rabbit with black olives, *pappardelle* pasta with sauce of young cock and *formaggio di fossa* cheese, Catria lamb with fried sage, barley-coffee and aniseed ice-cream. Finally, do not forget Montemaggiore, a small, hillside village converted into a hotel. You do not just get a room here but the key to a small house.

FANO. In the valley, with the hills behind you, you run along the last section of the via

The Eremo at Fonte Avellana

Flaminia which curves towards the sea. In the historical center with its strong Malatesta influence, you will find the Palazzo della Ragione (built 1299) which you must see along with the Renaissance Corte Malatestiana and the Loggia del Sansovino. The town is famous for its *pesce azzurro* (literally 'blue fish': various types of fish with blue coloring, e.g. sardines and anchovies). The "Comarpesca", a co-operative of Fano fishermen, runs the "Pesce Azzurro" self-service restaurant which is excellent value. The *brodetto di Fano* (Fano fish broth) is one of the four Marche variations of this ancient dish. Local specialties include the *salsiccia matta fanese* ("mad" Fano sausage), the *buzzotto* cheese, and the Moretta, a liquor made from brandy, aniseed and rum, which fishermen used to add to their coffee. Do not miss the lively market with its wonderful display of fish. In the modern resort side of town, you will find the "Corallo" hotel with nice modern well-furnished rooms. Also at the seafront, there is the seafood restaurant, "Ristorante no Da Giulio".

2. The Montefeltro area

URBINO. This was where the magical Italian Renaissance took place. It is in the heart of the province, the capital of the duchy of Montefeltro, and the birthplace of Raffaello. The Ducal palace, near Laurana, now houses the Galleria Nazionale delle Marche. Opposite the Palazzo Ducale, there is the "Il

Cortegiano" restaurant which carefully chooses and prepares the local dishes it serves. Also in the historical center, there is the "Vecchia Urbino" restaurant where mushrooms and truffles reign supreme. Typical dishes include the *braciola all'urbinate* (a type of roulade of pork, stuffed with omelette and a slice of ham, then cooked in oil, white wine and stock), *passatelli* (tube-shaped pasta made from breadcrumbs or semolina, eggs and milk), and *lumachelle di pasta* (snail-shaped pasta). In the town, as in the neighboring area, the production of quark has just started up again. Quark is a cheese of ancient origins, which does not contain rennet.

SASSOCORVARO. Known as the sentinel of Montefeltro, this town was a fortress from the tenth century. The Rocca Ubaldinesca, a masterpiece of military architecture with its singular vessel-shape topped with large towers and turrets, was, in fact, "a big mistake": its rounded forms and narrow loopholes meant that those being attacked could not see their attackers. "Le Logge" restaurant is small and welcoming, or there is the "Nido del Corvo" restaurant in the center.

SAN LEO. More landscape filled with fortresses and keeps built by the architect Francesco di Giorgio Martini at the wishes of Duke Federico. They include Sant'Agata Feltria, Mondavio, Cagli and San Leo, the latter also acting as prison to Giuseppe Balsamo detto

BIANCHELLO
DEL METAURO

COLLI METAURENSI
Cantine Produttori

HOTELS AND RESTAURANTS

Serrungarina
Villa Federici ¶¶ ★
at Bargni (km 2)
via Castello 19
☎ 0721891510
Urbania
Big Ben ¶
corso V. Emanuele 61
☎ 0722319795
Urbino
Bonconte ★☆★ ★
via delle Mura 28
☎ 07222463
Raffaello ★★★ ★
via S. Margherita 40
☎ 07224896
Il Cortegiano ¶¶ ★
via Puccinotti 13
☎ 0722320307
Vecchia ★
Urbino ¶¶
via dei Vasari 3/5
☎ 07224447

AGRITURISMI

Pesaro
Lo Limonale
di Muraglia
via Flaminia 305
☎ 072155577
Cagli
Ca' Belvedere
at Smirra di Cagli
strada Pigno-
M. Martello
☎ 0721799204
CasaleTorre del
Sasso ★
strada Civita 12
☎ 0721782655
Frescina Centro
Benessere
at Nero
☎ 0721708240

*White truffle
(Tartufo bianco)*

Cagliostro, to whom is attributed the invention of the Balsamo di Cagliostro, a liquorice-flavored digestive liquor. The *cotechino* (large spiced pork sausage for boiling) is famous here, and the nearby Romagna inspires great *cappelletti* (large, stuffed pasta like *ravioli*). One of the *pecorino* cheeses, *slattato*, is made in the area: it is matured for seven days and is then sold, wrapped in either cabbage or fig leaves. You must make a detour to Talamello for its *formaggio di fossa* cheese, which is called Ambra, due to its limpid golden color. At San Leo, there is the "Castello" hotel and restaurant serving good local cuisine.

PENNABILLI. It sits in a valley dominated by the rocky spurs of Penna and Billi, today called the Roccione (big rock) and the Rupe (cliff). The center comes alive in the summer during the Mostra Mercato dell'Antiquariato (antiques fair). For a gastronomic break, there is the "Piastrino" restaurant, set in a farmhouse surrounded by greenery, which serves local produce.

CARPEGNA. This mountain resort, physically in the center of the Montefeltro area, is famous for its hams which have the right balance of fat and lean – the meat is firm, compact and tasty. The Palazzo Carpegna, built in the late-Renaissance style, is situated in the center of the town. The "Silvana" and "Vecchio Montefeltro" restaurants not only serve the *piadine con prosciutto* (unleavened bread with ham) but also mushroom and truffle specialities. To stay over, there is the *agriturismo* establishment, "Il Biancospino".

3. The Metauro Valley

URBANIA. In a tight bend at the center of the Metauro Valley, you will find the ancient Castel Durante, famous in the sixteenth century for the production of maiolica earthenware. Its current name comes from Pope Urban VII. Black truffles are found here, and you can buy them and even taste fresh truffles and truffle delicacies at "Ravaldo Longhi". There are two villages in the area worth visiting. One is

Urbania. Barco Ducale

Piobbico, where they celebrate the mushroom, especially the *porcino* and the locally-marinated *spugnola* (morel). This village also plays host to the Castello dei Brancaleoni, an ancient fortress transformed into an elegant Renaissance home which has recently been restored and which you can visit. The other village is Borgo Pace, where you can stay at the "Oasi di S. Benedetto", a small hotel typical of the area, which has been built amongst ancient remains. The hotel's amenities are simple but good and its restaurant serves local food.

ACQUALAGNA. The Metauro Valley crosses the gorges of the Furlo and opens out at Acqualagna, one of the capitals of the white truffle. It is a largely modern town with an important commercial center where the famous Fiera del Tartufo (Truffle Festival) takes place in February. The "Furlo" restaurant serves truffle and mushroom dishes made by experts in the tradition. Another restaurant to try is the "Tartufo" where you can also buy truffle specialties.

CAGLI. The Mallio bridge at the entrance to the town tells of its Roman origins. It was an important town due to its position along the Via Flaminia. The imposing fortress, commissioned by the Montefeltros, was also destroyed by them so that it would not fall into the hands of the Borgias. From here, take a brief detour to Cantiano to taste its famous bread and the Acquacanina *pecorino* cheese. In the histori-

cal center, you will find simple local cuisine at the "La Guazza" restaurant.

PERGOLA. To get here, you travel along the Cesano Valley. It is of medieval origin and saw the rule of the Malatesta. It was destroyed by the Sforzas and rebuilt by the Montefeltros. 'Il Valentino' had Giulio Varano, the Lord of Camerino, strangled in the town's fort, which is famous for its gilded bronzes. A few kilometers away, in a lonely valley at the foot of the rocky wall of Mount Catria sits the Monastero di Fonte Avellana. This atmospheric hermitage was once host to Dante. The hotel-restaurant "Le Sorgenti" and the "Osteria della Pergola" can be found along the Statale Cesanese (Cesanese federal highway). We recommend the hotel-restaurant "Giardino" in San Lorenzo, for its excellent regional cuisine based on mushrooms and truffles when in season.

FOSSOMBRONE. The town covers the side of the hill with its harmonious lines, and the fort dominates the summit. It got its name from Gaius Sempronius Gracchus and was fortified by the Malatestas who then sold it to the Montefeltros, who used it for their holidays. The town consists of various historical quarters with buildings dating from the sixteenth and seventeenth centuries. There is an archaeological collection in the Corte Alta. The modern and welcoming "Al Lago" hotel is set in greenery at the foot of the Furlo Pass.

SHOPPING

Pesaro
L'Orto di famiglia
at Candelara (km 5)
via Valgelata
☎ 03683200550
Organically-grown vegetables.
Acqualagna
Tartufi Tofani
via Bellaria 37
☎ 0721798918
White and black truffles; truffle specialties.
Cantiano
Amarena Furiosi di A. Morelli
Ristorante Giardino
via dell'Industria 18
☎ 0721788073
Berry juice, honey, truffles and the typical wisner wine.
Cartoceto
Frantoio della Rocca
via Pandolfi 1
Olive oil producer.
Gastronomia Beltrami
via Umberto 124
☎ 0721898145
Typical cheeses (such as "formaggio di fossa") and Frantoio della Rocca olive oil.
Fano
Drogheria Enoteca Ricci
via Cavour 67
☎ 0721803252
Delicatessen, vast range of olive oils and the Moretta liquor.
San Lorenzo in Campo
Monterosso srl
via Costantinopoli 7
☎ 0721776511
Spelt and spelt flour.
Sant'Angelo in Lizzola
Salumificio Sauro Geminiani
via Serra 36/a
☎ 0721490593
Charcuterie.
Urbania
Ravaldo Longhi
corso V. Emanuele 55
☎ 0722319459
White and black truffles; truffle specialties.

UMBRIA WHERE EATING IS AN ART

The hills, mountains, vines, olive groves, woods, the streams
feeding Lake Trasimeno and charming farm houses,
as well as characteristic cities and surrounding villages,
all make up the gastronomic backdrop of Umbria.

U mbria, "Italy's holy land" is how the homeland of
Saints Benedict and Francis, Santa Chiara and
Santa Rita is most commonly known. But it has
other titles: "Umbria, the lush green heart of Italy" for its
great natural beauty with its mountains and beautiful countryside, or "Umbria, where eating is an art", for its daily devotion to the best of all that is edible.

Todi.
A typical
image of the
Tiber valley

SMALL IS BEAUTIFUL

Buried in the heart of the Apennines, Umbria follows the
rolling valleys of the Tiber, the Chiascio and the Nera and
unfolds into the 'inland sea' of lake Trasimeno. Its troubled

and ancient history is revealed in the Etruscan, Roman and medieval remains. The same is true of the harsh yet gentle landscape with its low quantity but high quality produce.

The hillsides are studded with myriad small towns, each with a bell tower that witnesses the poverty of their deeply traditional inhabitants. Each town has its church, fortifications and city gate, all redolent with history. The valleys are covered in poplars and oaks, with of course olive trees in every clearing. From Norcia to Lake Trasimeno, from Città del Castello to Orvieto, right down to Amelia and Narni, then back up North to Spoleto, Assisi and Gubbio, this difficult terrain is illuminated by remarkable vistas. And the local produce is as varied as the setting. Each area has its own specific flora and fauna, and the farmers, shepherds and goatherds use to them produce food as unique as its area of origin.

PEASANT COOKING

Umbrian traditional cuisine is dominated by olive oil, which features in everything from roast pork to the pride of the region – its luxurious truffle dishes. Local dishes are, as a result, simple and tasty. There are only a few local ways of cooking pasta, pulses, *polenta*, pork and game. The locals would have no time for soups or salads, but wherever possible preferred fuller dishes washed down with wines, which today are highly prized – the white Orvieto, the red Montefalcone Sagrantino and Torgiano Rosso wines. Umbrian

cooking is down-to-earth, putting the accent on the excellence of the raw materials, with very little over-the-top sophistication. You only need three things to make good Umbrian food: a fire or oven, local produce and plenty of time.

'TORTA AL TESTO' CAKE AND STRANGOZZI NOODLES

Torta al Testo cake is typical of the gastronomical approach of the area. Flour, water and salt (and a little lard) are its only ingredients. The dough is carefully kneaded and then cooked on a hot stone or in the corner of the fireplace. *Strangozzi* noodles are the result of making a virtue out of necessity. Made without eggs (which were expensive in times past) and roughly cut on a pastry board, these long pasta strings are ideal for soaking up a rich sauce or for enhancing the taste of mushrooms and truffles. Indeed, egg noodles were reserved for great occasions, in the same way that chicken broth or roast chicken were only produced for religious festivals and weddings, harvest, women after childbirth and convalescents. As the proverb puts it, "when the peasant eats a chicken, either the chicken's ill, or he is".

The symbol of Eurochocolate, a confectionery trade show held in Perugia

The Umbrian countryside

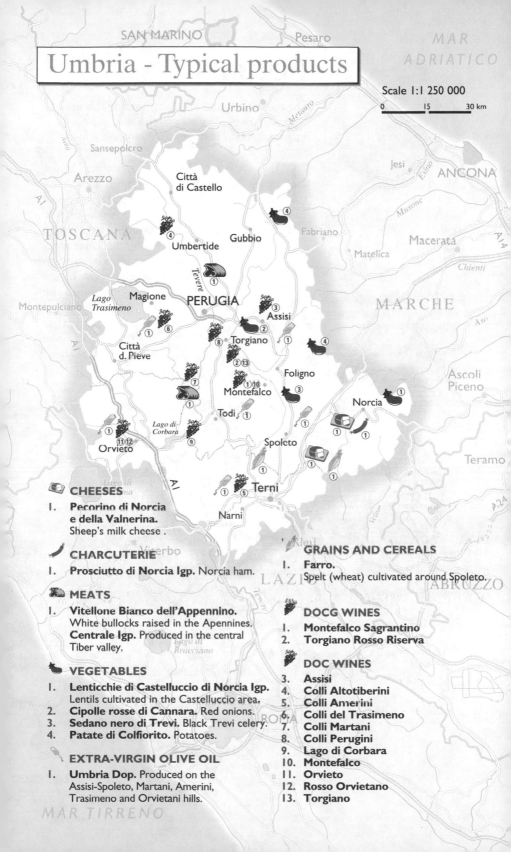

Umbria - Typical products

Scale 1:1 250 000

0   15   30 km

CHEESES

1. **Pecorino di Norcia e della Valnerina.** Sheep's milk cheese.

CHARCUTERIE

1. **Prosciutto di Norcia Igp.** Norcia ham.

MEATS

1. **Vitellone Bianco dell'Appennino. White bullocks raised in the Apennines. Centrale Igp.** Produced in the central Tiber valley.

VEGETABLES

1. **Lenticchie di Castelluccio di Norcia Igp.** Lentils cultivated in the Castelluccio area.
2. **Cipolle rosse di Cannara.** Red onions.
3. **Sedano nero di Trevi.** Black Trevi celery.
4. **Patate di Colfiorito.** Potatoes.

EXTRA-VIRGIN OLIVE OIL

1. **Umbria Dop.** Produced on the Assisi-Spoleto, Martani, Amerini, Trasimeno and Orvietani hills.

GRAINS AND CEREALS

1. **Farro.** Spelt (wheat) cultivated around Spoleto.

DOCG WINES

1. **Montefalco Sagrantino**
2. **Torgiano Rosso Riserva**

DOC WINES

3. **Assisi**
4. **Colli Altotiberini**
5. **Colli Amerini**
6. **Colli del Trasimeno**
7. **Colli Martani**
8. **Colli Perugini**
9. **Lago di Corbara**
10. **Montefalco**
11. **Orvieto**
12. **Rosso Orvietano**
13. **Torgiano**

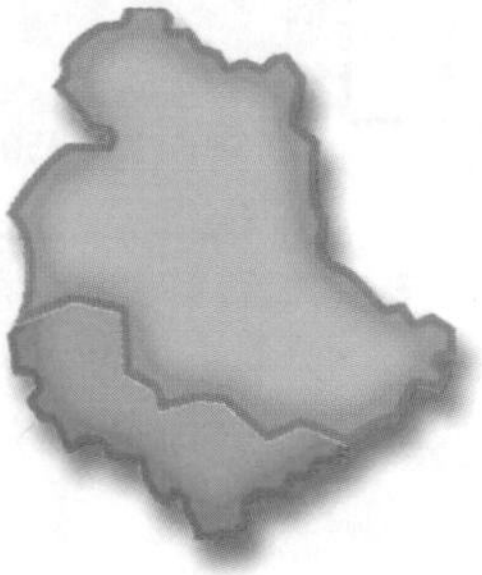

PERUGIA

The mountains and hills surrounding this major Umbrian town offer superb fish and game, mushrooms and truffles, olive oils and wines.

The province of Perugia is characterized by the spiky Appenines to the north-east and the fertile alluvial plains formed by the valleys of Spoleto and the Tiber, and the Gubbio/Gualdo and the Norcia basins, with their beautiful agricultural scenery, counterbalancing the Lake Trasimeno basin on the far north-western edge. These plains merge imperceptibly into the low hills and mountains that make up about

Opposite:
Castelluccio.
Fields of lentils

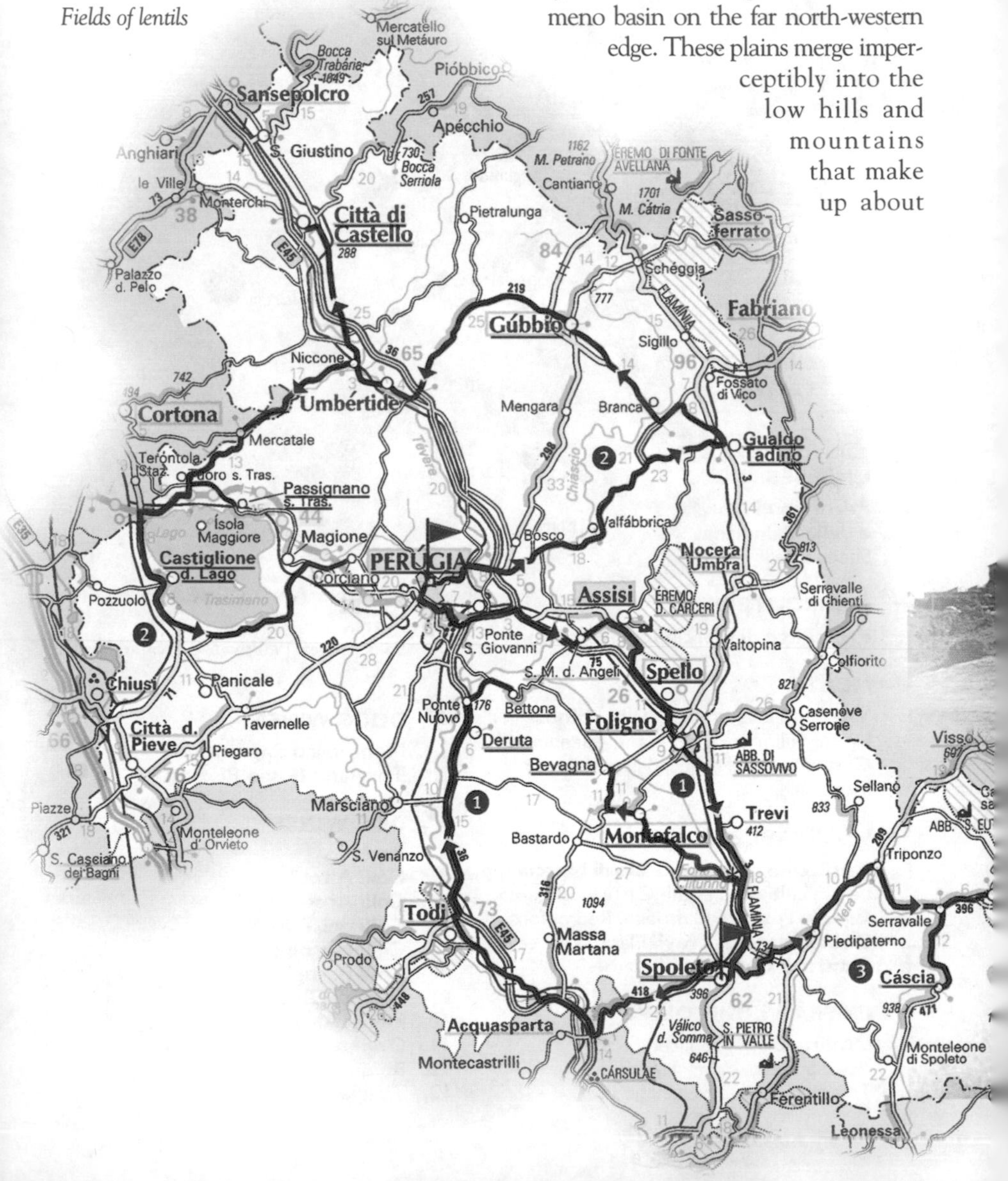

Mercatello sul Metáuro
Bocca Trabária 1049
Pióbbico
Sansepolcro
Apécchio
Anghiari
S. Giustino
Bocca Serriola
M. Petráno 1162
EREMO DI FONTE AVELLANA
le Ville
Monterchi
Cantiano
M. Cátria 1701
Pietralunga
Città di Castello 288
Sasso Ferrato
Palazzo d. Pelo
Schéggia
FLAMINIA
Niccone
Gúbbio
Sigillo
Fabriano
Cortona
Umbértide
Mengara
Branca
Fossato di Vico
Teróntola Staz.
Mercatale
Tuoro s. Tras.
Gualdo Tadino
Passignano s. Tras.
Ísola Maggiore
Magione
Bosco
Valfábbrica
Nocera Umbra
Castiglione d. Lago
Corciano
PERUGIA
Pozzuolo
Trasimeno
Assisi
EREMO D. CARCERI
Serravalle di Ghienti
Chiusi
Panicale
Ponte S. Giovanni
Valtopina
Colfiorito
Città d. Pieve
Tavernelle
Piegaro
Ponte Nuovo
Bettona
S. M. d. Angeli
Spello
Foligno
Casenóve Serrone
Visso
Piazze
Marsciano
Deruta
Bevagna
ABB. DI SASSOVIVO
Sellano
Monteleone d'Orvieto
S. Venanzo
Bastardo
Montefalco
Trevi
Triponzo
S. Casciano dei Bagni
Todi
Massa Martana
Serravalle
Piedipaterno
Prodo
Spoleto
Cáscia
Monteleone di Spoleto
Acquasparta
Válico d. Somma
S. PIETRO IN VALLE
Montecastrilli
CÁRSULAE
Ferentillo
Leonessa

80 percent of the surface area of the region.The produce of the region starts in the hills with the excellent Montefalcone Sagrantino and Torgiano Rosso Riserva wines. Next comes the olive oil, produced from ancient varieties of olive. More important are the regional herds, known especially for the meat of the Chianina breed, the charcuterie from Norcia and the cheeses particularly *pecorino*. The high plains are characterized by crops such as the famed lentil fields around Castelluccio. Gastronomically speaking, Perugia and the Valle Umbra are rightly renowned for their roast meats – pork, lamb and game – and musk of the truffle. Perugia's chocolate specialty is atypical of the region.

Gourmet Tours

PERUGIA. The slightly sloping 'theatrical' piazza is one of the most beautiful in Italy. On one side stands the Palazzo dei Priori (built 1293-1443), facing the cathedral (1345-1490). In the center lies the celebrated Fontana Maggiore fountain built by Nicola Pisano (1275-78). And where the center of power ends, the local neighborhoods begin. The Via Maestà delle Volte is lined with ancient houses and murky passageways. But once across the thresholds of the noble palazzos, the visitor stands amazed at the sight of the frescoes by Perugino on the Collegio del Cambio, the inlaid wood of the Collegio della Mercanzia and the paintings in the Galleria Nazionale. The first restaurant worth visiting is the "Locanda degli Artisti" near to the Scalette di S. Ercolano, with it simple but delicious food, such as the nettle *ravioloni* and steak with a *porcini* mushroom or truffle sauce. Another recommended eatery is the "Enoteca Giò", with its re-

HOTELS AND RESTAURANTS

Perugia
Giò Arte
e Vini ★★★ 🍴🛏
Enoteca Giò ¶¶🛏
via D'Andreotto 19
☎ 0755731100
Etruscan
Chocohotel ★★★
via C. di Marte 134
☎ 0755837314
Da Giancarlo
¶¶🛏
via dei Priori 36
☎ 0755724314
Fortebraccio¶¶🍴🛏
via Palermo 88
☎ 07534643
Grifone ¶¶🍴🛏
via Pellico 1
☎ 0755837616
Il Falchetto ¶¶
via Bartolo 20
☎ 0755731775
Dal Mi Cocco ¶
corso Garibaldi 12
☎ 0755732511
Locanda
degli Artisti ¶
via Campo Battaglia10
☎ 0755735851
Assisi
Umbra ★★★ ¶¶
via degli Archi 6
☎ 075812240
Buca di
S. Francesco ¶¶
via E. Brizi 1
☎ 075812204
Frantoio ¶¶🍴🛏
vicolo Illuminati
☎ 075812883
Medio Evo ¶¶
via Arco dei Priori 4/b
☎ 075813068
Taverna dell'Arco
- da Bino ¶¶
via S. Gregorio 8
☎ 075812383
Bevagna
Ottavius ¶
via del Gonfalone 4
☎ 0742360555
Enoteca Piazza
Onofri ¶
piazza Onofri 1
☎ 0742361920

markable wine list and local cuisine that follows the seasons. The specialty at the "Fortebraccio" restaurant is soup, notably the *imbrecciata* made from the rare *farro* flour and vegetables, but the most prized offering is the *strangozzi* with a goose sauce, a peasant dish typical of harvest time. Of the Buon Ricordo restaurants, we recommend medieval-style "Il Grifone" restaurant with its specialty of lamb with Colfiorito herbs. Another eatery providing a suitable mix of period interior and traditional gastronomy is "Il Fachetto", next to the cathedral. Two dishes not to be missed are the traditional *tagliatelle* with chicken innards and Perugia veal garnished with chicken liver paté and minced game. At "Da Giancarlo" in the main piazza, guests are treated to wonderful beef from local Chianina herds cut into steaks and cooked with rocket and balsamic vinegar. For more down-to-earth family cuisine, served in a peasant setting, the *locanda* (inn) "Dal Mi Cocco" serves a fixed price menu every night with strictly Perugia fare. For shopping, visit the "Magazzini Gio", which is as colorful as something out of Arabian Nights, and the ancient sweet and chocolate shop in the Via delle Volte, "Talmone". One last stop of note is at the "Etruscan Chocohotel", a hotel for "sweet" dreams, as the hotel slogan has it, which is also the venue for the annual Eurochocolate trade fair.

1. The Valle Umbra and the central Tiber region

ASSISI. Set in the folds of Mount Subasio, Assisi was initially Estruscan and then Roman, but is

Assisi. The Sacred Convent

best known in medieval guise for its most famous son and daughter, Saint Francis and Saint Clare. There is also the Basilica with its frescoes by Cimabue and Giotto, a high point in both an artistic and religious sense. Nor is the cuisine of the town to be ignored. There are several medieval theme restaurants, notably "Medio Evo" with its Chianina steak flavored with garden vegetables, the "Buca di San Francesco", where the Buon Ricordo dish is pigeon in the Assisi style. "Il Frantoio" is renowned for its truffles and freshwater shrimps. For mushrooms and truffles, gourmets should visit the "Taverna dell'Arco da Bino". If you want to try local dessert specialties, go for the *rocciata* (a cake made of *polenta*, chopped apples, pinenuts, hazelnuts, lemon peel and sugar) and *brustengolo* (a type of strudel made of almonds, nuts, dried fruits, apple and cinnamon) as sold at the "Sensi" pastry shop. For shopping, there are plenty of traditional local crafts to choose from, including traditional Assisi embroidery, pottery and wrought iron work. For a short visit out of town, Petrignano is worth the trip for its restaurant "Cavalieri", where they serve excellent *bottaccio* and *penchi* as well fine modern fish dishes.

SPELLO. The atmospheric Roman and Medieval town is renowned for masterpieces such as the frescoes by Pinturicchio on the walls of Santa Maria Maggiore. For those with food in mind, we recommend "Il Molino", the restaurant of the excellent Hotel "Palazzo Bocci". "La Bastiglia" is another fine hotel, both for its high quality cuisine and stupendous view. They offer jugged red onions from Cannara and an exceptional Vernaccia.

FOLIGNO. As it skirts the foothills of Mount Subasio, the Topino river bathes the outskirts of this town, which is rich in medieval history. The past is particularly in evidence every September with the Giostra Quintana (Quintana Medieval Tournament) with its chivalric jousting. During the festival, *taverne* serving medieval food open all over the town. This atmosphere can also be soaked up in the "Locanda del Cavaliere che non c'è". The specialties include potato *gnocchi* with melted cheese and a pasta sauce made of three meats, followed by chunks of steak cooked with chives and *porcini* mushrooms. "Da Remo" on the other hand offers a more familial style, with its *porcini/fagioli* bean and chickpea/chestnut soups. Don't forget to try the Sagrantino lamb and the honey and fig tartlets. At the "Villa Roncalli", experience the romantic atmosphere and the earthy cuisine.

BEVAGNA. A Roman town (then called Mevania) that hugs its central piazza, Bevagna has preserved intact its medieval surroundings with its Romanesque churches, San Silvestro and San Michele. Gastronomic recommendations include: "L'Enoteca Piazza Onofri", with its 400 – bottle wine list and powerful meat and game dishes (with comfortable rooms not far off). "Ottavius" offers fine home-made pasta first courses, notably *gnocchi* in a Sagrantino wine sauce. This should be followed by pork fillet cooked either in the rustic style or flavored with truffles. If you have time to go further, visit Cantalupo for its delicious snails.

MONTEFALCO. This is the home of the DOCG Sagrantino wine, rich in both art and atmosphere. The town is rightfully known as the 'Balcony of Umbria' because of the exceptional views that can be enjoyed from here. "Villa Pambuffetti" offers a refined version of traditional fare, including vegetable purée soup and lamb and beef cooked with truffles. One the menu at "Coccorone" are *pappardelle* noodles with a Sagrantino wine and mushroom sauce and grilled snail kebabs. Not to be missed are the two *cantina* associated with the Movimento Turismo del Vino (Wine tourism organisation), the "Rocca di Fabbri" and the "Val di Magio-Arnaldo Caprai". Visitors simply must return via the Flaminia with its views over Trevi, a place known for its celery fields. Also not to be missed are the exceedingly beautiful Fonti di Clitunno fountains, so redolent with literary memories.

SPOLETO. Small and austere on its

HOTELS AND RESTAURANTS

Foligno
Da Remo ¶
via F. Filzi 10
☎ 0742340679
Gubbio
Park Hotel ★ 🏨
ai Cappuccini ★★★
via Tifernate
☎ 0759234
Relais Ducale ★★★
via Galeotti 19
☎ 0759220157
La Fornace di ★ 🏨
Mastro Giorgio ¶¶¶
via Mastro Giorgio 2
☎ 0759221836
Taverna 🏨
del Lupo ¶¶¶
via Ansidei 6
☎ 0759274368
Villa ★ 🏨
Montegranelli ¶¶¶
at Monteluiano
☎ 0759220185
Montefalco
Villa ★ 🏨
Pambuffetti ★★★
viale della Vittoria 20
☎ 0742378823
Coccorone ¶¶
via N. Fabbri 7
☎ 0742379535
Norcia
Granaro ★ 🏨
del Monte ¶¶
via Alfieri 12
☎ 0743816513
Trattoria ★ 🏨
dal Francese ¶
via Riguardati 16
☎ 0743816290
Passignano
sul Trasimeno
La Fattoria ★★★
La Corte ¶¶
at Castel Rigone
☎ 075845322

393

CLEOS

rocky outcrop, Spoleto is renowned for its art and culture, as seen in the cathedral and its famous Festival of Two Worlds arts event, but it is also undeniably Umbria's most gastronomic town. Especially famous is its olive oil, the strong tasting Moraiolo variety. There are also some excellent meats and salamis together with the mushrooms and truffles of Monteluco. Indeed "Tartufo" (truffle) is the name of the first restaurant we recommend. Next door is the "Trattoria del Festival", housed in a sixteenth-century palazzo: here the specialties are the *strangozzi* noodles with a truffle sauce, sweet *caciottina* cheese in vol-au-vent-like pastry and pepper mousse. Shopping highlights include embroidery, leather goods and wrought iron. Visit Valnerina to taste the trout in a truffle sauce on the menu at the "Del Ponte" restaurant.

TODI. A Renaissance jewel perched on the side of a hill. 'Must sees' include the Santa Maria della Consolazione, designed by Bramante, the Piazza del Popola at the top of the town, the cathedral and the public palaces all juxtaposed to create one of the finest town views in the whole of Italy. Recommended restaurants include "Jacopone" with its specialties of *ricotta* trifle, meats and vegetables, not to mention pigeon cooked in the Todi style, and broad beans and bacon. Another tip for those interested in truffles is the restaurant "Umbria", particularly noted for its *pan nociato* dessert.

DERUTA. The locals are rightly proud of their church, San Francesco, and its frescoes, not to mention the Piazza dei Consoli. However, it has been renowned for its pottery since medieval times (most noted for the Madonna del Bagno votive offerings). Do not forget to try the suckling pig with fennel. The "Relais il Canalicchio" is a romantic hotel in a nearby neighborhood.

HOTELS AND RESTAURANTS

Petrignano
Cavalieri ♙♙
via Matteotti 47
☎ 0758030011
Scheggino
Del Ponte ♙
via del Borgo 11
☎ 074361131
Spello
Palazzo Bocci ★★★
⭐ 🔟 via Cavour 17
☎ 0742301021
Bastiglia ★★★
via dei Molini 17
☎ 0742651277
Il Molino ♙♙
piazza Matteotti 6/7
☎ 0742651305
Spoleto
⭐ 🔟 **Tartufo** ♙♙♙
piazza Garibaldi 24
☎ 074340236
⭐ 🔟 **Trattoria del Festival** ♙
via Brignone 8
☎ 0743220993
Todi
Umbria ♙♙
via S. Bonaventura13
☎ 0758942737
Jacopone ♙
piazza Jacopone 3
☎ 0758942366

Todi countryside

BETTONA. Hidden among the olive groves, the Etruscan walls enclose what is left of the medieval town. Art highlights include the church of Santa Maria Maggiore and the Pinacoteca art gallery. Here too the salamis and suckling pig are remarkable, and the olive oil is very refined, while in May the peas are particularly sweet.

TORGIANO. A small 'fine wine' town with its DOCG of the same name and the renowned *cantina* "Lungarotti". Indeed, it was this very *cantina* which furnished the Museum of Wine in Palazzo Baglioni, with its *osteria* nearby, and restored an olive press as part of an exhibition of olive oil. This *cantina* is also active on the tourist scene, offering wine tasting in its hotel restaurant "Le Tre Vaselle", beds and breakfast at its *agriturismo* establishment "Poggio alle Vigne", and selling olive oil, *grappa*, quince jam, grape juice and honey and crafts at "La Spola".

2. The high Tiber valley and Lake Trasimeno

GUALDO TADINO. Situated on the Roman Via Flaminia, Gualdo Tadino has lost much of its antique charm, but has retained its name for artistic gold and ruby pottery. The cuisine is typified by truffles, mushrooms, a very unusual type of wild asparagus used in frittata omelets and spring soups. Shopping highlights include hams and salamis. There are also some refined olive oils, notably the particularly smooth Nostrale di Rigali variety.

GUBBIO. Set at the foot of Mount Ingino, Gubbio is a center upon which history has left its mark, from the Romans right up to the Renaissance. Its steep streets are beautiful, as are the buildings that line them. In gastronomic terms, Gubbio is the truffle capital of an important truffle gathering area, Alto Chiascio. The local specialties are *risotto* with truffles and macaroni noodles with walnuts. For an overnight stay, go to the "Park Hotel ai Cappuccini" with its heavy monastic atmosphere. Eateries include the "Taverna del Lupo", famed for its generous cuisine of truffles, mushrooms and game. The Buon Ricordo dish is rabbit in the taverna-style, but this is accompanied by dishes of great sophistication, such as fanned pheasant in a juniper sauce. Also worthy of note, in terms of its *cantina*, cuisine and atmosphere, is the restaurant "Il fornace di Mastro Giorgio". In Monteluiano there is a hotel renowned for its food, namely the "Villa Montregranelli". A good souvenir from the city is Sant'Ubaldo's liquor, made from herbs picked on Mount Ingino.

Wine jug from the Wine Museum of Torgiano

HOTELS AND RESTAURANTS

Torgiano
Le Tre Vaselle ★★★ ¶¶¶
via Garibaldi 48
☎ 0759880447
Trevi
Taverna del Pescatore ¶¶
at Pigge (km 4)
via Chiesa Tonda 50
☎ 0742780920

AGRITURISMI

Perugia
Agricola Arna ★🔲
at Civitella d'Arna
☎ 075602896
Assisi
Casa Faustina ★🔲
at Mora 28
☎ 0758039377
Malvarina ★🔲
at Capodacqua
via Malvarina 32
☎ 0758064280
Bevagna
La Fonte ★🔲
at Torre del Colle
at Fiaggia
☎ 0742360968
Città di Castello
Villa Bice ★🔲
at Cerbara
Villa Zampini 43/45
☎ 0758511430
Deruta
Antica Fattoria del Colle ★🔲
strada del Colle delle Forche 6
☎ 075972201

CITTÀ DI CASTELLO. The artistic panorama spreads from the medieval cathedral and the Palazzo dei Priori to the figurative contemporary art of the Burri collection. The cuisine is centered around truffles, but the local pork is also a serious contender for top prize, especially when combined with haricot beans and broad beans. We recommend you eat at "Il Postale di Marco et Barbara", remarkable for its pleasant, unusual surroundings and cooking that is both traditional and original. Dishes to try here include the potato purée, leeks with *farro* flour and white truffles, and roast pigeon with potato cakes. Those keen on 'homey' cooking (and mushrooms) should aim for the "Bersaglio". For lodgings, go to the hotel "Tiferno" with its busy "Le Logge" restaurant. Shopping highlights include pottery and Umbrian textiles. A little outside the city, in Garavelle, there is an interesting Center for Peasant Traditions and, in San Lorenzo di Lerchi there is the unusual Museum of Tree Archeology with its 350 ancient fruit trees.

PASSIGNANO SUL TRASIMENO. Situated on the northern edge of the lake, this center of Etruscan origin has a strongly medieval look, with its intact city walls and network of small streets. Gourmets should head for "La Corte", a restaurant tacked onto the hotel "La Fattoria", where in addition to the oven-cooked pas-

Spoleto. "Hotel San Luca"

tas with various flavors they serve THE prized dish of Italian cuisine, *Medaglione all boscaiola*, a "pocket" of *provolone* cheese stuffed with *porcini* (boletus mushrooms) and garnished with asparagus. In this region famed for its olive oil, the Dolce Agogia variety is the best, and the top wine is the DOC label Colli del Trasimeno made from Umbrian and French grapes. From the village you can board a boat for Isola Maggiore, home to a small community dedicated to fishing and embroidery.

CORCIANO. On the Trasimeno Inferiore road, visit the Museo della Pesca peach museum and cross over by boat to the island of Polvese, these days an educational national park. Having reached Magione and completed the circumference of the lake, head for Corciano, a remarkable medieval open-air jewel. In Taverne, eat at the "Orchidea" restaurant and enjoy the classics of Umbrian cuisine, notably Chianina steak with rocket, roast lamb spiked with bacon and wild fennel. Don't miss the "Pieve del Vescovo" *cantina* in the picturesque town of the same name.

3. The Nera valley and the Monti Sibillini

CASCIA. The main Valnerina highway rises from Terni to the Fornaci pass in the heart of the Monti Sibillini. Following the path of the river Corno, you climb to Cascia, of Saint Rita fame. The village combines spiritual attractions with the delicious gastronomy of the Apennines with its heavy emphasis on *pecorino* sheep's milk cheese. It is also noteworthy for its meat, mushrooms and truffles, the fundamental elements of local dishes. A unique feature of the place is its almond and walnut production, which makes for interesting pastries. We recommend the restaurant "La Brace da Gualtiero", famous for its *pappardelle* noodles in the Cascia style and the lamb grilled with mountain herbs.

NORCIA. A town framed by soaring mountains and fourteenth-century city walls, Norcia is a must-see for art lovers and gourmets alike. In the heart of the town stands the church which is believed to have been built on the site of the house of the two great saints Benedict and Scolastica. A maze of streets rich in colors and tastes weaves around the church. It is hard to say whether truffles or charcuterie win the day, since both are synonymous with the name of the town. On the one hand, there is a truffle named after the town, the Tuber Melanospora, known as the Norcia truffle, and on the other certain salami are known throughout the whole of Umbria as *norcini*. But that is not all. The lower pastures produce *pecorino* and salted *ricotta* cheese, whilst the upper slopes, notably in Castelluccio, are renowned for their lentil cultivation – indeed the area has been rightly awarded the prestigious title of Indicazione Geografica Protetta. All that is best in the gastronomy of the region can be had at the "Granaro del Monte", a Buon Ricordo restaurant. Here they offer sophisticated dishes such as lentil purée with breast of pheasant, and truffle hunter's steak, a steak garnished with creamed minced beef, *caciotta* cheese and truffles (lentil tart with *ricotta* cheese is an unusual dessert served here). Another good address is the "Trattoria del Francese", where you can get *porcini* mushroom soup with truffles, sweet and sour pork filet with vinegar and cherries, baked custard with must (partially fermented grape juice) and quince.

SHOPPING

Perugia
Magazzini Giò
via R. D'Andreotto 19
☎ 0755726953
Typical products.
Talmone
via Maestà delle Volte 10
☎ 0755725744
Sweets and chocolates.
Assisi
Pasticceria Sensi
via Fontebella 20
☎ 075813689
Pastries and sweets.
Gubbio
Gastronomia Eugubina
via Porta Romana 95
☎ 0759276654
Delicatessen.
Pasticceria Le Delizie
via Fontevole
☎ 0759271329
Pastries and sweets.
Norcia
Cooperativa Lenticchia di Castelluccio
via del Lavoro 32
☎ 0743817073
Lentils from Castelluccio.
Spello
Azienda Agricola Biologica Cuore Verde
via Cavour 57
☎ 0742652346
Organic products.
Spoleto
La Terra dei Sapori
☎ 0233611691
Delicatessen, cheeses and charcuterie.
Torgiano
La Spola
via Garibaldi 46
☎ 0759880447
Olive oil, "grappa", jam, grape juice, honey.

Castiglione del Lago. A view over Lake Trasimeno

TERNI

The Tiber valley, with its varied landscapes, provides the perfect backdrop for the simple local cuisine and the excellent local oils and wines.

T he province of Terni crosses hills and valleys passing through beautiful natural features such as the lake of Piediluco, remarkable man-made sights such as the Marmore waterfall, and historical sites such as the Roman city of Carsulae, all lending excitement to the thrills of gastronomic discovery. The typical features of the countryside around Terni are the olive trees, the crops on the hillsides and the vines. It should therefore come as no surprise that the local Orvieto wine, which has for centuries graced the tables of pontiffs and governors alike, is a principal attraction.

Gourmet Tours

TERNI. Situated on the Nera river, Terni is renowned for its ancient crafts, modern look and simple but mouth-watering cuisine, notably the noodle dishes with pulses, quadrucci with a sauce and a soup- con of tomato, and ciriola noodles with their almost imperceptible sauce of oil, garlic and red chilli. Also typical of the Terni region is the roast pork, such as the *prosciutto porchettato*, suckling pig with fennel, and feathered game in the form of doves *alla leccarda*, today usually re-

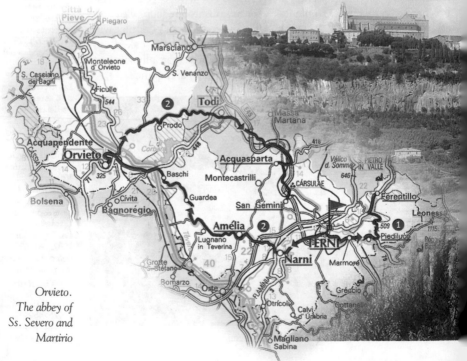

Orvieto.
The abbey of
Ss. Severo and
Martirio

placed by the more convenient guinea fowl. The standard-bearer of Norcia cuisine is the *mazzafegato*, a sausage made from liver mixed with sugar, raisins and pine nuts. Also of great renown is the trout from the Nera river and the Piediluco lake. The best-known of local desserts is *pampepato*, a sweet made from small grapes, walnuts and candied peal. One restaurant which serves all these dishes is "Lu Somaru", whose simple cuisine includes first courses such as, *tagliolini* noodles with truffle and tomato, and second courses such as the traditional 'somarello' (an envelope of filet steak filled with truffles). Shoppers should head for the first-class food and wine delicatessen "Galli", while "Massarini" is famous for its truffles and other delicacies. Visitors to Papigno should go to the "Villa Graziani" restaurant. There they will experience a eighteenth-century atmosphere with home cooking, including notably

chickpea soup and filet steak in a potato pie. Also not to be missed is "Lu Pilottu", where tradition goes hand in hand with creativity and intelligence. And however long you are staying, you simply cannot miss the Marmore falls.

1. The Valnerina

PIEDILUCO. About a dozen kilometres from Terni, Piediluco is a pleasant, lakeside town. Fishing is the main local activity, and this provides much material for the food-lover. The name, which means "at the foot of the wood", reflects the woodlands around the town and the mushrooms and game to be found in them. We recommend the family-run "Tavoletta", whose menu varies with the seasons and the markets.

FERENTILLO. Divided into two neighborhoods by the river, Ferentillo guards the entrance to the wooded Valnerina. The popular holiday resort is, however, best

HOTELS AND RESTAURANTS

Terni
Villa Graziani 𝅘𝅥𝅮𝅘𝅥𝅮𝅘𝅥𝅮
at Papigno (km 4)
Villa Valle
Papigno 11
☎ 074467138
Lu Somaru 𝅘𝅥𝅮𝅘𝅥𝅮
viale C. Battisti 106
☎ 0744300288
Lu Pilottu 𝅘𝅥𝅮
strada Grazie 5
☎ 0744274412
Acquasparta
Martini 𝅘𝅥𝅮 ⚜
via Marconi 26
☎ 0744943696
Amelia
Anita ★★★ ⚜
via Roma 31
☎ 0744982146
Il Carleni 𝅘𝅥𝅮𝅘𝅥𝅮 ⚜
via Carleni 21
☎ 0744983925
Baschi
Vissani 𝅘𝅥𝅮𝅘𝅥𝅮𝅘𝅥𝅮𝅘𝅥𝅮𝅘𝅥𝅮
at Civitella del Lago
(km 12) S.S. 448
☎ 0744950396
Ferentillo
Monterivoso ★★★
at Monterivoso
☎ 0744780772
Piermarini 𝅘𝅥𝅮𝅘𝅥𝅮 ⚜
via della Vittoria 53
☎ 0744780714
Vecchio Ponte 𝅘𝅥𝅮𝅘𝅥𝅮
via Circonvallazione 3
☎ 0744780333
Narni
Monte del Grano 𝅘𝅥𝅮𝅘𝅥𝅮
at San Vito (km 15)
☎ 0744749143
Cavallino 𝅘𝅥𝅮
via Flaminia 220
☎ 0744761020
Orvieto
I Sette Consoli 𝅘𝅥𝅮𝅘𝅥𝅮
piazza S. Angelo 1/a
☎ 0763343911
Maurizio 𝅘𝅥𝅮𝅘𝅥𝅮 ⚜
via Duomo 78
☎ 0763341114
Osteria dell'Angelo 𝅘𝅥𝅮𝅘𝅥𝅮
piazza XXIX
Marzo 8/a
☎ 0763341805

known for the Cemetery of Mummies at the Chiesa S. Stefano. On the hillside stands the remarkable monastery S. Pietro in Valle. The family-run restaurant "Piermarini" is a place of gastronomical pilgrimage for its valley specialties: trout from the Nera river, feathered game and truffles. Also worth trying are the romantic 'Vecchio Ponte", and the "Monterivoso" hotel set in an old mill.

2. The Orvieto region

NARNI. Set on a rise washed by the waters of the Nera river, Narni is a picturesque city with a medieval atmosphere and upon which every epoch has left its mark. The local wines are first rate and the local olive oil is the best in the region. The "Cavallino", previously an old hostelry, is a pleasant restaurant. In Otriocoli, the "Locanda Casole" has a fine wine cellar in its ancient

rooms. Nearby, in San Vito, you can find the restaurant "Monte del Grano", which offers sophisticated dishes such as *agnolotti* pasta (similar to *ravioli*) with borage and wild asparagus.

AMELIA. On the ridge between the Tiber and the Nera, Amelia has preserved its ancient look of a fortified city, first under the Umbrians and later under the Romans. It is renowned for its olive oil – indeed the Rajo variety is particularly notable for its fruity flavor –, its figs and its susine prunes, used frequently in local desserts. Amelia is also known for its game, and this can be enjoyed at the "Anita" restaurant, where dishes include *pappardelle* noodles with boar and dove *alla leccarda*. Also of note is "Il Carleni", with its sophisticated historical atmosphere and its "country" yet slightly French cuisine.

ORVIETO. Taking its name from the Latin words *Urbs* (city) and *Vetus* (old), Orvieto has origins which have been lost in the mists of time. It is set on an outcrop of the local volcanic rock towering

Vineyards in the Orvieto countryside

over the Paglia river valley. The most remarkable of its monuments is the legendary "Pozzo di S. Patrizio" well, which goes down 62 meters. As for the surrounding countryside, Orvieto has been not only a Città del Vino for many centuries but also a Città del Tartufo, set as it is in the center of the truffle picking regions of Monte Peglia and the Selva di Meano. The local cuisine is renowned for its *insaccati* sausages and its game cooked in a bread crust. The restaurant "I Sette Consoli" is renowned for its *lasagnotti* noodles with leeks, small onions and black truffles, not to mention the roast lamb loin cooked in a rosemary sauce with a bacon and potato pie. Also worthy of a mention is the "Osteria dell'Angelo", set within the city's medieval walls, with its inventive menu and studied wine list. As for the celebrated local white wine, "Decugnano dei Barbi" in Fossatello di Corbara offers excellent bottles of Orvieto Classico in its atmospheric underground wine cellars. Turn off the road in Baschi and head for Civitella del Lago, where the cuisine of the restaurant "Vissani" is an event in itself. Much discussed by critics, the cuisine here is loved by some and hated by others. But it is well though out and sometimes shows genius. The sampler menu is worth considering as it offers a taste of pretty much everything but at a reasonable price.

ACQUASPARTA. The splendid palace of prince Cesi housed the first deliberations of the famous Accademia dei Lincei. A stay here offers plenty of gastronomic possibilities, notably at "Martini", with the grilled meat, the specialties made with mushrooms and truffles, and the excellent wine list.

SAN GEMINI. This final stage on the road to Terni was once renowned for its mineral water. The atmospheric ruins of the Roman town of Carsulae, destroyed in the ninth century, make for an excellent visit. "Antica Carsulae" is a good restaurant with a good wine list.

WINE PRODUCERS

Ficulle
Castello della Sala - Marchesi Antinori
at Sala
☎ 076386491
Orvieto
Decugnano dei Barbi
at Fossatello
☎ 0763308255

OLIVE OIL PRODUCERS

Arrone
Bartolini
via della Grotta 16
☎ 0744389142
Stroncone
Malvetani
via S. Lorenzo 25
☎ 074460113

SHOPPING

Terni
Gastronomia Galli
via Cesare Battisti 44
☎ 0744403276
Delicatessen.
Massarini Tartufi
via Biblioteca 8
☎ 0744405286
Truffles..
Montecchio
Gastronomia Morelli Renzo
piazza Garibaldi 2
☎ 0744951204
Delicatessen.
Orvieto Scalo
La Boutique del Pane
via Paglia 20
☎ 0763300072
Bakery.

Orvieto. "Cantina Decugnano dei Barbi"

COMUNE DI AMELIA

TYPICAL WINES AND DISHES

The Amerino district is an excellent land for the cultivation of vines and olive trees. Thanks to the sunny hills rich of water and to the mild climate the production of wine and olive oil is among the best ones in central Italy. The wines of certificate quality- D.O.P. of the Amerini hills range from the traditional white , red and rosè to the delicate and superlative Malvasia and Novello. On the hill slopes a beautiful view is offered by the olive groves where is produced one of the most appreciated extravirgin olive oil since the ancient times.

Home-made dishes,tradition and old flavours are the characteristic ingredients of the local cuisine. The simplicity of the dishes prepared is based on the local agricultural products. Legume soups with ham bone are some of the best main dishes. "Fettucine"," polenta" and "strozzapreti", hand –made pasta with flour and water are also to be tasted. For centuries hunting has been a local pastime on these lands: on the tables there is a vast choice of meat ,wild boar, hare ,deer wild doves. The products made with pork meat are extremely tasty such as "mazzafegate",a kind of black pudding sausages made with pork liver and "sangui-nacci", made with pork blood and raisins. Finally typical cakes are the "Fichi Girotti",pride of Amelia, created in 1830 and well reputed everywhere: the figs are dried then stuffed with a mixture of almonds and walnuts. It is also worth remembering the "schiacciata" , a kind of focaccia bread with rosemary , onion and potatoes. Some typical recipes from Amelia: Wild doves with leccarda After preparing the wild doves or pigeons roast them slowly on the spike.The juice meat that comes out is collected in a terracotta pot and seasoned with oil , sage , salt , vinegar garlic and chopped olives.This sauce is spread on the wild doves and on the peasant bread toasts.

"Acciaccata" a kind of focaccia so called because, due to its flat shape, it allows the cooking of a lot of them in the wood burning ovens Biscotti al mosto: These are biscuits made with a mixture of flour and wine must to which is added sugar and anis seeeds :then they are shaped like small cylinders and baked. They are very tasty dipped in local wine. Among the wine producers it is worth remembering:... pasta manufacturers... honey producers... cakes producers restaurants... Hotels and restaurants Listed buildings

TRASIMENO LAKE

Comune di Castiglione del Lago

CASTIGLIONE DEL LAGO

Cittàslow

On the shores of the Trasimeno, historical sites offering art, culture, ancient traditions.

Here a good reception, a tasty cooking and a high quality life are waiting for you.

www.comune.castiglione-del-lago.pg.it
E-Mail: sviluppo.economico@libero.it

Montefalco

Montefalco, the highest hill in the area, is situated on the west side of the valley between the towns of Assisi and Spoleto. It was an important settlement during the Roman period. Several patrician villas were situated there, including the villa of Marco Curione, from which the old name of Montefalco – *Coccorone* – derives. The town's present name was given to it in 1249-1250, following the visit of the Emperor Federico II, who was a great lover of falconry.

A synthesis of the history, culture and traditions of Montefalco can be found at its **Museum of S. Francesco**. The Museum contains **frescoes by Benozzo Gozzoli showing scenes from the lives of S. Francis and S. Girolamo**, and there is also Perugino's fresco of the Nativity. Just outside the town walls, along religious itineraries combining natural beauty and Franciscan spirituality, ancient monuments such as the **Convent of S. Fortunato**, famous for its frescoes by Benozzo Gozzoli, are to be found.

Montefalco, which occupies a central position in an important wine-growing region, is an ideal destination for those interested in gastronomy, thanks to its wines and traditional local produce. **Sagrantino**, a D.O.C.G. wine made from an indigenous vine, was introduced to Montefalco by Franciscan friars returning from Asia Minor. While the *secco* (dry) version of Sagrantino is more common nowadays, it was originally made as a *dolce* (sweet) wine. In fact, Sagrantino was once produced exclusively as a *passito* wine, which was made by drying the grapes on wooden trellises. This technique was particularly suited to Sagrantino grapes, which could dry for months without rotting and could preserve their sugar content intact for a long time. It produces a wine whose colour is ruby - tending to garnet red, and it has a bouquet of blackberries and a warm, spicy flavour. Another Montefalco wine is the **Montefalco Rosso D.O.C.** It is made mainly from Sangiovese grapes, but the regulations require that these are mixed with other red-berry grapes, including Sagrantino. **Montefalco Bianco D.O.C.**, a wine made mainly from Grechetto and Trebbiano grapes, has a straw yellow colour with slightly greenish tinges, and a fresh, complex bouquet reminiscent of white flowers and fruit, apples in particular, giving it a fruity, fresh, well-balanced flavour. These wines are presented at many events such as **Terre del Sagrantino**, a market of gastronomical specialities and handcrafts from the Sagrantino area; **Open Wine Cellars**, on the last Sunday on May, when Montefalco wines can be tasted at the wineriess where they are made;

the **Settimana Enologica**, during the first half of June, which includes an exhibition of Montefalco wines, a presentation of the new Sagrantino, tasting sessions and meetings, Sagrantino cartoons and other entertainments; Goblets of Stars, on August 10th in the Town Hall Square; and the **Festa della Vendemmia** in the second half of September, which keeps the ancient custom of allegorical vineyard carts alive. Montefalco also produces the excellent **D.O.P. Umbria Colli Martani olive oil**, which is produced in old oil mills where the cold pressing technique is still used in order to guarantee the very highest quality of the product. It can be tasted at the local oil mills and during **Andar per Frantoi e Mercatini,** the market for the new olive oil held at the end of November or the start of December. Among the other local products are excellent honey, terracotta ornaments and traditional weaving.

AGRITURISMO TENUTA DI CORBARA

A vacation in the Agriturismo Tenuta di Corbara is just the occasion to discover Umbrian gastronomic tradition. We make all we offer to our hosts: meat, vegetables, extra virgin olive oil, Orvieto wine, honey, cheese, bread and pasta still hand made. Walking through ancient farms dominated bay large farmstead restructured following Umbrian peasant tradition, you'll discover our flavors and our nature. We are in Italy, near the city of Orvieto, in Umbria, an hour from Rome and Florence.

Orvieto - Terni - Umbria - Italy Tel. +39 0763.304003 Fax +39 0763.304152
Web: www.tenutadicorbara.it   e-mail: info@tenutadicorbara.it

---

From the green heart of Italy, Umbria, the great, world renowned oil from Trasimeno

Frantoio Faliero Mancianti s.n.c.
Via della Parrocchia 20
06060 S. Feliciano sul Trasimeno (PG) - Umbria
Tel. +39 075 84 76 045

Olearia Mancianti Distribuzione s.a.s.
28010 PISANO (NO) Via Duchessa di Genova 27
Tel./Fax +39 0322 58 92 01 Tel. +39 0322 58 91 70
Internet: http://www.mancianti.it - e-mail: oleman@tin.it

Hotel dei Consoli

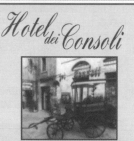

Via dei Consoli, 59 - 06024 Gubbio (PG)
Tel. +39 0759 220639 - Fax +39 0759 220639
A characteristic hotel in the historicalheart of the medieval town of Gubbio, situated under the majestic Palace of the Consuls

Agriturismo il Palazzaccio

Fraz. Montanaldo - 06024 Gubbio (PG)
Tel. +39 0759 258010 - Fax +39 0759 258062
An alternative tourism for people who desire relaxing moments among incontaminated nature

DOMINUS ***HOTEL

Via Matteotti - 06028 Sigillo (PG)
Tel. +39 0759 179074 - Fax +39 0759 178203
A marvellous hotel situated in one of the most interesting naturalistic park of the region, the regional park of Monte Cucco

Sporting Hotel ☆☆☆☆

Via Bottagnone - 06024 Gubbio (PG)
Tel. +39 0759 220753 - Fax +39 0759 220555
An elegant environment, ideal for meetings, conferences and banquets

URBANI
Ristorante IL CAMPANONE

Filosofia Ricettiva

Via Piccardi, 21 - 06024 Gubbio (PG)
Tel. +39 0759 276011 - Fax +39 0759 220555
An elegant restaurant where you can taste typical dishes of the Middle Age kitchen in an historical atmosphere

"Il Faro Rosso"
COMPLESSO TURISTICO RURALE

Fraz. Montanaldo - 06024 Gubbio (PG)
Tel. +39 0759 258010 - Fax +39 0759 258062
A tourist rural complex with swimming pool, ideal for banquets

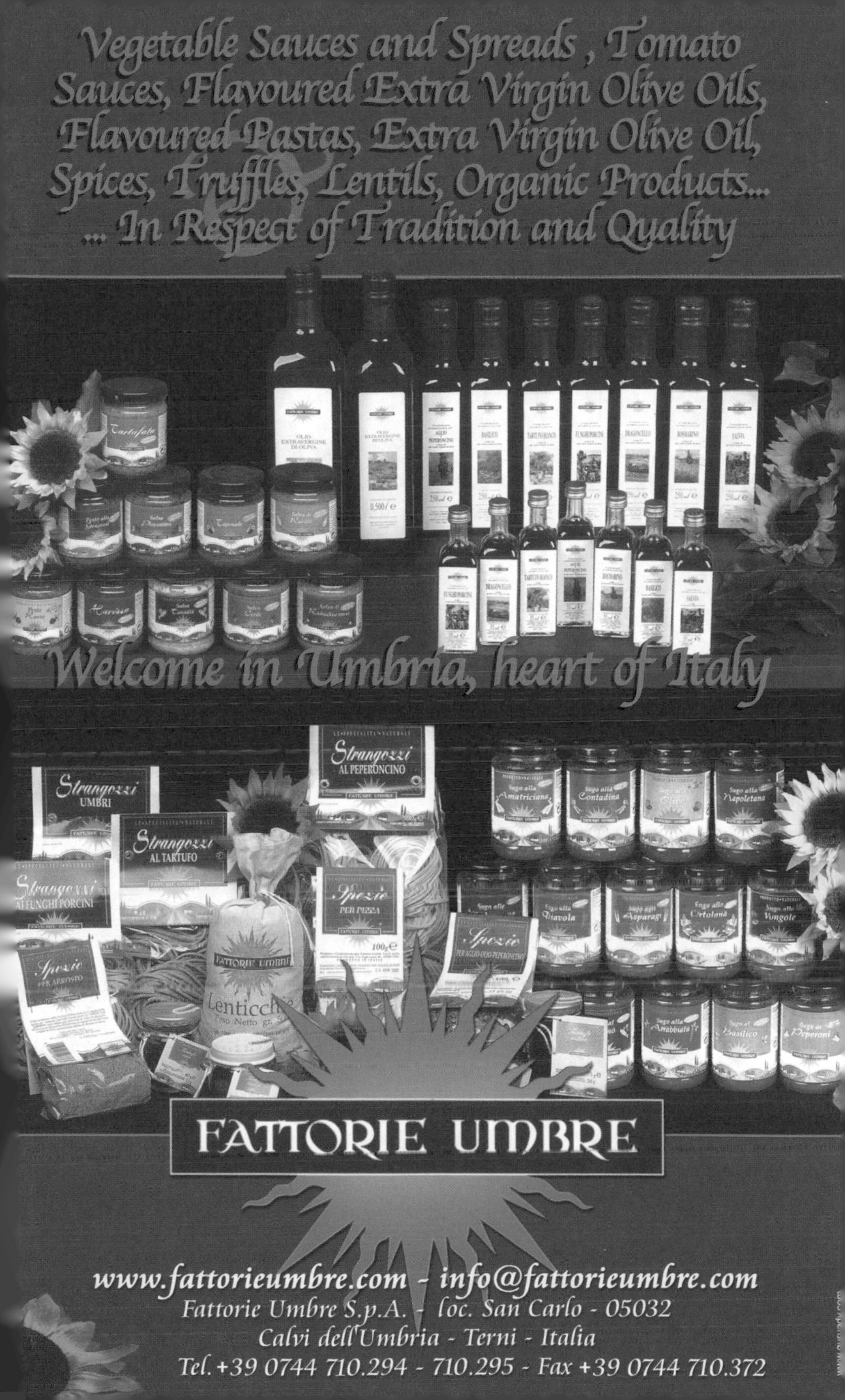

Vegetable Sauces and Spreads, Tomato Sauces, Flavoured Extra Virgin Olive Oils, Flavoured Pastas, Extra Virgin Olive Oil, Spices, Truffles, Lentils, Organic Products...
... In Respect of Tradition and Quality
Welcome in Umbria, heart of Italy
Strangozzi UMBRI
Strangozzi AL PEPERONCINO
Strangozzi AL TARTUFO
Strangozzi AI FUNGHI PORCINI
Spezie PER PIZZA
Spezie PER ARROSTO
Spezie PER AGLIO-OLIO-PEPERONCINO
Lenticchie
Sugo alla Amatriciana
Sugo alla Contadina
Sugo alla Napoletana
Sugo alla Diavola
Sugo agli Asparagi
Sugo alla Ortolana
Sugo alle Vongole
Sugo all'Arrabbiata
Sugo al Basilico
Sugo ai Peperoni
FATTORIE UMBRE
www.fattorieumbre.com - info@fattorieumbre.com
Fattorie Umbre S.p.A. - loc. San Carlo - 05032
Calvi dell'Umbria - Terni - Italia
Tel. +39 0744 710.294 - 710.295 - Fax +39 0744 710.372

ALTO CHIASCIO MOUNTAIN COMMUNITY

Communes of Costacciaro, Fossato di Vico, Gualdo Tadino,
Gubbio, Scheggia e Pascelupo, Sigillo and Valfabbrica.

06024 GUBBIO Via Matteotti, 17 - Tel. +39 075 923041 - Fax +39 075 9274720
E-mail: cmaltochiascio@libero.it

*T*he AltoChiascio: a spendid and generous nature at the foot of the Umbria Apennines, suggestive historic centre, synthesis of art, history, culture, good-quality handicraft, traditions and authentic folklore. A territory where the quality of life goes also through the pleasures of the table, where the white truffle of Gubbio makes precious a genuine and tasty gastronomy.

Gubbio *End of october - Beginning of november*
NATIONAL SHOW - MARKET OF THE WHITE TRUFFLE
and the agroindustrial products

"Il Croco di Pietro Perugino"
Saffron of Città della Pieve

Città della Pieve, fascinating town of Umbria,
at the borders with Tuscany, offers Renaissance specialities based
on saffron, a spice grown in its territory since the time
of its most illustrious son, Pietro Vannucci called "Il Perugino"
(c. 1450-1523), Raffaello's master.

Info: tel. 0578 299375 - 0578 291219
www.cittadellapieve.org - e-mail: promopieve.cittadellapieve.org

VARNELLI
THE FINISHING
TOUCH
TO ESPRESSO
COFFEE

Varnelli Distillery, since 1868 - U.T.F. licence no. 1
Tel. +39 0737 647000 - Muccia (MC) - E-mail: varnelli@varnelli.it

LAZIO THE LAND OF THE TRATTORIA

*The Lazio cuisine is strongly anchored in its peasant origins.
The same goes for Rome where, despite all its history and
the effects of tourism, the trattoria is the acknowledged
defender of traditional dishes.*

T he Roman countryside and the city's immediate surroundings
were once known for being completely untouched. Today it is
the opposite: the area is intensively farmed and full of towns.
There are five provinces in the region: Forsinone, Latina, Rieti, Viterbo and Rome, the latter representing 70% of Lazio's inhabitants. And
it is a cultural feast.

*Characteristic
countryside
in the Tiberina
Valley*

FROM THE TYRRHEANIAN SEA TO THE APENNINES

Lazio stretches inland from the Tyrrheanian coast through a variety of
landscapes: mountains, hills, plains, lakes and even an island, Ponza.
There is a strong tradition of horticulture and animal rearing (espe-

cially sheep). There are two wine-producing districts: the Castelli Romani and the Viterbese.

A WIDE CHOICE OF PEASANT DISHES

Three criteria characterize the Lazio and Roman dishes: they have few ingredients, they are simple, and they are often meager. It is a gastronomy of the common people despite the many great cooks who have come here from all over Italy. At one time, lard in particular, but also *guanciale* (pig's cheek), bacon and extra-virgin olive oil were the most commonly-used flavorings. The spices were (and still are) garlic, onion, basil, rosemary, parsley, bay leaf, marjoram, celery, sage and mint. In a land so rich, dishes remain plain; the main one being the *agnello di latte* (suckling lamb). First courses, too, are simple: *fettuccine* or *bucatini* pasta *all'amatriciana* (a sauce made with *guanciale* (cheek), olive oil and fresh tomatoes). Today, despite a greater attention to diet, the Lazio and Roman cuisines are still good and solid, e.g. the *gnocchi alla romana* (medallions of flour and potato) in a meat or tomato and basil sauce. Another top runner in the food stakes is the *carciofo* (artichoke), or *mammola*, cooked *alla giudia*, an ancient recipe from the Roman ghettos (originally a Jewish recipe whereby the artichokes are cooked twice in olive oil). Other important foods include the Romana lettuce, peppers, beans, peas and onions. The cuisine is not all vegetables, though, there is also seafood from the Lazio coastline; cheese primarily *pecorino* and *ricotta*; and the sweets, of course. Finally, the Lazio and Roman luxury food is the black truffle.

CHEESES

1. **Mozzarella di bufala campana Dop.** Buffalo milk cheese made in the provinces of Frosinone, Latina and Roma.
2. **Pecorino romano Dop.** Sheep's milk cheese produced throughout the region.
3. **Fiordilatte.** Fresh milk cheese made in the provinces of Frosinone and Latina.
4. **Ricotta romana.** Fresh cheese produced throughout Lazio.

CHARCUTERIE

1. **Coppiette.** Regional product.
2. **Mortadella di Amatrice.** Amatrice sausage.
3. **Salsiccia di Monte San Biagio.** Sausage from Monte San Biagio.

MEATS

1. **Abbacchio romano.** Suckling lamb found throughout the region.

FRUIT

1. **Kiwi del Lazio.** Kiwi.
2. **Fragole di Nemi.** Nemi strawberries.

VEGETABLES

1. **Carciofi.** Artichokes grown in the Cerveteri and Sezze areas.
2. **Lenticchie di Onano.** Lentils from Onano.
3. **Olive da tavola.** Eating olives from San Gregorio, Gaeta and Itri.

EXTRA-VIRGIN OLIVE OIL

1. **Canino Dop.** Produced in Viterbo province.
2. **Sabina Dop.** Produced in the provinces of Rieti and Rome.

VARIOUS

1. **Marroni di Vallerano.** Chestnuts from Viterbo, Antrodoco and the Tolfa Mountains.
2. **Nocciole del Lazio.** Hazelnuts from the Monti Cimini area.

BREAD AND SWEETS

1. **Pane casareccio di Genzano Igp**

DOC WINES

1. **Aleatico di Gradoli**
2. **Aprilia**
3. **Bianco Capena**
4. **Castelli Romani**
5. **Cerveteri**
6. **Cesanese del Piglio**
7. **Cesanese di Affile**
8. **Cesanese di Olevano Romano**
9. **Circeo**
10. **Colli Albani**
11. **Colli della Sabina**
12. **Colli Etruschi Viterbesi**
13. **Colli Lanuvini**
14. **Cori**
15. **Est! Est!! Est!!! di Montefiascone**
16. **Frascati**
17. **Genazzano**
18. **Marino**
19. **Montecompatri-Colonna**
20. **Orvieto**
21. **Tarquinia**
22. **Velletri**
23. **Vignanello**
24. **Zagarolo**
25. **Atina**

ROME

The capital is the Mecca for tourists and food lovers but the rest of this extensive and varied province should not be underestimated.

A common mistake of people staying in Rome is to exhaust their cultural and gastronomic curiosities within the city itself and underestimate the rest of the province. First of all, it has a long coastline with two interesting centers of seafood cuisine: Civitavecchia, bordering on Tuscany, and Anzio, bordering on Campania. Then there is the Campagna Romana running along the River Tiber, known for its beautiful countryside and its fruit and vegetables. Then there are the hills and some specific areas in between, such as the Monti della Tolfa to the north, the Sabatini around Lake Bracciano, and the Colli Albani with the Albano and Nemi lakes. The volcanic nature of the area, which favors agriculture, has also made it famous for producing wine (Frascati and Cerveteri being the most

Rome. The capital is a stage-set for popular traditional cuisine. Today, people in characteristic dress continue to enliven the piazzas of the capital, passing among the tables of cafés and trattoria for the benefit of tourists

widely-known), olive oil, fruit and vegetables. In the Apennines animal husbandry and cheese-making predominate. The cuisine is almost exactly that which is served in the most down-to-earth places in the capital: pasta flavored with vegetables or sauces made from meat or innards; suckling lamb or pig; fish from the sea or the lakes; peasant side dishes. Rome has an exceptionally high number and variety of restaurants; no less important are the more casual *trattoria* in the province.

Gourmet Tours

ROME. "If there is a city where you cannot possibly go and eat in a luxury hotel or a pretentious *trattoria*, it's Rome" says Paolo Monelli in the Ghiottone errante (The Misguided Glutton). "In Rome, you should only eat where the people eat; and if a tavern becomes fashionable, it would be better to find yourself another one. Rome, the capital of modern civilization, has the most plebeian cuisine in the world. However, this does not mean it is in-

sipid or bad. Roman cuisine is very tasty, aggressive, and varied but still rustic. And when the Rome of emperors, the Rome of Popes, the Rome of diplomats wants to eat well, it finds its recipes in the ghettos of the Jews and the alleys of the plebs." Taking up this idea, we have tried to find eating places which still have the *trattoria* atmosphere of fifty or a hundred years ago. Firstly, we recommend, for its history, the "Checchino dal 1887", which started life as a tavern for the old slaughterhouse and, as such, was the birthplace of the famous *coda alla vaccinara* (oxtail stewed with many seasonings and flavored

HOTELS AND RESTAURANTS

Rome
La Pergola ★★★
via Cadlolo 101
☎ 0635092211
La Terrazza ▯▯▯▯▯
via Ludovisi 49
☎ 06478121
Sans Souci ★▯
▯▯▯▯▯
via Sicilia 20
☎ 064821814
Alberto Ciarla ▯▯▯▯
piazza S. Cosimato 40
☎ 065818668
La Rosetta ▯▯▯▯
via della Rosetta 8
☎ 066861002
D'Inghilterra ★★★
via Bocca di Leone 14
☎ 0669981
Agata e Romeo ▯▯▯
via Carlo Alberto 45
☎ 064466115
Checchino dal 1887 ▯▯▯
v. Monte Testaccio 30
☎ 065746318
Enoteca ★▯
Capranica ▯▯▯
piazza Capranica 99/100
☎ 0669940992
Quinzi Gabrieli ▯▯▯
via delle Coppelle 5
☎ 06689389
Troiani ▯▯▯ ★▯
via dei Soldati 28
☎ 066869432
Al Bric ▯▯
via del Pellegrino 51
☎ 066879533
Al Moro ▯▯
vicolo delle Bollette 13
☎ 066783495
Antico Arco ▯▯
piazzale Aurelio 7
☎ 065815274
Asino Cotto ▯▯
via dei Vascellari 48
☎ 065898985

with sultanas, pine nuts and bitter chocolate). Today it is a Buon Ricordo restaurant and its specialty is the *abbacchio alla cacciatora* (suckling lamb cooked with garlic, rosemary, white wine, anchovies and red chili pepper). You must visit the incredible (and well-stocked) cellars dug out of the broken pieces of 86 million amphorae which made up the Monte Testaccio in Roman times. Not far away there is the "Felice" *trattoria*, which truly reflects the spirit of the common people with its honest, simple cuisine – and service – at an honest price. In places such as this, a truly Roman lunch should start with a *bruschetta* (home-made bread rubbed with garlic and spread with olive oil). When they are in season, you should try the fresh broad beans with *pecorino* cheese or salami. You then have *fettuccine* or *bucatini* pasta *all'amatriciana* (see earlier), or the more simple *spaghetti cacio e pepe* (spaghetti with cheese and pepper) or the *spaghetti alla carbonara* (spaghetti with egg, bacon and pepper sauce). Next, you eat the classic *abbacchio* (suckling lamb) served with *carciofi alla giudia* (see earlier). More eateries along traditional lines include the small and delicious "Mandragola", with two sisters who do great home-made cooking, and the "Sora Lella", in the characteristic setting of the Tiberina island, for its *rigatoni con la pajata* (rigatoni pasta with a

sauce of veal innards cut into pieces and cooked in oil, garlic, parsley, white wine, tomatoes and chili pepper), *trippa* (tripe) and *polpette* (meat balls). The latter place was named after Sora Lella Fabrizi, sister of the great Aldo; cook, actress and personality of the real Rome. In the same vein, but with a more innovative approach, there are the "Antico Arco" and the "Al Bric". More of the same but higher up the scale, there are the "Agata e Romeo" and "Troiani" which alternate peasant tradition with more inventive dishes so you get the typical *minestra di broccoli e arzilla* (broccoli and skate soup) and then the refined *spiedino di agnello* (lamb kebab with potatoes, black truffle and fried leeks). For fish cuisine (Roman style) in a city where the artless grill reigns, you should try the elegant and renowned "Quinzi Gabrieli", "La Rosetta", "Alberto Ciarla", and the less formal "Sangallo". Finally, in the realms of the great luxury restaurants, there are "La Pergola", "La Terrazza" and the "Sans Souci". The first two are in the magnificent settings of the grand hotels, the third is of a more unusual refinement. You will find that these three restaurants do feature Roman cuisine here and there but that the international taste of a cosmopolitan clientele prevails. Nonetheless, they are still worth mentioning. Getting back to a more accessible reality,

The historic "Checchino dal 1887"

there is another category of lively venues in the city, that of the *enoteche* and wine bars. These are places where a good wine is often accompanied by a taste of local delicacies and good food – Roman and otherwise – even outside the normal eating hours. The "Enoteca Capranica", the oldest *enoteca* in the capital, is in actual fact a restaurant serving all types of Mediterranean food. Places more faithful to the tavern idea include: the ancient "Trimani" with its long bar of English oak and a selection of 70 wines; the "Costantini" with over 2000 labels plus wines they produce themselves from the Castelli area; Anacleto Bleve's "Bottega del Vino" in the heart of the Ghetto; and the newer "Enoteca Ferrara" in its characteristic setting, where local dishes are also served. And last but not least, a place which contains a slice of Roman history, the "Caffè Greco" (established 1760): its famous 'Omnibus' room has seen Casanova, Goethe, Wagner, and many others, all remembered in busts and mementos. For food shopping, you really should try the Campo de' Fiori market, which is busy with stalls every morning, and has the added bonus of interesting shops all around the piazza. But best of all is the "Antica Norcineria Viola" with its amazing selection of charcuterie including *salsicce a punta di coltello* (sausages), *coralline, lonze, capicollo, pancette,* etc. etc. The smaller markets form little islands of color, like the one in Piazza delle Coppelle near the Pantheon, or the one in Piazza S. Cosimato in Trastevere. As you wander through the Ghetto, there are dozens of Jewish cakes to try. For somewhere to stay, there is one place worth recommending for its extraordinary atmosphere and memories and that is the "Albergo d'Inghilterra" (est. 1850), which started life as guest rooms for the Torlonia princes, and has been a refuge for many an unquiet spirit in the past. It is exceptional for its ancient rooms and elite service. In a city spilling over with museums, there is even one for our subject: the Museo Nazionale delle Paste Alimentari (National Museum of Pasta), set up by the Fondazione Agnesi in the fifteenth-century Scandeberg building: there are fifteen rooms covering the period from the Etruscans up to the present day, with various mementos.

1. Tivoli and the Aniene Valley

TIVOLI. Famous for its romantic associations with the Aniene waterfall, grandiose villas like the imperial Villa Adriana and the sixteenth-century Villa d'Este. The food-lover will have plenty to keep him happy with the renowned pasta all'uovo (egg pasta), the various types of meat, and wonderful ways of preparing trout. We vote for the "Adriano", set in an ancient building with a garden, where they have been cooking local food for a century: the hand-stretched house pastas include *ravioli di ricotta e spinaci alla primavera* (ravioli filled with *ricotta* cheese and spinach); main courses include the *cosciotto di abbacchio al ginepro* (leg of lamb with juniper berries). If you want to stay longer, there is the hotel "Torre Sant'Angelo" in a splendid setting with a good restaurant, the "Del Castello".

SUBIACO. A medieval village in the Simbruini mountains, it is

HOTELS AND RESTAURANTS

Civitavecchia
Scaletta ⁇
lungoporto Gramsci 65
☎ 076624334
Colonna
Osteria della
Colonna ⁇
via Casilina al km 25,5
☎ 069438816
Fiumicino
Bastianelli
al Molo ⁇⁇
via di Torre
Clementina 312
☎ 066505358
La Perla ⁇
via di Torre
Clementina 214
☎ 066505038
Frascati
Cacciani ⁇
via A. Diaz 13
☎ 069420378
Taberna
Mamilius ⁇
viale Balilla 1
☎ 069421559
Genzano di Roma
L'Infiorata ⁇
via I. Belardi 55
☎ 069399933
Grottaferrata
Park Hotel Villa
Grazioli ★★★
via Pavoni 19
☎ 06945400
Cavola d'Oro ⁇
via Anagnina 35
☎ 0694315755
Fico Vecchio ⁇
via Anagnina 257
☎ 0694315940
La Briciola ⁇
via D'Annunzio 12
☎ 069459338
Taverna dello
Spuntino ⁇
via Cicerona 22
☎ 069459366

415

home to the San Benedetto monastery and the Sacro Speco, both tourist destinations. Having met your spiritual needs, you can turn to your physical ones and enjoy good mushrooms and game, trout and suckling lamb, *caciotta* (type of cheese) and charcuterie. Famous throughout the past century, the hotel-restaurant, the "Belvedere", with its Art Nouveau rooms, will serve you *pappardelle alla lepre* (*pappardelle* pasta with hare), *filetto ai porcini* (steak with *boletus* mushrooms), and hot desserts.

2. From Cerveteri to Lake Bracciano

CERVETERI. The Etruscan necropolis of Banditaccia and the archaeological museum represent the cultural interest of this town. In the countryside, olives and vines are intensively cultivated and DOC wines are produced. You can taste and buy wine at the nearby "Cantina Sociale". The *trattoria* serve wild boar. In Ladispoli, by the sea, they have a special type of succulent artichoke without prickles. The best gastro-

nomic experience here is at the "Sora Olga" *trattoria* which serves simply but properly cooked fish. In Palo, there is the "La Posta Vecchia" country post-house of superlative quality. Further North is Santa Severa with its turreted Osdescalchi castle and the archaeological site of *Pyrgi*.

CIVITAVECCHIA. The largest seaside town in Lazio has its historical feature right in its port: the Michelangelo Fortress. The first place worthy of note is on the ramparts: the "Scaletta" is dedicated to a cuisine of the freshest fish – *tagliatelle di triglie* (*tagliatelle* pasta with mullet), *linguine alle cicale di mare* (*linguine* pasta with squilla), *fritto di paranza* (fry-up of fish caught in a *paranzella* net). For a less formal break, there is the "Vicolo di Bacco" with a wide choice of wines to go with charcuterie, cheeses and the odd hot dish. Inland in Tolfa, there is the "La Loggetta Più", a characteristic *trattoria* which offers dishes and produce from the Tolfa mountains, including charcuterie and Maremma meat.

BRACCIANO. From the walkway that runs round the top of the

HOTELS AND RESTAURANTS

Grottaferrata
La Villa di Lucullo ⁙
viale V. Veneto 93
☎ 069413778
Labico
Antonello Colonna ⁙⁙
via Roma 89
☎ 069510032
Ladispoli
La Posta Vecchia ★★★
at Palo (km 3)
☎ 069949501
★ 🚗 **Sora Olga** ⁙
via Odescalchi 99
☎ 0699222006
Lido di Ostia
Bizze del Tino ⁙
via dei Lucilii 17
☎ 065622778
Villa Irma ⁙
corso Regina M. Pia 67
☎ 065603877
Marino
G.H. Helio Cabala ★★★
via Spinabella 13/15
☎ 0693661235
Cantina Colonna ⁙
via Carissimi 22
☎ 0693660386
Monte Porzio Catone
Il Monticello ⁙
via Romolo 27
☎ 069449353
Da Franco ⁙
via Duca d. Abruzzi 19
☎ 069449205
I Titelloni ⁙
via Tinelloni 10
☎ 069447071

Bracciano. Lake fish and excellent garden vegetables star in the cuisine

Orsini-Odescalchi Castle, with its angular fifteenth-century architecture, you can see the whole lake. The water breeds pike and trout, the soft hills around give olives and vegetables. Of note is the "Vino e Camino", a pleasant *enoteca* where you can try smoked fish, goat's cheese, charcuterie, and sweets such as a cake made with ground almonds and pears, and *ricotta* and chocolate cake. Trevignano Romano is on the opposite side of the lake, framed by the Sabatini Mountains. Its oil, sausages, tomatoes and peaches are renowned. The "Archetto" restaurant serves *longarucci*, a local pasta, with fish from the lake, which can also be served as a main course, fried, grilled or *alla cacciatora* (with a sauce of rosemary, anchovies, garlic and vinegar). There is also the "Villa Valentina Giardino dell'Eden" restaurant, which serves a wide variety of food from farm, lake and sea.

3. Ostia Antica and the coast

OSTIA ANTICA. The River Tiber runs close by this medieval village gathered around the Renaissance castle of the Della Rovere family. Just a little further on is the ancient Roman port. The trip culminates in an excellent gastronomic surprise: the realization that all you have to do is reach Lido di Ostia to find some of the best places on the Lazio coast. "Villa Irma" and "Bizze del Tino" serve copious fish dishes which

will leave you feeling very satisfied. Beyond the Tiber, in Fiumicino, are two more restaurants: the "Bastianelli al Molo" and the "La Perla", both serving creative but sensible dishes. Dishes of the former include *spaghetti alla spigola* (spaghetti with sea bass) and *cernia col radicchio* (grouper with chicory); dishes of the latter include *polentina bianca con caponatina leggera di pesce* (white *polenta* with a light fish sauce with egg plant, celery, olives, capers and tomato) and *rombo in crosta ai carciofi* (turbot in a crust with artichokes).

ANZIO. The remains of Nero's villa reminds us of how long this place has been a seaside resort. Anzio is a Città del Pesce di Mare (City of Sea Fish), and offers many a gluttonous opportunity for good food. We recommend "Pierino" and "Sbarco di Anzio", simple family restaurants, sometimes over-full but always managing to be forgiven. The wine bar and *enoteca* "Franco del Gatto" is also worth a mention, and the super-busy "Nettuna". The medieval village and fort are worth a visit. The "Cacciatori" restaurant at the port has praiseworthy fish and prices, and a good selection of white wines.

ARDEA. The village, bordered on three sides by a rocky drop and on the fourth by a wall of volcanic rock, is built on the acropolis of the ancient capital of the Rutuli people. In this ancient setting, we

Marino. The grape harvest festival

HOTELS AND RESTAURANTS

Nemi
Diana Park 🏨 📺
Hotel ★★
via Nemorense 44
☎ 069364041
Nettuno
Cacciatori 🍴 🏨 📺
via Matteotti 27/29
☎ 069880330
Rocca Priora
Villa La Rocca ★★
via Castelli Romani 1
☎ 069471594
Subiaco
Belvedere 🍴
viale dei Monasteri 33
☎ 077485531
Tivoli
Torre
Sant'Angelo ★★
via Quintilio Varo
☎ 0774332533
Adriano 🍴 🏨 📺
via Villa Adriana 194
☎ 0774382235
Tolfa
La Loggetta Più 🍴
via U. Fondi
☎ 076693443
Trevignano
Romano
Villa Valentina 🍴
Giardino dell'Eden
via Settevene
☎ 069997647
Archetto 🍴
piazza V. Emanuele
☎ 069999580
Velletri
Benito al Bosco 🍴
via di Morice 20
☎ 069633991
Benito 🍴
via Lata 241
☎ 069632220

find the modern sculpture collection of Giacomo Manzù, and some of his S. Pietro church decorations. Return to Rome via Pomezia, near to which you will find the archaeological site of *Lavinum*, then coast the hunting estate of Castel Porziano.

4. The Albani Hills and the Castelli

CASTEL GANDOLFO. Amongst the Castelli, this is the one chosen by the Popes for their vacations. From the piazza, dominated by the papal palace, you can see Lake Albano. The "Antico Ristorante Pagnanelli" serves a good and varied cuisine of fish and meat. There are characteristic cellars carved out of the rock and the view is splendid. The area is famous for its peaches.

ALBANO LAZIALE. The Albani are the volcanic hills, of an intense green, on which the town is situated. Albano is the lake which opens out in front of the town. Both are the favorite destinations of those escaping the city. The town itself holds Roman and medieval remains. The "Antica Abbazia" is a very characteristic restaurant with tables arranged around the monastery's well. They serve *orecchiette ai ramolacci* (*orecchiette* pasta with a tasty local chicory) followed by classic meat dishes, *abbacchio* (suckling lamb) and *porchetta* (stuffed roast suckling pig), or the singular *grigliata di mozzarella affumicata ai carciofi* (grilled smoked *mozzarella* cheese with artichokes).

ARICCIA. On the Via Appia, on a rocky outcrop between two wooded valleys, and glowing with the sumptuous architecture of Bernini. For a break, there is the "Villa Aricia" with an outdoor

Porchetta, *or Ariccia specialty*

restaurant in the centuries-old park.

GENZANO DI ROMA. On the outer slope of the Lake Nemi crater, this is an active flower-growing town, famed for its picturesque Infiorata festival in the Spring. "Infiorata" is also the name of a *osteria* (tavern) serving very good local food, especially the grilled meats and mushrooms. They also serve asparagus dishes when in season. The landscape is beautiful, leading to Lanuvio, a partly-walled town with fourteenth-century tower.

VELLETRI. This little town, with its winding streets, perches on a rocky spur amongst the vines and olive trees on the southern side of the Albani hills. We recommend a stop at the "Benito al Bosco", with its wide-ranging cuisine covering land and sea food: *risotto alla provola* (*risotto* with *provola* – buffalo-milk cheese); *linguine con gamberi, pomodori e basilico* (*linguine* pasta with crayfish, tomato and basil); *starne alle erbe aromatiche* (partridge with aromatic herbs); and *spigola al cartoccio con porcini* (sea bass baked in foil with *porcini* mushrooms). One of the traditional dishes served is the *carciofi alla matticella cotti sulla brace di sarmenti di vite* (artichokes roasted on a fire made from the vine runners).

NEMI. For historical interest, there

AGRITURISMI

Cerveteri
Da Paolo
at Gricciano Quota 177
☎ 069941358
Genzano di Roma
Tre Palme
at Landi
I strada Muti 73
☎ 069370286
Velletri
Iacchelli
via dei Laghi al km 15
☎ 069633256

WINE PRODUCERS

Ariccia
Cantina Sociale
Colli Albani
at Fontana di Papa
via Nettunense km 10,8
☎ 069340071
Cerveteri
Cantina Coop.
Sociale
via Aurelia, km 42,7
☎ 069902407
Colonna
Principe Pallavicini
via Casilina, km 15
☎ 069438816
Frascati
Cantina Camilli
viale Balilla 1
☎ 069421559
Conte Zandotti
Tenimento S. Paolo
via Vigne Colle Mattia 8
☎ 0620609000
Casale Marchese
via di Vermicino 34
☎ 069408932
Casale Vallechiesa
via Prataporci 23
☎ 0695460086
Grottaferrata
Castel De Paolis
via Val De Paolis
☎ 069413648

is the Museum of Roman Ships dedicated to the worship of Diana, guardian of the lake. The high planes of Pratoni are very characteristic and renowned for their strawberries, apples and peaches. Note the "Diana Park Hotel" with its restaurant, the "Il Castagnone". ROCCA DI PAPA. On the northern side of Mount Cavo, there are villas, pleadant walks and restaurants where, thanks to an abundance of mushrooms, there is good cuisine to be found. The very old upper part of town is called the *quartiere dei Bavaresi* (Bavarian quarter) because a colony of German soldiers were said to have inhabited it. MARINO. The village is situated on a spur of light sandy volcanic rock and surrounded by the vines of the famous white wines of the area. There are two very different restaurants to note: the refined "Il Platina", part of the "Grand Hotel Helio Cabala", and the "Cantina Colonna" for an excellent *carbonara fumata col vino* (pasta with a sauce made from eggs, cheese and bacon, all smoked with wine), or the *fettuccine tirate in casa con le rigaglie di pollo* (home-made *fettuccine* pasta with chicken giblets).

GROTTAFERRATA. The name comes from the abbey founded by San Nilo in 1004, then given protecting walls and towers in the Renaissance period. There are good gastronomic experiences to be had at: the "Taverna dello Spuntino" with its tasty dishes from the Campagna Romana area, including handmade *fettuccine* and mushrooms; the "La Briciola" with its sensitively re-worked traditional dishes, its honest and carefully prepared food, and the excellent Velletri vegetables; the "La Villa di Lucullo", a small and pleasant townhouse with tables outside in the summer; the "Cavola d'Oro", a Castelli restaurant serving the classics; and the "Il Fico Vecchio" in the unusual setting of a Roman aqueduct. At the "Castel De Paolis" *cantina* (wine producers and sellers), you can taste the DOC 'Frascati' wines and the most recently produced table wines. The land is renowned for its olive oil. FRASCATI. Frascati is situated on the outside edge of the Albani hills, along the Appia Antica, the 'queen of roads', today an exceptional archaeological route. It has long been a pleasure-store and this is reflected in its sumptuous six-

WINE PRODUCERS

Marino
Azienda Vitivinicola Paola Di Mauro
at Frattocchie
via Colle Picchione 46
☎ 0693548440
Montecompatri
Tenuta Le Quinte
via delle Marmorelle 91
☎ 069438778
Velletri
Cons. Produttori Vini di Velletri
viale Oberdan 113
☎ 069625305

SHOPPING

Rome
Antico Caffè Greco
via Condotti 86
☎ 066791700
Historic cafe.
Antica Norcineria Viola B. & F.llo
Campo de' Fiori 43
☎ 0668806114
Typical charcuterie.
Bottega del Vino di Anacleto Bleve
via S. Maria
del Pianto 9/11
☎ 066865970
Wines.
Enoteca Costantini
piazza Cavour 16
☎ 063203575
Wines.
Enoteca Ferrara
via del Moro 1/a
☎ 065803769
Wines.
Enoteca Trimani
via Goito 20
☎ 064469661
Wines.
Gelateria San Crispino
via della Panetteria 42
☎ 066793924
Ice-creams.
Tazza d'Oro - La Casa del Caffè
via degli Orfani 84
☎ 066789792
Good selection of coffee varieties.
Albano Laziale
Macelleria Tavoloni
piazza Gramsci 9
☎ 069323815
Charcuterie and meat.

Frascati. The osteria at the Castelli Romani

SHOPPING

Anzio
Enoteca Franco
del Gatto
via XX Settembre 21
☎ 069846269
*Wines and typical
Italian products.*
Bracciano
Vino e Camino
via delle Cantine 11
☎ 0699803433
*Wines, cheeses,
charcuterie and sweets.*
Castel Gandolfo
Norcineria Ciociara
di Armando Mancini
at Villetta
via Appia Nuova 28
☎ 069325513
Typical charcuterie.
Civitavecchia
Al Vicolo di Bacco
piazza Fratti 10
☎ 076623260
*Wines, cheeses and
charcuterie.*
Frascati
Enoteca Frascati
via A. Diaz 42
☎ 069417449
*Wines and savoury
cookies.*
Genzano di Roma
Forno a legna
Ripanucci
corso Don Minzoni 29
☎ 069362033
Bakery.
Grottaferrata
Panificio Cerquozzi
via del Pratone 88
☎ 069410136
Bakery.
Marino
Umberto Zoffoli
via Roma 53
☎ 069387055
Regional specialties.
Velletri
Salumeria Pietro
Marinelli
viale Oberdan 26
☎ 069627287
Charcuterie.

teenth- and seventeenth-century villas with parks, centuries-old holm oaks, and fountains. All around, in Malvasia, Trebbiano and Greco, are over 1,000 hectares of vines, producing the grapes for the famous white wines of the area. There are many olive trees, too. To eat well, we recommend you try the "Cacciani" with its rich and varied cuisine and laudable home-made bread and cakes. You will find a family welcome and excellent wines at the picturesque "Taberna Mamilius" near the ancient "Camilli" *cantina*. Other cantinas, members of the "Movimento Turismo del Vino", are to be found in the area.

MONTE PORZIO CATONE. The panoramic road which rises on the northern side of the Colli goes through Monte Porzio Catone (known for its apricots, fish and olive oil), Montecompatri (known for its olive oil and mushrooms) and Rocca Priora, the highest of the Castelli (known for its *pecorino* cheese). The first of the restaurants has the good old name of "Da Franco". Dishes include *rigatoni al sugo di coda* (*rigatoni* pasta with ox-tail sauce), *abbacchio a scottadito* (just-roasted suckling pig), and the most delicate steak with *porcini* mushroom sauce. Alongside this restaurant, you will find "I Titelloni" and "Il Monticello" with

their home-made pastas, meats and mushrooms. The wine-tourist will find some exceptional places in Montecompatri: there is a seventeenth-century farm built on Roman ruins. Nearby Colonna merits two entries, one for the wine company "Principe Pallavicini", situated in an old post-house, and the other for the adjoining "Osteria della Colonna", frequented by illustrious travelers of the past, where you can taste the house Frascati Superiore and other wines, even some made from new strains of grape.

PALESTRINA. You are invited to lengthen your trip beyond the Casilina by what looks like a medieval site but which is actually dominated by Roman remains of the Fortuna Primigenia sanctuary, and the Baroque Barberini palace. You can also find an exceptional gastronomic excuse for a trip in the "Antonello Colonna" restaurant in Labico, with its elegant room and one of the best chefs in the region. Dishes include: *lardo con verza* (bacon with Savoy cabbage), *sformato di ricotta* (*ricotta* cheese soufflé), *capretto* (kid goat), various *pecorino* cheeses, good desserts and a wide choice of wines. In the *trattorie* the top dish is the *fettuccine con sugo di carne e rigaglie* (*fettuccine* pasta with meat and giblet sauce).

FROSINONE

A landlocked province, faithful to its farming and pastoral origins, whose flavors come from the vegetable garden, the meadow and the wood.

We are in the Ciociaria region, characterize agriculture and sheep-rearing. But that does are not good meats, charcuterie and a wide variety of dairy products. The cuisine does not vary greatly from the Roman one. Amongst the first courses, we can name the *maccheroni alla ciociara*, egg pasta with a meat and tomato sauce, and the *acqua cotta*, a vegetable soup with slices of bread. The local sweets and desserts are the *ciambelle* (circular cake with a hole in the center, made with flour sugar and egg), pizzas, and egg *frappe* and *pigne* (varieties of big *ciambelle*). Straddling the border with Rome is the vast wine-producing area of the DOC Cesanese del Piglio.

Piglio. The wine-producing center, known for the red Cesanese, set among the Ernici hills

HOTELS AND RESTAURANTS

Frosinone
Enoteca Pane e Vino ❜
via Tiburtina 11
☎ 0775872070
La Stella ❜
via Garibaldi 89
☎ 0775250085
Acuto
Colline Ciociare ❜❜❜
via Prenestina 27
☎ 077556049
Alatri
Rosetta ❜
via Duomo 35
☎ 0775434568
Anagni
La Floridiana ★★★
via Casilina al km 63,7
☎ 0775769960
❜❜ **Della Fontana** ❜
at Osteria della Fontana
via Casilina 23
☎ 0775768577
Lo Schiaffo ❜
via V. Emanuele 270
☎ 0775739148
Cassino
Forum Palace ★★★
v. Casilina N. km136,5
☎ 0776301211
❜❜ **Da Mario** ❜❜
via Di Biasio 53
☎ 077622558
La Colombaia ❜
via Di Biasio 200
☎ 0776300892
Ferentino
Bassetto ★★★ ❜❜
via Casilina al km 74,6
☎ 0775244931
Fiuggi
G.H. Palazzo della Fonte ★★★
via dei Villini 7
☎ 07755081
La Torre al Centro Storico ❜❜
at Fiuggi Città (km 4)
piazza Trento e Trieste 18
☎ 0775515382

Gourmet Tours

FROSINONE. There is an old part of this administrative center of Ciociaria up on the hill overlooking the Sacco plain. They have a fairly rich culinary tradition, including dishes like *timballo alla Boniface VIII* (*maccheronicini* pasta with chicken giblets, meat sauce, meat balls, mushrooms and truffles); *gnocchi* with *polenta*; *spiedini arrostiti* (roasts on spits); barbecued meats; and the sweet specialty, *ciambella cresciuta* (giant ciambella). The first restaurant to note in the area is "La Stella", which serves the classic dishes as well as some new ones. The *enoteche*, which also serve food, include the "Enoteca Pane e Vino" and the "Bar Enoteca Celani", the latter also offering local specialties. If you want to buy olive oil, we recommend the "Consorzio Provinciale Olivicoltori", which produces the Rosciola di Paliano, 80% of which is made from the olive of that name.

1. In the heart of Ciociaria

FERENTINO. Roman remains and Roman and Gothic monuments blend into the town plan created by the ancient Ernici people, which remains to this day. Do not miss the acropolis at the top of the hill, the Romanesque Duomo (cathedral) from the twelfth century, and the Gothic Cistercian church of S. Maria Maggiore. The local gastronomic specialties can be summed up in four foods: garlic, onion, and Porciano Pecorino cheese in both its young and matured forms. You can buy wine at both the "Mastrosanti" and "Pio Roffi Isabelli" *enoteche*. The hotel and restaurant "Bassetto" serves typical Ciociaria dishes, including *maiale al rosmarino* (pork with rosemary), *agnello pilottato* (lamb cooked on the spit), and truffles.

ANAGNI. The town has gone down in history as the place where Sciarra Colonna slapped Pope Bonifacio VIII during a long dispute following Bonifacio's insistence that he was superior to temporal rulers. It occupies a spur overlooking the Sacco valley. There is a very medieval feel to the place. Things to see include the famous Palace of Bonifacio VIII (where the slap was given) and the beautiful Romanesque cathedral. Good addresses include the "Villa La Floridiana" restaurants for fish and meat dishes, "Lo Schiaffo" for modern local cuisine and great choice of cheeses and, at the "Osteria della Fontana", the "Della Fontana" restaurant serving good local cuisine. Try red and white Romagnano wines and the Torre Ercolana.

FIUGGI. This well-known spa town on the heights of Mount Ernici is surrounded by woods. The first place to mention is the "La Torre al Centro Storico", characteristic for many reasons and possessing an excellent wine cellar and a memorable menu. Next is the renowned "G.H.Palazzo della Fonte". For wines, there are the "Enoteca Doc" and the "Bagatto", and "Sarandrea" in Fiuggi Fonte.

ALATRI. This ancient little town is situated on a hill of olive trees. It still has its Duomo in the square at the top of the acropolis, and two kilometers of city walls intact. If you want good honest food, go to the "Rosetta" *trattoria* (it is also a hotel), which serves local cuisine as well as a variety of pizzas. Do not miss the classic *fini fini con ragù alla ciociara* (*fini fini*

Isola del Liri. The celebrated waterfall, with the garden of Castello Boncompagni

pasta with Ciociaria sauce), the *fettuccine ai porcini* (*fettuccine* pasta with *porcini* mushrooms), the *abbacchio*, and the home-made sweets. For your shopping, try: the "Latteria Pomella" with an interesting production of cheeses: *mascarpone* and *bocconcini di latte vaccino*, *mozzarella di bufala*, *caciocavallo*, *ricotta*, and many other treats; and "Maria Letizia Roccasecca" in Fiura, for their home-made breads, pizza-bread, *ciambelle*, *crostate* (tarts), and the celebrated *amaretti di Guarcino*. In Mole Bisleti they have the "Fratelli Stirpe" butchers, the kings of all kinds of pork produce.

2. The River Liri and the abbeys
VEROLI. This medieval village is on a rise to the south of the Ernici mountains. The area's specialties are extra virgin olive oil, strawberries, *ricotta* cheese, *pecorino* cheese, sausages, mountain ham, and pastry and *ricotta* cheese balls. You can buy some of these things at "Sanità", a shop that also sells home-made bread baked in a wood oven, *pane di segale* (rye bread), *pane integrale* (wholemeal bread), and the traditional and much sought-after Ciociaria sweets: the *ciambella*, the

classic *pigna di Pasqua*, *amaretti* and *zuccherini al vino*. On the road to Isola del Liri, stands the solitary Benedictine abbey of Casamari with a church, cloisters and capitular room built in the Cistercian-Gothic style.
ISOLA DEL LIRI. The River Liri splits into two here and forms the Valcatoio and Grande falls. Along the road to Sora there is the "Il Negozietto" food shop which sells a good selection of local produce. It is worth eating at the "Ratafià".
SORA. Set on the edge of an intensively-cultivated crescent in the valley of the River Liri, the town boasts good black truffles, onions, cherries, trout, freshwater crayfish, *ciambelle* and sambuca.
ARPINO. Caio Mario and Cicero were born around this ancient land. It is a famous center for *pecorino* cheese and sausages.
CASSINO. This little town is at the foot of the famous abbey of Montecassino. The local cuisine is characterized by a strong Neapolitan influence. Local specialties are numerous and include Atina beans, Vallerotonda lentils, peas, trout and lamb. Stay at the "Forum Palace" and eat at "Da Mario" or "La Colombaia".

HOTELS AND RESTAURANTS

Isola del Liri
Ratafià ❘
vicolo Calderoni 8
☎ 0776808033

AGRITURISMI

Ferentino
Punto Verde ★
via Casilina al km 76,4
☎ 0775396596

OLIVE OIL PRODUCERS

Frosinone
Consorzio Provinciale Olivicoltori
via Brighindi 45
☎ 0775251681

SHOPPING

Alatri
Latteria Pomella
strada Statale 155
☎ 0775408363
Cheeses.
M.L. Roccasecca
at Fiura
via Capranica 20
☎ 0775442883
Bread and pizza-bread.
Macelleria Stirpe
via Mole Bisleti
☎ 0775409349
Pork.
Ferentino
Enoteca Mastrosanti
via Casilina 108
☎ 0775397721
Wines.
Enoteca P. Roffi Isabelli
piazza Matteotti 19
☎ 0775245737
Wines
Fiuggi
Enoteca Doc
via Casavetere 29/31
☎ 0775504312
Wines
Isola del Liri
Il Negozietto
corso Roma 67
☎ 0776806969
Local products.
Veroli
Sanità
via Colle del Bagno 71
☎ 0775238362
Home-made bread.

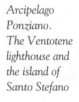

LATINA

*The seafood cuisine of Circeo and Gaeta,
and the farmhouse flavors of Agro Pontino
and the mountains leading up to Campania.*

T he province occupies a large part of the Agro
Pontino, a flat, marshy plain which was reclaimed between 1926 and 1935 by the Opera
Nazionale Combattenti, which employed over 13,000 workers to create
a triple system of drainage canals, and a network of roads and towns.
The area was then populated by people from the north, especially from
Venezia Giulia and Istria, so there are no particular local gastronomic
traditions, but the district is intensively cultivated. The cuisine of the
province is characterized by good quality local produce like the *mozzarella di bufala* in the Formia and Gaeta areas, and also *provola affumicata, caciocavallo* and *provolone* cheeses. Along the coast towards
Circeo, the sea has a good harvest of mullet, small cod, sea bass and
crayfish. In Gaeta, apart from the renowned olives, there is the traditional '*tiella*' – two disks of pasta cooked in the oven and stuffed with
young squid, garlic, olives, raisins, pine nuts, capers and, sometimes, also cheese, ham and eggs. Do not forget to visit Ponza Island whose culinary tradition featuring sea food and Ponza tomatoes. Finally, the land
is also interesting from the wine producing point of view, the most important being the Aprilia and white Cori DOC wines.

*Arcipelago
Ponziano.
The Ventotene
lighthouse and
the island of
Santo Stefano*

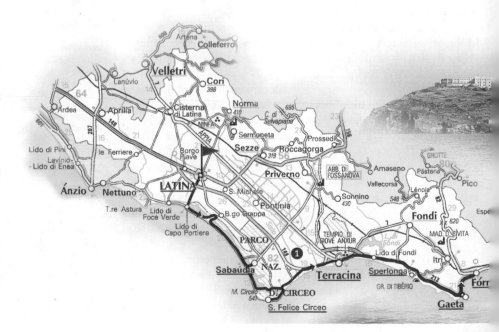

Gourmet Tours

LATINA. This is quite a new town which developed in 1932 as administrative center of the Pontino plain. For restaurants, you have the "Abaco" in the "Victoria Residence Palace Hotel" where they serve excellent first courses; there is also the "Assunta" restaurant, *enoteca*, food shop and bar. The shop has a good selection of cheeses from the Luca, Venice and Langhe areas, a wide choice of extra virgin olive oils and over 100 grappas. Do not miss the "Sezzi" *enoteca*.

1. From Circeo to Gaeta

SABAUDIA. Situated on the edge of Lake Sabaudia, this is a classic urban example of rationalism. Behind it lies the Parco Nazionale del Circeo. You can buy savory tarts, sausages, and *torta della nonna* in the "Danti" foodshop.

SAN FELICE CIRCEO. The town is in a panoramic setting on the slopes of the Circeo headland. It has an elegant beach, lots of grottos and beautiful views. All these elements unite to make the town quite unique. The cuisine is of sea food and rich pizzas which you can eat at the "Il Grottino" *trattoria*. For a more refined meal, there is the "Punta Rossa" restaurant belonging to the hotel of the same name, serving *tagliolini Punta Rossa* (*tagliolini* pasta with shellfish).

TERRACINA. This medieval village is situated on the site of a Roman forum with the remains of the Temple of Giove Anxur (Jupitur Anxur) at the top of Mount Sant'Angelo. For eating, there is the "Bottega Sarra 1932" in the historical center serving both seafood – *trenette con la bottarga* (*trenette* pasta with mullet roe) – and food from the land – *capra in umido* (stewed goat) and *polenta con le spuntature* (*polenta* with beef or pork from the rib ends). Then there is the

HOTELS AND RESTAURANTS

Latina
Victoria Residence Palace Hotel ★★★★
Abaco ¶¶ 🛏🚗
via Rossetti 24
☎ 0773663966
☎ 0773661923
Assunta ¶
via Pontina at km 74,5
☎ 0773241940
Aprilia
Focarile ¶¶¶
via Pontina at km 46,5
☎ 069280392
Fondi
Vicolo di Mblò ¶¶
corso Italia 126
☎ 0771502385
Formia
Chinappi ¶¶
via Anfiteatro 8
☎ 077179002
Sirio ¶¶
via Unità d'Italia
☎ 0771790047
Gaeta
Antico Vico ¶¶ 🛏🚗
vico del Cavallo 2/4
☎ 0771465116
Masaniello ¶
piazza Commestibili 6
☎ 0771462296
Itri
Grottone ¶
corso V. Emanuele II 2
☎ 0771727014
Ponza
Acqua Pazza ¶¶
☎ 077180643
Orèstorante ¶¶
via Dietro la Chiesa 3/4
☎ 077180338
**Lanterna -
da Silverio** ¶
corso Pisacane
San Felice Circeo
Punta Rossa 🛏🚗
★★★, at Quarto Caldo
via delle Batterie 37
☎ 0773548085
Il Grottino ¶¶
piazza V. Veneto 6
☎ 0773548446

"Geranio" which only serves fish which "have not been farmed". SPERLONGA. White medieval houses are piled on the headland. This is a fishing village which is particularly lively in the summer. For a delicious restorative break, there is the "Gli Archi" and the "Il Laocoonte", the former with its tables arranged along the steps and the latter on the sea front. For the sweet-toothed, there is the cake shop, "Dolce e Gelato" which sells Neapolitan desserts.
GAETA. In between Gaeta and Tore Capovento, there is the Tiverius Grotto where he may have once lived. The ancient part of the village, with its very strong Mediterranean feel, is situated on a small peninsula. Walking through the streets of Gaeta, it is easy to get an idea of how important it was as a port and stronghold. The rich local gastronomy includes olives, tomatoes, artichokes, fennel, melon, sole and crayfish. For a meal there is the "Antico Vico" and the "Masaniello", both of which offer fish dishes which change with the season and availability at market.
FORMIA. The town of lemons and mandarins still has two medieval quarters, Mola and Castellone, and many Roman remains. For wine and food shopping, there is the "La Botte" *enoteca*, and the "Alessandro Recco e C." food store with a wide choice of local produce, such as the *formaggio monaco dei monti Lattari* cheese and the *pecorino romano* cheese. The restaurants "Chinappi" and "Sirio" are both worth a mention. The

first serves rich fish dishes: starters with *ricci di mare* (sea urchins), and *frittelle di bianchetti e gamberetti del golfo di Gaeta* (griddlecakes with whitebait and shrimp from the Gaeta Gulf). The second has more land-based dishes, though there are some fish dishes, too: tasty *insaccati* (sausages), game, and *fiorentine di carne chianina* (grilled top quality beef-steak from Val di Chiana). It is worth making a detour north to Itri, where you can buy kid goat, suckling lamb, free-range chicken, sausages and salamis at "Da Scherzerino". The "Grottone" restaurant serves typical Lazio dishes. A little further on, in Fondi, you will find one of the most important fruit and vegetable markets in the southern-central region of Italy. Restaurants include "Da Cima" with its farmhouse foods made from local produce, and the "Vicolo di Mblò" where you can eat *pisellini freschi con cipollotti* (fresh peas with onions), *baccalà con peperoni secchi* (baccala with dried peppers), *rombo al forno* (baked turbot) and *pastiera* (tart made with short pastry, filled with *ricotta* cheese, ground maize and candied peel).

2. Ponza Island

PONZA. This is the biggest island in the Ponza archipelago which is made up of two groups of volcanic islands (Ponza, Gavi, Zannone and Palmarola to the West, and Ventotene and Santo Stefano to the East). For a seafood restaurant, go to "Acqua Pazza" with its specialties of *linguine alla ricciola* (linguine pasta with sea-urchins).

RIETI

*Spaghetti all'amatriciana (spaghetti with a sauce
made from guanciale (cheek), olive oil and fresh
tomatoes) symbolise this cuisine*

I n the province of Rieti, synonymous with the
historic Sabina area (now north-west Lazio), pig
and cattle-rearing prevails, so you get excellent charcuterie (especially the Leonessa and di Amatrice labels),
pork *mortadella*, and the Rieti dried sausage. The town's
history and Umbrian traditions are even reflected
in its cuisine, though some of the local
dishes have been assimilated from the
Lazio cuisine, e.g. the *bucatini all'a-
matriciana* (*bucatini* pasta with a
sauce made from *guanciale*
(cheek), olive oil and
fresh tomatoes).

*Rieti.
Lake Turano*

427

Gourmet Tours

RIETI. This town is the historical center of Sabina and sits on the River Velino on a plain dotted with vegetable gardens and wheat fields. Its monuments reflect its intense medieval past. Do not miss the Palazzo Vescovile (Bishop's Palace), the Bishop's cellars with their imposing two-nave gallery, and the Piazza Vittorio Emanuele II. For eating, the best restaurant is the "Bistrot" in the pedestrian area, serving local cuisine which is good value for money. The "Checco-al Calice d'Oro" restaurant belonging to the "Miramonti" hotel is also worth a try. A little out of the center, you will find the "Pecora Nera" restaurant, also serving local cuisine and with an excellent wine list. Local specialties on sale include *terzitti* made from flour, eggs, honey, pepper and chopped walnuts. At the "Sorgi" bakery, you can buy *sciapo* bread, *focaccia, pane al latte* (soft bread made with milk), *rosette romane* bread rolls, and other treats. Near Rieti, in Poggio Moiano, there is the "Società Cooperativa Olivicola dell'Alta Sabina" where you can buy olive oil.

The olive harvest

1. The River Velino and the Laga Mountains

CITTADUCALE. This small medieval town, situated in the Velino valley, is surrounded by town walls that were built by order of Carlo II d'Angiò in 1309. In the main square, there is the late-Romanesque church of S. Maria del Popolo. The local gastronomic specialty is the charcuterie, especially the *porchetta*, which you can buy at "Ennio Pasquini" near Caporio. Here you can also buy *salamelle* (horse-shoe-shaped salami eaten when not too matured), *coralline* salami and the *caporini*, the house special, which is a thin, mild salami made from lean pork meat.

ANTRODOCO. It is worth stopping at Borgo Velino to visit the interesting Museo Civico (Civic Museum) where, amongst other things, they have old agricultural tools. You reach Antrodoco, the "town between the mountains", through a gentle landscape of woods and slopes. This well-known spa and holiday town has many tourist attractions, from its cathedral (Duomo) to the Velino gorges. If you want to try the famous Antrodoco *stracci* (thin, warm omelets served with cheese) and other local dishes, we recommend the "Dionisio". The town has a good crop of chestnuts from the trees in the surrounding mountains. There are also plenty of the much-sought-after *caci* cheeses and *pecorino* cheeses, liver sausages, mountain ham and *porchetta*. Good quality examples of these foods can be found at "Riccardo Guerci" in the center of town and in Cittareale.

AMATRICE. This little town in the mountainous area not far from the Laga mountains was built according to a very well-ordered town plan which may have been designed by Cola dell'Amatrice some time after 1529. It is the home of the traditional *bucatini all'amatriciana* (see earlier) which you can try at the "La Conca" *trattoria*, which also serves excellent *spaghetti alla carbonara* (spaghetti with a sauce of eggs, bacon, cheese and pepper)and barbecued pork. The place is known for its fine production of *caciotte* (type of cheese produced in central Italy), *ricotta*, *pecorino* – fresh and mature – and the finer grain *mortadella* made from pork meat, similar to those found in Campotosto in Abruzzo. You can buy *stracchino* (a kind of soft cheese), yogurt, *ricotta*, *pecorino* and local cheese at the "Cooperativa Produttori Latte".

LEONESSA. This holiday town is at the edge of the Reatini mountains. Founded long ago, its still has some medieval houses. For a gastronomic stop, we suggest the "Leon d'Oro" restaurant where you can eat barbecued meats and home-made desserts. The town's main specialty is the *fiore molle* cheese, which is doughy and flavorsome with a yellowish color which comes from the saffron used in it. There are also plenty of *caciottelle marzo-*line (little cheeses made from sheep's or buffalo milk), sausages, little salamis, *capocollo* salamis (made from meat high up on the neck), *sanguinacci* (blood sausages) and *pan pepati* (gingerbread).

TERMINILLO. This is the mountain where Romans go skiing in the winter. Nearby Pian de' Valli and Campoforogna are central Italy's largest winter resorts.

2. Sabina

MAGLIANO SABINA. This little town is on a hill on the border with Umbria. It overlooks the River Tiber from on high. The "Degli Angeli" restaurant serves local food with dishes such as: *strangolapreti con asparagi* (pasta with asparagus), *arrosticini di castrato* (mutton roast) and *pollo alla diavola* (broiled chicken). Magliano is known for its extra virgin olive oil, though production is not huge.

FARFA. Half way between the Tiber and Salaria, on the right-hand side of the Farfa Valley, there is an abbey which was one of the biggest religious and cultural centers of medieval times. The area is also known for its extra virgin olive oil.

ROCCA SINIBALDA. You must cross the Sabini mountains to reach this small typical town clustered around a castle designed by Baldassarre Peruzzi. It specializes in sheep meat, particularly lamb from the Vallecupola area.

OLIVE OIL PRODUCERS

Castelnuovo
di Farfa
Azienda Agricola A.M. Billi
at Mercato Vecchio
☎ 076536388
Coltodino
E. e F. Rosati
☎ 0765370 51
Fara Sabina
**Azienda Agricola ARCI
di Laura Fagiolo**
at Passo Corese
☎ 0765487036
Poggio Moiano
Società Cooperativa Olivicola Alta Sabina
via Licinese
☎ 0765876770

SHOPPING

Rieti
Forno Sorgi
via S. Rufo 37
Vast range of breads, "focaccia" and pizza.
Amatrice
Cooperativa Produttori Latte
at Sommati (km 4)
contrada Ponte
☎ 074685065
Typical cheeses and yogurt.
Cittaducale
Ennio Pasquini
at Caporio
via Salaria per L'Aquila 3
☎ 0746602267
Traditional charcuterie.

VITERBO

The Lazio Maremma, the Bolsena Lake and the Cimini mountains give this province its flavors, which come from water as much as the earth.

The Viterbo province between Tuscany and Umbria has a variety of landscapes, with its Maremma zone, the Bolsena Lake and the Cimini mountains. The agriculture is equally diverse, with the production of the DOP oil Canino; wine, beginning with Est! Est!! Est!!! from Montefiascone; chestnuts and hazelnuts from the Cimini mountains; cheeses and charcuterie; and vegetables such as the renowned Onano lentils. Consequently, the cuisine is also diverse, with soups and home-made pastas, meats and game, and fish from the sea and lake. Viterbo, once a papal town, still plays a crucial role as a place to meet and exchange ideas.

Cows at grass along the shores of the volcanic lake of Mezzano

430

Gourmet Tours

VITERBO. The Palazzo dei Papi, the cathedral and the medieval quarter take you back to the times of the pilgrims on the Via Francigena. The food is also very evocative, with things such as: rustic spaghetti (*lombricelli*); meat dishes eaten at court – *pollo al pomodoretto* (chicken with tomato) and *coniglio alla cacciatora* (rabbit cooked with garlic, rosemary, white wine, anchovies and chili peppers); the *pignattaccia* (pork stewed in an earthenware pot with potatoes and celery); food from the woods – especially *porcini* mushrooms, served in soups, pastas, and with *polenta* and stews. And from the bakeries, there are the *tozzetti*, hazelnut biscuits for dunking in Aleatico di Gradoli. Restaurants worth trying include "La Zaffera" with its atmosphere of long ago, local food and a menu which allows you to taste a good variety of dishes. There is also the "Richiastro" restaurant. When shopping, you should really try the delicious *porchetta*. On the cheese side, it is traditional to eat fresh broad beans and pears with *pecorino*, either the Roman variety with *la goccia* (the larger grained type) or the local one, *del pastore* (from the shepherd). Then there are the *caciotte* cheeses made from different milks. On the charcuterie side, there are the 'mountain' hams – *capocolli* and *lombetti* – and the more unusual sausages such as black and white sausages, *cotechino* (spiced pork sausage for boiling) and *coppe di*

Tarquinia. The Leonesse tomb

testa (meats from the head of the pig, which are cooked and pressed). For the classic tourist excursion, visit the sanctuary of S. Maria della Quercia and the sixteenth-century Villa Lante di Bagnaia which has a restaurant, the "Villa Gambara" where you can eat outside in the summer, and a well-stocked *enoteca*.

1. The Lazio Maremma

VETRALLA. From this town, situated along the Cassia road, you can catch sight of medieval splendors and the nearby important Etruscan remains of Norchia and Blera. The gastronomy is connected to the olive oil and truffles which are named after the town.
TARQUINIA. This Etruscan town, founded by the legendary Tarconte, lives on in the Palazzo Vitelleschi Museum and in the painted tombs of the Monterozzi family. Today's town has kept its medieval layout, the church of S. Maria di Castelo marking the oldest part. Around the town are the DOC vines of the Trebbiano and Malvasia wines, the artichoke and water melon fields, and the pasture for the livestock necessary for local meat and cheese production. The eating places offer Maremma cuisine: home-made pastas, *abbacchio* (suckling lamb) and, when in season, game, *ferlenghi* mushrooms and snails. Seafood cuisine is also prevalent. Restaurants to note in town are the "Bersagliere" and the "Arcadia"; and at the seafront, in Tarquinia Lido, the "Gradinoro" and the "Velcamare".
MONTALTO DI CASTRO. The town

near the Tuscan border was built up around a medieval castle. It is the starting point for Abbadia and the Vulci archaeological site. Here, we have more Maremma specialties made with excellent locally-grown vegetables, *pecorino* cheese and olive oil. To name just a few of the specialties, there is *acquacotta* (a farmhouse soup made from vegetables and herbs), various types of *abbacchio* – even in soup form, called *giubba e calzoni* – and game, especially wild boar. Two hotels with restaurants are worthy of note: the "Vulci" and the "Enterprise", the latter being in Montalto Marina.

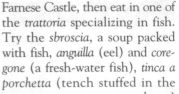

TUSCANIA. This walled village sits on a ridge of tuff, bordered by ravines. Just outside its walls, there are two Romanesque churches, S. Pietro and S. Maria Maggiore, which made the town famous. There are various Etruscan necropolises in the surrounding area. For somewhere to stay, there is the "Al Gallo" in the heart of the village, whose restaurant follows the seasons and has an interesting wine list. The most important things in the local gastronomy are game – this can be wild boar, wood pigeon or woodcock – snails in a sauce, tripe, *quarantini* beans (beans with a short growing cycle), and wild asparagus. Local produce includes olive oil which supplies the central producer of DOP olive oil in the ancient village of Canino.

2. Lake Bolsena

CAPODIMONTE. This town gives you a panoramic foretaste of Lake Bolsena and a foretaste of its gastronomy. You should visit the Farnese Castle, then eat in one of the *trattoria* specializing in fish. Try the *sbroscia*, a soup packed with fish, *anguilla* (eel) and *coregone* (a fresh-water fish), *tinca a porchetta* (tench stuffed in the same way as *porchetta*) served with potatoes and wild fennel, and the mixed fish grill with *lattarini* (fresh-water fish), fillets of *persico* (perch) and *luccio* (pike).

VALENTANO. On the west side of the Volsini mountains, there are many towers and an important Farnese fort. *Porchetta* and excellent chestnuts are the pride of the local cuisine. Moving on down to Castrense Statale you reach Gradoli, famous for its Aleatico red wine and for a particular white bean which is small and round with a thin skin and used in the traditional Purgatory meal in Dante's Divine Comedy.

ACQUAPENDENTE. Up on the Cassia you can see the River Paglia running down between the Volsini mountains and Mount Rufeno towards Tuscany. Today the area is classified as a nature reserve together with its ancient farmhouses. In the town center, you can visit the Romanesque cathedral and then the *trattoria*. Local specialties include *zuppa di fagioli* (bean soup), *abbacchio con le lenticchie di Onano* (suckling lamb with Onano lentils), and *fregnacce* which are farmhouse griddlecakes. Also good are the vegetables and tasty sausages.

BOLSENA. This Mediterranean village looks out onto the lake. In the background are the mountains whose name comes from the Roman *Volsinii*. Umbria and Orvieto are a stone's throw away. The landscape is dominated by vines and olive groves, interrupted by areas of peach trees and *scatoloni* tomatoes. The cuisine is mostly lake-based, including the famous eels which earned Pope Martin IV a mention as one of Dante's condemned, "to be purged by fasting" after his dependence became such that he had eels in his bedroom in order to eat them any time he wanted. We recommend the "Da Picchietto" restaurant with its traditional atmosphere and cuisine. A final detour to Bagnoregio with picturesque Civita, and Castiglione in Teverina, a wine town at the southern edge of the Orvieto wine district.

MONTEFIASCONE. This town on a hill, overlooking the lake, is the home of Est! Est!! Est!!!, the famous wine (Giovanni Fugger, buried in S. Flaviano, created the name as a sign of triple excellence). The cuisine is from the lake – *brodo di tinca* (tench broth), *coregoni alla bisentina* and *luccio al forno* (baked pike) – but also from the land with wild boar ham and *tordi allo spiedo* (thrush kebabs).

3. The Cimini Mountains

RONCIGLIONE. From Viterbo you travel along the mouth of the ancient Cimino volcano. In the green mouth of the crater, there is Lake Vico and the solitary cone of Mount Venere. Take a detour to Caprarola where you must visit the Palazzo Farnese with its sixteenth century architecture full of wonderful shapes and decoration, in a superb setting of gardens and fountains. Next you reach Ronciglione, a medieval village with valuable Renaissance and Baroque additions. The area is famous for its chestnuts and hazelnuts. The *pecorino* cheeses are also excellent.

In the restaurants, you get perch and roast pike.

SUTRI. This medieval village, set on a spur of light volcanic rock, reveals Roman and Etruscan relics at every step. Just outside it, on the Cassia, there is a huge necropolis and an Etruscan amphitheater. Go a little further to Capranica, a picturesque little town with its renowned *trattoria* "I Vitigni".

NEPI. The medieval walls of Nepi, the town hall, the cathedral and the Farnese fort are built on the Etruscan remains of *Nepet*.

CIVITA CASTELLANA. This picturesque site, set amongst rocks and raging waters, was that of *Falerii Veteres*, the capital of the Faliscans, destroyed in 241 BC and abandoned for a thousand years. The thirteenth century cathedral and the renaissance fort are the symbols of its re-birth. The ruins of nearby *Falerii Novi* tell of the thousand years in between. We highly recommend "L'Altra Bottiglia" set in a seventeenth-century building in the center, with good cuisine and top wines from all around the world.

ORTE. This little town with its Etruscan name looks out onto the rough and, in some parts, bleak landscape of the Tiber valley. Its specialty is roast lamb with peas, the pride of the local farmers.

SORIANO NEL CIMINO. This little hill town is set tightly around the imposing Orsini castle. The fanciful Papacqua fountain is the well-known image of the town. On the hillside, there are lovely beech and chestnut woods and many hazel trees. Restaurant ideas include "La Rosa Blu" in Vitorchiano and, right outside it, "Nando Al Pallone" which is particularly good in the summer.

WINE PRODUCERS

Bolsena
Italo Mazziotti
largo Mazziotti 5
☎ 0761799049
Castiglione in Teverina
Trappolini
via del Rivellino 65
☎ 0761948381
Gradoli
Cantina Oleificio Sociale di Gradoli
via Roma
☎ 0761456087
Montefiascone
Cantina di Montefiascone
via Cassia 22
☎ 0761826148
Falesco
S.S. Cassia km 94
☎ 0761826332
Vignanello
Cantina Sociale Colli Cimini
at Piano Trosce
☎ 0761754591

OLIVE OIL PRODUCERS

Viterbo
Santa Caterina
strada Tuscanese 54
☎ 0761360085
Canino
Archibusacci
via del Boschetto 3
☎ 0761437213

SHOPPING

Viterbo
Enogastronomia Menghini
via Dobici 33
☎ 0761340676
Wine, distilled spirits, jams and sweets.
Enoteca La Torre
via della Torre 5
☎ 0761226467
Wines, olive oil, delicatessen.
Gastronomia Cencioni
via Cairoli 18
☎ 0761325281
Typical charcuterie and cheeses; home-made pasta.

ABRUZZO FROM THE APENNINES TO THE SEA

The Adriatic flavors of Pescara, the vines and olives of Chieti and Teramo, and the mountain cuisine of L'Aquila shape the gastronomic character of this scenic central Italian region.

olden beaches give way to olive-clad slopes as the visitor goes inland to the Abruzzo Apennine mountains, which reach their highest point with the Gran Sasso. It is a difficult land which farmers, shepherds, livestock breeders and fishermen work hard to exploit for corn, beet, tobacco, fruits, vines and, in the valleys around L'Aquila, saffron. The ancient seasonal rhythm of moving from high summer pasture to low winter pasture and back every six months is in decline, but nature still rules in the three large local national parks.

THE FOOD OF SHEPHERDS AND FISHERMEN

Wine pitcher

Typical countryside

The gastronomy of the Abruzzo region is 'no-nonsense' and has two manifestations, coastal and mountain. The coastal cuisine essentially comprises anchovies, sardines and mackerel, and deep-water varieties such as scorpion fish, skate and angler fish, with fish broth a typical dish. The mullet, whelks and shellfish are also very good. The traditional countryside dishes are based on lamb and goat, while pork is mostly used for salamis. Hot red chilli is a fundamental ingredient in almost every Abruzzo dish. No description of Abruzzo gastronomy could be given without the almost mythical *panarda*. Traditionally supposed to comprise 50 dishes, the *panarda* was a meal at which the participants were not allowed to leave the table until everything was eaten. It began with a broad bean soup, followed by sardines, trout and lentils as appetizers, then thistle soup, *maccheroni alla chitarra* (pasta made with an implement resembling a guitar), timbale, sausages, goat and lamb dishes in various guises, finishing with desserts and a copious supply of wine.

Abruzzo - Typical products

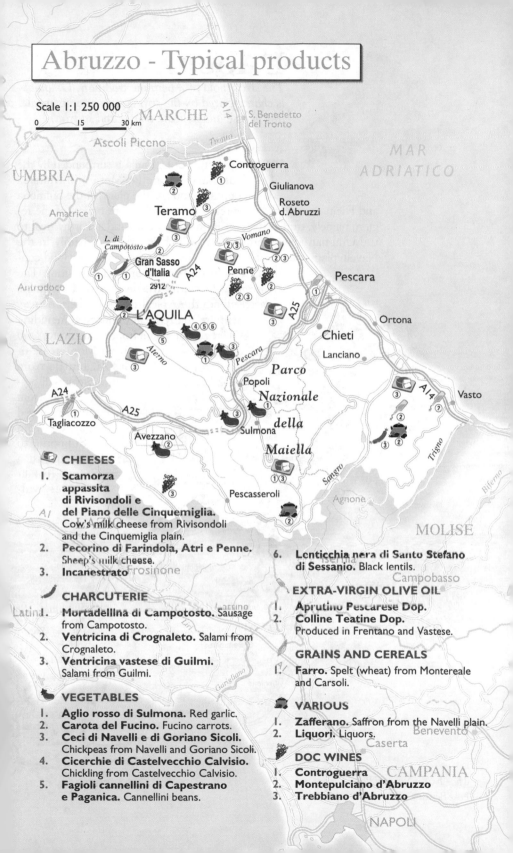

Scale 1:1 250 000

0   15   30 km

MARCHE

S. Benedetto del Tronto

Ascoli Piceno

MAR ADRIATICO

UMBRIA

Amatrice

Controguerra

Giulianova

Roseto d.Abruzzi

Teramo

Vomano

L. di Campotosto

Gran Sasso d'Italia
2912

Penne

Pescara

L'AQUILA

Aterno

Pescara

Chieti

Ortona

LAZIO

Lanciano

A24

A25

Tagliacozzo

Parco

Popoli

Nazionale

Vasto

Avezzano

Sulmona

della

Maiella

Pescasseroli

Agnone

MOLISE

Campobasso

CHEESES

1. **Scamorza appassita di Rivisondoli e del Piano delle Cinquemiglia.** Cow's milk cheese from Rivisondoli and the Cinquemiglia plain.
2. **Pecorino di Farindola, Atri e Penne.** Sheep's milk cheese.
3. **Incanestrato**

CHARCUTERIE

1. **Mortadellina di Campotosto.** Sausage from Campotosto.
2. **Ventricina di Crognaleto.** Salami from Crognaleto.
3. **Ventricina vastese di Guilmi.** Salami from Guilmi.

VEGETABLES

1. **Aglio rosso di Sulmona.** Red garlic.
2. **Carota del Fucino.** Fucino carrots.
3. **Ceci di Navelli e di Goriano Sicoli.** Chickpeas from Navelli and Goriano Sicoli.
4. **Cicerchie di Castelvecchio Calvisio.** Chickling from Castelvecchio Calvisio.
5. **Fagioli cannellini di Capestrano e Paganica.** Cannellini beans.

6. **Lenticchia nera di Santo Stefano di Sessanio.** Black lentils.

EXTRA-VIRGIN OLIVE OIL

1. **Aprutino Pescarese Dop.**
2. **Colline Teatine Dop.** Produced in Frentano and Vastese.

GRAINS AND CEREALS

1. **Farro.** Spelt (wheat) from Montereale and Carsoli.

VARIOUS

1. **Zafferano.** Saffron from the Navelli plain.
2. **Liquori.** Liquors.

DOC WINES

1. **Controguerra**
2. **Montepulciano d'Abruzzo**
3. **Trebbiano d'Abruzzo**

CAMPANIA

NAPOLI

L'AQUILA

The stronghold of Apennine tradition, L'Aquila is characterized by the strong flavors of its meat and cheese and delicate truffle and saffron.

The province of L'Aquila is surrounded by the Gran Sasso, Maiella, Meta and Marsica mountains and has the plains of the Sulmona and Fucino rivers in the center. Two specialties are typical of the region, namely, truffles (present in many varieties and a worthy rival to the Umbrian truffle) and saffron, which is produced mainly in the Navelli plain and whose quality is renowned the world over (and consequently a stong feature in Italian haute cuisine). The *maccheroni alla chitarra*, thistle soup and vegetable *gnocchetti* are the typical dishes of the province. There are many local delicacies, including *mortadellina* salami from Campotosto, *farro* grain from Montereale or Casoli, lentils from Santo Stefano di Sessanio, carrots from Fucino, and red garlic from Sulmona, to name just a few. In fact every val-

The Abruzzo National Park.
Lake Barrea

ley, almost every hamlet, has its own typical food, whether it be salami, cheese or an alcoholic drink. Indeed, if you think that you can manage a lunch of thirty to fifty dishes, then go to any restaurant offering local cuisine and the traditional *panarda* is for you.

Gourmet Tours

L'AQUILA. In the heart of the most mountainous part of Abruzzo, L'Aquila is a town known for it environmental and artistic beauties. Some of its historical monuments are unique examples of their type in Italy. The town offers a great variety of local hotels and restaurants. Those worth trying include the "Grand Hotel del Parco", the "Duca degli Abruzzi" and the "Duomo". Not far from the cathedral, the "Tre Marie" restaurant has for five generations offered its customers the best of local food and wine. Close to the Law Courts, the "Osteria Antiche Mura" serves rabbit in saffron, and near the castle at the wine bar "Cantina del Boss", visitors can taste Abruzzo wines at very reasonable prices.

1. On the slopes of the Gran Sasso

SAN VITTORINO. On leaving L'Aquila to visit the ancient Sabine settlement of *Amiternum*, the birthplace of the ancient Roman historian, Sallust (68-35 BC), visitors can go a little further to the small town of San Vittorino with its Romanesque church of San Michele, which, together with its ancient catacombs, is one of Abruzzo's most famous monuments.

CAMPOTOSTO. If you climb the thickly-wooded winding road from Arischia to the Capanelle pass, from the top you get a remarkable panorama of the Apennines, stretching from the Corni Grande and the Piccolo del Gran Sasso mountains to the Velino and Simbruini mountains. Descending through grassy valleys you come to the forked road leading to Campotosto. The town is by a man-made lake full of fish, used for hydro-electric power (most used source of energy in the area). We recommend the "Trattoria del Pescatore" for its

HOTELS AND RESTAURANTS

L'Aquila
G.H. del Parco ★★★
corso Federico II 74
☎ 0862413248
Duca degli Abruzzi ★★★ 🍴🖳
viale Giovanni XXIII 10
☎ 086228341
Duomo ★★★ 🍴🖳
via Dragonetti 6/10
☎ 0862410893
Tre Marie 🍴🍴🍴
via Tre Marie 3
☎ 0862413191
Osteria Antiche Mura 🍴🍴
via XXV Aprile 2
☎ 086262422
Assergi
Fiordigigli ★★★ 🍴🖳
at Fonte Cerreto
(km 4), base funivia
del Gran Sasso
(cableway station)
☎ 0862606171
Elodia 🍴🍴 🖳
at Camarda (km 4)
S.S. 17/bis Gran Sasso
☎ 0862606219
Avezzano
Il Gioco dell'Uva 🍴
corso Garibaldi 133
☎ 086325441
Campotosto
Trattoria del Pescatore 🍴
via Rio Fucino
☎ 0862900227

Mortadellina di Campotosto salami, although this can also be bought in the shops in the center of town.

ASSERGI. Just before the Capanelle pass, you turn off towards Assergi. Nearby is the hotel "Fiordigigli" (the cableway which goes to the summit of the Gran Sasso starts here). For typical Abruzzo dishes, we recommend the "Elodia" restaurant.

2. Heading for Marsica

ROCCA DI CAMBIO. The highest municipality in Abruzzo is perched on the side of Monte Cagno and dominates a vast 'alpine' meadow. It is popular with holiday-makers, notably skiers and mountain walkers on Monte Sirente and Monte Velino, and they often stay in the "Albergo Crystall". The nearby village of Rocca di Mezzo, with its attractive historic houses, is renowned for the local specialty, black lentils.

OVINDOLI. An excellent summer and winter resort, Ovindoli also has good hotels. Restaurants of note include "Il Pozzo" with its family cuisine and local produce making extensive use of saffron,

The Fucino plain

truffles and *porcini* mushrooms. The surrounding countryside offers excellent *scamorza*, a cheese typical of the region with its numerous dairy cattle.

CELANO. The visitor to Calano, the historical center of the Marsica region, has to take winding mountain roads through thick woods to get to this destination. The sturdy Piccolomini castle towers over the fertile Fucino plain, which used to be a lake.

AVEZZANO. The town of Avezzano once derived its wealth from the Fucino lake as a result of fishing rights granted to it by the Duke Alessandro Torlonia in 1875. Today the town is mostly modern, having suffered heavy damage from an earthquake in 1915. Of the many good restaurants in town we recommend "Il Gioco dell'Uva" with its broad selection of excellent Abruzzo cheeses. Here, the gourmet visitor should try the Fucino potato, widely cultivated in the area.

TAGLIACOZZO. Renowned as a summer and winter tourist resort and set slightly to the north of the Simbruini mountains, Tagliacozzo is not only famous for the historic battle in which the last of the Svevi, Corradino II, was defeated

by Carlo d'Angiò, but also for the fifteenth-century church of San Francesco and the fourteenth-century Palazzo Orsini. We recommend the "Albergo Miramonti" for a night's stay. From there visitors can visit the piazzas in the center of town, the Marsi Arch and perhaps try some of the biscuits produced by the nearby Benedictine monastery.

3. Between the Maiella and the Abruzzo National Park

SULMONA. In the center of the Peligna valley – rendered fertile by the Vela and Gizio mountain streams – stands ancient *Sulmona*, the birthplace of the Roman poet Publius Ovidius Naso, better known as Ovid. Visitors are immediately drawn by the sight of the splendid Medieval aqueduct which runs around Piazza Garibaldi. But their attention soon turns to the palace, the Annunziata church and the many eateries and shops in the town center. The restaurants "Rigoletto", "Cesidio" and "Clemente" are worth visiting, most notably for their takes on the local cuisine. One of the best-stocked wine bars in the region is "Di Loreto Vinattieri", and here you should try the excellent "Centerbe della Maiella" from the Cesaroni winery. Last but not least, Sulmona is also famous for its sweet *confetto* pastries, and you can even visit the *confetto* museum, itself part of the *confetto* bakery "Pelino", which, along with "Di Carlo", is one of the oldest in town. Those with a very sweet tooth should not leave without getting some *scarponi* – tasty candies filled with walnuts, almonds, sugar, chocolate and cooked must

(partially fermented grape juice).

PESCOCOSTANZO. The local slopes of Monte Calvario offer excellent opportunities both for winter sports and for visits to Renaissance and Baroque churches. Local traditional crafts include embroidery (with many specialist shops), gold leaf work (the "Domenicano", "Macino", Rinaldi", "Sciullo" and "Tollis" workshops are known throughout the region) and wrought iron work by celebrated artist/craftsmen such as "Donatelli" and "Zappa".

RIVISONDOLI. At Christmas time locals create a "live" crib, and the sporting and hotel facilities here provide for excellent holidays. We recommend the restaurant "Da Giocondo" as the best place to taste the local specialties such as *ricotta* cheese *ravioli*, *mortadella* sausage and *scamorza* cheese.

ROCCARASO. Another site beloved of skiers, Roccaraso also has excellent hotels, notably the "Iris", and restaurants such as "Tratturo" and "Galleria", which offer fine local cuisine.

CASTEL DI SANGRO. Descending from the Piano delle Cinquemiglia plain, visitors arrive at the high Valle del Sangro, described by many as "The gate to the Abruzzi" because it let ancient Roman soldiers pass in one direction and the Abruzzo flocks in search of fresh pastures in Puglia in the other. Chocolate lovers should not under any circumstances miss the exquisite *mostaccioli* candies, on sale at "Sammarone".

ALFEDENA. Along the road to-

Sausage from Campotosto

AGRITURISMI

Barete
Casa Colonia
at Teora
via Forcella 22
☎ 0862976322
Cagnano
Amiterno
Cupello ★
at Fossatillo
☎ 0862978820
Cansano
Agripark
at Renaro
☎ 0863412657
Montereale
Montorselli ★
at Cesaproba
at Ranaglie
☎ 0862908319
Navelli
Casa Verde
at Civitaretenga
corso Umberto I
☎ 0862959163
Scanno
Le Prata
at Le Prata
☎ 0864747263

SHOPPING

L'Aquila
La Cantina del Boss
via Castello 3
☎ 0862413393
Wine tasting.
Anversa
degli Abruzzi
Cooperativa ASCA - Nunzio Marcelli
via Fonte di Curzio
☎ 086449354
Organic products.

SHOPPING

Anversa degli
Abruzzi
**Panificio Anversa
D'Intino e Ciofani**
via Duca degli Abruzzi
☎ 086449251
Bakery.
Castel di Sangro
**Di Benedetto -
Sammarone**
via XX Settembre 25
☎ 0864845046
"Mostaccioli" candies.
Navelli
**Coop. Altopiano
di Navelli**
at Civitaretenga (km 3)
via Umberto 17
☎ 0862959163
*Saffron and organic
products: chickling,
cicerchie lentils, spelt,
olive oil.*
Prezza
**Forno Bruno
De Santis**
via Corfinio
☎ 086445201
*Home-made
"focaccia" and cookies.*
Sulmona
**Liquorificio
Artigianale di
Luigino Cesaroni**
via Leopoldo
Dorrucci 16
☎ 086451383
*"Centerbe della
Maiella" liquor.*
Confetti Pelino
via St. Introdacqua 55
☎ 086452741
*Since 1783, a vast range
of "confetto" pastries.
Closed to the shop, the
"confetto" museum
(Museo Pelino dell'Arte
e della Tecnologia
Confettiera).*
**Confetteria
Di Carlo**
via M. Barbato 6
☎ 086452393
*Historic address for
"confetto" pastries.*
**Di Loreto
Vinattieri**
via Gramsci 41
☎ 086451919

wards the Abruzzo National Parks you find the village of Alfedena, best known for its Iron Age necropolis. The region also produces wonderful cheeses.

VILLETA BARREA. In Barrea and Villetta Barrea, just inside the national park, visitor can stay in the "Il Pescatore" hotel situated on the lake shore and ideally placed for easy mountain walks.

PESCASSEROLI. Set in the heart of the park, Pescasseroli has several good hotels and is perfect for both winter and summer holidays, whether for sport or for relaxation. The restaurant "Plistia", on the town's main street and connected to the hotel of the same name, has an excellent menu of local specialties.

SCANNO. This old town is marked by its narrow streets, flights of steps and courtyards, whilst the new town is perfectly equipped for holiday-makers and skiers. The tasty salamis and lamb dishes typical of the Abruzzo region should be sampled in the "Agli Archetti" restaurant, and those eating in "Lo Sgabello" should not miss the Scanno candy specialty, *mostaccioli scannesi.*

4. In the land of saffron

CASTELVECCHIO SUBEQUO. Perched on the slopes of Monte Sirente and alongside the Forca Ceruso pass (which leads to the

Scanno. Traditional dress

Marsica region), Castelvecchio Subequo is an old town facing the Navelli plain, source of that rare and fragrant spice, saffron.

CORFINIO. Dropping down into the Aterno valley, visitors reach the remains of the ancient city of the Peligni people, who used to live in the area. More recent is the interesting eleventh-century complex of monuments. The apricots are very good when in season.

CAPESTRANO. Perched on a hill, Capestrano dominates the Tirino valley. It is renowned for its ancient necropolis and for the fact that in 1934 the Capestrano Warrior, a statue representing King Nervius Pompuledius (sixth-century BC) was found here. Today it is held in the Museo Nazionale in Chieti. For a lunch of trout and freshwater shrimp, we recommend the "La Sorgente" restaurant in the nearby village of Presciano.

BOMINACO. The small town of Bominaco is a historical treasure trove with its thirteenth-century castle on Monte Buscito and its fascinating churches.

PRATA D'ANSIDONIA. Set in the high plains near L'Aquila, this town is medieval in character. Here and in neighboring Navelli, Civitaretenga and Camporciano visitors can enjoy a view of the crocus fields from which saffron is produced.

CHIETI

Mixing the taste of its olive oils and wines with the flavors of sea and land, the Chieti region is a gourmet's dream.

From the south-eastern slopes of the Maiella to the coast, and from Vasto almost to Pescara, the province of Chieti boasts a wealth of gastronomic pleasures, notably vegetables, pulses and high-quality meat. Local dishes worth trying include thistle soup, Chieti-style rabbit, *turcenelle* in tomato sauce and fried fish. Three renowned local wines are the principal DOC labels of the Abruzzo region, namely Montepulciano d'Abruzzo, Trebbiano d'Abruzzo and Cerasuolo. The Teatino region also boasts many fine *cantine*, where we recommend you try out the local wines.

The coast at Fossacesia. View from the abbey of S. Giovanni Venere.

441

Gourmet Tours

HOTELS AND RESTAURANTS

Chieti
Venturini ¶¶
via De Lollis 10
☎ 0871330663
Nonna Elisa ¶
via P. Bentivoglio 2
☎ 0871684152
Fara San Martino
Del Camerlengo
★★★
at Macchia del Fresco
☎ 0872980136
Francavilla al Mare
★ ¶¶ **Sporting Hotel**
Villamaria ★★★
at Pretaro (km 4)
☎ 0854511001
Marianna ¶¶
via D'Annunzio 62
☎ 085810131
La Nave ¶¶
viale Kennedy 2
☎ 085815688
Guardiagrele
★ ¶¶ **Villa Maiella** ¶¶
via Sette Dolori 30
☎ 0871809319
Lanciano
Corona di Ferro ¶¶¶
corso Roma 28
☎ 0872713029
Ai Vecchi Sapori ¶
via Ravizza/c.
Roma 16
☎ 0872712184
Ortona
Miramare ¶
largo Farnese 15
☎ 0859066556
San Buono
Francoforte ¶
contrada Cantarelli 23
☎ 0873930288

CHIETI. From its vantage point atop a steep hill, Chieti looks out over a vine-clad valley and the nearby coast. There is a great deal to see, including Roman remains, churches, more recent palazzos and the Abruzzo Archaeological Museum with its many exhibits , which were originally found in nearby mountain caves and necropolises. For traditional local cuisine, eat at "Nonna Elisa", although the lamb dish *coratelle d'agnello* is very good at the restaurant "Venturini". One of the Abruzzo's venerable bars, the "Gran Caffè Vittoria" in the center of Chieti, is not to be missed.

1. Along the coast

FRANCAVILLA AL MARE. The town is split in two, with the old town on a hill and the port area by the sea. Don't miss the famous *brodetti*, dishes based on scampi and calamari. The best of Abruzzo seafood cuisine can be had in the restaurants "Nave" and "Marianna". For the best DOC wines, visit the "Pasetti" and "Aprutine" wineries. Also worth a visit, in the nearby town of Pretaro, is the "Sporting Hotel Villamaria".

ORTONA. Following the line of the coast, visitors must at all costs visit Ortona, the ancient capital of the Frentani people. There, the twelfth-century cathedral of San Tommaso, the Baglioni tower and the Aragonese castle are the only ancient buildings to have survived the Second World War. Not far from the interesting Palazzo Farnese stands the restaurant "Miramare" which serves

typical local fish dishes. The "Citra" consortium, a company specializing in the world-wide distribution of "Montepulciano d'Abruzzo", offers one of the best opportunities to taste Teatino wine. In the village of Caldari there is an *azienda* specializing in local organic produce, of which their extra-virgin olive oil is an outstanding example.

VASTO. This small town almost on the border with Molise looks down upon the Adriatic from its cliff-top vantage point. Visitors should not miss the mediaeval castle and the church Santa Maria Maggiore with its paintings by Titian and Veronese. For a sea-food lunch, why not try the famous Vasto specialty *zuppa Vastese* in the *trattoria* "Zì Albina"? If you want to buy some of the celebrated local salami – the *ventricina Vastese* – "Fratelli Bruno" in the town center is the place for you. Food shops in Vasto offer another local specialty, the *scapece di Vasto*. Other out-of-town gastronomical addresses include "Il Corsaro" in Porto di Vasto and "Villa Vignola" (with its excellent cuisine) in a villa in nearby Vignola.

2. Around the Maiella National Park

LANCIANO. Romans, Longobards, Angevins, Kings of Naples – many have ruled Lanciano, as can be seen from the four relief plaques in the center of the new town, and they have all left their mark. There are several noteworthy churches, including the cathedral and the church of Santa Maria Maggiore. Gourmets will enjoy the pleasant central "Cortona di Ferro" restaurant, with its

Villa Santa Maria. Panorama

fish-oriented cuisine. For a good grain and chick-pea soup, go to the small "Ai Vecchi Sapori" restaurant, which also offers other traditional dishes. And you cannot leave without trying the traditional Christmas dessert, *Crespelle di Lanciano* crêpes.

GUARDIAGRELE. Set in the Maiella National Park, Guardiagrele is renowned for its crafts, notably wrought iron, copper and gold and, in the first half of August, an important craft fair. Just outside the city center stands the excellent "Villa Maiella" restaurant with its cuisine of local specialties, using truffles and mushrooms. The farm winery "Santoleri" offers good "Montepulciano d'Abruzzo" and "Trebbiano d'Abruzzo" wines, which should be accompanied with the local specialty biscuits, *tarallucci*. Finally, for snail lovers, "Palombaro" is a must.

FARA SAN MARTINO. Home to Abruzzo pasta making, Fara San Martino. is famed for the typical Abruzzo pasta, *maccheroni alla chitarra*. All the famous pasta making companies are here – "Delverde", "Pastificio cav. Cocco" and "F.lli

De Cecco" – and on the same industrial estate you can buy pasta, extra-virgin olive oil and other products. For an excellent restaurant in the green heart of the Maiella National Park, there is the "Del Camerlengo" hotel, celebrated for its local specialties.

VILLA SANTA MARIA. Driving down the low Sangro valley, you come to the town of Villa Santa Maria, a town of chefs. And it is no accident that the patron saint of chefs, Francesco Caracciolo, founded perhaps one of the first ever cooking schools here. Today it plays host to an institute of hotel management. For excellent local cuisine (particularly home-made salamis) and a warm welcome, visit the *agriturismo* establishment "Olimpo" in Montebello.

SCHIAVI D'ABRUZZO. Almost on the border with Molise and on one side of the Frentani mountains, Schiavi d'Abruzzo is a pleasant tourist resort. In the nearby village of San Buono con Atessa, the *trattoria* "Francofonte" is well worth the detour, offering *sagne*, *frascarielli* and desserts (strictly home-made).

HOTELS AND RESTAURANTS

Vasto
Corsaro 🍴🍴🍴
at Porto di Vasto
via Osca 51
☎ 0873310113
Villa Vignola 🍴🍴🍴
at Vignola, S.S. 16
☎ 0873310050
Zi' Albina 🍴🍴
via Marchesani 15
☎ 0873367429

AGRITURISMI

Ortona
Agriverde ⭐️🏠
at Villa Caldari
via Monte Maiella 118
☎ 0859032101
Villa Santa Maria
Olimpo
contrada Montebello 4
☎ 0872940425

WINE PRODUCERS

Francavilla al Mare
Az. Agr. Aprutine
via Adriatica Sud 92
☎ 0854919343
Pasetti
via S. Paolo 21
☎ 08561875
Ortona
Citra Vini
contrada Cucullo
☎ 0859031288

PASTA PRODUCERS

Fara San Martino
Pastificio Delverde
via Roma
☎ 08729951
Pastificio cavalier Cocco
Zona Industriale 55
☎ 0872984121
Fratelli De Cecco
Zona Industriale
☎ 0872980425

SHOPPING

Chieti
Gran Caffè Vittoria
corso Marruccino 89
☎ 0871330844
Historic cafe.

PESCARA

It is only a short ride from the "brodetto" of the Adriatic to the 'hearty' Apennine cuisine typical of the Gran Sasso and Maiella regions.

The province of Pescara runs from the ridge of hills on the southern slopes of the Gran Sasso to the northern hills of the Maiella, and from the Pescara river to the Coast. Its cuisine (as with the whole of the Abruzzo region) is a happy marriage of sea and land, ranging from the Pescara *brodetto* and baby squid preserved in oil to the *coda di rospo* (a fish whose name literally means "toad's tail") flavored with rosemary and *maccheroni alla chitarra*. Also in these hills some of the Abruzzo region's best extra-virgin olive oil is produced, not only at Loreto Aprutino – the most prestigious of the DOP oils – but also at the nearby towns of Penne, Pianella and Moscufo.

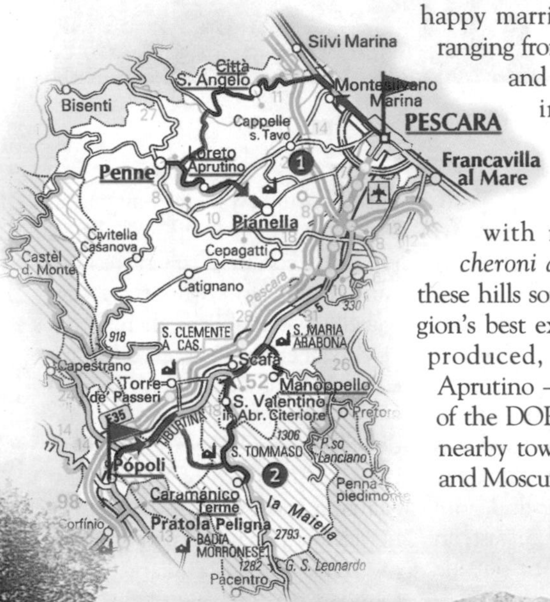

The Maiella range

444

Gourmet Tours

PESCARA. The wealthiest and most modern city in the region, Pescara has taken great care to diversify, mixing craft shops with modern boutiques, industry with holiday bathing facilities and night clubs. The city is also the birthplace of not only the great poet and writer Gabriele D'Annunzio (his house and the connected D'Annunzio Institute are worth a visit) but also Ennio Flaiano, the Italian writer and journalist. The well-stocked fish market and the exuberant fruit and vegetable market of Porta Nuova (offering the produce of the entire region) are interesting to visit. The town also plays host to various types of event, but most notably the "Dieta Mediterranea" (Mediterranean Diet) food trade fair which takes place at the beginning of August. For those in search of luxury, the hotel "Carlton" is the place, and visitors wishing to try the classic *virtù* and *agnello a cutturo* lamb dish should

visit "La Cantina di Jozz" not far from D'Annunzio's house. Also not to be missed is the "Taverna 58" restaurant with its local cuisine. For those seeking home-made pasta, such as *maccheroni alla chitarra*, the historic gourmet restaurant "La Chittara Antica" is a must, and it also serves other Pescara specialties. Finally in Via Tinozzi stands the history eatery "Luigi d'Amico" where they serve Pescara's best-known dessert, the celebrated *parrozzo*.

1. In the olive oil hills

CITTÀ SANT'ANGELO. Renowned even in antiquity for its wines and salt flats, Città Sant'Angelo still has many palaces and a splendid collegiate church of San Michele Arcangelo. In the local restaurant, "Locanda dell'Arte", situated in the center of town in the remarkable "Palazzo Zuccari", visitors can try the best local specialties, especially those made with *farro* (spelt) grain, game, and

It was the poet D'Annunzio who gave this name to the flavoured liquor

HOTELS AND RESTAURANTS

Pescara
Carlton ★★★
viale della Riviera 35
☎ 085373125
La Cantina di Jozz ¶¶
via delle Caserme 61
☎ 085690383
Taverna 58 ¶¶
corso Monthonè 58
☎ 085690724
Caramanico T.me
La Réserve Hotel Terme ★★★
via Santa Croce
☎ 08592391
Maiella Terme ★★★
via Roma 29
☎ 08592301
Città Sant'Angelo
Locanda dell'Arte ¶
vico II Santa Chiara 7
☎ 0859666?
Civitella Casanova
Bandiera ¶¶
contrada Pastini 32
☎ 085845219
Loreto Aprutino
Castello Chiola ★★★
via degli Aquino 12
☎ 0858290690
La Bilancia ★★★
contrada Palazzo
(km 5)
☎ 0858289321
Popoli
Tre Monti ★★★
via Tiburtina al km 181
☎ 08598481

AGRITURISMI

Città Sant'Angelo
⭐ 🏨 **La Bigattiera**
contrada San Pietro
☎ 08596796
Loreto Aprutino
La Casina Rosa
contrada Sgariglia 6
☎ 0858289744

WINE PRODUCERS

Bolognano
Zaccagnini
contrada Pozzo
☎ 0858880195
Nocciano
Bosco
contrada Casali 7
☎ 085847345

OLIVE OIL PRODUCERS
Loreto Aprutino
Ai Calanchi di Alberico D'Intino
contrada Fiorano
☎ 0854214473

SHOPPING

Pescara
La Chitarra Antica
via Sulmona 2
☎ 0854224010
Home-made fresh pasta.
Luigi D'Amico "Parrozzo"
via Tinozzi 44
☎ 08561869
"Parrozzo"and typical sweets.
Taberna Imperiale
via De Amicis 6/8
☎ 0859351724
Regional charcuterie and cheeses ("formaggio di fossa").
Bussi sul Tirino
Itticoltura Di Carlo
via dell'Aquila 1
☎ 085980371
Fish-breeding.
Civitella Casanova
Frantoio Coletta
contrada S. Benedetto
☎ 085845441
Olive oil.

desserts made with *farro* grain flour. Another must is a visit to Elice to taste the local *caciotta* cheese or to buy the local delicacies of stuffed duck and stuffed lamb prepared at the butcher's "Macelleria Di Lodovico".

PENNE. Further inland lies the ancient and once important town of *Pinna Vestinorum*, or Penne. It boasts eight old churches in its historical center set on four hills and looks out over the lake, which these days is a nature reserve in one of the most charming corners of the region. In addition to producing olive oil, they also smoke hams here in the hills. One of the best local dishes is "perazze", large pears marinated in vinegar and served as a side dish. Cheese lovers must not miss nearby Farindoli where they serve excellent fresh *pecorino* sheep's milk cheese.

LORETO APRUTINO. Surrounded by vineyards and olive groves, Loreto Aprutino was one of the first locations in Italy where olive producers were awarded a DOP for their produce. This olive oil is called "Aprutino Pescarese". As for other gourmet attractions, the restaurant "La Bilancia" offers tasty local dishes, whilst the *agriturismo* establishment, "La Casina Rosa" serves home-made pasta. Also worth visiting is the hotel

"Castello Chiola" in an eleventh-century castle and museum.

PIANELLA. Beyond the river Tavò, the village of Pianella (with its many farming establishments) has many gastronomic delights to offer, not least its exquisite olive oil, its local wines and its excellent charcuterie, which is frequently made of wild boar.

2. West of the Maiella

POPOLI. At the cheese manufacturers "Tre Monti", you can buy *caciotta*, *caciocavalli* and *ricotta* cheeses of the best Abruzzo tradition. "Tre Monti" is also the name of a modern hotel along the Via Tiburtina. Other local specialties include goat's meat, river trout from the Pescara river and spaghetti with freshwater crayfish.

CARAMANICO TERME. The ideal starting point for any excursions into the Maiella National Park or the Nature Reserve of the Ofento Valley. Here we recommend the restaurant "Il Cervo" with its wild boar specialties and dishes cooked in the local *cutturo* style. There are also excellent hotels. "La Réserve Hotel Terme" and "Maiella Terme" cater specifically for those who come to take the waters. In the shops in the center of town and in the *agriturismo* establishments on the outskirts visitors can get smoked mountain ham, *pecorino* cheese, *ricotta* for grating and wild boar sausages.

MANOPPELLO. On your return to the valley we recommend that you take a detour via the panoramic routes towards Manoppello and San Clemente a Casuaria.

Typical charcuterie

TERAMO

On the frontier of the Marche, excellent olive oil and wine enhances a cuisine influenced by good land and sea produce.

The province of Teramo covers the northern part of Abruzzo, where the land from the Gran Sasso to the coast is one vast hilly area punctuated by three large valleys – those of the Tordino, the Tronto and the Vomano. The province as a whole is almost entirely devoted to wine, including the Montepulciano d'Abruzzo, which can be found throughout the zone, the Colline Teramesi and the most recent DOC label, Controguerra, named after the nearby hamlet where it is made. All the local peasant dishes can be found in most restaurants in the Teramo area, particularly lamb *a cacio e uova* (with *cacio* cheese and egg) and lamb *a cutturo*. In this zone you can also find "Ventricina di Crognaleto", a soft spreadable meat paste made from smoked ham, pig's cheek, bacon and suet mixed with hot red pepper and rosemary.

Teramo. Panorama

Salsicciotto salami

Gourmet Tours

TERAMO. The rivers Vezzola and Tordino run either side of the ancient city of the Pretuzi. The ancient Roman theater exists today and is used for cultural and theatrical events. Also worthy of note is the twelfth-century cathedral. The central restaurant "Il Duomo" offers the local Teramo pizza as well as tasty dishes using asparagus and truffles. Classic local cuisine can also be had at the restaurant "Sotto le Stelle", along with regional wines and charcuterie. Wine lovers should visit "L'Enoteca Centrale" which has hundreds of different wines, all matched with local specialties.

1. From Tronto to the Sea

CAMPLI. Set in the hills between the river Tronto and the river Tordino, Campli boasts many prestigious buildings, most notably the Palazzo Farnese. This is Controguerra wine country, and we recommend you try it in one of the local *aziendas*.

CIVITELLA DEL TRONTO. This town is instantly recognizable from the imposing fortress and the high walkways which connect the palazzos along the narrow local streets. Of the local restarants, we would choose "Zunica" for its *pietanze* lamb dish and local salamis, and "Le Rocche di Carletto" for its local specialties.

ALBA ADRIATICA. In this modern seaside resort you can have an excellent fish lunch at the restaurant "Mediterraneo". In the hills between Alba and Civitella, in the Nereto region, they serve goat's meat *alla*

Gran Sasso. The Corno Grande

neretese, in the Nereto style. Not far from here, at Torano, you can get excellent *salsiciotto* salami and the *farro* (spelt) grain typical of the region.

GIULIANOVA. Visitors to this coastal town should eat the sole, the *marinara* in the Giulianova style, and stuffed calamari in the town restaurants "Beccaceci" and "Il Gabbiano". The local delicacy of squill can be eaten at the "Lo Stracciacocc".

ROSETO DEGLI ABRUZZI. Another key gastronomic high point is the *antipasto* di mare marine appetizer at "Aprodo". The restaurant "Per Bacco" has an excellent wine list, perhaps to drink with their *farro* grain soup.

PINETO. Before leaving the coast, visit Pineto to taste roast kid and other Teramo specialties at the restaurants "Bacucco d'Oro" and "Pier delle Vigne".

ATRI. To get to Atri, you have to cross the local *calanchi* or clay hills. Points of interest include the cathedral, the archaeological museum, Muséo Capitolare, and the Museo delle Tradizione Popolari, a folk museum. On the belvedere, there stands the "Locanda del Duca d'Atri" restaurant which serves lamb *mazzarelle* in the Teramo style, and in the town center visitors can buy the tasty *pecorino* cheese and local candy specialties.

2. The Vomano valley

MONTORIO AL VOMANO. At the bottom of the valley between the Monte della Laga and the Gran Sasso, following the route of the highway to Teramo, you come to Montorio al Vomano. The village has preserved its medieval center, with the remains of a fine fort and a beautiful parish church. Lovers of liqueurs should visit the "Paesani" *azienda* to try the Amaro Gran Sasso bitters.

PIETRACAMELA. Once over the peak of the Vomano mountain you come to a small lake and from here the road rises to the foot of the Corno Piccolo, a mountain set in beautiful countryside. Pietracamela lies here and is an excellent base for those wishing to use the nearby ski establishments at Prati di Tivo, or simply to take mountain walks.

ISOLA DEL GRAN SASSO D'ITALIA. This village, set in the Mavone valley, is dominated by the peaks of the Gran Sasso and is perhaps one of the best starting points for those wishing to scale the Adriatic side of this mountain group. Of note is the Romanesque church outside the village, San Giovanni al Mavone, with internal frescoes in the apse and the crypt. Nearby, in the village of San Pietro you can try some *ventricina* paté and local cheeses.

CASTELLI. Once back in the valley, be sure to visit Castelli with its excellent ceramics. Buildings of the past, such as the parish church and the cloister of a disused Franciscan monastery, rub shoulders with the shops of ceramic craftsmen. There is also a Ceramics Museum and a Ceramics Exhibition/Market open all summer long.

HOTELS AND RESTAURANTS

Roseto degli
Abruzzi
L'Approdo ¶¶
via Napoli 5
☎ 0858930464

AGRITURISMI

Morro d'Oro
Ponte Murato 🏠☞
at Ponte Murato 26
☎ 0858041171
Sant'Omero
La Meridiana 🏠☞
at S. Maria
at Vico
☎ 0861786336

WINE PRODUCERS

Notaresco
Nicodemi
contrada Veniglio
☎ 085895493

OLIVE OIL PRODUCERS

Controguerra
**Azienda Agricola
Monrori**
via Piane Tronto 23
☎ 0861809943

SHOPPING

Montorio
al Vomano
Distilleria Paesani
S.S. 80 al km 66
☎ 0861593103
Distilled spirits.
Roseto degli
Abruzzi
Enoteca Per Bacco
via Nazionale 150
☎ 0858943300
Wines.

INCOMING ABRUZZO
Società Cooperative a r.l.

Always a land of agriculture and sheep-farming traditions, Abruzzo, but especially our areas, the Altopiano delle 5 Miglia, the National Abruzzo Park and the Valle del Sagittario, offer visitors a wide choice of "infinite sensations", of scents and flavours. As you sit down for a meal you'll directly experience the delights of simple and genuine food.

The oil is smooth and balanced, perfect for seasoning and for cooking.

The pasta, home made the way our grandmothers used to, can make any recipe tastier and more appetizing.

Exquisite salami and cheese are a sin of gluttony you can afford.

Vegetables and greens, raw or cooked for delicious starters, tasty side dishes or unusual decorations.

Truffle, the "black gold", to sprinkle over any dish, satisfies even the most demanding palates.

Honey, in its different varieties, is a perfect accompaniment to both sweet and savoury food, enhancing its organoleptic qualities.

But Abruzzo tradition does not stop here. You can rediscover old time flavours by participating to events like the "Panarda del Giubileo". The first edition, organized by the "Incoming Abruzzo" hoteliers association in collaboration with the local hoteliers school, took place in January 2000. A sumptuous 73 courses banquet, complete with fireworks, was laid out in remembrance of old Medieval splendours, to relaunch the strong relationship between food & wine and the tourist industry with typical, traditional dishes, local uses and customs.

Come and see us, you won't regret it!

Booking and Information Office:
Incoming Abruzzo
Via Claudio Mori, 1 - 67037 Roccaraso (AQ)
Tel. 0864 602122 - Fax 0864 619782
Pescasseroli office: Tel. 0863 912216 - Fax 0863 911797
Scanno office: Tel. 0864 747774 - Fax 0864 749955
www.incomingabruzzo.com - e-mail: segreteria@incoming.com

BOSCO

dal 1897

*T*hanks to the quietness of the country, the mild climatic, the displacement of the hills and the perfect selection of grapes the final product is the undisputed king on our tables. The high quality of this wine arises from a real, even though still concealed, better skill in producing wine which undoubtedly characterizes the present generation of the Bosco family.

*L*ong buried corridors where, in porpose-built niches, vintage after vintage, the bottles for aging of Montepulciano are placed; the attention given to both aesthetic and building details makes this new winery and the wines themselves the expression of a timeless passion.

*T*he English oak barrels are the symbol of Bosco's tradition. They have always been used in the production process, and are able to add the finishing touches to the already rapresentative Montepulciano d'Abruzzo.

AZIENDA VINICOLA BOSCO NESTORE & C. s.n.c.

C. da Casali, 7 - 65010 Nocciano - PE - Italy
Tel. 0039 085 847345 - Fax 0039 085 847585 - www.nestorebosco.com

MOLISE
FLAVORS OF OLD

This is a region whose beauty and flavors are not widely known.
The flavors come from the hillside wheat fields and olive
groves, the mountain cheeses and charcuterie and
a surprising treasure store of truffles from the woods.

M olise has always been a land of farmers and shepherds, with mountains that soften into hills sloping down to the Adriatic coast. The people, not yet accustomed to mass tourism, are very hospitable and the region as a whole is an exciting discovery.

FROM THE MOUNTAINS TO THE SEA
We begin our journey from the southern spurs of the Abruzzi Apennines where the Sannio mountains reach over 2000 meters. Here an area rich in truffles has recently been discovered. Then we slope down to the rounded hills of the sub-Apennines. The River Trigno marks the region's limit to the north, the River Fortore to the south and the River Biferno runs across the middle. These are torrential rivers which take us through the characteristic villages of the region - many of these being Città dell'Olio (Cities of Olive Oil) with limited but excellent produce. The Pentro d'Isernia, nestled between the hills, has recently been awarded the DOC label for its wine. This joins another DOC wine, the Biferno, named after the river along which the vines grow. After the last range of hills, you reach the little-known but typical beaches of the Adriatic: Termoli, Campomarino and Petacciato.

The Volturno plain ### A DOWN-TO-EARTH CUISINE
Molise cuisine is enriched by that of its neighbors Abruzzi and Puglia, but the Molise recipes have their own particular twist. The whole region has excellent charcuterie. The vegetables and pulses are prized (especially the famous Capracotta lentils) and used in many dishes – even desserts such as the Christmas *caucione*, a soft mixture of chick-peas flavored with *Milk*, a common Molise liqueur. The tasty vegetables remind us of the down-to-earth nature of typical Molise cuisine.

Molise - Typical products

MAR ADRIATICO

Scale 1:800 000

0   10   20 km

ABRUZZO

Lanciano
Guardiagrele
Sulmona
Atessa
Vasto
Lago d. Sangro
Roccaraso
Agnone
Termoli
Guglionesi
Lago di Guardalfiera
Larino
Castel di Sangro
Trivento
Casacalenda
Pescolanciano
Bagnoli del Trigno
LAZIO
Isernia
CAMPOBASSO
Lago di Occhito
PUGLIA
Venafro
Matese
Lago d. Matese
Daunia
Sannio
S. Bartolomeo in Galdo

CHEESES

1. **Burrino.** Strong cheese wrapped around butter found in the Apennine regions.
2. **Caciocavallo di Agnone.** Strong cheese from Agnone.
3. **Fiordilatte di Bojano.** Fresh milk cheese from Bojano.
4. **Mozzarella di Venafro**
5. **Pecorino.** Sheep's cheese renowned in Maiella and Matese.
6. **Scamorza.** Firm, mild cheese at its best in Alto Molise.

CHARCUTERIE

1. **Sagicciotto di Montenero di Bisaccia.** Matured smoked-pork salami.
2. **Salsicce di fegato di Rionero Sannitico.** Liver sausage from.

3. **Sfarriccio.** Produced throughout the region.
4. **Soppressata.** Renowned in Castel del Giudice, Macchiagodena, Montenero di Bisaccia and Rionero Sannitico.
5. **Ventricina.** Salami seasoned with fennel and paprika.

EXTRA-VIRGIN OLIVE OIL

1. **Olio extravergine di oliva.** Produced in Campobasso province.

DOC WINES

1. **Biferno**
2. **Molise**
3. **Pentro d'Isernia**

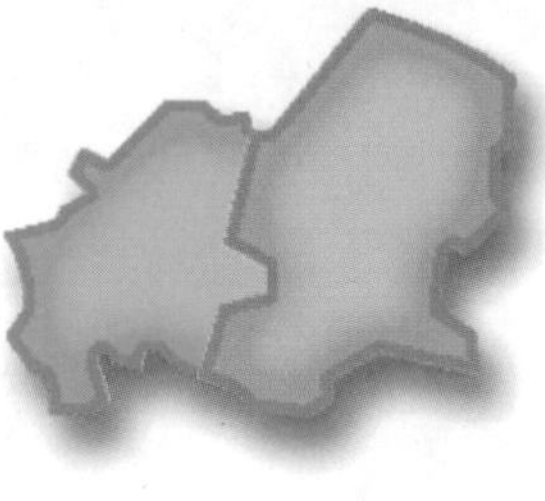

CAMPOBASSO

The River Biferno accompanies visitors as they discover an old and simple gastronomy which extends from the sea to the Matese mountains.

The Campobasso province starts from the mountainous area characterized by splendid natural landscapes and the archaeological remains of ancient *Saepinum*, which mark the border with Campania. It stretches to the valleys made fertile by the numerous rivers and torrents and then slopes down to the sea. The plain is intensely cultivated with wheat, olive trees, exuberant fruit trees and vines that produce Molise's most prestigious DOC wine, the Biferno. In the hill areas, there is extensive agricultural land intermingled with pasture for sheep and goats. Along the Adriatic coast, there is extensive fishing. Gastronomically speaking, pasta dominates the first courses, in all its various forms, often accompanied by the excellent local pulses and vegetables. For a main course, lamb is the predominant dish and as for fruit, there are the exquisite sour *limoncelle* apples, and delicious figs from Acquaviva Collecroce and Montefalcone.

Opposite: view of Fossalto

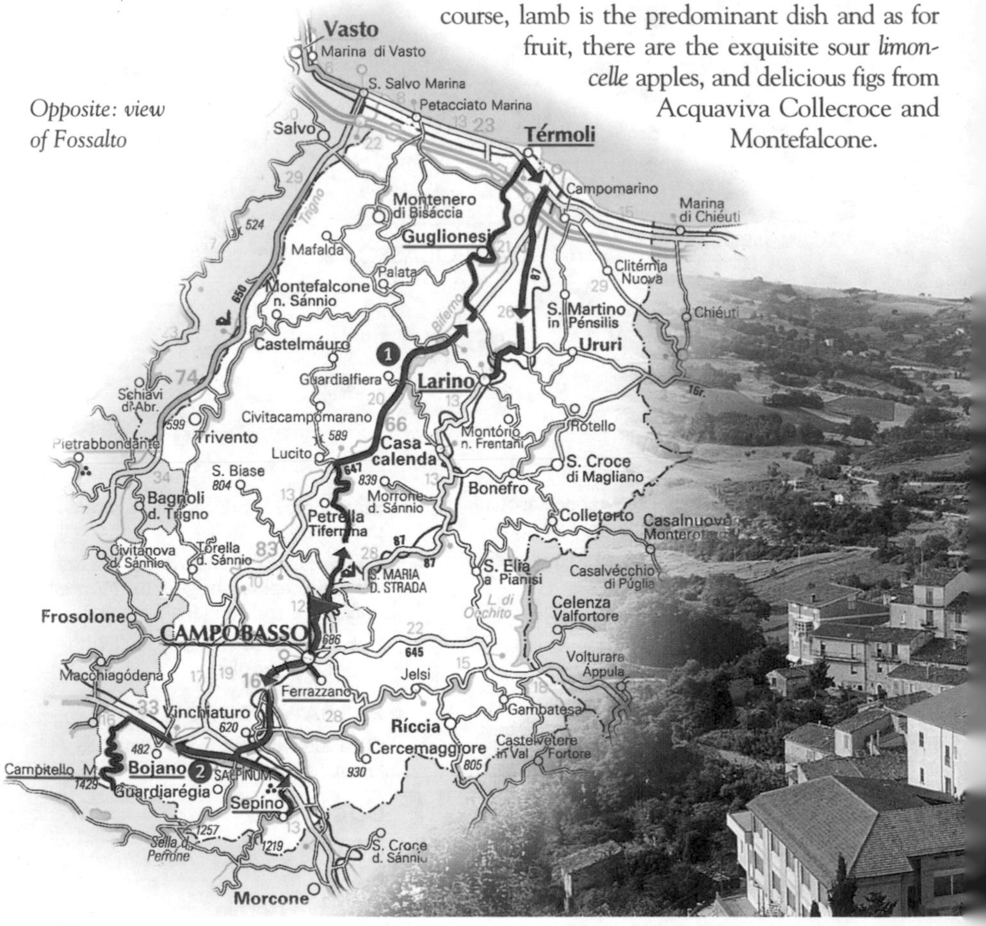

454

Gourmet Tours

CAMPOBASSO. The old town, whose fifteenth-century castle towers over the new town, is full of *trattorie* where you can try the *baccalà* griddlecakes and finish your meal with a glass of *Milk* or *poncio*, both typical Campobasso liqueurs. For a good meal based on local cuisine, we recommend the "Vecchia Trattoria da Tonino". In the S. Pietro quarter there is the *osteria* S. Pietro, which specializes in grilled meats. For a tour just outside town there is Ferrazzano, but it is also worth going further afield to try the pizzas of San Martino; the local charcuterie, cheeses and *polenta* with meat sauce at Baranello; the famous bread of Ripalimosani; and the *pollo all'oratinese* (a good fried chicken) at Oratino.

1.The Biferno valley

GUGLIONESI. From Campobasso you reach Petrella Tifernina, where there is a Romanesque parish, then continue alongside the River Biferno, which will take you across the most fertile valley of the region. You will pass through the vineyards of Trebbiano, Montepulciano, Sangiovese and Aglianico before reaching the Molise vines and wine-producing area. Pushing on towards the sea you reach Guglionesi. Here you will find the excellent "Ribo" restaurant, which includes local cheeses, wines and charcuterie on its menu. For salami-lovers we recommend the "Berchicci" butchers in San Giacomo degli Schiavoni. When in Montenero di Bisaccia, be sure not to

BIBLOS

DI MAJO NORANTE

HOTELS AND RESTAURANTS

Campobasso
Vecchia Trattoria da Tonino ¶¶¶ ★
corso V. Emanuele 8
☎ 0874415200
Osteria S. Pietro ¶
rione S. Pietro 17/19
☎ 08/465826
Bojano
Pleiadi's ★★★
via Molise 40
☎ 0874773088
Filomena ¶¶
via Garibaldi 16
☎ 0874773078
Ferrazzano
Da Emilio ¶¶
via Spensieri 21
☎ 0874416576
Guglionesi
Ribo ¶¶¶ ★
contrada Malecoste 7
☎ 0875680655
Termoli
Z' Bass ¶¶
via Oberdan 8
☎ 0875706703
Da noi tre ¶
corso F.lli Brigida 34
☎ 0875703639

Extra-virgin olive oil produced in Molise

AGRITURISMI

Montenero
di Bisaccia
⭐🏠 Masseria
Bisaccia
contrada Piscone
☎ 0875966972
Sepino
⭐🏠 La Taverna
contrada Piana
d'Olmo 6
☎ 087479626

WINE
PRODUCERS

Campomarino
Di Majo Norante
contrada Ramitello 4
☎ 087557208

OLIVE OIL
PRODUCERS

Rotello
Oleificio
Cooperativa
Tre Colli
via Dante Alighieri 2
☎ 0874839100

SHOPPING

Bojano
Antonio Pulsone
via S. Bartolomeo 31
☎ 0874773263
*Typical cheeses such
as "mozzarella".*
San Giacomo
degli Schiavoni
Macelleria
Berchicci
largo del Tempio 23
☎ 087551344
Meat

miss the *sagicciotto* and the *ventricina* salamis, the first made with smoked pork and matured for 3-4 months, the second seasoned with paprika and fennel. In town we recommend the *agriturismo* establishment "Masseria Bisaccia".

TERMOLI. In this sweet little town the gastronomy turns to the sea. Right in the middle of the historical center the "Z'Bass" restaurant serves excellent food in a jovial atmosphere. For a dinner based on fresh fish there is nothing to beat the "Da noi tre". Not far from the town, there is Molise's only Città del Vino (City of Wine), Campomarino. Here, you can try the Biferno wine and buy local wines from the "Di Majo Norante" *cantina*.

LARINO. This inland town, once ancient *Larinum*, is a good base for trips out to the Fortone valley, the shores of Lake Occhito or to two of the most important Città dell'Olio of Molise: Colletorto and Casacalenda.

2. The Sannio and the Matese mountain ranges

FERRAZZANO. In the narrow medieval streets of this town you can buy the characteristic sausage *alla ferrazzanese* before going on to a meal at the "Da Emilio" restaurant. In the nearby town of Mirabello Sannitico, the markets

sell the sour and juicy *limoncella* apple, excellent wild strawberries and, at the right time of year, the *fett'onta*, the home-made bread rubbed with garlic – a practice used in the olive presses to taste the new oil.

SEPINO. This town is near the ancient site of *Saepinum*. You will find cuisine that is typical of the region at "Taverna", an *agriturismo* business in an eighteenth-century farmhouse.

BOJANO. You must stop here before you go up to the Matese peaks. The "Pleiadi's" hotel offers an excellent welcome, while the dishes at the "Filomena" *osteria* take you back to the pastures. Lovers of *mozzarella* and *fior di latte* cheeses will not be disappointed if they go to "Antonio Pulsone".

CAMPITELLO MATESE. The town is situated at the center of the Matese – one of the biggest of the peninsular massifs. It is a recently-created holiday resort with good hotels, self-catering hotels and winter sports facilities. It is also known for its cheeses: the *burrino*, a *caciocavallo* wrapped around a heart of butter, the Matese *pecorino* and the Molise *scamorza*, which is firm and mild, and eaten cooked on a grill.

ISERNIA

This province offers the most authentic flavors of the Apennines, including wine, olive oil and, most importantly, the white truffle.

The province of Isernia is protected by the high Matese hills and mountains which are crossed by the River Voltunro, the Mainarde, the Meta mountains and the Frentani mountains. It is a landscape that seems to want to hide the land of the ancient *pentri* people, where produce is of excellent quality but of limited quantity. The wine is good: Pentro d'Isernia, covering the area around Agnone and Venafro, has recently been awarded the DOC label. The truffles are excellent and there are several Città del Tartufo (Cities of Truffles). Most truffles are found in Alto Molise in the Comunità Montana area. The olive oils, too, are of high quality and there are five Città dell'Olio. The charcuterie is excellent. History plays a large part in the province, with the ancient ruins of Pietrabbondante and Isernia, where the stone constructions date back more than 700,000 years.

View of Agnone

Lace weaving with a tombolo

Gourmet Tours

HOTELS AND
RESTAURANTS

Isernia
⭐🏠 **G.H.**
Europa ★★★
S.S. 17 uscita Isernia
Nord
☎ 0865411450
La Tequila ★★★
⭐🏠**Taverna** 🍴
via S. Lazzaro 85
☎ 0865412345
⭐🏠 **Taverna**
Maresca 🍴
corso Marcelli 186
☎ 08653976
Agnone
⭐🏠 **Sammartino**
★★★
largo P. Micca 44
☎ 086577577
Da Casciano 🍴
viale Marconi 29
☎ 086577511
Carovilli
Da Adriano 🍴
via Napoli 14
☎ 0865838688
Frosolone
Colombina 🍴
via Dante 10
☎ 0874890456
La Tana dell'Orso 🍴
at Colle dell'Orso
☎ 0874890785
Trivento
⭐🏠 **Meo** 🍴
at Fondo Valle Trigno
☎ 0874871430

ISERNIA. This town of ancient origins offers both decent food and hospitality. The "Grand Hotel Europa" is worth mentioning for its restaurant "Pantagruel", which serves dishes inspired by Molise cuisine. Equally good are "Taverna" – part of the "La Tequila" hotel –, which combines local dishes with international ones, and the "Taverna Maresca". *Mostacciolo* (rich fruit cake) made with short pastry and covered in chocolate is just one of the treats in the "Dolciaria Valentino" in Pettoranello del Molise (sales to the public are made in Isernia from October through Easter). From the city, you can reach Venafro, also known for its *mozzarella di bufala* (*mozzarella* cheese made from buffalo milk); Cerro al Volturno; and Rionero Sannitico, a production center for smoked hams, fennel sausages and *soppressate* (sausage of choice meats, eaten after six months).

FROSOLONE. This town with wide-ranging views was rebuilt after the 1805 earthquake. Among places of note there is the family-run hotel-restaurant "Colombina", and the bar-restaurant "La Tana dell"Orso", complete with riding school, in Colle dell'Orso. Along the road to Isernia, in Carpinone, you can still fish for excellent crayfish in the River Carpino.

PESCOLANCIANO. This village is in the heart of the Pentria region in an area dedicated to sheep-rearing. It is an excellent base for trips to Agnone and to Rionero Sannitico where, just a few kilometers away in Carovilli, you will find the *trattoria* "Da Adriano" which serves snails – in May and June – and roast wild boar.

PIETRABBONDANTE. The interest of visitors here usually focuses on the remains of one of the religious centers of the ancient *sanniti pentri* people at the foot of Mount Caraceno. However, for the food-lover it is not difficult to recognize the special flavor which distinguishes the local dishes in this Città del Tartufo. We can recommend the family-run "Meo" restaurant, on the other side of the river, in Trivento.

AGNONE. This is the principal vine/wine center of the DOC wine Pentro di Isernia. It is also known for the Pontificia Fonderia Marinelli, the oldest bell foundry in the world. In the "Da Casciano" restaurant, apart from the excellent charcuterie, you can

also try the wafers filled with walnuts, chocolate, honey and cooked must (partially-fermented grape juice). Other places to remember include the hotel-restaurant "Sammartino", the *agriturismo* farm "Selvaggi" which offers regional cuisine and, for agricultural treks, the "Alto Molise".

CAPRACOTTA. This Città del Tartufo is a holiday resort on the slopes of Mount Campo (1421m). In the *trattorie* you can eat the local *pecorino* cheese, with its strong, aromatic smell and slightly spicy taste, as well as well-matured lamb and other sheep meat in traditional Molise style.

Tipical Molise products: cheeses, charcuterie

AGRITURISMI

Agnone
Agritrekking Alto Molise
contrada Maranconi 15/a
☎ 0865770361
Selvaggi
at Staffoli
km 1 of the strada Provinciale Montesangrina
☎ 086577177

SHOPPING

Agnone
Dolciaria Pasticceria Carosella
corso Vittorio Emanuele 235
☎ 086578247
Sweets and pastries.
Carovilli
Profumi di Bosco dell'Alto Molise
via Fonteritana
☎ 0865838330
Truffles and boletus mushrooms.
Pettoranello del Molise
Dolciaria Valentino
corso Risorgimento
☎ 0865460294
Pastries; from October to Easter, sales to the public in Isernia.
Vastogirardi
Coop. Allevatori di Vastogirardi
via Re d'Italia 3
☎ 0865836363
Typical cheeses.

CAMPANIA
THE NOBLE CUISINE
OF THE POOR

*The good climate, the rich sea and the fertile land make
this one of the richest gastronomic districts in Italy.
Its cuisine is a mixture of the 'making do' attitude of the
common folk, and the culinary traditions of the nobility.*

*Amalfi.
The Penisola
Sorrentina coast*

This land has been greatly admired for centuries by such figures as
the poet Goethe, who wrote of "delirious joy" and "marvellous
beauty" while describing Naples. The Romans called it *Campania
felix*, the fortunate, which it still is despite its very public problems.

A REGION STRETCHING OUT TO SEA

Campania is inextricably linked with the sea, and most of its activities
and pleasures are to be found at the coast. The fishing ports enjoy rich
waters, and the fertile soil of the plains of
Gargliano, Sele, Volturno and Sarno, cou-
pled with advanced technology, allows
for intensive fruit and vegetable

growing. Local produce includes tomatoes, apricots, apples, artichokes and green figs. Local specialties include lemons and *mozzarella
di bufala* cheese (*mozzarella* made with buffalo milk). Inland, there
are olives on the lower mountain slopes, and mush-
rooms, truffles and chestnuts in the woods. There is
also pasture, leading to the production of meat, charcuterie and a wide range of cheeses. Vines are everywhere,
from the islands to the furthest point inland. The leading
red wine Taurasi is a descendant of the Falerno
wine drunk in Imperial Rome, and today it carries the DOCG label (*Denominazione di Origine Controllata e
Garantita*). There are other ancient wines and many DOC (*Denominazione di Origine Controllata*) ones.

THE CUISINE OF CAMPANIA IS POOR ONLY IN NAME.

It is a mixture of two extremes: that of the poor people and that of the
various nobility who have reigned in Naples over the centuries, from
the Austrians and French right back to the Romans and Greeks. The
extremely simple pizza is set against the elaborate *sartù* (ring of rice
filled with meat balls, sausage, chicken giblets, *mozzarella*, mushrooms,
peas and possibly other things, too) eaten on special occasions. The star
of every meal is the pasta dish. The renowned pasta of Campania is
made locally from top quality ingredients, and comes in many shapes
and sizes ready for the chefs' equally wide variety of sauces. Although
these are mainly fish-based, the classic *ragù* (ragout) is one of the great
institutions of Neapolitan cuisine. Finally, there is the very important
tradition of cakes and sweets, as well as many local specialties. As far as
restaurants are concerned, Naples and the touristic 'prima donnas'
(Capri, Ischia and Amalfi) have establishments of the very highest
quality but also many lively *trattorie* in the smaller streets, serving specialties hard to find anywhere else. Inland, you can find farmhouse
cooking with the emphasis on vegetables, mushrooms and black truffles. There is also a welcome growth in the *agriturismo* business.

CHEESES

1. **Caciocavallo silano Dop.** Strong cheeses from the provinces of Avellino, Benevento and Salerno.
2. **Mozzarella di bufala campana Dop.** Buffalo milk cheese made in the area from Paestum to the Lazio borders.
3. **Burrino in corteccia (incamiciato).** Strong cheese wrapped around butter made in Penisola Sorrentina, Monti Alburni, Cilento, Matese, Terminio-Cervialto.
4. **Provola affumicata** Smoked cheese from the Sele valley and Caserta province.
5. **Provolone del monaco.** Cheese typical of the Sorrenta Peninsula.

CHARCUTERIE

1. **Salame tipo Napoli.** Salami produced throughout the region.
2. **Capocollo campano**
3. **Cervellatine.** Produced in Naples.
4. **Salsiccia di Napoli.** Sausage produced in Avellino, Benevento and Nola.

FRUIT

1. **Albicocca vesuviana.** Vesuvius apricots.
2. **Fico bianco del Cilento.** White figs.
3. **Limoni di Amalfi e di Massa.** Lemons.
4. **Melannurca.** Small red apples.
5. **Pera spadona di Salerno.** Pears.

VEGETABLES

1. **Pomodoro San Marzano dell'Agro Sarnese-Nocerino Dop.** San Marzano tomatoes.
2. **Carciofo di Paestum.** Artichokes.

EXTRA-VIRGIN OLIVE OIL

1. **Cilento Dop.**
2. **Penisola Sorrentina Dop.**
3. **Colline Salernitane Dop.**
4. **Irpinia.**
5. **Sannio Beneventano.**

VARIOUS

1. **Castagna di Montella Igp.** Montella chestnuts.
2. **Nocciola di Giffoni Igp.** Giffoni hazelnuts.
3. **Castagna di Serino.** Serino Chestnuts.
4. **Castagna di Roccamonfina.** Roccamonfina chestnuts.
5. **Marrone di Roccadaspide.** Roccadaspide chestnuts.
6. **Noce di Sorrento.** Sorrento walnuts.
7. **Torrone di Benevento.** Nougat.
8. **Liquore Strega.** Liqueur from Benevento.

DOCG WINES

1. **Taurasi**

DOC WINES

2. **Aglianico del Taburno**
3. **Aversa**
4. **Campi Flegrei**
5. **Capri**
6. **Castel San Lorenzo**
7. **Cilento**
8. **Costa d'Amalfi**
9. **Falerno del Massico**
10. **Fiano di Avellino**
11. **Galluccio**
12. **Greco di Tufo**
13. **Guardia Sanframondi o Guardiolo**
14. **Ischia**
15. **Penisola Sorrentina**
16. **Sannio**
17. **Sant'Agata dei Goti**
18. **Solopaca**
19. **Taburno**
20. **Vesuvio**

NAPLES

The setting is the most beautiful bay in the world, while the cuisine, starting from the humble pizza, is honest and unique.

The Gulf of Naples, with its crown of islands, has always been a place of fascination and contradiction. The one-time capital of a kingdom is an important cultural center and a land of contrasts and cohabitation, which is reflected in its cuisine. The poorest and most authentic cuisine is intermingled with that of the nobility, in the *monzù* tradition (the word comes from a dialect version of the French 'monsieur'). More than any other cuisine, the Neapolitan cuisine has creat-

Naples. The ancient village of Marechiaro

ed dishes (pizza and spaghetti) that are part of not only the national but also international gastronomy.Not all specialties seem very original but their flavor, which comes from the use of lots of fresh local produce, makes them unique. Alongside the vegetable dishes, there are also the fish dishes, and the variety of inviting ways in which they are prepared is surprising. In conclusion, we cannot pass over the various vines of historical importance which are used in the DOC wines of Ischia, Capri, Vesuvio, Penisola Sorrentina and Campi Flegrei.

Gourmet Tours

NAPLES. The former capital of the Kingdom of the Two Sicilies is known world-wide, not only for its Gulf waters, Vesuvius, and the palaces, but also for the poorer quarters with their market places and narrow streets which remind us of the Orient, and whose emblem is the *Spaccanapoli*, named after a district of Naples . Naples is rich in history, the most impressive proof of which is the Maschio Angioino, which Charles I of Angiò wanted as the nucleus of his royal palace. There is a vast choice of food here, from the traditional pizza and spaghetti to dishes that satisfy the demands of the most exigent palate. One of the very best eating places is"La Sacrestia", unequalled for its fish, the *orecchiette con cozze e zucchine* (*orecchiette* pasta with mussels and zucchini), *spigola in dadolata di pomodori* (sea bass with seasoned bread and tomato sauce) and the *tortine calde di mela annurca* (hot *annurca* apple cakes), not to mention the

Typical market in Naples

excellent wines. Do not miss the "Cantinella", also up there with the best, with its *enoteca* "La Mia Cantina" which offers a choice of extraordinary wines. In the bay, overhanging the sea, there is the "'A Fenestella" which appears in Salvatore Di Giacomo's song, "A Marechiaro". In the center of the city, there are a variety of eating places, including the historical "Ciro a Santa Brigida", and the "San Carlo". One of the best is the very busy "Mimì alla Ferrovia" whose cuisine concentrates on the flavors of the vegetable garden with its tasty *involtini di peperoni* (roulades of peppers) and a classic *parmigiana di melanzane* (layers of eggplant with tomato and parmesan cheese sauce, baked in the oven). For dining with a great view of the Gulf, there is the "Sbrescia Antonio", a characteristic restaurant with very fresh fish. If you like eating good food to the sound of Neapolitan melodies, try "Girulà". Fish, and only fish, is served at the "Poeta", situated on a hill in a residential district of

HOTELS AND RESTAURANTS

Naples
Cantinella ¶¶¶¶
via Cuma 38/42
☎ 0817648684
Sacrestia ¶¶¶¶
via Orazio 116
☎ 081664186
'A Fenestella ¶¶¶
calata Ponticello
a Marechiaro 25
☎ 0817690020
**Ciro a
S. Brigida** ¶¶¶ ⬛
via S. Brigida 71/73
☎ 0815524072
Enot. Gra.Pa.Lù. ¶¶¶
via Toledo 16
☎ 0815522114
Girulà ¶¶¶
via Vetriera a Chiaia 7/a
☎ 081425511
San Carlo ¶¶¶ ⬛
via Cesario Console 18
☎ 0817649757
La Bersagliera ⬛ ¶¶
borgo Marinari 10
☎ 0817646016
Mimì alla Ferrovia ¶¶
via Alfonso d'Aragona 21
☎ 0815538526
Poeta ¶¶
piazza S. Di Giacomo 133
☎ 0815756936
Sbrescia Antonio ¶¶
rampe S. Antonio
at Posillipo 109
☎ 081669140
Taverna dell'Arte ¶¶
rampe S. Giovanni
Maggiore 1/a
☎ 0815527558
Vadinchenia ¶¶ ⬛
via Pontano 21
☎ 081660265
Masaniello ¶
via Donnalbina 28
☎ 0815528863

Posillipo. Make a special note of "La Taverna ll'Arte", a *trattoria* typical of the region with excellent cuisine (land-based), including *bucatini di ricotta e pecorino* (*bucatini* pasta with *ricotta* and *pecorino* cheese sauce), and *salsiccia ripiena alla griglia* (grilled, stuffed sausages). The traditions of Campania and Luca are combined at the "Vadinchenia". The family-run "Masaniello" is set in the stables of a historical building. You can have a break in the shadow of Castel dell'Oro at "La Bersagliera", a time-honored-meeting place for artists, intellectuals and politicians. At the end of your meal, you could order an ice-cream or local pastry from the famous old "Caffè Gambrinus". Do not miss the "Gay Odin", founded by a Swiss confectioner, which makes chocolates and sugared almonds sold in six shops around the city, many of which still have their original Art Nouveau décor. There is also the delicious dairy products store, "Mandara". Finally, when you cross the old center, you must stop at the top-quality food store, "Scaturchio". If you want to buy wine, we recommend the "Enoteca del Buon Bere", the "Partenopea" and the *enoteca* of the restaurant "Enoteca Gra.Pa.Lù".

1. Sorrento and Capri

ERCOLANO. Partly built on ancient *Hercolanum*, Ercolano was, until the end of the nineteenth century, a holiday resort for the Neapolitan aristocracy. This is reflected in the buildings in Corso Resina. You absolutely must go to the hotel-restaurant, "Punta Quattroventi" on the seafront.

TORRE DEL GRECO. This was called the kingdom's *spugna d'oro* (golden sponge) by Ferdinand IV of Bourbon because of the wealth that came from its fishing and its

Naples. Vesuvius at dawn

coral workmanship. To combine the pleasures of relaxation and those of the palate you should try the hotel "Sakura" and its restaurant, the "Caruso", set in a pine forest.

TORRE ANNUNZIATA. Famous in Roman times for its waters, ancient *Oplonti* came back into the limelight in 1964, when archaeological digs unearthed the villas of Poppea and Crasso. The town is known for its pasta. You can visit the pasta-makers "Setaro" and watch pasta being made the old-fashioned way with machines from the beginning of the twentieth century. For relaxing and dining, try the hotel "Grillo Verde".

POMPEI. Two things attract visitors to Pompei: its famous excavations, and the sanctuary of the Madonna del Rosario, a place of constant pilgrimage. Near the church, there is the elegant restaurant, "Il Principe", serving interesting experimental cuisine. At the "President", in the evening, its Neapolitan dishes are accompanied by the sounds of the classic Neapolitan guitar. In the town center, there is the "7i' Caterina" with a wood oven for pizza and a well-stocked winery. "Peluso" does great cakes. The restaurant "Da Andrea" in Pompei Scavi serves shell-fish, fresh fish and good pizzas.

CASTELLAMMARE DI STABIA. Today, this is a modern industrial town and the headquarters of important shipyards and a cut glass factory. Stabiae, as it was called in ancient times, was not spared the devastation of the eruption of Vesuvius. It was later rebuilt around a castle: *Castrum ad mare de Stabiis.* You can enjoy a romantic atmosphere at the hotel-

Pompei. Millstones

restaurant, "La Medusa", set in a nineteenth-century villa. There is another good hotel-restaurant, the "Stabia", on the seafront.

VICO EQUENSE. This ancient Etruscan center (Acqua) is, today, a beach resort (Marina di Equa) and holiday destination. You can find refined Campania cuisine inside "Nonna Rosa", whose walls are made of volcanic ash rock, and a cuisine of quality and imagination at the "Torre del Saraceno". For good home-made ice-cream, we recommend the "Exotic Ice Cream" and for local milk-based products, go to "Alimentari Italia" and "Caseificio Savarese". Lovers of fresh pasta should stop at the pasta-makers "Punto e Pasta".

SORRENTO. Originally the Greek Surrentum, home of ancient luxury Roman villas, it is situated on a terrace overhanging the sea. For the most demanding of palates, there is the "Caruso" restaurant serving its *ravioli di cicala ai pomodorini* (*ravioli* of squill with baby tomatoes), *calameretti riepieni di zucchine e scamorza* (young squid stuffed with zucchini and *scamorza* cheese) and *delizie al*

limone (lemon-flavored delicacies). The restaurant "Favorita-'O Parrucchiano", set out in terraces surrounded by greenery and one of the oldest in Italy, is also good. Those who love seafood should go to "La Vela Bianca" which is frequented by stars of the theater. On a more rustic note, there is "L'Antica Trattoria" set under a flowering pergola. In addition, there is the *agriturismo* establishment, "La Pergola", set amongst citrus plantations and olive groves, which serves good local cuisine. Do not miss the "Apreda", a renowned cheese store on the coast, "Pollio", "Primavera" and "O Funzionista" for top quality cakes, "Davide" for the best ice-

cream and "Piemme" for home-made sweets, *limoncello*, and mint and basil liqueurs.

MASSA LUBRENSE. At the very end of the Sorrento peninsula, this town is high above the sea and looks over towards the island of Capri. The restaurant "Antico Francischiello Da Peppino" is in a good panoramic setting and has a terrace overlooking the sea. You can also enjoy a lovely view of the Gulf of Naples and Capri at the century-old "Riccardo Francischiello" restaurant in the "Bellavista" hotel. There are also a few detours you could make to some good restaurants. Go to Marina del Cantone for "La Taverna del Capitano" where you can eat home-made dishes of tuna in oil, *zuppa di gamberi e cicoria* (crayfish and chicory soup), and *pesce in*

Procida. The Mediterranean architecture of the port and the castle

crosta (fish en croute), to Nerano for the "I Quattro Passi", where they always have fresh fish, and to Sant'Agata sui Due Golfi for the ultra-famous hotel-restaurant, "Don Alfonso-1890", for excellent Mediterranean cuisine.

CAPRI. This magical island surrounded by lapping turquoise waters provides a wide choice of restaurants. The top class restaurant "Quisi" in the "Grand Hotel Quisisana" is set in a nineteenth-century palace looking out onto the Faraglioni (crags in the sea). The service is suitably refined and the wine very well chosen. The "Capri Moon" is set in another nineteenth-century villa and serves genuine Campania cuisine. The "Canzone del Mare" is situated in an exclusive beach club in a park. For imaginative cuisine, try the "Da Paolino", set in a sunny lemon grove. The celebrated "La Pigna" restaurant is over one hundred years old, "La Capannina" is famous for its fish and "La Scogliera" in the "Palatium" hotel is also good. For your visit to Anacapri, we recommend "Il Cucciolo", "Gelsomina alla Migliara" and "Rondinella" for their exquisite Campania cuisine served with a good choice of wines. The "Enoteca La Capannina Più" also has excellent wines. To buy local produce, go to the organic farm

CASA D'AMBRA
ISCHIA
BIANCOLELLA
FRASSITELLI
1995

SHOPPING

Naples
Caffè Gambrinus
via Chiaia 1/2
☎ 081417582
Pastries and ice-creams.
Cremeria Mandara
via Cilea 135
☎ 0815604651
Typical dairy products.
Enot. del Buon Bere
via Marino Turchi 15
☎ 0817647843
Wines.
Gay Odin
via Vetriera 12
☎ 081417843
Chocolates and "confetto" pastries.
Pasticceria Gelateria Scaturchio
piazza S. Domenico Maggiore19
☎ 0815517031
Pastries and ice-creams.
Enoteca Partenopea
viale Augusto 2
☎ 0815937982
Wines.
Capri
La Capannina più
via Botteghe 39/41
☎ 0818378899
Wines.
Pasticceria Alberto
via Roma 9/11
☎ 0818376524
Sweets and pastries.
Limoncello di Capri
via Roma 79
☎ 0818375561
Ischia (island of)
Pasticceria Calise
via A. Sogliuzzo
☎ 081991270
Sweets and pastries.
Ischia Sapori
via Morgione 88
☎ 081984213
via Gianturco 2
☎ 081984482
Local specialties.

shop, "Elio ed Erika". For the best Capri cakes, visit the "Alberto" cake shop. At "Limoncello di Capri" you will find various liqueurs, including the famous *limoncello*.

2. The Campi Flegrei and Ischia

POZZUOLI. You must stop at the ancient Roman colony of *Puteolis* in the volcanic area of the Campi Flegrei (between Naples, Cuma and Capo Miseno), today a busy tourist destination. At the "Piazzetta Serapide", which actually faces the Temple of Serapide, the menu depends on the fish caught that day and is accompanied by the wines of Campania. You can find regional cuisine and fish at the "Ninfea". It is worth stopping at Bacoli for the restaurant "La Misenetta", and sampling its Buon Ricordo dish, *pennette al pesto napoletano* (*pennette* pasta with Neapolitan-style pesto sauce – basil, garlic and cheese).

PROCIDA. This small island at the mouth of the Gulf of Naples has interesting gastronomic fare. Try "Crescenzo", a restaurant typical of the area, set in the center of the port, and the "Osteria del Gallo" where you can eat popular traditional dishes. You really must stop at "Dal Cavaliere" for a *granita al limone* (lemon-flavoured crushed ice), and do not miss the honey from the honey shop "Il Miele dei Campi Flegrei".

ISCHIA. This island is covered in citrus groves, vineyards and chestnut trees, and is home to many spas and beauty centers. As soon as you arrive, you will notice the "Damiano", a relaxing restaurant serving good local cuisine. In the center, "Gennaro" serves good fish dishes. Right on the sea, there is the "Giardini Eden" which you can reach by boat. Those wanting wines produced by the "Casa Perrazzo" stop at "Appuntamento Vino". You can also find the island's DOC wines at "Cenatiempo Vini", "Lo Chef" and "Enoteca D'Ambra". The latter is involved in the creation of new wines, like the sparkling wine, Kalimera. For eating, there are also "Da Cocò", " 'O Padrone d'O Mare", and "La Villarosa", which specializes in mushrooms, cereals and snails. In Forio, you will find the excellent restaurants "Da Peppina di Renato" and "Il Melograno" with unforgettable food from land and sea, including *mezzemaniche alla ricciola* (pasta with curly endive salad), and capers, olives and rabbit Ischia-style (the rabbit is cut into pieces and browned in olive oil, then cooked in white wine, tomatoes and rosemary). But the gourmet's true temple is the "Bar Calise". At the "Ischia Sapori" store, you will find all the island's flavors under one roof: extra virgin olive oil flavored with lemon, citrus jams and jellies, honey, spices and local wines.

AVELLINO

The area offers mountain flavors – mushrooms, meats, truffles, charcuterie and cheeses – largely unknown in Campania cuisine.

B road green landscapes of woods and hills, that is the nature of the Avellino area. Nature itself was not disturbed by the strong earthquake of 1980, unlike the "signs" of man, whose injuries are taking a long time to heal. The gastronomy reflects the countryside and comprises simple traditional farmhouse dishes, often meat-based – especially lamb and rabbit –, and salamis and mountain hams, chestnuts, hazelnuts and excellent fruit and vegetables. The wines are top quality, the best being the DOCG Taurasi then the DOC wines Aglianico del Taburno, Greco di Tufo and Fiano di Avellino.

Rural landscape of Irpinia

Gourmet Tours

AVELLINO. The modern look to the town is due to its reconstruction after bombings in 1943 and then the earthquake of 1980. In the old center, Irpinia cuisine is the fare at the "Antica Trattoria Martelle", with cheeses, charcuterie, and a selection of Campania and national wines. Even though the sea is far off, you still get the freshest of fish at "Malaga". The "Caveja" restaurant serves specialties from the Romagnese area. You will be very comfortable at the "Hotel De La Ville" which has three restaurants: "Il Cavallino", the "Rosa" and the "Lilla". The restaurant "Ippocampo" in the "Jolly" hotel is very innovative. On the wine side, try the "Wine Bar Evoè" which has a country feel to it but is also elegant; the "Enoteca Garofalo" which serves all types of wine; and the "Marianna", which also produces wine including the DOC Aglianico, Fiano and Greco di Tufo. A brief detour will bring you to Moschiano and the "Santa Cristina" restaurant, serving adapted farmhouse recipes. A little further on, in Lauro, you will find the "Dente d'Oro" fish restaurant, which also has excellent desserts. Just outside Avellino, in Mercogliano, there is a restaurant worth trying at the "Green Park Hotel Titino" where you will get a really traditional meal. Finally, for wine-tasting, there is the "Mastroberardino" in Atripalda (try their Greco di Tufo) and the "Di Marzo" in Tufo.
MIRABELLA ECLANO. This town, in

the heart of the historic Irpinia region, boasts a wooden ceiling and wooden crucifix in its church, S. Maria Maggiore. In September, there is the festival of the obelisk . At the hotel-restaurant "Mirabella" enjoy *stringozzi con porcini* (pasta with *porcini* mushrooms) and *capretto all'irpina* (kid goat Irpinastyle). Do not miss nearby Taurasi, a Città del Vino (City of Wine) where you can drink Taurasi wine (shop at "Antonio Caggiano" and "Cantina Antica Irpinia"), and the "Antico Torronificio Nardone" in Dentecane.
ARIANO IRPINO. Marked by earthquakes, this town stands on the three hills which separate the river basins of the Ufita and Cervaro. You should visit the cathedral and the Museo degli Argenti. The modern hotel "Incontro" has a good restaurant, so too does the "Terrazze Hotel Giorgione", which serves local food. It is worth pushing on to Vallesaccarda so as not to miss one of the best of the inland restaurants, "Oasis Antichi Sapori" and the excellent "Minicuccio".
BAGNOLI IRPINO. First, you pass Sant'Angelo dei Lombardi which was badly hit by the 1980 earthquake. Then you arrive at Bagnoli, an important center for truffles – the black, *mesentericum* variety, the so-called Bagnoli truffle. Dishes of the area include *ravioli di ricotta* (*ravioli* stuffed with *ricotta* cheese) and *insalata di tartufi* (truffle salad). Traditional dishes served with the best local DOC wines can be found at the *trattoria* "Lo Spiedo".

BENEVENTO

From the hills up to the mountains, the area is a land of wines, olive oil, artichokes and apples, meats and mushrooms, and cheeses and hams.

The Benevento area, and particularly the Caudina Valley, was strategically important in Roman times. The Benevento part of the Sannio was even forced into isolation for a long period under the papal reign. This led to an economy based primarily around agriculture and sheep farming, which is reflected in its cuisine of simple foods, vegetables, Matese cheeses (*ricotta* and *pecorino*), and charcuterie, including *soppressate*, *capocolli*, salamis and hams. The area is known for its wine production, including the DOC wines Guardia Sanframondi, Sannio, Solopaca, and Sant'Agata de' Goti. And you simply cannot leave Benevento without trying the famous *torrone* (nougat), an ancient tradition of excellent quality.

Sant'Agata de' Goti

Gourmet Tours

BENEVENTO. You can see from the town's Museo del Sannio and the monuments of Imperial Rome what an important merchant town this was. It is worth stopping at some of the restaurants here, especially the "Enoteca del Sannio" which serves not only the precious wines of the area but also local dishes and produce. Here you can also try the famous Liquore Strega made from herbs. For good food, we highly recommend "Pedicini", for its fresh pastas with sauces made from woodland produce (but also fish), grilled meats  and, in the evening, excellent pizzas. Two other dependable restaurants are the "Traiano" and the "Pina e Gino". The Benevento Torrone (nougat) is to die for – you can buy it at "Sassano" and "Ambrosino". Another great store is "Da Soccio", selling *mozzarella, scamorza* and *provola* cheeses, and all the local specialties you can imagine. At the "Vecchie Carrozze" restaurant, on the hill in Piano Cappelle, you can have a traditional drink with your meal in an old-fashioned atmosphere.

MONTESARCHIO. At the foot of wooded Taburno Mountain, there is a castle which watches over the valley. Back in 321 B.C., it witnessed the humiliation of Rome by the Samnites. In the ancient piazza, there is the fountain of Hercules from which the town got its name (*Mons Herculis*). For a break, try the "Cristina Park Hotel", with flowers everywhere and substantial dishes such as the *gnocchetti al ragù d'agnello* (small *gnocchi* with lamb

sauce) and the *tagliata di filetto con verdure e pecorino* (steak with vegetables and *pecorino* cheese).

SANT'AGATA DE' GOTI. The village sits on a spur bordered by the River Isclero. Its name tells of its Germanic past. Stop at the "Locanda dei Goti" for a table laden with charcuterie and stuffed grilled vegetables, *orecchiette* pasta with asparagus and veal cutlets with mushrooms. We highly recommend the "Mustilli" *cantina* with its top wines (Falanghina, Aglianico, Greco, etc.) and *agriturismo* establishment.

TELESE TERME. The Roman town, *Telesia*, owed its fortune to an earthquake which created a spring of spa water. The feel of the town is reflected in the nineteenth-century "Grand Hotel Telese" and the refined "Villa Gioia" in San Salvatore Telesino. Wine tourists should continue to Solopaca where they will find the famous labels at the "Cantina Sociale".

CERRETO SANNITA. This town was rebuilt in Baroque style after an earthquake in 1688. It is know for its fabrics and ceramics. Another good reason to stop here is "Masella", a simple restaurant serving good, traditional food. In Faicchio, you can choose between the *agriturismo* establishment "Antico Frantoio" and the *trattoria* "Fontanavecchia", serving *pasta e fagioli* (pasta and bean soup), *pappardelle con la lepre* (pasta with hare sauce), game and meat

GUARDIA SANFRAMONDI. Once a strategic town, it is now known for its Santuario dell'Assunta and the DOC wines of Guardiolo, which you can try at "De Lucia".

CASERTA

This is a province with a variety of resources, which come from the sea, the Terra di Lavoro and the Matese mountains.

The province of Caserta occupies the section of the Campania region that the Romans called *Campania Felix* (i.e. blessed). It is a land of undulating hills crossed by the River Volturno and made exceptionally fertile by the mild climate and the Roccamonfina and Campi Flegrei volcanoes. On the gastronomic side, it is a province perhaps more devoted to land food than seafood, where you can find dishes ranging from the poorest to the richest, like the *sartù* and the *lasagne di Carnevale* (eaten on Shrove Tuesday, the strips of *lasagna* pasta are layered with sausage, meat balls, *mozzarella*, *ricotta* and other cheeses, and boiled eggs). The vines also benefit from the volcanic ash, supplying the DOC wines of Asprinio di Aversa, Galluccio and Falerno del Massico.

The village of
Pietravairano

Gourmet Tours

CASERTA. The original medieval center of the town is now known as Casertavecchia, and is on a hill right opposite today's town, which was built during the famous rule of the Bourbons. Near the latter is the "Ciacco" fish restaurant, serving food made in the regional style. Close to the historical center, there is the "Adamo Bistrot", in a modern building but serving traditional dishes. In Casertavecchia, mushrooms and local cuisine tempt your taste buds at the inviting, rustic "La Castellana". In the most characteristic part of the old medieval village you can find good food at reasonable prices at the "Mastrangelo". There is a feeling of history at the "Le Colonne" restaurant, with its Art Nouveau decor and traditional cuisine. In Casagiove, just before you reach town, you will find the *enoteca* "La Botte" which sells excellent wines, extra virgin olive oil, cheeses, and exquisitely-made sweets and cakes. It is also worth making a note of "Massa", "Il Pappagallo" (part of the "Belvedere" hotel) and "La Reggia" – all good restaurants. A little further on, in Leucio, you will find traditional Campania fare at the "Antica Locanda". An even more traditional menu is offered at the "Leucio".

AVERSA. This highly-populated town has seen a lot of development in modern times but has kept reminders of its Norman past in the cathedral and castle, both in the historical center. We recommend visitors go to the "Ristorante del Sole", with its innovative cuisine specialising in seafood. Moving on along the coast, you pass Mondragone in the heart of ancient Agro Falerno, from where the most well-known Caserta wine gets its name. Have a wine tasting stop at the nineteenth-century "Cantina Moio". The area has excellent and much-sought-after vegetables – tomatoes, string beans and beans. The charcuterie is also worth buying.

SESSA AURUNCA. This town is set in the ancient *Suessa* region, center of the Aurunci people, in a landscape of orchards and olive groves. You must see the ducal castle, the Romanesque cathedral and, a little further away, the bridge of the Aurunci, a Roman structure with 21 arches. The land is used for the intensive growing of high quality

Sheep-breeding in the Matese plateau

fruit and vegetables. It also produces quality cheeses, hams and sausages, and the red wines of the DOC Falerno del Massico, brimming full of character. Do not miss the "Cantine Fontana Galardi", set in an area where they successfully cultivate vines and olives alongside chestnut trees.

ROCCAMONFINA. The ash from the dead volcano acts as fertilizer for the young chestnut trees which surround the Parco Regionale del Roccamonfina e Foce Garigliano. For good food and a good view, there is the "Il Castagneto" restaurant which specializes in Campania and Mountain cuisine. Try the thistles, which are cooked in a variety of different ways, and the local charcuterie. Further inland, on the road to the Matese, we recommend a break in Pietravairano which is worth the trip both for its local produce (especially the cheeses) and the excellent restaurant "La Caveja", with its rustic ambiance and a cuisine typical of the area – griddlecakes filled with tomato, potato and mushrooms; chicory soup with meatballs; and boned lamb stuffed with *pecorino* cheese.

PIEDIMONTE MATESE. At the foot of the Matese plateau, you will find ancient houses and a sumptuous seventeenth-century sanctuary. Here the farming and cheesemaking traditions of the Matese are alive and strong, giving us everything from mushrooms and potatoes through to sausages and cheeses (*caciottine, scamorze, pecorino* and *mozzarella*). Nearby Alife, which you should visit, has provided good vegetables for a century, especially string beans and beans. From Piedimonte you can also take a pleasant trip out to

San Gregorio Matese, a town traditionally devoted to the rearing of cattle, which has recently enjoyed a boost in tourism. A good dinner with a Castelvenere or Solopaca wine can be found at the "San Donato" restaurant. On the way back to Caserta, you can make a scenic detour to Gioia Sannitica and get a good meal at the "Borgo Antico" which serves *tagliatelle condite alla rustica* (*tagliatelle* pasta with country sauce) and different meats with various types of mushroom.

CAPUA. The town was built on the ruins of *Casilinum* by refugees from the fire in Roman Capua, from where it took its name. On the gastronomic side, there is the *agriturismo* establishment, the "Giò Sole", set in an ancient group of houses. Typical examples of their produce are: *frutta sciroppata* (fruit preserved in syrup), conserves, and vegetables preserved in oil. The "Romano" restaurant, run by a family which put the restaurant on the map, serves Campania dishes as well as the classics, and, in the evening, makes wonderful pizzas using an ancient recipe.

SANTA MARIA CAPUA VETERE. This is the Capua of classical antiquity and still has some Roman remains. The fertile soil means there is extensive cultivation of fruit and vegetables. In the cake shops, you can buy the *torroni* (nougats) and a variety of different types of *pastiera* (cake made of short pastry and filled with *ricotta* and candied fruit) made with corn or rice. From the selection of restaurants we have picked out the "Ninfeo" known for its pasta first courses, grilled fish and home-made *limoncello*. And "Milano" is a good hotel in a quiet area.

AGRITURISMI

Capua
Masseria Giòsole
via Giardini 31
☎ 0823961108
Ciorlano
Il Teologo
contrada Castagna
☎ 0823944832
San Potito Sannitico
Quercete
contrada Quercete
☎ 0823913881
Sessa Aurunca
Aria Nova
at S. Castrese, S.S. 430,
via Campo Felice
☎ 0823706249

WINE PRODUCERS

Mondragone
Moio
viale Margherita 6
☎ 0023970017
Sessa Aurunca
Fontana Galardi
via Provinciale San Carlo
☎ 0823708034

SHOPPING

Caserta
Green Garden
piazzetta Gramsci
☎ 03396348407
Ice-creams.
Casagiove
Enoteca La Botte
via Nazionale Appia 178
Wines.

SALERNO

This province stretches from the Amalfi coast to the Cilento national park, taking in sea and mountain, town and undiscovered lands.

The province of Salerno occupies the lower part of Campania and is made up of coastline, the Vallo di Diano plain, the Sele plain and the Cilento mountains. Inland the cooking is typical of the countryside with dishes such as *patàne e cicci* (potatoes and beans). At the coast, fish prevails, mostly fresh fish but also dried, salted and preserved. Alongside fishing, the other main resources of the province are olive oil (DOP extra-virgin olive oils from Colline Salernitane and Cilento), DOC wines (Costa d'Amalfi, Cilento and Castel San Lorenzo), lemons from Amalfi and Massa, Giffoni IGP hazelnuts, and many other fruits and vegetables.

Opposite: the Amalfi coast and one of the villages between vineyards and citrus orchard

Gourmet Tours

SALERNO. The modern quarters which greet the tourist on arrival then give way to the old center towards the slopes of the hill. The first important gourmet stop is right at the entrance of the town, at the excellent "Al Cenacolo" restaurant which serves house specialties including *cortecce Antica Salerno con zucchine* (pasta old-Salerno style with zucchini) and *pici con patate* (pasta with potatoes). In the old part of town, there is the "Antica Pizzeria del Vicolo della Neve", the oldest pizzeria in Salerno. The "Hostaria del Brigante" serves dishes made from ancient recipes. Another gallery of flavors is provided by the restaurant-pizzeria, "Santa Lucia", "La Brace" serves excellent dishes from the cuisine of the poor, while "Il Timone" and "Del Golfo" are also worth trying. You should get your aperitif and dessert from the "Caffè dei Mercanti" or at the "Pasticceria Napoleone". To buy fresh dairy products, go to "La Contadina". The two "Alimento Manzoni" stores are *enoteca*, cake shop and bakery rolled into one, where you can find local *grappa* and liqueurs, including the Amalfi *limoncello*.

1. The Amalfi Coast

VIETRI SUL MARE. This little town which looks out onto the Gulf of Salerno is famous for its majolica which you can admire in the Museo della Ceramica and buy at the many little shops around the town. The first gastronomic stop is the "La Lucertola", where you can also stay the night. Next, there is the "La Locanda" where the owner will greet you with an aperitif before you pass through to one of the two tastefully decorated dining rooms.
CAVA DE' TIRRENI. In the past this ancient village was important for its monopoly of silk

HOTELS AND RESTAURANTS

Salerno
Al Cenacolo ¶¶
piazza Alfano I 4
☎ 089238818
Brace ¶¶
lungomare Trieste 11/13
☎ 089225159
Del Golfo ¶¶ ★
via Porto 57
☎ 089231581
Timone ¶¶
via Generale Clark 29/35
☎ 089335111
Antica Pizzeria del Vicolo della Neve ¶
vicolo della Neve 24
☎ 089225705
Hostaria il Brigante ¶
via Fratelli Linguiti 4
☎ 089226592
Santa Lucia ¶
via Roma 182
☎ 089225696
Agropoli
Ceppo ¶¶ ★
via Madonna del Carmine 31
☎ 0974843036
'U Saracino ¶
via Trentova
☎ 0974824063
Amalfi
Il Saraceno ★★★ ★
via Augustariccio 25
☎ 089831148
Santa Caterina ★★★
at Pastena (km 1)
S.S. Amalfitana 9
☎ 089871012
Eolo ¶¶¶
via P. Comite 3
☎ 089871241
La Caravella ¶¶¶
via M. Camera 12
☎ 089871029
Da Gemma ¶¶
via Fra' G. Sasso 10
☎ 089871345
Smeraldino ¶¶
piazzale dei Protontini 1
☎ 089871070

tapestries. It still has its original colonnaded streets, which are unique in the south of Italy. "L'Incanto" (The Enchantment) is both the name and character of the villa immersed in greenery, where you should dine. For lovers of cooking 'the way it used to be', the ideal place is "La Taverna Scacciaventi" – the vegetables in season are served in a huge variety of different ways. In Via Mazzini, the "Gran Caffè Respighi" is a meeting place for local artists. Country cuisine is served at the "Saura" and "Country Club Santa Lucia" *agriturismo* establishments.

MAIORI. The great majolica dome of S. Maria a Mare dominates the town and its sandy cove. The town is full of excellent hotels aimed at relaxation. For a gastronomic stop, there is the choice of "Le Ninfee" in the "Panorama" hotel, the "Mammato" with home cooking and seafood, and the cake shop, "Gambardella", which sells local specialties.

RAVELLO. Stretched between two valleys going down to the sea, the place will enrapture you with the intense colors of its landscapes and the luxurious gardens. The thirteenth-century Arab-Sicilian architecture is also very atmospheric. The best Campania cuisine is to be found at "Confalone", set in the house of a twelfth-century nobleman. Note also the refined "Rossellinis" restaurant in the elegant "Palazzo Sasso" hotel, a building with medieval origins. Those wishing to buy a good *limoncello* should go to "Profumi della Costiera". Also note the liqueur producers, "Giardini di Ravello".

AMALFI. The white houses of this popular holiday destination are dotted between the azure sea and the green vegetation. One of the best stops here is the "Eolo" whose modernised Campania cuisine can be eaten on a balcony with a panoramic view. We also recommend "Da Gemma", where seafood – but not exclusively – is on the menu every day, with dishes such as *zuppa di pesce* (fish soup) and *paccheri di Gragnano* with shrimp and angler fish. "La Caravella" serves excellent Amalfi and fish specialties, and has made a name for itself over the years for being serious and dedicated about its food. For a family atmosphere, there is the "Smeraldino" with panoramic views. There are also the hotel, "Il Saraceno", with

restaurant on the beach, and the two elegant restaurants of the hotel "Santa Caterina". Finally, we recommend you try the *spaghetti al cartoccio* (spaghetti cooked in paper) at "Ciccio Cielo, Mare e terra". You can buy local syrups and liqueurs at "La Valle dei Mulini", and the cake shop, "Pansa", also sells the liqueur Villa Paradiso. POSITANO. White houses cling to a steep slope that descends into the old seaside village, once frequented by elegant artists. Ancient and modern are combined in the nineteenth-century noble building that is home to the "Le Sirenuse" hotel, one of the best-kept in Italy. You should try the *diavoletti alla griglia* or the *aragosta con salsa 'remoulade'* (lobster with remoulade sauce) at its restaurant, "La Sponda". For fresh pasta with shellfish, go to the "Le Tre Sorelle", facing the sea. There are also other good restaurants, including "La Donna Rosa", for those wanting to escape the busy seafront, "Chez Black" which looks like a ship on the inside, "Cambusa" and "La Buca di Bacco". We highly recommend the hotel-restaurant, "San Pietro". In the quiet Piazzetta di Montepertuso, you will get value for money at the recently-opened "Il Ritrovo" *trattoria*. Visit the interesting *enote-*

The deep valley of Furore

ca corner in the "Bar Internazionale". And don't forget the restaurant, "Le Agavi", with its cascade of flower-filled terraces on the sea. For dessert, there is the "De Martino" bar which has excellent sweet dishes, and "La Zagara".

2. The Cilento and its coastline

PAESTUM. Here you will find the exceptionally complete ruins of Magna Graecia *Poseidonia*, one of the most thriving towns of the southern Italian peninsular. On the archaeological site, with a panoramic view, there is the "Il

HOTELS AND RESTAURANTS

Paestum
Esplanade ★★★
via Sterpina
☎ 0828851043
Gelso d'Oro-Da Nonna Sceppa ¶¶
via Laura 53
☎ 0828851064
Nettuno ¶¶
via Principe di Piemonte 2
☎ 0828811028
Palinuro
Carmelo ¶¶ 🛏
at Isca (km 2)
S.S. 562
☎ 0974931138
Pertosa
Càfaro - Zi' Marianna ¶
via Nazionale 6
☎ 0975397044
Positano
San Pietro ★★★£
via Laurito 2
☎ 089875455
Le Agavi ★★★ 🛏
via G. Marconi 127
☎ 089875733
Le Sirenuse ★★★
La Sponda ¶¶¶¶
via C. Colombo 30
☎ 089875066
Buca di Bacco ★★★ 🛏
via Rampa Teglia 4
☎ 089875699
Cambusa ¶¶ 🛏
piazza A. Vespucci 4
☎ 089812051
Chez Black ¶¶
via del Brigantino 19/21
☎ 089875796
Donna Rosa ¶¶
via Montepertuso 97/99
☎ 089811806
Le Tre Sorelle ¶¶ 🛏
via d. Brigantino 23
☎ 089875452
Il Ritrovo ¶
via Montepertuso 77
☎ 089875453
Ravello
Palazzo Sasso 🛏
★★★£, **Rossellinis** ¶¶¶¶
via S. G. del Toro 28
☎ 089818181
Palumbo ★★★
Confalone ¶¶¶¶
via Toro 16
☎ 089857244
Palazzo della Marra ¶¶
via della Marra 7/9
☎ 089858302

HOTELS AND
RESTAURANTS

Santa Maria
di Castellabate
Due Fratelli ¶¶
via S. Andrea
☎ 0974968004
La Taverna
del Pescatore ¶¶
via Lamia
☎ 0974968293
Sapri
⭐ℍ Tirreno ★★★
corso Italia 73
☎ 0973391006
'A Cantina 'i
Mustazzo ¶
piazza Plebiscito 27
☎ 0973392066
Teggiano
Osteria
Sant'Andrea ¶
via S. Andrea
☎ 097579201
Vietri sul Mare
La Lucertola ★★★
via C. Colombo 29
☎ 089210837
⭐ℍ La Locanda ¶
corso Umberto I 52
☎ 089761070

AGRITURISMI

Capaccio
Azienda
Agricola Seliano
via Seliano
☎ 0828723634
Cava de' Tirreni
Saura - Country
Club Santa Lucia
via S. Felice 2
☎ 089342366
Palinuro
⭐ℍ Sant'Agata
at Sant'Agata Nord
☎ 0974931716

WINE
PRODUCERS

Santa Maria di
Castellabate
Maffini
at San Marco (km 3)
at Cenito
☎ 0974966345
San Giovanni
at Punta Tresino
☎ 089237331

Rural landscape of Cilento

Nettuno" restaurant, serving Campania seafood cuisine. The "Gelso d'Oro-Da Nonna Sceppa" restaurant serves honest country cuisine. Also worth noting is the well-looked-after restaurant of the "Esplanade" hotel. Inland, in Capaccio, the "Seliano" farm invites you to try its produce. In Capaccio Scalo, the "La Pergola" restaurant combines seafood with ingredients from the vegetable garden.
AGROPOLI. In this ancient village high above the sea, the ruins of the castle tell of its Byzantine origins. The best cooking in this seaside resort can be found at the "'U Saracino", and the "Il Ceppo", a rustic place serving both Campania cuisine and classic Italian dishes, especially fish.
SANTA MARIA DI CASTELLABATE. This is one of the first places in the Cilento to become involved in the seaside resort industry. The "Taverna del Pescatore" has just a few tables for its excellent fish cuisine, while the "Due Fratelli" serves

Campania and seafood dishes. Do not miss the "Maffini" and "San Giovanni" *cantinas* in Castellabate.
PALINURO. This well-known seaside resort gets its name from the helmsman of Enea, who drowned himself in the desperation of unrequited love. The jewel in Palinuro's crown is the "Sant'Agata" farm dating from the eighteenth century and now restored. The "Carmelo" restaurant, which has been run by the same family for years, serves the most typical Cilento dishes.
MARINA DI CAMEROTA. The beauty of the coast and the town's grottos attract visitors who are well accommodated at the tourist establishments, including the TCI holiday resort. We recommend a meal at the hotel-restaurant, "Bolivar", for some traditional specialties (open from June to September). Open all year round, there is "Pepè", which is on the seafront and specializes in seafood, and "Da Valentone" which only

serves Cilento home-cooking. SAPRI. This little town was made famous when writer and patriot Carlo Pisacane came here in 1857. From then, it experienced a rapid growth in tourism. There is no doubt that the fish is fresh at "L'Uorto". The restaurant, "'A Cantina 'i Mustazzo", serves vegetables, meats and wine grown by the family business, whilst the other foods come from small local producers. The "Il Tirreno" restaurant and hotel (open in the summer only) is just a few meters from the sea.

Giffoni hazelnuts

PADULA. The huge Carthusian monastery of S. Lorenzo is a good example of southern Italian Baroque architecture, even though building only started in the fourteenth century. In town, at the foot of the Monti della Maddalena, we recommend you eat at the "La Sosta del Priore". In the historical center, the tavern, "Il Lupo", serves the best traditional

The wide range of mozzarella cheese

dishes, while on the border between Sole and Padula there is the *agriturismo* establishment, "Il Castagneto". And finally, you will find down-to-earth cuisine for an honest price at the "La Capatina", situated at the fork in the road to Padula and Sassano.

TEGGIANO. The town with its castle is situated high up on the hill. Two restaurants share top billing – the classic "La Romantica", and the "Osteria Sant'Andrea", where ancient flavors mingle with the house wine. EBOLI. It is worth stopping at the Grotta di Pertosa along the road to Eboli, the reason being the delicious "Càfaro-Da Zi' Marianna" restaurant. Then go on to Eboli. This town is known thanks to the writer Carlo Levi, and has enjoyed healthy agricultural and industrial development, spreading from the Sele plain to the foot of the hill where the medieval village is situated. To dine, go to the hotel "Grazia" for its well-run restaurant.

SHOPPING

Salerno
La Contadina
via Picenza 153
☎ 089330834
Fresh dairy products..
Alimento Manzoni
via P. De Granita 11
☎ 089227465
via Lembo 46
☎ 089332242
Sweets, biscuits, wines and distilled spirits.
Pasticceria Pantaleone
via Mercanti 75
☎ 089227825
Sweets and pastries.
Amalfi
La Valle dei Mulini
via L. d'Amalfi 11
☎ 089872603
Good selection of liquors.
Pasticceria Pansa
piazza Duomo 40
☎ 089871065
Sweets and pastries.
Capaccio
Agriseliano
at Seliano
☎ 0828725456
Typical products.
Cava de' Tirreni
Gran Caffè Respighi
corso Mazzini 5
☎ 089343039
A meeting place.
Minori
Pasticceria Gambardella
corso V. Emanuele 37
☎ 089877299
Sweets and pastries.
Positano
Bar Internazionale
via Marconi 298
☎ 089811089
Wine tasting.
Bar De Martino
viale Roma 28
☎ 089875082
Sweets and pastries.
Bar Pasticceria La Zagara
via dei Mulini 10
☎ 089875964
Sweets and pastries.
Ravello
Giardini di Ravello
at Castiglione (km 5)
via Civita
☎ 089872264
Typical liquors.

PUGLIA
FARMING COUNTRY

The big isolated farms dotted around the Puglia countryside
conceal a world of flavors and traditions. The land, bordered
by the sea and the Apennines, is a mosaic of vegetable
gardens, fields of crops, vines, olive groves and pasture.

P uglia, with its vast plain second only to that of the Po valley, attracts the visitor with its landscape, sea and sun. The region is split into five provinces. Bari, the administrative center, has always been considered the commercial center opening out to the east, followed by Brindisi and Taranto (which are more industrial) and Foggia and Lecce (which are more agricultural). Agriculture is still the region's principal resource, the main produce being durum wheat, tomatoes, table grapes, olive oil and artichokes.

THE LANDS OF BARI, CAPITANATA AND OTRANTO
It is not easy to describe the Puglia cuisine because of the richness of the recipes, primary products, traditions, and habits, which differ from area to area. In 1222 Frederick II separated the Terra di Bari (Land of

Bari) from the Capitanata and the Terra d'Otranto. This division can still be felt today through the three different cuisines, even though the same ingredients are used throughout the region. One of the differences is in the use of garlic, which, as you descend to the Salento Peninsular, grows less important and, in some cases, even disappears, giving way to the onion. On the other hand, the chilli pepper is used in nearly all dishes and pasta dishes abound. The wheat produced in the Tavoliere is one of the main ingredients in pasta dishes such as *lasagne* and *orecchiette (rècchie)*. The rich variety of pasta is matched by an equally rich range of sauces, often based on vegetables.

THE WELL-BALANCED CUISINE OF SEA AND COUNTRY
The richness of Puglia cuisine can be seen in the ragout made with veal or horse meat, tomatoes and *pecorino* cheese. The *tielle* are a reminder of the period of Spanish dominion (the most common mussel tiella consists of layers of rice, potatoes, onions and parsley, and mussels, baked in the oven). The main dish is often lamb and during the hunting season there are some interesting game dishes. Then there are the cheeses made from cow's and sheep's milk. After the meal it has become fashionable to eat raw vegetables with a dip based on extra-virgin olive oil. Lovers of sweet desserts can try the classic *carteddate* (strips of puff pastry fried in olive oil, and covered in honey, sugar and cinnamon). Or the *taralli*, *zeppole* or *caciuni*, all types of cake filled with a paste of cooked chick peas, chocolate, must (partially-fermented grape juice), cinnamon and vanilla-flavored sugar and fried in oil.

Li Cucchi. Prized wines are stored in clay jars - a centuries-old custom

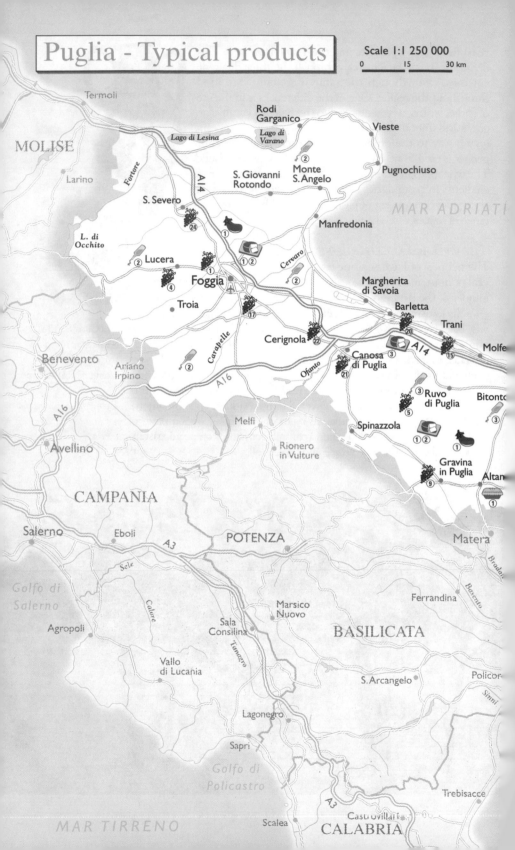

CHEESES

1. **Canestrato Dop.** Produced in the province of Foggia and part of Bari province.
2. **Fiordilatte.** Fresh milk cheese produced throughout the region.
3. **Burrata di Andria.** Strong cheese wrapped around butter from Andria.

CHARCUTERIE

1. **Capocollo di Martina Franca Dop.** Martina Franca salami.
2. **Soppressata**
3. **Salsiccia leccese**
4. **Tarantello.** Tuna sausage from Taranto.

VEGETABLES

1. **Lampascioni.** Onions produced throughout the region.

EXTRA-VIRGIN OLIVE OIL

1. **Collina di Brindisi Dop.**
2. **Dauno Dop.** High Tavoliere,

Low Tavoliere, Gargano and Sub-Appennine.
3. **Terra di Bari Dop.** Castel del Monte, Bitonto, Murgia of the Trulli and of the Grotte.
4. **Terra d'Otranto Dop**

BREAD AND SWEETS

1. **Pane d'Altamura**

DOC WINES

1. **Aleatico di Puglia**
2. **Alezio**
3. **Brindisi**
4. **Cacc'e mmitte di Lucera**
5. **Castel del Monte**
6. **Copertino**
7. **Galatina**
8. **Gioia del Colle**
9. **Gravina**
10. **Leverano**
11. **Lizzano**
12. **Locorotondo**
13. **Martina o Martina Franca**
14. **Matino**
15. **Moscato di Trani**
16. **Nardò**
17. **Orta Nova**
18. **Ostuni**
19. **Primitivo di Manduria**
20. **Rosso Barletta**
21. **Rosso Canosa**
22. **Rosso di Cerignola**
23. **Salice Salentino**
24. **San Severo**
25. **Squinzano**

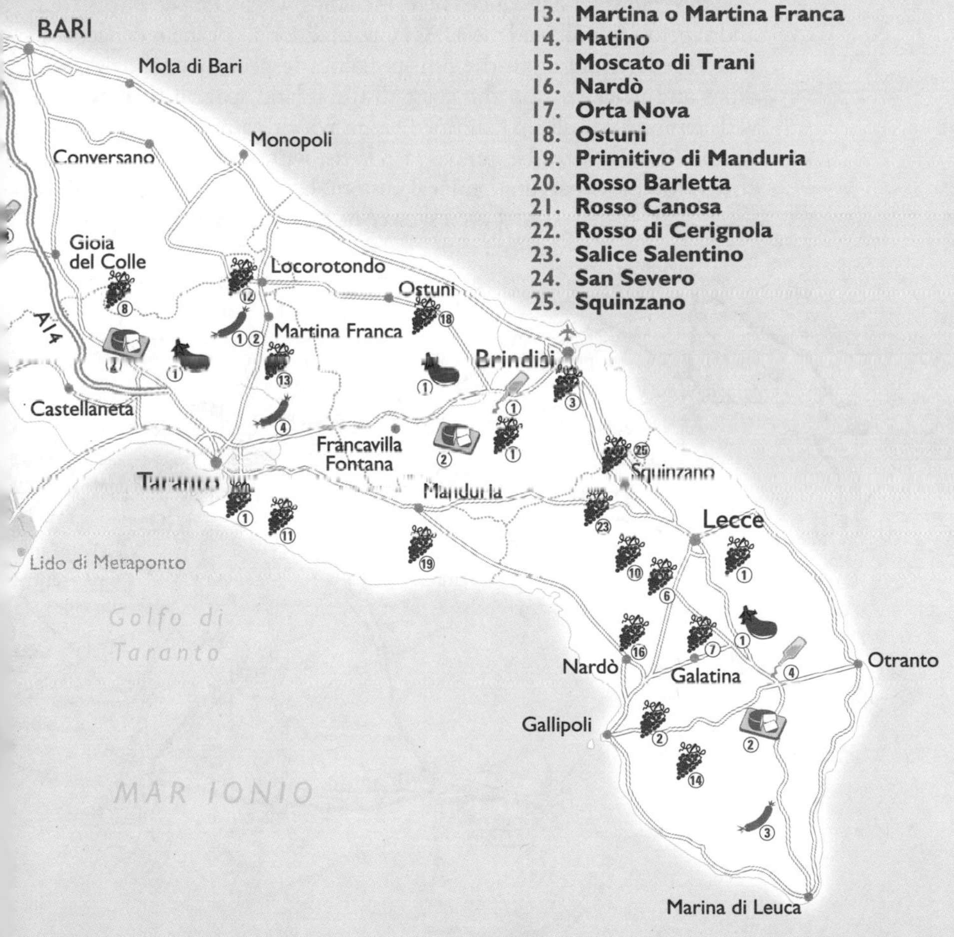

BARI

Mola di Bari

Monopoli

Conversano

Gioia del Colle

Locorotondo

Ostuni

Martina Franca

A14

Brindisi

Castellaneta

Francavilla Fontana

Taranto

Manduria

Squinzano

Lido di Metaponto

Lecce

Golfo di Taranto

Nardò

Galatina

Otranto

Gallipoli

MAR IONIO

Marina di Leuca

BARI

This land is filled with cultural pleasures, from architecture – trulli and Romanesque cathedrals – to cuisine, which is sometimes exceptional.

The province includes the so-called Terra di Bari and a large part of the Murge plateau. It is a fertile land and intensively cultivated along the coast, which is rich with tree plantations. Inland the earth is rather arid, but woods and meadows still grow and provide for the thriving sheep-rearing industry. A characteristic of the Bari province is the concentration of its population in big towns (14 towns have over 25,000 inhabitants each and 35 have over 10,000) with appropriately large monuments to match (think of all the Romanesque cathedrals) and well-delineated production activities. There are fewer people in the countryside nowadays. They used to live in tiny settlements dotted about the area, usually farms arranged around a courtyard and fortified against frequent invasions by sea marauders. All the seasonal products would be grown and produced here, including wheat, grapes, olives, fruit and vegetables, milk and meat. As far as traditional cuisine is concerned, there is everything from the fish specialties (especially anchovies, sardines and mackerel) on the coast to the inland specialties associated with farming and sheep country. Durum wheat pasta is popular everywhere, starting with the famous *orecchiette*, with shellfish, vegetable or cheese sauces, depending on local custom. Lamb is the most prevalent meat, cooked on a skewer or in a frying pan, and often enhanced with mushrooms from the Murge. All can be accompanied by the top-quality wines of Castel del Monte or Locorotondo, the two best-known.

Gourmet Tours

BARI. The historical center of Bari, with its narrow, twisted streets, and the new town Bari, with its grid pattern design, lie between the sea and vineyards. The S. Sabino Cathedral, the S. Nicola Basilica and the Svevo Castle are very interesting to visit. There are plenty of places to sample the pastas and vegetables, all of them a source of local pride. Start with the *orecchiette* topped with *cime di rapa* (turnip tops) or *sugo di soffritto* (lightly fried mixture of onions, herbs and bacon). Then there is the fish course (*pesce azzurro* – anchovies, sardines and mackerel – and *pesce bianco* – with white flesh) served in a multitude of ways, for instance the tasty *alici arracanate* (boned anchovies layered with breadcrumbs and chopped garlic, mint and capers, seasoned with oregano and oil and baked in the oven), or the *dentice alle olive* (dentex – a kind of sea bream – with olives). In town our favorite restaurants are

the cosy and welcoming "Alberosole", and the simple but brilliant "Terranima" with its wide range of shellfish first courses. There are also two Buon Ricordo restaurants which are really worth trying: the "Nuova Vecchia Bari", in the heart of the Murattiano quarter, and "Piccinni", not far from the Porto Vecchio (old port) with a lovely enclosed garden. The historical café-cake shop, "Stoppani" (established 1860) offers delicacies such as the *cassatine* (small sponge cake filled with *ricotta* cheese, sugar, candied fruit, chocolate and liqueur), *cremini* (chocolates that melt in the mouth), and many others. In the stores, such as "De Carne", and on the stalls, you will find an excellent variety of Terra di Bari flavors. First and foremost, there is the slightly bitter and spicy olive oil, flavored with herbs and fresh almonds, then the vegetables, such as *popone serpentino* (checombre-musk melon) and *cime di crescione* (*cimescazzìtte* – water-

Giovinazzo. The fifteenth-century town walls

HOTELS AND RESTAURANTS

Bari
Mercure
Villa Romanazzi Carducci ★★★
via Capruzzi 326
☎ 0805427400
Palace H. ★★★
Murat ¶¶
via Lombardi 13
☎ 0805216551
Boston ★★★
via Piccinni 155
☎ 0805216633
Windsor ★★★
via Amoruso Manzari Mauro 62/7
☎ 0805610011
Alberosole ¶¶
corso V. Emanuele 13
☎ 0805235446
Nuova Vecchia Bari ¶¶
via Dante 47
☎ 0805216496
Piccinni ¶¶
via Piccinni 28
☎ 0805211227
Taberna ¶¶
at Carbonara di Bari
via Ospedale di Venere 6
☎ 0005650557
Terranima ¶¶
via Putignani 213/215
☎ 0805219725
Acquaviva delle Fonti
Del Ghiottone ¶¶
vicolo II Piergentile 13
☎ 080762253

489

cress tops), then the pastas such as *taralli al pepe* (with pepper), *frise* and *zeppole*, and finally, the Murge wines, Canosa, Castel del Monte, Gioia del Colle, Locorotondo and, best of all, Moscato di Trani. In Carbonara di Bari, look out for the "Taberna", which serves tomatoes, artichokes and mushrooms preserved in oil, *minestra di cicorielle e polpette* (chicory and meatball soup) as a change from the more common *orecchiette col ragù* (orecchiette pasta with ragout), lamb and goat, and the exceptional local cheeses, of which, together with *ricotta*, you will also find a lot used in pastries in the cake shops.

1. A trip round the cathedrals

GIOVINAZZO. This town, at the edge of the sea, has its own cathedral and a historical center set inside fifteenth-century town walls. Inland extensive olive groves make Giovinazzo one of the Puglia Città dell'Olio (Cities of Olive Oil). There are also citrus groves (mostly mandarins) and vegetable gardens (mostly cauliflower, chicory, endive and fennel). For a meal, we recommend "La Luna nel Pozzo", a small, romantic oasis of elegant cuisine of land- and seafood. The "Chiodo Fisso" is a more traditional restaurant, set in the Spinelli Sagarriga building. Dishes include *tiella barese* and *orecchiette* with horse meat ragout; then there are the meat dishes and a fine selection of cheeses. The town is famous for its cake made with cooked wheat ('*u grane cuotte*).

MOLFETTA. The Duomo Vecchio with its three cupolas and its two bell towers standing side by side rises out of this ancient port. The fishing supplies an important fish market and a cuisine that showcases mullet and shellfish. The countryside provides olive oil, almonds and cherries. For good

Molfetta with the Duomo Vecchio in the background

seafood, try the "Borgo Antico" restaurant, with its *spaghetti al torchio con aragostine e peperoni dolci* (spaghetti with small lobsters and sweet peppers), which you can follow with a *pescatrice ai cardoncelli e pomodori secchi* (angler fish with sun-dried tomatoes and *cardoncelli* – boiled and roasted thistles flavored with black olives, anchovies and oil, or fried with egg, cheese and spices). Another good restaurant is "Bufi" with its refined interpretation of traditional dishes plus some innovative ones, and with a nice balance between land- and seafood.

BISCEGLIE. Bisceglie features olives and vines, vegetable gardens and citrus groves, plus a cathedral. The big fruit and vegetable market provides daily entertainment. The area is famous for its table grapes, oil, tomatoes and cherries. The restaurants have excellent fish; some serving raw squid salad, others serving tasty dishes of mutton. The "Villa" and the "Salsello" are good hotels, and both have restaurants.

TRANI. Standing alone with the sea as its backdrop, the cathedral leaves you with an unforgetable image of this little town, which also lends its name to a famous Moscato wine. The good food is equally divided between land and sea produce. First courses include *pesce azzurro* ('blue' fish - anchovies, sardines and mackerel), small fried mullet, cuttlefish and squid. A good place to eat is the "Torrente Antico" combining shellfish dishes with a top-rate wine cellar. Note also the "Osteria Cacciainferno" which serves simple farmhouse dishes, such as *orecchiette con le cime di rapa* (orecchiette pasta with turnipstops),

which are given a lift by the excellence of the local produce. The figs here are renowned.

BARLETTA. Its 'Literary Park' is dedicated to the famous 'Disfida' (a story involving a mercenary who challenges French knights after they insult Italy's honour) and its writer, Massimo d'Azeglio. The park starts from the building where the real-life mercenary, Ettore Fieramosca, gave orders for the Sant'Elia battle and extends to the district of Sant'Elia – incidentally, he won the battle, which took place in 1503. The historical center, rich in reminders of the Normans and the Crusaders, also has an elegant nineteenth-century colonnade dedicated to the painter, Giuseppe De Nittis. On the food side, Barletta is a Città del Pesce di Mare (City of Salt Water Fish). To put this reputation to the test, you could try the "Antica Cucina" with its wonderful mussel soup, the very new "Baccosteria", with its excellent *pescatrice in salsa di carciofi* (angler fish in artichoke sauce), and the *capretto murgiano ai funghi cardoncelli* or *al "Moscato di Trani"* (Murge goat with *cardoncelli* mushrooms or with Moscato di Trani wine). You should also visit the fantastic *cantina* and the local biscuit- and cake-makers. For a really good DOC Rosso Barletta, ask for the Falcone label.

CANOSA DI PUGLIA. The town is situated on the slope of one of the Murge hills, looking over the Ofanto Valley and the Tavoliere. The cathedral is remarkable and contains the tomb of Boemondo, prince of Antioch. Local produce includes the DOC wine Rosso Canosa, olive oil and various fruits and vegetables. In Montegrosso, in Andria territory,

HOTELS AND RESTAURANTS

Bisceglie
Salsello ★★★
via Siciliani 31
☎ 0803955953
Villa ★★★ ⬲
S.S. 16 al km 765
☎ 0803980212
Bitonto
Nuovo ★★★
via E. Ferrara 21
☎ 0803751178
Castellana-Grotte
Relais ⬲
Le Jardin ★★★ ¶¶¶
contrada Scamardella 59
☎ 0804966300
Fontanina ¶ ⬲
S.P. Alberobello 33
☎ 0804968010
Corato
Mulino ¶¶
via Castel del Monte 135
☎ 0808723925
Gioia del Colle
Svevo ★★★ ¶¶ ⬲
via Santeramo 319
☎ 0803481212
Giovinazzo
La Luna ⬲
nel Pozzo ¶¶
via G. Sasso 6
☎ 0803946554
Chiodo Fisso ¶
via S. Maria degli
Angeli 18
☎ 0803948131
Gravina in Puglia
Madonna
della Stella ¶¶
via Madonna della Stella
☎ 080856383
Osteria di S. Cucco ¶¶
piazza Pellicciari 4
☎ 0803261872

the "Antichi Sapori" *trattoria* serves old-fashioned dishes of charcuterie, country pizza, vegetable soup with *capunti* (mushrooms and sausage), lamb with potatoes, and stuffed rabbit.

ANDRIA. This town is also situated on the slopes of the Murge. It has a cathedral and plenty of medieval architecture, and was dear to Frederick II's heart. Today it is a flourishing rural center, producing *burrata* (a creamy *mozzarella*-type cheese) - a truly regional product - olives, and a famous olive oil. In town, note the historical "Rivera" *azienda* which is associated with the Movimento Turismo del Vino (Wine Tourism Movement). DOC wines include Castel del Monte and the excellent Rosso Riserva il Falcone, aged in French oak barrels. There are also some good places to eat, at the "Arco Marchese" in the center, and the "Tenuta Cocevola", which has a wonderful view.

CASTEL DEL MONTE. The solitary, octagonal castle of Frederick II is the most important symbol of the region. It is surrounded by the vines of the town's DOC wine, and by the DOP olives, Terra di Bari. The farms produce lentils and potatoes and the cheese-makers produce *pecorino* and *ricotta*. Ask for *muscicchia*, sheep's meat that has been dried in the sun.

RUVO DI PUGLIA. On the cultural side, you must not miss the cathedral - a masterpiece of the Puglia

Romanesque style - and the Museo Nazionale Jatta, containing some exceptional ceramics. The produce from the land includes olive oil (this is a Città dell'Olio) and dairy products such as *mozzarella*, *treccia*, *ricottina*, *scamorza* and *provole* cheeses. Try the "Pineta" hotel for its views, its proven track record, its calm, family-run atmosphere, and a top-rate restaurant. Corato, which is not far away, is a center for good wine and food. Note the "Mulino" restaurant.

BITONTO. Last in our tour of the cathedrals, this Romanesque cathedral is considered the most complete and beautiful of the region. The town's other merits are its renowned olive oil and its almonds, which are used in the cakes.

Trani. The port

2. In the land of the Trulli

MOLA DI BARI. This medieval village with its cathedral and castle is situated on the headland, behind the fishing port. It is surrounded by olive groves and vegetable gardens. The refined restaurant, "Niccolò Van Westerhout", (note that it also has guest rooms) offers both land- and seafood, in dishes such as *battuto di scampi crudi* (chopped vegetables with bacon and raw scampi), *spaghetti al nero di seppia* (spaghetti with black ink from cuttlefish) and *polpo di scoglio fritto o alla brace* (fried or grilled rock octopus). You can finish your meal with

HOTELS AND RESTAURANTS

Mola di Bari
Niccolò Van Westerhout ¶¶
via De Amicis 3/5
☎ 0804744253
Molfetta
Bistro 86 ¶¶
via Dante 33
☎ 0803975812
Borgo Antico ¶¶
largo Municipio 20
☎ 0803974379
Bufi ¶¶
via V. Emanuele 17
☎ 0803971597
Monopoli
Il Melograno ★★★
contrada Torricella 345
☎ 0806909030
★ **Lido Bianco** ¶¶
via Procaccia 3
☎ 0808876737
Pietrantica ¶¶
contrada Larghezza 132
☎ 080803676
Noci
L'Antica Locanda ¶
via Santo Spirito 49
☎ 0804972460

the curious home-made *rosoli*.
CONVERSANO. A lovely road takes you up from the sea to the crest of the Murge hills where cherry trees brighten the landscape. The historical center holds a Norman castle, a fourteenth-century cathedral and the S. Benedetto church. You must try the cherry jam while you are there. In neighboring Rutigliano, there is the thirteenth-century church of S. Maria della Colonna, where there is a polyptych by the fifteenth-century painter Antonio Vivarini.
POLIGNANO A MARE. This little town is arranged along a rocky outcrop, sheer to the sea. It has a pretty church - its founding church - and renowned vegetables and *fioroni* figs. There are lots of good restaurants, particularly along the seafront, where the "Da Tuccino" serves raw food starters, mussel *tiella*, and the best fish served in the best possible ways. There are two fairytale hotel-restaurants here - the "Grotta Palazzese", with the charm of the

blue-green waters lapping on the rocks, and the "Castellinaria" in the atmospheric Cala San Giovanni amphitheater.
MONOPOLI. The fort and cathedral testify to the importance of this little town, which used to be one of the prime commercial ports. Today fishing is important, and this is strongly reflected in the cuisine. For proof, try the rich cuisine of the "Il Melograno" hotel, set in a seventeenth-century farm. As far as cultivation is concerned, the strong points are olive oil, vegetables and fruit (oranges, mandarins and figs). To fully appreciate these flavors, go up the hill to the "Pietrantica" restaurant, where the most interesting dishes are first courses of vegetables and meat combined with the herbs or mushrooms that are in season. Game is also served when in season.
ALBEROBELLO. The *trulli*, ancient constructions with conical roofs, dotted around the countryside make up this town

Castel del Monte

HOTELS AND RESTAURANTS

Polignano a Mare
Castellinaria ★★★ ¶¶
at Cala San Giovanni
☎ 0804240233
Grotta Palazzese ★★★
via Narciso 59
☎ 0804240677
Da Tuccino ¶¶¶
via S. Caterina 69/F
☎ 0001211560
Ruvo di Puglia
Pineta ★★★
via Carlo Marx 5
☎ 0803611578
Upedippe ¶¶
vico S. Agnese 2
☎ 0803613879
Hostaria Pomponio ¶
vico Pomponio 3
☎ 0803629970
L'Angolo Divino ¶
corso Giovanni Satta 11
☎ 0803628544
Trani
Torrente Antico ¶¶¶
via Fusco 3
☎ 0883487911
Osteria Cacciainferno ¶¶
vicolo S. Nicola 9
☎ 0883585978

AGRITURISMI

Noci
⭐🏠 **Le Casedde**
S.S. 604 per Gioia
☎ 0804978946
Poggiorsini
⭐🏠 **Il Cardinale**
contrada Capoposto
☎ 0803237279

**WINE
PRODUCERS**

**Andria
Rivera**
S.S. 98 km 19,8
☎ 0883541310
**Barletta
Falcone**
via Discanno 21/a
☎ 0883531142
**Corato
Torrevento**
S.S. 170 km 28
☎ 0808980929

**OLIVE OIL
PRODUCERS**

**Bari
Agricole di
Cagno Abbrescia**
piazza Massari 6
☎ 0805214195
S.Croce & S.Aloja
corso V. Emanuele 10
☎ 0805216730)
**Barletta
Tenuta Rasciatano**
contrada Rasciatano
S.S. 93 km 13
☎ 0883510999

which UNESCO has deemed a World Heritage site. The area's olive oil and cheeses (*cacio-ricotta* and *pecorino*) are little works of art, which the stores serve together with flavored *taralli* (O-shaped unsweetened biscuits). The restaurant for the gourmet is the "Il Preta Contadino" (which is also a Buon Ricordo restaurant), with prized specialties like *zuppetta di frutti di mare* (shellfish soup) and *spigola alla Leonardo* (Leonardo-style sea bass), and a sensational wine cellar. The "Lanzillotta" hotel has a good reputation, especially for its restaurant. A few kilometers away you will find Locorotondo, a Città del Vino with a wine named after it. It is set in a lovely position in the Valley of Itria. The town is also known for its table grapes, lamb and *cardoncelli* mushrooms.

NOCI. The town's celebrated Literary Park is set in a nineteenth- century mill. It is dedicated to the writer Tommaso Fiore (1884-1973), and to the Murgia dei Trulli, described in his book, *Formiche di Puglia*. In the fourteenth-century collegiate church, there is a seventeenth-century polyptych in multicolored stone. The "Antica Locanda" provides the culinary

interest of this trip, with *cicorielle in brodo* (young chicory in broth), *orecchiette al ragù* (orecchiette with ragout), *braciole al sugo* (chops with gravy), rabbit, game and mushrooms when in season, and, for dessert, the *sospiri di Nunzia* (Nunzia's light sponge cake covered with sugar or chocolate).

CASTELLANA-GROTTE. The marvels of this underground complex, one of the most important in Italy, are enough to enchant even those who know little or nothing about caves. It is, therefore, an unmissable town in our itinerary; but it also presents us with an opportunity to appreciate the refined and welcoming restaurant, the "Relais le Jardin" and taste its *sformatino di melanzane con filetti di pomodoro* (eggplant soufflé with tomato), *cavatelli con funghi cardoncelli e pomodorini* (cavatelli pasta with *cardoncelli* mushrooms and little tomatoes), *terrina di capretto, patate e lampascioni* (terrine of goat, potatoes and onions). And that is just the food from the land; their wine and liqueur list is also very good.

3. Altamura and the Murge
ACQUAVIVA DELLE FONTI. The town's name tells of its everlasting springs which water the vegetable gardens in the countryside. The cathedral, well worth a visit, is one of Puglia's four Palatine basilicas. Then you can try out the seafood cuisine at the "Del Ghiottone". The sweet red onions of the area are renowned, and used in the preparation of a characteristic pizza.

GIOIA DEL COLLE. The Swabian castle, previously a

Byzantine fort, marks the town's position up on a saddle in the Murge hills, halfway between Bari and Taranto. The town is most famous for its cheeses – *mozzarella, scamorza* and *caciocavallo* – and DOC Gioia del Colle wines. You must try the *zampitti*, a poor man's sausage flavored with chilli peppers. The excellent hotel-restaurant, "Svevo", is good for a break, with its *tegame di agnello al forno* (roast lamb), game, and Primitivo red wine.

ALTAMURA. This is an ancient town, built in one of the prettiest rural parts of the Murge. It has a cathedral, winding streets and secret courtyards. It is famous in all Italy for its unique bread, cooked in a wood oven in the traditional way. The lentils from the countryside are very well-known, too, and also good are the olive oil, turnip tops, and other vegetables, as well as the *ricotta forte* and *ricotta soppressata* cheeses. Wild ingredients include wild chicory and mushrooms. Make a rendez-vous at the "Del Corso" restaurant whose specialty is *agnello allo orbo (u cutturidd)*

The distinctive 'trullo' houses

(lamb with herbs).
GRAVINA IN PUGLIA. The town gets its name from the deep Carso canal which runs past the cathedral and the oldest part of the town. There are many good foods here: the bread and olive oil, some cheeses called *palloni*, mutton, lamb and sausages. In addition, there is a good DOC white wine. The two top restaurants are the "Madonna della Stella", set in a natural grotto, and the "Osteria di Salvatore Cucco", which is welcoming and relaxing. Both have excellent dishes of pasta with vegetables, and meat from the Murge, especially lamb and pork.

BITETTO. On the road back to Bari, before you go down the last step of the Murge, you should make one more stop to look around this village overflowing with medieval drawings, and its remarkable late-Romanesque cathedral. It is a Città del Olio with presses where you can buy well-priced olive oil. It also produces good eating olives. Peaches and almonds are grown locally.

Altamura bread

OLIVE OIL PRODUCERS

Bisceglie
Fratelli Galantino
via Corato 2
☎ 0803921320
Bitetto
Olio Beato
via Palo 80
☎ 0809921358
Bitritto
Frantoio Diesse
via XXIV Maggio 54
☎ 080630767
Corato
Del Console
piazza XX Settembre 2
☎ 0808724788
Gioia del Colle
Agrigioia
strada provinciale
Acquaviva 1707
☎ 0803481359

SHOPPING

Bari
Gastronomia De Carne
via Calefati 120
☎ 0805219676
Delicatessen.
Caffè Stoppani
via Roberto da Bari 79
☎ 0805213563
Historical café-cake shop.
Andria
Caseificio Baffone
via Malpighi
☎ 0883597492
Cheeses.
Bisceglie
Puma Conserve
S.S. 16 Km 771
☎ 0803951531
Preserves.

BRINDISI

The capital of the province and the inland towns of Ostuni and Francavilla have specialties that perfectly combine the cuisine of sea and land.

The cuisine of this province does not really have its own identity, but rather reflects that of the other Puglia provinces. Vegetables feature strongly, especially the famous Brindisi chicory which is particularly big, tender and sweet. Other typical products are melon and cucumber. But do not overlook the turnip tops, cauliflower, black cabbage (famously known as *mugnolicchi*), lettuce, broad beans, chick peas, capers, figs and almonds. Since the town is situated on the coast, fish characterizes the Brindisi cuisine,

An olive grove near Ostuni

giving rise to the *zuppe alla marinara* (seafood soups), *zuppe di cernia* (grouper soups) and *vermicelli con le vongole* (*vermicelli* pasta with clams). Much-prized specialties include the *grattapuepoli*, a type of bivalve shellfish. Inland they make interesting charcuterie, especially the fresh sausages. No less interesting are the cheeses, especially the *pecorino*, *ricotta*, *cacio-ricotta* and *mozzarella*. Wine is represented by the Brindisi and Ostuni DOCs.

Gourmet Tours

BRINDISI. In Roman and Norman times this was an important center for maritime exchanges, thanks to its natural port. You should see the Piazza del Duomo and the cathedral itself, the Museo Archeologico Provinciale Francesco Ribezzo, the Romanesque S. Giovanni al Sepolcro, and the Roman columns which mark the end of the Via Appia. Typical produce includes the extra virgin olive oil, the Brindisi chicory, the *scamorza*, and the pepper *taralli*. At the delicatessen, "Arte della Carne", you can find some delicious examples of the good food in their salamis, foods preserved in oil, jams and meats. For wine, note the *enoteca* "Delizie di Anelli" and the "Cantina Cooperativa Brundisium". For those wanting to try Brindisi cuisine, there is the "La Lanterna" in the historical center, set in a fifteenth century building, where you can eat *spaghetti ai ricci di mare/alla bottarga* (spaghetti with sea urchins or mullet roe), *maccheroncini alla contadina* (*maccheroncini* pasta 'farmer's-wife' style) and *grigliate miste di pesce* (mixed grills of fish). Another restaurant for the gourmet is the "Pantagruele" which serves *trucioletti con anelli di calamari* (*trucioletti* pasta with squid rings), *cozze e basilico* (mussels and basil), *spaghetti al torchio con frutti di mare* (spaghetti with shellfish), *tagliolini al pecorino di fossa* (*tagliolini* pasta with *pecorino di fossa* cheese), baked fish and classic fish soup. For a peaceful stay, try the "Majestic" hotel.

MESAGNE. Olive groves, vines and tobacco plantations dominate the landscape around Mesagne. You should visit the Museo Civico Archeologico Ugo Granafei. Local produce includes extra virgin olive oil, melons, peaches, artichokes, *cartellate* (Christmas specialties: fried pastry ribbons covered with honey or cooked in must - partially-fermented grape juice - then scattered with icing sugar and cinnamon), and *taralli*. Along the road to Oria you will pass Latiano. It is worth stopping here to visit the Museo di Arti e Tradizioni Popolari (Museum of Folk Art and Popular Traditions), and the "Vinicola Lomazzi & Sarli" for tasting and buying wine.

ORIA. A castle built by Frederick II towers over this ancient town of the Messapico (ancient inhabitants of Puglia), which boasts a rich cuisine. The main produce here are artichokes, beans, chick peas, broad beans, Catalonia chicory, mulberries, cucumbers and dried figs. You can find tasty

HOTELS AND RESTAURANTS

Brindisi
Majestic ★★★
corso Umberto 151
☎ 0831597941
La Lanterna
via Tarantini 18
☎ 0831564026
Trattoria Pantagruele
salita di Ripalta 1/3
☎ 0831560605
Carovigno
Osteria già sotto l'Arco
corso V. Emanuele 71
☎ 0831996286
Ceglie Messapica
La Fontanina
★★★, contrada Palagogna
☎ 0831380932
Fornello-da Ricci
contrada Montevicoli
☎ 0831377101
Cibus
via Chianche di Scarano 7
☎ 0831388980
Francavilla Fontana
Al Piccolo Mondo
via S. Francesco 98/100
☎ 0831853618
Marina di Ostuni
Masseria S. Lucia ★★★
at Costa Merlata
S.S. 379 al km 23,5
☎ 08313560
Oria
Vecchia Oria
vico Rotto Milizia 3
☎ 0831845880

**HOTELS AND
RESTAURANTS**

Ostuni
Osteria Cantone ⍾
contrada Fantese
☎ 0804446902
Vecchia Ostuni ⍾
largo Lanza 9
☎ 0831303308
**Osteria
del Tempo Perso** ⍾
via Tanzarella Vitale 47
☎ 0831303320
Savelletri
⭐🏨 **Masseria
San Domenico** ✪✪✪
☎ 0804827990

AGRITURISMI

Fasano
⭐🏨 **Masseria
Marzalossa**
contrada
Pezze Vicine 65
☎ 0804413780
Ottava Piccola
at Montalbano
☎ 0804810902
Ostuni
⭐🏨 **Lo Spagnulo**
contrada Spagnulo
☎ 0831350209
Il Frantoio
S.S. 16 al km 874
☎ 0831330276
⭐🏨 **Masseria
Salinola**
contrada Salinola 134
☎ 0831330683
**San Vito dei
Normanni**
Tenuta Deserto
☎ 0831983062

**WINE
PRODUCERS**

Brindisi
**Cantina
Cooperativa
Brundisium**
viale E. Majorana
☎ 0831546543
Latiano
Lomazzi & Sarli
contrada Partemio
S.S. 7 ter
☎ 0831725898

examples of the cooking at the "Vecchia Oria" restaurant which serves local cuisine heavily influenced by Tuscany, where the owners come from.

FRANCAVILLA FONTANA. The town still has lovely Baroque architecture, including the Imperial palace, which is now the town hall. We suggest you stop to eat at the restaurant, the "Piccolo Mondo", which has dishes of fresh fish, meat, and pizzas cooked in a wood oven. Extra virgin olive oil, almonds and figs are the main local produce. Travelling back up north towards Ostuni, you will come across the town of Ceglie Messapica. You absolutely must not miss the "Fornello da Ricci" restaurant here, with dishes such as *fave e pecorino* (broad beans and *pecorino* cheese), *fiori di zucca con ricotta* (pumpkin flowers with *ricotta* cheese), *costolette di capretto fritte* (fried goat's ribs) and the *grigliata di carni* (mixed grilled meats). Then there is the *trattoria* "Cibus" with its *enoteca*, serving local dishes that vary with the

Ostuni. Masseria Lo Spagnulo

seasons. Dishes to try include the *sagna penta* (fried bread with *ricotta forte* cheese), and the *grano in zuppa con verdure e carni arrosto* (soup with wheat, vegetables and roast meats).

OSTUNI. This little town, set between olive groves and the sea, has given its name to a DOC wine. Its late-Gothic cathedral at the top of a hill is the first you

Grapes in bright sunshine

see of it. We suggest you eat at the "Osteria Cantone" with its *tortino di grano* (wheat cake), *fave novelle in minestra* (new broad beans in soup) and *capretto in coccio* (baked kid goat) or the "Osteria del Tempo Perso" with its *fusilli con carciofi e pomodorini* (*fusilli* pasta with artichokes and baby tomatoes), *timballi di uova con verdure* (timbale of eggs with vegetables) and *caciocavallo alla brace* (grilled *caciocavallo* cheese). Another alternative is the "Vecchia Ostuni" restaurant with its *verdure fritte gratinate* (gratin of fried vegetables), *polpo alla Luciana* (Luciana-style octopus), and *cavatelli ai frutti di mare e pesce* (*cavatelli* pasta with shellfish and fish). If you want to buy the local produce, go to "Antichi Sapori di Puglia" which sells *cacio-ricotta* cheese, fresh goat's and sheep's milk cheeses, *orecchiette* pasta, salamis, *cavatelli* and other specialties. To buy wine, go to the "Drink Shop" or

the "Enoteca Apulia". Not far away, in Carovigno, there is the excellent restaurant, "Osteria già sotto l'Arco" with a light, elegant cuisine including the best local dishes.

FASANO. The town is situated at the foot of the Murgia del Trulli embankment. It is know for its wildlife park but also for its produce: rocket, turnips, extra virgin olive oil and fennel, especially fennel from Torre Canne. In town you should visit its founding church with its High-Renaissance façade. For shopping, we recommend "Renna", which sells fish products, such as octopus, anchovies, sardines and mackerel preserved in oil. The historical town of *Egnazia* is situated on land belonging to the municipality. It has been cited by Strabo and Pliny, and you really should not miss it. The acropolis and the excavation area are on a wide headland of rock. You should also visit the Museo Archeologico Nazionale.

OLIVE OIL PRODUCERS

San Vito dei Normanni
Masseria Iacucci
via Latiano km 4
☎ 0831982648

SHOPPING

Brindisi
Delizie di Anelli
via Rubini 5
☎ 0831563507
Wines.
Ceglie Messapica
Forno a legna di Lucia Urso
via Fedele Grande
☎ 0831380736
Sweet and savoury cookies such as "frise", "tarallini" and "panzerottini".
Latteria Caliandro Azienda Agricola Fragnite
via Ceglie-Ostuni 102
☎ 0831376365
Local cheeses and charcuterie.
Orto Da Maria
contrada Fragnite
via Ceglie-Ostuni 96
☎ 0831379655
Organically grown fruits and vegetables.
Fasano
Renna
via Mandorlara
☎ 0804426250
Fish preserved in oil.
Ostuni
Antichi Sapori di Puglia
viale Pola 1
☎ 0831336412
Local products.
Drink Shop
piazza Italia 27
☎ 0831302132
Sweets and liquors.

FOGGIA

The great variety of landscapes – rocky coasts, fertile plains, wooded hills – are all reflected in the equally varied cuisine of this province.

The Foggia area, indeed the Capitanata (from 'Catapani' or 'Catepani' meaning territorial administrator) is without a doubt the area with the highest production of the region. Not only is there durum wheat, but also many vegetables, which are all used in the local cuisine. Mushroom production is exceptional, especially the Cardoncelli, Prataioli and Prugnoli varieties. Do not forget the cheeses which come from a territory near Abruzzo where they still have separate summer and winter pastures. At table they strongly favor fresh, home-made pasta. The wines include a good production of DOCs such as San Severo and Cacc'è mmitte from Lucera, and Orta Nova.

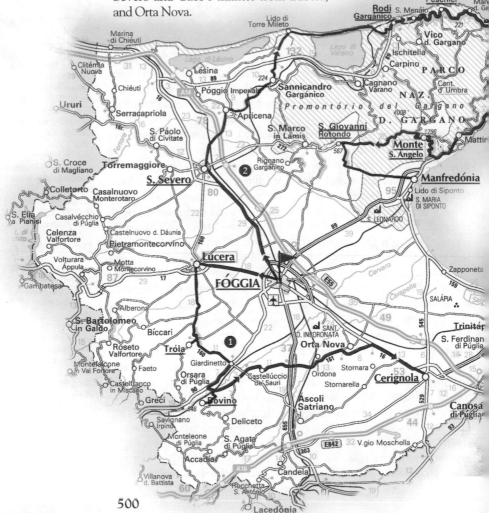

Gourmet Tours

FOGGIA. The town is in the center of the Tavoliere area; a vast, flat plain - the biggest in mainland Italy. Earthquakes and bombings have meant that this is a modern-looking town, despite its ancient origins. You should visit the Romanesque cathedral and the Museo Civico (Civic Museum). For wine and food shopping, there is the old town's local market, the "Gastronomia Arbore", selling cheeses, charcuterie and specialties such as jams, spices and wines, and the "Enoteca della Nuvola" (note the wonderful décor) selling a good selection of national and regional wines and spirits. You can buy cakes and *taralli* at the "Cupo" cake shop. If you want to eat out, there is the "Cicolella in Fiera" restaurant, where you can try *troccoli alla foggiana* (Foggia-style *troccoli* pasta), *pancotto rucola e patate* (bread soup with rocket and potatoes) and *carni alla brace*

(grilled meats); and the "Ventaglio", with its *cozze gratinate* (mussel gratin), *cavatelli con frutti di mare* (cavatelli pasta with shellfish) and *triglie al cartoccio* (mullet cooked in paper).

If you need a hotel, choose from the central "Cicolella" hotel, the modern, fully-equipped "President" hotel and the simple but exceptional "Salice" hotel.

1. The Tavoliere

LUCERA. This little town is situated on a spur of the Dàunia mountains, and is renowned for having kept 600 Roman cavalrymen prisoner after taking them hostage at Forche Caudine. You should see the cathedral, the castle and the amphitheater. Lucera is the home of extra virgin olive oil, thistles, fennel, sausages and the DOC wine Cacc'è mmitte which is mostly made from Troia grapes. At the "Monticella" store you can buy

Cavatelli pasta

Olive groves on the Gargano coast

HOTELS AND RESTAURANTS

Foggia
Cicolella ★☆★ 🍴 🏨
viale XXIV Maggio 60
☎ 0881688890
President ★☆★
viale degli Aviatori 130
☎ 0881618010
Salice ★★★
S.S. per Bari al km 4
☎ 0881680407
In Fiera-Cicolella 🍴
viale Fortore 155
☎ 0881632166
Ventaglio 🍴
via G. Postiglione 6
☎ 0881661500
Cerignola
Il Bagatto 🍴
via G. Gentile 7
☎ 0885427850
Lucera
Alhambra 🍴
via De Nicastri 10/14
☎ 0881347066
Manfredonia
Gargano ★★★
Gargano 🍴
viale Beccarini 2
☎ 0884587621
Il Gabbiano ★★★
at Lido di Siponto
viale Eunostides 20
☎ 0884542554
Panorama
del Golfo ★★★
at Lido di Siponto
lungomare del Sole 34
☎ 0884542843
Il Baracchio 🍴
corso Roma 38
☎ 0884583874

**HOTELS AND
RESTAURANTS**

Monte
Sant'Angelo
Rotary ★★★
via per Pulsano
☎ 0884562146
Li Jalantuùmene ❚❚
piazza De Galganis
☎ 0884565484
Medioevo ❚❚
via Castello 21
☎ 0884565356
⭐❚❚ **Al Grottino** ❚
corso V. Emanuele 179
☎ 0884561132
⭐❚❚ **La Caravella** ❚
via Reale Basilica 84
☎ 0884561444
Peschici
⭐❚❚ **La Collinetta** ❚❚
at Madonna di Loreto
☎ 0884964151
Rodi Garganico
⭐❚❚ **Baia Santa
Barbara** ★★★
at Santa Barbara
☎ 0884965253
⭐❚❚ **Gabbiano** ❚
via Trieste 16
☎ 0884965283
San Giovanni
Rotondo
**Masseria
Agropolis** ★☆★
at S. Egidio
☎ 0882452754
Da Costanzo ❚❚
via S. Croce 9
☎ 0882452285
San Severo
⭐❚❚ **Arcate** ❚
piazza Cavallotti 29
☎ 0882226025
Vieste
**Pizzomunno
Vieste Palace** ★★★
Il Trabucco ❚❚❚
lungomare di
Pizzomunno
☎ 0884708741

sauces, jams, vegetable patés and more. Try the "Alhambra" restaurant with both new and traditional cuisine of the area.

TROIA. Once the ancient town of *Aecae*, Troia has one of the most beautiful Romanesque cathedrals in Puglia. Here you can find excellent olive oil, dairy products, mutton or lamb, and almonds.

BOVINO. In this small town near the Irpinia mountains they produce extra virgin olive oil, turnip tops (known as *bruocchele*), durum wheat, onions and chicken. Local specialties include thin sausages for cooking, and hams.

CERIGNOLA. To reach this town, you have to pass through Orta Nova, an agricultural colony leased out on a profit-sharing basis. Of interest here is the red DOC wine, the olive oil and the good food. In Cerignola – a famous production center for corn and olive oil - you discover the immensity of the Tavoliere plain, which is like a sea of corn dotted with farms. The cathedral houses the thirteenth-century icon, *Madonna di Ripalta*. To buy local products, try the "Merlicco" store, selling olives for eating (the famous Bella di Cerignola variety comes from here), little

artichokes preserved in oil, and eggplants; the "Gianni dell'Olio" *enoteca*; and the "Antica Enotria" *cantina*. If you are looking for a restaurant, try the long-established family-run "Bagatto".

2. The Gargano

SAN SEVERO. This town is situated at the edge of the Tavoliere plain, between olive groves and vineyards. Extra virgin olive oil, common wheat, durum wheat, *mozzarella* and DOC wine are the most renowned products of this important agricultural market. You can buy the pasta from the pasta-makers, "Cara Nonna" who have a wide choice of local durum wheat pastas (*orecchiette, fusilli, cavatelli*), egg pastas (*cannoncini del Gargano, conchigliette*), and flavored pastas. For a culinary stop, there is the "Arcate" restaurant, offering local home cooking featuring plenty of vegetables. To taste and buy wine, there is the "Torretta Zamarra" *azienda* and the "L'Antica Cantina" *azienda*, while in the Sant'Antonio quarter, you should stop at the "Giovanni D'Alfonso del Sordo" *cantina*.

RODI GARGANICO. To reach Rodi

Deliceto

502

Foggia. Masseria Palmieri

Garganico you must cross Apricena and Sannicandro Garganico, then go round Lake Varano. The best local products are extra virgin olive oil and lots of fruit (oranges, lemons, mandarins, figs and carob beans). In order to try the seafood and other local dishes, go to the "Gabbiano" restaurant by the sea. To stay over, there is the "Baia Santa Barbara" hotel, which also has 100 small chalets.

PESCHICI. In the village, surrounded by the old town walls, you will find the "La Collinetta" restaurant which serves home-made pasta dishes, fresh fish and extra virgin olive oil. It also has rooms.

VIESTE. Characterized by alleyways, white houses and steps, this is the easternmost town of the Gargano massif, and has a splendid cathedral. Extra virgin olive oil, durum wheat, barley and oats are produced locally. At the "Mimmo Forte" store in the center of town, you can buy *cacio-ricotta, caciocavallo, pecorino* and *mozzarella* cheeses (some even stuffed), olive oil, food preserved in oil, and jams. At the "Casa della Bruschetta", you can eat *bruschetta* with vegetables , *orecchiette* with tomato, *cacio-ricotta*

cheese, and other specialties. Remember, also, the "Vesta" *enoteca*, with a list of wines exclusively from Puglia, and good seafood dishes. For an overnight stay, there is the "Pizzomunno Vieste Palace" with its own restaurant. We also recommend the "Il Trabucco" restaurant, which serves local food, the fish restaurant, "Box 19" and the "Locanda Dragone" in the old center.

MONTE SANT'ANGELO. The town has a splendid view and is known for the S. Michele Arcangelo sanctuary, one of the oldest sites of Christianity, and the Rotari tomb. The main features of its cuisine are extra virgin olive oil, celery, *cavallucci di caciocavallo* cheese, pork, *copate* (cakes made with honey and chopped dried fruit squashed between two biscuits) and *tarallucci*. The best restaurant is the "Li Jalantuùmene" in the old center, with a careful selection of traditional wines and dishes. Also good are "Medioevo", "Al Grottino", and "La Caravella", all of which serve local specialties. For an overnight stay there is the peaceful and modern "Rotary" hotel.

SAN GIOVANNI ROTONDO. This town, immersed in vineyards and almond groves, is known because Padre Pio lived and worked here. The area is noted for its chestnuts, walnuts and potatoes. To try the traditional dishes, go to the "Da Costanzo" restaurant, renowned for its *tronchetti alla pugliese* (Puglia-style *tronchetti* pasta), *agnello al cartoccio* (lamb

Troia grapes

HOTELS AND RESTAURANTS

Vieste
Al Dragone ¶
via Duomo 8
☎ 0884701212
Box 19 ¶
via S. Maria di Merino 13
☎ 0884705229
Enoteca Vesta ¶
via Duomo 14
☎ 0884706411

AGRITURISMI

Mattinata
Monte Sacro
contrada Stinco
☎ 0884558941
Vieste
Francesco Azzarone
contrada Piano Grande
☎ 0884701332
Fara del Falco
at Delfino
☎ 0884705796

WINE PRODUCERS

San Severo
D'Alfonso del Sordo
contrada S. Antonino
S.S. 89
☎ 0882221444

OLIVE OIL PRODUCERS

Mattinata
Azienda Agricola Bisceglia
via C. Battisti 74
☎ 0884551003
Torremaggiore
GR.A.C.O. di Bosco
contrada Pagliaravecchia
at km 17
☎ 0882383339

cooked in paper) and *spigola al-l'acquapazza* (sea bass in a light broth).

MANFREDONIA. Founded by King Manfredi in 1256, this town produces plenty of food (extra virgin olive oil, yellow carrots, prickly pears, *mozzarella*, gilthead bream, cuttlefish, sardines and *gnummerieddi*, made from minced lamb's innards). Do not miss the Museo Nazionale del Gargano, with its fine collection of Dàunia stele, and the Baroque cathedral. Shop at "Borrelli" for marinated fish such as rock octopus, cuttlefish, squid, anchovies,

A dairyman

and more. To try the local cuisine, visit the "Gargano" restaurant in the hotel of the same name, serving *zuppa di pesce* (fish soup), *spiedini di mazzancolle* (skewered crayfish) and *frittura mista* (mixed fry-up). As an alternative, try the *trattoria* "Il Baracchio", serving *zuppetta alla marinara* (seafood soup), *linguine ai frutti di mare* (linguine pasta with shellfish), *seppie ripiene* (stuffed cuttlefish), and grilled meats.

For an overnight stay at Lido di Siponto, there are the hotels "Il Gabbiano" and the "Panorama del Golfo".

Field of corn in Foggia area

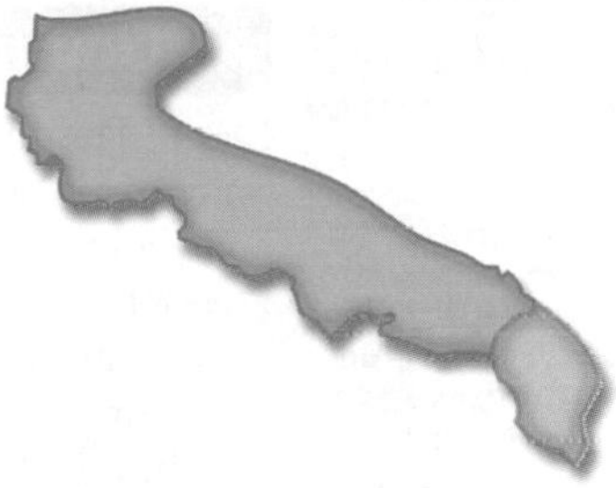

LECCE

The farmhouse cooking of this province draws on the flavors of the sea and the inland vegetable gardens and pastures.

The province boasts quite a varied and well-known cuisine. As with the rest of the region, vegetables are often used in the cooking and bring several recipes to life. No less important is the role of the dairy products and white meats, which are mostly roasted or baked. The most well-known local dishes include *pasta e ceci* (pasta and chick peas), *ciceri e tria* (*tagliatelle* pasta made from durum wheat, with onions fried in olive oil), the *frisedde* (crackers made with corn flour, softened and seasoned with oil, salt and tomatoes), country pizza and the *carteddate*. And that is not forgetting the rich range of wines, the best being the rosés and reds. These include the DOC wines Alezio, Copertino and Salice Salentino.

Lighthouse at Capo d'Otranto. The easternmost point of Italy

505

Gourmet Tours

LECCE. This town is the capital of Salento, a sub-region of Puglia, and has grown up over an ancient Messapico site. The old town, enclosed within ancient walls, is full of twisting roads and little piazzas which, together with the lovely Lecce Baroque architecture, make the old center quite unique. The Piazza del Duomo is a fine example of the harmony and beauty of the setting. The piazza contains the Seminario, the Palazzo Vescovile (Bishop's palace) and the cathedral. Do not miss the Basilica di Santa Croce, the Palazzo del Governo, the Roman amphitheater and the church of Ss. Nicolò and Cataldo. The best food here includes the traditional *taralli*, the no less typical *pesce dolce* , the *pasticciotto*, the *puccie* (small bread rolls filled with olives or raisins) which are made on 7th December ready for the vigil of the Immaculate Conception, the *cotognata* (a jam made from Cotogna apples) and the Gran Liquore di San Domenico. If you wish to buy cakes, go to "Franco Alvino" where you can also find the classic Carnival sweet *sanguinaccio* , re-worked to give a

modern version without the pig's blood used originally. Other cake shops include "Citiso", a traditional Lecce cake shop, and "Cotognata Leccese". If you wish to buy the local *gnummerieddi* (oven-cooked or grilled intestines), you will find it at the butchers, "Gianfrate"; if you wish to buy *puccia*, you will find it at the bakers, "Boulangerie". Those who prefer wine should go to "Rollo", an *enoteca* in the center of town, and the "Agricole Vallone" *cantina*. The restaurant "Picton" is excellent, with its *zuppa di farro alla salentina* (*farro*, or spelt, soup Salento-style), *cavatelli con fagioli* (*cavatelli* pasta with beans), *tagliata di calamaretti farciti* (slices of stuffed squid), *zuppa alla galipollina* (Gallipoli-style soup) and *padellata di scamorza affumicata* (fried smoked *scamorza* cheese). Also extremely good is the restaurant in the hotel "President", with its *maccheroncini di farro* (spelt macaroni pasta), *fritture di mare* (mixed fish fry), and *carello di pesce* (filet of fish). The "Enoteca Caffetteria Carlo V", with over 300 wine labels and the chance to try some local dishes, is worth a visit, as is the simpler "Casareccia" with its Salento cuisine. In Acaia you will find the

Gallipoli. The port

"La Locanda del Gallo", which offers cuisine that follows the rhythms of the seasons and of the market. For a quiet hotel, there is the modern "Cristal" and the "Grand Hotel Tiziano e dei Congressi" near to the entrance of the superhighway to Brindisi, and the Art Nouveau style "Grand Hotel" near the railway station.

1. The Western Coast of Salento

COPERTINO. This town is situated halfway between Lecce and Porto Cesareo. Copertino is also the name of red and rosé DOC wines. The locality also produces extra virgin olive oil, figs, onions and fresh cheeses. You can buy wine at the "Cantina Sociale di Copertino" and at the "Masseria Monaci". PORTO CESAREO. This fishing village is set on a small headland on the jagged and low-lying western coast of Salento. Try the "L'Angolo di Beppe" for traditional cuisine and hotel, and the "Veliero" fish restaurant.

NARDÒ. This is an ancient rival of Lecce for the position of artistic and cultural center. The little town has a Benedictine cathedral and the Piazza Salandra, which is surrounded by Baroque buildings with balconies, loggias, arches and the Immacolata spire. Nardò also has a rich gastronomic heritage, which includes the local Celline olives, extra virgin olive oil, the classic country pizza, and the copeta (a cake made with almond paste). And do not forget the riches of the sea: mussels, sardines, lobster and grouper fish are commonly used. For shopping, there is the "Delicatezze" cake shop offering a vast selection of cakes, bocconotti, sweet biscuits, Puglia wines, and so on.

Picking table grapes

GALLIPOLI. This ancient Messapica town, then called *Anxa*, has a beautiful cathedral and the Castle of Angioini, which kept watch over the port. The fish (mullet, lobster, crab, swordfish and tuna) together with almond milk and asparagus, are the culinary mainstays of the area. Several restaurants stand out, including the "Marechiaro", which serves local cuisine on terraces overlooking the sea, "Da Olga", a long-established *trattoria* which offers a huge variety of fish dishes and the "Da Sarino" *trattoria* with home-made local dishes. If you want to stay over, there is the lovely "Grand Hotel Costa Brada" in Baia Verde, which is surrounded by greenery and has direct access to the beach. Then there is the modern "Le Sirenuse" hotel which should not be underestimated. That, too, is surrounded by greenery and is next to the sea. CASARANO. Leaving the coast, we go inland to Casarano at the foot of the Murge Salentine hills. This is the agricultural center of Salentino. At the southern edge of the town there is the Casaranello

HOTELS AND RESTAURANTS

Maglie
Bel Ami ❢
via Manzoni 7
☎ 0836428554
Otranto
Degli Haethey ★☆★
via F. Sforza 33
☎ 0836801548
Albania ★★★ 🛏
via S. F. di Paola 10
☎ 0836801183
Valle dell'Idro ★★★
🛏, via G. Grasso 4
☎ 0836804552
Acmet Pascià ❢❢
lungomare degli Eroi
☎ 0836801282
Porto Cesareo
L'Angolo di Beppe
★☆★, at Torre Lapillo
via Zanella 24
☎ 0833565333
Veliero ❢❢
litoranea S. Isidoro-
Gallipoli
☎ 0833569201
Santa Cesarea Terme
Le Macine ★★★
via Fontanelle 37
☎ 0836949941
Uggiano la Chiesa
Masseria Gattamora ❢❢ 🛏
via Campo Sport. 33
☎ 0836817936

AGRITURISMI

Castrignano del Capo
Serine 🛏
contrada Serine
☎ 0833751337
Otranto
La Fattoria 🛏
S.S. Otranto-Uggiano
☎ 0836804651

WINE PRODUCERS

Lecce
Agricole Vallone
viale XXV Luglio 9
☎ 0832308041
Copertino
Cantina Sociale
via M. del Risorgimento 6
☎ 0832947031
Masseria Monaci
via Galatina
☎ 0832947512

OLIVE OIL PRODUCERS

Lecce
Alberti di Catenaya srl
via Ribezzo 2/b
☎ 0832318415
Merine
Frantoio A. Bianco
corso Italia 24
☎ 0832623002
Tricase
Sapori del Salento - Stefanicò srl
via Madonna di Fatima 6
☎ 0833544759
Tuglie
Michele Calò & F.
via Masseria Vecchia 1
☎ 0833596242

SHOPPING

Lecce
Enoteca Rollo
via C. Battisti 23
☎ 0832302832
Wines.
La Cotognata Leccese
via Marconi 51
☎ 0832302800
Traditional cakes.
Maglio
Arte Dolciaria
via Templari 16
☎ 0832243816
one shop in Maglie:
via S. Giuseppe 54
☎ 0836423831
Sweets and pastries.
Panetteria Boulangerie
via Oberdan 10!/12
☎ 0832340944
Bakery.
Pasticceria F. Alvino
piazza S. Oronzo 30
☎ 0832247436
Sweets and pastries.
Pasticceria Citiso
viale Japigia 12
☎ 0832312996
Sweets and pastries.
Galatina
Pasticceria Dulcedo
via Galateo 19
☎ 0836561114
Sweets and pastries.
Maglie
Antico Pastificio Cavalieri
via Garibaldi 64
☎ 0836484144
Bakery.

Repairing fishing nets

church, which is all that is left of the ancient town of that name.

For a meal, go to the "Buongustaio" restaurant. For shopping, there are the pasta-makers, "La Contrada del Re", a co-operative which aims to recover and rediscover the gastronomic traditions of seventeenth-century Salento.

GALATINA. This town, in the heart of the Salento peninsular, still has a late Romanesque church, S. Caterina d'Alessandria. Local specialties are the *taralli* and mutton. You can buy rich cakes at the "Andrea Ascalone" cake shop (e.g. *fruttoni*, Sicilian *cassata* and *pastiera*) and at the "Dulcedo" cake shop, deemed by many to be the best makers of almond paste. They also sell *tronchetti* (log cakes which can also be made with ice-cream), *pesce dolce*, Easter lamb cake, *fruttoni*, *amaretti* and much else besides. You get good prices and wine tasting at the "Valle dell'Asso" farm. To stay over, we recommend the "Hermitage" hotel set in a large park.

2. The Eastern Coast of Salento

OTRANTO. The easternmost point of Italy is in the history books for having suffered a sustained attack by the Turks in 1480 . The town's main monument is the cathedral, which has a beautiful mosaic floor. A large part of the old town is still enclosed by a wall, and there is a castle higher up. The area produces good extra virgin olive oil, Otranto chicory, sweet peppers, watermelon and almond milk. We recommend the "Castellana" restaurant, which belongs to the "Club Nike", and the "Acmet Pascià", serving dishes in season, and with a terrace overlooking the sea. To stay over, there is the new hotel "Degli Haethey", the "Albania" in the town center, and the "Valle dell'Idro", immersed in greenery.

The "Masseria Gattamora" near Uggiano La Chiesa, is worth a trip. It is very typical of the area and serves good combinations of fish and vegetables.

SANTA CESAREA TERME. If you follow the rocky coast, dotted with prehistoric caves, you will get to Santa Cesarea Terme. Here the main produce is melons and wheat, both durum and common. The hotel "Le Macine" is good. A little before Castro, there is a road which goes down to the Zinzulusa grotto, the most interesting marine cave in Puglia.

MARINA DI LEUCA. The town is situated on the headland dividing the Jonio Sea from the Adriatic. Maglie is at the extreme tip of Santa Maria di Leuca, and is known for its museum of mammoth fossils, as well as fossils of other Pleistocene animals. The cuisine's main ingredients include extra virgin olive oil, *cappella* corn, peaches, stuffed dried figs and almond milk. For excellent vegetable dishes, pizzas and desserts, try the "Bel Ami" restaurant.

TARANTO

The city of two seas is the gastronomic heart of a province with a highly developed coastline and excellent inland agriculture and sheep farming.

Oysters and mussels are Taranto's specialties, thanks mostly to the particularly good position of this ancient sea town. You should, therefore, make the most of the fish, in general, but also of the fruit, vegetables, extra virgin olive oil, goat's meat and lamb, and the cheeses. Wine production includes the DOC wines Lizzano, Martina Franca and Primitivo di Manduria.

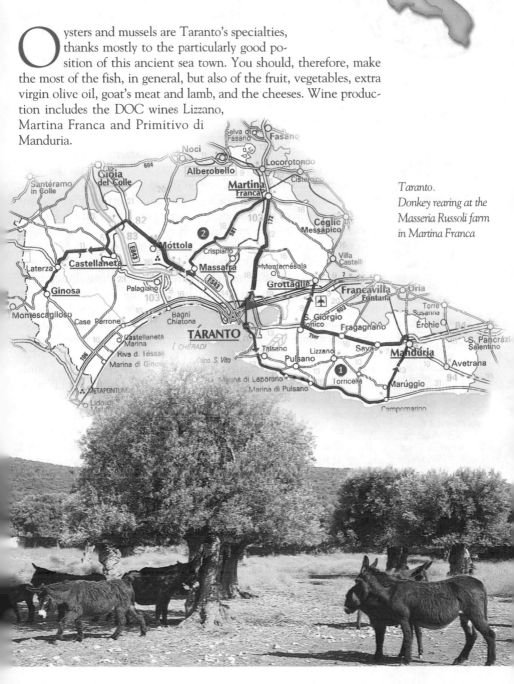

Taranto.
Donkey rearing at the
Masseria Russoli farm
in Martina Franca

Gourmet Tours

TARANTO. This town is a little island between two peninsulas, separating nearly completely the Mar Grande from the further inland Mar Piccolo. The town is nearly all based on the island and the southeastern peninsula. In the Museo Archeologico Nazionale you can learn about the glittering past and the attachment of the town to Magna Grecia , the ancient Greek colony on Italian soil that included Puglia and Sicily. You should also visit the castle and the cathedral. Taranto boasts a rich culinary tradition, with local specialties including the *tarantello* (a tuna sausage), the *cervellata* (a sausage made with meat, brain and flavorings), Taranto mussels and the *scattiata* (a sort of *peperonata* – sweet peppers cooked with tomatoes and onions). Local produce includes extra virgin olive oil, *mozzarella*, gilthead bream, yellow carrots, cuttlefish, sardines, prickly pears, and *gnummerieddi* (intestines).To try these foods, we recommend the restaurant "Le Vecchie Cantine", which also serves *tortino di rape stufate* (baked turnip pie), *linguine ai calamaretti e rucola* (*linguine* pasta with baby squid and rocket), *cavatelli ai frutti di mare* (*cavatelli* pasta with shellfish), and grilled meats and fish. Also good is "Il Golfo", with its *tubettini ai frutti di mare* (*tubettini* pasta with shellfish), *strozzapreti con melanzane* (strozzapreti pasta with eggplant), and *sella di vitello* (saddle of veal), "La Fattoria", which serves *cozze gratinate* (mussel gratin), *spaghetti alle von-*

gole (spaghetti with clams), fresh fish cooked in salt or in paper, or fried; and the "Al Faro" with its *risotto di mare* (seafood *risotto*) and *bucatini in brodetto di pesce* (*bucatini* pasta in fish broth). Finally, for a pleasant stopover, go to the "Grand Hotel Delfino", the "Palace" in the town center, or the "Park Hotel Mar Grande" on the seafront. At the delicatessen "Torio", you can buy salamis, hams, *soppressate* sausage, sausages and cheese.

1. The Taranto Murge
MANDURIA. This Città del Vino is the administrative center of the "Primitivo" district. See the ancient cathedral, late medieval ghetto, Imperial palace, Messapica walls and the Fonte Pliniano. The "Cantine Pervini" wine producers have been lauded for bringing back the Primitivo wine. "Felline" are also good. In addition, there is the "Cantina Sociale" in Sava. You should try the restaurant, "Castello", which serves local dishes. A hotel worth trying is the modern "Dei Bizantini", set in greenery.
GROTTAGLIE. The town is known for its ceramics and wines. Extra virgin olive oil, almonds and dried figs can be found in abundance. You can get some good buys at the "Cantina Sociale Pruvas".

2. Amongst the gorges
MARTINA FRANCA. The name of this Città del Vino is also that of a DOC wine. The town got its name from the exemptions (*franchigia*) given to it by the Prince of Taranto, Filippo d'Angiò. At the "Ritrovo degli Amici", you can eat *baccalà fritto* (fried stockfish), *arancini* (rice balls

HOTELS AND RESTAURANTS

Taranto
G.H. Delfino ★★★
viale Virgilio 66
☎ 0997323232
Palace ★★★
viale Virgilio 10
☎ 0994594771
Park Hotel Mar Grande ★★★
viale Virgilio 90
☎ 0997351713
Al Faro ❙❙
via Galeso 126
☎ 0994714444
Il Golfo ❙❙
viale Virgilio 66
☎ 099339981
La Fattoria ❙❙
via Abruzzo 9
☎ 0997362560
Vecchie Cantine ❙❙
at Lame, via Girasoli 23
☎ 0997772589
Castellaneta Marina
Jonico ★★★
S.S. 106, at km 464
☎ 0998433082
★❙☎❙ **Riva dei Tessali Golf Hotel** ★★★
at Riva dei Tessali
☎ 0998439251
Cisternino
★❙☎❙ **Aia del Vento** ★★★
via Locorotondo 7
☎ 0804448388
Villa Cenci ★★★
via per Ceglie Mess.
☎ 0804413668
Manduria
Dei Bizantini ★★★
at S. Pietro in Bevagna
via Borraco 264
☎ 0999729820
Martina Franca
★❙☎❙ **Park Hotel San Michele** ★★★
viale Carella 9
☎ 0804807053

with cheese), *orecchiette al po-modoro, basilico e cacio-ricotta* (*orecchiette* pasta with tomato, basil and *cacio-ricotta* cheese), *stufato di manzo* (pork stew) and *cosciotto di agnello* (leg of lamb). Other restaurants worth trying are the "Dell'Erba", which serves local dishes including *orecchiette alla martinese* (Martinese style *orecchiette* pasta) and *grigliate miste* (mixed grills), the "Villaggio In", where you can get local and traditional dishes such as *fusilli al nero di seppia* (*fusilli* pasta with the black ink from cuttlefish), *puré di fave* (broad bean purée) and *agnello con patate e lampascioni* (lamb with potatoes and onions). For overnight stays, places range from the *agriturismo* establishment "Il Vignaletto" to the "Park Hotel San Michele". To buy excellent local produce, you can start at the butchers "Fratelli Ricci", for their charcuterie (*soppressata, capocollo, salsiccia fresca*), kid goat, beef, pork and lamb. Then there is the "Miali" *cantina*, and, for the gourmets, there is the old café, "Caffè Tripoli", where you can buy chocolate nougat, *mostaccioli* (cake made of flour, sugar, dried figs, candied fruit and raisins) and *bocconotti all'amarena*.
MASSAFRA. In this landscape marked by olive groves and prickly

pears, you can see a thick line of grottos and the crypts of San Basilio il Grande, deep in the gorges which divide the town. On one side you have the Borgo di Terra with its ancient tangle of twisted alleyways, and on the other side there is Borgo Santa Caterina.
MOTTOLA. The town and its cathedral dominate the last step of the Murge hills before they slope down to the Gulf of Taranto. At the "Le Rocce" restaurant they serve excellent *orecchiette al ragù di carne e ricotta forte* (*orecchiette* pasta with meat ragout and *ricotta forte* cheese), *cavatelli ai frutti di mare* (*cavatelli* pasta with shellfish) and grilled meats and fish. Try the "Delfino" hotel, with a swimming pool filled with sea water; and the *agriturismo* establishment, "Masseria Il Porticello".
CASTELLANETA. Situated on the edge of a deep gorge, this town is characterized by the Sacco and the Muricello quarters. Do not miss the Museo Rodolfo Valentino which is dedicated to the famous actor. For a pleasant stay, try the "Jonico" hotel.
GINOSA. This ancient agricultural center specializes in olive growing and is surrounded by a deep gorge. Go food shopping at "Genusia" and "Apicoltura Jonica".

The Ionian coast

**Azienda Agricola Vitivinicola
LOMAZZI & SARLI**

C.da Partemio s.n. - Latiano (BR)
Tel. e Fax +39 0831725898
www.vinilomazzi.it
E-mail: vinilomazzi@quipo.it

BRINDISI
DENOMINAZIONE DI ORIGINE CONTROLLATA

SOLISE®
1998

ROSSO RISERVA

The excellence of Salento wines

GOLD MEDAL
at the XXI Banco
D'Assaggio
dei Vini d'Italia
Torgiano (PG)

**CANTINE
DUE PALME**

GREAT
GOLD MEDAL
at 36° Vinitaly
International Wine
Competition
2002

Cellino San Marco (Br)
tel. 0831 617865
fax 0831 617866
E-mail: duepalme@tin.it
www.cantineduepalme.it

GOLD MEDAL AT VINITALY 2001

frantoio
GALANTINO

Leone
d'Oro
1997-2001

Ercole
Olivario
1997

Montiferru
1996

*Ancient oil-press using traditional granite mills since 1860,
produces extra virgin olive oil, organic oil,
aromatised oils, elegant gift sets.*
**Open to the public for retail sale and guided visits
on weekdays, 9-12 a.m. and 4-7 p.m. with tasting
of "bruschette" snacks.**

Premio Biol
2001

Frantoio F.lli Galantino s.n.c. - *70052 Bisceglie (Ba) Italy - Via Corato, 2*
Tel. ++39 080 3921320 - Fax ++39 080 3951834
E-mail: oliogalantino@oliodioliva.net - www.galantino.it

APOLLONIO®

In one of the regions of Italy best known for its wines, Puglia, was founded at the end of the 19th century the Apollonio Company.

The symbol for the great vocation and love for the "art of making wine" of the four Apollonio generations who followed each other at the helm of the company is a little bottle of red wine going back to 1816, the birth year of the founder. In our days, this little treasure is jealously kept at the company premises and it has become the emblem of the great passion shared by all members of the family for high quality wine.

The Apollonio wine owes its noble character to the attention given to every single production step, to the direct selection of vines and grapes, and to bottling according to the latest technologies, but also to the excellent wine area: North Salento, home to wines which have become famous all over the world.

The Company is now run by Marcello and Massimiliano Apollonio. Marcello takes care of marketing and often joins the company's sales representatives to hear opinions and advice directly from the clients. Massimiliano, an oenologist and sommelier, after studying at a very renowned oenology college in Locorotondo (BA) and developing his professional expertise through several stages in Italian, French and Spanish companies, takes care with great professionalism of the selection of grapes and the whole production cycle.

Another characteristic, which singles out the Apollonio company, is the welcoming given to anyone who wishes to visit the processing centre.

Numerous Italian and foreign delegations visit the vineyards every year, and can see for themselves the quality of wines and follow the whole production cycle.

In particular, Marcello and Massimiliano are glad to play host to foreign guests who wish to know not only about the Apollonio Company but also about Salento, a south Italian area rich in history and traditions.

For this reason, every year in May the company organizes the "Salento week", dedicated to foreign operators coming from all over the world, who are given a chance to visit places of great tourist and cultural attraction.

APOLLONIO®

Casa Vinicola Apollonio S.n.C. di Marcello e Massimiliano Apollonio & C.
73047 Monteroni di Lecce (LE) Italy - Via S. Pietro in Lama, 6
Tel. 0039 0832 327182 • Fax 0039 0832 325238
web-site: www.apolloniovini.it - e-mail: info@apolloniovini.it

BASILICATA FLAVORS OF LUCANIA

The ancient name of Lucania brings to mind a mountainous area covered in woods and sheep farms. The Tirreno and Ionian coastlines, though extremely short, guarantee a typically Mediterranean culture and cuisine.

This is a largely mountainous region encompassing the peaks of the Lucane Dolomites and woods stretching from the Vulture area to the Pollino area. There is a great tradition of cheeses and charcuterie, and the hills provide crops which contribute to exceptionally high quality pasta. The olive oil and wine are excellent, and the vegetables are renowned. Basilicata's best dishes are its pasta first courses with vegetable, meat or cheese sauces, often benefiting from the addition of olive oil and chilli peppers. Then there are the meats: lamb is the most popular, then pork from the local breed of black pigs. The region has some outstanding restaurants in touristic areas, and a good network of family-run trattorias.

The little port of Maratea

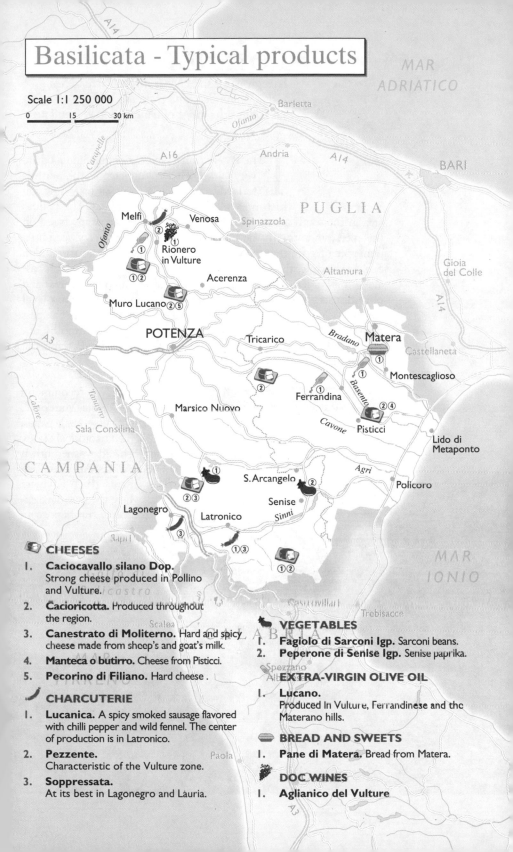

Basilicata - Typical products

Scale 1:1 250 000

0   15   30 km

MAR ADRIATICO

PUGLIA

BARI

Barletta

Andria

Spinazzola

Gioia del Colle

Altamura

Melfi   Venosa

Rionero in Vulture

Acerenza

Muro Lucano

POTENZA

Tricarico

Matera

Castellaneta

Montescaglioso

Ferrandina

Marsico Nuovo

Pisticci

Lido di Metaponto

Sala Consilina

CAMPANIA

S.Arcangelo

Agri

Policoro

Senise

Lagonegro

Latronico

MAR IONIO

CHEESES
1. **Caciocavallo silano Dop.** Strong cheese produced in Pollino and Vulture.
2. **Cacioricotta.** Produced throughout the region.
3. **Canestrato di Moliterno.** Hard and spicy cheese made from sheep's and goat's milk.
4. **Manteca o butirro.** Cheese from Pisticci.
5. **Pecorino di Filiano.** Hard cheese .

CHARCUTERIE
1. **Lucanica.** A spicy smoked sausage flavored with chilli pepper and wild fennel. The center of production is in Latronico.
2. **Pezzente.** Characteristic of the Vulture zone.
3. **Soppressata.** At its best in Lagonegro and Lauria.

VEGETABLES
1. **Fagiolo di Sarconi Igp.** Sarconi beans.
2. **Peperone di Senise Igp.** Senise paprika.

EXTRA-VIRGIN OLIVE OIL
1. **Lucano.** Produced in Vulture, Ferrandinese and the Materano hills.

BREAD AND SWEETS
1. **Pane di Matera.** Bread from Matera.

DOC WINES
1. **Aglianico del Vulture**

POTENZA

This province stretches from the Tirreno Sea to the Ionian Sea, and from the Vulture area to the Pollino. Its range of wine and food is unique.

The Potenza landscape, agriculture and food are very varied. The Vulture area in the north is formed from a volcanic massif providing soil which is excellent for grapes and olives. The Pollino area in the south is sheep-rearing country with an economy based on the cheese industry. In the hills, the Agri and Sinni rivers open up a prime area for fruit and vegetables on their way down to the Ionian Sea. Meanwhile, the Ofanto, Basento and Bradano rivers, which pass along the borders with Campania, mark out an important cereal and olive district. There is a brief stretch of Tirreno coastline on a level with the Gulf of Policastro. In the space of a few kilometers you pass from the citrus groves on the coast to the woods of the Sirino Mountains. The cuisine is equally varied, the best being found in Potenza, the administrative center, and Maratea.

Gourmet Tours

POTENZA. The old town rises up between the mountains and woods of the high Basento valley and is centered around the Via Pretoria. It has been hit by several earthquakes, but has managed to stay vibrant with the culture and politics of the day. We recommend the "Antica Osteria Marconi", with a menu of home-made pastas, nicely re-worked traditional dishes, including fish, all washed down with Vulture wines. Another place worth trying is the "Taverna Oraziana" where the Lucania dishes - the *strascinati con salsiccia* (a

type of *gnocchi* with sausage) and the *agnello con lampascioni* (lamb with onions) - are never disappointing. Finally, the "La Fattoria", a Buon Ricordo restaurant, is excellent value.

In the stores you can buy all the Potenza mountain produce, including Pecorino di Filiano cheese, charcuterie (Soppressata and Ventresca di Picerno), sausage and Bella-Muro goat's cheeses. You can also buy tomato, artichoke and eggplant preserves. Cakes include the *mostazzuoli di Avigliano*. Vaglio Basilicata is a place worth visiting and, once here, you should have a break at the "Locanda di Eolo".

1. In Aglianico territory

RIONERO IN VULTURE. When you go past the castle of Lagopesole, you will see the old volcanic cone of the Vulture like a backdrop to the little town. Today the cone is green with vines and chestnut trees. We are in Aglianico country - Aglianico the red wine which needs a long time to mature, and Aglianico the top quality olive oil. If you want a break, try "La Pergola", known for its mushrooms and game. The "Armando Martino" *cantina* is worth trying for its Aglianico Canneto wine. You should buy the Atella cheeses and the *salsiccia pezzenta* (a poor man's sausage made with the discarded bits of meat from pork, veal, lamb and mutton, flavored with garlic, chili pepper and spices, and added to sauces). Nearby Barile is full of Albanian traditions. The top wine-makers are "Paternoster" with their esteemed Aglianico del Vulture Don Anselmo.

MELFI. Just beyond Rapolla, this characteristic Byzantine village is marked out by its huge four-sided

castle and the Baroque profile of the cathedral. Frederick II of Swabia loved it. We recommend the "Novecento" restaurant here, with its scrumptious *maccheronata* (big serving of macaroni pasta), lamb and the rare *mozzarella avvolta nell'asfodelo* (*mozzarella* cheese wrapped in asphodel). "Vaddone" is a good *trattoria*. From the mountains you get chestnuts, the so-called *marroncini di Melfi*, which are used in certain cakes and desserts. From the plains you get vegetables, including the San Marzano tomatoes which are excellent in sauces.

Lagonegro. The old town

HOTELS AND RESTAURANTS

Potenza
Antica Osteria Marconi ¶¶
viale Marconi 233/235
☎ 097156900
Due Torri ¶¶
via Due Torri 6/8
☎ 0971411661
⭐🏠 **La Fattoria** ¶¶
via Verderuolo Inferiore 13
☎ 097134680
Taverna Oraziana ¶¶
via O. Flacco 2
☎ 097134044
Fuori le Mura ¶
via IV Novembre 34
☎ 097125409
Acerenza
Il Casone ★★
at Bosco S. Giuliano Nord-Ovest (km 6)
☎ 0971741141
Brienza
La Perla ¶
viale Stazione
☎ 0975381375
Castelmezzano
Al Becco della Civetta ¶¶
vicolo I Maglietta 7
☎ 0971986249
Chiaromonte
⭐🏠 **Ricciardi** ★★★
via Calvario 27
☎ 0973571031

VENOSA. This Città del Vino, or city of wine, is situated in the bed of an ancient lake. It was once a town of ancient Apulia, and then a Roman colony on the Via Appia and home to the poet Horace. The main street runs from the castle to the cathedral. Then, taking the Ofantina road, you pass the Abbazia della Trinità, one of the most interesting medieval monuments in the whole of southern Italy. It is in the middle of a vast archaeological site. You will find excellent examples of Lucania specialties at the "Cantina della Riforma Fondiaria" and the restaurant "Cistercensi".

ACERENZA. The town, with its cathedral of charming shapes and colors, dominates the high valley of Bradano. In the stores you can buy excellent *salsiccia* (sausage) from the area, and Forenza cheeses. The popular "Cooperativa Basilium" sells Aglianico del Vulture wine under the Valle del Trono and I Portali labels. For a break, try "Il Casone" in the peaceful woods of Bosco San Giuliano.

2. The Pollino area and the Val d'Agri

LAGONEGRO. From the eighteenth-century Piazza Grande you climb up a long set of steps to the old village, which is perched on rocky cliff tops. The vis-

HOTELS AND RESTAURANTS

Lagonegro
Baita Laudemio ❢
at Lago Laudemio
☎ 097322135
Maratea
La Locanda delle Donne Monache ★★★
via C. Mazzei 4
☎ 0973877487
Zà Mariuccia ❢❢❢
a Fiumicello-S.Venere
via Grotte 2
☎ 0973876163
Maratea
Il Giardino di Epicuro ❢❢
contrada Massa Piano
☎ 0973870130
Taverna Rovita ❢❢ 🍴
via Rovita 63
☎ 0973876588
Melfi
Vaddone ❢
contrada S. Abruzzese
☎ 097224323
Novecento ❢❢
contrada Incoronata
☎ 0972237470
Moliterno
Vecchio Ponte ★★
at Piano di Maglie
☎ 097564969
Némoli
Da Mimì ❢
at Lago Sirino
☎ 097340586
Rionero in Vulture
La Pergola ★★★
via Lavista 27/31
☎ 0972721179

it offers some good *trattoria* stops, some of the best *soppressate* (salami made from the leanest and best pork, with black pepper) in the region and some excellent cheeses. For the more adventurous, there is a climb up Mount Sirino, rewarded by the "Baita Laudemio" restaurant.

RIVELLO. Little streets come off the main crescent-shaped road in this picturesque village, with the S. Nicola dei Greci church as a reminder of the ancient Byzantine people who once lived there. For a meal, try the "La Panoramica" in town, and the "Mimì" at Lake Sirino.

Aglianico

MARATEA. This little town nestled between rocks and grottos, looking out onto the beautiful Tirreno Sea, is rich in history. The ancient village with the mountain behind has preserved its medieval churches and streets. We recommend you try the "Taverna Rovita" restaurant, with its wholesome *strascinati alle mille verdure* (a type of *gnocchi* with vegetable sauce), *involtini di carne* (slices of meat stuffed and rolled up) and, to finish, the *cassata* (either sponge cake filled with *ricotta*, sugar, candied fruit, chocolate and liqueur or ice-cream in a cake shape filled with cream and candied fruit). The "Il Giardino di Epicuro" restaurant is also good, with its home-made pastas and grills served on a pretty terrace. To stay over, there is the "Locanda delle Donne Monache" set in a former eighteenth-century convent. In the coastal town of Fiumicello-Santa Venere you will find the "Zà Mariuccia", a Buon Ricordo restaurant famous for a century, with its specialty of *ravioli di ricotta dolci in ragù d'agnello* (*ravioli* filled with mild *ricotta* in a lamb sauce). Things to buy include the *soppressate di Lauria* and the *limoncello* and *rosolio* liqueurs.

ROTONDA. This is home to the Pollino National Park. It has a beautiful medieval center and a top gastronomic attraction in the restaurant "Peppe", with its starters of charcuterie, mushroom and vegetables in oil, its first course of *gnocchetti con le erbe di monte* (little *gnocchi* with mountain herbs) and its second course of *capretto in padella* (pan-fried kid goat). Apart from the great variety of beans to be found in the countryside, you also get the exclusive red eggplant, which is small and has a spicy, exotic taste. Next, follow the twisting but atmospheric road crossing the Pollino via the towns of Viggianello, San Severino Lucano and Francavilla in Sinni. We recommend you go still further to Terranova di Pollino, at 926meters. Here you will be rewarded for your efforts at the "Luna Rossa" restaurant, which serves Alpine cuisine. The *foglie verdi del buon pastore* (shepherd's salad) and the *maiale con cipolla dolce e uva sultanina* (pork with sweet onions and sultanas) are exceptional. You can have a grand finale of forest fruit ice-cream and Pollino grappa.

HOTELS AND RESTAURANTS

Rivello
La Panoramica
at Valle del Noce
☎ 097346221

Rotonda
★ **Da Peppe**
corso Garibaldi 13
☎ 0973667838

Terranova di Pollino
Luna Rossa
via Marconi 18
☎ 097393254

Vaglio Basilicata
Locanda di Eolo
S.S. 7 al km 471
☎ 0971481110

Venosa
Cistercensi
via S. Giorgio
☎ 097232724

AGRITURISMI

Latronico
Valpollino
contrada Cornaleta 1
☎ 0973851593

Pignola
★ **Fattoria sotto il Cielo**
contrada Petrucco
☎ 0971420166

Viggiano
Azienda Agricola Biologica Pisani
at San Lorenzo
☎ 0975354054

Throughout your journey you will have the opportunity to buy mountain produce such as *Paddraccio* (a soft sheep and goat's milk cheese with quite an acidic taste), charcuterie and mushroom preserves.

CHIAROMONTE. Once over the River Sinni, you should stop in Senise to buy *zafarani* and sweet peppers in either their fresh or *cruschi* (dried and fried) form. Once in Chiaromonte, an ancient walled village, you can stop at the family-run hotel-restaurant, "Ricciardi".

LATRONICO. This spa town has been popular since ancient times. It is broadly agreed that you can buy the best Lucanica here (spicy sausage, lightly smoked and flavored with chili pepper and wild fennel). "Valpollino" serves simple local cuisine.

MOLITERNO. It is known for its DOP Canestrato (a hard, spicy cheese the color of straw made from sheep and goat's milk) and its *casieddu* cheese, similar to the *cacio-ricotta* (a type of salted *ricotta* made from sheep and goat's

cheese). At nearby Sarconi, the quality of the beans is certificated. For a break, there is "Il Vecchio Ponte".

GRUMENTO NOVA. This town, set in the high Agri valley, descends from one of the most important towns in ancient Lucania. Typical products of the area are vegetables, including the San Marzano tomato, the local variety of apples, *limoncella* and *ghiaccio*, and forest fruits – wild strawberries, gooseberries, etc.

VIGGIANO. This town, set on the slopes of the Volturino, has been known since ancient times for its Sacro Monte sanctuary, its musical instrument making, and its ham. Those looking for good wine should go to the "Azienda Agricola Biologica Pisani", producers of the popular Basilicata Rosso Concerto, a mixture of Bordeaux wines matured in the barrel.

BRIENZA. This town has a picturesque center with a castle looking over the wild Ripe delle Balze. The "La Perla" *trattoria* brings the trip to a pleasant close.

Olive trees in the province of Potenza

WINE PRODUCERS

Acerenza
Cooperativa Vitivinicola Basilium
contrada Pipoli
☎ 0971741449
Barile
Azienda Vinicola Paternoster
via Nazionale 23
☎ 0972770658
Rionero
in Vulture
Armando Martino
via Lavista 2/a
☎ 0972721422
Venosa
Cantina Cooperativa Riforma Fondiaria
contrada Vignale
S. Felice
☎ 097236702

SHOPPING

Potenza
Forno Lucia Pace
contrada Dragonara 75/bis
☎ 0971449260
Regional sweets and bread.
Maratea
Il Patriarca
at Marina di Maratea
☎ 0973879016
Liquors and distilled spirits.

MATERA

Matera goes from the rocky terrain of Sassi through inland olive groves and wheat fields to the Magna Graecia remains on the Ionian coast.

The province of Matera is divided between the downward slopes of the Murge on the border with Puglia, which is dotted with villages and Norman castles, and the plain formed by the rivers running down to the Ionian Sea, where there are still the remains of some important cities from the Magna Graecia period. Inland the landscape is characterized by the golden wheat fields and the contrasting green of the olive groves. Sheep farming is also a well-developed industry, as is the cultivation of fruit and vegetables, thanks to the fertile valley and strip of coastline. Pasta dominates the cuisine, and is served with vegetable and other sauces. There is also sheep and goat's meat, particularly the *gnumaridd*, a type of sausage made from innards. There are plenty of pleasant *trattorie* and *agriturismo* establishments for eating out.

Matera.
Sasso Barisano

Gourmet Tours

MATERA. In order to admire the famous Sassi (groups of ancient habitations carved out of rock), you need to go up the cathedral, a fine Puglia-Romanesque building which towers over the town. The town, carved out of volcanic rock, is spread out below on the edge of the gorge. Once an embarrassment because of its poor state, today it is one of UNESCO's sites of International Heritage. You can follow the Sassi road which skirts round them, absorbing the evidence revealing how ancient but how full of life they are. You can visit the Carlo Levi Center in the Palazzo Lanfranchi, which shows paintings and writings of the author of *Cristo si è fermato a Eboli*. A restaurant with a very distinguished past, the "Il Terrazzino", with three rooms set in the cellars of an ancient building, is also famous for its unparalleled view. Its food is strictly traditional, with *grano e ceci* (grain and chick peas), *cavatelli alla boscaiola* (little gnocchi with forest sauce), grills and roasts, all accompanied by a good Aglianico wine. In the newest parts of town there are two more restaurants worth noting, the "Da Mario", with an excellent reputation, situated within the ancient town walls, and the "Trattoria Lucana", run by the Sanrocco family for over fifty years, and to be recommended to all those who love home cooking. Dishes include *orecchiette con spinaci e ricotta* (orecchiette pasta with spinach and *ricotta* cheese), *involtini al ragù* (ragout of rolled strips of stuffed meat) and *scamorza alla griglia* (grilled *scamorza* cheese). For those wanting fish, follow the road to Altamura and after a few kilometers you will find the

"Venusio" serving *cavatelli alle cime di rapa e frutti di mare* (little *gnocchi* with turnip top and shellfish sauce), *pesce in crosta con spezie della Murgia* (fish en croute with Murgia spices), a good selection of wines, and home-made *sfogliatine di crema e nocino* (puff pastry layered with confectioner's custard and walnut liqueur). If you go shopping, apart from all the Lucana charcuterie and cheeses, don't forget the unique local bread and the olive oil from the Colline Materane. Once you have finished visiting the town, think about a trip to the Parco Archeologico Storico e Naturale delle Chiese Rupestri del Materano, a nature park. To reach it, you follow the Appia route towards Laterza. Do not miss the Murgia Timone village and its view of the gorge and Matera.

MONTESCAGLIOSO. The town is on a hill with a broad view of the Bradano valley, filled with olive groves and wheat fields, and the gorge. In medieval times it was home to one of the oldest and richest Benedictine communities of the region, the Abbey of S. Michele Arcangelo, which dominates the old part of the town. You should visit the ethnographic museum of the S. Francesco convent. You will find local cuisine at the "Contangelo" farm in the Pratolino quarter, and imaginative food at "Doganella".

METAPONTO. The remains of a large Doric temple mark the start of the ruins of *Metapontum*, one of the most powerful cities of the Magna Graecia. You should visit the vast excavations, complete with theater and Temple of Apollo Licio, and the archaeological

HOTELS AND RESTAURANTS

Matera
Venusio 🍴 ★ 🏧
at Venusio (km 7)
via Lussemburgo 2
☎ 0835259081
Da Mario 🍴 ★ 🏧
via XX Settembre 14
☎ 0835336491
Il Terrazzino sui Sassi 🍴
vico S. Giuseppe 7
☎ 0835332503
Moro 🍴 ★ 🏧
vico IV Capelluti 2
☎ 0835332652
Tommaso 🍴
via degli Aragonesi 31
☎ 0835261971
Trattoria Lucana 🍴
via Lucania 48
☎ 0835336117
Accettura
Pezzolla 🍴
via Roma 14
☎ 0835675008
Bernalda
Fifina 🍴
corso Umberto 63
☎ 0835543134
Ferrandina
Degli Ulivi ★★★
S.S. 407 Basentana at km 68, Borgo Macchia
☎ 0835757020
Nova Siri
Ai Tre Limoni 🍴🍴
viale Siris 134
☎ 0835877178
Al Torchio 🍴
viale Siris
☎ 0835877410
La Trappola 🍴
viale Marittimo 6
☎ 0835877021
Policoro
Heraclea Hotel Residence ★★★
at Lido di Policoro
☎ 0835910144

museum. Today's town is divided between the Borgo, mainly an agricultural center, and the Lido, a well-organized beach resort. The countryside produces top quality fruit, including apricots, peaches, oranges, mandarins, clementines, strawberries and grapes (Italia, Regina and new seedless varieties).

BERNALDA. This ancient village is made up of rows of houses with sloping roofs and little eighteenth-century houses, all overlooked by a castle with two towers and the sixteenth-century parish church. You can take a walk along the Corso Umberto then try the home cooking of the *trattoria* "Fifina", with its home-made pasta with sauces of garden vegetables and local cheeses. You can buy products from the countryside at "Casa Ricotta", including wine, oil, conserves and food preserved in oil or vinegar.

POLICORO. You reach this agricultural center by passing through roads bordered with oleander. The town is full of memories from Byzantine *Polychorion* and the two Magna Graecia towns of *Siris* and *Heraclea*, which were the previous occupiers of the plain between the mouths of the Agri and Sinni rivers. For a gastronomic break there is the "Ragno Verde", offering fish and fresh pasta specialties.

NOVA SIRI. Once across the Pantano di Policoro, formed out of the waters of the Sinni river, and now a nature reserve, you arrive at Marina di Nova Siri, a walled

town with a tower, the Torre Bollita. The town has recently been turned into a seaside resort and spa and offers some good opportunities for excellent food, including the "Ai Tre Limoni", a fish restaurant which occasionally cheats by adding some land-base'cuisine such as pasta with shellfish and beans. The restaurants "La Trappola" and "Al Torchio" also have good fish. Inland is the administrative center, created after the original community escaped from repeated floods. The castle and the Madre church are also here.

TURSI. On the road going up inland you will find the S. Maria d'Anglona church which is all that is left of the village dating from Frederick II's time. A stop here is well worth it for the beauty of the area and the frescoes which decorate the inside of the church. Further on, in a position which has been occupied since prehistory, is Tursi, probably founded by the Saracens. The characteristics of the Rabatana quarter, dominated by the castle, would seem to confirm this. The church of S. Maria Maggiore is full of valuable paintings, including a triptych from the end of the fourteenth century. The area is renowned for its apricots, the *percoco* - a special type of peach - and stàccio, a unique rose-colored orange. We recommend the "Il Caminetto" restaurant.

PISTICCI. The white houses of Pisticci, with their pointed façades can be found in the midst of olive groves, vineyards and strawberry fields. The town, afflicted by landslides, possesses the exclusive and secret recipe for the Amaro Lucano bitters. Its cheeses are also renowned, especially its *ricotta* fresca and its *butirri*. It is worth prolonging your journey to visit their centers of production: Stigliano, Gorgoglione and Accettura (where you should remember the "Pezzolla" restaurant). There are also many bakeries where, apart from the excellent bread, you can buy fresh pasta, biscuits, candies and hand-made *taralli*. On the seaward road you should stop at the huge farm-castle of S. Basilio, virtually intact in terms of both its farming activities and its architecture.

FERRANDINA. This walled town, which has a castle founded by Frederick of Aragon at the end of the fifteenth century, can first be seen through the olive groves producing the extra virgin olive oil Colline Ferrandinesi. Churches, monasteries and ancient houses enrich the urban landscape of whitewashed houses. In the shops you get the famous baked Maiatiche olives and the excellent cheeses of Salandra (a town worth the extra journey for the beauty of the trip and the unmatched view from the castle there). For eating we recommend the "Hotel degli Ulivi" on the Statale Basentana.

MIGLIONICO. The massive but compact structure of the Malconsiglio castle with its seven towers crowns this ancient town. The Chiesa Madre church will surprise you with a polyptych of the Venetian school, the *Madonna in trono con Bambino e S. Giovanni Battista*, one of Cima da Conegliano's masterpieces. Another discovery, this time a tasty one, is the prickly pears traditionally cultivated here and center of the Madonna della Porticella festival held on the second Sunday in September.

TRICARICO. This picturesque town, set at the top of a calcareous spur, faces the Busento valley, and can be seen from miles away thanks to its Norman towers. In the town there are many buildings of artistic interest, including the convent of S. Chaira, the Chiesa Madre and the Palazzo Ducale. For a gastronomic break, we recommend three restaurants: "Centoducati", "Tre Cancelli" and "Tomacci". Do not forget to ask for the *latedda* pizza, a *ricotta* cake which is the local specialty, and the renowned *soppressata*.

Pastoral landscape

AGRITURISMI

Miglionico
San Giuliano
contrada Foggia di Lupo at Caldone
☎ 0835559183
Montescaglioso
⭐🛏 **Emilia Pierro**
at Menzone Fiumicello
☎ 0835200406
Masseria Contangelo
at Pratolino
☎ 0835200677
Pisticci
Torretta di Silvana Panetta
contrada S. Basilio
☎ 0835470021

SHOPPING

Matera
Antico Frantoio Loperfido
via Casalnuovo 154
☎ 0835331331
Excellent olive oil and spiced olive paté since 1928.
Il Buongustaio
piazza Vittorio Veneto 1
☎ 0835331982
Typical products such as cheeses and preserves.
Gorgoglione
Caseificio Viola
contrada S. Maria
☎ 0835560500
Typical cheeses.
Montescaglioso
Azienda Agricola La Doganella
via Masseria La Doganella
☎ 0835207008
Preserves, tomato sauces and dried tomatoes.

REGIONE BASILICATA
Dipartimento Agricoltura e Sviluppo Rurale

**Per adesioni
ed informazioni:**

REGIONE BASILICA▮
*Dipartimento Agricoltura
e Sviluppo Rurale*
Via Anzio • 85100 Poter▮

telefono:
+39.0971.668657
+39.0835.284299
+39.0835.284297

fax:
+39.0835.284250
+39.0971.668751

e-mail:
agromktg@regione.basilica▮
anpandol@regione.basilica▮

sito web:
http://ristoranti.regione.basili▮

RISTORANTE LUCANO NEL MONDO

*... un viaggio virtuale nella
cucina lucana*

In 1992 the region Basilicata set up, in accordance with Regional Law, the Sapori Lucani (Flavours of Basilicata) Prize. The aim of this Prize was to promote, by means of typical regional restaurants, the use of the typical products of Basilicata both in Italy and throughout the world. The awarding of this prize made it possible to identify those restaurants, scattered throughout the world, which offer the typical cuisine of Basilicata. Over 650.000 people have emigrated from Basilicata and have settled in numerous countries, allowing the local cuisine to reach the four corners of the globe.

This recognition has enabled others to discover unthinkable culinary realities in which the recipes, handed down from generation to generation, are strictly adhered to and prepared with ingredients imported directly from Basilicata.

Paradoxically, some restaurateurs abroad offer recipes that have almost disappeared within the region of Basilicata and continue to identify them using their original name in dialect. Today these same recipes, offered after so many years and thousands of miles away, tie the Region's emigrants to their native territory.

This publication is aimed at thanking and encouraging the restaurateurs originating from our Region to carry on and improve their work in order to become a reference point for our regional gastronomy, tradition and culture.

This work is aimed at drawing up an initial map of Lucanian Restaurants in the World which will be continually updated with the name and address of restaurateurs who wish to join or convert themselves to the typical cuisine of Basilicata. The next step will be to establish a brand which will certify the typical features and unite the restaurants throughout the world.

The restaurants listed in this Guide will be recognised by a symbol which shows a picture of early 20th century country life as painted by Guido Spera.

Carmine Nigro
Country Councillor

The logo Lucanian Restaurants in the World is taken by a lithography of Guido Spera. Guido Spera (Tito 1886 – Matera 1956) studied at the Faculty of Agriculture in Portici. He was Director of the "Regia Cattedra Ambulante" of Agriculture in Matera and Manager of the Agricultural Inspectorate in Matera.
In his youth, due to his passion for art, he wrote for various Italian and foreign periodicals and was a student at the "Accademia delle Belle Arti" in Naples. He also worked as stage designer in the S. Carlo Theatre in Naples.
A man of many talents, he wrote plays, poetry and literary works in dialect. He published some monographs on the origins of Lucanian tradition and culture. He published a work under the title: "The history and evolution of a farm in Basilicata". His figurative artist work was entirely dedicated to the Basilicata rural world.

LUCANIAN RESTAURANTS IN ITALY

GENOVA - L'ANGOLO DELLA LUCANIA - Address: Via della Libertà, 112 - Tel. and Fax 010.540063

In the year 2001 the "L'Angolo della Lucania" was awarded the recognition of being the best "Lucanian Restaurant in Italy"; a just reward for offering an "integral" Lucanian cuisine.

This 40-seater restaurant, situated in the centre of Genova, has been offering the typical Lucanian cuisine of the Vulture area.

The owner, Mr. Donato Leopardi, buys directly from Lucanian producers the most typical products of the Region's food industry. In fact, here we can find goat's and sheep's milk cheese as well as the Pecorino cheese from Filiano and the Cacioricotta cheese, salami from Picerno, home-made preserves in olive oil respecting the age-old traditions of Lucanian families. Here it is possible to savour the real and exclusive specialities from Lucania such as the Cruschi (crisp) sundried peppers fried in extra virgin olive oil, mashed broad beans with chicory, Cavatelli (home-made pasta) with pulses, Lagane (home-made pasta) and grasspeas, chicory and beans. The unique quality of the Lucanian cuisine expresses itself through the second courses of lamb, roast kid or mutton in casserole, roast pork, braised ass, all seasoned with the precious extra virgin olive oil of Basilicata of the Vulture area, the same area which supplies the natural sparkling mineral water. Cakes and sweets are the traditional Tarallucci biscuits and Ravioli filled with chestnut purée and soaked in mulled (brulé) wine. The wine list includes approximately 40 diferent wines including, for the best part, wines of Basilicata; most of which Aglianico of the Vulture DOC.

BOLOGNA - DROGHERIA DELLA ROSA - Address: Via Cartoleria, 10 - Tel. 051.222529 - Fax 051.227216

This restaurant in Bologna, with 40 places, has, since 1988, been purchasing Lucanian products directly from producers in Basilicata; this restaurant offers recipes deriving from the gastronomic tradition of Basilicata and enhanced by the creativity of the owner Mr. Emanuele Addone. In this restaurant the cuisine of Basilicata blends together with the cuisine of Bologna. Here it is possible to taste products such as goat's milk cheese, sausages and salami, dried peppers and extra virgin olive oil from Basilicata.

BOLOGNA - RISTORO DEL MERIDIONE - Address: Via Belle Arti, 6F - Tel. 051.267648 - Fax 051.2511397

The gastronomic proposal of this restaurant, set up in 1999, is the classical cuisine of Basilicata: Orecchiette (home-made pasta) in tomato sauce, Strascinati (home-made pasta) in tomato sauce, chicory and broad beans, Lagane and chickpeas; bread-soup; lamb (stew) alla Cutturiddu; Arraganate (oven baked) potatoes, vegetable pies. The salami comes from the area of Tricarico and the goat's and sheep's milk cheese from Stigliano. Guido Onorato, born in Calciano (MT), also offers extra virgin olive oil from the area of Ferrandina and of the Vulture. The choice of wines is also excellent including not only the prestigious Aglianico del Vulture DOC but also lesser known wines and the IGT Grottino di Roccanova. In this restaurant it is possible to buy typical products such as bread, pasta, olive oil and wine.

BOLOGNA - SCACCO MATTO - Address: Via Broccaindosso, 63B - Tel. 051.263404

From the very day in which this restaurant was set up in 1986 the restaurateur, Mario Ferrara, has always had the been intent on offering the best of the Mediterranean cuisine; a cuisine based on old flavours, though made with innovative techniques and particular care in order to obtain "lighter" dishes. Most of the products come directly from Basilicata such as the fresh hand-made pasta, the food preserved in olive oil, the salami and the fresh sausage. From the recipes, it is quite clear that the cook originates from the Sant'Arcangelo area. The wine list contains a good number of wines coming from Basilicata in the wine card.

BOLOGNA 40138 - L'AMALFITANA - Address: Via G. Massarenti, 350 - Tel. 051.530213

This restaurant with 50 places, founded 1986 by Agostino Caputo, offers the typical cuisine of the Viggianello (PZ) area. The first courses are include pastas with mushrooms from the Pollino area, Lagane and chickpeas, Orecchiette and turnips (a particular kind of green turnips which are peculiar to Southern Italy) and Penne all'arrabbiata an Italian pasta in spicy tomato sauce. To follow one can choose from Spezzatino (meat stew), roast and barbecued lamb. The Pecorino cheese is made in Moliterno, the Caciocavallo, a strong cheese, in Filiano, the Mozzarella cheese in Cancellara, and the peppers come from Senise. In this restaurant, the wine offered is the Aglianico del Vulture DOC and the after-dinner liqueur is specific to the region of Basilicata.

40068 SAN LAZZARO DI SAVENA (BO) - TRATTORIA LA CAMPANA
Address: Via Emilia, 560 - Tel. e Fax 0516255051

Matera born Antonio Targiani set up this restaurant 1993. The cuisine, expertly carried out by his wife Maria from Tursi (MT) is reminiscent of Matera. The restaurant seats approximately 80 people, and the gastronomic delights range from Cavatelli in a tomato and meatball sauce, to Ferretti with broccoli with green turnip or wild mushrooms and sausage. The chicory and bean purée dish has tradition links with Basilicata, while the Orecchiette are prepared alla contadina with bacon and potatoes or alla Materana baked in the oven in a tomato-based sauce.

The second courses are characterised by pork fillets with Aglianico wine, oven-baked lamb and kid with potatoes and wild mushrooms, and mixed grill. The desert menu is composed of traditional dishes such as Ricotta cheese cake and a blood based chocolate sauce. The ingredients derive from the Targiani area of the Basilicata, while the extra virgin olive oil is home-made. The wine list boasts about ten different brands of Aglianico del Vulture DOC.

PERUGIA - LA LOCANDA DEGLI ARTISTI
Address: Via Campo battaglia, 10 - Tel. 075.5735851 - Fax 075. 5720125

This is a typical restaurant which offers the cuisine of the Alto Bradano area. It seats about 80 people, and this number doubles during the summer months thanks to the use of a terrace. Since 1992, Giacomino the owner, buys pastas, sausages, olive oil, and food preserves from the producers of Basilicata; he also sells these products under his own brand and uses them in the restaurant to prepare the typical first courses such as pasta and green turnips, chicory and broad beans, Cavatelli and Cacioricotta cheese and home-made Ferrettini alla Contadina. The wines also come from Basilicata and are marketed under the restaurant's own brand name. The restaurant represents an important gastronomic meeting point in Umbria owing to the possibility to buy products originating from the region of Basilicata.

MEDESANO (PR) 43014 - LA CORNACCINA - Address: Via Cornaccina, 36 - Tel. 0525.420481
Mr. Salvatore Stellato, born in Sant'Arcangelo (PZ), set up this restaurant in 1997 with 80 places (and in summer 160). Here we can find the typical cuisine of Basilicata of the Sant'Arcangelo area. In this restaurant it is possible to savour first courses such as Orecchiette with green turnips, Maccheroni ai ferri (home-made pasta) with mutton sauce or with radish, and second courses of barbecued lamb and kid, stew of pork with peppers, roast meat with fried peppers, mutton with spicy red peppers. Mr. Stellato buys his ingredients, extra virgin olive oil, salami, and pastas, directly from the area where he was born.

MILANO - TRATTORIA LUCANA DA MARIO
Address: Via Gluck, 13 - Tel. and Fax 02.6694438 - e-mail: franco.giordanelli@tin.it
The Trattoria Lucana has since 1975 been offering traditional recipes such as Fusilli (home-made pasta) and Orecchiette and lamb and kid on request. This restaurant uses ingredients such as the extra virgin olive oil, flour and the different kinds of cheese, all deriving from Basilicata. The wine list contains only one type of Aglianico del Vulture, nevertheless, contains Limoncello (a typical liqueur made from lemons) coming from the Maratea area.

MODENA - TRATTORIA DA MALGAREIN - Address: Via san Damaso, 3 - Tel. and Fax 059.469611
In 1996 Mr. Domenico Lionetti, born in Matera, set up this restaurant with the clear aim of making it a reference point for Lucanian cuisine in Emilia Romagna. This aim has been achieved; once a week all the ingredients arrive from Matera and province. The gastronomic offer is original for this part of Italy, and consists of Gnummariedd (rolls of lamb filled with lamb giblets), lamb, meat roulades in tomato sauce, Cavatelli, Strascinate and bread from Matera. The first courses are also highly typical; lamb meat sauce, chicory and broad beans stew and oven-baked Orecchiette. In addition, just to put the icing on the cake, Mr. Lionetti offers starters such as wild Cardoncelli mushrooms, Lampascioni (little tasty onions peculiar of the Southern Italy), sundried tomatoes and salted olives. The wine list contains the Aglianico del Vulture DOC and wines from Matera.

MARANELLO (MO) 41053 - OSTERIA IL POSTIGLIONE
Address: Via Abetone Superiore, 143 - Tel. and Fax 053.6945307
Mr. Domenico Lionetti, owner of another Lucanian restaurant in the same area, inaugurated the opening of the Osteria Il Postiglione on January 2002. The restaurant seats 550, and the cuisine is typical of the province of Matera where Mr. Lionetti was born : for example chicory and broad beans, Crapiata (dish of mixed pulses), Cavatelli alla Materana, Strascinati with lamb sauce, Orecchiette with meatballs and Scamorza cheese. Once a week the restaurant receives deliveries from Basilicata; biscuits, Friselle (dried bread rounds) and bread from Matera. The meat for the second courses also comes from Basilicata and includes Pignata (mutton or lamb meat), lamb and potatoes, Gnumuredde (rolls of lamb filled with lamb giblets) and meat roulades in tomato sauce. Peppers and aubergine fried in olive oil are offered as a side dish. A wide variety of wines is available and the after-dinner liqueurs come from the region of Basilicata.

RIOLO TERME (RA) - RISTORANTE VILLA GOLINI - Address: Via Bologna, 78 - Tel. 054.671867
The cuisine proposed by Mr. Nicola Russo, born in San Chirico Nuovo, is based on the culinary traditions of the Potenza area. Here both salami and various kinds of goat's milk cheese are offered with pomegranate. Here it is possible to savour Orecchiette with lamb sauce topped with slivers of Ricotta cheese, Cavatelli with beans or with porcini mushrooms, lamb loin alla Pastorale, wild chicory Lucanian style, chickpeas and thyme in extra virgin olive oil. The restaurant, set up in 1990, seats 180 and offers an interesting cuisine enriched with aromatic herbs.

PIOSSASCO (TO) - RISTORANTE IL CASTELLETTO - Address: Via Zivalta, 15 - Tel. 011.9065402
Thanks to the initiative of Mr. Domenico Lisanti, born in Salandra (MT), the cuisine of Basilicata has achieved widespread success in Piemonte. This restaurant, set up in 2000 and seating 80 people, provides first courses made with pasta and pulses, and Tagliatelle (home-made Italian pasta) with bread crumbs and peppers. The second courses are particularly typical: giblets lightly fried in olive oil, sausages, Capicollo, lamb cooked with potatoes and tomatoes or cooked alla Pastorale - obviously all cooked in extra virgin olive oil coming from Basilicata. Pecorino cheese, typical of the region, is also readily available. The wine list contains Aglianico del Vulture.

TYPICAL LUCANIAN RESTAURANTS ABROAD

USA - WASHINGTON DC 20036 - RISTORANTE AL TIRAMISU
Address: 2014 P. St. N.W. - Tel. 001.202.467.4466 - Fax 001.202.467.4468
e-mail: luigi@altiramisu.com   Web Site: www.altiramisu.com
In 2001 the restaurant "Al tiramisu" was awarded the prize as the best Lucanian Restaurant in the World due to the attention given to the regional gastronomy and to the service offered. In this restaurant, in the very hearth of Washington DC and in the culinary district par excellence, Mr. Dupont Circe Luigi Diotaiuti born in Lagonegro (PZ), offers an exquisite cuisine deeply tied to his own home town. The use of Fusilli, salami, and kid, and the presence of Aglianico del Vulture DOC in the rich wine list of the restaurant makes this place a meeting point for admirers of the Lucanian cuisine in the United States. Professional training courses in Basilicata, enhanced by va-

rious experiences in Italy and abroad, allow the chef to propose typical Lucanian dishes enriched by his own international experience. Frequent collaboration with culinary institutes, journals, and TV programmes have helped diffuse the knowledge of the Lucanian cuisine on the other side of the Ocean.

USA - NEW YORK - LIDO RISTORANTE & CATERERS
Address: 101 CITY ISLAND AVENUE - Tel. 001.718.8852177 - Fax 001.718.8853017
Mr. Piero Mellante, born in Stigliano, runs both the restaurant and the catering activity with passion and care. This 680 seater restaurant is an important meeting point and is also available to clients for parties and private functions. It offers the typical Lucanian menu from Mr. Mellante's home-town with dishes such as tripe alla Stigliano, Strangolapreti (home-made pasta) alla Materana, chicken alla Potentino and Migliulatiello (lamb stew). The majority of the ingredients used are imported from the region Basilicata including food preserved in oil and in vinegar, extra virgin olive oil and coffee. The wine offered is Aglianico del Vulture DOC.

USA - ROCHESTER - RISTORANTE LUCANO
Address: 1815 EAST AVE - Tel. 001.716.2443460 - e-mail: pisticci@aol.com
The true Lucanian cuisine is proposed in the US by Mr. Giovanni Lopassio, born in Pisticci in the province of Matera. The restaurant, set up in the year 2000, seats 50. The gastronomic proposal includes the basic recipes of the cuisine of Basilicata such Orecchiette in lamb sauce, Orecchiette with green turnips and broad beans with vegetables. The starters are the typical of the Basilicata region and the extra virgin olive oil comes from Montescaglioso (MT). In his careful selection of typical products we can find Aglianico del Vulture DOC, the bitter after-dinner liqueur of the Vulture and the mineral water.

USA - CHICAGO - ANNA MARIA PASTERIA
Address: 3953 N. BROADWAY - Tel. 001.773.929.6363 - Fax 001.773.929.1553
This restaurant, with 99 places to sit and set up in 1986, is run by Maria and Anna Picciolini Spinelli both born in Ripacandida (PZ). The cuisine offered is typical of Southern and Central Italy and of the Vulture area of Basilicata. Among the first courses there are pasta with beans, pasta with meat roulades in a meat sauce, Calzoni (home-made pasta) filled with Ricotta cheese in a tomato sauce. Among the second courses there we can choose from dried peppers with olives and codfish and spicy chicken casserole. The extra virgin olive oil comes from Ripacandida (PZ) and the wine list contains a selection of Aglianico del Vulture DOC coming from different producers.

SOUTH AFRICA - CAPE TOWN - TI AMO RISTORANTE
Address: HAMILTON HOUSE CHIAPPINI STREET 2001 C. - Tel. 0027.214218677 - e-mail: ashmurray@hotmail.com
This 50 seater restaurant was set up in 2001 by Matera born Fabrizio Perrone who proposes the typical regional cuisine of his home-town. Genuine and simple, this cuisine expresses itself in the most far away horn of Africa where it is possible to taste soups made with pulses or vegetables, pasta with meat sauce, barbecued mixed grill. All these recipes are made with local ingredients but, nevertheless, fully respect of the original recipes of Basilicata.

COLOMBIA - BOGOTA D.C. - SAN GIORGIO TRATTORIA
Address: CALLE, 81#8-83 - Tel. and Fax 0057.1.2123962 - e-mail: zitomario@latinmail.com
Mr. Macario Mario Zito set up this restaurant in 1987 and called it after his native town: San Giorgio Lucano (MT). In spite of the difficulties encountered in finding original ingredients due to the considerable distance, the recipes closely follow Lucanian traditions. One can choose from grilled Scamorza and Provolone cheese, pasta and chickpeas, bread soup, beetroot and peppers, pasta with bread crumbs and anchovies, lamb stew and roasted kid, dried cod stew, and meatballs in a meat sauce. All these recipes, immediately recall the gastronomic tradition of Basilicata. One of Mr. Zito's main passions is to establish a distribution network for Lucanian products in Colombia.

LUXEMBOURG 2327 - LUXEMBOURG - IL FRAGOLINO
Address: Montée de la Petrusse L. - Tel. 00352.26480267 - Fax 00352.26480268 - Web Site: www.il-fragolino.lu
This restaurant, set up in 1999 by Mr. Vincenzo Lauria, born in Salandra (MT), has 100 places which increase to 170 during the summer months. The chef offers the typical cuisine of the Salandra area in the province of Matera. As a starter we can choose from, among others, sundried tomatoes and courgettes preserved in oil, followed by either Strascinati alla crudaiola (pasta with uncooked vegetables, beans and prawns), Orecchiette with green turnips, Cavatelli in a tomato and ham sauce with Mozzarella cheese. The second courses comprise Salandra-made sausage, meat roulades, lamb in a tomato sauce, oven-baked peppers and breaded aubergines. The extra virgin olive oil comes from Basilicata and the desserts are made by hand in accordance with Lucanian traditions.

SWITZERLAND - 6440 BRUNNEN - BAHNHOFBUFFET
Address: ALTE KANTONSSTR,11 - Tel. 0041.418203369 - e-mail: bahnhofbuffet@gmx.ch
This recently opened restaurant was set up in 2001 by Salvatore and Luigi Gallicchio both natives of Calvello in the province of Potenza. The gastronomic offer consists of home-made salami, both in the fresh and seasoned varieties of Soppressata, Salsiccia and Pezzente. The home-made pastas are directly imported from the inland areas of Basilicata and are offered together with typical regional dressings. Extremely typical is the dried cod with peppers and potatoes and stuffed rind. The starters consist mainly of food preserved in oil while the wine list offers a wide choice of Aglianico del Vulture DOC.

GERMANY - 80939 MUNCHEN - LA LUCANIA
Address: FLORIANS MUHL STRASSE,1 - Tel. 0049.893226796 - Fax 0049.893233448 - e-mail: denigris1@aol.com
Mr. Michele De Nigris, born in Palazzo San Gervaso (PZ), set up this restaurant in 2001. The name of the place suggests, being inspired by the region, aims at being a meeting point for gastronomic admirers of the cuisine of Basilicata. The restaurant, with 115 seats, offers as first courses Orecchiette with green turnips, Cavatellialla al Lucano, Strascinati in a with meat sauce and spicy Pennette, an Italian pasta dish with tomatoes and spicy red chilli peppers. The second courses also follow a regional theme; for example mixed beans with meat, vegetable soups, grilled fillet, grilled pork chops and mixed grills. Bruschette (roasted bread seasoned with olive oil, salt, garlic and tomatoes) are also served together with vegetable pies, peppers, spices and cheeses from the Vulture area of Basilicata. A

good choice of extra virgin olive oil and Aglianico del Vulture DOC is also available.

GERMANY – TROISDORF - RISTORANTE AI PARIOLI G.B.R.
Address: MENDENESTR, 4 - Tel. 0049.2241.82666 - Fax 0049.228.455958
Mr. Giuseppe Viola bought this 95 seater restaurant in 2001 with the intention of changing it into a symbol of Lucanian cuisine. Mrs Giuseppina is in charge of the cooking and prepares dishes typical of the hills of Matera as she comes from Gorgoglione (MT). The first courses consist of home-made pasta made with the durum wheat coming from Basilicata: Lagane and chickpeas, Orecchiette with green turnips, pasta with cauliflower and pasta with beans. The different kinds of cheese, salami and olives come from Gorgoglione. The wine list, almost entirely Lucanian, includes the Aglianico del Vulture DOC, IGT wines from Basilicata and wines from the Metaponto area.

GERMANY - 10777 BERLIN - TRATTORIA A' MUNTAGNOLA
Address: FUGGER STRASSE, 27 - Tel. 0049.302116642 - Fax 0049.302139761
e-mail:trattoria@muntagnola.de - Web Site: www.muntagnola.de
This restaurant represents one of the best examples of the typical Lucanian cuisine overseas. Mr. Pino Bianco set up this restaurant in 1991 with the intention of match uniting the culinary art with the culture of his region. The restaurant accommodates 90 people and here we can savour the most typical and traditional dishes prepared Mr. Bianco's mother Angelina from Cirigliano in the province of Matera. (MT). All the dishes, broad beans and chicory, Fusilli with bread crumbs, Orecchiette with green turnips, Ravioli (home-made pasta) filled with Ricotta cheese, are made with original ingredients imported from Basilicata. The extra virgin olive oil comes from Aliano and the salami come from the middle Valley of Sinni. The second courses such as lamb alla Contadina, Mutton alla Pastorale and all the sweets including the Apostle's Fingers, belong to the traditions of Basilicata. This origin is forever evident on the menu and clearly illustrated in the recipe books printed by the restaurant in German. The wine list is made up of Lucanian brands: from the numerous Aglianico del Vulture DOC wines of those of the Metaponto area and the regional typicality is completed by the natural sparkling water of the Vulture.

GERMANY - BERLIN - AL CONTADINO SOTTO LE STELLE
Address: AUGUSTRASSE, 34 - Tel. 0049.302819023 - Fax 0049.3028097558
e-mail: cosimobianco@tiscali.it - Web Site:www.soleluna.net
This restaurant was set up by Mr. Lucio Massaro and by Mr. Cosimo Bianco, the former born in Pietragalla and the latter in Scanzano. The restaurant seats 60 people and as the name demonstrates, the cuisine is typical and traditional of the rural cuisine of Basilicata. The dishes on offer are Orecchiette with meat roulades, kid alla Pastorale, roast lamb with potatoes, green turnips and salami stew, broad beans and chicory and Ciambotta a typical dish with vegetables. The ingredients are imported directly from Basilicata such as extra virgin olive oil from Montalbano, wines from Nova Siri, goat milk and sheep milk cheese from Stigliano, while the pasta is home-made in accordance with regional recipes.

GERMANY - BERLIN - LA RUSTICA
Address: KLEINE PRASIDENTENSTR - Tel. 0049.302189169 - Fax 0049.3028096268
E-mail: cosimobianco@tiscali.it - Web Site:www.soleluna.net
This restaurant shows that it is possible to combine a modern and elegant atmosphere with the regional typical cuisine. The restaurant seats 150 people and was set up in 1998 by Mr. Giovanni Massaro and Mr. Cosimo Bianco, the former born in Guardia Perticara and the latter in Scanzano. The regional dishes are characterised by Ravioli filled with Ricotta cheese and spiced with cinnamon, Mutton, lamb with potatoes, dried cod with ground pepper, and stuffed squids. It is possible to find fresh and grilled goat's and sheep's milk cheese coming from Stigliano. The home-made pasta is made following regional recipes ad all the ingredients are imported from Basilicata and include extra virgin olive oil from Montalbano, and wine from Nova Siri.

GERMANY - 10587 BERLIN - TRATTORIA MARINELLI
Address: ABBESTRASSE, 15 - Tel. 0049.303414324 - Fax 0049.3089725431
This restaurant was set up in 1989 by Mr. Michele Marinelli, born in Calvello in the province of Potenza. It comfortably accommodates 50 people and its home-made pasta is particularly typical of Basilicata : Fusilli, Cavatelli, Strascinati and Ravioli, all of which are served with typical sauces of the region. Among the recipes we can find fusilli with dried cod, dried cod in a tomato sauce, rabbit chasseur, and roast leg of lamb with potatoes. Moreover, fresh Ricotta cheese with honey, and goat's milk cheese with honey and walnuts are also on the menu. Finally, it is also possible to savour pickled peppers and vegetables, Caciocavallo cheese from Filiano and Pecorino cheese from the Calvello and Moliterno. The wine list includes various brands of Aglianico del Vulture DOC.

GERMANY - 10777 BERLIN - RISTORANTE PETROCELLI
Address: MOTZ STR., 68 - Tel. 0049.1714181616 - Fax 0049.302176422 - Web Site: www.petrocelli-berlin.de
Mr. Enzo Petrocelli started this business together with some family members, in fact, his sister Pina is in charge of the cooking. One of the restaurant's strong points is its home-made pasta, made by Mr. Petrocelli's mother, and comprising Fusilli, Orecchiette, Ravioli, as well as a wide range of filled pastas. Served with numerous with typical Lucanian sauces including a simple tomato sauce, meat sauce, in small meatballs, and pesto (a sauce made with a mixture of chopped herbs, oil, basil, garlic, pine seeds and cheese).

GERMANY - 14612 FALKENSEE - TRATTORIA LUCANA
Address: SPADAUER STRASSE 112 - Tel. 0049.3322240861 - Fax 0049.3322240862.
In the year 2000, after twenty years' experience of managing restaurants in Germany, Mr. Francesco Bellomo set up this new restaurant with the intention of making it a type of meeting place for admirers of the Lucanian cuisine, hence the restaurant's name. The restaurant comfortably accommodates 100 people with an additional 50 places being added during the summer months. The cuisine offered is of the area of Potenza. Fresh home-made pasta is made in its most traditional shapes and varieties; Fusilli or Cavatelli in a sausage sauce and Orecchiette or Strascinate with green turnips. The typical starters include salami from Picerno, birthplace of the owner, and grilled vege-

tables. The second courses feature sausage with peas, roast lamb or kid. The different kind of cheeses come from the Filiano area, in the province of Potenza. The extra virgin olive oil, the numerous wines and the after-dinner bitter liqueurs all come from the region Basilicata.

GERMANIA - 12277 BERLIN - NUOVA MASSERIA
Address: MARIENFELDER ALLEE, 20 - Tel. 0049.3072019307 - Fax 0049.306399558
The Nuova Masseria seats 90 guests and was set up in 2001. The aim of the restaurant is to follow the traditional cuisine of Basilicata by offering the typical regional pasta in all its different shapes and varieties and served with traditional dressing. Lamb and other types of meat are offered as second courses. The salami comes from Picerno (PZ), where the owner of the restaurant Mr. Mario Tripaldi was born. The wine list includes Aglianico del Vulture DOC.

GERMANY - 10587 BERLIN - IL POZZETTO
Address: HELMHOLTZSTRASSE, 30 - Tel. 0049.30.3996780
The owner, Mr. Domenico Diroma, set up this restaurant in 2001. Born in Abriola (PZ), his intention was to introduce the cuisine and the flavours of his home-town to this area of Germany. The restaurant opens only for lunch and the majority of its clients are young business men. The typicality cuisine of Basilicata is represented by the first courses which are substantial enough to be considered as main courses, therefore catering for those clients who have limited time for lunch. The menu includes Calzoncelli filled with Ricotta cheese, Fusilli and Orecchiette in a sausage or Pezzente sauce. In addition, there are also Cruschi peppers with fried bacon, lamb giblets lightly fried in oil, cheeses from Potenza, salami from Picerno and extra virgin olive oil bought directly from the producers of Basilicata. As far as the wine list is concerned, there is a good selection of regional wines including Aglianico del Vulture DOC.

GERMANY - 10551 BERLIN - LA TETTOIA
Address: WALDSTRASSE, 55 - Tel. 0049.244366733 ; 0049.24436006 - Fax 0049.24436982
Mr. Giuseppe Di Vitto was one of the first people from Basilicata to come to this area. He started this business in 1977 and offered a choice of recipes linked to the province of the Potenza. Subsequently, other people joined him from the region of Basilicata and worked with him to later open their own business activities. The restaurant accommodates 67 people with approximately another 15 places being added on the terrace during the summer months. There are numerous recipes whose names are geographically linked to Basilicata: Strascinati, Orecchiette or Gnocchi al Potentino (with Mozzarella cheese, tomatoes and basil), black Spaghetti and Fettuccine al Potentino (with cuttlefish, prawns and red chilli peppers), Basilicata pie (with Mozzarella cheese, ham and parmesan). The restaurant offers sundried tomatoes preserved in oil, Caciocavallo cheese and Pecorino cheese from Fialiano together with traditional second courses such as lamb cutlets with potatoes and rosemary. Other regional dish are available on request. The wine list includes Aglianico del Vulture and the regional after-dinner bitter liqueur.

GERMANY - 53894 MECHERNICH - KOMMERN - LA FATTORIA AM SEE
Address: ERNST - BECKER - WEG - Tel. 0049.24436733 ; 0049.24436006 - Fax 0049.24436982
e-mail: info@la-fattoria-am-see.com - Web Site: www.la-fattoria-am-see.com
This restaurant with 160 places was set up in 1998 by Mr. Antonio Tucci, born in Cirigliano (MT). Mr. Tucci's intention was to use the restaurant as a vehicle for the genuine and typical cuisine of Basilicata. Here it possible to sample first courses such as Orecchiette with salted Ricotta cheese, fresh home-made pasta with porcini mushrooms, pastas and beans, cauliflower with pork rind, hot salami sauce. The traditional second courses include the Pastorale (roast kid) and roast lamb. Alternatively we can savour pizzas with fresh tomatoes, olives, Cruschi peppers, goat's milk and sheep's milk cheeses Gorgoglione (MT). All these typical dishes remind us of the flavours of the hills of Matera. The extra virgin olive oil is produced directly in Basilicata by the owner of the restaurant. The ingredients used, and in particular the salami, are imported between January and February from Basilicata, the reason for which the restaurant closes during these months in order to allow Mr. Antonio Tucci to return to Cirigliano so that he can witness the slaughtering of the pigs which are bred on the spot. The wines, such as the Aglianico del Vulture DOC and wines from the Metaponto area, are sold directly to clients by Mr. Tucci who also distributes them to other restaurants.

GERMANY - COLOGNE - RISTORANTE AL DELFINO
Address: GOLDSTEINSTRASSE, 68 - Tel. 0049.221.342140 - Fax 0049.221.3401025
Mr. Anio Delfino set up this restaurant in 1986 and brought the typical cuisine of Pisticci (MT) to Cologne. In this 80 seater restaurant, it is possible to choose from Maccheroni al ferro with basil and fresh tomatoes, Cavatelli with garlic and breadcrumbs, broad beans Pisticci style, stuffed aubergines and peppers as a first course. To follow, the Pastorale is worthy of attention – goat meat cooked following the old traditional recipe of Basilicata. Among the sweets the fig mousse is worthy of note. The food preserved in oil, the extra virgin olive oil, the wine and the after-dinner bitter liqueur all come from Basilicata.

GERMANY - BERG - GLADBACH - RISTORANTE GRAPPOLO D'ORO
Address: NITTUMBERWEG, 7 - Tel. 0049.22.028730 - Fax 0049.22.02802046

Mr. Emilio Lattarulo represents, in this area of Germany, an important reference point for the gastronomy of Basilicata. In the last twenty years he has started up many successful Italian restaurants and set up the Grappolo d'oro in 1992. This 72 seater restaurant proposes Italian dishes which are prepared with ingredients deriving from Basilicata. The typical regional dishes on offer include Taglierini (thin home-made noodles) with chickpeas, extra virgin olive oil and black truffle; pork meat and chestnut purée. The ingredients arrive directly from the region of Basilicata with the food preserved in oil, the olives and the extra virgin olive oil coming from area of Montescaglioso (MT). Approximately 10 different brands of Aglianico del Vulture DOC and other regional wines are available.

GERMANY - BONN - DA GINO
Address: FRIDERICH EBERT ALLE, 69 - Tel. 0049.228231332 - Fax 0049.228.230110
Mr. Carmine Di Vincenzo and Mr. Salvatore Di Vincenzo started this business in 1998. The majority of the restaurant's clients are business men due to the restaurant's location which is in the Parliament area in the centre of Bonn. The gastronomic offer is represented principally by regional fresh home-made pasta such as truffle filled Ravioli and Ravioli filled with Ricotta cheese. Among second courses we can find roast lamb and kid stew with peas, potatoes and herbs. The Pecorino cheese is typical of Basilicata, the strong Provolone cheese, and the fresh cheeses come from Calvello where the restaurant's owners were born. The wine list includes Aglianico del Vulture DOC.

GERMANY - 84347 PFARRKIRCHEN - NEL CANTUCCIO
Address: FRANZSTELZEBERGER STR. 56 - Tel. 0049.856171949 - Fax 0049.856171931
Basilicata and its regional traditions are well represented in this area of Germany by Mr. Raffaele Fortunato, born in Paterno di Lucania (PZ). The restaurant, which caters for 100 people, offers traditional recipes such as bean soup, Fusilli with pesto, made with Rucola (a typical herb from Basilicata), Penne lucanian style (with mixed meat sauce), Fusilli della nonna (with bread crumbs, pecorino cheese and extra virgin olive oil). The second courses also have a regional flavour ; cod fillet stew with Cruschi peppers, (dried peppers fried in extra virgin olive oil), lamb alla Pastorale. All the pasta is imported directly from the producers in Basilicata. The wine list offers Aglianico del Vulture DOC and the regional after-dinner bitter liqueur.

GERMANY - 84130 - DINGOLFING - IL GIARDINO
Address: FISCHEREI, 20 - Tel. 0049.8731.40875 - Fax 0049.8731.60293
This restaurant, set up in 1997 by Matera-born Cesare Colazzo, seats 85 people with this number reaching 300 during the summer season. The main chef, Mr. Vincenzo Dandrea, born in Moliterno (PZ), specialises in offering the traditional cuisine of Potenza. The Ravioli, Ferricelli, and Orecchiette, served with meat or game sauce, are all home-made and obtained using traditional methods. The second courses include boar and hare while the salami comes from Moliterno and the cheeses come from Metaponto. To complete the regional gastronomic offer we can also find extra virgin olive oil from Ferrandina and Aglianico del Vulture DOC wine.

GERMANY - 72213 ALTENSTEIG - GOLDENER-STERN
Address: POSTSTRASSE, 73 - Tel. 0049.7453.910435
The restaurant, set up in 1998 by Mr. Giuseppe Allegretti, born in san Martino D'Agri (PZ), accommodates 90 customers. Mr. Allegretti's wife is in charge of the cooking which consists of typical dishes characteristic of the entire region. Great care and attention is taken in the preparation of the home-made pastas and the traditional first courses made in accordance with the recipes of Basilicata. Among the first courses the restaurant offers Orecchiette with green turnips, Fusilli in a sausage sauce, Ravioli with Ricotta cheese, and Cavatelli with Rucola. Most of the second courses are meat based for example meat stew with peas and potatoes, and roast lamb with potatoes. All the cakes are hand-made and all dishes are cooked with extra virgin olive oil from Agri Sauro with the different kinds of cheeses and salami coming from the same area.
The wine offered is Aglianico del Vulture DOC and the regional after-dinner liqueur is also available.

GERMANY - 36037 FULDA - TOMATE
Address: HEINRICHSTR., 13 - Tel. 0049.661.21366 - Fax 0049.661.9011419
Mr. Nicola M. Tedesco, born in Sant'Arcangelo (PZ), set up this restaurant in 1986, with the clear intention of introducing the cuisine of his home-town to this area. The restaurant accommodates approximately 50 clients and offers a wide range of first courses including Lagane and chickpeas, Cavatelli with green turnips, Cavatelli with bread crumbles, Fusilli with radish, fried crisp peppers and the Pastorale. The restaurant uses ingredients such as flour, extra virgin olive oil, cheeses, etc which come directly from Sant'Arcangelo and from the surrounding area. Aglianico del Vulture DOC wine is also served.

TYPICAL LUCANIAN RESTAURANTS IN BASILICATA

In each town of Basilicata there are restaurants worthy of representing the typical regional cuisine, however, this guide lists in detail only those which have been given a special mention in acknowledgement in the awarding of the Lucanian Flavours 2001 Regional Prize (Premio Regionale Sapori Lucani 2001). Each year this guide will be updated with the names of restaurants which receive such acknowledgement in subsequent editions of this initiative.

CASTELMEZZANO (PZ) - AL BECCO DELLA CIVETTA
Address: Vico 1° Maglietta, 7 - Tel. and Fax 0971.986249
e-mail: beccodellacivetta@tiscalinet.it
In the year 2001 this restaurant was judged as being the best "Ristorante Lucano in Basilicata" (the best Lucanian Restaurant in Basilicata) and the aim of this award was to reward the owner for the careful attention taken in offering the very best of the typical regional cuisine. This restaurant can be considered as the best among those restaurants which offer a territorial cuisine and has been doing so for over a decade. Its strong links with the territory are not only found in its preparation of typical dishes, but are also evident in the restaurants decor and hospitality. The Dolomiti Lucane (Lucanian Dolomites) provide a breathtaking backdrop to the restaurant and this spectacular landscape extends to the beginning of the town.
This 40 seater restaurant, set up in 1990, is named after of the rock which towers over road leading to the town. Mrs. Antonietta Santoro and her husband run the business and take the greatest care in preparing the dishes they serve and in providing a hospitable environment for their guests. In a crescendo of colours and flavours, you can taste delicious and high quality dishes in full respect of local traditions. Starters of salami, grilled vegetables in oil, wild chicory and Pecorino cheese hot pot - all made on the premises - whet your appetite for delicious first courses such as Cavatelli with bread crumbs or with Cacioricotta cheese, crisp peppers, Ferricelli with sausage and radish, and Calzoncelli with Ricotta cheese. To follow we can choose from pork with peppers, roast lamb with potatoes, Pastorale, stuffed free-range chicken. A wide range of regional, high-quality cheese is offered and the wine list includes

the names of almost all of the wine producers of the region and obviously Aglianico del Vulture DOC. Finally, there is even a list of carefully selected regional oils.

BARILE (PZ) - LOCANDA DEL PALAZZO - Address: Piazza Caracciolo, 7 - Tel. 0972.771051

This restaurant, set up in 2001, has already been awarded with the special mention in the "Re-discovery of Basilicata's culinary tradition in modern cuisine" (rivisitazione della tradizione culinaria lucana nella cucina moderna). Mr. Rino Botte and his wife Lucia, after having worked for several years in Cremona, have seen their dream come true: today they have a refined and elegant restaurant and offer a cuisine rich in regional culture which is enhanced by imaginative recipes and international dishes. Meat and fish dishes managed to satisfy any request: roast stuffed squid served with aubergines, finely cut lamb dressed with vinegar and served on a bed of potato purée, sweet Ravioli with cinnamon and mint, Tagliatelle with prawns, pumpkin flowers with basil. The second courses follow the same line: rhombus fillet with tomato and aubergine fondue, or a more traditional roast lamb with vegetables. There is also a good selection of cheeses and sweets and the wine list contains the best of the Vulture area and other wines.

TERRANOVA DI POLLINO (PZ) - RISTORANTE PICCHIO NERO

Address: Via Mulino, 1 - Tel. and Fax 0973.93170 - e-mail: picchionero@picchionero.com

Terranova del Pollino is 15th century historical town in the territory of the National Park. This place is the gate to some of the most important peaks of the Pollino. The Picchio Nero, situated in the heart of the town, is an annex to the three star hotel run by the Golia family. Set up in 1970 by Mrs. Maria Carmela Genovese, most of its customers are keen mountaineers. Many foreign tourists, mainly English and American, visit the restaurant all year round, and for this reason it received the Hospitality and Development Award (Premio Ospitalità e Valorizzazione del Territorio) - an accolade reserved to those who have continually offered not only good cuisine and hospitality but also the entire territory, thus promoting culture and tourism within the inland areas of the territory.
As a starter we can choose from among ham from the mountains, Ciambotta egggs with sausage and peppers, grilled Scamorza cheese with truffles.
The first courses consist of fresh home-made pasta (Ferrazzuoli, Cavatelli, Tagliorelli, and Mischigli, the latter made with ground pulse flour) dressed with bread crumbs and peppers, mushrooms, boar sauce, hare sauce, or black truffles. Among the second courses we can savour chopped beef, veal with mushrooms and truffle, and pork chops. Also worth trying is the selection of local cheeses served with honey and the strawberries (or blackberries) of the Pollino. The wine list offers a good variety of wines from Basilicata. A list of the regional oils is also available.

MATERA - RISTORANTE LUCANERIE - Address: Via S. Stefano, 61 - Tel. 0835.332133

The choice of proposing the typical cuisine of the inland areas of Basilicata is evident from the name of this restaurant which translates as "things from Lucania". Mr. Francesco Abbondanza and his wife Enza, both born in Gorgoglione (MT), offer recipes strongly linked to the inland areas of Basilicata which include the Rafanata (dish of radishes), minced sausage, Lampascioni with eggs and sausage, the Ciambotta", Pezzente sausage sauce, Gorgoglione roulades, Sarconi bean soup, and home-made pastas. Only typical, local ingredients are used in the preparation of the dishes. Despite the fact that the restaurant has just recently begun to offer typical cuisine and local recipes, it was awarded the special mention as "Emerging business" reserved for those restaurateurs who have exploited the characteristic features of their surroundings in order to satisfy the expectations of gourmet lovers. The restaurant offers a good choice of goat's and sheep's milk cheese and the wine list includes a wide range of wines from Basilicata. An extensive choice of oils is also available.

MATERA - TRATTORIA LUCANA - Address: Via Lucana, 48 - Tel. 0835.336117

The Trattoria Lucana, set up in 1950 by the Sanrocco family, has been offering a very good traditional cuisine based on typical products for over 40 years. The special mention of Fedeltà alla Tradizione (Adherence to tradition) given in 2001 was a just reward for the quality and care offered to clients during their many years of activity. The restaurant offers a rich variety of starters: salami, fresh cheese, Bruschette, Parmigiana (aubergines cooked with tomatoes and cheese), omelettes with vegetables. Among the first courses there are Orecchiette alla Materana with aubergines and peppers, Lasagna (home-made pasta) with layers of aubergines, Orecchiette and green turnips, and Cavatelli in a mushroom and sausage sauce. Among the second courses there are meat roulades in a meat and tomato sauce, veal stew with mushrooms, lamb alla Cutturiello, grilled lamb and sausages, and stuffed artichokes. A good wine list, made up only of regional brands, is also available.

SARCONI - AZIENDA AGRITURISTICA AL FAGIOLO D'ORO

Address: C/da Cava - Tel. 0975.66053 / 66400 - e-mail: dimarian@tiscalinet.it

Mr. Antonio di Maria gave the bean of Sarconi IGT a new dignity when, in 1995, he set up this restaurant together with his daughter Nicla and gave the restaurant this name (The Golden Bean – Restaurant and Farm). The family-run business, as well as growing and cultivating the beans, offers a wide range of dishes based on their most exclusive bean variety including soups and recipes served together with typical pastas of the Agri Valley. More innovative recipes are also on offer such as Ravioli filled with bean purée or fresh pasta with wild chicory and bean purée (the purée is obtained by mixing three different varieties of local beans). The menu is largely seasonal as it is elaborated using only the home-grown products of the farm. The second courses are based on local lamb and kid, and fried fresh cheeses while the side dishes consist of seasonal vegetables. The sweets are made with home-grown raspberries, blackberries and strawberries and peach and apple tarts are also served.
Even though the farm produces its own wine, Aglianico del Vulture DOC and a range of organic wines produced in the Agri Valley are served. Finally the farm also sells its produce directly to customers.

OTHER PARTICIPATING RESTAURANTS IN THE PREMIO REGIONALE SAPORI LUCANI 2001

AGRITURISMO DA ZIA ELENA
CTR. SCARNATA - 85010 ARMENTO PZ
Tel. 0971.751381- e-mail: agri.daziaelena@tiscalinet.it

AGRITURISTICA SAPORI DEL PARCO
CTR BATTAGLIA - 85010 PIETRAPERTOSA PZ - Tel. 0971.983085

AZIENDA AGRITURISTICA SANT'AGATA
CTR. TOPPO SANT'AGATA - 85025 MELFI PZ - Tel. 0972.238294

GROTTA DELL'EREMITA
CTR. CALCESCIA - 85010 CASTELMEZZANO PZ - Tel. 0971.986314

HOTEL KRISTALL
P.ZZA MUNICIPIO - 85013 GENZANO PZ - Tel. 0971.775284

LA ROMANTICA
CTR. SANGUE SOMARO - 85053 MONTEMURRO PZ
Tel. 0971.753573 - e-mail: aulix99@yahoo.it

L'INCONTRO
VIA RISORGIMENTO, 2-4 - 75015 PISTICCI MT
Tel. 0835.582467 - e-mail: l'incontro@tiscalinet.it

OASI - VIA FALASCOSO - 85040 VIGGIANELLO PZ
Tel. 0973.576292 - oasi.viggianello@tiscalinet.it

RISTORANTE 2 TORRI
VIA DUE TORRI - 85100 POTENZA - Tel. 0971.411661

RISTORANTE FARO EUROPA LIDO - DI I SASSI SRL.
VIA LIDO TORRE, 25 - 75020 SCANZANO J. MT
Tel. 0835.950882

RISTORANTE IL CASTELLO TRAMONTANO
VIA CASTELLO - 75100 MATERA - Tel. 0835.333752
Sito web: www.castellotramontano.tiscali.it

RISTORANTE LA BUCA
VIA S. PARDO, 95 - 75100 MATERA
Tel. 0835.261984 - e-mail: buca1@tiscalinet.it

RISTORANTE LA SOPPRESSATA
VIA LAGO TOTARO, 12 - 85059 VIGGIANO PZ
Tel. 0975.61520 - e-mail: soppressata@tiscalinet.it

RISTORANTE MARVIGNA
VIA S. BIAGIO, 12 - 75100 MATERA
Tel. 0835.344145 - e-mail: marvigna@tiscalinet.it

RISTORANTE MONTEPIANO
VIA BOSCO MONTEPIANO S.S. 277
75011 ACCETTURA MT - Tel. 0835.675005

RISTORANTE NATURA
CTR. ABETINA - 85056 RUOTI PZ   Tel.0971.82185

RISTORANTE O GIARDINELL
CTR. COSTA DELLA GAVETA - 85100 POTENZA
Tel. 0971.50045

RISTORANTE PANAINO
VIA ROCCO SCOTELLARO, 150 - 85045 LAURIA PZ
Tel. 0973.823920 - e-mail: panaino@tiscalinet.it

RISTORANTE PIZZERIA DA MARIO
VIA XX SETTEMBRE, 14 - 75100 MATERA - Tel. 0835.336491

RISTORANTE PIZZERIA L'INCONTRO
VIA VITTORIO VENETO, 14
75012 BERNALDA MT - Tel. 0835.543291

RISTORANTE PIZZERIA S. MICHELE
VIA S. CROCE, 53 - 85037 SANT'ARCANGELO PZ
Tel. 0973.619828 - e-mail: mssanmichele@tiscalinet.it

RISTORANTE RIVELLI
VIA CASALNUOVO, 27 - 75100 MATERA - Tel. 0835.311568

RISTORANTE TIPICO LUNA ROSSA
VIA MARCONI, 18 - 85030 TERRANOVA DI P. PZ
Tel. 0973.932544 - e-mail: federicoval@libero.it
Sito web: www.pollino.com/basilicata

RISTORANTE TOMMASO
VIA DEGLI ARAGONESI - 75100 MATERA - Tel. 0835.261971

ANTICA GOLA
S.S. 598 KM 71 - 85010 MISSANELLO PZ - Tel. 0971.955263

RISTORANTE LE SPIGHE
VIA LUCREZIO - 75100 MATERA - Tel. 0835.388844
e-mail: info@hoteldelcampo.it - Sito web: www.hoteldelcampo.it

RISTORANTE IL GATTO E LA VOLPE
V.CO VIALE DELLA VITTORIA
85021 AVIGLIANO PZ - Tel. 338.3936938

RISTORANTE IL PIZZICOTTO
VIA SICILIA, 21 - 85100 POTENZA - Tel. 0971.25508

RISTORANTE VECCHIA MATERA
V.CO LOMBARDI, 52 - 75100 MATERA

Tel. 0835.336910 - e-mail: vecchiamatera@libero.it

VECCHIO FRANTOIO
C.SO UMBERTO, 70 - 75012 BERNALDA MT - Tel. 0835.543546

RISTORANTE A CASA TUA
CTR. MACCHIA - 85050 TITO PZ - Tel. 0971.651256

IL POGGIO
CTR. PUPOLI - 85024 LAVELLO PZ - Tel. 0972.877112

TAVERNA ORAZIANA - VIA ORAZIO FLACCO, 2 - 85100 POTENZA
Tel. 0971.34044 - e-mail: micheleso@tiscalinet.it

RISTORANTE IL GIUBILEO
S.S. 92 RIFREDDO - 85010 PIGNOLA PZ - Tel. 0971.479910
e-mail: hgiubile@tin.it - Sito web: www.giubileohotel.cjb.net

LA FONTANA
VIA CARMINE, 79 - 75029 VALSINNI PZ - Tel. 0835.817076

RISTORANTE CAVALLINO BIANCO
VIA PROFESSOR BASTANZIO - 85038 SENISE PZ - Tel. 0973.686559

LA FATTORIA
VIA VERDERUOLO INF., 13 - 85100 POTENZA
Tel. 0971.34680 - e-mail: ristorantelafattoria@tiscalinet.it

AGRITURISTICA PUNZI MARIA
STR. VALLONE DEI PIOPPI - 85055 PICERNO PZ
Tel. 0971.795010 - e-mail: info@agriturismopunzi.it
Sito web: www.agriturismopunzi.it

LA FATTORIA SOTTO IL CIELO
CTR. PETRUCCO, 9/A - 85010 PIGNOLA PZ
Tel. 0971.486000 - e-mail: fattoriasottoilcielo@libero.it

RISTORANTE IL TERRAZZO - VIA ROMA - 75020 NOVA SIRI MT
Tel. 0835.505513 - e-mail: vitnicola@libero.it

LA PICCOLA FATTORIA
CTR. CUCONE - 85033 EPISCOPIA PZ
Tel. 0973.655072 - e-mail: piccola.fattoria@tiscalinet.it

AGRITURISTICA LA VILLA
CTR. CAVALLERIZZA - 85025 MELFI PZ - Tel. 0972.236008

LA CAPANNINA - ANTICA OSTERIA BANTINA
VIA CAIROLI, 8 - 85010 BANZI PZ - Tel. 0971.947526

L'ORIZZONTE - CTR. SETA - 85044 LAURIA PZ - Tel. 0973.822312

AI PIOPPI - VIA COMMISERAZIONE
75018 STIGLIANO MT - Tel. 0835.565053

AGRITURISTICA MASSERIA S. GIULIANO
CTR. FOGGIA DI LUPO - 75010 MIGLIONICO MT
Tel. 0835.559183

MASSERIA DEL PANTALEONE
CTR. CHIANCALATA - 75100 MATERA - Tel. 0835.335239

RISTORANTE TAVERNA ROVITA
VIA ROVITA, 13 - 85046 MARATEA PZ - Tel. 0973.876688

OLIVARA
S.P. CARRERA - 75024 MONTESCAGLIOSO MT
Tel. 0835.201040 - e-mail: olivara@libero.it Sito web: www.olivara.it

OSTERIA DEL GALLO
L.GO NAZIONALE, 2 - 85050 MARSICO VETERE PZ - Tel. 0975.352045

RISTORANTE DA PEPPE
C.SO GARIBALDI - 85048 ROTONDA PZ
Tel. 0973.661251 - e-mail: dapeppe@bridge.net - Sito web: www.ristodapeppe.it

LE BOTTEGHE - P.ZZA S. PIETRO BARISANO, 22
75100 MATERA - Tel. 0835.344072
e-mail: lebotteghe@hotmail.com - Sito web: www.materaweb.it

RISTORANTE VENUSIO
VIA LUSSEMBURGO, 2 - 75100 MATERA - Tel. 0835.259081
e-mail: info@ristorantevenusio.it - Sito web: www.ristorantevenusio.it

HOTEL DELLE COLLINE
VIA BELVEDERE, 1 - 85054 MURO LUCANO PZ - Tel. 0976.2284
e-mail: hoteldellecolline@tiscalinet.it
Sito web: www.aziendelucane.org/hoteldellecolline

TRATTORIA FIFINA
C.SO UMBERTO - 75012 BERNALDA MT - Tel. 0835.543134

AZIENDA AGRITURISTICA VENTRICELLI
CTR. DIGA S. GIULIANO - 75100 MATERA - Tel. 0835.307312

HOTEL PIERFAONE
CTR. PIERFAONE - 85010 ABRIOLA PZ - Tel. 0971.722972

LA CUCINA CASERECCIA DI FRANCO STANO
VIA S. CESAREA, 67/69 - 75100 MATERA Tel. 0835.344101
e-mail: lacucinacasereccia@virgilio.it
Sito web: www.materacittà.com/stano

AGRITURISMO L'ASSIOLO - LOCALITA' OASI S. GIULIANO
75010 MIGLIONICO MT - Tel. 0835.559678

CALABRIA
POWERFUL FLAVORS
FROM LAND AND SEA

From the ridges of Aspromonte, Calabria offers that most
unmistakable of qualities, authenticity, and its cheeses,
charcuterie, oils, wines, preserves and citrus fruits
are all firmly routed in the area's ancient traditions.

Calabria, the heel of Italy's boot, has two coastlines of more than 700 kilometers and yet has no maritime history to speak of. The coast was settled by the ancient Greeks but was soon abandoned in favor of the mountains. The hills are harsh and rocky, preventing communication and leading to isolation, and this has fed the legend of the rough, tough, proud and yet hospitable Calabrian. However, whilst this situation has prevented much economic growth, it has led directly to the preservation of culinary traditions which are the pride of the inhabitants.

Sangineto.
The Castle

A BROAD MOSAIC OF ENVIRONMENTS AND CULTURES

Calabria is a wild country with incomparable views: emerald seas, snow-peaked mountains, citrus and oleander trees everywhere, ancient olive groves and vineyards, woods and rushing torrents. But the cultivated land is just as varied with its cereals and vegetables, notably eggplants and bell peppers. And then there are the olive trees (an industry on a national scale) and citrus fruit trees, including citron and bergamot. As for grapes, the ancients called the place *Calabria Enotria*, or 'Wine-producing Calabria', and today this quality can be seen in the DOC (*Denominazione di Origine Contollata*) wines Cirò and Greco di Bianco, to mention only the most important. There is also a great deal of livestock breeding, notably pigs, sheep and goats, which in turn lead to unusual charcuterie and cheese, often with a generous pinch of hot red chilli pepper. As for the produce of the sea, the ports of Pizzo, Palmi and Scilla provide swordfish, tuna and anchovies, sardines and mackerel – what the Italians call 'blue' fish – from which they make the distinctive festival preserve, Rosamarina.

Citrus fruits, an important product of Calabria's agriculture

A WINNING COMBINATION OF HISTORY AND TASTES

The rich gastronomy of Calabria is the result of its varied history. Against a general Greek backdrop, food has been influenced by the Americas, invading Arabs, Normans, Spanish and French, as well as the Greek and Albanian communities still present in Calabria today. Calabrian cuisine is fundamentally vegetarian, using not only cultivated vegetables but also wild ones, such as mushrooms. The principal dishes are, therefore, salads, soups, vegetables and above all pulses, the poor man's meat. There is a great deal of food preservation, whether in oil, vinegar or salt, particularly the *a scapece* method, that is, with oil, vinegar and onion. As for cereals, in addition to pasta, *cuccìa* is noteworthy – a grain-based dish made in different ways according to the area, sometimes in salads with meat and lard, sometimes as a dessert with chocolate and peanuts. Which brings us to meat, once the preserve of the rich (or often eaten only at festivals). Pork dishes include *vrasciole* (pork chops), *frisulìmiti* and *cìcculi*, whilst lamb features in the typical *trattoria* dish, *morseddhu*, a spicy fricassee of lamb's innards. The salamis are highly varied and often very spicy, and include the smoky capocolli, the chewy salsiccia di Calabria, the chunky soppressata and the celebrated '*nduja* salami, soft and red-coloured from the hot red chili pepper. Last but not least, there is fish, predominantly swordfish and tuna, often in dishes of Sicilian origin. One final note: the best and most authentic Calabrian cuisine can more often than not be found in the *trattorie* and *rosticcerie*.

Calabrian cheeses

537

CAMPANIA   BASILICATA

Calabria - Typical products

MAR IONIO

Scale 1:1 750 000

0   20   40 km

A3

Trebisacce

Verbicaro

Castrovillari

Belvedere Marittimo

A3

Crati

Rossano

Luzzi

Paola

Cosenza

Cirò

Melissa

MAR TIRRENO

Neto

Crotone

Tacina

Isola di Capo Rizzuto

Nicastro

Lamezia Terme

CATANZARO

Golfo di Squillace

Soverato

Vibo Valentia

Mesima

Bivongi

Palmi

A3

Messina

Locri

Reggio di Calabria

Bianco

SICILIA

A20 A18

Melito di Porto Salvo

🍐 FRUIT
1. **Clementina di Calabria Igp.** Calabrian clementines.
2. **Bergamotto.** Bergamot.
3. **Cedro.** Cedro, or citron, grown in Cetraro and S. Maria del Cedro.
4. **Zibibbo di Pizzo Calabro.** A grape often used for sweet white wine.

🍆 VEGETABLES
1. **Cipolle rosse di Tropea.** Red onions.

🫒 EXTRA-VIRGIN OLIVE OIL
1. **Bruzio Dop.**
2. **Lametia.**

🍶 VARIOUS
1. **Liquirizia.** Liquorice produced in the Rossano Calabro area.
2. **Torrone di Bagnara.** Bagnara nougat.

🧀 CHEESES
1. **Caciocavallo silano Dop.** Strong cheese produced throughout the region.
2. **Abbespata.** Salted and smoked cheese from Sila and Crotonese.
3. **Butirro.**
4. **Giuncata.** Curds and whey made in Sila.
5. **Pecorino crotonese.**
6. **Ricotta calabrese.**

🥓 CHARCUTERIE
1. **Capocollo di Calabria Dop.** A Calabrian salami.
2. **Pancetta di Calabria Dop.** Calabrian bacon.
3. **Salsiccia di Calabria Dop.** Calabrian sausages.
4. **Soppressata di Calabria Dop.**
5. **'Nduja.** A spicy salami from Spilinga and Poro.

🍇 DOC WINES
1. Bivongi
2. Cirò
3. Donnici
4. Greco di Bianco
5. Lamezia
6. Melissa
7. Pollino
8. Sant'Anna di Isola di Capo Rizzuto
9. San Vito di Luzzi
10. Savuto
11. Scavigna
12. Verbicaro

CATANZARO

From the Ionian to the Tyrrhene sea, stretching as far as Sila Piccola, the cuisine of Calabria juxtaposes the flavors of land and sea.

The mountainous region around Catanzaro includes the whole of the Sila Piccola and the bands of hills in the Marchesato. Wherever the woods give way the land is cultivated: fruit, grapes, cereals and olives are just some of the produce grown in the area around Catanzaro. Livestock breeding (cattle and sheep) is done for the most part in the Sila region, which gives the region its two main forms of fresh meat and its *pecorino* and *ricotta* cheeses. Pork is ubiquitous, used directly in cooking or made into processed forms marked with an IGP (*Indicazione Geografica Protetta*) label. The dish most typical of the area is *morseddhu* or *morzello*, a unique dish of its type, made of slices of beef innards, tripe, pieces of intestine, heart and lungs, all braised in wine mixed with herbs and spices, and a great deal of red hot chilli. This is eaten in the tasty local *pita* bread, which should allow the sauce to slip easily down the

Lamezia Terme. The Angitola plain

throat, "*gargi, gargi*" as they say in these parts. Another local dish is the *tiana* (named for the clay dish it is cooked in), made of goat's meat with roast potatoes, artichokes or fresh peas. On the coast fish is grilled or served in the *guazzetto* style. All these should be eaten with a generous DOC (*Denominazione di Origine Controllata*) wine such as the red Lamezia, and Scavigna, produced exclusively in the Catanzaro region. Other local wines (also produced in Cosenza) are Melissa, Savuto, Sant'Anna di Isola di Capo Rizzuto and the Bivongi label (also produced in Reggio Calabria).

HOTELS AND RESTAURANTS

Catanzaro
⭐☑ **Guglielmo** ★★★
via A. Tedeschi 1
☎ 0961741922
Brace ¶¶
at Catanzaro Marina
via Melito di Porto
Salvo 102
☎ 096131340
Da Pepè ¶
piazza Roma 6, vico 1
☎ 0961726254
Da Salvatore ¶
salita 1 del Rosario 28
☎ 0961724318
Trattoria Nisticò ¶
at Catanzaro Marina
piazza Stazione 19
☎ 096133027
Copanello
⭐☑ **Villaggio
Guglielmo** ★★★
via Nazionale
☎ 0961911321
**Gizzeria Lido
Marechiaro** ¶¶
S.S. 18
☎ 096851251
**Lamezia Terme
Al Tempo Perso** ¶¶
via A. d'Ippolito 22
☎ 096825883
**Soverato
San Domenico** ★★★
via della Galleria
☎ 096723121
Palazzo ¶¶
corso Umberto 1 40
☎ 096725336
**Squillace
Castrum** ¶¶
via G. Rhodio 10
☎ 0961912588
**Taverna
Parco delle Fate** ★★★
at Villaggio Mancuso
☎ 0961922057
Sila ★★★
at Villaggio Mancuso
☎ 0961922032

Gourmet Tours

CATANZARO. Set on three hills overlooking the Bay of Squillace, Catanzaro was founded by the Byzantines, and has winding lanes and medieval architecture. The local culinary tradition can be sampled in the *trattorie, osterie* and *putiche* (small stores where you can sample local food) both in the center of town and on the outskirts. Dishes include pasta with fried eggs and *pecorino* cheese, a local specialty, which normally precedes the celebrated *morseddhu*. Of the many restaurants, one of the oldest is "Da Pepe" with its homemade pasta, and wine from a barrel. "Da Salvatore" offers *baccalà* (dried stockfish) with olives and potatoes. Slightly more refined is "Guglielmo", offering a broad range of fish dishes, including smoked swordfish, spaghetti with anchovies, and sea bass "alla diavola". For those who wish to "shop till they drop", "Lanzo" is the place for you; but curiosity hunters will not be able to resist the Saturday morning market in the Piazzale dello Stadio. The candy shops all stock the typical local candies, most notably the very soft *cumpittu* nougat of Arab origin. On the Catanzaro marina "La Brace" next to the "Stillhotel" specializes in fish, with excellent shellfish and various types of fish

in bell pepper and tomato sauce. Another good address at which to try the *morseddhu* is "Nisticò", also on the marina.

1. From the Ionian to the Tyrrhenian Sea

SQUILLACE. Set back from the coast of the gulf of the same name, Squillace looks very much like a medieval town, but it is studded with large sixteenth – and seventeenth-century buildings. At the highest point in the city stand the ruins of the Norman castle, which guards the coast from Capo Rizzuto to the Sila region. In the historical center of town lies the restaurant "Castrum". Here you should try the local charcuterie, the homemade pasta with salami sauce and the mixed grill. Heading inland, on the road to Maida, stands the town of Cortale. Here they grow borlotti beans and make *provole* buffalo milk cheeses, which draw in customers from the whole of the nearby region. On the coast, at Copanello, we recommend the "Villaggio Guglielmo".

SOVERATO. Facing the Gulf of Squillace, Soverato is a fishing port, a market town and also a seaside resort with a long beach and excellent promenade, all of which goes to make it popular with holiday makers and food and wine enthusiasts. "Il Palazzo" is a

540

restaurant with a good reputation throughout the region, combining quality with good presentation. Dishes to try include vegetables with smoked tuna and fig pancakes, *trofie* pasta with swordfish and eggplant, and roasted endives with *porcini* mushrooms. As for places to stay, we strongly recommend "San Domenico", excellently positioned as it is on the sea front. Don't forget when shopping to buy some *mustica*. The best wines are those inland, namely the DOC Bovingi label made with Greco and Gaglioppo grapes.
LAMEZIA TERME. Set on the Tyrrene coast, Lamezia Terme grew out of the fusion of the three towns Nicasrto, Sambiase and Sant'Eufemia. Nicastro was a Byzantine settlement and is known for its eighteenth-century cathedral and its Norman/Svevo castle, which you reach via the picturesque S. Teodoro neighborhood. Sambiase on the other hand, with the nearby Terme Caronte, is a wine center and the home of the DOC wine Lamezia (with reds made from Nerello, Gaglioppo and Greco grapes, and whites from Greco, Trebbiano and Malvasia grapes) and the "Valdamato" (reds, whites and rosés), which has been awarded the IGP quality control mark. For wine tasting we recommend you try the "Cantine Lento", whose production ranges from modern whites to heavy reds, and the "Cantina Statti", which also sells its prestigious Olio del Barone and other market garden produce. Finally, Sant'Eufemia is a modern town served by a nearby airport. Take a detour here to Gizzeria Lido to eat the excellent sea food dishes at the hotel restaurant "Marechiaro".

2. The Sila Piccola
TIRIOLO. Set on a hill and buttressed by the Sila Piccola, Tiriolo is an ancient town straddling two Calabrian seas (to get a view you have to scale the Monte, which is also an archaeological site). The town is best known for its textile craftwork, notably shawls called *vancali*. As for the food, the "Coniglio d'oro" serves excellent mushroom and mountain game dishes. Driving along the beautiful "Strada delle Calabrie" road you come to Serrastretta, renowned for its smoked hams and *soppressate* and *capocolli* salamis. At nearby Gimigliano, you should try the local pastries made with *passolina* grapes.
TAVERNA. Buried deep in the heart of the Sila Piccola, Taverna is also an ancient resting place, and today still provides food and lodging for weary travelers. Its tranquillity, fresh mountain air and hearty country cuisine make it a favorite with holidaymakers. Pine mushrooms are frequently the stars of the cuisine. Taking the state highways towards the principal town of the region you come to Villagio Mancusio, where the Calabria National Park begins. Here, you can buy some marvellous food – notably *caciocavallo* and *pecorino* cheeses and *capocollo* and *salsiccia* salamis – and have a very agreeable holiday at the local "Parco delle Fate" hotel or the *locanda* "Sila", which offers simple dishes of *tagliatelle* noodles with *porcini* mushrooms and roast goat's meat. For those bitten by the Calabrian bug, we recommend a detour to Buturo, a holiday resort in one of the most beautiful parts of the Sila.

541

COSENZA

Demarcated by land and sea, the Cosenza area glitters with the ancient capital of the Bruzi and the richness of old culinary traditions.

The land around Cosenza is almost completely mountainous, apart from the valley of the river Crati, the Sybaris plain and certain coastal stretches. As for the food, the key ingredients are grain, corn, olives, the ubiquitous grape, excellent potatoes and market garden vegetables. The soil in the Pellino region is very chalky and consequently par-

Foresters' road through the Campotenes Pass

ticularly favorable to vines. The three principal DOC wines of the area are (together with Donnici) the best to be found locally. To these should be added San Vito di Luzzi, the muscat wine from Saracena and Frascineto, and many others. The Gaglioppo grape variety comes from the Cosenza region; it is the most widespread there and used particularly for full-bodied wines. The black grapes are blended to make red wines of great character and the white grapes create good table wines. The milk produced from local herds was praised even in antiquity, as was the characteristic salami of the Sila High Plain. The cuisine, traditionally simple, is based on meat and fish combined with garden vegetables and wild elements such as mushrooms. Typical dishes include *làgane* (*tagliatelle* noodles) and chick peas, *mazzacorde* (fried lamb's innards), *'mbacchiuse* (sticky potatoes with onion and bell peppers), and *frascàtula* (a sort of *polenta*). Good desserts include *buccunotti* from Mormanno, *chjinulille* (a Christmas specialty), *cuddhureddhi* and *pitta 'mpigliata*.

Gourmet Tours

COSENZA. Founded by the Bruzi at the confluence of the Busento and Crati rivers, Consenza was for centuries the first city of the plain, described with admiration by the Greek historian and geographer Strabo. Also powerful in Longobard and Norman times, Cosenza continued to be illustrious, at least in terms of culture, thanks to the unbroken academic tradition from the ancient Accademia Cosentina to the modern University of Calabria. The atmospheric medieval old town is packed tightly all around the Pancrazio hill in the shade of the Svevo castle. Corso Telesio, previously the "street of merchants and goldsmiths", is the main town artery, off which runs a dense web of tiny streets, alleys and steps, all crossing over and under each other, punctuated from time to time by small palaces. For those wishing to indulge in the

HOTELS AND
RESTAURANTS

Cosenza
Executive ★★★ 🍴🅔
at Rende (km 10)
via Marconi 59
☎ 0984401010
L'Arco Vecchio 🍴
piazza Archi
di Ciaccio 21
☎ 098472564
La Calavrisella 🍴
via De Rada 11/a
☎ 098428012
**Pantagruel nella
Vecchia Rende** 🍴
🍴🅔
at Commenda (km 3)
via Pittor Sant'Anna 2
☎ 0984443508
Giocondo 🍴
via Piave 53
☎ 098429810
**Il Setaccio:
Osteria del Tempo
Antico** 🍴 🅔
at Santa Rosa (km 4)
☎ 0984837211
Luna Rossa 🍴
via Sicilia 94
☎ 098432470
Altomonte
Barbieri ★★★ 🍴 🍴🅔
via S. Nicola 30
☎ 0981948072
Amantea
La Tonnara 🍴🅔
★★★, via Tonnara 13
☎ 0982424272
Comfortable ★★★
at Campora S. Giovanni
S.S. 18
☎ 098246048
Camigliatello Sil.
**Aquila &
Edelweiss** ★★★ 🍴
viale Stazione 11
☎ 0984578044
Castrovillari
**La Locanda di
Alia** ★★★ 🍴🍴
via Jetticelle 69
☎ 098146370
Cerisano
La Stalla del Duca 🍴
via S. Pietro 17
☎ 0984473968

**HOTELS AND
RESTAURANTS**

Cetraro
⭐🏨 G.H. San
Michele ★★★
at Bosco (km 5)
☎ 098291012
Il Casello ⑪
via Porto
☎ 0982971355
Civita
Agorà ⑨
piazza Municipio 30
☎ 098173410
Kamastra ⑨
piazza Municipio 3/6
☎ 098173387
Diamante
⭐🏨 Ferretti ★★★
via Lungomare
☎ 098581428
Lo Scoglio ⑪
via Colombo
☎ 098581345
Dipignano
Osteria dal Cugino ⑨
via G.M. Serra 6
☎ 0984621103
Falconara Albanese
Elios ⑨
viale Paradiso
☎ 098282299
Frascineto
⭐🏨 Scanderbeg ⑪
via Arcuri 13
☎ 098132117
Morano Calabro
La Cantina ⑨
piazza Croce 21
☎ 098131034
Il Nido del Falco ⑨
at Crocifisso
☎ 03474671657
Praia a Mare
⭐🏨 Casetta
Bianca ★★
at Fiuzzi (km 3)
☎ 0985779265
Rogliano
Disagre ⑨
via P. Nicoletti 15
☎ 0984961998

typically Italian evening promenade or *passeggiata*, the "Gran Caffè Renzelli", with its Art Nouveau interior and famous pastries, is a must. Not far from there is the "Arco Vecchio" restaurant, recommended for its careful approach to local cuisine. Once across the bridge over the river Busento, you come to the new town, a lively center in which they produce countryside fare, such as the typical liquorice and dried figs which local pastry cooks stuff and coat with chocolate. The first restaurant that we recommend is "La Calavrisella", where they serve the classic *antipasti* centered around the local charcuterie, or preserved in local Sila oil. They also offer homemade pasta with tomato and *caciocavallo* cheese or a boar sauce. Then you should try the goat in oregano. And those a little more adventurous should attempt the *mazzacorda* (lamb's innards). Other recommended local eateries include "Giocondo", which is both modern and convenient, and "Luna Rossa", which is simple but lively, and where you should have a pizza. You can also eat well on the road to Dipignano, a town set in an area full of ancient medieval communes. At the entrance to the town, the "Osteria del Cugino" provides a comfortable local atmosphere and leaves the visitor well satisfied. Climbing up through the woods, you can visit the *agriturismo* center "Foresta Sottana", with its rustic lodgings and cuisine studded with organic

homegrown produce (vegetables, olive oil, preserves, sauces and candies). For home cooking and excellent wines "La Stalla del Duca" in nearby Cerisano is also worth trying. We recommend that lovers of fish should lengthen their journey a little to include Rende. Here in the old part of this historical town, perched on a hill, is the interesting Palazzo Zagarese museum, which should be followed by a visit to the restaurant "Pantugruel nella Vecchia Rende". Within its ancient walls you can taste peppered rosemary, home-made pasta with mussels and rocket or zucchini flowers with scampi, and tuna in the Calabria style, *i.e.*, grilled with paste made of capers, oregano, vinegar and hot red chilli. If you wish to stay, you should check into the "Executive" hotel in the new part of town, a hyper-modern structure with a lively restaurant, "Nabucco". In Santa Rosa we make one final recommendation; "Il Setaccio-Osteria del Tempo Antico", a rustic location offering simple but attractive dishes.

Mozzarella *making*

1. The "Via dei Casali" and the Tyrrhennian coast

ROGLIANO. There are several reasons for staying in Rogliano, set as it is in the central Savuto valley. Among these is the Renaissance church of San Giorgio, and for food lovers there is the restaurant "Disagre" with its celebrated *papardelle ravioli* stuffed with *porcini* mushrooms. The quickest route there is Statale 19, Via delle Calabrie, but we recommend that you try the narrow, winding minor roads which take you past the "Casali di Cosenza", set amongst the vineyards of the Crati valley. Here Donnici is important. It is the key location in the area which produces the DOC wine of the same name. Also of note is Figline Vegliaturo; a tiny village of narrow streets set on a hill, it is also a Città del Vino and a busy tourist center. To sample some of the local produce visit the "Cooperative San Michele" in Piane Crati and the *azienda* "Vigne Piccole" in Aprigliano.

AMANTEA. The church of San Bernardino in the upper town and the walls which descend to the port are the principal features of this market and fishing town. Two hotels are notable for their mixture of land-oriented and marine cuisine, "La Tornata" and "Il Comfortable" '(which, among other things, also organizes fishing trips for enthusiasts).

PAOLA. High above the sea, Paola has a double prospect, one looking out towards the Tyrrhenian coast and the other towards the shrine of San Francesco, both set in the cliff top scenery of the Catena Costiera coastal ridges. Here the local tomatoes are renowned. At Torremezzo di Falconara you should eat fish at the restaurant "Elios" – they also have a huge selection of appetizers, including the remarkable specialty *capicollo*, an octopus paste.

CETRARO. From the height of a single spur, Cetraro dominates the surrounding sunny coastline. As the name suggests, cedro or citron trees grow here, although

today the place is primarily a holiday resort with hotels and good restaurants, notably "Grand Hotel S. Michele", in a villa on the seafront, and "Casello", a somewhat more relaxed venue.

2. From the Ionian Sea to the Sila Grande

CASSANO ALLO JONIO. Although principally a place for taking the waters, Cassano is today a place where people stay because of the archaeological park of Greek *Sybaris* and the nature reserve of the Fosce del Crati. On the marina, we recommend "Il Cavallino" as a good fish restaurant. Travel along the coast to Trebisacce with its old central town and the Baroque parish church of San Nicola di Mira. Shop at "Garoppo Giovanni" for your charcuterie, cheeses, and land and sea preserves. For rooms and food, the "Trattoria del Sole" is never disappointing. Near the fishing port and the modern bathing resort, "Il Canneto" and "Da Raffaele" are two excellent fish restaurants.

SAN DEMETRIO CORONE. Those interested in something different should take an excursion to the Sila Greca to see the ancient Al-

Morano Calabro

HOTELS AND
RESTAURANTS

Rossano
Antiche Mura ❦
via Prigioni 40
☎ 0983520042
Stella dello Jonio ❦
at Rossano Scalo
at Momena
☎ 0983516983
San Giovanni in Fiore
Al Cariglio ❦
contrada Olivaro
☎ 0984970944
Sibari
Cavallino ❦❦
at Marina di Sibari
contrada Salicette
☎ 0981784869
Trebisacce
Il Canneto ❦
viale Riviera delle Palme
☎ 0981500409
Raffaele ❦
via Lungomare
☎ 098157472
Trattoria del Sole ❦
via Piave 14 bis
☎ 098151797

AGRITURISMI

Acri
Santa Maria di Macchia ⭐▣
contrada Macchia di Baffi 73
☎ 0984946165
Dipignano
Foresta Sottana
at Foresta
☎ 0984621574
Morano Calabro
La Locanda del Parco ⭐▣
contrada Mazzicanino
☎ 098131304
Rossano
Cozzo di Simari ⭐▣
at Crocicchia
☎ 0983520896
Il Giardino di Iti ⭐▣
at Amica
☎ 0983512448

WINE
PRODUCERS

Aprigliano
Vigne Piccole
contrada S. Nicola
delle Vigne
☎ 0360759044
Frascineto
Cantina Sociale
Vini del Pollino
contrada Ferrocinto-
-Castrovillari
☎ 098138035
Azienda Miraglia
via Corvo 11
☎ 098132016
Mandatoriccio
Cantine Igt
Condoleo
via Nazionale 149
☎ 0983994004
Piane Crati
Cooperativa San
Michele
via Nazionale
☎ 0984422021
Rossano
Cantina Marinelli
via S. Bartolomeo 87
☎ 0983521333

SHOPPING

Cosenza
Azienda Vinicola
Spadafora
at Donnici
contrada Muraglione
☎ 0984780738
Wine producer.
Bar Caffè Renzelli
piazza XX Settembre
☎ 098427005
corso Telesio 8
☎ 098426814
Historic cafe
and pastry shop.
Caffè Telesio
via Ant. Serre 6
☎ 098422099
Cafe and pastry shop.
Altomonte
Bottega di
Casa Barbieri
via S. Nicola 30
☎ 0981948072
Wines.

banian community at its liveliest. Not only do the church of San Adriano and the name of the town bear witness to the town's Greek origin, there are also *trattoria* and pastry shops which still carry a vague aroma of the East. Go a little further and you reach Acri, a base for visiting the Sila. We recommend the organic *azienda* "Santa Maria di Macchia", which offers dishes such as home-made pasta, meat and mushrooms.

ROSSANO. A Byzantine center, Rossano was known for its religious associations, with seven Basilian monasteries and hermitages in nearby valleys. The best way to approach the town is to have a coffee in the long-established cafe "Tagliaferri". Then, when you are ready to eat, the *trattoria* "Antiche Mura" offers exceedingly tasty meat and vegetable dishes. In the surrounding area, not only are the olive oil and cheese renowned, there is also liquorice, as sold in the *azienda* "Amarelli", founded more than a hundred years ago. Finally, at Rossano Scale, the restaurant "Stella dello Ionio" is rustic yet refined and offers elegant dishes redolent of both the land and sea.

SAN GIOVANNI IN FIORE. Starting at the sea, the Statale 383 at Mandatoriccio rises through olive groves and vineyards towards the Sila Grande. Following the boundary of the Crotone region near Savelli, you come to San Giovanni in Fiore; a picturesque spot with a medieval abbey. Today it is not only much frequented by vacationers but also by art and crafts artisans. The key gastronomic address is "Al Cariglio", a traditional venue. Essential buys include Abate bitters and Paesanella *grappa*.

CAMIGLIATELLO SILANO. Set in the heart of the Sila Grande among deep forests of pines and larches, Calmigliatello is a modern holiday resort, particular popular with those in search of snow. We strongly recommend that you stay at "Aquila & Edelweiss", an elegant hotel restaurant whose culinary highlights include *porcini* mushroom soup, grilled lamb and roast freshwater trout, accompanied by a fine wine list.

3. Around Mount Pollino

CASTROVILLARI. Built in a large basin at the foot of Mount Pollino, Castrovillari is a city with two faces: one modern and lively, set in the plain, the other picturesque and silent in the central old town – Civita – which is set on a spur. For gourmets, the venue "Locanda di Alìa", based in an elegant country house, is a must. The cuisine is traditional yet imaginative, including dishes such as mullet roe salad with dried figs, *panzerotti* pastry envelopes stuffed with spinach, *ricotta* and aniseed and lamb with strawberry grape *mostarda* chutney. Climbing to Pollini, visitors should stop at Frascineto, famed for its smoked hams, *soppressate* salamis and cheeses, particularly the *caciocavallo* and the salted *ricotta*. The hotel/restaurant "Scanderbeg" provides an excellent cuisine of meat and mushrooms for first courses. You then come to Civita, source of the noble *arbëresh* (Italian-Albanian) traditions. The ethnic cuisine in the atmospheric *trattoria* "Agorà" and "Kamastra" has a quality of yesteryear.

ALTOMONTE. Set on a hill in the Esaro valley, Altomonte has a strongly medieval feel, with its narrow streets and flights of steps which converge up towards the Chiesa della Consolazione. Pliny the Elder was thinking of Altomonte when he praised Calabria wines, which are indeed exactly the same wines, in terms of grapes and traditions, as those which can today be found at the vintners "Bottega di Casa Barbieri". And this is perhaps the best way to be introduced to the familial and yet highly professional world of the "Barbieri" hotel/restaurant. Dishes of note include Albanian-style dishes such as macaroni with spicy tomato sauce and leg of mountain mutton with juniper.

DIAMANTE. Perched high on a rocky cliff, Diamante is famous for its crystal-clear sea, its gardens perfumed with lime, and its murals, all of which go to make the town a riot of colour. The town boasts a rich fish cuisine, and gourmets should look out for the *jujume* patties (made from sea anemones). First in the list of recommended restaurants is the "Pagoda" in the hotel "Ferretti", right on the beach, with its *pignatiellu* specialty, a dish of fried fish coated in lime flour. A more down-to-earth venue is "Lo Scoglio", which serves excellent sea food including *linguini* noodles and a very tasty *orata* or gilt head fish cooked in salt. In the

countryside, the specialty is preserves. Some of the most unusual include little *lampascione* onions and wild baby chicory preserved in oil, small peppered sardines in a spicy sauce, red chili and onion 'jam', and bergamot and lime marmalade. Just in from the coast is Verbicaro, a serious agricultural and livestock rearing area with its own DOC wine and a celebrated young salted *pecorino*.

PRAIA A MARE. The ultimate Tyrrhenian beach, with its bays cut into the high rocky cliffs and its green limes. This is one of Calabria's best known bathing resorts. Amongst the many offerings provided for tourists, we recommend the nice family-run hotel/restaurant "Casetta Bianca", with its view of the island of Dino and its fish specialties.

MORANO CALABRO. Take the Statale 504 from Mormannò up the valley of the Lao until it joins the Strada delle Calabrie. This then leads to the picturesque village of Morano Calabro, perched on the side of a hill, above which soars a ruined castle. The town is famous for its *giuncata*, or curds and whey, produced according to ancient methods. Two establishments are worth trying: "La Cantina", for local dishes and produce, and "Nido del Falco", for its *mazzacorde* salami specialty.

Villa with vineyards at Castrovillari

CROTONE

Wines famed since antiquity and one of the best known pecorinos of the south are the highlights of the gastronomy of Crotone.

A young province, but whose principal town dates back to the Magna Graeca settlement *Kroton* – the site of the school of Pythagoras. The most significant Greek remains today are the solitary ruins of the temple of Hera Lacinia, where the compact clay is interspersed with hard sandy rocks. A network of rivers, including the Neto, irrigates the hills, and on the border with the Cosenza region, among the pines of the Sila, there is the winding Lake Ampollino. These carefully channeled watercourses feed a flourishing agriculture, the jewel of which is the exceedingly sweet watermelon, as well as the cereals and vines. Here the celebrated Cirò grape is grown and the prestigious wines Melissa and Crucoli are made. The meadows produce cheeses of character, such as the *abbespata*, a salted and smoked *ricotta*, and Crotone Pecorino, the principal cheese in the region.

Olive grove in the region of Crotone

Crotone. The Castle bridge

Gourmet Tours

CROTONE. The castle high up on the promontory occupies the site of the ancient acropolis of Crotone, one of the principal cities of Magna Graecia. And squeezed inside the Spanish bastions are the winding streets of the historic center with its cathedral and archaeological museum. Outside the antique center there is all the bustle of a primary business and maritime center in Ionian Calabria. In this modern context it is nice to see that the great local cheese traditions have not died out. These include the making of *pecorino* (both fresh and matured) and salted *ricotta*. Another source of local pride is the remarkably sweet local watermelon. As for good restaurants, we recommend "La Casa di Rosa", set between the Molo Vecchio and the castle, with its creative fresh fish cuisine (the fish are all there in the tank). You should try the *sette delizie di mare* appetizer, then have the excellent *tagliatelle* noodles with salted grouper fish and various fried fish with vegetables in batter. Among the enormous selection of restaurants in Crotone,

there is something for everyone, from the refined venue, such as "La sosat da Marcello", to the rustic *trattoria* – namely, "'A Pignata" and "Zio Emilio" – which offer the traditional local classics such as the fish soup *quadaro* and the spicy tripe *morseddhu*. If you take the touristic trip to Capo Colonna, the site of the ancient temple to Hera Lacinia, you should eat in the restaurant "Lido degli Scogli" and in the *trattoria* "A Quadrara". Further inland visitors are presented with the harsh and romantic landscape of the Marchesato region. To get a taste of the peasant cuisine – the meat, cheese and salami – you should call in at the *agriturismo* establishment "Ada Fazzolari" in Papanice.

1. From the sea to the Sila

ISOLA DI CAPO RIZZUTO. This principal town in the region is a noted agricultural center, with its DOC wine produced in the Sant'Anna zone, and a seaside resort with beaches and holiday resorts all down the coast. The most famous view of the area is the castle "Le Castella" (built by the Spanish Aragon dynasty), set alone at the water's edge. Of

HOTELS AND RESTAURANTS

Crotone
Casa di Rosa ⁜
via C. Colombo 117
☎ 096221946
**La Sosta
da Marcello** ⁜
via C. Alvaro
☎ 0962902243
'A Pignata ⁜
vico Orfeo 4
☎ 096229742
Lido degli Scogli ⁜
via Capo Colonna
☎ 096228625
A Quadara ⁜
via Capo Colonna
☎ 096222150
Zio Emilio ⁜
via M.Nicoletta 79
☎ 096227283
Cirò
L'Aquila d'Oro ⁜
via Sant'Elia
☎ 096238550
**Isola di Capo
Rizzuto**
Annibale ⁜
at Le Castella
via Duomo 35
☎ 0962795004
La Scogliera ⁜
at Le Castella
via Scogliera
☎ 0962795071
Santa Severina
**La Locanda
del Re** ⁜
discesa V. Emanuele III
☎ 096251734
Savelli
Il Ritrovo ⁜
contrada Coste Lese
☎ 0984996722

S. Severina

AGRITURISMI

Crotone
Ada Fazzolari
at Papanice
via Pietà
☎ 0330356704
Marina di
Strongoli
Brasacchio
contrada Serpito
☎ 096288320
Dattilo
contrada Dattilo
☎ 0962865613
Mesoraca
Badessa
contrada Badessa
☎ 096248135
Santa Severina
**Biologica
Sant'Anastasìa**
at Cocina
☎ 096251161

**WINE
PRODUCERS**

Cirò Marina
Librandi
contrada San
Gennaro S.S. 106
☎ 096231518

SHOPPING

Crotone
**Gastronomia
Buscema**
at Papanciano, Z.I.
☎ 096229992
*Typical wines
and delicatessen.*

the many local restaurants, the best ones are to be found in this locality. The first of note is the hotel restaurant "Annibale" which offers home cooking that is often pork-based and usually made from their own produce and ingredients, including home-made charcuterie, *maccaruni* noodles with ragù, grilled meat, and to finish *pittanchiusa*, a dessert made with sultanas, almonds and walnuts. For fish dishes, we recommend the restaurant "La Scogliera".

SANTA SEVERINA. The "Strada della Sila Piccola" leaves the coast and rises into the uplands of the Marchesato. Set in the Neto valley, Santa Severina appears in a landscape of cliffs scattered amongst olive and citrus fruit trees. And the visitor is presented with many opportunities to enjoy not only Byzantine and Norman sites of historical interest, but also the local wines and dishes. Near the castle stands the excellent restaurant "La Locanda del Re". Also worthy of interest is the *agriturismo* establishment "Biologica Sant'Anastasia" in Cocina, just below Santa Severina.

SAVELLI. After passing through Cerenzia, a small place known as a Citta dell'Olio (City of Olive Oil), and passing along the Cosenza region at San Giovanni in Fiori, you come to Savelli, a delightful resort set amongst the oaks and elms of the Sila around Crotone. We recommend you

eat at the restaurant "Il Ritrovo" – the flavors are those of the mountains, in other words, meat, charcuterie and cheese, and also mushrooms and game when in season.

CIRÒ MARINA. Via a winding road, you descend through hills just inland of the Ionian Sea. These hills have been famous since ancient times for their grapes, Greco Bianco and Gaglioppo, which have brought renown to the local DOC wines. First you come to Cirò, a town simply steeped in history, where you should eat in the small *trattoria* "Aquila d'Oro". The key features are the charcuterie, the mushrooms, the *cavatelli* noodles in the *cirò* style, rabbit and kid goat. You should then descend to Marina, a fishing port which recently became a tourist resort. The *cantina* not to be missed is "Librandi", where you simply must try the Rosso Riserva Duca S. Felice red. The town is also known for its olive oil production.

STRONGOLI. Previously the ancient town of *Petelia*, first Greek and later Bruzi, Strongoli perches on the slopes of an isolated hill. The place is interesting first and foremost for its wine production and the innovative (for Calabria, at any rate) Chardonnay and Cabernet varieties. We recommend that you stretch your journey a little further to include Melissa and you wil come across the vines used for the DOC wine of the same name, another remarkable product whose creation is lost in the mists of time. For a bite to eat, take some country time out in the *agriturismo* establishments "Dattilo" and "Brasacchio".

REGGIO DI CALABRIA

Blessed with an excellent climate and beautiful scenery, Reggio is a mix of delicate aromas carried by sea breezes and strong flavors.

Reggio sits on the southernmost end of the region and is dominated by the wooded Aspromonte mountain. In the central parts, especially on the edges of the Gioia Tauro plain, olive trees ensure a significant local olive oil output. Grapes also grow here, providing the wines Greco di Bianco DOC. Along its short coastline, and only there, grows the region's singular citrus fruit, bergamot, from which a perfume fragrance is produced. As for the cuisine, the Sicilian influence can be strongly felt, notably in the pasta with eggplant and in the *cannoli* and *cassata* pastries.

Scilla. The sheer drops from the castle to the Strait of Messina

551

Everywhere the first course is fish, including anchovies in Reggio style, swordfish in Bagnara style and also *alalunga* (a rare type of tuna) served in a sweet and sour sauce. As for desserts, the *torrone* nougat is greatly appreciated, particularly in Bagnara and Taurianova, as are the *passulate* crunchy Christmas specialties from Ardore.

HOTELS AND RESTAURANTS

Reggio di Calabria
★☎ **Fata Morgana** ★★★
at Gallico Marina
via Lungomare
☎ 0965370009
☎ **Baylik** ¶¶
vico Leone 3
☎ 096548624
Bonaccorso ¶¶
via Bixio 5
☎ 0965896048
Bagnara Calabra
★☎ **Kerkyra** ¶¶
corso V. Emanuele 217
☎ 0966371088
Bianco
Vittoria ★★★
via C. Alvaro 2
☎ 0964911015
Bivongi
La Vecchia Miniera ¶
contrada Perrocalli
☎ 0964731869
Canolo
Da Cosimo ¶
at Canolo Nuova
strada XVI 5
☎ 0964385931
Gambarie
Miramonti ★★★
via degli Sci 10
☎ 0965743048
Gerace
A Squella ¶
via della Resistenza 8
☎ 0964356086
La Tavernetta ¶
at Azzuria
☎ 0964356020
Lo Sparviero ¶
via L. Cadorna 3
☎ 0964356826
Gioiosa Jonica
Enoteca Micu 'i Cola ¶
at Gioiosa Marina
via C. Maria 189
☎ 0964415912
RicaRoka ¶
at Gioiosa Marina
corso Carlo Maria 11
☎ 0964415860
Locri
★☎ **La Fontanella** ¶
at Moschetta (km 4)
☎ 0964390005

Gourmet Tours

REGGIO DI CALABRIA. Positioned between Aspromonte and the Straits of Messina, the city of Reggio di Calabria has a significant antique history. An earthquake in 1908 has also left its mark on the physical aspect of the place today. The exotic plants and the view of Etna give the seafront promenade a completely unique feeling. The *Museo archeologico* is also not to be missed, with the Riace *Bronzes* and certain other treasures. You should begin the morning in one of the cafes with a *brioche* (or sweet croissant) filled with ice-cream. Then as the hours go by, allow yourself to be tempted by the delights of the *rosticceria*, sampling *arancini*, deep fried balls of *risotto* with a blob of *mozzarella* in the center, *panzerotti* crepes filled with spinach and *ricotta*, *fritelle*, pizzas and *focaccia* pizza bread. Almost every *osteria* still serves *morseddhu*. When you sit down to eat, pasta always plays a significant role, particularly the homemade types such as *maccaruni 'e casa*. In restaurants you can try a selection of local dishes, which often feature fish, particularly swordfish. We recommend the handy restaurant "Baylik", with its bewildering array of seafood *antipasti*, such as *maccheroncini* pasta with fish ragù and grilled bread-crumbed crayfish. Nearby is "Bonaccorso", a stylish but completely unpretentious place. In

Reggio di Calabria. National Museum

the stores don't forget to buy the ultimate Calabrian delicacies, namely *mustica*, stuffed olives, eggplant preserved in oil, and as regards desserts, orange marmalade, dried figs with almonds and different types of *torrone* nougat, some with ice-cream.

1. Aspromonte and the Jasmin Coast
GAMBARIE. From Gallico Marina (not far from Reggio) you take the road for Aspromonte. Before turning your back on the sea, you must make a detour to the restaurant "Fata Morgana", with its stupendous view over the Straits of Messina. Then there is the very beautiful steep course of the Gallico river, whose exposed river bed is divided up into *nasiti*, used as places to grow citrus fruits and protected from the river by mud walls. Carry on along the road and visit "Da Nunziatina", an intimate and welcoming *trattoria* in Sant'Alessio. On the other hand, you could always go from Santo Stefano towards Aspromonte but stopping at Schiccio, where the

restaurant "Villa Rosa" has a colonial atmosphere, with a fireplace for the winter and open air dining in summer; their specialty is mushrooms. Thus you eventually reach Gambarie, which is a summer holiday resort situated between the forest and the National Park – and there is even a ski slope. We recommend the chalet "Miramonti".

BIANCO. The winding but spectacular road across the Aspromonte mountain passes by Delianuova and Platì and brings the visitor finally to Jonio a Bovalino and then almost immediately to Bianco. The fame of this ancient village is connected to the wine of the same name, and we recommend you try it at "Stelitano", which has an organic wine *cantina*. For those wishing to stay, an excellent combination of good food and comfort can be had at the hotel "Vittoria". Here artichokes are the local specialty.

BOVA MARINA. Traveling along the Jasmin Coast with its fields of jasmin, you come to the flourishing center of Bova Marina, a green heaven full of gardens, palms and bergamot plants. For those wishing to take an excursion out in the Aspromonte, you should go to Mount Scafi where the town of Condofuri stands, the last bastion of the *grecanica* (Greekanic) language, itself a direct descendent of Ancient Greek. In the village of Amen-

dola, sited inside the National Park, the restaurant "Il Bergamotto" offers excellent rural cuisine.

MELITO DI PORTO SALVO. On the southernmost end of the coast, Melito di Porto Salvo is best known for its bergamot cultivation, which was introduced into the area in the 1400s. Try the restaurant "Casina dei Mille". The cuisine is divided equally between sea and mountain, and includes home-made pasta with swordfish, eggplant, pork ragù and other Aspromonte meats. For spectacular views visit to Pentedattilo, a semi-abandoned village at the foot of a limestone cliff.

2. From coast to coast

SCILLA. Scilla is famed for the mythical monster with six heads from which Odysseus only just escaped. Today the peak is crowned by a castle, and the seashore plays host to boats fishing for swordfish. For haute fish cuisine, of all the sea-front restaurants you should visit "U Baìs-La Grotta Azurra" and "La Pescatora". Other local specialties are the rare *verdello* lemon and the *zibibbo* grape, from which a sweet white wine is made.

BAGNARA CALABRA. Set in the center of the "Purple Coast", Bagnara is known for its variations on the swordfish theme, including macaroni with swordfish sauce, swordfish steaks roasted or broiled and swordfish crepes in different

AGRITURISMI

Condofuri
★🏠 Il Bergamotto
at Amendolea
☎ 0965727213
Siderno
Da Zio Salvatore
at Siderno Superiore
via Annunziata 1/3
☎ 0964385330

WINE PRODUCERS

Casignana
Francesco
Stelitano
contrada Palazzi 1
☎ 0964913023

SHOPPING

Reggio di
Calabria
Giuseppe Fazia
viaTommasini 26
☎ 096523823
Bakery.
Pasticceria
G. Malavenda
via S. Caterina 87
☎ 096548638
Sweets and pastries.
Pasticceria
P. Caridi
via Sbarre Centrali 263
☎ 0965591796
Sweets and pastries.
Pratticò
via Saracinello 42
☎ 0965640477
Cheeses and
dairy products.
Cittanova
Sapori di Calabria
via D. Cavaliere 54
☎ 0966661702
Olive oil and typical
products.
Gioiosa Jonica
Golosìa
at Gioiosa Marina
piazza Zaleuco
☎ 0964416463
Ice-creams.
Gelateria
Pisciuneri
at Gioiosa Marina
piazza Plebiscito 10
☎ 096451272
Ice-creams.

guises. The "Kerkyra" restaurant is interesting for the Greek dishes which it serves and its moderately creative approach. Bagnara is also renowned for its sweets, such as *mostaccioli* or *'nzuddi* (honey cookies) and *torrone* nougats.

PALMI. The town is on a high plateau, the Marina is at sea level, and there is small beach in between the rocks. In Rizziconi, on the way towards Gioia Tauro, in the Audelleria neighborhood, you should sample the excellent cuisine offered by the "Osteria Campagnola della Spina".

POLISTENA. A timeless town, Polistena has checkerboard streets and eighteenth – and nineteenth-century houses in abundance. Take the road from here to San Giorgio Morgeto to eat the excellent food offered by the *trattoria* "La Scaletta".

GIOIOSA JONICA. In Mammola, an ancient town with closely-packed houses, you should eat in the gourmet "Da Ettore" restaurant, which serves a lovely leg of boar roast in a wood oven. The next town, Gioia Jonica, with its seventeenth- and eighteenth-century buildings – including a fabulous ice-cream parlor, "Pisciuneri" – is a fortified village on a cliff. Go to the marina to drink some wine and to try the local "Micu 'i Cola". Have lunch at "Rica-Roka", and ice-creams at "Golosìa".

STILO. Take a detour to the north to Roccella Jonica to visit the ancient, uninhabited town and the remains of the castle. Go further in, and on to Stilo, an old town with its one solitary Byzantine church, La Cattolica. At Bivongi eat at the "Vecchia Miniera" restaurant, espe-

cially the homemade pasta with olives and sausage or goat's meat sauce, followed by a Marmàrico trout.

Calabria Bergamot

SIDERNO. Medieval in origin, Siderno has narrow streets and old houses. Facing the valley, the homely "Sa Zio Salvatore" restaurant offers cheeses, charcuterie, good farmhouse bread and wine from the cellar. In the countryside there is the restaurant "Al Rifugio", offering solid farmhouse cooking. For a sea view, eat at "Il Gabbiano", and for atmosphere, try "L'Antica Hostaria".

LOCRI. A farming center on the northernmost edge of the bergamot cultivation area, Locri has recently become a bathing resort. Don't forget to visit the excavations of *Locri Epizefiri* and the museum. As for cuisine, dishes related to sheep and goat farming are excellent, notably cheeses (*pecorino* and *ricotta* from Ciminà) and lamb and goat's meat.

GERACE. Positioned high on a cliff and set back from the sea, Gerace has preserved its medieval atmosphere and the ancient arts of ceramics and weaving. The cathedral, the biggest in the whole of Calabria, has survived a thousand years of earthquakes. In midsummer in the countryside, they have exceedingly sweet and pleasant table grapes. The *soppressate* salamis are excellent. There are two fine *trattorie* in town: the popular "Lo Sparviero", with its many preserves and cask served wines, and "A Squella", which serves country cuisine. In "La Tavernetta" in Azzùria, they serve *maccheruni 'e casa* and crepes.

VIBO VALENTIA

A land and a cuisine which spans the mountains and the sea, and incorporates traditions and flavors from beyond its borders.

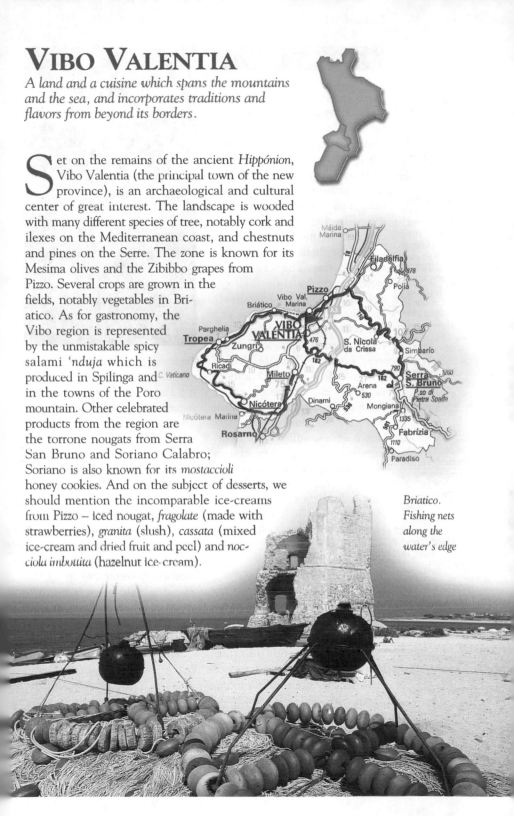

S et on the remains of the ancient *Hippónion*, Vibo Valentia (the principal town of the new province), is an archaeological and cultural center of great interest. The landscape is wooded with many different species of tree, notably cork and ilexes on the Mediterranean coast, and chestnuts and pines on the Serre. The zone is known for its Mesima olives and the Zibibbo grapes from Pizzo. Several crops are grown in the fields, notably vegetables in Briatico. As for gastronomy, the Vibo region is represented by the unmistakable spicy salami *'nduja* which is produced in Spilinga and in the towns of the Poro mountain. Other celebrated products from the region are the torrone nougats from Serra San Bruno and Soriano Calabro; Soriano is also known for its *mostaccioli* honey cookies. And on the subject of desserts, we should mention the incomparable ice-creams from Pizzo – iced nougat, *fragolate* (made with strawberries), *granita* (slush), *cassata* (mixed ice-cream and dried fruit and peel) and *nocciola imbottita* (hazelnut ice-cream).

Briatico.
Fishing nets
along the
water's edge

Gourmet Tours

HOTELS AND
RESTAURANTS

Vibo Valentia
501 Hotel ★★★
Il Corallo ¶¶¶
loc. Madonnella
☎ 0963439 51
Approdo ¶¶
a Vibo Marina
via Roma 22
☎ 0963572640
Maria Rosa ¶¶
a Vibo Marina
via Toscana 13/15
☎ 0963572538
Daffinà ¶
via S. Ruba 20
☎ 0963592444
Il Fortino ¶
via Vespucci 39
☎ 0963572515
Drapia
L'Uliveto ¶¶
a Brattirò
c.da Catafari
☎ 096368006
Mileto
Il Camino ¶
a Lenzo della Corte
☎ 0963338505
Il Normanno ¶
via Duomo 12
☎ 0963336398
San Pietro ¶
S.S. 18, loc. S. Pietro
☎ 0963367756
Nicotera
Gabbiano ¶
viale Stazione 35
☎ 096381732
Pizzo
🔲 Grillo ★★★
riviera Prangi 10
☎ 0963531632
Marinella ★★★
riviera Prangi
☎ 0963534864
Isolabella ¶¶
riviera Prangi
☎ 0963264128
🔲 Medusa ¶
via M. Salomone
☎ 0963531203
Ricadi
Punta Faro ★★★
via Grotticelle
☎ 0963663139
Fattoria ¶
at Torre Ruffo (km 5)
☎ 0963663070

VIBO VALENTIA. Descendant of the Greek *Hippónion*, Vibo Valentia dominates the Tyrrhenian Sea from the vantage point of its high plain. On what in ancient times used to be the acropolis (now surrounded by the attractive medieval quarter) stands the Norman castle, from which you get some remarkable views. Inside the castle is the museum which recounts the thousand years of the town's history. The surrounding areas are renowned for their excellent cheeses, particularly *pecorino*. The local cuisine is a fine balance of sea and land. We recommend "Il Corallo" (in the very good "501 Hotel") and "Daffinà", for simple and authentic dishes. But you must not miss the elegant restaurant "L'Approdo" in Vibo Marina. On offer here is some stunning fish cuisine, most notably anchovy and eggplant tart, grouper soup in the Vibo style, and tuna with Tropea onions. In the port, "Maria Rosa" is well known. It has three Art Nouveau dining areas with al fresco dining in summer.

1. From the Serre to the two Gulfs

SERRA SAN BRUNO. The name tells the story of the place, set as it is in the Serre mountain chain and with its Certosa (charterhouse), founded in 1091 by the Benedictine, Bruno di Colonia. Today Serra San Bruno is characterized by its fir and beech trees and is a pleasant holiday resort which offers robust mountain cuisine, predominantly mushroom dishes (they still use the, now rare, growing process of cultivat-

Pizzo. View from the Gulf of Sant'Eufemia

ing the mushrooms on certain porous mycelium-bearing rocks). The exception to the mountain rule is the spaghetti noodles in the Serre style with tuna and anchovies, derived from the Certosa's connections with the towns on the coast below. Other typical features of the place are its desserts and candies, including *cumpittu*, a soft nougat covered with sesame seeds, *'nzullo*, almond cookies baked in the shape of San Biagio's bishop's crook, and the Amaro dei Certosini, a remarkable herbal liquor sold at the priory. For those in search of a good meal, the two best places are "Certosa" and "Kursaal". At Spadola, on the road which descends to the Angitola plain, you could try the "Taverna dei Borboni".

PIZZO. The Aragonese towers survey the gulf of Sant'Eufemia with its fishing boats and bathers, representing the fishing and tourism that have sustained the local economy for some time. From Pizzo you should visit the Matrice church with its Gagini sculptures, and the castle. In addition to this, there are several opportunities to taste the local fish cuisine; at the "Medusa" restaurant, for example, which serves old tunny recipes reworked and adapted to modern tastes. "L'Isola Bella", one of the most chic addresses in the area, faces the sea at Riviera Prangi. We particularly recommend you try "Casa Janca", an *agriturismo* restaurant set in pleasant surroundings and offering good peasant dishes, including vegetarian options and some fish dishes, for example *licurdia* (onion soup), *fileza* (homemade *fusilli* noodles) with eggplant and *struncatura* with tuna roe. And do not miss the ice-cream for which Pizzo is so famous – indeed its truffle ice- cream has been exported to all the nearby regions. As for gourmet shopping, you should take home with you the salted tuna preserved in oil, and the fish roe.

TROPEA. This is a place of unimaginable beauty, with Monte Poro in the background and a seafront of rocks and beaches. Coming down from the Piazza Ercole to the cathedral, and then continuing down into the old town, you are treated to picturesque corners and breath-taking views of the Tyrrhenian Sea. This is the spectacle that can be enjoyed from "Pimm's", a celebrated local venue situated in a fourteenth-century palace, with an excellent low-price menu and good local wines. Of the many local hotels, "Virgilio" is especially worth visiting for its convenience

and the stylishness of the restaurant. When walking through the center of town, you absolutely must sample the *granita* in the bar "Ariston", and also the eclairs stuffed with *crema* at "Filiardi". In the midst of all this sophistication, the local red onions (greatly enjoyed and widely exported) and the very sweet local table grapes provide a pleasant touch of color and tradition. In the shops you should ask for '*nduja*, the distinctive red pepper salami, produced at Spilinga and in the towns around Poro. We strongly recommend that you lengthen your visit slightly to include Capo Vaticano. It has excellent, well- served beaches and good opportunities for eating well, at the restaurants "Punta Faro" and "La Fattoria", which is at San Nicolò di Ricadi. In the coastal hinterland, at Brattirò, there is the *trattoria* "Uliveto".

NICOTERA. From this vantage point, above a sharp drop down into the sea, you get a spectacular view that stretches from Aspromonte to Sicily. All around the village there are vines, citrus fruit trees, olives trees and vegetable gardens. Here the restaurant "Il Gabbiano" offers simple and authentic cuisine.

MILETO. The town's vast central piazza and the broad, rectilinear streets are clear signs of the reconstruction which took place after the earthquake of 1783. You can get good home cooking at the restaurants "Normanno" and "San Pietro".

Malvasia Bianca

HOTELS AND RESTAURANTS

Serra San Bruno
Certosa ★★
via Alfonso Scrivo 6
☎ 096371538
Kursaal ⍾
piazza Guido
☎ 096371089
Spadola
**Taverna
dei Borboni** ⍾⍾
via Conte Ruggero
☎ 096374300
Tropea
Virgilio ★★★ 🚗📺
viale Tondo
☎ 096361978
Pimm's ⍾⍾
largo Migliarese 2
☎ 0963666105

AGRITURISMI

Drapia
Torre Galli 🚗
contrada S. Rocco
Moccina 1
☎ 096367254
Pizzo
Agrimare 🚗📺
at Colamaio
☎ 0963534880
Casa Janca
riviera Prangi
☎ 0963264364

SHOPPING

Tropea
Bar Ariston
corso V. Emanuele 8
☎ 096362820
Excellent "granita".
Bar Filardi
largo S. Giuseppe
☎ 096361106
Sweet and pastries.

SICILY
THE FLAVORS OF THE MEDITERRANEAN

A land of contrasts at the crossroads of civilization, whose cuisine is also one of its treasures – from the coast with its tuna and swordfish to the interior with its mountain flavors, each part of the island offers memorable food.

S icily is more than one island and has many souls and many regions – the fruits of multiple influences. And yet its geographical isolation makes it unique and immediately identifiable.

Trapani.
Scopello

LAND OF CONTRASTS
Although the product of a wild and occasionally deadly natural environment, Sicily seems to have been tamed by man, whilst at the same time torn apart by the ravages of time. There are many con-

trasting climates, from mountain snow to sunny beaches. Locals fish for tuna in the deep waters of the Mediterranean and swordfish from the straits. The vines on the hills provide excellent wines, the mountains are used as pastures for sheep, whose milk is used in cheese. In the mountainous land around Etna, with its vines and DOC wines, they also harvest almonds, pistachios, pine nuts and hazelnuts, as well as mushrooms, honey and citrus fruits. Near Syracuse, the chalky soil produces not only olives but also carob and figs, whilst in Ragusa it is the cattle, sheep and cereals which form the focus of cooking. The river valleys and plains are also favorite spots for growing olives and garden vegetables.

Sicilian blood oranges

SICILIAN CUISINE IS COMPLETELY HYBRID

Many of the dishes can be traced back to a single source, but there is a multitude of variations on each one. With couscous they eat fish, while *baccalà* (dried cod) and stockfish are cooked in unusual ways, and in mixed vegetable *caponata* the usual chicken is replaced with eggplant. In addition to new ways of cooking old dishes, there are also many different national traditions which can be recognized in the mixing of the flavors. From the Arabs came the use of sweet and sour, the use of dried fruit such as sultanas and pine nuts in first course pastas, and the appearance of almonds and honey in dessert recipes, and from the Spanish a Baroque taste for excess, and colored desserts. From Greece came the traditional country dishes typical of Ragusa and Syracuse. And from the French came the introduction of the onion. Local desserts and candies can be divided up into three basic fundamental groups – desserts made in convents (such as those prepared for religious festivals), the Arab tradition centering on almonds, with the addition of other ingredients such as sugars and sorbets, and the introduction of cream and stuffings was the work of the Swiss.

STREET FOOD AND FAMOUS CHEFS

With a tradition of French chefs or "Monsu" as cooks for the island's high society, and of English wine merchants (such as the inventor of Marsala), Sicilian cuisine has always had a sense of adventure, especially in the cities. Today this innovation rests upon a recently discovered taste for forgotten traditional recipes, which good chefs know how to embellish. However, food sold on the streets plays a big part in the culinary traditions here. There is a public desire to have dishes available all the hours of the day and to be able to eat them in the street. These dishes include *polipari* from the Palermo marina, *panellari* and *friggitorie, focaccia* bread from Messina, plus *scacciate* from Catania and *scaccie* from Ragusa and Syracuse, and traditional selz drinks which can be had in the booths and piazzas of Catania.

Sicily - Typical products

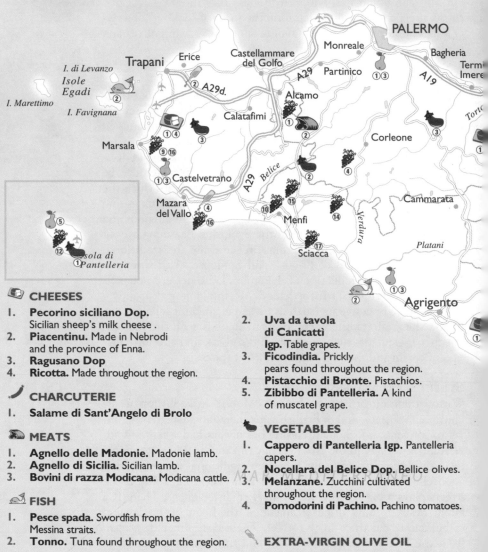

I. di Ustica

Scale 1:1 250 000

0   15   30 km

MAR TIRRENO

PALERMO

Monreale · Bagheria · Term Imere

Trapani · Erice · Castellammare del Golfo · Partinico · A19

I. di Levanzo
Isole Egadi
I. Marettimo
I. Favignana

A29d. · Alcamo · Corleone

Calatafimi

Marsala

Castelvetrano

Mazara del Vallo · Belice · Menfi · Cammarata

Sciacca · Platani

Isola di Pantelleria

Agrigento

CHEESES

1. **Pecorino siciliano Dop.** Sicilian sheep's milk cheese .
2. **Piacentinu.** Made in Nebrodi and the province of Enna.
3. **Ragusano Dop**
4. **Ricotta.** Made throughout the region.

CHARCUTERIE

1. **Salame di Sant'Angelo di Brolo**

MEATS

1. **Agnello delle Madonie.** Madonie lamb.
2. **Agnello di Sicilia.** Sicilian lamb.
3. **Bovini di razza Modicana.** Modicana cattle.

FISH

1. **Pesce spada.** Swordfish from the Messina straits.
2. **Tonno.** Tuna found throughout the region.

FRUIT

1. **Arancia rossa di Sicilia Igp.** Sicilian blood oranges.

2. **Uva da tavola di Canicattì Igp.** Table grapes.
3. **Ficodindia.** Prickly pears found throughout the region.
4. **Pistacchio di Bronte.** Pistachios.
5. **Zibibbo di Pantelleria.** A kind of muscatel grape.

VEGETABLES

1. **Cappero di Pantelleria Igp.** Pantelleria capers.
2. **Nocellara del Belice Dop.** Bellice olives.
3. **Melanzane.** Zucchini cultivated throughout the region.
4. **Pomodorini di Pachino.** Pachino tomatoes.

EXTRA-VIRGIN OLIVE OIL

1. **Monti Iblei Dop**
2. **Valli Trapanesi Dop**
3. **Valdemone**
4. **Val di Mazara**

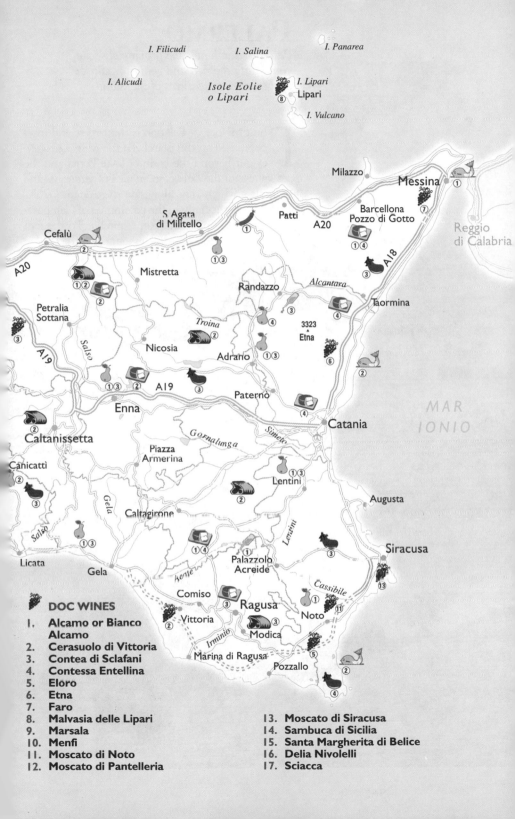

I. Stromboli

I. Filicudi   I. Salina   I. Panarea

I. Alicudi

Isole Eolie
o Lipari   I. Lipari
Lipari

⑧

I. Vulcano

Milazzo

Messina ①

S Agata
di Militello   Patti   A20   Barcellona
Pozzo di Gotto   ⑦

Cefalù ①④

②

A20

Mistretta   ①③

Randazzo   Alcantara   A18

①② ②   ③   Taormina

Petralia
Sottana   Troina   ④ ④   3323
Etna

③   Salso   ②

A19   Nicosia   Adrano ①③   ⑥ ②

①③ ② A19   Paternò

Enna   ④

Caltanissetta   Gornalunga   Simeto   Catania

②   Piazza
Armerina   MAR
IONIO

Canicattì   Gela   Lentini ①③   Augusta

② ③   ②

Caltagirone

Salso   ③

①③   ①④   Palazzolo
Acreide ①   ③   Siracusa

Licata   Gela   ⑬

Comiso   Cassibile   ①

DOC WINES   Vittoria   Ragusa   Noto ⑪

1. **Alcamo or Bianco
   Alcamo**   ②   ③   Modica
2. **Cerasuolo di Vittoria**   Marina di Ragusa   ⑤
3. **Contea di Sclafani**   Pozzallo   ②
4. **Contessa Entellina**
5. **Eloro**   ④
6. **Etna**
7. **Faro**
8. **Malvasia delle Lipari**
9. **Marsala**
10. **Menfi**
11. **Moscato di Noto**
12. **Moscato di Pantelleria**

13. **Moscato di Siracusa**
14. **Sambuca di Sicilia**
15. **Santa Margherita di Belice**
16. **Delia Nivolelli**
17. **Sciacca**

Reggio
di Calabria

PALERMO

Palermo dominates the provincial scene, combining the rich and genuin tradition of the culinary features of the island.

Below: panorama of the Madonie

The province of Palermo is the largest and most populated on the island. To the west it stretches out beyond the basin of Lake Poma and the upper valleys of the Belice, in an area of vineyards and olive groves which runs alongside the Alcamo DOC region, particularly in the communes of Camporeale, Partinico and San Cipirello. To the east lie the Madonie mountains – the land of the olive, which aims to add a DOC to the DOP for olive oil. Here lamb

562

and mutton form the nucleus of the cuisine. To the south of the Madonie lie the DOC area known as Contea di Sclafani. Along the coast, from Termini Imerese to Palermo, olive trees are interspersed with fruit (occasionally citrus) trees, with Bagheria as the main commercial center. To the south, the territory includes other olive growing areas, along the San Leonardo and Mendola valleys, and wine producing areas such as the DOC Contessa Entellina on the border with Agrigento. Palermo's unforgettable dishes include pasta with sardines, anelletti pasta cooked in the oven, tuna with *sfinciuni focaccia* and desserts such as *cassata* cake, *cannoli* (cream-stuffed pastries), *Martorana* fruits, and the savory *arancini* (rice balls with *mozzarella* in the center), *sfinciuni focaccia*, vegetables in batter and *guastedde* breads.

Gourmet Tours

PALERMO. The city of Norman churches, red domes amidst the palms, and glimmering mosaics, has many beautiful sights to offer.. You can also admire the sculpture of the Kouros of Selinunte, the famous bust of Eleanor of Aragon by the fifteenth-century sculptor Francesco Laurana, and the Serpotta stuccos in the churches of San Domenico and San Cita. Other lovely sights include the Italian gardens of the Villa Giulia; the exotica of the Botanical Gardens; the long boulevards at La Favorita with Monte Pellegrino in the background; the Piazza dei Quattro Canti, in the heart of the old town, and the Vucciria, the oldest and liveliest of the city's markets. Gourmets should try the fare at the *rosticcerie* and booths, such as *arancini* rice balls, and *pani ca' meusa*, stuffed with tasty beef innards. There is also no shortage of good restaurants. We recommend "Santandrea", a new restaurant, with its exceedingly light fried fish, its carefully chosen pastas and main course fish to suit all tastes. "Dal Maestro del Brodo" offers the traditional menu of meat and fresh fish. Then there are the older eateries immersed in the town's history. First of all comes "L'Antica Focacceria San Francesco" (established 1834), the place where the Italian Risorgimento was planned and where Garibaldi sat

HOTELS AND
RESTAURANTS

Palermo
Villa Igiea G.H.
- 1905 ★★★
salita Belmonte 43
☎ 091543744
Charleston ¶¶¶¶
piazzale Ungheria 30
☎ 091321366
Grande Albergo
e delle Palme
- 1874 ★★★
via Roma 398
☎ 091583933
Charleston -
Le Terrazze ¶¶¶
at Mondello (km 10)
viale Regina Elena
☎ 091450171
Il Ristorantino ★🐜
¶¶¶, piazzale
De Gasperi 19
☎ 091512861
Scuderia ¶¶¶
viale del Fante 9
☎ 091520323
Bye Bye Blues ¶¶
at Mondello (km 10)
via del Garofalo 23
☎ 0916841415
Santandrea ¶¶
piazza S. Andrea 4
☎ 091334999
Trattoria Piazza
Magione ¶¶
via Castrofilippo 10
☎ 0916162024
Ai Cascinari ¶
via Di Ossuna 43/45
☎ 0916519804
Dal Maestro
del Brodo ¶
via Pannieri 7
☎ 091329523
Il Delfino ¶
at Sferracavallo (km 13)
via Torretta 80
☎ 091530282
Bagheria
Don Ciccio ¶
via del Cavaliere 87
☎ 091932442
Bolognetta
Mulinazzo ¶¶
contrada Mulinazzo
☎ 0918724870

HOTELS AND RESTAURANTS

Castelbuono
⭐🍴 **Vecchio Palmento** 🍴
via Failla 4
☎ 0921672099

Cefalù
La Brace 🍴
via XXV Novembre 10
☎ 0921423570

Isnello
⭐🍴 **Piano Torre Park Hotel** ★★★ 🍴
at Piano Torre (km 8)
☎ 0921662671

Monreale
La Botte 🍴
S.S. 186
contrada Lenzitti
☎ 091414051

⭐🍴 **Taverna del Pavone** 🍴
vicolo Pensato 18
☎ 0916406209

Santa Flavia
⭐🍴 **La Grotta** 🍴🍴
Parco Archeologico
di Solunto
☎ 091903213

Muciara - Nello El Greco 🍴🍴
at Porticello
via Roma 105
☎ 091957868

⭐🍴 **Antica Trattoria dell'Arco** 🍴
at Porticello
largo Pescheria 16
☎ 091957758

Ustica (island of)
Mamma Lia 🍴
via S. Giacomo 1
☎ 0918449594

Mario 🍴
piazza Umberto 121
☎ 0918449505

together with the anti-Bourbon Francesco Crispi. For sweets, there is the pastry shop "Mazzara" (est. 1911), one of whose regulars used to be Tomasi di Lampedusa, the author of The Leopard. Next to this is the restaurant "Charleston", with its Art Nouveau atmosphere and refined cuisine, including grilled roulade of swordfish as its Buon Ricordo dish. As for lodgings, the highest expression of Palermo hotel chic is the "Grande Albergo e delle Palme" (est. 1874), designed by Basile, an architect of the Belle Epoque. Next comes the "Villa Igeia Grand Hotel" (est. 1905), another Belle Epoque mecca, with sea-view terraces and a surrounding park. Simply on its gastronomic merits, "Il Ristorantino", a quiet and discreet venue not far from the soccer ground, is a must. The cuisine features mostly fish. Next door near the Pulci market is the trattoria "Ai Cascinari", a reference point for lovers of folk cuisine. "La Scuderia", in the La Favorita zone, is a classy Buon Ricordo restaurant with the specialty merluzzetti alla ghiotta (cod cooked in a drip tray pan). As for shopping, there is a vast choice of bakeries offering everything from everyday bread, made with durum wheat flour to give the bread a strong golden crust, to sfinciuni focaccia topped with anchovies, tomato, primosale cheese, and black olives. Then, in addition to the complete range of island cheeses, there are specific preparations such as mulberry jam or apples with ginger, jams made from mandarin oranges and other much rarer citrus fruits such as

small lumia limes. Palermo is also famed for its anchovies preserved in salt and its "tuna milk"(dried tuna sperm sacs). For wines, we recommend the wine specialists "Picone", for their excellent selection and reasonable prices. Olive oil should be bought at the azienda "M. Barbera & Figli". And to close, there are the desserts, offered in all their remarkable varieties by the hundreds of bakeries here. Those staying in Palermo cannot leave without visiting Mondello, once a fishing village but now a garden city with elegant bathing establishments. Here you can eat in the restaurant "Bye Bye Blues" set on the sea front, with its excellent appetizers. Another restaurant worth visiting is "Charleston - Le Terrazze", the summer address of the previously-mentioned restaurant in town. A little further along the coast, at Sferracavallo, the "Delfino" restaurant is excellent value for money.

1. In the Palermo hinterland

MONREALE. On a spur towering over the Conca d'Oro, the settlement of Monreale not only has a Norman cathedral with Sicilian/Venetian mosaics and a Benedictine monastery, but is also one of the most spectacular sites in Sicily. In an eighteenth-century palazzo, there is the "Taverna del Pavone", where the Puppella family offers traditional cuisine. In a nearby hamlet in the countryside, "La Botte" is a beautifully restored establishment for selling wine. In the nearby Virzì neighborhood stands the local grape and vine research laboratories, the "Cantina Sperimentale Istituto Regionale della Vite e del Vino".
PIANA DEGLI ALBANESI. The Alba-

nians in question are descendants of those who fled the Turkish invasion of Albania in 1488. The culture of the founders can still be seen in the local dialect and in the Greek rites at the church of S. Demetrio. On the main avenue there is the Anthropological Museum. The "Di Noto" cake shop is a good point of reference for those who wish to get in contact with the locals. Those taking a detour via Camporeale can visit the "Adelkam" *cantina* at Rapitalà. CORLEONE. Set on the road to Agrigento in the local uplands, Corleone is an important farming center, known to the outside world as the home town of the Mafia family in the Godfather films. Peeking out from the strangely eroded yellow rocks are the "Castello Soprano" – on which stands the Saracen Tower – and the "Castello Sottano", alone on the bank of the river that flows around the town. The area itself is renowned for its *caciocavallo* cheese, made from full milk, for both grating and for eating. "Il Mulinazzo" in Bolognetta provides an excellent culinary experience. The restaurant sets itself apart through its wine, the service and some of the lightest and most modern cooking on the island. The menu includes fish dishes, such as *timballetti di tagliolini*

con filetti di triglia e finocchietti (small timbales of *tagliolini* noodles with fillets of mullet and small bulbs of fennel), *involtini di pesce con caponata croccante* (envelopes of fish with succulent *caponata* vegetable stew), and millefeuille *sfoglina* with cold custard and vanilla ice-cream.

2. Along the coast to the Madonie

BAGHERIA. At the peak of Mount Catalfano, which stands as a boundary to the gulf of Palermo, amidst citrus, medlar and olive trees you can see the country houses of the nobility of Palermo, still splendid despite the ravages caused by the surrounding modern constructions. Villa Palagonia and Villa Valguarnera are the most famous, whilst the Villa Cattolica (where the painter Renato Guttuso is buried) has a gallery of contemporary art. In the surrounding countryside there is one *trattoria* which keeps very close to old traditions – "Don Ciccio". Here the hearty dishes (which used to be served to passing carriages) include an unforgettable *pasta con le sarde* (pasta with sardines). In Porticello, a seaside village successfully converted to tourism, there are two good resturants: the "Muciara – Nello el Greco", an elegant rus-

Mondello

AGRITURISMI

Castellana Sicula
Feudo Tudia
at Borgo Tudia
☎ 0934673029
Montelepre
Don Vito - La Fattoria del Sorriso
at Piano Aranci
☎ 0918784111
Partinico
Arabesque
at Manostalla
☎ 0918787755
Petralia Sottana
Monaco di Mezzo 🏠 📷
contrada Monaco
☎ 0934673949

WINE PRODUCERS

Camporeale
Adelkam
contrada Rapitalà
☎ 092436115
Casteldaccia
Duca di Salaparuta
via Nazionale S.S. 113
☎ 0919451 1
Monreale
Cantina Sperimentale Istituto Regionale della Vite e del Vino
contrada Virzì
☎ 0916278223

OLIVE OIL PRODUCERS

Palermo
M. Barbera & Figli
via E. Amari 55
☎ 091582900
Scillato
Sausa
contrada Firrione
☎ 0921663028
Ventimiglia di Sicilia
Manzella Iannello
via Garibaldi 18
☎ 0918209735

SHOPPING

Palermo
Antica Focacceria
S. Francesco - 1834
via A. Paternostro 58
☎ 091320264
Bread and "focaccia".
Enoteca Picone
via Marconi 36
☎ 091331300
Wines.
I Peccatucci di
Mamma Andrea
via Principe di Scordia 67
☎ 091334835
Jams, distilled spirits,
almond sweets.
Panificio Ingrassia
via Dante 42
☎ 091584092
Bakery.
Pasticceria Cappello
via Colonna Rotta 68
☎ 091489601
Sweets and pastries.
Pasticceria
Mazzara - 1911
via Generale
Magliocco 15
☎ 091321443
Sweets and pastries.
Pasticceria
Scimone
via V. Miceli 18/b
☎ 091584448
another shop in
Mondello,
viale Regina Elena 61
☎ 0916841788
Sweets and pastries.
Marineo
Macelleria
G. Pulizzotto
via Falcone e
Borsellino 30
☎ 0918725040
Local meat and
charcuterie.
Piana degli
Albanesi
Pasticceria
Di Noto
via Portella della
Ginestra 79
☎ 0918571195
Sweets and pastries.
Ustica (island of)
Bar Centrale
piazza Umberto 18
☎ 0918449
Cakes and pastries.

tic venue with a seafood menu and serious wine list, and "Antica Trattoria dell'Arco", also with a menu of very fresh fish served by the family that owns the establishment. In Santa Flavia, near the Salunto archaeological site, "La Grotta" restaurant is excellent value for money. Further on, in Casteldaccia, the "Duca di Salaparuta" *cantina* is especially worth visiting, most notably because "Corvo", the first modern Sicilian wine (invented in 1824 by Giuliano Alliata), comes from here. His descendants still carry the torch by making excellent wine, from the aristocratic reserve labels to the sparkling whites, and an ancient bitter liqueur called Ala.

CEFALÙ. On the road to Messina the first town of note is Termini Imerese, descended from the Greek *Himera*. Further inland, in the olive growing region, stands Caccamo, a fortified town in a beautiful setting. Beyond that a towering cliff informs visitors that Cefalù is next, with its ancient houses on the sea front and the Norman cathedral, which houses breathtaking golden mosaics. Another remarkable sight, in the Barone di Mandralisca's collection, is the *Ritratto ignoto* (Portrait of an unknown man) by Antonello da Messina. As for fine eating, the central restaurant "La Brace" stands out. It is small, refined and famed for its wonderful cuisine.

CASTELBUONO. In the valley of the Castelbuono torrent stands Isnello. Here we recommend the "Piano Torre Park Hotel", set as it is within an old building. The restaurants offers the savors of the hinterland, and the *pasta fresca al ragu di maiale*

(fresh pasta with pork ragout) is not to be missed. At the foot of Pizzo Carbonara stands Castelbuono. In the surrounding countryside, you simply must stay at the "Vecchio Palmento", a fine eighteenth-century building with a remarkable garden featuring citrus fruits and jasmin plants. The cooking features the excellent produce of the *azienda*, notably the white meat, game and mushrooms.

PATRALIA SOTTANA. A holiday resort and starting point for visits to the Madonie National Park, Patralia Sottana takes its name Sottana (lower) from the fact that its sister town Petralia Soprana, which affords good views, is higher up. Lower Petralia is famous for the charcuterie made from the black pigs reared in semi-domesticity in the woods of the Madonie. The road back goes via Collesano before reaching the coast. Olive oil enthusiasts should make a detour via Scillate to visit the master oil makers at the "Sausa" *azienda*.

3. Ustica

The highest point on Ustica island is the peak of Monte Guardia dei Turchi (248 m.). Amongst the rocky outcrops you can spot vines, fig trees and areas where vegetables are cultivated. All around the island there are pockets of deep sea packed with underwater life – indeed Ustica plays host to Italy's first marine park. Naturally, the cuisine is almost entirely based on the produce of the sea, although wild rabbit also figures on menus. "Mamma Lia" and "Mario" are two obligatory *trattorie*. And in Piazza Umberto, the "Bar Centrale" offers a formidable array of pastries and cakes.

AGRIGENTO

The wheat and almonds of the Valley of the Temples, and the sea provide the quintessential image of this fertile and confident province.

I n a diagonal line set on the coast, very much resembling Lazio, the province of Agrigento is wedged between Palermo and the Nisseno region. And the province boasts numerous towns famed for their grapes and DOC wines (Sambuca di Sicilia, Menfi, Santa Margherita dei Belice) and the whole of the Agrigento area forms part of the Inzolia wine-growing region, the source of many white wines. Given the broad local spread of sheep and goat rearing, sheep's milk *ricotta*, *caciu* and *casccavallu all' argintera* cheeses can be found almost everywhere. The zone is also known for its olive oil, particularly that of the DOP Nocellara de Belice variety, and for its shelled and peeled almonds, known as *mandorla 'ntrita'*.

Signorio

VINO DA TAVOLA BIANCO

750 ml e ITALIA 11,5% vol

HOTELS AND RESTAURANTS

Agrigento
★🍴 **Foresteria Baglio della Luna** ★★★
contrada Maddalusa
☎ 092251 1061
★🍴 **Le Caprice** 🍴
strada Panoramica
Templi 51
☎ 092226469
Leon d'Oro 🍴
viale Emporium 102
☎ 0922414400
Castrofilippo
Osteria del Cacciatore 🍴
contrada Torre
☎ 0922829824
Menfi
Vittorio 🍴
at Porto Palo (km 4)
via Friuli Venezia Giulia
☎ 092578381
Il Vigneto 🍴
at the cross-road to
Porto Palo
☎ 092571732
Montevago
Terme
Acqua Pia ★★
contrada Acque Calde
☎ 09539026
Pelagie (Islands)
★🍴 **Gemelli** 🍴
at Lampedusa
via Cala Pisana 2
☎ 0922970699
Caffè dell'Amicizia 🍴
at Lampedusa
via V. Emanuele 60
☎ 0922970149
Errera 🍴
at Linosa
Scalo Vecchio
☎ 0922972041
Sciacca
★🍴 **Hostaria del Vicolo** 🍴
vicolo Sammaritano 10
☎ 092523071

Gourmet Tours

AGRIGENTO. Tourists' attention is inevitably drawn to the large Doric temples which tower over the sea amidst the corn fields and almond trees. But there is also an important medieval town center and, at Porto Ercole, a monument in homage to Luigi Pirandello. The renowned playwright's body rests in the shade of the Mediterranean pine which marks his house in the village of Caos. The candy and cake shops are well-stocked with *cannoli*, *cassata* and *mostaccioli*. "Le Caprice" on the scenic Temple route is worth stopping at for its Agrigento cuisine. In the village of Maddelena, we recommend the "Foresteria Baglio della Luna", an old country residence with terraces commanding a panoramic view of the Valley of the Temples. On the Porto Ercole sea front (not far from the center) stands the "Leon d'Oro" restaurant, with its very reasonably- priced fish dishes and enormous selection of specialties, both local and otherwise. On the Statale 115, there is the *cantina* "Settesoli" with its DOC and IGT (*Indicazione Geografica Tipica*) label wines, which include the Bianco di Menfi, Feudo dei Fiori and Rosso Bonera.

The Almond Blossom Festival

1. From inland to Licata

RACALMUTO. Dominated by the castle of Chiaramontano, Racalmuto is the home town of the twentieth-century writer Leonardo Sciascia and renowned for its table grapes. In the same area, there are sulphur and rock salt mines, including the ancient Ghibelline sulphur mine.

CANICATTÌ. This agricultural village is famous for its eating grapes, which have earned an IGP (*Indicazione Giografica Protetta*) mark. At Castrofilippo the "Osteria del Cacciatore" serves meat grilled on a spit, and an excellent dish of tripe and potatoes.

NARO. Perched high on a hill with its solid fourteenth-century castle, Naro dominates the fertile Naro river valley. The medieval center is well worth a visit, with its buildings of golden sandy stone. Local products include citrus fruit, peanuts, almonds and excellent olive oil.

LICATA. Built on the right bank of the Salso river, Licata is an active commercial port, shifting tons of corn and sulphur every day. In the town visitors should not miss the main church and the Castel S. Angelo. In the village of Castel Pozzillo, the restaurant "Tenuta Barone La Lumìa" serves many local DOC wines.

2. From Eraclea to the Belice valley

SCIACCA. Passing back up the coast, visitors reach the excavations of Eraclea Minoa. Continuing along the Statale 115 you come to Sciacca, completely surrounded by its sixteenth-century walls and a maze of central streets, lanes and closed courtyard reminiscent of Arab countries. Here the famous products are preserved tuna, anchovies in salt and dwarf squids (*capuccetti*) preserved in oil and traditional almond sweets – the famed *cucchiteddi*. In the center of town, we recommend the "Hostaria del Vicolo", a simple but welcoming venue which serves updated traditional dishes, such as *sampietro panato al forno o alla mentuccia* (breaded John Dory roasted or with mint). Good wine is produced here. In the village of Scunchipani there is "Montalbano", a good *agriturismo* establishment.

MENFI. The town of the DOC wine of the same name, this Citta del Vino still possesses a medieval tower, although it has been greatly damaged by many earthquakes. But this does not diminish tourist interest in the zone, which also has its beaches at Porto Palo and its high quality wines. Excellent extra-virgin olive oil of the Biancolilla and Cerasuola variety can be found at the *azienda* "Ravidà". At the crossroads for Porto Palo stands the "Il Vigneto" restaurant (with "Vittorio" lodgings), which serves excellent fish dishes and has a reasonably-priced tourist menu.

SANTA MARGHERITA DI BELICE. A Città del Vino and worthy owner of a DOC label with a grand piazza full of monuments, Santa Margherita and its surroundings produce excellent must and prickly pear *mostarda* (preserve) which can be bought at the "Cooperativa Agricola Gattopardo". You can have a pleasant stay at the thermal waters known as "Acqua Pia". The hills and countryside are covered with olive, fig and prickly pear trees.

SAMBUCA DI SICILIA. The place renowned for its DOC label, Sambuca di Sicilia, has one of the best preserved Arab settlements on the island. In between the town and Menfi lies the *cantina* "Pianeta", one of the most interesting representatives of modern Sicilian wine producers. In the ancient *baglio* building, you can taste their wines, hybrids of traditional and international grape varieties.

CALTABELLOTA. This is the ancient Greek town of *Triocala* ('three fine things'). The three have been identified as the abundant fresh water springs, the grape- and olive-bearing land, and the impregnable cliffs. The principal church and the S. Pellegrino hermitage are of particular interest. If you take a short excursion to Burgio, you can buy the excellent olive oil of the Biancolilla, Cerasuola and Nocellara varieties from the "Piazza" *azienda*.

3. The Isole Pelagie

LAMPEDUSA. The island is a huge flat surface which slopes into the sea, with a rocky coastline and several caves. Once known for its sponges, Lampedusa is best known these days for its fishing. A restaurant worth visiting is "Gemelli", a pleasant venue in the Arab style with carefully presented dishes. "Caffè dell'Amicizia" is also worth a visit.

LINOSA. Of volcanic origin, the island of Linosa is dotted with brightly-colored houses. The restaurant "Errera" offers a cuisine matched to the seasons, including couscous, fish soup and lentil soup.

Cataratto grapes

AGRITURISMI

Sciacca
Montalbano 🍴
at Scunchipani
☎ 092580154

WINE PRODUCERS

Agrigento
Settesoli
S.S. 115
☎ 092577111
Licata
Barone La Lumia
contrada Castel Pozzillo
☎ 0922891709
Sciacca
Planeta
contrada Ulmo
☎ 091327965

OLIVE OIL PRODUCERS

Menfi
Azienda Agricola Ravidà
via Roma 173
☎ 092571109

SHOPPING

Santa Margherita di Belice
Cooperativa Agricola Gattopardo
contrada Luni
☎ 092538886
Preserves.
Santo Stefano Quisquina
La Casa del Formaggio
via Maranzano 11
☎ 0922982035
Typical cheeses.
Sciacca
Licata Conserve Alimentari
contrada Scunchipani
☎ 092521815
Preserves.

CALTANISSETTA

From the high Caltanissetta plain, in the heart of the island, to the southern coast, this province offers the whole range of Mediterranean flavors.

Cut in half at its narrowest point by the river Salso, Caltanissetta is made up of two completely different parts. The northern, internal side is hilly (indeed mountainous) and populated by hares, partridges and wild ducks stopping as they fly elsewhere, and is full of pastures, olive groves, vines and nut trees. To the south-west the hills drop down to the sea, and on the coast there are citrus fruit groves as well as olive groves and vines. Around the principal town, itself at an altitude of 568 meters above sea level, they grow the highly prized Nero d'Avala grapes, whilst around Riesi there is another wine producing area which has its own DOC, itself part of the larger Cerasuolo di Vittoria wine making area. The Caltanissetta specialties which you should not miss are as follows: *pollo con cacciocavallo* (chicken with *caciocavallo* cheese), baked *pangrattato* and lemon, *cavati* or *cavatiddi* (a sort of durum wheat gnocchi) and *tochetti* (small pieces of nougat).

Vineyards on the Caltanissetta high plains

Gourmet Tours

CALTANISSETTA. Set amongst the hills of the mining area, the city has a fine central piazza and baroque architecture. To begin with, you should visit the pastry shop "Romano". You should eat in the "Cortese" restaurant, with its typical Sicilian fish and mushroom cuisine. The *azienda* "Fratelli Averna" is based in the city, and they have been making their famous bitters since 1868, using a recipe handed down by a monk from the S. Spirito monastery.

1. The Valley of the Plane Trees

SAN CATALDO. This solid town nestles amongst olive groves, almond groves and vines. There are many olive oil presses in the area which are renowned for the quality of their product. At the station exit from the superstrada highway heading towards Agrigento there is a particularly good restaurant called "Al 124", where they serve excellent fresh fish. At Milena, a town in the center of the sulphur and rock salt mining area (but also studded with almond and olive trees), there is the restaurant "La Lanterna", a traditional *trattoria* serving authentic local cuisine.
VALLELUNGA PRATAMENO. Vallelunga is set in an enclave of the province of Caltanissetta, between the Palermo and Agrigento regions. The nearby village of Regaleali is the site of excellent vineyards belonging to the Tasca d'Almerita family, which has been making wines with Sicilian grapes since the middle of the nineteenth-century – but these days they allow admixtures of Chardonnay and Cabernet Sauvignon. You can sample excellent country cui-

sine in the village of Piraino at the "Al Castello" restaurant.
MUSSOMELI. A town with an interesting medieval center (known as the "Terravecchia"), Mussomeli is surrounded on all sides by fertile areas of olive, grape and almond cultivation.

2. Towards the sea

RIESI. A City of Wine, Riesi is one of the principal production centers of the DOC wine Cerasuolo di Vittoria. It is particulaly abundant in fruits, notably wine (Nero d'Avola and Frappato) and table grapes, peaches and pears. Excellent sweets are also on offer, notably: *pupi di zucchero* (sugar puppets), *cuccia* and marzipan fruits. From 20 August to 10 September they hold their fish and grape festival.
BUTERA. A picturesque town on a rocky hilltop dominating the Gela plain with and eleventh-century castle and a Palazzo Comunale with a fifteenth-century portal, Butera is also renowned for its sheep and cattle rearing.
GELA. It was only in 1929 that this town took the name Gela, after the ancient Greek colony which was founded in 689 BC. The petrochemical plants and the archaeological excavations sum up the extremes of the town's history. Indeed, in the area there is a great deal of interest in archaeological matters. In the center of town the "Aurora" restaurant serves excellent food and has *al fresco* dining in summer. On your return to Caltanissetta, it is possible to go through the large agricultural villages around Niscemi – where they grow *mallesi* almonds and cork trees – and through Mazzarino, with its citrus fruit trees, olive groves.

HOTELS AND RESTAURANTS

Caltanissetta
Cortese ¶¶
viale Sicilia 166
☎ 0934591686
Gela
Aurora ¶¶
piazza Vittorio Veneto 1
☎ 0933917711
Milena
La Lanterna ¶
via P. Nenni 8
☎ 0934933478
San Cataldo
Al 124 ¶¶
at the cross-road to
to the railway station
☎ 0934569037

AGRITURISMI

Resuttano
Al Castello
at Castello
☎ 0934673815
Santa Caterina Villarmosa
Al Castello
contrada Piraino
☎ 0934671699

WINE PRODUCERS

Vallelunga Pratameno
Tasca d'Almerita
contrada Regaleali
☎ 0921544011

SHOPPING

Caltanissetta
Fratelli Averna
via Xiboli 345
☎ 093472111
Famous for their bitters
("Amaro Averna").
Pasticceria Romano-Rair
corso Umberto 147
☎ 093421402
Sweets and pastries such as "cassate" and "cannoli".

CATANIA

Our journey takes us from the town, the epicenter of culinary interest, to the sea at Riviera dei Ciclopi, then through the vines and woods around Etna.

The Simeto river splits the province in two as it runs down into the broad and fertile plain of Catania. This natural land of the citrus fruit has left room for the cultivation of the prized Sicilian eggplant, celery, artichokes, sweet peppers, dwarf kidney beans, *bastardo* (purple cauliflower) and other vegetables. South of the river, between Ramacca, Palagonia and Scordia, is the land of blood oranges (which have the IGP label). Even further south, the province slopes down towards the Iblei mountains to the east and the Erei mountains to the west. North of the river Simeto rises the restless Etna, the biggest volcano in Europe, on whose slopes grow the Adrano sweet almond, the Bronte pistachio and

Catania.
Isola dei Ciclopi

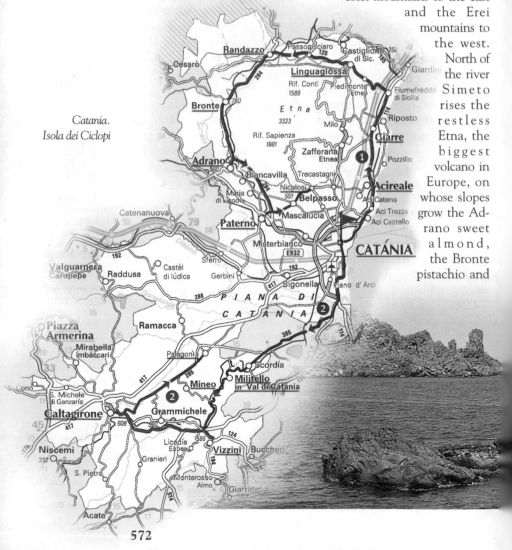

the Randazzo, Castiglione and Linguaglossa hazelnuts. But the land also gives the prized DOP olive oil, Val Demone and some ancient wines (from before 5B.C.) that come under the DOC Etna and are full-bodied and perfumed. They are made from indigenous vines (the Nerello Mascalese and Nerello Cappuccio reds, and the Carricante white). You always get reds from Randazzo and Linguaglossa, dry whites from Linguaglossa and Piedimonte Etneo, and the Bianco Superiore from Milo. Provincial dishes you must try include *maccheroncini alla Norma* (*maccheroncini* pasta with fried eggplant, tomato sauce and salted *ricotta*) dedicated to the great composer Bellini (for his opera Norma), *ripiddu nivicatu* (snowy lapillus) and *risotto nero con ricotta fresca e salsa di peperoncino* (black *risotto* with fresh *ricotta* cheese, and chili pepper sauce) served piled up on the plate to look like Etna. Also try *caponata* (mixed vegetables fried in olive oil, sprinkled with vinegar, then once on the plate sprinkled with olives, anchovies and capers), anchovies and sardines *a beccafico* (the fish are marinated in vinegar, stuffed with *pecorino* cheese and egg, coated in breadcrumbs and deep fried) and savory *sfinci* (*focaccia*) with *ricotta* or anchovies. The cakes to eat here include *olivette* and *torrone* (nougat) *di Sant'Agata*, *minni 'i virgini* (made between the 3rd and 5th February), marzipan, *ossi di morto*, pasta reale and many more treats.

Gourmet Tours

CATANIA. The Baroque face of the town is seen in the churches and buildings, all similarly decorated with the contrasting black lava stone and white marble, particularly noticeable in the cathedral and the Liottru (elephant) Fountain. There are plenty of classical ruins (the Roman theater, the Greek odeum) and medieval ones (the Ursino castle). In the heart of the town, the bakeries and *rosticcerie* sell rustic products (*siciliane*, *carocciate*, *scacciate*, *cipolline* and *arancini fritti* and *al forno*), the refreshment kiosks sell traditional drinks with selz, the bars sell fresh almond milk (also with a dash of coffee) and *granita*, which, in Catania, are worked to

HOTELS AND RESTAURANTS

Catania
La Siciliana ﹗﹗﹗
viale Marco Polo 52/a
☎ 095376400
Cantine del Cugno Mezzano ﹗﹗
via Museo Biscari 8
☎ 0957158710
Don Saro ﹗﹗
viale Libertà 129
☎ 095539836
Poggio Ducale - da Nino ﹗﹗
via Paolo Gaifami 5
☎ 095330016
Antica Marina ﹗
via Pardo 29
☎ 095348197
Sicilia in Bocca ﹗
via Pietro Lupo 16/18
☎ 0957461361
Aci Castello
Villa delle Rose ﹗﹗
via XXI Aprile 79
☎ 095271024
Acireale
La Brocca du Cinc'Oru ﹗﹗
corso Savoia 49/a
☎ 095607196
Aci Trezza
Cambusa del Capitano ﹗﹗
via Marina 65
☎ 095276298
Caltagirone
San Giorgio ﹗﹗
via Altobasso S. Luigi 2
☎ 093355228
Cannizzaro
Alioto ﹗﹗﹗
via Mollica 24/26
☎ 095494444

make the ice dense and compact. The markets are colorful and noisy. Try the 'a Piscaria' market between the cathedral and the sea, and the 'a Fera' market in the little streets of the town center. You should visit the "Grillo" stores, in Piazza Lincoln and Piazza Stesicoro, selling charcuterie and other local products. The best cake shop is "Savia" in Via Etnea. The "Il Carato" in Via S. Gaetano is a wine club. As far as restaurants are concerned, we recommend "Poggio Ducale – Da Nino", which is also a hotel, with innovative cuisine often inspired by Sicilian traditions. The dishes sometimes involve unusual combinations of foods, but are rarely disappointing. "La Siciliana" is also good, and was made famous by an unforgettable *ripiddu nivicatu*. As for *trattorie*, there is the "Sicilia in Bocca", the "Antica Marina" and the "Don Saro" at the station.

The ceramics of Caltagirone

1. From the Riviera to the Lemons of Etna

ACIREALE. In Cannizzaro, which is on the road to Taormina, the restaurant "Alioto" offers traditional Sicilian cuisine and fish. Travelling along the coast, you will reach Aci Castello with its Norman castle. You can dine in the park of the "Villa delle Rose" with Sicilian and classic cuisine – especially fish dishes – plus pizzas. Then there is Aci Trezza which provided the picturesque background to the book 'I Malavoglia', by Giovanni Verga. The "Cambusa del Capitano" restaurant in this town has a nautical feel to it which goes well with the good fish cuisine. You will get an excellent *granita* and ice-creams at the "Eden" bar. Next is Acireale, the most important of the nine Aci towns. It is a Baroque town set between 'gardens' of lemon groves (including the special *verdelli*, or summer, lemons). We recommend the "La Brocca du Cinc'Oru" restaurant. Set in a small ancient building in the center, it is atmospheric and elegant, with creative dishes, mostly of fish. Don't miss their pistachio ice-cream. In July and August the staff are transferred to the camping site "La Timpa" in Santa Maria La Scala. Whichever cake shop you try, you will get the very best marzipan, nougat, *nucatole, pasta reale, cassata, zeppole di riso* and more. Note also the "Panoramico" restaurant in nearby Santa Maria Ammalati, along Statale 114. From Acireale you can take an alternative route to Zafferana Etnea, a Sicilian mountain tourist destination for the rich (where they have excellent mushrooms, and honey, orange and lemon are typical flavors). In the bakeries, they have special *scacciate* (pastry normally filled with cheese, anchovies, tomatoes and onion, or with meat instead of anchovies, or with *ricotta* and coffee for the sweet version) and seasoned *cunsatu* bread. Every Sunday in October, there is a festival with a huge number of local products available. In the surrounding area, there are the Città del Vino (Cities of Wine) of Milo, Sant'Alfio and Santa Venerina. In Milo the *cantina* "Barone di Villagrande" produces of the DOC wine Etna, and in the town itself you will find *mostarda* (spiced, preserved fruit) and hazelnut paste. In Santa Venerina you will get cheeses, the wine of the *azienda* "S. Michele del barone Scamacca del Murgo", and the *limoncello* liqueur from the distillery, "F.lli Russo".

GIARRE. This modern town on the lower slopes of the volcano is in an area where there is intensive cultivation of citrus trees and other fruit trees, even exotic ones such as mango and kiwi. In the little town of Riposto, which now adjoins Giarre, you will find the wine producers, "Vincenzo Russo". In Trepunti, in the Comune

of Giarre, there is the *agriturismo* establishment, "Codavolpe", with vegetarian and Sicilian cuisine.

Sicilian lemons

LINGUAGLOSSA. This is the first town along the Etna road and its name ('shiny tongue') tells of the lava trails that licked it centuries ago. The route leading up to the crater is one of the easiest to negotiate in the Parco dell'Etna. At table, there is game, cheeses and mushrooms with the characteristic dish of broad bean flour *polenta* with mushrooms. There is a local *cantina*, the "Valle Galfina". With a brief detour you will reach Castiglione di Sicilia where you should try the *sciauni*, a typical *ricotta* cake. In this area, the *ricotta* can come fresh, baked, or with honey and pepper. In the Solicchiata district, the "Coop. Patria" offers wine and food-tasting with typical local produce

Aci Trezza. Fishermen

but you must book in advance.

RANDAZZO. This medieval town overlooking the Valley of Alcantara is all built from volcanic rock. In town, the "Trattoria Veneziano" has a cuisine inspired by the woods, and includes mushrooms, wild asparagus and wild herbs. The cake shops are excellent and sell sweets with almonds, pistachio or *ricotta*. In the Montelaguardia quarter you will find the *agriturismo* firm, "L'Antica Vigna", selling wine, olive oil, conserves, cheeses and fruit.

BRONTE. This is an agricultural center known for its pistachios, pine nuts, hazelnuts, *a cuore* (heart) almonds, shelled Nostre Contrade almonds, and honey (the most typical being the green *pumma maiurina*). Not far away is the Maniace abbey.

ADRANO. This town is on the south-western side of Etna. It has a Norman castle, the former monastery of Santa Lucia, and a section of town walls from ancient-Greek *Adranon*. Here they rear the typical Etna dog, from the most ancient Cirneco breed, and they produce oranges, honey, pistachios and *a cuore* almonds.

PATERNO. This town, surrounded by orange groves, and overlooked by a Norman castle, has one of the richest culinary traditions in Sicily. Its foods include *arancini*, the whole range of island pastas, stuffed eggplant, and eggplant *alla parmigiana* (baked with tomatoes and cheese). Local production includes olive oil, preserved olives, *ricotta* cheese (mostly the drier version) and *caciocavallo* cheese.

NICOLOSI. In Nicolosi, at the foot of Parco dell'Etna, there is the "Grotta del Gallo" restaurant which serves Sicilian and classic dishes, especially fresh pasta and fish, in a villa with a garden and a view of the sea. In the same

WINE PRODUCERS

Caltagirone
Azienda Agricola Imakara
contrada
Valle delle Ferle
☎ 0933992483
Giarre
Vincenzo Russo
via Ariosto 17
☎ 095939650
Linguaglossa
Valle Galfina
S.P. Linguaglossa-
Zafferana (km 2)
contrada Arrigo
☎ 095933694
Milo
Barone di Villagrande
via del Bosco 25
☎ 0957894339

SHOPPING

Catania
Il Carato
via S. Gaetano 1
☎ 0957159247
Wine club; hot dishes on Sunday.
Grillo
piazza Lincoln 15
☎ 095430035
piazza Stesicoro 54
☎ 095327070
Charcuterie and typical products.
Pasticceria Svizzera Caviezel
via Cervignano 48
☎ 0957223686
One of the best address for Sicilian sweets.
Pasticceria Savia
via Etnea 204
☎ 095322335
Traditional sweets and pastries since 1897.
Salumeria Carlo Dagnino
via Etnea 179
☎ 095312169
Regional cheeses and charcuterie.

Vineyards lining the route from Nicolosi to Etna

Comune, you will find the "Rifugio Sapienza" of the CAI (Club Alpino Italiano) at 1910 meters. It is the last outpost for excursions to the volcano. We can recommend the fresh pastas and Etna mushrooms of the nearby *trattoria*, "Corsaro". On the journey back to Catania, you go past San Giovanni La Punta where you can stop at the "Giardino di Bacco" restaurant, set in an old Etna house, serving seasonal food with traditional flavors. It is well worth staying at the "Villa Paradiso dell'Etna", a restored Thirties villa with an excellent restaurant, "La Pigna".

2. From Val di Catania to Caltagirone

MILITELLO IN VAL DI CATANIA. From Catania take Statale 385 then veer off to Scordia, known for its citrus fruits (the "Oranfrizer" firm produces excellent blood orange juice without preservatives). Moving on, you reach Militello in the Val di Catania (home to the physicist Ettore Maiorana). Situated on the edge of the Catania plain and near Etna, this is the headquarters of a famous producer of prickly pears, from which an excellent *mostarda* is made. The quality of the fruit is guaranteed by traditional organic cultivation methods, made possible thanks to special soil climate conditions which prevent parasites living there. Locally, the almond cakes and *vino cotto* (fortified wine) are excellent. Note the *trattoria*, "'U Trappitu", set in an ancient olive mill, where you can discover local dishes, such as pasta with wild fennel.

VIZZINI. This picturesque town

on the edge of a hill is the setting for the novel, *Mastro don Gesualdo*, by Giovanni Verga . In town, note the *trattoria*, "A Cunziria", set in a grotto. Nearby, in the Tana Calda quarter, in the Comune of Licodia, there is the *agriturismo* establishment, "Dain", set in an eighteenth-century villa.

CALTAGIRONE. This ancient market town is the headquarters of ceramic industries specializing in the production of wine amphorae. There is a wonderful flight of steps leading to S. Maria del Monte, with 142 steps all covered in polychrome clay. The local produce is the Sicilian *mostarda* made with grape must. You should eat at "San Giorgio", set in an eighteenth-century convent. The cake shop, "Scivoli", in Via Milazzo, was founded in the 1920s, and sells excellent cakes with *ricotta*. The DOC wine Cerasuolo di Vittoria is also produced in the area. You can visit the agricultural firm, "Imakara", in the Valle delle Ferle quarter.

MINEO. Back on the *Statale* 385, you travel to Mineo, on the north-western side of the Iblei mountains, and home to the writer Luigi Capuana (who was once also the town mayor). There are two Baroque churches, S. Agrippina and S. Pietro. The town's *cannoli* (a roll of crusty pastry filled with sweetened *ricotta*, and candied fruit or pistachios) and olive oil are both extremely famous, the olive oil being the best in the area. Lastly, you reach Palagonia where they produce blood oranges.

SHOPPING

Bronte
Bronte Dolci
via G. Falcone 85
☎ 0957724090
Sweets and pastries.
Caltagirone
G. Cannizzaro
via Ronco Venezia 4
☎ 0933520081
Vast range of honey varieties.
Pasticceria Scivoli
via Milazzo 123
☎ 093323108
Sweets and cakes with "ricotta" since 1920's.
Castiglione di Sicilia
Coop. Agr. Patria
at Solicchiata
via Naz. Passopisciaro (km 194,500)
☎ 0942983143
Sicilian delicatessen.
Linguaglossa
Pasticceria
L'Alhambra di Rosaria Barone
via Marconi 76
☎ 095643156
Almonds, pistachios and and hazelnuts sweet specialties.
Santa Venerina
Az. Agr. S. Michele
Barone Scamacca del Murgo
☎ 0957130090
Typical wines and cheeses.
Distilleria
Fratelli Russo
via D. Galimberti 70
☎ 095953321
Distilled spirits such as "limoncello".
Scordia
Oranfrizer
contrada Cittadino
S.P. 99
☎ 095659229
Excellent blood orange juice without preservatives.

ENNA

This is a mountainous inland province, faithful to its pastoral traditions, as reflected in the simplicity of its flavors.

A *solitary carob tree*

I t is the only province of the island without a coastline, in the heart of *Sicilia fredda* (cold Sicily), as Sciascia defined it. The ancient granary of Italy, it is dominated by high plains with some very bleak areas and the wooded area of Erei. The provincial capital, at 931m, is the center of a traditionally farmhouse cuisine which reflects the whole province's gastronomy. The cuisine is marked by honest foods and local variations in side-dishes which can be anything from vegetable omelettes, through *focaccia*, and from pasta *ncasciata* (*maccheroni* with meat ragout, meat balls, boiled eggs salami, *caciocavallo* cheese, fried eggplant and peas; baked in a pot and served with fresh ragout) through Sicilian cutlets. You will find the *pecorino piacintinu* (flavored with black pepper grains and saffron) almost everywhere.

Gourmet Tours

ENNA. The highest provincial capital in the whole of Italy, Enna is situated in the heart of the island on a plateau overlooking olive groves, almond tree plantations and fields of corn. It is a farming town with rich and tasty culinary traditions. Do not miss the *focaccia* filled with salami and elderflowers, or the local cakes *ditini, zuccarini* and *cubbaita* (Arab nougat). If you wish to go to a restaurant, try the "Centrale" and the "Ariston", where you can try both Sicilian cuisine and the local specialties.

1. The 'Lombardy' towns
LEONFORTE. The town was founded in the seventeenth century. Here you can find prized embroidery and good meat.
NICOSIA. This is a typical inland Sicilian town, set on the lower slopes of four mountains. In the dialect you can still hear traces of Lombardy and Piedmont sounds dating from the eleventh and twelfth-century immigration from those provinces. In the surrounding area, they rear animals, especially sheep, and produce *provole, ricotta, pecorino* and *primo sale* cheeses, meat, sausage, *supprissatu* salami, hams and oregano-flavored pig's intestines, cured for eating raw or, more often, cooked with broad beans in the spring. You can buy these products direct from the *massarie* (farms), including the *agriturismo* establishment "Masseria Mercadante" in Mercadante, and in the food shops. In Portelle, near the turn-off for Mistretta, there is the typical Nebrodi mountains restaurant, "La Vigneta" whose

specialties are cheese and lamb. From Nicosia you will soon be in Sperlinga, which opens out on a landscape of woods and pasture, overlooked by the remains of a castle. The typical local dish is the *frascatela*, a soup of broccoli and bran flour.
TROINA. This town, previously an Arab and Norman stronghold, stands out on a rocky crest at 1121 meters. Horses and cattle are reared here.

2. From the Pergusa Lake to Pietraperzia
LAGO DI PERGUSA. The basin is surrounded by eucalyptus trees, set in a landscape partly ruined by a motor-racing track. You can stay over in the "Giara Park Hotel" or the "Riviera".
AIDONE. The town has panoramic views and you can see the ruins of the ancient *Morgantina*, a flourishing town in the Hellenistic Roman period.
PIAZZA ARMERINA. Surrounded by woods, this town is famous for the nearby Roman villa of Casale (late third – early fourth century). You can get excellent cheeses and cakes here. We recommend dinner at "Al Fogher", set in an old railway gatekeeper's lodge, serving excellent *fusilli alla siciliana* (Sicilian-style *fusilli* pasta).
PIETRAPERZIA. Once past Barrafranca, you will reach Pietraperzia, wedged between mountain tops, where they cultivate olives, almonds and pistachios. The local specialty is a pizza uniting land and sea food (with tomatoes, garlic, *pecorino* cheese and oregano plus salted sardines). You can get extra virgin olive oil from the "Fattoria Serra di Mezzo".

HOTELS AND RESTAURANTS

Enna
Giara Park Hotel ★★★
at Pergusa (km 10)
via Nazionale 125
☎ 0935541687
Riviera ★★★
at Pergusa (km 10)
via Autodromo
☎ 0935541260
Centrale ❨❨
piazza VI Dicembre 9
☎ 0935500963
Ariston ❨
via Roma 353
☎ 093526038
Nicosia
La Vigneta ❨
contrada S. Basilio
☎ 0935638940
Piazza Armerina
Al Fogher ❨❨
contrada Bellia 1
☎ 0935684123

AGRITURISMI

Nicosia
Masseria 🛏🚗
Mercadante
contrada Mercadante
☎ 0935640771
Piazza Armerina
Savoca 🛏🚗
contrada Polleri
☎ 0935683078

OLIVE OIL PRODUCERS

Pietraperzia
Fattoria
Serra di Mezzo
contrada
Serra di Mezzo
☎ 0934401294
Troina
Az. Agr. Le Querce di Cota di C. Rundo
via S. Pietro 96
☎ 0935654888

SHOPPING

Enna
Formaggi Di Dio
via Mercato
S. Antonio 34
☎ 093525758
Typical cheeses.
Piazza Armerina
Pasticceria Restivo
via Mazzini 112
☎ 0935680048
Sweets and pastries.

MESSINA

The Nebrodi and Peloritani mountain ranges, wedged between two seas, give shape to a province with a dual culinary identity.

S tretching out as if a natural extension to the mainland, this province has a varied landscape thanks to two mountains ranges, the Peloritani and the Nebrodi, and a fragmented coastline divided between two seas. Mountain and sea also make their mark on the cuisine – the mountain regions are rich in charcuterie, sausages, grilled lamb and mutton, while in the Tyrrhenian valleys and the Milazzo plain locals cultivate citrus and other fruits, olives, vegetables and vines. The grapes from these vines make excellent wine, even though the most prized, and to-day rare, wine is the DOC Faro from the Messina hills. The province also has a tradition of beer – it has the highest consumption in Italy – with local beer being produced in the *azienda* "Birra Messina".

Stromboli, Aeolian Islands. Preparing to fish

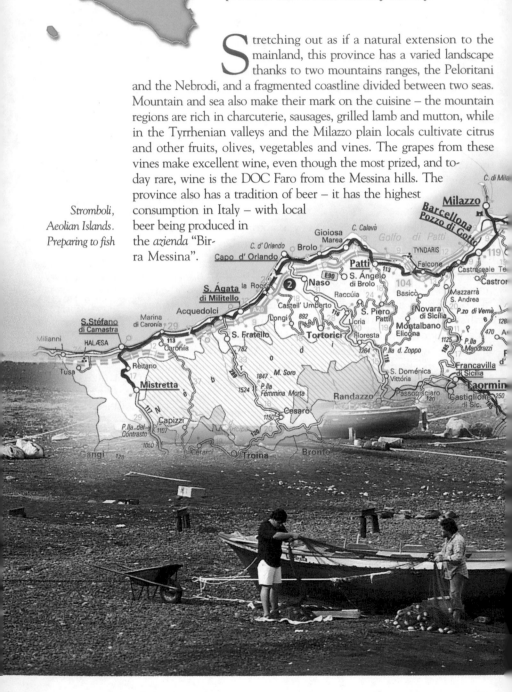

In addition to its fishing, the Aeolian archipelago is renowned for its capers and the liqueur-like wine, Malvasia delle Lipari. The large proportion of coastline means that cuisine is fish-based. Fish is prepared in various ways, and this is particularly true for swordfish, which is grilled with *salmoriglio, a ghiotta* (with tomato, olives and capers), and served in filets which are rolled and stuffed. Other food you should not miss includes the eggplant, the *maccu* (broad bean purée) and the *arancini* (balls of rice filled with minced meat, gravy, peas, soft cheese and other things)

Gourmet Tours

MESSINA. The town was destroyed by an earthquake in 1908 but retained its cathedral, the church of SS. Annunziata dei Catalani and paintings by Antonello and Caravaggio, now in the regional museum. In town, you get bread with sesame seeds, the characteristic soft *pane di cena* (dinner bread) and the *zuccherata* (toasted bread), and the typical *focaccia* with capers, tomato, cheese and endive. The *arancini* and *pidoni* (*arancini* with vegetables and cheese) are excellent. You can try the Messina cakes at "Irrera" and "Doddis". You must have a *granita* for breakfast (the preferred morning *granita* is coffee with whipped cream) and a *brioche* (croissant). We recommend the "Bar Progresso", on the Viale S. Martino, for this. As far as restaurants go, the "Savoja" is excellent, with its famed *risotto agli agrumi* (*risotto* with citrus fruits). Then there is the typical Messina

HOTELS AND
RESTAURANTS

Messina
Savoja ¶¶
via XXVII Luglio 36/38
☎ 0902934865
Al Padrino ¶
via S. Cecilia 54/56
☎ 0902921000
Capo d'Orlando
La Tartaruga
★★★ ¶¶¶ ★
at Lido S. Gregorio
☎ 0941955012
La Tettoia ¶
contrada Certari 80
☎ 0941902146
Castel di Tusa
Atelier
sul Mare ★★★
via C. Battisti 4
☎ 0921334295
Cesarò
Villa Miraglia ★★
at Portella della
Miraglia S.S. 289
☎ 0957732133
Eolie (Islands)
Filippino - 1910 ¶¶¶
★
Lipari, piazza Municipio
☎ 0909811002
La Piazza ★★★ ★
Panarea, via S. Pietro
☎ 090983151
Ai Gechi ¶¶
Stromboli, via Salina 12
☎ 090986213
E Pulera ¶¶ ★
Lipari, via Diana
☎ 0909811158
La Ginestra ¶¶
Lipari, via Stradale 10
☎ 0909822285
A Cannata ¶ ★
Santa Marina Salina
via Umberto 113
☎ 0909843161
Maria Tindara ¶
Vulcano,
via strada Provinciale 38
☎ 0909853004

trattoria, "Al Padrino", whose *maccu riposato* (broad bean purée) you must try. Stores to visit include "Il Salumaio – Doddis" in Via Garibaldi for charcuterie, and the refined "Enoteca Abbate", offering a huge range of Sicilian wine. Don't miss the salt lakes, Ganzirri and Faro, to the north of the town, with their rich mussel fields. You can try produce from the lakes, cooked in the traditional way, at "Napoletana – Da Salvatore", which has a view of the lakes. The cheese shop "Calogero" sells very good *provole*, *ricotta*, *scamorza*, *tume* and *pecorino pepato*. In Lido di Mortelle you will find the famous Sicilian cuisine of "Alberto – Sporting Mortelle" in an elegant Mediterranean dining room. In the surrounding hills, they produce the DOC wine Faro. Note the "Bagni" *cantina*.

1. The Ionic coast

TAORMINA. On the way to Taormina, travelling along Statale 114, you will arrive in Letojanni, where you will find the "Da Nino" restaurant which serves imaginative fish dishes. In Taormina itself, suspended between rock and sea, there is a lovely walk along the elegant Corso (main street) where you can enjoy the beautiful landscape of jagged cliffs and Etna in

the distance. There are many restaurants, not all of them good value for money. We can recommend "Maffei's", an elegant place with a sweet-smelling garden of citrus fruits, bananas and jasmine, where traditional fish cuisine is served. Don't miss their *ravioli neri con ripieno di cernia* (black *ravioli* filled with grouper fish). "'A Zammara" is also worth a visit, with its nice atmosphere, a garden, and good, genuine Sicilian cuisine. The "Al Duomo" fish restaurant is also worth trying. On the way up to Castelmola, you should not miss sampling the almond wine with biscuits at the unusual "Turrisi" bar. Whilst in the bay of Mazzarò, go to the "Pescatore" restaurant with typical Messina dishes. From Taormina, take the coastal road to Giardini-Naxos where there are many choices of places to stay we recommend the "Ramada Hotel" and the "Nike Hotel".

FRANCAVILLA DI SICILIA. The Statale 185 will take you up the Valley of Alcantara. Before reaching the Gole dell'Alcantara, take a detour to Graniti where the cuisine of the *trattoria*, "Paradise", is based on dry *ricotta*, pork ragout and *falso magro* (a large slice of lean veal covered in boiled egg, cheese, ham and sausage, which is then rolled up and cooked in a

Lipari. Marina Corta seen from the castle

tomato sauce). In Francavilla di Sicilia you can stay at the hotel "D'Orange Alcantara", where you can eat outside in the summer. You could then come back via a section of the Tyrrhenian coast and then cross inland via Novara di Sicilia, an area renowned for the cultivation of almonds, hazelnuts and walnuts.

2. From Milazzo to the Nebrodi mountains

MILAZZO. The town is at the base of a long, thin peninsula, bordered with little beaches, which stretches out into the Tyrrhenian Sea. For an excellent introduction to local cuisine, we recommend the restaurant "Villa Esperanza". In town there is the "Grasso" *cantina* with a large range of labels, including the full-bodied red wine, Mamertino, heir to a famous Roman wine, the refined Capobianco, the liqueur-like Malvasia, Moscato and Zibibbo, and the almond wine made from an ancient island recipe. In Via Cavour there is the wine and liqueur store, "Boutique Vini e Liquori". In Torregrotta, in the Scala district, you can stay at "Redebora" which is simple, convenient and has good food. In Valdina, you will find the "Giovi" distillery.
BARCELLONA POZZO DI GOTTO. This large village was founded in the seventeenth century and is renowned for its *riso nero* (black rice) ice-cream, which is, in fact, chocolate ice-cream. Once past the Terme di Castroreale, make a brief detour to Mazzarà Sant'An-

drea – here, along the river, there is abundant plant life. On the way up to Furnari, on the other side of the Mazzarà torrent, you see the famous vines from which must and wine are produced. In Tripi they make an excellent dry *ricotta*, and in Montalbano they are famous for their *provole sfoglie* and *provole piccanti* cheeses.
PATTI. In front of this little town is the pleasant landscape of the Marinello lakes with the Tindari fortress and the evocative ancient Greek theater. You should visit the cathedral and the excavations of a Roman villa. In Saliceto, which is in the neighborhood, there is the restaurant "Cani Cani" with a Sicilian cuisine of vegetables and fish. Going back through Capo Calavà, you then leave the *Statale* and proceed to Sant'Angelo di Brolo, which is famous for its hand-sliced charcuterie – try the "Cooperativa La Collina".
CAPO D'ORLANDO. This modern little seaside resort sits at the foot of a bare cone of rock, sheer to the sea. We recommend a stop at the "Tartaruga" restaurant in the enchanting bay of Lido di San Gregorio. You will find a good quality, good-priced *trattoria* in the "La Tettoia", where you can taste Sicilian flavors. In the San Gregorio district, there is the "Milio" *agriturismo* establishment which produces organic citrus fruits, olives, oil, hazelnuts and berries.
SANT'AGATA DI MILITELLO. This coastal town is a good place to start trips to inland areas. Alcara

Fishermen at Stromboli

HOTELS AND RESTAURANTS

Taormina
Pescatore ❦❦
at Mazzarò (km 4)
via Nazionale 107
☎ 094223460
Torregrotta
Redebora ★★
at Scala
via Siracusa 7
☎ 0909981182

AGRITURISMI

Capo d'Orlando
Milio ★
at San Gregorio
☎ 0941955008
Pettineo
Casa Migliaca ★
contrada Migliaca
☎ 0921336722
Tusa
Borgo degli Olivi ★
contrada Aielli
☎ 090712430

WINE PRODUCERS

Messina
Bagni
at Santa Margherita
via Bellone 10
☎ 090633944
Eolie (Islands)
Caravaglio
Salina, at Malfa
via Provinciale 33
☎ 0905844368
Carrà
Salina, at Malfa
via Umberto I 7/9
☎ 0909044051
Milazzo
Grasso
via Albero 5
☎ 0909201002

SHOPPING

Messina
Bar Progresso
viale S. Martino 33
☎ 090673734
Excellent "granita" with brioche
Enoteca Abbate
via Garibaldi 62
☎ 090774064
Sicilian wines.
Pasticceria Doddis
via Garibaldi, block 414
☎ 09043943
Sweets and pastries.

SHOPPING

Messina
Caseificio
D. Calogero
via S. Cecilia 17
☎ 0902921460
Cheeses.
Il salumaio-Doddis
via Garibaldi 317,
block 414
☎ 09040257
Charcuterie.
Pasticceria Irrera
viale Boccetta 4
block 377
☎ 090344209
Sweets and pastries.
Castelmola
Bar Turrisi
via Pio IX 16
☎ 094228181
*Almond wine
with biscuits.*
Eolie (Islands)
Bar Alfredo
Salina, at Lingua
☎ 0909843050
Regional specialties.
Cosi Duci
Salina, at Malfa
via S. Lorenzo 9
☎ 0909844358
Aeolian cakes.
Pasticceria Subba
- 1930, Lipari
via V. Emanuele 92
☎ 0909811352
Historical cake shop.
S. Onofrio
Delizie Eoliane
Malfa, at Pollara
via Leni 10
☎ 0909843951
Local products.
Milazzo
Boutique
Vini e Liquori
via Cavour
Wines and liquors
Valdina
Distilleria Giovi
v. Valdina Fondachello
☎ 0909942256
Distilled spirits.

Li Fusi is not far off. It is a medieval village, and produces ham, *pancetta arrotolata* (rolled bacon) and *supprissatu* (*soppressato*-style salami) which is highly prized if made from the local breed of black pigs. Moving on across San Fratello, in the land where they rear the Sanfratellani horses, you reach Portella della Miraglia (1464m) and the refuge "Villa Miraglia", where you can stay overnight and eat mountain cuisine of charcuterie, meat and mushrooms.

SANTO STEFANO DI CAMASTRA. This is an artisan town producing splendid ceramics. Make a special note of the "Atelier sul Mare", in Castel di Tusa which is a little further on. It is an unusual hotel-museum with surroundings reinvented by famous contemporary artists. From Santo Stefano, take the road to Mistretta where the women still make prized lace by hand, and where the cheeses and pasta reale (a typical Sicilian sweet with marzipan) are excellent. In Capizzi, an isolated little town in the woods, they rear Sanfratellani horses and produce *provole sfoglie* cheese, charcuterie (especially *prosciutto crudo* – dry-cured ham) and durum wheat.

Ceramic of Santo Stefano di Camastra

3. The Aeolian Islands

VULCANO. The Gran Cratere (volcano) dominates this island whose landscape is made up of broom, cliffs, and a terrain of ash and lapillus. On the heights of the Vulcano Piano area , it is worth stopping at "Maria Tindara" for its traditional Sicilian cuisine.

LIPARI. Archeological excavations and imposing architecture reflect the history of this, the largest of the Aeolian islands. The historical bar and cake shop, "Subba" (established 1930) is worth trying. Another top tip is for "Filippino" (est. 1910), originally a wine tavern also serving food, today an elegant restaurant. The "E Pulera" restaurant is also excellent, its specialty being fish-based island cooking. In Pianoconte, on a hill covered in vineyards, you will find "La Ginestra" which also serves fish, excellently matched with home-grown vegetables.

SALINA. This is an island of wine, but here capers, olives and vegetables are also cultivated. This is the realm of the Malvasia, especially famous in Malfa where it is made by the "Carrà" *cantina* only from local grapes. In Malfa, there is also the "Caravaglio" *cantina.* For Aeolian cakes – *vastidduzzi, giggi, pipareddi* and more – go to "Cosi Duci". In Pollara, in a volcanic amphitheater, the co-operative association "Sant'Onofrio-Delizie Eoliane" sells typical local produce, including capers. In Santa Marina Salina, near the lake of Lingua, there is the "A Cannata" restaurant, serving regional and fish cuisine and excellent wine, and the "Alfredo" with fresh fruit *granita* and salads with tuna.

PANAREA. This is the smallest Aeolian island, and the tourist destination of the rich and fashionable. To stay over, there is the hotel "La Piazza", with Aeolian architecture. STROMBOLI. We thoroughly recommend the restaurant "Ai Gechi" for its meticulous service, Aeolian cuisine, creative dishes, and fresh, home-made pasta.

RAGUSA

Pastures, cereals, olive groves and vineyards color this area of ancient beauty where the technology of greenhouse cultivation gives early produce.

T he province is triangle-shaped, and its northern tip rises to Mount Lauro, the peak of the Iblei mountains at 986 meters. This is the source of the River Irminio, which descends towards the coast, cutting the whole province in two. The provincial capital Ragusa, and nearby Modica, form the heart of the local cuisine which has traditions that are very different from those of other Sicilian towns. The province is very agricultural, the most important vegetables being the artichoke and tomato, but there are also the DOP olives, "Monti Iblei". Also renowned are the sheep farming products, including *pecorino* and *ricotta* cheeses, whilst cattle-rearing gives *provole* and *caciotte* cheeses, and butter. Fishing is also important, reflected in the fresh fish dishes. All over the province, they cultivate the Nero d'Avola vine, whose grapes form the basis of many of the red Sicilian wines. When mixed with Frappato, it gives the DOC wine Cerasuolo di Vittoria.

Agricultural landscape in the Ragusan province

Gourmet Tours

HOTELS AND RESTAURANTS

Ragusa
★🍴 **Eremo Giubiliana** ★★★ 🍴🍴🍴
contrada Giubiliana
☎ 0932669119
★🍴 **Mediterraneo Palace** ★★★
via Roma 189
☎ 0932621944
La Pergola 🍴🍴
piazza L. Sturzo 6/7
☎ 0932255659
Antica Macina 🍴
at Ibla
via Giusti 129
☎ 0932248096
Chiaramonte Gulfi
★🍴 **L'Antica Stazione** 🍴
contrada Santissimo
☎ 0932928083
★🍴 **Majore** 🍴
via Mart. Ungheresi 12
☎ 0932928019
Marina di Ragusa
Terraqua ★★★
via delle Sirene 35
☎ 0932615600
Alberto 🍴🍴
lungomare Doria 48
☎ 0932239023
Modica
Fattoria delle Torri 🍴🍴
vico Napolitano 14
☎ 0932751928
Vittoria
Sakalleo 🍴🍴
at Scoglitti (km 13)
piazza Cavour 12
☎ 0932871688

AGRITURISMI

Acate
Il Carrubo ★🍴
contrada Bosco Grande-Canalotti
☎ 0932989038
Modica
Villa Teresa ★🍴
contrada Bugilteza
☎ 0932771690

RAGUSA. This town lies at the southern end of the Iblei mountains. It has two distinct parts – one part is designed in the modern take on the eighteenth-century chess-board layout, with long, parallel roads and pretty buildings, while the other part is ancient Ibla, clinging to the hill, with narrow, medieval alleys and characteristic staircases, overlooked by the church of S. Giorgio. In the town bakeries, you will find *pastizzu* and *vasteddi* (patterned bread flavored with elderflower). Stores to note include the cheese shop, "La Casa del Formaggio", where you can buy the Ragusa *caciocavallo* and other local specialties, and the "Enoteca Ristorvip – Lo Presti". We can recommend a stay in the central hotel, "Mediterraneo Palace" with its restaurant, the "Splendid". "La Pergola" is excellent for its menu of traditional dishes and some more modern items. In the summer the restaurant also has an outlet in Marina di Ragusa, where they serve fish and pizzas. We also recommend the hotel-restaurant, "Eremo Giubiliana" on the road to Marina, set in a restored fifteenth-century hermitage, serving Ragusa cuisine, with fresh pastas, roasts, home-grown organic specialties, and local wines. Also worth a visit is the *trattoria*;

Pedalino. The grape festival

"Antica Macina", in Ibla, set in an old water mill.

1. From Modica to Camarina

MODICA. The town is made up of an upper and lower part. The upper town is on a wedge of plateau, the lower in the basin formed by two torrents, now covered over. There are glimpses of the Baroque, the best being the wonderful cathedral of S. Giorgio. It is worth visiting the Cava d'Ispica, a cave excavated in the limestone rock where there are many remains dating from the Aeneolithic period through the beginning of the twentieth century. Modica is situated between two Sicilian towns rich in gastronomic traditions. We recommend the "Fattoria delle Torri", rustic and welcoming, set in an eighteenth-century building. The food here truly represents traditional cooking. In the street Corso Umberto I, there is the cake shop, the "Antica Dolceria Bonajuto", which sells excellent *gelo di carrube* (carob frosting) and *mpanatigghie*. In town they use an ancient recipe for chocolate which is worked cold, without melting the sugar. You can buy honey, vegetables and charcuterie at "Giorgio Cannata". In the countryside they rear cattle and make cheese.

ISPICA. This is an agricultural center set on the edge of the south-western plateau of the

Iblei mountains. It has an eighteenth-century town plan and an ancient center, which is uninhabited and now an archaeological site, the Parco archeologico della Forza. You should visit the church, S. Maria Maggiore.

SCICLI. Past Pozzallo on the coast, you reach Scicli with its pretty eighteenth-century buildings and Baroque churches. Olive groves are everywhere. You can get very fine olive oil at the "Fratelli Aprile" *azienda* in the Sant'Agata quarter.

MARINA DI RAGUSA. This is a small port and seaside resort. We recommend the hotel "Terraqua" in a pretty building with a restaurant set in a garden with a pool. You get Sicilian fish cuisine at the restaurant "Alberto", in a wooden building on the sea front. Near Punta Secca, there are the archaeological excavations of Caucania with the remains of a town from between the fourth and sixth centuries. Further north, at the source of the river Ippari, there is the Syracuse colony of Camarina, founded in five B.C. You can see the town walls, and the remains of the theater and a Hellenistic quarter. Locally, they produce water melons, melons and greenhouse vegetables.

2. From Comiso to the Macconi and the Iblei mountains

COMISO. This is a Baroque town which was reconstructed after the 1693 earthquake. The landscape is marked by the typical limestone buildings (Comiso stone). It is one of the few towns in the province which preserves part of its original medieval town plan.

Prickly pear

VITTORIA. In the Sabuci quarter, between the greenhouses of early produce, you will find the *cantina* "Giovanna Cortese Presti" where you can try the Cerasuolo di Vittoria DOC wine. Giuseppe Coria will serve you the unusual Solicchiato. In Scoglitti, a seaside resort, there are many places to stay. To the north, there is the plain of Macconi with sand dunes and a Mediterranean vegetation.

ACATE. The town is on the border with the province of Caltanissetta. They produce olive oil and wine here. The *cantina* "Valle dell'Acate" sells local wines, the table wine Bianco di Sicilia Bidis, and the DOC wine Cerasuolo di Vittoria. You can also find the latter in the *cantina* "Torrevecchia" on the Statale 115.

CHIARAMONTE GULFI. There are two places where you can sample local cuisine: "L'Antica Stazione" set in an old railway station, and "Majore". They produce the excellent DOP olive oil Monti Iblei in the hills. Visit the "Poggio di Bortolone" *azienda* where you can buy olive oils and also Cerasuolo wine.

WINE PRODUCERS

Ragusa
Az. Agricola G. Cortese Presti
contrada Sabuci
piazza Mons. Arezzi 5
☎ 0932874077
Acate
Torrevecchia
contrada Torrevecchia
☎ 0932990996
Valle dell'Acate
contrada Bidini
☎ 0932874166
Comiso
Vinicola Avide
S.P. Comiso-
Chiaramonte
☎ 0932967456

OLIVE OIL PRODUCERS

Scicli
AgroIndustria F.lli Aprile srl
contrada S. Agata
S.P. Scicli-Sampieri km 2,5
☎ 0932833828

SHOPPING

Ragusa
La Casa del Formaggio
corso Italia 330
☎ 0932227485
Cheeses.
Enoteca Ristorvip-Lo Presti
via Corbino 23
☎ 0932652990
Wines.
Chiaramonte Gulfi
Azienda Agricola Poggio di Bortolone
contrada Bortolone 19
☎ 0932921161
Wines and olive oil.
Modica
Antica Dolceria Bonajuto
corso Umberto I 159
☎ 0932941225
Sweets and pastries.
Giorgio Cannata
via March. Tedeschi 5
☎ 0932946192
Honey, vegetables and charcuterie.

SYRACUSE

The Iblei mountains form the backdrop to one of the island's most interesting agricultural districts, in terms of both product variety and cuisine.

To the east of Mount Lauro, the highest point of the Iblei Mountains, this province stretches along a limestone plateau which slopes down northwards towards the Catania plain, and southwards towards the most southerly point of the island, Cape Passero. The land is famous for its citrus fruits, vegetables, almonds (from Avola), olive oil and olives. The fish is of top quality and there is a vast range of fish dishes available, from a rich and tasty variety of Sicilian fish soup, through the pastas with sauces of clams, fresh tuna, black squid ink, and more. The Syracuse cakes are based on the regional cakes but stand out for the quality of their ingredients and the deftness with which they are made. Last but not least, are the four important DOC wines of Eloro, Eloro Pachino, Moscato di Noto and Moscato di Syracuse.

Syracuse.
Promenade

Gourmet Tours

SYRACUSE. This historical center is hemmed in by Ortigia Island. It is full of little roads and steep drops to the sea. It is a modern town built where the remains of the one of the most powerful cities of the ancient world can still be seen in the archaeological park. In the bakeries the specialityes are the *impanate* (a type of very rich pizza or savory tart often filled with vegetables and meat or fish), made with rustic bread dough, and the *sparacelli* with sausage, *primosale* cheese and chili pepper. We can recommend the elite restaurant, "Don Camillo" in the town center, with its modern, light cuisine and truly excellent dishes based on sea urchins.. And don't overlook "Jonico 'a Rutta 'e Ciauli", in a villa with a terrace over the cliffs, this restaurant is famous locally. There is also "Minosse", specializing in fish and mushrooms. For good ice-cream, try the "Gran Caffè del Duomo", and for cakes, the "Artale" cake shop near the cathedral. You get an excellent choice of wines at the "Enoteca Solaria" in Via Roma. In Fontane Bianche, there is the "Spiaggetta" restaurant

where you can get an excellent fish soup. Not far away in inland Floridia, in the Fegoro district, you will find the *trattoria* "Da Nunzio Bruno" set in a very unusual house-museum.

1. From Augusta to Pantalica

AUGUSTA. This port and industrial center is an island off the main island, joined to it by two bridges. There is the castle built at the same time as the town (by Frederick II in 1232). In the surrounding area, there are the excavations of the ancient Greek towns of *Tapsos* and *Megara Hyblaea*. In Faro Santa Croce, there is the good restaurant, "Donna Ina", serving fish in a variety of successful ways, including grilled and *in guazzetto* (cooked in broth).
LENTINI. This was one of the agricultural colonies belonging to the ancient Chalchidean people of Naxos, and renowned for the fertility of its land. It makes cheeses, including *pecorino* and *primusali*, and there are extensive citrus groves where the famous Tarocco oranges of Lentini are grown. In nearby Carlentini, there is the good *agriturismo* establishment, "Tenuta di Roccadia", with its own *caciocavallo* and *pecorino* cheeses, the *limoncello* liqueur and different jams.

HOTELS AND RESTAURANTS

Syracuse
Jonico-'a Rutta 'e Ciauli ❙❙❙
riviera Dionisio il Grande 194
☎ 093165540
Don Camillo ❙❙
via Maestranza 92/100
☎ 093167133
Minosse ❙❙
via Mirabella 6
☎ 093166366
Spiaggetta ❙❙ 📷
at Fontane Bianche
via Mazzarò 1
☎ 0931790334
Augusta
Donna Ina ❙❙
at Faro Santa Croce
☎ 0931983422
Floridia
Da Nunzio Bruno ❙
S.P. Floridia-Canicattini
☎ 0931949301
Noto
Trattoria del Carmine ❙
via Ducezio 1
☎ 0931838705
Palazzolo Acreide
Il Portico ❙❙
largo Senatore Italia
☎ 0931881532
La Trota ❙❙ 📷
contrada Pianette
☎ 0931883433
Anapo da Nunzio ❙
corso V. Emanuele 7
☎ 0931882286
Il Camino ❙ 📷
v. Martiri di via Fani 13
☎ 0931881860
Portopalo di Capo Passero
Alta Marea ❙❙
via L. Tasca 1
☎ 0931842979

PALAZZOLO ACREIDE. Once past Buccheri, in the heart of the Iblei mountains, you reach this Baroque Città del Vino which was reconstructed after the 1693 earthquake. The historical center is wonderful, despite being rather run down. A little outside the current residential area you will find the ruins of *Akrai*, a Greek theater, the stone caves Intagliata and Intagliatella, and the Santoni (big saints) sculpted out of the rock. There are several good quality restaurants, including "Il Portico", which serves fish, "Il Camino" serving mushrooms and game, and "Anapo da Nunzio". The "La Trota" restaurant, in Pianette on the Statale 287, has a dining hall carved out of the rock, and serves trout, which it breeds itself. For a scenic route, travel down the Anapo valley as far as Ferla. Here you will find the "S.I.G.S." farm which produces excellent extra virgin olive oil. Very close by, in Cassaro, there is the "Michele Costanzo" *azienda* which produces limited quantities of the excellent olive oil Hyblon.
SORTINO. Once past the pre-Greek Necropolis of Pantalica, dug out of the limestone rock, you will reach Sortino, which is renowned for its citrus fruits, olive oil and cheeses.

2. From Avola to Capo Passero

AVOLA. Built on a hexagonal eighteenth-century plan, the town has five squares laid out in the shape of a cross. The central square contains the bar "Finocchiaro", known for its ice-creams.
NOTO. Known as the 'World Capital of Baroque Architecture', it is very evocative with its splendid buildings. The "Cantina Inter-

provinciale Elorina" is based here. On the Cantina's lands and towards Palazzolo and Pantalica, they produce the wine Moscato di Noto which carries the DOC label for its sparkling and fortified varieties. You can sip or buy at the "Cantina Sperimentale di Noto". The "Caffè Sicilia" is worth trying for its excellent cakes and *granita* (flavored crushed ice), and specialties such as honey flavored with various aromatic herbs and conserves of citron and pistacchio. If you go to a *rosticceria* (selling roasted foods ready to eat), you should try the *scaccie* (*focaccie* stuffed with tomatoes, eggplant, cheese and chilies), the *lumera* (a type of *focaccia* full of basil) and the cheese wheel. In the area, there are also fortified wines made with carob beans, and quince jam. Another specialty is the flower-flavored ice-cream. The "Trattoria del Carmine" has good food. In Roveto, which is not far away, in the *Oasi naturalistica di Vendicari* (a protected national park) there are some nice walks, and also the *agriturismo* establishment "Il Roveto".
PACHINO. This town is near Capo Passero and is an important fishing and wine center. It is well-suited to tourism with its coastline bordered with lovely beaches, pools and rich fauna. The Pachino cherry tomatoes are excellent, as are the melons and the red wine which was recently awarded the DOC label under the name Eloro. This comes in many varieties, including the Bianco and Rosso Pachino. All the wine is producedù by the local *cantina sociale* (co-operative wine-growers' association). Look out for the "Cooperativa Enoagricola" in the Camporeale quarter.

TRAPANI

This western part of the island together with the Egadi Islands and the island of Pantelleria has a seafood cuisine influenced by the Arabs.

This province on the sea is connected to the African Continent by far-away Pantelleria, the "windy island". Closer to the coast, the archipelago of the Egadi Islands, with the two little islands, Maraone and Formica, face the salt fields to the south of mainland Trapani. Sailors from the Baltics, in need of salt, would come here, leaving their gift of *baccalà* (partially dried salt cod) to the local cuisine. The cuisine came about as a result of continual Arab, French and Spanish influences. The province is also gifted with superb wines – from the Marsala Vergine and Superiore to the DOC Alcamo – and prized olive oils. The DOP olive variety, Nocellara del Belice, from which the DOP olive oil Valli Trapanesi is produced, grows here.

Alcamo A farmhouse

Gourmet Tours

TRAPANI. The town is situated on a crescent-shaped headland at the western-most point of Sicily. The historical center is very Arabian in style. Along the ancient road, the Rua Grande, today called the Corso Vittorio Emanuele, are the cathedral and beautiful buildings dating from the eighteenth century. From the coastal road, Regina Elena, you can see the salt fields and the Egadi islands. Fish couscous is the most prominent local dish. The "Giovanni Renda" store and the "La Chiazza" market stalls sell typical produce from the tuna-fishing industry: smoked steaks, *tonnina* (a type of tuna sausage) and products made from all parts of the fish. You should try the pizza, without *mozzarella*, called *rianata* (with oregano) – for this we recommend the "Pizzeria Calvino", established in 1947. For sweets, try the cake shop "Vanella" for its *cassate* (sponge cake, *ricotta*, sugar, candied fruit, all wrapped up in green marzipan), *cannoli* (tube of pastry filled with a mixture of *ricotta* sweetened with sugar and either pistachios or candied fruit) and *pasta reale* (a marzipan sweet); and "Colicchia" for its '*scarzonera*' ice-creams (jasmine-flavored), *granite* (flavored crushed ice – here the mulberry flavor is very good), and *cannoli*. The "Trattoria del Porto" serves *tonno in agrodolce* (sweet and sour tuna), *seppie farcite* (stuffed cuttlefish) and fish couscous. There is also good seafood

to be found at the "P & G", "Meeting" and "Peppe" restaurants. A little out of town, in Xitta, you will find the *agriturismo* establishment, "Duca di Castelmonte", set in a building that once belonged to the nobility. The Comune di Paceco, once part of land belonging to an ancient salt town, is today an unusual ecological museum. The area produces yellow melons, the DOP Valli Trapanesi olive oil – one of the best in western Sicily – and handmade cheeses. The olive oil produced by "Case Sparse" of Guarrato is excellent – you will find them along the road to Marsala.

Trapani. Saltpan

1. From Erice to Alcamo

ERICE. This fascinating ancient city is situated on an isolated mountain of limestone. The cuisine of the hotel "Moderno" has been inspired by Arabian traditions, the fish couscous being its Buon Ricordo dish. The cakes, based on almonds, chocolate, lemon, rum and citron pulp, are excellent. The cake shops "Antica Pasticceria del Convento" and "Grammatico" sell *ericini* whose recipe dates back to the nuns of the S.Carlo convent, and *mustazzoli di Erice* (biscuits). Locally they also produce the liqueur *amaro ericino*, which is a deep green color. Good eateries include the seafood restaurant, "Monte San Giuliano", and the "Osteria di Venere" with Trapani cuisine based on fresh pasta. In Valderice, you will find the hotel-restaurant, "Baglio Santa Croce", set in a seventeenth-century farm, whose dining-room is carved out of a grotto.

SAN VITO LO CAPO. This is a typical tuna-fishing village, whose cuisine reflects various influences. There are almond plantations in the area and the nuts are used in cakes. You will find both Trapani and traditional cuisine in the restaurants "Alfredo" and "Tha'am".

CASTELLAMMARE DEL GOLFO. The waters and beaches around the castle tempt you to stop a while and the hotel-restaurant, "Al Madarig", provides you with the perfect excuse. The Riserva Naturale Regionale dello Zingaro (regional park) is situated on the Mediterranean. Near the Riserva in the Badia quarter, is the *agriturismo* establishment, "Camillo Finazzo". The "Torre Bennistra" restaurant in Scopello is good. Set around an eighteenth-century *baglio* (farm of feudal origins), it comes complete with ancient tuna-fishery.

ALCAMO. This Città del Vino has an Arab name and origins. It is famous for its DOC Alcamo wine, but also produces olive oil, pre-

served olives and excellent watermelons. You will find the "Enoteca" on the street called Via Madonna del Riposo. In the countryside you will find the *bagli* which, in the nineteenth century, were used to produce the must for Marsala. The "Cantina Sperimentale dell'Istituto Regionale della Vite e del Vino", near Camporeale, cultivates 40 different varieties of grape, and there you can taste the local wines.

CALATAFIMI. On the road to Calatafimi, you will pass Segesta, an archaeological site whose origins date back to the times of the ancient Elimi people who lived in western Sicily. The Doric temple, which has been saved from the ravages of the weather, looms out of the landscape. A little further on, ancient *Kalat al-Fin* (the ancient name for Calatafimi) stands out amongst the vines. You should stop at the "Marzuko" *cantina* where they make Müller Thurgau and Chardonnay wines, as well as the local wines, Cataratto, Inzolia and Nero d'Avola.

HOTELS AND RESTAURANTS

Pantelleria (island of)
I Mulini ¶¶
contrada Tracino
☎ 0923915398
Favarotta ¶
contrada Favarotta
☎ 0923915347
San Vito lo Capo
Alfredo ¶¶ ★🄒
zona Valanga
☎ 0923972366
Tha'am ¶¶ ★🄒
via Abruzzi 32
☎ 0923972836
Pocho ¶
contrada Maccari
☎ 0923972525
Selinunte
Pierrot ¶ ★🄒
at Marinella (km 1)
via Marco Polo 108
☎ 092446205
Valderice
Baglio Santa Croce ★★★
S.S. 187 (km 12,300)
☎ 0923891111
Sirena ¶¶
contrada Bonagia
via Lungomare 41
☎ 0923573176

AGRITURISMI

Trapani
Duca di Castelmonte
via S. Motisi Xitta 3
☎ 0923526139
Castellammare del Golfo
C. Finazzo ★🄒
contrada Baida
☎ 092438051

San Cusumano.
The tuna killing.

2. From Marsala to the Belice Valley

MARSALA. Even though its name is Arabic (from *Marsa Alì*, meaning Port of Allah), its origins are Phoenician and its architecture Renaissance and Baroque. Towards Capo Boeo, there are Roman remains and further on there are the archaeological excavations of Mozia Island. Marsala is the most highly populated town of the province and is known for its famous "Marsala" (a fortified wine). The drink comes from a Roman wine which was refined by the Spanish and then reworked by the Englishman, Woodhouse, in the last quarter of the eighteenth century. We recommend the restaurant, "Delfino" with its *carpaccio di tonno al basilico* (raw tuna with basil), *pennette alla bottarga* (*pennette* pasta with roe) and the unmissable fish couscous. In the *trattorie*, you will find good cooking, fresh fish and seafood couscous. For shopping, note the "Gerardi" store selling charcuterie and typical Sicilian and Italian products, and the cake shop "Pasticceria e&n". In this area, we highly recommend the *cantine* "Florio" and "Donnafugata" and the nineteenth-century "Cantine Rallo", where you will find everything from the Marsala Superiore and Vergine to the *moscati* (Muscat wines), and from the *passiti* (wine made from raisins) of Pantelleria to the DOC wines of Contessa Entellina. Note also Mr De Bertoli's Marsala Vecchio

Samperi, in the Fornara Samperi Quarter. On the coast, there are wine-making establishments dating from the nineteenth and twentieth centuries, some still using the traditional *baglio* structures. The wine and agricultural museum of Montalto, on the road to Mazara, is dedicated to the wine-producing activities of Marsala.

MAZARA DEL VALLO. The town, founded by the Phoenicians, has little streets which testify to the Arabic period when it was the capital town of the Mazara Valley. It is a Città del Pesce di Mare (City of Salt-Water Fish) and its cuisine combines fish with vegetables. The *trattoria*, "Pescatore", serves *caserecci con zucchin e e cernia* (*caserecci* pasta with zucchini and grouper) and *gamberetti marinati alle alghe* (shrimp marinated in seaweed). You really should try *the mazaresi al pistacchio* which you can buy in the cake shops. The town is renowned for its anchovies preserved in salt.

Pantelleria. Arco dell'Elefante

CASTELVETRANO. This Città dell'Olio, like is neighbor Campobello di Mazara, is situated amongst vineyards, olive groves and vegetable gardens in the Belice Valley. Towards the sea lies Selinunte, an ancient Greek town with magnificent temples. We can recommend the cuisine at "Pierrot" in nearby Marinella.

GIBELLINA NUOVA. To reach this town, you will go through Partanna and Santa Ninfa, vineyards and olive groves interspersed with vegetable gardens (especially artichokes), where the DOP olive,

Nocellara del Belice, grows. The new town was built after the 1968 earthquake and includes some important modern architecture and the ghostly abandoned remains of Gibellina Vecchia.

SALEMI. This Città del Vino was ancient Halyciae, an Elimo town, and then became Arab (Salam). The tradition of bread-making lives on through the festival of San Giuseppe. The breads come in various forms, including stairs, nails, the crown of thorns, and fish. In the surrounding hills, there are corn fields, vineyards, olive groves and citrus groves.

3. The Egadi and Pantelleria islands

FAVIGNANA. This is the largest island in the archipelago, and a fishing center with the most well-known tuna fishery in Sicily. On the plateaus, there are also corn fields, vineyards and pastures. We can recommend the "Sorelle Guccione" restaurant with excellent seafood and a superb couscous.

MARETTIMO. Mount Falcone, which rises to 686 meters, is the highest point on the islands. Marettimo has a Bourbon fort and a Marine Reserve. The restaurant "Il Veliero" serves cuscus con la 'ghiotta' di pesce (fish couscous with a sauce of tomato, olives, capers and celery).

LEVANZO. Set on a high plateau with steep cliffs, the town cultivates vines and cereals. At the "Paradiso" restaurant you will get seafood cuisine, including couscous, and you can also stay overnight.

PANTELLERIA. This island is situated in the middle of the Mediterranean Sea. Its coastline is fragmented and its landscape is studded with dammusi (cubic houses made of lava stone). Here locals cultivate capers (buy them at the "Cooperativa Agricola) in holes in the ground to protect them from the wind. They produce raisins, sweet wines – the "Passito" and Moscato of Pantelleria – and also red wines, dry whites and the sparkling "Solimano". Many aziendas take part in wine tourism. Try the "I Mulini" restaurant set in some ancient dammusi or the "Favarotta" trattoria with its spaghetti al pesto pantesco (spaghetti with Pantelleria-style pesto sauce) and its coniglio selvatico (wild rabbit). You can buy passiti wines and extra virgin olive oil at the "Murana" azienda.

SHOPPING

Trapani
Pasticceria Colicchia
via Arti 6/8
☎ 0923547612
Sweets and pastries.
Pasticceria Vanella
via Fedra 27
☎ 0923535804
Sweets and pastries.
Salumeria Renda
via G.B. Fardella 82
☎ 092322270
Charcuterie.
Alcamo
Enoteca Manfrè
v. S. Maria del Riposo 43
☎ 092426596
Wines.
Erice
Antica Pasticceria del Convento
via Guarnotta 1
☎ 0923869777
Sweets and pastries.
Il Tulipano
via V. Emanuele 10
☎ 0923869672
Almond sweets and nougat.
Maria Grammatico
via V. Emanuele 14
☎ 0923869390
Traditional sweets.
Tonnara
Nino Castiglione
contrada S. Cusumano
☎ 0923562088
Tuna.
Marsala
Gerardi Alimentari
piazza Mameli 14
☎ 0923952240
Typical products.
Pasticceria Aloha
via Mazzini
Palazzo Giattino
☎ 0923715460
Sweets and pastries.
Pasticceria e&n
via XI Maggio 130
☎ 0923951969
Sweets and pastries.
Pantelleria (island of)
Cooperativa Agricola Produttori Capperi
contrada Scauri Basso
☎ 0923916079
Capers.

Egadi Islands. The small port of Marettimo

★★★★

Hotel Aloha D'Oro

The Aloha D'Oro Hotel is adjacent to the city centre of Acireale and, im the mean time, at a stone throw from the sea. It is located within a park gradually descending to our private beach below, made of lava stones, and to our outfitted platforms, reached by a private 500 Mt long road. The hotel also disposes two swimming pools, one of which is heated from 21 March until 31 October.

Unusual for a modern hotel, it is characterized by a main area called "Il Castello" (The Castle). It is build with materials and techniques typical of this area, enriched with wooden window frames, red tiles, arches, towers and wrought iron decorations.

As for the architecture, our cuisine is highly influenced by local traditions of good food; our restaurant "Le Torri" (The Towers) displays every evening on its menu at least one main course and one second course, both based on fresh Mediterranean fish.

Via de Gasperi, 10 - 95024 Acireale
Tel +39 095 7687001 - Fax +39 095 606984
e-mail: Info@hotel.aloha.it
web: www.hotel-aloha.com

Once again La Dispensa di Ulisse (Ulisse's Pantry) comes to you with a choice selection of foods and wines from prestigious Sicilian producers.
We invite you to visit our Site, from which you can order directly a wide range of quality products from all over Sicily.
Many of our products bear important brand names, while others are produced from small firms renowned among connoisseurs and refined palates.
Ours is a showcase you can explore comfortably from home or office, from which to create your own "Pantry" or choose exquisite gifts for Friends or Customers.
Your choice of products will be delivered with speed to the recipients indicated by you, together with a personal message you can send us or on one of our cards with the wording of your choice.
Hoping to number you among our Customers, if you aren't one already, we wish to thank you for the time you have taken to read this message.

www.dispensa.com

La Dispensa di Ulisse

Enogastronomia Mediterranea di Qualità

e-mail: info@dispensa.com
FAX: +39 0922 870441

SARDINIA AN ISLAND OF ANCIENT FLAVORS

Sardinian culture has a strong respect for agricultural and pastoral traditions, something that is reflected in the local gastronomy. This is also a reason why Sardinia has been able to resist the pull of seaside resort tourism.

A reporter for the Touring Club Italiano who was visiting the island in 1929 was impressed with how the old traditions, in every aspect of life, had been kept for centuries. Now, at the beginning of the third millennium, the cult of all things traditional, and independenc has changed very little. This is also true of culinary customs, which have remained simple by rejecting certain foods that would need to be imported by sea and, consequently, be expensive.

Costa Smeralda. Capriccioli beach and Cala di Volpe

A PASTORAL ISLAND

When you talk about an island, you think first of the sea and consequently of a fish-based cuisine. But Sardinia, even if well-known for its tuna and lobster, is different because most foods come from inland, including fruit, vegetables and cereals. Goats, sheep and cattle are also reared in the hinterland, which means that dairy products are good. And although Sardinia's cuisine is mainly land-based, its climate and situation in the Mediterranean give its foods a special flavor.

TYPICAL FLAVORS FROM THE HINTERLAND

The traditional gastronomy is characterized by farming and sheep-rearing, which strongly influence the pasta and soups. Meats also feature prominently, especially lamb and kid goat. Cooking methods are simple: meats are mostly grilled or skewered, and aromatic herbs are used in abundance. In the autumn come the game and mushrooms. None of this means detracts from the quality of the fish, quite the opposite, in fact. The varieties of fish range from tuna to shellfish, and there are many canning factories whose specialty is the *bottarga* made from mullet eggs. Restaurants are more developed on the coast because of the tourists. There are many high-class restaurants, and of these, the "Corsaro" in Cagliari is especially good. The hinterland restaurants are less sophisticated and pleasantly unpretentious.

Sardinia - Typical products

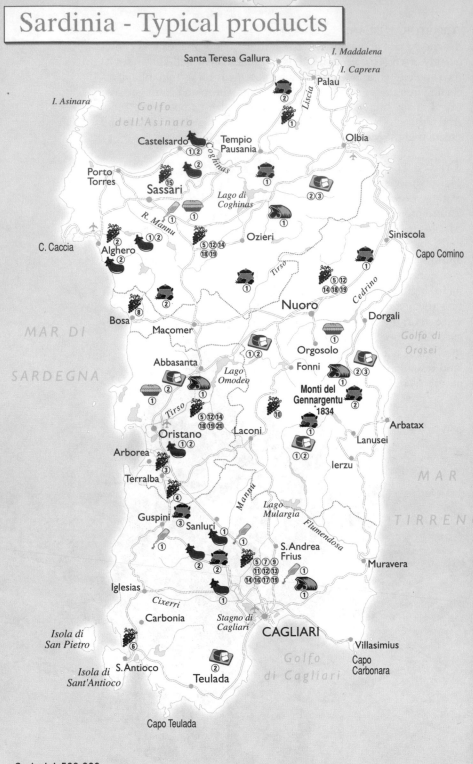

I. Maddalena
Santa Teresa Gallura
I. Caprera
Palau
Liscia

I. Asinara
Golfo
dell'Asinara

Olbia

Castelsardo
Tempio
Pausania
Coghinas

Porto
Torres

Sassari
Lago di
Coghinas

R. Mannu
Siniscola
Capo Comino

C. Caccia
Alghero
Ozieri

Tirso
Cedrino

Nuoro

Bosa
Dorgali

Macomer
Golfo di
Orosei

MAR DI
Abbasanta
Lago
Omodeo
Orgosolo
Fonni

SARDEGNA
Tirso
Monti del
Gennargentu
1834

Oristano
Laconi
Arbatax
Lanusei

Arborea
Ierzu

Terralba
MAR

Guspini
Mannu
Lago
Mulargia
TIRRENO

Sanluri
S.Andrea
Frius

Iglesias
Cixerri
Muravera

Isola di
San Pietro
Carbonia
Stagno di
Cagliari
CAGLIARI

S.Antioco
Villasimius
Capo
Carbonara

Isola di
Sant'Antioco
Teulada
Golfo
di Cagliari

Capo Teulada

Scale 1:1 500 000
0   15   30 km

CHEESES

1. **Fiore Sardo Dop.**
   Produced in central Sardinia.

2. **Pecorino Sardo Dop.**
   Sheep's milk cheese exclusive to the region.

3. **Pecorino Romano Dop.**
   Sheep's milk cheese produced in Sassari
   and Nuoro.

MEATS

1. **Agnello di Sardegna.**
   Sardinian lamb found across the region.

VEGETABLES

1. **Carciofo di Sardegna.**
   Artichokes grown in Samassi, Serramanna,
   Decimoputzu, Oristano, Ittiri and Valledoria.

2. **Pomodoro camone di Sardegna.**
   Tomatoes grown in Campidano di Cagliari,
   Oristano, Alghero, Nurra, Valledoria
   and Anglona.

EXTRA-VIRGIN OLIVE OIL

1. **Sardegna.** Produced in Sassari,
   Gonnosfanadiga, Igleslente, Dolianova
   and Campidano di Cagliari.

VARIOUS

1. **Miele di Sardegna.**
   Sardinian honey especially good in the
   mountainous areas.

2. **Mirto di Sardegna.**
   Sardinian myrtle found throughout
   the region.

3. **Zafferano di Sardegna.**
   Sardinian saffron cultivated in Cagliaritano,
   in San Gavino Monreale.

BREAD AND SWEETS

1. **Pane carasau.**
   Found in the northern part of the island.

DOCG WINES

1. **Vermentino di Gallura**

DOC WINES

2. **Alghero**
3. **Arborea**
4. **Campidano di Terralba**
5. **Cannonau di Sardegna**
6. **Carignano del Sulcis**
7. **Girò di Cagliari**
8. **Malvasia di Bosa**
9. **Malvasia di Cagliari**
10. **Mandrolisai**
11. **Monica di Cagliari**
12. **Monica di Sardegna**
13. **Moscato di Cagliari**
14. **Moscato di Sardegna**
15. **Moscato di Sorso-Sennori**
16. **Nasco di Cagliari**
17. **Nuragus di Cagliari**
18. **Sardegna Semidano**
19. **Vermentino di Sardegna**
20. **Vernaccia di Oristano**

CAGLIARI

This is a large province, rich in resources, with Cagliari, the provincial capital, being the culinary highlight.

The province of Cagliari includes all the southern part of the island and a good part of the plain of Campidano, and stretches from the Gulf of Cagliari to the Oristanese area and the mountain districts that flank it: the Iglesiente to the west, and Sarrabus, Trexenta and others to the east. The agricultural production is intense, particularly in Campidano, with the cultivation of vegetables, artichokes and tomatoes, and many vineyards and olive groves (Dolianova, Gonnosfanadiga), citrus groves (Villacidro), almond trees (Sanluri) and peaches (San Sperate, Villacidro).

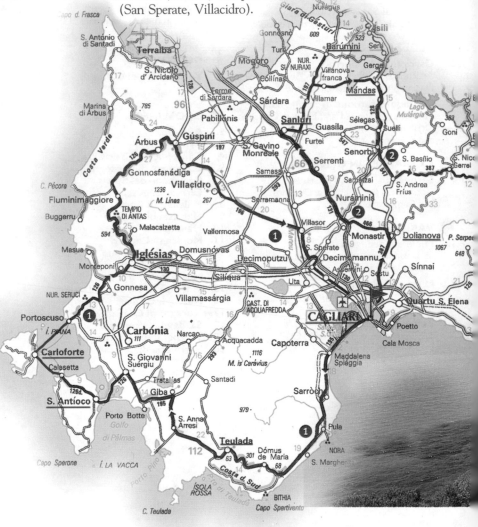

One unique specialty is the cultivation of saffron in San Gavino Monreale, which accounts for 19 of the 25 hectares of the entire national production. The rest of the province is dedicated to vineyards and orchards but, most of all to the rearing of sheep and goats which produce the area's renowned dairy products. What really typifies the Cagliari province is the wine - with wines exclusive or specific to the area, such as Carignano del Sulci, Girò, Malvasia, Monica and Nasco di Cagliari, and regional wines such as Nuragus and Cannonau. Completing the picture is the fishing, with the *tonnare* (fixed places for fishing tuna) of the Sulci Islands, and the preparation of preserved fish such as *bottarga* and *musciame*. The cuisine, heavy with many primary ingredients, is firmly grounded in tradition, with tourist areas providing most of the innovation. The most notable examples of cooking can be found in the provincial capital, because of the long-lasting influences of Liguria, Spain and Piedmont, and in the Sulcis Islands where North African and Genoese ideas have been superimposed. Restaurants are of a good standard, the "Corsaro" in Cagliari being an institution.

Gourmet Tours

CAGLIARI. This is an old port with a wealthy agricultural hinterland: flavors of the sea and countryside combine to make the cuisine exceptional. The history of the town is represented in the Pisan churches and towers, a castle of Spanish influence, and districts with Ligurian and Piedmont aspects (there is an important museum dedicated to the Punic origins and Nuraghic prehistory of the island). The cuisine is singular because of the merging of different influences. On the subject of restaurants, the first one we recommend is the very central "Dal Corsaro", managed for many

The south coast

HOTELS AND RESTAURANTS

Cagliari
Dal Corsaro ¶¶¶
viale Regina Margherita 28
☎ 070664318
Flora ¶¶¶
via Sassari 45
☎ 070664735
Spinnaker del Corsaro di Marina Piccola ¶¶¶
at Poetto (km 5)
☎ 070370295
Antica Hostaria ¶¶
via Cavour 60
☎ 070665870
Lo Scoglio ¶¶
borgo S. Elia
at La Spiaggiola
☎ 070371927
La Balena ¶
via S. Gilla 123/125
☎ 070288415
Lillicu ¶
via Sardegna 78
☎ 070652970
Barumini
Su Nuraxi ¶¶
strada Provinciale
☎ 0709368305
Sa Lolla ¶
via Cavour 49
☎ 0709368419
Calasetta
Da Pasqualino ¶
via Roma 99
☎ 078188473

generations by the Deidda family. The atmosphere is classic and pleasant, the service and standards are excellent, and the wine cellar exceptional. Their Buon Ricordo dish is the *minestr' e cocciula*, a soup with mussels. During the summer the Deidda family have an additional restaurant at Poetto, with a menu exclusively of fish. Next to this restaurant is the "Spinnaker", open all year round and specializing in fish dishes at cheaper prices. Not far away, by the sea near the lighthouse of St. Elia, there is another restaurant we can recommend, the "Lo Scoglio". In the town another choice is the "Flora", with typical cuisine of the district, such as *spaghetti al cartoccio con frutti di mare* (spaghetti with shell fish cooked in paper) and *cinghiale in umido marinato con la cannella* (stewed wild boar marinated in cinnamon). Still in the center, try the "Antica Hostaria",

a small but elegant place, or the "Lillicu", which offers simple and traditional flavors in the popular district of Marina. For those searching for something truly typical of the area, there is "La Balena", serving no first courses, no vegetables, just fresh grilled fish. For a sweet conclusion to your meal, there is the old cafe, "Genovese", in the very central Piazza della Costituzione, and the cake shop "Piemontese" in front of the lively town market. In the shops you will find the typical foods of the island, from seasonal sausages to a variety of cheeses, from the traditional bread to the renowned cakes and nougat. You can find wines and spirits at "Zeddo Piras"; founded in 1854, it is the oldest wine merchant on the island. Turning to the west, in Quartu Sant'Elena we recommend the restaurant "Hibiscus", known for its imaginative cuisine, which is good value for money. In Sinnai they produce cheese from sheep's milk. In Capoterra there is the Buon Ricordo

HOTELS AND RESTAURANTS

Capoterra
**Sa Cardiga e
Su Schironi** ¶¶
at Maddalena
Spiaggia (km 5)
☎ 07071652
Carloforte
Hieracon ★★★
Lo Sparviero ¶¶
corso Cavour 62
☎ 0781854028
**Al Tonno di
Corsa** ¶¶
via Marconi 47
☎ 0781855106
Costa Rei
★ ⌨ **Sa Cardiga
e su Pisci** ¶¶
piazza Sardegna 10
☎ 070991108
Iglesias
Pan di Zucchero ¶
at Nebida (km 15)
via Centrale 365
☎ 078571699
Portoscuso
La Ghinghetta
★★★
★ ¶¶¶
via Cavour 28
☎ 0781508143
Quartu
Sant'Elena
★ ⌨ **Hibiscus** ¶¶
via Dante 81
☎ 070881373
Villa San Pietro
Terrarancio ¶¶
at Su Cunventeddu
☎ 070907519

The Giara di Gesturi

restaurant, "Sa Cardiga e su Chironi", serving the specialty '*cassola de pisci*' (a rich fish soup flavored with tomato sauce, garlic, oil and chilli pepper).

1. The Iglesiente area

TEULADA. From Cagliari take the Sulcitana road. The first road sign points you to Villa San Pietro and the popular restaurant "Terrarancio", part of a small country hotel. Then there is Pula where you will find the ruins of the Punic town of Nora and the beautiful beaches of Santa Margherita. Further ahead the road divides. One fork follows the south coast to the archaeological site of *Bithia*, the other fork goes on to Teulada, an unusual-looking village renowned for its work with stones and textiles. For those interested in wine, the "Cantina Sociale di Santadi " is a good landmark between the coast and the hills. The best product here is Carignano, both in grape and wine form.

SANT'ANTIOCO. Heir to the Phoenician town of *Sulcis*, Sant'Antioco is the capital of the island bearing the same name, which can be reached by a narrow isthmus. In the village you can visit the church dedicated to the patron saint. All around there are the "Carignano" and "Monica" vineyards. In Calasetta, from where you can take a boat to the island of S. Pietro, there is the

The Iglesiente landscape

trattoria "Da Pasqualino" which serves a good range of fish. A short distance away, there is the "Sardegna Market" offering popular produce from land and sea.

CARLOFORTE. This is the capital of the Island of S. Pietro. It was founded at the end of the eighteenth-century by a Piedmont military engineer and populated by Ligurian sailors released from prison in Tabarka, Tunisia. Specialties are the *capponata* (a sort of starter salad) and the North African *cascà* clearly originating from couscous. The prime dish is tuna, fresh, canned or smoked. At the restaurant "Al Tonno di Corsa", you can eat tuna in all its different sauces, served with the best wines of the island. We also recommend the Art Nouveau "Hieraçon" hotel with its restaurant "Lo Sparviero". In the stores you can find all sorts of preserved fish, while in the cake shops you can find the *amarettoni carlofortini* almond biscuits. When you cross the Canale delle Colonne by ferry to Portoscuso, you will be tempted by "La Ghinghetta", a small hotel in a beautiful setting, which serves very good food and specializes in fish and shellfish.

IGLESIAS. *Villa Ecclesiarum* is the old name of this town, with reference ot the second-century cathedral. On the coast at Nebi-

VERMENTINO
di Sardegna

SERRAMANNA

HOTELS AND RESTAURANTS

Villasimius
Il Giardino ⫲
via Brunelleschi 4
☎ 070791441
Il Ragno Blu ⫲
at Santo Stefano II
☎ 070797061
Le Zagare ★★
provinciale per
Villasimius, km 19
☎ 070791581

AGRITURISMI

Arbus
La Quercia
at Riu Martini - Sibiri
☎ 0709756035
Capoterra
Fratelli Piga
at Baccalamanza
☎ 070728131
Pula
**Consorzio
Agriturismo
di Sardegna**
at Villa San Pietro
☎ 078373954
Villacidro
Monti Mannu
at Bassella
via Stazione 57
☎ 0709329369

WINE PRODUCERS

Cagliari
Zedda Piras
via Ciusa 125
☎ 070502351

WINE PRODUCERS

Santadi
**Cantina
Sociale Santadi**
via Su Pranu 8
☎ 0781950127
**Senorbi
Cantina Sociale
della Trexenta**
viale Piemonte 28
☎ 0709808863
**Serdiana
Argiolas**
via Roma 56
☎ 070740606

SHOPPING

Cagliari
Caffè Genovese
piazza della
Costituzione 12
☎ 070654843
*Home-made pastries
and ice-creams.*
Il Formaggiaio
via Cocco Ortu 11
☎ 070492167
*Goat's and sheep's milk
cheeses, sausages,
"bottarga" and honey.*
Latteria Italiana
viale Diaz 162
☎ 070306453
*Cheeses, charcuterie,
wines, "bottarga", olive
oil, preserves, "carasau"
bread and sweets.*
**Pasticceria
Piemontese**
via Cocco Ortu 39
☎ 07041365
Sweets and pastries.
Piras Carni
via Pessina 95
☎ 070303272
*Sardinian meat
and charcuterie.*

da it is worth considering a visit to the rustic *trattoria* attached to the hotel "Pan di Zucchero". Back in town visit the cake shops to buy the typical *suspiros* (biscuits made of a sugar and almond paste which, once baked, are covered in lemon-flavored sugar icing) . You then have a choice of a quick return to Cagliari, or the spectacular tour of Mount Linas. In the latter case, the first stop is at Fluminimaggiore for olive oil and good wine, then comes Guspini, the gateway to Campidano, where you can buy the best products of the Arburese area: meat, cheese, sausage and honey. Finally you come to Villacidro, renowned for its artichokes and saffron. On the road, in the various *trattorie*, you get lamb, goat and *porceddu* (pork cooked on a spit).

2. The Campidano, Trexenta and Sarrabus areas

DOLIANOVA. The evocative Romanesque church of S. Pantaleo is a pleasant surprise. Important products of this district are vegetables, olive oil, wine and cheese. In Serdiana, we especially recommend the *cantina* "Argiolas" and its ample stock of DOC wines (Nuragus, Vermentino, Cannonau and Monica) as well as good table wines. For olive oil, try the "Cooperativa Olivicoltori del Parteolla", which also offers specialties such as olives in brine, pressed, and *a scabecciu* (marinated in olive oil, vinegar, salt, parsley and garlic).

SANLURI. This is the agricultural center which has grown up around the Castle of Eleonora d'Arborea, the only well-pre-

served medieval Sardinian castle, and now a museum. In the shops there is sausage, cheese and traditional bread.

BARUMINI. There are two points of interest for the tourist: the prehistoric site of *Su Nuraxi*, the royal palace of the Nuraghic period, surrounded by a village, and the Giara di Gesturi, a high plain with steep cliffs, covered in cork (oak) trees, and with roaming wild ponies. The gastronomic offerings range from vegetables, cheeses and lamb to salt pork and sausages. "Su Nuraxi" is also the name of a good restaurant which serves traditional cuisine.

MANDAS. This is a pastoral and agricultural village. The wines produced in this district are Vermentino, Nuragus, Malva-

A traditional costume.

Rural landscape of the hinterland

sia, Moscato Bianco and Monica – see the "Cantina Sociale della Trexenta" in Senorbì. Not far away is the town of Gesico, a Città delle Lumache (City of Snails) with a well-known festival at the end of October.

MURAVERA. The famous local wine, Cannonau, is the equal of Villaputzu and Capoferrato. Also renowned are the thistles, tomatoes and oranges. To end the journey, you can go by the internal Orientale Sarda road that crosses the mountains of Sarrabus, otherwise, take the panoramic coastal road which also offers good eating places along the way. In Costa Rei the restaurant "Sa Cardig e su Pisci" specializes in grilled fish. In Villasimius there are three restaurants: "Il Ragno Blu", on the road to Capo Carbonara, the quaint "Il Giardino" and "Le Zagare" , a hotel which is good value for money.

SHOPPING

Calasetta
Sardegna Market
via Roma 110
☎ 0781899000
Regional specialties.
Dolianova
**Cooperativa
Olivicoltori
del Parteolla**
via E. Lussu 43
☎ 070741329
*Olive oil and typical
specialties made
from olives.*
Maracalagonis
**Famiglia
Corvetto-Garia**
via Dante 20
☎ 070700524
*Typical home-made
sweets and pastries.*
Su Sirboni
via Fani 11
☎ 070789535
*Charcuterie made
from pork and wild
boar.*
Quartu
Sant'Elena
Il Dolce Antico
via Cagliari 10
☎ 070884734
*Typical sweets from
Campidano: "gueffus",
"papassinas",
"pastissus".*
Sorelle Piccioni
viale Marconi 312
☎ 070810112
*Regional sweets
and pastries.*

NUORO

This is the virtually inaccessible and picturesque heart of the island where the pastoral traditions and the flavors of the past are best preserved.

The province of Nuoro is on the central-eastern part of Sardinia. It is mostly mountainous and hilly, culminating in the Gennargentu massif. Near the Tirreno Sea to the east, there are the Baronie and Ogliastra districts, whilst on the west coast there is Planargia, which ends in the town of Bosa. The economy is based on the breeding of goats and sheep, and the production of cheeses and meat, especially hams, in Ogliastra and Barbagia. The valleys are cultivated with cereals, potatoes and vegetables, while on the hills there are vines (in Bosa, Oliena, Dorgali, Jerzu and Sorgono), olive groves (Dorgali) and oranges (in Tortolì). The harvest of mushrooms and chestnuts is important, as is the production of honey. The DOP cheeses, Pecorino Sardo, Pecorino Romano and Fiore Sardo are the most typical of the province. Among the wines, we must mention the sweet white Malvasia di Bosa, the red wine, Mandrolisai

The cliffs of the Bosa coast

from Bovale, Cannonau and Monica grapes, and the Cannonau di Sardegna in Oliena, Dorgali and Jerzu. The cuisine of Nuoro draws on the traditions of the Barbagia area in central Sardinia. The starters are composed of various sausages and hams, the first courses consist of vegetable soups flavored with wild fennel, or pasta dishes with meat sauces and cheese, and the main courses are roast or stewed lamb, goat or pork. For dessert, there is usually nougat made with orange peel and toasted almonds.

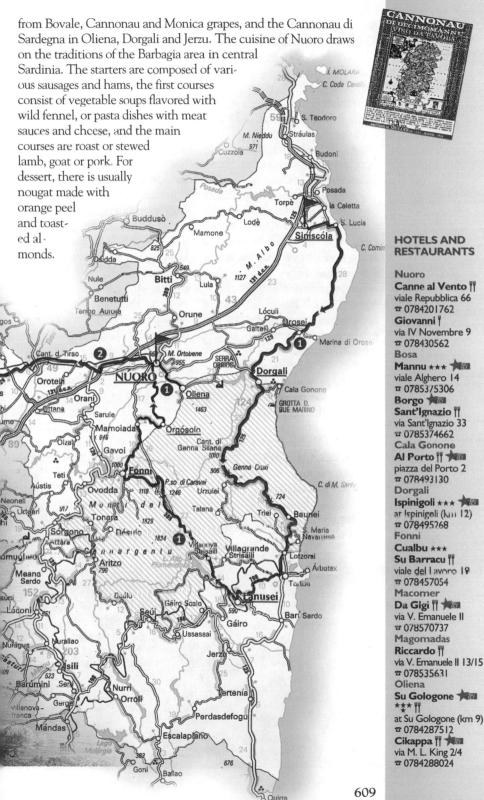

HOTELS AND RESTAURANTS

Nuoro
Canne al Vento ⑪
viale Repubblica 66
☎ 0784201762
Giovanni ⑨
via IV Novembre 9
☎ 078430562
Bosa
Mannu ★★★ 🏨
viale Alghero 14
☎ 0785375306
Borgo 🏨
Sant'Ignazio ⑪
via Sant'Ignazio 33
☎ 0785374662
Cala Gonone
Al Porto ⑪ 🏨
piazza del Porto 2
☎ 078493130
Dorgali
Ispinigoli ★★★ 🏨
at Ispinigoli (km 12)
☎ 078495268
Fonni
Cualbu ★★★
Su Barracu ⑪
viale del Lavoro 19
☎ 078457054
Macomer
Da Gigi ⑪ 🏨
via V. Emanuele II
☎ 078570737
Magomadas
Riccardo ⑪
via V. Emanuele II 13/15
☎ 078535631
Oliena
Su Gologone 🏨
★★★ ⑪
at Su Gologone (km 9)
☎ 0784287512
Cikappa ⑪ 🏨
via M. L. King 2/4
☎ 0784288024

Gourmet Tours

NUORO. In Nuoro you can visit the house where the writer Grazia Deledda was born, in the S. Pietro district (the tomb of the writer is in the church of Nostra Signora della Solitudine). You should also visit the Museo della Vita e Tradizioni Popolari Sarde (Museum of Traditional Sardinian life) situated on the hill of Sant'Onofrio. As for the food, the flavors are those of the *Barbaricini* (that is, from Barbigia): *porceddu* (roast pork), stewed mutton and a few seafood dishes. Two restaurants to try are the "Canne al Vento" and "Giovanni". In the local stores you can find all the products of the Sardinian mountains. In the cake shops – we recommend "Maria Francesca Fogheri" – you can buy nougat and *aranzada* (nougat made with orange peel and toasted almonds mixed with honey).

1. Baronia, Ogliastra and Supramonte

OROSEI. Taking you along the coast is the Statale 125 Orientale Sarda which you can join in

Siniscola or, more directly in Orosei, the old capital of Baronia. It has a central square, Piazza del Popolo, with four churches. The hotel "Su Barchile", in the historical center, has good family cuisine, especially fish.

DORGALI. The sea is just a short distance away behind a mountain, but the local economy is based on agriculture – it is a Città del Vino (City of Wine)– and the many craft shops along the main road, including goldsmiths, pottery and leather goods. The cuisine is also land-based and renowned for game, especially wild boar. You can try this a dozen kilometers away at the panoramic hotel-restaurant, the "Ispinigoli" near the grotto of the same name. Also to be recommended is the local olive oil, cheese and Cannonau wine. For fish go to Cala Gonone on the Gulf of Orosei – the "Al Porto" restaurant is a good example, as well as being a good hotel.

LANUSEI. This is the capital town of the Ogliastra area. In Tortolì there is the well-known restaurant, "Da Lenin", serving *bottarga* (mullet eggs), *spaghetti con le arselle* (spaghetti with mussels) and

The Gennargentu massif

HOTELS AND
RESTAURANTS

Oliena
Monte Maccione
at Monte Maccione
☎ 0784288363
Orgosolo
★ Ai Monti del
Gennargentu
at Settiles
☎ 0784402374
Orosei
Su Barchile ★★★
via Mannu 5
☎ 078498879
Tortolì
Da Lenin
via S. Gemiliano 19
☎ 0782624422

AGRITURISMI

Atzara
Zeminariu
at Zeminariu
☎ 078465235070
Bitti
Demurtas
at Ertila
via Deffenu 33
☎ 0784414558
Gavoi
Speranza
Todde Ibba
via Cagliari 192
☎ 078452021
Oliena
Camisadu
at Logheri
☎ 03683479502
Posada
★ Guparza
via Nazionale 26
☎ 0784854528

fried and grilled fish. To enhance the pleasure of the food, there is a good local Cannonau wine, which you can buy at the "Cantina Sociale dell'Ogliastra". Those wishing to venture further afield can visit Jerzu (a Città del Vino), Isilì and Laconi in the Sarcidano area, and Aritzo in the heart of the Gennargentu mountains, or Sorgono in the Mandrolisai area.

FONNI. This is the highest town in the island at 1000 meters, in the heart of Barbagia . The forests provide mushrooms and chestnuts, and you can also buy very good cheeses, sausages and hams here. The specialty of the area is pickled pears (*pire in cuffettu*). In the town the hotel "Cualbu" has a good restaurant, "Su Barracu", which is typical of the area.

ORGOSOLO. The town represents the pastoral side of Sardinia. We recommend the hotel-restaurant "Ai Monti del Gennargentu" which will introduce you to the Barbaricina cuisine.

OLIENA. At the foot of the limestone cliffs of Supramonte is this Città del Vino, known for the Nepente wine, an exceptional

Cannonau. The restaurants serve good food, particularly "Su Gologone" and "Cikappa".

2. The Bosa coast

MACOMER. The province of Nuoro opens out onto the western coast through a narrow corridor, with Macomer as the main town there. There is large-scale production of cheeses and agricultural products in general. The bread, including the famed *carta da musica*, is renowned. For a break, try the family-run hotel-restaurant, "Da Gigi".

BOSA. In the shops you can find the products of the ancient arts of filigree worked in gold and silver, embroidery, coral-working and wood-carving. In the surrounding area are the vineyards of the celebrated Malvasia as well as olive groves and vegetable gardens. Cuisine is land- and sea-based. For the former, go to the "Borgo Sant'Ignazio" restaurant with its warm welcome and typical Barbaricina food; for the latter, try "Mannu" on the seaward road, which is also a hotel. Halfway there, in Magomadas, there is another good restaurant, "Da Riccardo"

WINE PRODUCERS

Tortolì
Cantina Sociale Ogliastra
via Baccasara 39
☎ 0782623228

SHOPPING
Nuoro
Latteria Sociale Cooperativa
regione Biscollai
☎ 0784202416
Typical cheeses.
Pasticceria Fogheri
vico Giusti 21
☎ 078434300
Sweets and pastries such as "amuretti", "bianchini" and "aranzada".
Bosa
Costantino Brisi
viale della Repubblica 16
☎ 0785374591
Good selection of honey varieties.
Oliena
L'Elysée
via Managhesi 4
☎ 0784287390
Vast range of typical pastries from Oliena and "carasau" bread.
Villanova Strisaili
Agriturismo S'Arroali Manna
at Sarcerì
☎ 078230067
Cured ham, sausages, sheep's milk cheeses, good "carasau" bread and olive oil.

ORISTANO

Small and self-contained, Oristano extends from the sea to the market gardens of Campidano, and from the vine covered hills to the inland pastures.

This young province, comprising 77 comuni (municipalities) taken from the Cagliari and Nuoro provinces, occupies the central-western part of the island, including the highest side of the Campidano area overlooking the Gulf of Oristano, and the smaller mountains (Marmilla, Arborea, and the plateau of Abbasanta) at the foot of the Gennargentu massif. The largely agricultural economy is concentrated on fruit and vegetables (tomatoes, artichokes, cucumbers, melons and strawberries) grown on reclaimed land, and on vines and oranges grown on the sunlit hills. In the areas which are difficult to cultivate, the animal breeding and and cheese-making predominate. Fish (eels and mullet) are caught in the lakes of Sinis; a practise that links in with the preserving of *bottarga* (mullet roe). The most typical product is wine, characterized by the DOC production of traditional wines, such as the white Vernaccia di Oristano or the red Campidano di Terralba from Bovale, Pascale, Greco and Monica; and of new wines such as Arborea, with reds from Sangiovese and whites from Trebbiano Toscano grapes . The cuisine is firmly rooted in the farmhouse and pastoral traditions of the island,

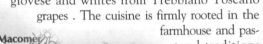

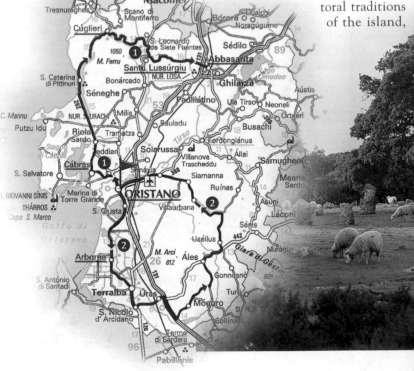

with pastas, vegetables and meats. But there is also an important seafood component in the lagoon areas, which varies according to local tastes, with grilled mullet and eels as well as the delicate flavor of *bottarga* enhancing a dish of spaghetti. Restaurants are limited, as is normal for a district not overly developed for tourism, with the exception of the excellent restaurant "Faro" in Oristano.

MONICA
DI SARDEGNA
SERRAMANNA

Gourmet Tours

ORISTANO. This town has its origins in the Punic town of *Tharros*, whose ruins are situated on the peninsula which encloses the gulf. The medieval tower of Mariano II records the territory of Arborea, of which Oristano was the capital. The landscape changes from the sea to the lagoons, then to the cultivated fields of the Campidano and the vineyards on the hills. All these result in a cuisine of fish – from freshwater fish to eels and mullet from the sea – and vegetables and meat from the farms. The first restaurant worth trying is the "Faro", a classic place with traditional dishes such as *spaghetti alle arselle* (spaghetti with

mussels), *fettuccine al sugo di cinghiale* (*fettuccine* pasta with wild boar sauce), followed by *cosciotto di maiale di montagna al Cannonau* (leg of mountain pig cooked in Cannonau wine). You will also eat well at the "Giovanni" restaurant, which offers seafood and the very best of pastas and fried dishes. A more simple stop would be at the *trattoria* "Da Gino" serving traditional dishes (mostly fish but also mushrooms, artichokes and asparagus). For accommodation there is the hotel "Cocco e Dessì", noted for its cuisine based on old recipes. In the shops, you can find preserved fish, at the "Cantina Sociale della Vernaccia", the local wine, and in the cake shops, nougat and cakes.

HOTELS AND RESTAURANTS

Oristano
Da Renzo ❢❢❢
sulla S.S. 131, al bivio
per Siamaggiore
☎ 078333658
Faro ❢❢❢
via Bellini 25
☎ 078370002
Cocco e Dessì ★★
via Tirso 31
☎ 0783300720
Da Gino ❢
via Tirso 13
☎ 078371428
Da Giovanni ❢
at Marina di Torre
Grande (km 8)
via Colombo 8
☎ 078322051
Arborea
Ala Birdi ★★★
L'Aragosta ❢❢
at the see (km 5)
☎ 0783801084
Cabras
Sa Funtà ❢❢
via Garibaldi 25
☎ 0783290685
Casas is
Carrogas ❢
at San Giovanni
di Sinis (km 12)
☎ 0783370071
Cuglieri
Meridiana ❢❢
via Littorio 1
☎ 078539400
Desogos ❢
via Cugia 6
☎ 078539660
Ghilarza
Al Marchi ❢
via Concezione 1
☎ 078552280
Santu Lussurgiu
La Bocca del Vulcano ❢
via Alagon 27
☎ 0783550974
Terralba
Cibò Qibò ❢❢ ★
via Marceddì 193
☎ 078383730

Pasture in the province of Oristano

Milking time for the productin of pecorino cheese

AGRITURISMI

Oristano
Consorzio
Agriturismo di
Sardegna
via Duomo 17
☎ 078373954
Arborea
Le Mimose
strada 24 Ovest
☎ 0783800587
Cabras
Da Nino e
Anna Maria
via De Castro 188
☎ 0783290595
Cuglieri
Pittinuri
at Santa Caterina
di Pittinuri
via Case Sparse
☎ 078538314

WINE
PRODUCERS

Oristano
Cantina Sociale
Cooperativa
della Vernaccia
at Rimedio (km 3)
via Oristano 149
☎ 078333860
Cabras
Attilio Contini
via Genova 8
☎ 0783290806

SHOPPING

Oristano
Dolce e Piccante
via Figoli 41
☎ 078372552
*Typical sweets and
wines; sheep's milk
cheeses and
"carasau" bread.*
Pasta Fresca
Cuozzo
via Figoli 87
☎ 078378292
*Home-made fresh
pasta such as
"malloreddus".*

1. The Sinis and the plateau of Abbasanta

CABRAS. It is worth making an extra visit to the lagoons of Cabras, often frequented by flocks of flamingos, and fishermen using the old bamboo boats. Here you can buy mullet fish roe at the firm "Anser". In the restaurants you will find the rare *merca,* which is a fillet of mullet conserved in salt between the stems of the Salicornia plant. The best restaurant in the district is "Da Renzo", which serves good fresh fish, particularly shell fish, and pasta with lobster sauce. "Sa Funtà" also has a good reputation and serves the classic *spaghetti con la bottarga* (spaghetti with fish roe) or *anguilla cotta con pecorino e pomodori secchi* (eels cooked with goat's cheese and sun-dried tomatoes). In the village you

can visit the *cantina* "Attilio Contini", which sells the prestigious Vernaccia wines but also the Cannonau, Vermentino and Moscato wines, and table wines from the indigenous Nieddera vines. In San Giovanni di Sinis, where you can visit the excavations of *Tharros,* the restaurant "Casas is Carrogas" specializes in grilled fish.

CUGLIERI. Going along the coastal road, the Nord Occidentale Sarda, you come to Santa Caterina di Pittinuri – a lovely place where you can swim amongst the rocks in the shadow of a Spanish tower – then carry on into the country towards the capital of the rural district of Muntiferru. We recommend the restaurant "Meridiana", set in an old road-mender's house with a big sundial, and a cuisine which juggles the traditional flavors well. Next comes the *trattoria*-inn, the "Desogos", with its specialties of wild boar and stewed meat with vegetables.

SANTU LUSSURGIU. The village is a tempting stop, set amongst olive groves and chestnut trees, with a fine fifteenth-century church and a lively craft industry. In the stores you can find carpets, knives, carved wood, wrought-iron work and a strong spirit called *filuferru*. You can find a culinary synthesis of the mountain region at the restaurant "La Bocca del Vulcano", with ham and sausages, *tagliatelle al sugo di cinghiale* (*tagliatelle* with wild boar sauce), *maialetto al mirto* (suckling pig with myrtle) and, for dessert, cakes made with *ricotta* cheese. In Seneghe note the "Frantoio Cosseddu"

olive press, whose organic extra virgin olive oil has earned it great fame.

ABBASANTA. This is an agricultural and pastoral village. Not far away there is the evocative Losa – an ancient stone-built settlement. In Ghilarza, you can visit the house, now a museum, of the communist writer and thinker Antonio Gramsci, and stop at the "Al Marchi" *trattoria* to eat the very good meat from their own farm, together with game and mushrooms. By traveling around Lake Omodeo, you descend into Fordongianus, the secluded spa town whose waters have been attracting visitors for thousands of years.

2. Campidano and Arborea

ARBOREA. This town was founded in 1928 in the middle of reclaimed land and was, at that time, called Mussolinia; it is one of the best examples of rational urbanism of its period. In the center there is the Piazza S. Maria Ausiliatrice (formerly Vittorio Emanuele III), with the neo-Gothic church, while the town hall is a mixture of medieval and Renaissance styles. In the hotel and sports complex "Ala Birdi", there is the "L'Aragosta" restaurant serving pasta with shell fish, grilled fish and *spigola all'oristanese* (sea bass Oristano-style – stewed in Vernaccia wine). Further on, in Terralba, still in the land of vineyards and vegetable gardens, there is the restaurant "Cibò Qibò" where they make land-based and seafood dishes and pizzas from the local primary ingredients. On the way back to Oristano, you cross the wine district of Arborea via Mogoro, where you will find some *cantinas*.

SHOPPING

Oristano
S'Antiga Bontade
via Campania 61
☎ 0783211756
Vast range of typical sweets such as "pippias de zuccuru", "mostaccioli", "gueffus".
Cabras
Anser
via Tharros 115
☎ 0783290738
"Bottarga" made from mullet.
Azienda Agricola Francesco Atzori
strada Provinciale 4 Km 2,500
☎ 0783290576
Excellent olive oil, and typical "Vernaccia di Oristano" white wine.
Fratelli Manca
via Bovio 30
☎ 0783290848
"Bottarga" and "merca" made from mullet, smoked mullet.
Seneghe
Frantoio Fratelli Cosseddu
via Iosto 13
☎ 0783310390
Sartos and Livarios olive oils.
Siamanna
Cooperativa Allevatori Ovini
via Satta 3
☎ 078552150
one shop in Ghilarza, via Tirso 21
Sheep's milk cheeses, "ricotta" and dairy products.

SASSARI

This is the golden Sardinia of upmarket tourism, with rocky coastlines providing plenty of lobster. But it is also a land full of farmhouse.

The province of Sassari is the largest in Sardinia. Situated at the northern part of the island, it is defined on three sides by a rocky coastline and many islands sculptured by the wind. It is divided into districts of varying types of landscape: the undulating Logudoro planted with cork oaks; the granite landscape of Gallura, two-thirds of which are hills; and, at the core, the mountain group of Limbara. The flat lands of Sassari and Alghero are ideal for the cultivation of cereals, vines, olive groves and citrus fruits while, on the slopes of the hills, the ground is also good for growing artichokes and tomatoes. The cultivation of vines for wine-making is very important, and the Vermentino di Gallura wine excels, recently attaining the DOCG (*Denominazione di Origine Controllata e Garantita*) standard. Other exclusive DOC (*Denominazione di Origine Controllata*) productions are the traditional Moscato di Sorso-Sennori from inland Castelsardo, and the innovative Alghero with its single-variety grape wines from either indigenous grapes (Torbato and Cagnulari) or imported grapes (Chardonnay, Sauvignon, Cabernet, and Sangiovese). The less productive land is used for the breeding of animals, so there are good cheeses and charcuterie. The fishing trade is important at Alghero and Porto Torres on one side of the province, and Palau and Olbia on the other. The cooking of the Sassari district is very similar to that of the rest of the island, with dishes such as the *favata*, a winter dish with broad beans, meat, bacon, sausage and local herbs. On the coast, the fish is the main food, with a preference for lobster, which is also used in many different sauces. In Alghero the influence of Catalan cuisine is very noticeable. As far as the restaurants are concerned, tourism has helped a lot, so top quality chefs can be found, especially in the more elegant towns, including some excellent female chefs at the "Gallura" restaurant in Olbia.

Stintino. Pelosa beach

HOTELS AND RESTAURANTS

Sassari
Giamaranto ¶¶
via Alghero 69
☎ 079274598
Senato ¶¶
via Alghero 36
☎ 079277788
L'Assassino ¶
vicolo Ospizio
Cappuccini 1/b
☎ 079235041
Alghero
La Lepanto ¶¶¶ ★🖾
via Carlo Alberto 135
☎ 079979116
Pavone ¶¶¶ ★🖾
piazza Sulis 3/4
☎ 079979584
Al Tuguri ¶¶ ★🖾
via Maiorca 113
☎ 079976772
Palau Real ¶¶ ★🖾
via Sant'Erasmo 14
☎ 079980688
Baia Sardinia
Grazia Deledda ¶¶¶¶
at Tilzitta
☎ 078998988
Club Hotel ★🕇★
Casablanca ¶¶¶
☎ 078999006
Castelsardo
Riviera ★🕇★ ★🖾
Fofò ¶¶ ★🖾
lungomare Anglona 1
☎ 079470143
Sa Ferula ¶¶ ★🖾
at Lu Bagnu (km 5)
corso Italia 1/b
☎ 079474049
La Maddalena
La Grotta ¶ ★🖾
via Principe di Napoli 3
☎ 0789737228
Sottovento ¶
via Indipendenza 1
☎ 0789727792
Olbia
Gallura ¶¶¶
corso Umberto 145
☎ 078924648

617

Gourmet Tours

SASSARI. Cagliari's historical opponent for control of the island, Sassari is an ancient town rich in culture and traditions. The Museo Nazionale Sanna reflects this, as does the urban architecture, including the Corso Vittorio Emanuele II and the Duomo. The cuisine fully encompasses the traditions of the north of the island, making use of fish from the coast and all the inland produce. We recommend the elegant restaurant, "Senato", situated in the center of the commercial district. It serves *gnocchi d'asino* (gnocchi with donkey-meat sauce) *carne d'asino ai ferri* (grilled donkey meat), and a tasty *torta della suocera* (mother-in-law cake) to finish, the whole washed down with the best wines of the region. Another recommend restaurant is the "Giamaranto", whose menu ranges from fish to mushrooms. And finally, there is the "Trattoria Assassino" for those who love barbecued food. The "Martinez" *enoteca* offers a good selection of regional wines and you can sample sausage, cheese or seafood. At "Fratelli Rau",you can get cakes and liqueurs, such as the *mirto rosso* (red myrtle) and the *filuferru*.

View of the Costa Smeralda

1. Nurra, Meilogu and Logudoro

PORTO TORRES. This is the old city of Turris Libisonis, which was a Roman grain port before it became the capital of the barony of Nurra; it contains the important Roman basilica of S. Gavino. From Sassari take the Carlo Felice road, but you must make a detour to the prehistoric sanctuary of Monte d'Accoddi, then take a break at the rustic family-run tavern, "Li Lioni", or at the nearby *trattoria*, "S'Appentu", with its enticing barbecued food. We very much recommend the excursion to Stintino, with the Pelosa beach and the tower of Capo del Falcone. There are many chances to eat well, obviously involving seafood cuisine, but also pizzas. At the restaurant "Sarago" we recommend the *coccio d'aragosta alla stintinese* (lobster Stintino style), at "Silvestrino" the *zuppa di pesce* (fish soup) and at "Pelosetta" the *spigola al Vermentino* (sea bass Vermentino style) and *gamberoni alla Vernaccia* (crayfish cooked in Vernaccia wine).

ALGHERO. A town typical of the area, which, even today, has the influences and dialect of the Catalans. It has a cathedral with a majolica cupola, and town walls. It is

HOTELS AND RESTAURANTS

Olbia
⭐🖭 **Nino's** ¶¶¶
at Lido di Pittulongu (km 7)
strada Panoramica km 4,8
☎ 078939027
⭐🖭 **Bacchus** ¶¶
via D'Annunzio 2/b
☎ 078921612
Leone e Anna ¶¶
via Barcellona 90
☎ 078926333
Palau
Franco ¶¶¶¶
via Capo d'Orso 1
☎ 0789709310
Gritta ¶¶¶
at Porto Faro
☎ 0789708045
Porto Cervo
Cala di Volpe ★★★L
at Cala di Volpe
☎ 0789976111
Pitrizza ★★★L
at Liscia di Vacca
☎ 0789930111
Romazzino ★★★L
at Romazzino
☎ 0789977111
Porto Rotondo
Da Giovannino ¶¶¶
piazza Quadrata
☎ 078935280
Porto Torres
Li Lioni ¶¶
at Li Lioni
☎ 079502286
S'Appentu Club ¶¶
regione Li Lioni
S.S. 131, km 224
☎ 079502080

a lively working town, well-known for its wine and good food, thanks to the fishing fleet and fertile agricultural hinterland. The most important local specialty is the lobster prepared either oven-baked, in a sauce, in a salad or in the Catalan style. A variety of other seafood specialties make the cuisine even better, including mullet roe, or the rarer molva roe, conger eel in vinegar, pickled tuna filets and other big fish. All this food is further enhanced by top quality olive oils and wines. For you to try all this, we recommend the restaurant the "Al Tuguri", a romantic place which seats just 30, and serves Catalan cuisine. Other top class restaurants include the refined "Palau Real", with the specialty of *ravioli di carciofo alla crema di bottarga* (artichoke *ravioli* with fish roe sauce), the strongly traditional "Pavone", which serves an exquisite *zuppa di cozze* (mussel soup), and the "La Lepanto", with its celebrated *aragosta algharese* (lobster Alghero style). Don't miss a visit to the "Tenute Sella e Mosca", deservedly the most important vineyard of the island, which promotes local grapes and the development of international vines in Sardinia. The best traditional wines of the vineyard are the Cannonau and the liqueur-like Anghelu Ruju. Then there are the newly-created wines and a single-variety wine, the Torbato, from an ancient indigenous vine. Adjoining the vineyard is the house museum with an archaeological section inside the property devoted to the necropolis Anghelu Ruiu. If you want to go shopping, the "Cooperativa Allevatori e Produttori Latte" in Fertilia sells *ricotta* and *pecorino* cheeses, and the "Consorzio Oleario Sardo" sells olive oil and olives. Another place to buy olive oil is at the olive press "Manca". In the stores ask for the local *bottarga* (fish roe) and *musciame*. Not to be missed is the excursion to Porto Conti and Capo Caccia among the steep cliffs and grottos, where you can see flying griffon vultures. The same goes for the spectacular coastline which extends down to Bosa.

TORRALBA. Two winding and scenic roads lead to this Logudoro village, one goes via Ittiri, the other via Villanova Monteleone. The object of this journey is the valley of Nuraghi with the

HOTELS AND RESTAURANTS

Santa Teresa Gallura
S'Andira ⅋⅋
at Santa Reparata
via Orsa Minore 1
☎ 0789754273
Canne al Vento ⅋
via Nazionale 23
☎ 0789754219
Riva ⅋
via Galliano
☎ 0789754283
Stintino
La Pelosetta ⅋⅋
at La Pelosa
☎ 079527140
Sarago ⅋⅋
at Cala Lupo
☎ 079523370
Silvestrino ⅋⅋
via Sassari 12
☎ 079523007

AGRITURISMI

Alghero
Consorzio Agriturismo di Sardegna
at Santa Maria La Palma
☎ 078373954
Arzachena
Ca' la Somara
at Sarra Balestra
☎ 078998969
Pattada
Matteo Crasta
at S'ispasularzu
☎ 079755686

**WINE
PRODUCERS**

**Alghero
Tenute Sella
e Mosca**
at I Piani
☎ 0789997700
**Arzachena
Tenute
Capichera**
at Capichera
☎ 078980612
**Berchidda
Cantina Sociale
Cooperativa
Giogantinu**
via Milano 30
☎ 079704163
**Monti
Cantina Sociale
del Vermentino**
via S. Paolo 1
☎ 078944494
**Olbia
Cantina delle
Vigne di Piero
Mancini**
at Cala Saccaia
☎ 078950717
**Tempio Pausania
Cantina Sociale
Gallura**
via Val di Cossu 9
☎ 079631241

SHOPPING

**Sassari
Caffè Enoteca
Martinez**
via Porcellana 23
☎ 079210247
*Cheeses, chracuterie,
fish preserves
and local wines.*
Fratelli Rau
via Gorizia 7
☎ 079292264
Sweets and liquors.

spectacular complex of Santu Antine and the unmissable Pisan church. This is a zone for excellent cheese which can be bought directly from local cheese-makers. A more adventurous trip is to Ozieri, situated in the hills. Opposite is a fertile plain ideal for the breeding of farm animals. Local food includes wild boar and feathered game.

PLOAGHE. The last place to visit before returning to Sassair has the most celebrated Romanesque building on the island, the SS. Trinità di Saccargia. In the village you can sample hams and sausages at "La Genuina".

2. Anglona and Gallura

CASTELSARDO. From Sassari, travelling along the Anglona Statale 200, you see the vineyards which produce the rare and prized Moscato di Sorso-Sennori. Going a little further along the coastline, you reach the capital town of this district, set in a semi-circle facing the Gulf of Asinara. The village, of ancient importance, has a cathedral and a castle up high, overlooking the harbor. The craft here is the weaving of palm leaves and raffia. Inland, there are huge fields of artichokes, and the rest

of the land is bush with stones shaped by the wind. The Roccia dell'Elefante (Elephant Rock) is famous. In the shops you find the special salame di Tergu, made with top quality lean meat and bacon, preserved in ash. On the seafront there is the Hotel Riviera with its restaurant, the "Fofò", specializing in the best traditional fish dishes and large meat roasts. In Lu Bagnu we recommend the restaurant "Sa Ferula" with its terrace overlooking the sea.

SANTA TERESA GALLURA. The town was founded in 1808 by the King of Savoy (Teresa was the wife of Vittorio Emanuele I); the town was a checkpoint to control smuggling, and also a stronghold against Napoleon. Here we recommend the restaurant "Riva", traditionally patronized by the local gourmets, and the "Canne al Vento". In the shops you should ask for the *supressada*, a type of salami made with top quality lean meat and bacon, mixed with salt and flavorings, and ready to eat after about a month. The mushrooms in oil are also worth a mention. In Santa Reparata we can recommend the well-tended, family-run restaurant, "S'Andira", which is very welcoming and has an enticing fish menu. Don't miss the trip to Capo Testa.

PALAU. The place was not inhabit-

*Alghero.
Town walls and historical center*

ed until the nineteenth century when it became the ferry pick-up point for the island La Maddalena. Good restaurants include the "Gritta", in a splendid position on the sea, and the elegant "Franco", a Buon Ricordo restaurant specializing in *branzino al vapore su credités in salsa aromatica* (steamed sea bass on a bed of crudités with an aromatic sauce).

LA MADDALENA. This is a naval base which was built in the nineteenth century. "La Grotta" is a restaurant renowned for fish and shellfish dishes, and "Sottovento" for its large choice of starters and home-made pastas. You can reach the island of Caprera, the last home of Giuseppe Garibaldi, by bridge.

Traditional customes of Ittiri

ARZACHENA. The town has grown up in an area full of prehistoric remains, Tombs of the Giants (2,500-3,000-year-old huge stone monuments) and necropoli. The charcuterie is renowned (buy ham and salamis from "Paolo Azaro") as is the Vermentino wine (from the "Tenute Capichera"). From here you can take an excursion along the beautiful Costa Smeralda, the 'emerald coast'. Good restaurants worth mentioning are the "Grazia Deledda" and "Casablanca" in Baia Sardinia, and "Da Giovannino" in Porto Rotondo.

OLBIA. This has been the chief port of the eastern coast since the Carthaginian period, and the church of S. Simplicio recalls its medieval history. The stop here provides the opportunity for a visit to the excellent hotel-restaurant "Gallura", where Rita Denza skil-

fully interprets the flavors of Sardinia and its sea. The gourmet menu should not be missed, particularly the *ostriche alle erbe e zafferano* (oysters with herbs and saffron), the *maltagliati alla cernia* (*maltagliati* pasta with grouper), the *risotto mantecato con zucchine e gamberi* (*risotto* with zucchini and crayfish) and the *pesce con le erbe* (fish with herbs). That is just the seafood, then there is the 'land' food, with pastas with vegetable sauces, and meat cooked in a wood oven, or in red wine. Other good restaurants include "Bacchus", "Leone e Anna" and "Nino's". To buy Vermentino wine, go to the "Cantina delle Vigne di Piero Mancini".

TEMPIO PAUSANIA. There are two roads you can take: the Settentrionale Sarda which is shorter but winding, or the Statale 199 which is a good road up to Oschiri but becomes very difficult around Lake Coghinas. Wine-lovers will not have a problem choosing because the southern (latter) route passes by the two little Citta del Vino of Monti and Berchidda where you can find the "Cantina del Vermentino" and the "Cantina Sociale Giogantinu", respectively. The area is also renowned for its charcuterie, cheeses and honey. Whichever road you take, the objective is Tempio Pausania and here, too, you can find the Vermentino wine at the "Cantina Sociale Gallura", and the town's renowned honey.

SHOPPING

Alghero
Consorzio Olcario Sardo
at Fertilia (km 6)
☎ 079261179
Olive oil producer.
Cooperativa Allevatori Produttori Latte
at Santa Maria La Palma (km 14)
☎ 079261070
Milk products.
Frantoio Manca
via Carrabuffas
☎ 079977215
Olive oil producer.
Arzachena
Paolo Azara
via Genova 1
☎ 078981366
Typical charcuterie.
Soliana
Stazione Marittima Isola Bianca
☎ 078925297
Organic products, "carasau" bread, wines and liquors.
Ploaghe
La Genuina
corso G. Spano 306
☎ 079449223
Typical charcuterie.
Porto Torres
La Bottega
piazza XX Settembre 1
☎ 079514834
Cheeses and charcuterie.
Stintino
Biscottificio S. Nicola
pozzo S. Nicola
☎ 079534016
Biscuits producer.
Enoteca Vabes
via Sassari 32
☎ 079523072
Wines.

Dorgali and Cala Gonone
The good food itineraries

Dorgali and Cala Gonone are a must for all lovers of good food. Within a wonderful natural environment, you can enjoy the recipes of Barbagia food tradition, going back a thousand years and passed on from generation to generation, continuously renewed with creativity and skill.

The Cannonau wine, the pecorino cheese, the carasau bread, the typical sweets, the olive oil, the fish all invite you to an enjoyable visit to the numerous local restaurants, shops and farms.

Foto e dir. creativa: Antonio Fancello

by the Dorgali Tourist Board
www.dorgali.it

For Information:
Pro Loco 0784/96243
Uff.Inf. Cala Gonone 0784/93696
Centro Serv. Turistici 0784/920149

Hotel PORTOCONTE

The Portoconte Hotel, overlooking the sea, is situated in the wonderful Porto Conte bay, only 12 km far from Alghero. All 144 rooms, with 6 junior suites and 16 family rooms, have bathroom, independent air conditioning, balcony, direct line telephone, hair dryer, colour TV and satellite. All common areas, restaurant, bar, play and entertainment room, TV room and boutique, are air conditioned. The hotel is also equipped with 2 swimming pools (one for children), 2 tennis courts, minigolf, bowls, amusement park and a pier for private boats. Our restaurant's diverse offers include a rich breakfast buffet and typical menus with Sardinian and Catalan specialities. Wide choice of leisure activities: windsurf, sailing, diving, water-ski, mountain bike, trekking, etc.

Località Porto Conte
04041 Alghero (SS) - Sardegna (Italia)
Tel. +39 079942035 - Fax +39 079942045
www.hotelportoconte.com - E-mail: info@hotelportoconte.com

GLOSSARY

ACRONYMS

D.O.C. (Denominazione di Origine Controllata) A quality-control label which according to Italian legislation indicates the viticultural area and the method of production.

D.O.C.G. (Denominazione di Origine Controllata e Garantita) A more stringent quality category than D.O.C., the wine is subjected to tighter cultivation and processing controls, and the title is awarded only after a taste test by a specially appointed commission.

D.O.P. (Denominazione di Origine Protetta) An official seal given to outstanding foods with an exclusively regional importance.

I.G.P. (Indicazione Geografica Protetta): Denotes 'typical' wines from broad areas, such as an entire region or province.

I.G.T. (Indicazione Geografica Tipica) The wine equivalent of the IGP title, it refers to the area in which the grapes are grown and made into wine. This is less restrictive than D.O.C.

CHARCUTERIE

MAIN TYPES *Salumi* (cured pork products); prosciutto (cured ham); *prosciutto cotto* (cooked hams).

Bresaola, cotechino, ciasculo, lardo, mortadella, pancetta, porchetta, soppressata, speck and *mortadella* are all charcuterie products.

CHEESES

MAIN TYPES Parmigiano (Parmesan) and Grana Padana are medium-fat hard cheeses; *pecorino* denotes a group of sheep's milk cheeses and *mozzarella* (like *provolone*, *scamorza* and *caciocavallo*) is a buffalo's milk cheese that has been rolled into a dough-like paste and drawn out like a ribbon to get its distinctive texture.

Cacioricotta, fontina, gorgonzola, ricotta, mascarpone and *scamorza* are all typical Italian cheeses.

FOOD

GNOCCHI (singular gnocco) Dumplings made of flour, semolina, or potatoes, boiled or baked and served with grated cheese or a sauce.

POLENTA A thick maize porridge served with meat or vegetables and popular in northern Italy.

RISOTTO A creamy rice dish with many variations depending on the region.

MISCELLANEOUS

CITTÀ DEL VINO (or Olio etc) Towns belonging to the national association of wine producers (or olive oil producers etc).

STATALE Main state road – a smaller road than the Autostrada.

PASTA

VARIETIES include egg pastas such as *tagliatelle* and *fettuccine*; filled pastas such as *ravioli, tortellini, cappelletti* and *cannelloni* as well as durum wheat pastas such as *spaghetti* or the hollow *bucatini*.

Maccheroni, maccheroncini, orrecchiette, pappardelle, strangozzi and *tagliolini* are all typical Italian pasta varieties.

PLACES TO STAY AND EAT

AGRITURISMO A farm establishment offering holiday lodgings where guests can eat local food and buy farm produce.

AZIENDA A winery that also produces other products such as jams, cheeses or cured hams. These products can be tasted and bought here.

CANTINA A wine-producing co-operative where several associated growers contribute grapes to a common product. Wine can be tasted and bought.

ENOTECA A wine bar and shop which sells wine by the bottle or by the glass with snacks.

FATTORIA A Tuscan term denoting a vineyard with its own wine production facilities.

LOCANDA An inn.

OSTERIA A tavern or inn, where you can eat meals and sometimes stay the night.

SALUMERIA A shop dedicated only to the retail of cold cuts and cured meats.

TRATTORIA A family restaurant with a relaxed atmosphere.

INDEX

Page numbers printed in italic indicate useful information provided in the left and right margins of the pages.

PICTURE CREDITS

The majority of the labels reproduced belong to the AICEV's (Associazione Italiana Collezionisti Etichette del Vino) Giacomo Prato Collection

Archivio Fotografico TCI: 27; M. Cresci: 375, 385; Fumagalli: 92; Gamba: 96; T. Nicolini: 86/87, 95, 98/99, 101, 106, 114, 120, 121, 122; F. Radino: 81, 82, 490, 498 bottom, 502, 504, 508, P510.

Agenzia Laura Ronchi: V. Lombardo: 600/601; R. Meazza: 348/349.

Agenzia Marka: M Albonico: 192/193; L. Barbazza: 180/181; Bavarie: 161; D. Donadoni: 132, 178, 258; L. Fioroni: 260; M. Mazzola: 171; V. Pcholkin: 137; F. Rho: 253.

Agenzia Realy Easy Star: 144/145, 206, 212/213, 216/217, 257, 330, 331, 335, 338, 602/603, 604; G. Alberghina: 312; B. Allaix: 46/47; P. Bertoli: 113; E. Carli: 306/307, 337, 339; C. Concina: 128 bottom, 148/149, 350/351, 565, 566; G. Corte: 436/437, 447, 408/409, 427; M. Di Paolo: 112; F. Ferraris: 231; G. Furghieri: 141, 176/177, 270, 112, 390/391, 441; P. Gislimbcerti: 147, 596/597; G. Giusta: 572; G. Iacono: 440, 459, 556, 576; F. Iorio: 449, 493, 507, 539; M. La Tona: 166/167, 557; M. Marchetti: 605, 289; G. Orlando: 560, 563 top, 568, 578/579; G. Ottolenghi: 59; A. Penco: 573; L. Pessina: 26, 29, 77, 83, 473, 538, 107, 369; A. Picone: 537 bottom, 544; A. Pitrone: CA. 3; 558; G. Pontari: 536, 542/543; N. Reitano: 582, C. Rizzi: 186/187, 190, 227, 236/237; G. Rodante: 139, 151, 314, 475, 126/127, 392; V. Rossato: 438, 503, A 8, 428; M. Rubino: 413, 418, 419; A. Safina: 583; Samperi: 155; M . Sandri: 179; L.A. Scatola: 50/51, 134/135, 555; L. Sechi: 610; Soneca: 53 top; T. Spagone: 27, 37 top, 37 bottom, 30, 31, 32/33, 36, 40/41, 45, 57, 62/63, 65, 67, 74, 110, 160, 231, 288, 308, 310, 311, 327, 330, 367, 377, 379, 384, 397, 454/455, 457, 459, 492 top, 492 bottom, 501, 504, 516/517, 518/519, 521, 611; P. Viola: 595, 598/599; C.A. Zabert: 222, 240; A. Zaven: 565.

Agenzia White Star: M. Bertinetti: 77; G. Veggi: 52/53.

Buysschaert&Malerba/Iconotec: 104, 162, 306, 318/319, 329, 460/461, H. Canabi 162, M. Yon Aulock 170.

Photo by D. Di Corato: 490 top.

Photo by Mairani: 34, 35, 69, 78/79, 130/131, 163, 169, 202, 205, 207, 209, 211, 214, 218, 220/221, 222/223, 225, 228, 234, 239, 242, 248/249, 282 bottom, 261, 262, 271, 300/301, 316/317, 317 top, 318 top, 320/321, 325, 328, 332/333, 342, 373, 374, 380/381, 382, 386/387, 388, 394/395, 398/397, 400, 416, 417, 420, 421, 423, 424/425, 426, 430, 431, 434, 439, 443, 444/445, 452/453, 464, 465, 466, 467, 468/469, 470, 473, 476, 479, 480 top, 480/481, 484/485, 489, 496, 498 top, 505, 506, 509, 514, 520, 522, 525, 539, 542, 537, 541, 562/563, 572/573, 564, 566, 570/571, 574 top, 584, 585, 574, 588/589, 592/593, 606/607, 608/609.

Photo by F. Soletti: 90, 93, 102 103, 104, 108, 118/119, 123, 128 top, 152/153, 154, 155, 158/159, 174, 182, 188, 191, 192/193, 195, 197, 198/199, 215, 255, 263, 276, 279, 283, 285, 286, 287, 296/297, 305, 310 top, 344, 346/347, 548, 577, 575, 581, 115

TRAVEL NOTES

TRAVEL NOTES

TRAVEL NOTES

TRAVEL NOTES

MADAMA OLIVA

**The pleasure of eating
Selection of quality olives
Ongoing research**

Madama Oliva bases its activity on centuries-old experience in the processing and packaging of table olives. The company boasts a highly technological plant – unique in its sector. – specifically designed to optimise processing procedures and product quality.
The uniqueness of Madama Oliva lies in its offer to consumers of a fresh product that is tested daily in our on location laboratory so as to ensure guaranteed hygienic and healthy product conditions and compliance with superior quality standards.
In addition to the vast assortment of the best varieties of table olives, our range of products includes salted lupins, vegetables preserved in olive oil, capers, hot peppers and olive spreads of various types.
Dedication and know-how have also led to innovative products and packagings capable of meeting and of anticipating consumer needs.

New products

PENTAGUSTO

aperitif

hot

hors-d'oeuvre

STERILIZED PRODUCTS

Green Mild Olives

Black Mild Olives

Salted Lupins

MINCE OF OLIVES AND VEGETABLES

UNI EN ISO 9002

www.madamaoliva.it - E-mail: info@madamaoliva.it
MADAMA OLIVA s.r.l.
Zona industriale Località Recocce - 67061 CARSOLI (AQ) - Tel. +39 0863 995498 - Fax +39 0863 995727

Col Sandago, il Wildbacher.

Martino Zanetti

Pieve di Soligo (Treviso) - Telefono +39 0438.841608 - info@martinozanetti.it

Rediscover Lombardy.

ONE REGION, ONE THOUSAND FLAVOURS

Cheese, salami, wines, oil, vegetables
the genuine good old food of Lombard tradition.

237 traditional regional products

9 DOP cheeses

6 DOP and IGP salamis

14 DOC and **2** DOCG wine areas

DOP extravirgin olive **oil** from the Garda Bresciano

DOP extravirgin olive **oil** from the Lombardy Lakes

IGP Mantua **pears**

500 farm guesthouses

Over **900** organic food producers

Flavours of Lombardy.
Let's be tempted.

Ente Regionale di Sviluppo Agricolo
della Lombardia

RegioneLombardia
Agricoltura

HOTEL OLEGGIO
MALPENSA
★ ★ ★

VIA VERBANO, 19 - 28047 OLEGGIO (NOVARA)
S.S. 32 del Lago Maggiore
TELEFONO +39 0321-93301 - PRENOTAZIONI +39 0321-94890 - FAX +39 0321-93377
E-mail: holeggio@starnova.it
INTERNET: www.comet.it/hoteloleggio • www.paginegialle.it/holeggio
www.hoteloleggiomalpensa.it - E-mall: Info@hoteloleggiomalpensa.it

Numero Verde TOLL FREE
800-233643
INFORMAZIONI - PRENOTAZIONI

family hotels
and
restaurants

SNACK BAR
COLD MEALS
AIR CONDITIONING
CARS CARE
LONGTERM - AIRPORT PARKING
ON PAYMENT:
WEEKLY CHARGE

"PARK and FLY"

24 HOURS FREE SHUTTLE SERVICE
TO AND FROM MILAN MALPENSA AIRPORT - TO AND FROM NOVARA RAILWAY STATION

HOTEL OLEGGIO = USCITA-EXIT-SORTIE
NOVARA EST → LAGO MAGGIORE

BOOKING BY E-MAIL

SURROUNDINGS: LAKE MAGGIORE - LAKE OF ORTA - LAKES OF VARESE - PARK OF TICINO RIVER - PARK OF MERCURAGO - PARK OF TORBIERA - GOLF CLUB CONTURBIA - FREE AND GUIDED RIDING - SWIMMING POOL - TENNIS COURT - POLO CLUB MILAN - ICE SKATING - BOWLING - DISCOS - GO KART SPORTS FISHING (LITTLE LAKES)

VISIT AND BRIEF TRIPS: EARLY ROMANTIC S. MICHAEL CHURCH - BASILICA AND WORKS BY ARCHITECT ANTONELLI ETNOGRAPHIC MUSEUM - CIVILIZATION AND PREHISTORIC RUINS OF GOLASECCA - RUINS OF ROMANTIC NECROPOLIS - RUINS OF KING'S ARDUINO CASTLE RUINS OF VISCONTI'S CASTLE S. CHARLES MONUMENT (COLOSSUS) - ANGERA FORTRESS - ORTA S. MOUNT - S. DONATO CHAPEL - BELLINZAGO OLD MILL - DULZAGO ABBEY - MILL "WATER CHANNEL" AND OLD MILL - VARALLO SESIA S. MOUNT NOVARA OF THE RISORGIMENTO - NOVARA HILLS.

OENOLOGY AND GASTRONOMY ROUTES: MONFERRATO HILLS AND ASTI SURROUNDINGS - NOVARA HILLS - SESIA VALLEY VERBANO AREA.

DAY TRIPS: ALAGNA AND MACUGNAGA - ARONA - LOCARNO (SWITZERLAND) BY BOAT - MOTTARONE MOUNT (STRESA) SKIING FACILITIES - FORMAZZA VALLEY (TOCE'S FALLS) BORROMEE ISLES - S. GIULIO ISLE.

CLOSE TO:

MALPENSA TERMINAL 1	= 10 MIN.
MALPENSA TERMINAL 2	= 15 MIN.
LINATE AIRPORT	= 60 MIN.
RS NOVARA	= 15 MIN.
RS MAILAND	= 50 MIN.
MILAN FAIR	= 40 MIN.

PARMIGIANO-REGGIANO:

A cheese with centuries of history still

Its origins can be traced back to the 13th century in the Po Valley or, more specifically, in the valley of the Enza River that marks the border between the provinces of Parma and Reggio Emilia. This was an area where agriculture flourished even centuries ago, mainly centred land reclamation undertaken by Benedictine and Cistercian monks. It was thanks to these monks and their industriousness that today we have Parmigiano-Reggiano: early monasteries possessed extensive farmlands where at the time cows were used to till the fields and also as a source of milk and meat. In the monastic background, where the Benedictine motto "ora et labora" was a rule of life, they had also the necessary passion and technical skills for making large-sized cheeses, an art that required - and still does - considerable experience, dedication and care. Parmigiano-Reggiano is the fruit of history, tradition and industriousness. A strict regulation, providing that cows must be fed using locally grown fodder and vegetable feed and forbidding the use of additives, is the grounding for a completely natural product: a raw milk cheese, matured for about two years in order to achieve the excellence in terms of taste and aroma that give its typical characteristic.

Information on guided tours:

Parma Office
Viale Gramsci, 26/b - 43100 Parma - Italy
tel. +39.0521.292700 - fax +39.0521.293441
e-mail: sezionepr@parmigiano-reggiano.it

Reggio Emilia Office
Via San Rocco, 3 - 42100 Reggio Emilia - Italy
tel. +39.0522.430844 - fax +39.0522.439291
e-mail: sezionere@parmigiano-reggiano.it